THE COMPLETE BOOK OF

YOGA

KARMA YOGA | BHAKTI YOGA | RĀJA YOGA | JNĀNA YOGA

SWAMI VIVEKANANDA

PRAKASH

Reprint 2023

PRAKASH
An imprint of Prakash Books India Pvt. Ltd.

113/A, Darya Ganj, New Delhi-110 002,
Tel: (011) 2324 7062 – 65, Fax: (011) 2324 6975
Email: info@prakashbooks.com/sales@prakashbooks.com

facebook www.facebook.com/fingerprintpublishing
twitter www.twitter.com/FingerprintP
www.fingerprintpublishing.com

ISBN: 978 81 9493 233 8

Processed & printed in India

Born Narendranath Datta on January 12, 1863, in Calcutta, capital of British India, Swami Vivekananda belonged to a traditional aristocratic Bengali Kayastha family. He was one of the nine children of Vishwanath Datta, an attorney, and Bhubaneswari Devi, a pious housewife. While his mother was religious, his father was rational and progressive.

Spiritual from an early age, Vivekananda was fascinated by wandering monks and used to practise meditation. But he was also very restive and energetic and his mother had a hard time controlling him. From 1871 to 1877, before his family moved to Raipur, he attended Ishwar Chandra Vidyasagar's Metropolitan Institution. On his return, he joined the Presidency College in January 1880.

Vivekananda was a passionate reader. He had an appetite for subjects ranging from art, literature, philosophy, and religion to history and social science. Owing to his deep interest in Hindu mythology and Sanskrit scriptures, he read the Ramayana, the Mahabharata, the Bhagavad Gita, the Vedas, the Upanishads, and the Puranas. Along with being studious, he was also a sports enthusiast and took an active part in physical exercise.

Vivekananda joined Keshab Chandra Sen's social group called 'Nava Vidhan' where he became familiar with Western esotericism. He also became a member of the Sadharan Brahmo Samaj, a division of Brahmoism. The concepts of the Samaj shaped his beliefs. He opposed idolatry and believed in a formless God.

It was during one of his literature classes at the Scottish Church College that he came to know about Ramakrishna. Vivekananda visited Dakshineswar with his friends sometime around the end of 1881 or beginning of 1882. His meeting with Ramakrishna came about as a life-changing experience for him.

In the beginning, he did not completely accept Ramakrishna's ideologies and even dismissed the Advaita Vedanta. But as he continued visiting him, especially after his father's death in 1884, he eventually accepted Ramakrishna as his guru, his spiritual teacher, and became his notable disciple.

Ramakrishna passed away in 1886 in Cossipore. Vivekananda, along with other disciples, set up their first monastery at Baranagar, the Ramakrishna Math. In December 1886, they all took monastic vows. It was then that he had taken the name 'Swami Vivekananda'. In the years that followed, he travelled extensively across India as a wandering monk.

During his travels, he came across people with diverse backgrounds and from various walks of life. He also familiarized himself with different social and religious customs, beliefs, and traditions. Vivekananda grew empathetic towards those who were suffering and decided to bring a change and uplift the country.

On May 31, 1893, he began his first journey abroad.

He visited Japan, China, and Canada, before reaching Chicago, United States, on July 30, 1893. He participated in the Parliament of World's Religions in September 1893. On the opening day, September 11, 1893, he represented India and Hinduism in his short welcome address. The speech is still remembered for it's opening line—"Sisters and Brothers of America."

In the following days, he gave speeches explaining why there were disagreements between the various sects and religions. Vivekananda's 'Paper on Hinduism', delivered on September 19, 1893, was an introduction of Hinduism. He enlightened the audience about the Vedanta philosophy and the concepts of god, soul, and body.

His speeches and addresses had an immediate effect not just on America but on the whole world. He became a hero, a celebrity in no time and was reported as "the greatest figure in the Parliament of Religions" by the American newspapers. In the words of Parliament President John Henry Barrows, "India, the Mother of religions was represented by Swami Vivekananda, the Orange-monk who exercised the most wonderful influence over his auditors."

He spent the next couple of years travelling across the United States delivering lectures and speeches. In 1894, he established the Vedanta Society of New York. In 1895 and 1896, he lectured in the UK. Here he met Margaret Elizabeth Noble (who later became Sister Nivedita) and Max Müller. He also travelled to various European countries.

Vivekananda came up with a 'four yoga' model. This included Karma Yoga, which is "purifying the mind by means of work"; Bhakti Yoga, which is "a real, genuine search after the Lord, a search beginning, continuing, and ending in love"; Rāja Yoga, which includes an interpretation of Patanjali's *Yoga Sutras*; and Jnāna Yoga, which is about realizing the truth.

He set up the Ramakrishna Mission, a twin organization of Ramakrishna Math, in Calcutta on May 1, 1897. Both the Ramakrishna Math and the Ramakrishna Mission were headquartered at Belur Math. Vivekananda also established the Advaita Ashrama in Mayavati, Uttrakhand.

In June 1899, he toured abroad with Swami Turiyananda and Sister Nivedita despite his declining health, establishing Vedanta societies in cities in the US and delivering lectures in Europe. On December 9, 1900, he came back to Calcutta.

While he continued his service and work for the Vedanta society and the Math, his health kept deteriorating. He breathed his last on July 4, 1902, while meditating. His disciples believe that he attained *mahasamadhi*.

Sangeet Kalpataru (1887), *Karma Yoga* (1896), *Rāja Yoga* (1896), *Vedanta Philosophy: An address before the Graduate Philosophical Society* (1896), *Lectures from Colombo to Almora* (1897), *Bartaman Bharat* (1899), *Jnāna Yoga* (1899), and *My Master* (1901) and are some of his literary works published during his lifetime.

Vivekananda played a major role in introducing yoga and the Vedanta philosophies to the West. It is because of him that Hinduism gained the status of a major world religion. His birthday is observed as the National Youth Day in India and the day he delivered his famous speech at the Parliament of World Religions, September 11, is commemorated as the World Brotherhood Day.

CONTENTS

FOUR PATHS OF YOGA*

Our main problem is to be free. It is evident then that until we realise ourselves as the Absolute, we cannot attain to deliverance. Yet there are various ways of attaining to this realisation. These methods have the generic name of Yoga (to join, to join ourselves to our reality). These Yogas, though divided into various groups, can principally be classed into four; and as each is only a method leading indirectly to the realisation of the Absolute, they are suited to different temperaments. Now it must be remembered that it is not that the assumed man becomes the real man or Absolute. There is no becoming with the Absolute. It is ever free, ever perfect; but the ignorance that has covered its nature for a time is

---

* Written by the Swami during his first visit to America in answer to questions put by a Western disciple.

to be removed. Therefore the whole scope of all systems of Yoga (and each religion represents one) is to clear up this ignorance and allow the Ātman to restore its own nature. The chief helps in this liberation are Abhyasa and Vairagya. Vairagya is non-attachment to life, because it is the will to enjoy that brings all this bondage in its train; and Abhyasa is constant practice of any one of the Yogas.

Karma Yoga. Karma Yoga is purifying the mind by means of work. Now if any work is done, good or bad, it must produce as a result a good or bad effect; no power can stay it, once the cause is present. Therefore good action producing good Karma, and bad action, bad Karma, the soul will go on in eternal bondage without ever hoping for deliverance. Now Karma belongs only to the body or the mind, never to the Ātman (Self); only it can cast a veil before the Ātman.

The veil cast by bad Karma is ignorance. Good Karma has the power to strengthen the moral powers. And thus it creates non-attachment; it destroys the tendency towards bad Karma and thereby purifies the mind. But if the work is done with the intention of enjoyment, it then produces only that very enjoyment and does not purify the mind or Chitta. Therefore all work should be done without any desire to enjoy the fruits thereof. All fear and all desire to enjoy here or hereafter must be banished for ever by the Karma Yogi. Moreover, this Karma without desire of return will destroy the selfishness, which is the root of all bondage. The watchword of the Karma Yogi is "not I, but Thou", and no amount of self-sacrifice is too much for him. But he does this without any desire to go to heaven, or gain name or fame or any other benefit in this world. Although the explanation and rationale of this unselfish work is only in Jnāna Yoga, yet the natural divinity of man makes him love all sacrifice simply for the good of others, without any ulterior motive, whatever his creed or opinion. Again, with many the bondage of wealth is very great; and Karma Yoga is absolutely necessary for them as breaking the crystallisation that has gathered round their love of money.

Next is Bhakti Yoga. Bhakti or worship or love in some form or other is the easiest, pleasantest, and most natural way of man. The natural state of this universe is attraction; and that is surely followed by an ultimate disunion. Even so, love is the natural impetus of union in the human heart; and though itself a great cause of misery, properly directed towards the proper object, it brings deliverance. The object of Bhakti is God. Love cannot be without a subject and an object. The object of love again must be at first a being who can reciprocate our love. Therefore the God of love must be in some sense a human God. He must be a God of love. Aside from the question whether such a God exists or not, it is a fact that to those who have love in their heart this Absolute appears as a God of love, as personal.

The lower forms of worship, which embody the idea of God as a judge or punisher or someone to be obeyed through fear, do not deserve to be called love, although they are forms of worship gradually expanding into higher forms. We pass on to the consideration of love itself. We will illustrate love by a triangle, of which the first angle at the base is fearlessness. So long as there is fear, it is not love. Love banishes all fear. A mother with her baby will face a tiger to save her child. The second angle is that love never asks, never begs. The third or the apex is that love loves for the sake of love itself. Even the idea of object vanishes. Love is the only form in which love is loved. This is the highest abstraction and the same as the Absolute.

Next is Rāja Yoga. This Yoga fits in with every one of these Yogas. It fits inquirers of all classes with or without any belief, and it is the real instrument of religious inquiry. As each science has its particular method of investigation, so is this Rāja Yoga the method of religion. This science also is variously applied according to various constitutions. The chief parts are the Pranayama, concentration, and meditation. For those who believe in God, a symbolical name, such as Om or other sacred words received from a Guru, will be very helpful. Om is the greatest, meaning the Absolute. Meditating on the meaning of these holy names while repeating them is the chief practice.

Next is Jnāna Yoga. This is divided into three parts. First: hearing the truth—that the Ātman is the only reality and that everything else is Maya (relativity). Second: reasoning upon this philosophy from all points of view. Third: giving up all further argumentation and realising the truth. This realisation comes from (1) being certain that Brahman is real and everything else is unreal; (2) giving up all desire for enjoyment; (3) controlling the senses and the mind; (4) intense desire to be free. Meditating on this reality always and reminding the soul of its real nature are the only ways in this Yoga. It is the highest, but most difficult. Many persons get an intellectual grasp of it, but very few attain realisation.

KARMA YOGA

CHAPTER 1

KARMA IN ITS EFFECT ON CHARACTER

The word Karma is derived from the Sanskrit Kri, to do; all action is Karma. Technically, this word also means the effects of actions. In connection with metaphysics, it sometimes means the effects, of which our past actions were the causes. But in Karma Yoga we have simply to do with the word Karma as meaning work. The goal of mankind is knowledge. That is the one ideal placed before us by Eastern philosophy. Pleasure is not the goal of man, but knowledge. Pleasure and happiness come to an end. It is a mistake to suppose that pleasure is the goal. The cause of all the miseries we have in the world is that men foolishly think pleasure to be the ideal to strive for. After a time man finds that it is not happiness, but knowledge, towards which he is going, and that both pleasure and pain are great teachers, and that he learns as much from evil as from good. As pleasure and pain pass before his soul they have upon it different pictures, and the result of these combined impressions is what is called man's "character". If you take the character of any man, it really is but the aggregate of tendencies, the sum total of the bent of his mind; you will find that misery and happiness are equal factors in the formation of that character. Good and evil have an equal share in moulding character, and in some instances misery is a greater teacher than happiness. In studying the great characters the world has produced, I dare say, in the vast majority of cases, it would be found that it was misery that taught more than happiness, it was poverty that taught more than wealth, it was blows that brought out their inner fire more than praise.

Now this knowledge, again, is inherent in man. No knowledge comes from outside; it is all inside. What we say a man "knows", should, in strict psychological language, be what he "discovers" or "unveils"; what a man "learns" is really what he "discovers", by taking the cover off his own soul, which is a mine of infinite knowledge.

We say Newton discovered gravitation. Was it sitting anywhere in a corner waiting for him? It was in his own mind; the time came and he found it out. All knowledge that the world has ever received comes from the mind; the infinite library of the universe is in your own mind. The external world is simply the suggestion, the occasion, which sets you to study your own mind, but the object of your study is always your own mind. The falling of an apple gave the suggestion to Newton, and he studied his own mind. He rearranged all the previous links of thought in his mind and discovered a new link among them, which we call the law of gravitation. It was not in the apple nor in anything in the centre of the earth.

All knowledge, therefore, secular or spiritual, is in the human mind. In many cases it is not discovered, but remains covered, and when the covering is being slowly taken off, we say, "We are learning," and the advance of knowledge is made by the advance of this process of uncovering. The man from whom this veil is being lifted is the more knowing man, the man upon whom it lies thick is ignorant, and the man from whom it has entirely gone is all-knowing, omniscient. There have been omniscient men, and, I believe, there will be yet; and that there will be myriads of them in the cycles to come. Like fire in a piece of flint, knowledge exists in the mind; suggestion is the friction which brings it out. So with all our feelings and action—our tears and our smiles, our joys and our griefs, our weeping and our laughter, our curses and our blessings, our praises and our blames—every one of these we may find, if we calmly study our own selves, to have been brought out from within ourselves by so many blows. The result is what we are. All these blows taken together are called Karma—work, action. Every mental and physical blow that is given to the soul, by which, as it were, fire is struck from it, and by which its own power and knowledge are discovered, is Karma, this word being used in its widest sense. Thus we are all doing Karma all the time. I am talking to you: that is Karma. You are listening: that is Karma. We breathe: that is Karma. We walk: Karma. Everything we do, physical or mental, is Karma, and it leaves its marks on us.

There are certain works which are, as it were, the aggregate, the sum total, of a large number of smaller works. If we stand near the seashore and hear the waves dashing against the shingle, we think it is such a great noise, and yet we know that one wave is really composed of millions and millions of minute waves. Each one of these is making a noise, and yet we do not catch it; it is only when they become the big aggregate that we hear. Similarly, every pulsation of the heart is work. Certain kinds of work we feel and they become tangible to us; they are, at the same time, the aggregate of a number of small works. If you really want to judge of the character of a man, look not at his great performances. Every fool may become a hero at one time or another. Watch a man do his most common actions; those are indeed the things which will tell you the real character of a great man. Great occasions rouse even the lowest of human beings to some kind of greatness, but he alone is the really great man whose character is great always, the same wherever he be.

Karma in its effect on character is the most tremendous power that man has to deal with. Man is, as it were, a centre, and is attracting all the powers of the universe towards himself, and in this centre is fusing them all and again sending them off in a big current. Such a centre is the real man—the almighty, the omniscient—and he draws the whole universe towards him. Good and bad, misery and happiness, all are running towards him and clinging round him; and out of them he fashions the mighty stream of tendency called character and throws it outwards. As he has the power of drawing in anything, so has he the power of throwing it out.

All the actions that we see in the world, all the movements in human society, all the works that we have around us, are simply the display of thought, the manifestation of the will of man. Machines or instruments, cities, ships, or men-of-war, all these are simply the manifestation of the will of man; and this will is caused by character, and character is manufactured by Karma. As is Karma, so is the manifestation of the will. The men of mighty will the world has produced have all been tremendous workers—gigantic souls, with wills powerful enough to overturn worlds, wills they got by persistent work, through ages, and ages. Such a gigantic will as that of a Buddha or a Jesus could not be obtained in one life, for we know who their fathers were. It is not known that their fathers ever spoke a word for the good of mankind. Millions and millions of carpenters like Joseph had gone; millions are still living. Millions and millions of petty kings like Buddha's father had been in the world. If it was only a case of hereditary transmission, how do you account for this petty prince, who was not, perhaps, obeyed by his own servants, producing this son, whom half a world worships? How do you explain the gulf between the carpenter and his son, whom millions of human beings worship as God? It cannot be solved by the theory of heredity. The gigantic will which Buddha and Jesus threw over the world, whence did it come? Whence came this accumulation of power? It must have been there through ages and ages, continually growing bigger and bigger, until it burst on society in a Buddha or a Jesus, even rolling down to the present day.

All this is determined by Karma, work. No one can get anything unless he earns it. This is an eternal law. We may sometimes think it is not so, but in the long run we become convinced of it. A man may struggle all his life for riches; he may cheat thousands, but he finds at last that he did not deserve to become rich, and his life becomes a trouble and a nuisance to him. We may go on accumulating things for our physical enjoyment, but only what we earn is really ours. A fool may buy all the books in the world, and they will be in his library; but he will be able to read only those that he deserves to; and this deserving is produced by Karma. Our Karma determines what we deserve and what we can assimilate. We are responsible for what we are; and whatever we wish ourselves to be, we have the power to make ourselves. If what we are now has been the result of our own past actions, it certainly follows that whatever we wish to be in future can be produced by our present actions; so we have to know how to act. You will say, "What is the use of learning how to work? Everyone works in some way or other in this world." But there is such a thing as frittering away our energies. With regard to Karma Yoga, the Gita says that it is doing work with cleverness and as a science; by knowing how to work, one can obtain the greatest results. You must remember that all work is simply to bring out the power of the mind which is already there, to wake up the soul. The power is inside every man, so is knowing; the different works are like blows to bring them out, to cause these giants to wake up.

Man works with various motives. There cannot be work without motive. Some people want to get fame, and they work for fame. Others want money, and they work for money. Others want to have power, and they work for power. Others want to get to heaven, and they work for the same. Others want to leave a name when they die, as they do in China, where no man gets a title until he is dead; and that is a better way, after all, than with us. When a man does something very good there, they give a title of nobility to his father, who is dead, or to his grandfather. Some people work for that. Some of the followers of certain Mohammedan sects work all their lives to have a big tomb built for them when they die. I know sects among whom, as soon as a child is born, a tomb is prepared for it; that is among them the most important work a man has to do, and the bigger and the finer the tomb, the better off the man is supposed to be. Others work as a penance; do all sorts of wicked things, then erect a temple, or give something to the priests to buy them off and obtain from them a passport to heaven. They think that this kind of beneficence will clear them and they will go scot-free in spite of their sinfulness. Such are some of the various motives for work.

Work for work's sake. There are some who are really the salt of the earth in every country and who work for work's sake, who do not care for name, or fame, or even to go to heaven. They work just because good will come of it. There are others who do good to the poor and help mankind from still higher motives, because they believe in doing good and love good. The motive for name and fame seldom brings immediate results, as a rule; they come to us when we are old and have almost done with life. If a man works without any selfish motive in view, does he not gain anything? Yes, he gains the highest. Unselfishness is more paying, only people have not the patience to practice it. It is more paying from the point of view of health also. Love, truth, and unselfishness are not merely moral figures of speech, but they form our highest ideal, because in them lies such a manifestation of power. In the first place, a man who can work for five days, or even for five minutes, without any selfish motive whatever, without thinking of future, of heaven, of punishment, or anything of the kind, has in him the capacity to become a powerful moral giant. It is hard to do it, but in the heart of our hearts we know its value, and the good it brings. It is the greatest manifestation of power—this tremendous restraint; self-restraint is a manifestation of greater power than all outgoing action. A carriage with four horses may rush down a hill unrestrained, or the coachman may curb the horses. Which is the greater manifestation of power, to let them go or to hold them? A cannonball flying through the air goes a long distance and falls. Another is cut short in its flight by striking against a wall, and the impact generates intense heat. All outgoing energy following a selfish motive is frittered away; it will not cause power to return to you; but if restrained, it will result in development of power. This self-control will tend to produce a mighty will, a character which makes a Christ or a Buddha. Foolish men do not know this secret; they nevertheless want to rule mankind. Even a fool may rule the whole world if he works and waits. Let him wait a few years, restrain that foolish idea of governing; and when that idea is wholly gone, he will be a power in the world. The majority of us cannot see beyond a few years, just as some animals cannot see beyond a few steps. Just a little narrow circle—that is our world. We have not the patience to look beyond, and thus become immoral and wicked. This is our weakness, our powerlessness.

Even the lowest forms of work are not to be despised. Let the man, who knows no better, work for selfish ends, for name and fame; but everyone should always try to get towards higher and higher motives and to understand them. "To work we have the right, but not to the fruits thereof:" Leave the fruits alone. Why care for results? If you wish to help a man, never think what that man's attitude should be towards you. If you want to do a great or a good work, do not trouble to think what the result will be.

There arises a difficult question in this ideal of work. Intense activity is necessary; we must always work. We cannot live a minute without work. What then becomes of rest? Here is one side of the life-struggle—work, in which we are whirled rapidly round. And here is the other—

that of calm, retiring renunciation: everything is peaceful around, there is very little of noise and show, only nature with her animals and flowers and mountains. Neither of them is a perfect picture. A man used to solitude, if brought in contact with the surging whirlpool of the world, will be crushed by it; just as the fish that lives in the deep sea water, as soon as it is brought to the surface, breaks into pieces, deprived of the weight of water on it that had kept it together. Can a man who has been used to the turmoil and the rush of life live at ease if he comes to a quiet place? He suffers and perchance may lose his mind. The ideal man is he who, in the midst of the greatest silence and solitude, finds the intensest activity, and in the midst of the intensest activity finds the silence and solitude of the desert. He has learnt the secret of restraint, he has controlled himself. He goes through the streets of a big city with all its traffic, and his mind is as calm as if he were in a cave, where not a sound could reach him; and he is intensely working all the time. That is the ideal of Karma Yoga, and if you have attained to that you have really learnt the secret of work.

But we have to begin from the beginning, to take up the works as they come to us and slowly make ourselves more unselfish every day. We must do the work and find out the motive power that prompts us; and, almost without exception, in the first years, we shall find that our motives are always selfish; but gradually this selfishness will melt by persistence, till at last will come the time when we shall be able to do really unselfish work. We may all hope that some day or other, as we struggle through the paths of life, there will come a time when we shall become perfectly unselfish; and the moment we attain to that, all our powers will be concentrated, and the knowledge which is ours will be manifest.

CHAPTER 2

EACH IS GREAT IN HIS OWN PLACE

According to the Sānkhya philosophy, nature is composed of three forces called, in Sanskrit, Sattva, Rājas, and Tamas. These as manifested in the physical world are what we may call equilibrium, activity, and inertness. Tamas is typified as darkness or inactivity; Rājas is activity, expressed as attraction or repulsion; and Sattva is the equilibrium of the two.

In every man there are these three forces. Sometimes Tamas prevails. We become lazy, we cannot move, we are inactive, bound down by certain ideas or by mere dullness. At other times activity prevails, and at still other times that calm balancing of both. Again, in different men, one of these forces is generally predominant. The characteristic of one man is inactivity, dullness and laziness; that of another, activity, power, manifestation of energy; and in still another we find the sweetness, calmness, and gentleness, which are due to the balancing of both action and inaction. So in all creation—in animals, plants, and men—we find the more or less typical manifestation of all these different forces.

Karma Yoga has specially to deal with these three factors. By teaching what they are and how to employ them, it helps us to do our work better. Human society is a graded organization. We all know about morality, and we all know about duty, but at the same time we find that in different countries the significance of morality varies greatly. What is regarded as moral in one country may in another be considered perfectly immoral. For instance, in one country cousins may marry; in another, it is thought to be very immoral; in one, men may marry their sisters-in-law; in another, it is regarded as immoral; in one country people may marry only once; in another, many times; and so forth. Similarly, in all other departments of morality, we find the standard varies greatly—yet we have the idea that there must be a universal standard of morality.

So it is with duty. The idea of duty varies much among different nations. In one country, if a man does not do certain things, people will say he has acted wrongly; while if he does those very things in another country, people will say that he did not act rightly—and yet we know that there must be some universal idea of duty. In the same way, one class of society thinks that certain things are among its duty, while another class thinks quite the opposite and would be horrified if it had to do those things. Two ways are left open to us—the way of the ignorant, who think that there is only one way to truth and that all the rest are wrong, and the way of the wise, who admit that, according to our mental constitution or the different planes of existence in which we are, duty and morality may vary. The important thing is to know that there are gradations of duty and of morality—that the duty of one state of life, in one set of circumstances, will not and cannot be that of another.

To illustrate: All great teachers have taught, "Resist not evil," that non-resistance is the highest moral ideal. We all know that, if a certain number of us attempted to put that maxim fully into practice, the whole social fabric would fall to pieces, the wicked would take possession of our properties and our lives, and would do whatever they liked with us. Even if only one day of such non-resistance were practiced, it would lead to disaster. Yet, intuitively, in our heart of hearts we feel the truth of the teaching "Resist not evil." This seems to us to be the highest ideal; yet to teach this doctrine only would be equivalent to condemning a vast portion of mankind. Not only so, it would be making men feel that they were always doing wrong, and cause in them scruples of conscience in all their actions; it would weaken them, and that constant self-disapproval would breed more vice than any other weakness would. To the man who has begun to hate himself the gate to degeneration has already opened; and the same is true of a nation.

Our first duty is not to hate ourselves, because to advance we must have faith in ourselves first and then in God. He who has no faith in himself can never have faith in God. Therefore, the only alternative remaining to us is to recognise that duty and morality vary under different circumstances; not that the man who resists evil is doing what is always and in itself wrong, but that in the different circumstances in which he is placed it may become even his duty to resist evil.

In reading the Bhagavad Gita, many of you in Western countries may have felt astonished at the second chapter, wherein Shri Krishna calls Arjuna a hypocrite and a coward because of his refusal to fight, or offer resistance, on account of his adversaries being his friends and relatives, making the plea that non-resistance was the highest ideal of love. This is a great lesson for us all to learn, that in all matters the two extremes are alike. The extreme positive and the extreme negative are always similar. When the vibrations of light are too slow, we do not see them, nor do we see them when they are too rapid. So with sound; when very low in pitch, we do not hear it; when very high, we do not hear it either. Of like nature is the difference between resistance and non-resistance. One man does not resist because he is weak, lazy, and cannot, not because he will not; the other man knows that he can strike an irresistible blow if he likes; yet he not only does not strike, but blesses his enemies. The one who from weakness resists not commits a sin, and as such cannot receive any benefit from the non-resistance; while the other would commit a sin by offering resistance.

Buddha gave up his throne and renounced his position, that was true renunciation; but there cannot be any question of renunciation in the case of a beggar who has nothing to renounce. So we must always be careful about what we really mean when we speak of this non-resistance and ideal love. We must first take care to understand whether we have the power of resistance or not. Then, having the power, if we renounce it and do not resist, we are doing a grand act of love; but if we cannot resist, and yet, at the same time, try to deceive ourselves into the belief that we are actuated by motives of the highest love, we are doing the exact opposite. Arjuna became a coward at the sight of the mighty array against him; his "love" made him forget his duty towards his country and king. That is why Shri Krishna told him that he was a hypocrite: Thou talkest like a wise man, but thy actions betray thee to be a coward; therefore stand up and fight!

Such is the central idea of Karma Yoga. The Karma Yogi is the man who understands that the highest ideal is non-resistance, and who also knows that this non-resistance is the highest manifestation of power in actual possession, and also what is called the resisting of evil is but a step on the way towards the manifestation of this highest power, namely, non-resistance. Before reaching this highest ideal, man's duty is to resist evil; let him work, let him fight, let him strike straight from the shoulder. Then only, when he has gained the power to resist, will non-resistance be a virtue.

I once met a man in my country whom I had known

before as a very stupid, dull person, who knew nothing and had not the desire to know anything, and was living the life of a brute. He asked me what he should do to know God, how he was to get free. "Can you tell a lie?" I asked him. "No," he replied. "Then you must learn to do so. It is better to tell a lie than to be a brute, or a log of wood. You are inactive; you have not certainly reached the highest state, which is beyond all actions, calm and serene; you are too dull even to do something wicked." That was an extreme case, of course, and I was joking with him; but what I meant was that a man must be active in order to pass through activity to perfect calmness.

Inactivity should be avoided by all means. Activity always means resistance. Resist all evils, mental and physical; and when you have succeeded in resisting, then will calmness come. It is very easy to say, "Hate nobody, resist not evil," but we know what that kind of thing generally means in practice. When the eyes of society are turned towards us, we may make a show of non-resistance, but in our hearts it is canker all the time. We feel the utter want of the calm of non-resistance; we feel that it would be better for us to resist. If you desire wealth, and know at the same time that the whole world regards him who aims at wealth as a very wicked man, you, perhaps, will not dare to plunge into the struggle for wealth, yet your mind will be running day and night after money. This is hypocrisy and will serve no purpose. Plunge into the world, and then, after a time, when you have suffered and enjoyed all that is in it, will renunciation come; then will calmness come. So fulfil your desire for power and everything else, and after you have fulfilled the desire, will come the time when you will know that they are all very little things; but until you have fulfilled this desire, until you have passed through that activity, it is impossible for you to come to the state of calmness, serenity, and self-surrender. These ideas of serenity and renunciation have been preached for thousands of years; everybody has heard of them from childhood, and yet we see very few in the world who have really reached that stage. I do not know if I have seen twenty persons in my life who are really calm and non-resisting, and I have travelled over half the world.

Every man should take up his own ideal and endeavour to accomplish it. That is a surer way of progress than taking up other men's ideals, which he can never hope to accomplish. For instance, we take a child and at once give him the task of walking twenty miles. Either the little one dies, or one in a thousand crawls the twenty miles, to reach the end exhausted and half-dead. That is like what we generally try to do with the world. All the men and women, in any society, are not of the same mind, capacity, or of the same power to do things; they must have different ideals, and we have no right to sneer at any ideal. Let every one do the best he can for realising his own ideal. Nor is it right that I should be judged by your standard or you by mine. The apple tree should not be judged by the standard of the oak, nor the oak by that of the apple. To judge the apple tree you must take the apple standard, and for the oak, its own standard.

Unity in variety is the plan of creation. However men and women may vary individually, there is unity in the background. The different individual characters and classes of men and women are natural variations in creation. Hence, we ought not to judge them by the same standard or put the same ideal before them. Such a course creates only an unnatural struggle, and the result is that man begins to hate himself and is hindered from becoming religious and good. Our duty is to encourage every one in his struggle to live up to his own highest ideal, and strive at the same time to make the ideal as near as possible to the truth.

In the Hindu system of morality we find that this fact has been recognised from very ancient times; and in their scriptures and books on ethics different rules are laid down for the different classes of men—the householder, the Sannyāsin (the man who has renounced the world), and the student.

The life of every individual, according to the Hindu scriptures, has its peculiar duties apart from what belongs in common to universal humanity. The Hindu begins life as a student; then he marries and becomes a householder; in old age he retires; and lastly he gives up the world and becomes a Sannyāsin. To each of these stages of life certain duties are attached. No one of these stages is intrinisically superior to another. The life of the married man is quite as great as that of the celibate who has devoted himself to religious work. The scavenger in the street is quite as great and glorious as the king on his throne. Take him off his throne, make him do the work of the scavenger, and see how he fares. Take up the scavenger and see how he will rule. It is useless to say that the man who lives out of the world is a greater man than he who lives in the world; it is much more difficult to live in the world and worship God than to give it up and live a free and easy life. The four stages of life in India have in later times been reduced to two—that of the householder and of the monk. The householder marries and carries on his duties as a citizen, and the duty of the other is to devote his energies wholly to religion, to preach and to worship God. I shall read to you a few passages from the Mahā-Nirvāna-Tantra, which treats of this subject, and you will see that it is a very difficult task for a man to be a householder, and perform all his duties perfectly:

The householder should be devoted to God; the knowledge of God should be his goal of life. Yet he must work constantly, perform all his duties; he must give up the fruits of his actions to God.

It is the most difficult thing in this world to work and not care for the result, to help a man and never think that he ought to be grateful, to do some good work and at the same time never look to see whether it brings you name or fame, or nothing at all. Even the most arrant coward becomes brave when the world praises him. A fool can do heroic deeds when the approbation of society is upon him, but for a man to constantly do good without caring for the approbation of his fellow men is indeed the highest sacrifice man can perform. The great duty of the householder is to earn a living, but he must take care that he does not do it by telling lies, or by cheating, or by robbing others; and he must remember that his life is for the service of God, and the poor.

Knowing that mother and father are the visible representatives of God, the householder, always and by all means, must please them. If the mother is pleased, and the father, God is pleased with the man. That child is really a good child who never speaks harsh words to his parents.

Before parents one must not utter jokes, must not show restlessness, must not show anger or temper. Before mother or father, a child must bow down low, and stand up in their presence, and must not take a seat until they order him to sit.

If the householder has food and drink and clothes without first seeing that his mother and his father, his children, his wife, and the poor, are supplied, he is committing a sin. The mother and the father are the causes of this body; so a man must undergo a thousand troubles in order to do good to them.

Even so is his duty to his wife. No man should scold his wife, and he must always maintain her as if she were his own mother. And even when he is in the greatest difficulties and troubles, he must not show anger to his wife.

He who thinks of another woman besides his wife, if he touches her even with his mind—that man goes to dark hell.

Before women he must not talk improper language, and never brag of his powers. He must not say, "I have done this, and I have done that."

The householder must always please his wife with money, clothes, love, faith, and words like nectar, and never do anything to disturb her. That man who has succeeded in getting the love of a chaste wife has succeeded in his religion and has all the virtues.

The following are duties towards children:

A son should be lovingly reared up to his fourth year; he should be educated till he is sixteen. When he is twenty years of age he should be employed in some work; he should then be treated affectionately by his father as his equal. Exactly in the same manner the daughter should be brought up, and should be educated with the greatest care. And when she marries, the father ought to give her jewels and wealth.

Then the duty of the man is towards his brothers and sisters, and towards the children of his brothers and sisters, if they are poor, and towards his other relatives, his friends and his servants. Then his duties are towards the people of the same village, and the poor, and any one that comes to him for help. Having sufficient means, if the householder does not take care to give to his relatives and to the poor, know him to be only a brute; he is not a human being.

Excessive attachment to food, clothes, and the tending of the body, and dressing of the hair should be avoided. The householder must be pure in heart and clean in body, always active and always ready for work.

To his enemies the householder must be a hero. Them he must resist. That is the duty of the householder. He must not sit down in a corner and weep, and talk nonsense about non-resistance. If he does not show himself a hero to his enemies he has not done his duty. And to his friends and relatives he must be as gentle as a lamb.

It is the duty of the householder not to pay reverence to the wicked; because, if he reverences the wicked people of the world, he patronizes wickedness; and it will be a great mistake if he disregards those who are worthy of respect, the good people. He must not be gushing in his friendship; he must not go out of the way making friends everywhere; he must watch the actions of the men he wants to make friends with, and their dealings with other men, reason upon them, and then make friends.

These three things he must not talk of. He must not talk in public of his own fame; he must not preach his own name or his own powers; he must not talk of his wealth, or of anything that has been told to him privately.

A man must not say he is poor, or that he is wealthy—he must not brag of his wealth. Let him keep his own counsel; this is his religious duty. This is not mere worldly wisdom; if a man does not do so, he may be held to be immoral.

The householder is the basis, the prop, of the whole society. He is the principal earner. The poor, the weak, the children and the women who do not work—all live upon the householder; so there must be certain duties that he has to perform, and these duties must make him feel strong to perform them, and not make him think that he is doing things beneath his ideal. Therefore, if he has done something weak, or has made some mistake, he must not say so in public; and if he is engaged in some enterprise and knows he is sure to fail in it, he must not speak of it. Such self-exposure is not only uncalled for, but also unnerves the man and makes him unfit for the performance of his legitimate duties in life. At the same time, he must struggle hard to acquire these things—firstly, knowledge, and secondly, wealth. It is his duty, and if he does not do his duty, he is nobody. A householder who does not struggle to get wealth is immoral. If he is lazy and content to lead an idle life, he is immoral, because upon him depend hundreds. If he gets riches, hundreds of others will be thereby supported.

If there were not in this city hundreds who had striven to become rich, and who had acquired wealth, where would all this civilization, and these alms-houses and great houses be?

Going after wealth in such a case is not bad, because that wealth is for distribution. The householder is the centre of life and society. It is a worship for him to acquire and spend wealth nobly, for the householder who struggles to become rich by good means and for good purposes is doing practically the same thing for the attainment of salvation as the anchorite does in his cell when he is praying; for in them we see only the different aspects of the same virtue of self-surrender and self-sacrifice prompted by the feeling of devotion to God and to all that is His.

He must struggle to acquire a good name by all means. He must not gamble, he must not move in the company of the wicked, he must not tell lies, and must not be the cause of trouble to others.

Often people enter into things they have not the means to accomplish, with the result that they cheat others to attain their own ends. Then there is in all things the time factor to be taken into consideration; what at one time might be a failure, would perhaps at another time be a very great success.

The householder must speak the truth, and speak gently, using words which people like, which will do good to others; nor should he talk of the business of other men.

The householder by digging tanks, by planting trees on the roadsides, by establishing rest-houses for men and animals, by making roads and building bridges, goes towards the same goal as the greatest Yogi.

This is one part of the doctrine of Karma Yoga—activity, the duty of the householder. There is a passage later on, where it says that "if the householder dies in battle, fighting for his country or his religion, he comes to the same goal as the Yogi by meditation," showing thereby that what is duty for one is not duty for another. At the same time, it does not say that this duty is lowering and the other elevating. Each duty has its own place, and according to the circumstances in which we are placed, we must perform our duties.

One idea comes out of all this—the condemnation of all weakness. This is a particular idea in all our teachings which I like, either in philosophy, or in religion, or in work. If you read the Vedas, you will find this word always repeated—fearlessness—fear nothing. Fear is a sign of weakness. A man must go about his duties without taking notice of the sneers and the ridicule of the world.

If a man retires from the world to worship God, he must not think that those who live in the world and work for the good of the world are not worshipping God: neither must those who live in the world, for wife and children, think that those who give up the world are low vagabonds. Each is great in his own place. This thought I will illustrate by a story.

A certain king used to inquire of all the Sannyāsins that came to his country, "Which is the greater man—he who gives up the world and becomes a Sannyāsin, or he who lives in the world and performs his duties as a house holder?" Many wise men sought to solve the problem. Some asserted that the Sannyāsin was the greater, upon which the king demanded that they should prove their assertion. When they could not, he ordered them to marry and become householders. Then others came and said, "The householder who performs his duties is the greater man." Of them, too, the king demanded proofs. When they could not give them, he made them also settle down as householders.

At last there came a young Sannyāsin, and the king similarly inquired of him also. He answered, "Each, O king, is equally great in his place." "Prove this to me," asked the king. "I will prove it to you," said the Sannyāsin, "but you must first come and live as I do for a few days, that I may be able to prove to you what I say." The king consented and followed the Sannyāsin out of his own territory and passed through many other countries until they came to a great kingdom. In the capital of that kingdom a great ceremony was going on. The king and the Sannyāsin heard the noise of drums and music, and heard also the criers; the people were assembled in the streets in gala dress, and a great proclamation was being made. The king and the Sannyāsin stood there to see what was going on. The crier was proclaiming loudly that the princess, daughter of the king of that country, was about to choose a husband from among those assembled before her.

It was an old custom in India for princesses to choose husbands in this way. Each princess had certain ideas of the sort of man she wanted for a husband. Some would have the handsomest man, others would have only the most learned, others again the richest, and so on. All the princes of the neighbourhood put on their bravest attire and presented themselves before her. Sometimes they too had their own criers to enumerate their advantages and the reasons why they hoped the princess would choose them. The princess was taken round on a throne, in the most splendid array, and looked at and heard about them. If she was not pleased with what she saw and heard, she said to her bearers, "Move on," and no more notice was taken of the rejected suitors. If, however, the princess was pleased with any one of them, she threw a garland of flowers over him and he became her husband.

The princess of the country to which our king and the Sannyāsin had come was having one of these interesting ceremonies. She was the most beautiful princess in the world, and the husband of the princess would be ruler of the kingdom after her father's death. The idea of this princess was to marry the handsomest man, but she could not find the right one to please her. Several times these meetings had taken place, but the princess could not select a husband. This meeting was the most splendid of all; more people than ever had come to it. The princess came in on a throne, and the bearers carried her from place to place. She did not seem to care for any one, and every one became disappointed that this meeting also was going to be a failure. Just then came a young man, a Sannyāsin, handsome as if the sun had come down to the earth, and stood in one corner of the assembly, watching what was going on. The throne with the princess came near him, and as soon as she saw the beautiful Sannyāsin, she stopped and threw the garland over him. The young Sannyāsin seized the garland and threw it off, exclaiming, "What nonsense is this? I am a Sannyāsin. What is marriage to me?" The king of that country thought that perhaps this man was poor and so dared not marry the princess, and said to him, "With my daughter goes half my kingdom now, and the whole kingdom after my death!" and put the garland again on the Sannyāsin. The young man threw it off once more, saying, "Nonsense! I do not want to marry," and walked quickly away from the assembly.

Now the princess had fallen so much in love with this young man that she said, "I must marry this man or I shall die"; and she went after him to bring him back. Then our other Sannyāsin, who had brought the king there, said to him, "King, let us follow this pair"; so they walked after them, but at a good distance behind. The young Sannyāsin who had refused to marry the princess walked out into the country for several miles. When he came to a forest and entered into it, the princess followed him, and the other two followed them. Now this young Sannyāsin was well acquainted with that forest and knew all the intricate paths in it. He suddenly passed into one of these and disappeared, and the princess could not discover him. After trying for a long time to find him she sat down under a tree and began to weep, for she did not know the way out. Then our king and the other Sannyāsin came up to her and said, "Do not weep; we will show you the way out of this forest, but it is too dark for us to find it now. Here is a big tree; let us rest under it, and in the morning we will go early and show you the road."

Now a little bird and his wife and their three little ones lived on that tree, in a nest. This little bird looked down and saw the three people under the tree and said to his wife, "My dear, what shall we do? Here are some guests in the house, and it is winter, and we have no fire." So he flew away and got a bit of burning firewood in his beak and dropped it before the guests, to which they added fuel and made a blazing fire. But the little bird was not satisfied. He said again to his wife, "My dear, what shall we do? There is nothing to give these people to eat, and they are hungry. We are householders; it is our duty to feed any one who comes to the house. I must do what I can, I will give them my body." So he plunged into the midst of the fire and perished. The guests saw him falling and tried to save him, but he was too quick for them.

The little bird's wife saw what her husband did, and she said, "Here are three persons and only one little bird for them to eat. It is not enough; it is my duty as a wife not to let my husband's effort go in vain; let them have my body also." Then she fell into the fire and was burned to death.

Then the three baby-birds, when they saw what was done and that there was still not enough food for the three guests, said, "Our parents have done what they could and still it is not enough. It is our duty to carry on the work of our parents; let our bodies go too." And they all dashed down into the fire also.

Amazed at what they saw, the three people could not of course eat these birds. They passed the night without food, and in the morning the king and the Sannyāsin showed the princess the way, and she went back to her father.

Then the Sannyāsin said to the king, "King, you have seen that each is great in his own place. If you want to live in the world, live like those birds, ready at any moment to sacrifice yourself for others. If you want to renounce the world, be like that young man to whom the most beautiful woman and a kingdom were as nothing. If you want to be a householder, hold your life a sacrifice for the welfare of others; and if you choose the life of renunciation, do not even look at beauty and money and power. Each is great in his own place, but the duty of the one is not the duty of the other.

CHAPTER 3

THE SECRET OF WORK

Helping others physically, by removing their physical needs, is indeed great, but the help is great according as the need is greater and according as the help is far-reaching. If a man's wants can be removed for an hour, it is helping him indeed; if his wants can be removed for a year, it will be more help to him; but if his wants can be removed for ever, it is surely the greatest help that can be given him. Spiritual knowledge is the only thing that can destroy our miseries for ever; any other knowledge satisfies wants only for a time. It is only with the knowledge of the spirit that the faculty of want is annihilated for ever; so helping man spiritually is the highest help that can be given to him. He who gives man spiritual knowledge is the greatest benefactor of mankind and as such we always find that those were the most powerful of men who helped man in his spiritual needs, because spirituality is the true basis of all our activities in life. A spiritually strong and sound man will be strong in every other respect, if he so wishes. Until there is spiritual strength in man even physical needs cannot be well satisfied. Next to spiritual comes intellectual help. The gift of knowledge is a far higher gift than that of food and clothes; it is even higher than giving life to a man, because the real life of man consists of knowledge. Ignorance is death, knowledge is life. Life is of very little value, if it is a life in the dark, groping through ignorance and misery. Next in order comes, of course, helping a man physically. Therefore, in considering the question of helping others, we must always strive not to commit the mistake of thinking that physical help is the only help that can be given. It is not only the last but the least, because it cannot bring about permanent satisfaction. The misery that I feel when I am hungry is satisfied by eating, but hunger returns; my misery can cease only when I am satisfied beyond all want. Then hunger will not make me miserable; no distress, no sorrow will be able to move me. So, that help which tends to make us strong spiritually is the highest, next to it comes intellectual help, and after that physical help.

The miseries of the world cannot be cured by physical help only. Until man's nature changes, these physical needs will always arise, and miseries will always be felt, and no amount of physical help will cure them completely. The only solution of this problem is to make mankind pure. Ignorance is the mother of all the evil and all the misery we see. Let men have light, let them be pure and spiritually strong and educated, then alone will misery cease in the world, not before. We may convert every house in the country into a charity asylum, we may fill the land with hospitals, but the misery of man will still continue to exist until man's character changes.

We read in the Bhagavad Gita again and again that we must all work incessantly. All work is by nature composed of good and evil. We cannot do any work which will not do some good somewhere; there cannot be any work which will not cause some harm somewhere. Every work must necessarily be a mixture of good and evil; yet we are commanded to work incessantly. Good and evil will both have their results, will produce their Karma. Good action will entail upon us good effect; bad action, bad. But good and bad are both bondages of the soul. The solution reached in the Gita in regard to this bondage-producing nature of work is that, if we do not attach ourselves to the work we do, it will not have any binding effect on our soul. We shall try to understand what is meant by this "non-attachment to" to work.

This is the one central idea in the Gita: work incessantly, but be not attached to it. Samskāra can be translated very nearly by "inherent tendency". Using the simile of a lake for the mind, every ripple, every wave that rises in the mind, when it subsides, does not die out entirely, but leaves a mark and a future possibility of that wave coming out again. This mark, with the possibility of the wave reappearing, is what is called Samskāra. Every work that we do, every movement of the body, every thought that we think, leaves such an impression on the mind-stuff, and even when such impressions are not obvious on the surface, they are sufficiently strong to work beneath the surface, subconsciously. What we are every moment is determined by the sum total of these impressions on the mind. What I am just at this moment is the effect of the sum total of all the impressions of my past life. This is really what is meant by character; each man's character is determined by the sum total of these impressions. If good impressions prevail, the character becomes good; if bad, it becomes bad. If a man continuously hears bad words, thinks bad thoughts, does bad actions, his mind will be full of bad impressions; and they will influence his thought and work without his being conscious of the fact. In fact, these bad impressions are always working, and their resultant must be evil, and that man will be a bad man; he cannot help it. The sum total of these impressions in him will create the strong motive power for doing bad actions. He will be like a machine in the hands of his impressions, and they will force him to do evil. Similarly, if a man thinks good thoughts and does good works, the sum total of these impressions will be good; and they, in a similar manner, will force him to do good even in spite of himself. When a man has done so much good work and thought so many good thoughts that there is an irresistible tendency in him to do good in spite of himself and even if he wishes to do evil, his mind, as the sum total of his tendencies, will not allow him to do so; the tendencies will turn him back; he is completely under the influence of the good tendencies. When such is the case, a man's good character is said to be established.

As the tortoise tucks its feet and head inside the shell, and you may kill it and break it in pieces, and yet it will not come out, even so the character of that man who has control over his motives and organs is unchangeably established. He controls his own inner forces, and nothing can draw them out against his will. By this continuous reflex of good thoughts, good impressions moving over the surface of the mind, the tendency for doing good becomes strong, and as the result we feel able to control the Indriyas (the sense organs, the nerve-centres). Thus alone will character be established, then alone a man gets to truth. Such a man is safe for ever; he cannot do any evil. You may place him in any company, there will be no danger for him. There is a still higher state than having this good tendency, and that is the desire for liberation. You must remember that freedom of the soul is the goal of all Yogas, and each one equally leads to the same result. By work alone men may get to where Buddha got largely by meditation or Christ by prayer. Buddha was a working Jnāni, Christ was a Bhakta, but the same goal was reached by both of them. The difficulty is here. Liberation means entire freedom—freedom from the bondage of good, as well as from the bondage of evil. A golden chain is as much a chain as an iron one. There is a thorn in my finger, and I use another to take the first one out;

and when I have taken it out, I throw both of them aside; I have no necessity for keeping the second thorn, because both are thorns after all. So the bad tendencies are to be counteracted by the good ones, and the bad impressions on the mind should be removed by the fresh waves of good ones, until all that is evil almost disappears, or is subdued and held in control in a corner of the mind; but after that, the good tendencies have also to be conquered. Thus the "attached" becomes the "unattached". Work, but let not the action or the thought produce a deep impression on the mind. Let the ripples come and go, let huge actions proceed from the muscles and the brain, but let them not make any deep impression on the soul.

How can this be done? We see that the impression of any action, to which we attach ourselves, remains. I may meet hundreds of persons during the day, and among them meet also one whom I love; and when I retire at night, I may try to think of all the faces I saw, but only that face comes before the mind—the face which I met perhaps only for one minute, and which I loved; all the others have vanished. My attachment to this particular person caused a deeper impression on my mind than all the other faces. Physiologically the impressions have all been the same; every one of the faces that I saw pictured itself on the retina, and the brain took the pictures in, and yet there was no similarity of effect upon the mind. Most of the faces, perhaps, were entirely new faces, about which I had never thought before, but that one face of which I got only a glimpse found associations inside. Perhaps I had pictured him in my mind for years, knew hundreds of things about him, and this one new vision of him awakened hundreds of sleeping memories in my mind; and this one impression having been repeated perhaps a hundred times more than those of the different faces together, will produce a great effect on the mind.

Therefore, be "unattached"; let things work; let brain centres work; work incessantly, but let not a ripple conquer the mind. Work as if you were a stranger in this land, a sojourner; work incessantly, but do not bind yourselves; bondage is terrible. This world is not our habitation, it is only one of the many stages through which we are passing. Remember that great saying of the Sānkhya, "The whole of nature is for the soul, not the soul for nature." The very reason of nature's existence is for the education of the soul; it has no other meaning; it is there because the soul must have knowledge, and through knowledge free itself. If we remember this always, we shall never be attached to nature; we shall know that nature is a book in which we are to read, and that when we have gained the required knowledge, the book is of no more value to us. Instead of that, however, we are identifying ourselves with nature; we are thinking that the soul is for nature, that the spirit is for the flesh, and, as the common saying has it, we think that man "lives to eat" and not "eats to live". We are continually making this mistake; we are regarding nature as ourselves and are becoming attached to it; and as soon as this attachment comes, there is the deep impression on the soul, which binds us down and makes us work not from freedom but like slaves.

The whole gist of this teaching is that you should work like a master and not as a slave; work incessantly, but do not do slave's work. Do you not see how everybody works? Nobody can be altogether at rest; ninety-nine per cent of mankind work like slaves, and the result is misery; it is all selfish work. Work through freedom! Work through love! The word "love" is very difficult to understand; love never comes until there is freedom. There is no true love possible in the slave. If you buy a slave and tie him down in chains and make him work for you, he will work like a drudge, but there will be no love in him. So when we ourselves work for the things of the world as slaves, there can be no love in us, and our work is not true work. This is true of work done for relatives and friends, and is true of work done for our own selves. Selfish work is slave's work; and here is a test. Every act of love brings happiness; there is no act of love which does not bring peace and blessedness as its reaction. Real existence, real knowledge, and real love are eternally connected with one another, the three in one: where one of them is, the others also must be; they are the three aspects of the One without a second—the Existence-Knowledge-Bliss. When that existence becomes relative, we see it as the world; that knowledge becomes in its turn modified into the knowledge of the things of the world; and that bliss forms the foundation of all true love known to the heart of man. Therefore true love can never react so as to cause pain either to the lover or to the beloved. Suppose a man loves a woman; he wishes to have her all to himself and feels extremely jealous about her every movement; he wants her to sit near him, to stand near him, and to eat and move at his bidding. He is a slave to her and wishes to have her as his slave. That is not love; it is a kind of morbid affection of the slave, insinuating itself as love. It cannot be love, because it is painful; if she does not do what he wants, it brings him pain. With love there is no painful reaction; love only brings a reaction of bliss; if it does not, it is not love; it is mistaking something else for love. When you have succeeded in loving your husband, your wife, your children, the whole world, the universe, in such a manner that there is no reaction of pain or jealousy, no selfish feeling, then you are in a fit state to be unattached.

Krishna says, "Look at Me, Arjuna! If I stop from work for one moment, the whole universe will die. I have nothing to gain from work; I am the one Lord, but why do I work? Because I love the world." God is unattached because He loves; that real love makes us unattached. Wherever there is attachment, the clinging to the things of the world, you must know that it is all physical attraction between sets of particles of matter—something that attracts two bodies nearer and nearer all the time and, if they cannot get near enough, produces pain; but where there is real love, it does not rest on physical attachment at all. Such lovers may be a thousand miles away from one another, but their love will be all the same; it does not die, and will never produce any painful reaction.

To attain this unattachment is almost a life-work, but as soon as we have reached this point, we have attained the goal of love and become free; the bondage of nature falls from us, and we see nature as she is; she forges no more chains for us; we stand entirely free and take not the results of work into consideration; who then cares for what the results may be?

Do you ask anything from your children in return for what you have given them? It is your duty to work for them, and there the matter ends. In whatever you do for a particular person, a city, or a state, assume the same attitude towards it as you have towards your children—expect nothing in return. If you can invariably take the position of a giver, in which everything given by you is a free offering to the world, without any thought of return, then will your work bring you no attachment. Attachment comes only where we expect a return.

If working like slaves results in selfishness and attachment, working as master of our own mind gives rise to the bliss of non-attachment. We often talk of right and justice, but we find that in the world right and justice are mere baby's talk. There are two things which guide the conduct of men: might and mercy. The exercise of might is invariably the exercise of selfishness. All men and women try to make the most of whatever power or advantage they have. Mercy is heaven itself; to be good, we have all to be merciful. Even justice and right should stand on mercy. All thought of obtaining return for the work we do hinders our spiritual progress; nay, in the end it brings misery. There is another way in which this idea of mercy and selfless charity can be put into practice; that is, by looking upon work as "worship" in case we believe in a Personal God. Here we give up all the fruits our work unto the Lord, and worshipping Him thus, we have no right to expect anything from man kind for the work we do. The Lord Himself works incessantly and is ever without attachment. Just as water cannot wet the lotus leaf, so work cannot bind the unselfish man by giving rise to attachment to results. The selfless and unattached man may live in the very heart of a crowded and sinful city; he will not be touched by sin.

This idea of complete self-sacrifice is illustrated in the following story: After the battle of Kurukshetra the five Pāndava brothers performed a great sacrifice and made very large gifts to the poor. All people expressed amazement at the greatness and richness of the sacrifice, and said that such a sacrifice the world had never seen before. But, after the ceremony, there came a little mongoose, half of whose body was golden, and the other half brown; and he began to roll on the floor of the sacrificial hall. He said to those around, "You are all liars; this is no sacrifice." "What!" they exclaimed, "you say this is no sacrifice; do you not know how money and jewels were poured out to the poor and every one became rich and happy? This was the most wonderful sacrifice any man ever performed." But the mongoose said, "There was once a little village, and in it there dwelt a poor Brahmin with his wife, his son, and his son's wife. They were very poor and lived on small gifts made to them for preaching and teaching. There came in that land a three years' famine, and the poor Brahmin suffered more than ever. At last when the family had starved for days, the father brought home one morning a little barley flour, which he had been fortunate enough to obtain, and he divided it into four parts, one for each member of the family. They prepared it for their meal, and just as they were about to eat, there was a knock at the door. The father opened it, and there stood a guest. Now in India a guest is a sacred person; he is as a god for the time being, and must be treated as such. So the poor Brahmin said, 'Come in, sir; you are welcome,' He set before the guest his own portion of the food, which the guest quickly ate and said, 'Oh, sir, you have killed me; I have been starving for ten days, and this little bit has but increased my hunger.' Then the wife said to her husband, 'Give him my share,' but the husband said, 'Not so.' The wife however insisted, saying, 'Here is a poor man, and it is our duty as householders to see that he is fed, and it is my duty as a wife to give him my portion, seeing that you have no more to offer him.' Then she gave her share to the guest, which he ate, and said he was still burning with hunger. So the son said, 'Take my portion also; it is the duty of a son to help his father to fulfil his obligations.' The guest ate that, but remained still unsatisfied; so the son's wife gave him her portion also. That was sufficient, and the guest departed, blessing them. That night those four people died of starvation. A few granules of that flour had fallen on the floor; and when I rolled my body on them, half of it became golden, as you see. Since then I have been travelling all over the world, hoping to find another sacrifice like that, but nowhere have I found one; nowhere else has the other half of my body been turned into gold. That is why I say this is no sacrifice."

This idea of charity is going out of India; great men are becoming fewer and fewer. When I was first learning English, I read an English story book in which there was a story about a dutiful boy who had gone out to work and had given some of his money to his old mother, and this was praised in three or four pages. What was that? No Hindu boy can ever understand the moral of that story. Now I understand it when I hear the Western idea—every man for himself. And some men take everything for themselves, and fathers and mothers and wives and children go to the wall. That should never and nowhere be the ideal of the householder.

Now you see what Karma Yoga means; even at the point of death to help any one, without asking questions. Be cheated millions of times and never ask a question, and never think of what you are doing. Never vaunt of your gifts to the poor or expect their gratitude, but rather be grateful to them for giving you the occasion of practicing charity to them. Thus it is plain that to be an ideal householder is a much more difficult task than to be an ideal Sannyāsin; the true life of work is indeed as hard as, if not harder than, the equally true life of renunciation.

CHAPTER 4

WHAT IS DUTY?

It is necessary in the study of Karma Yoga to know what duty is. If I have to do something I must first know that it is my duty, and then I can do it. The idea of duty again is different in different nations. The Mohammedan says what is written in his book, the Koran, is his duty; the Hindu says what is in the Vedas is his duty; and the Christian says what is in the Bible is his duty. We find that there are varied ideas of duty, differing according to different states in life, different historical periods and different nations. The term "duty", like every other universal abstract term, is impossible clearly to define; we can only get an idea of it by knowing its practical operations and results. When certain things occur before us, we have all a natural or trained impulse to act in a certain manner towards them; when this impulse comes, the mind begins to think about the situation. Sometimes it thinks that it is good to act in a particular manner under the given conditions; at other times it thinks that it is wrong to act in the same manner even in the very same circumstances. The ordinary idea of duty everywhere is that every good man follows the dictates of his conscience. But what is it that makes an act a duty? If a Christian finds a piece of beef before him and does not eat it to save his own life, or will not give it to save the life of another man, he is sure to feel that he has not done his duty. But if a Hindu dares to eat that piece of beef or to give it to another Hindu, he is equally sure to feel that he too has not done his duty; the Hindu's training and education make him feel that way. In the last century there were notorious bands of robbers in India called thugs; they thought it their duty to kill any man they could and take away his money; the larger the number of men they killed, the better they thought they were. Ordinarily if a man goes out into the street and shoots down another man, he is apt to feel sorry for it, thinking that he has done wrong. But if the very same man, as a soldier in his regiment, kills not one but twenty, he is certain to feel glad and think that he has done his duty remarkably well. Therefore we see that it is not the thing done that defines a duty. To give an objective definition of duty is thus entirely impossible. Yet there is duty from the subjective side. Any action that makes us go Godward is a good action, and is our duty; any action that makes us go downward is evil, and is not our duty. From the subjective standpoint we may see that certain acts have a tendency to exalt and ennoble us, while certain other acts have a tendency to degrade and to brutalise us. But it is not possible to make out with certainty which acts have which kind of tendency in relation to all persons, of all sorts and conditions. There is, however, only one idea of duty which has been universally accepted by all mankind, of all ages and sects and countries, and that has been summed up in a Sanskrit aphorism thus: "Do not injure any being; not injuring any being is virtue, injuring any being is sin."

The Bhagavad Gita frequently alludes to duties dependent upon birth and position in life. Birth and position in life and in society largely determine the mental and moral attitude of individuals towards the various activities of life. It is therefore our duty to do that work which will exalt and ennoble us in accordance with the ideals and activities of the society in which we are born. But it must be particularly remembered that the same ideals and activities do not prevail in all societies and countries; our ignorance of this is the main cause of much of the hatred of one nation towards another. An American thinks that whatever an American does in accordance with the custom of his country is the best thing to do, and that whoever does not follow his custom must be a very wicked man. A Hindu thinks that his customs are the only right ones and are the best in the world, and that whosoever does not obey them must be the most wicked man living. This is quite a natural mistake which all of us are apt to make. But it is very harmful; it is the cause of half the uncharitableness found in the world. When I came to this country and was going through the Chicago Fair, a man from behind pulled at my turban. I looked back and saw that he was a very gentlemanly-looking man, neatly dressed. I spoke to him; and when he found that I knew English, he became very much abashed. On another occasion in the same Fair another man gave me a push. When I asked him the reason, he also was ashamed and stammered out an apology saying, "Why do you dress that way?" The sympathies of these men were limited within the range of their own language and their own fashion of dress. Much of the oppression of powerful nations on weaker ones is caused by this prejudice. It dries up their fellow-feeling for fellow men. That very man who asked me why I did not dress as he did and wanted to ill-treat me because of my dress may have been a very good man, a good father, and a good citizen; but the kindliness of his nature died out as soon as he saw a man in a different dress. Strangers are exploited in all countries, because they do not know how to defend themselves; thus they carry home false impressions of the peoples they have seen. Sailors, soldiers, and traders behave in foreign lands in very queer ways, although they would not dream of doing so in their own country; perhaps this is why the Chinese call Europeans and Americans "foreign devils". They could not have done this if they had met the good, the kindly sides of Western life.

Therefore the one point we ought to remember is that we should always try to see the duty of others through their own eyes, and never judge the customs of other peoples by our own standard. I am not the standard of the universe. I have to accommodate myself to the world, and not the world to me. So we see that environments change the nature of our duties, and doing the duty which is ours at any particular time is the best thing we can do in this world. Let us do that duty which is ours by birth; and when we have done that, let us do the duty which is ours by our position in life and in society. There is, however, one great danger in human nature, viz that man never examines himself. He thinks he is quite as fit to be on the throne as the king. Even if he is, he must first show that he has done the duty of his own position; and then higher duties will come to him. When we begin to work earnestly in the world, nature gives us blows right and left and soon enables us to find out our position. No man can long occupy satisfactorily a position for which he is not fit. There is no use in grumbling against nature's adjustment. He who does the lower work is not therefore a lower man. No man is to be judged by the mere nature of his duties, but all should be judged by the manner and the spirit in which they perform them.

Later on we shall find that even this idea of duty undergoes change, and that the greatest work is done only when there is no selfish motive to prompt it. Yet it is work through the sense of duty that leads us to work without any idea of duty; when work will become worship—nay, something higher—then will work be done for its own sake. We shall find that the philosophy of duty, whether it be in the form of ethics or of love, is the same as in every other Yoga—the object being the attenuating of the lower self, so that the real higher Self may shine forth—the lessening of the frittering away of energies on the lower plane of existence, so that the soul may manifest itself on the higher ones. This is accomplished by the continuous denial of low desires, which duty rigorously requires. The whole organisation of society has thus been developed, consciously or unconsciously, in the realms of action and experience, where, by limiting selfishness, we open the way to an unlimited expansion of the real nature of man.

Duty is seldom sweet. It is only when love greases its wheels that it runs smoothly; it is a continuous friction otherwise. How else could parents do their duties to their children, husbands to their wives, and vice versa? Do we not meet with cases of friction every day in our lives? Duty is sweet only through love, and love shines in freedom alone. Yet is it freedom to be a slave to the senses, to anger, to jealousies and a hundred other petty things that must occur every day in human life? In all these little roughnesses that we meet with in life, the highest expression of freedom is to forbear. Women, slaves to their own irritable, jealous tempers, are apt to blame their husbands, and assert their own "freedom", as they think, not knowing that thereby they only prove that they are slaves. So it is with husbands who eternally find fault with their wives.

Chastity is the first virtue in man or woman, and the man who, however he may have strayed away, cannot be brought to the right path by a gentle and loving and chaste wife is indeed very rare. The world is not yet as bad as that.

We hear much about brutal husbands all over the world and about the impurity of men, but is it not true that there are quite as many brutal and impure women as men? If all women were as good and pure as their own constant assertions would lead one to believe, I am perfectly satisfied that there would not be one impure man in the world. What brutality is there which purity and chastity cannot conquer? A good, chaste wife, who thinks of every other man except her own husband as her child and has the attitude of a mother towards all men, will grow so great in the power of her purity that there cannot be a single man, however brutal, who will not breathe an atmosphere of holiness in her presence. Similarly, every husband must look upon all women, except his own wife, in the light of his own mother or daughter or sister. That man, again, who wants to be a teacher of religion must look upon every woman as his mother, and always behave towards her as such.

The position of the mother is the highest in the world, as it is the one place in which to learn and exercise the greatest unselfishness. The love of God is the only love that is higher than a mother's love; all others are lower. It is the duty of the mother to think of her children first and then of herself. But, instead of that, if the parents are always thinking of themselves first, the result is that the relation between parents and children becomes the same as that between birds and their offspring which, as soon as they are fledged, do not recognise any parents. Blessed, indeed, is the man who is able to look upon woman as the representative of the motherhood of God. Blessed, indeed, is the woman to whom man represents the fatherhood of God. Blessed are the children who look upon their parents as Divinity manifested on earth.

The only way to rise is by doing the duty next to us, and thus gathering strength go on until we reach the highest state. A young Sannyāsin went to a forest; there he meditated, worshipped, and practiced Yoga for a long time. After years of hard work and practice, he was one day sitting under a tree, when some dry leaves fell upon his head. He looked up and saw a crow and a crane fighting on the top of the tree, which made him very angry. He said, "What! Dare you throw these dry leaves upon my head!" As with these words he angrily glanced at them, a flash of fire went out of his head—such was the Yogi's power—and burnt the birds to ashes. He was very glad, almost overjoyed at this development of power—he could burn the crow and the crane by a look. After a time he had to go to the town to beg his bread. He went, stood at a door, and said, "Mother, give me food." A voice came from inside the house, "Wait a little, my son." The young man thought, "You wretched woman, how dare you make me wait! You do not know my power yet." While he was thinking thus the voice came again: "Boy, don't be thinking too much of yourself. Here is neither crow nor crane." He was astonished; still he had to wait. At last the woman came, and he fell at her feet and said, "Mother, how did you know that?" She said, "My boy, I do not know your Yoga or your practices. I am a common everyday woman. I made you wait because my husband is ill, and I was nursing him. All my life I have struggled to do my duty. When I was unmarried, I did my duty to my parents; now that I am married, I do my duty to my husband; that is all the Yoga I practice. But by doing my duty I have become illumined; thus I could read your thoughts and know what you had done in the forest. If you want to know something higher than this, go to the market of such and such a town where you will find a Vyādha (The lowest class of people in India who used to live as hunters and butchers.) who will tell you something that you will be very glad to learn." The Sannyāsin thought, "Why should I go to that town and to a Vyādha?" But after what he had seen, his mind opened a little, so he went. When he came near the town, he found the market and there saw, at a distance, a big fat Vyādha cutting meat with big knives, talking and bargaining with different people. The young man said, "Lord help me! Is this the man from whom I am going to learn? He is the incarnation of a demon, if he is anything." In the meantime this man looked up and said, "O Swami, did that lady send you here? Take a seat until I have done my business." The Sannyāsin thought, "What comes to me here?" He took his seat; the man went on with his work, and after he had finished he took his money and said to the Sannyāsin, "Come sir, come to my home." On reaching home the Vyādha gave him a seat, saying, "Wait here," and went into the house. He then washed his old father and mother, fed them, and did all he could to please them, after which he came to the Sannyāsin and said, "Now, sir, you have come here to see me; what can I do for you?" The Sannyāsin asked him a few questions about soul and about God, and the Vyādha gave him a lecture which forms a part of the Mahābhārata, called the Vyādha Gita. It contains one of the highest flights of the Vedanta. When the Vyādha finished his teaching, the Sannyāsin felt astonished. He said, "Why are you in that body? With such knowledge as yours why are you in a Vyādha's body, and doing such filthy, ugly work?" "My son," replied the Vyādha, "no duty is ugly, no duty is impure. My birth placed me in these circumstances and environments. In my boyhood I learnt the trade; I am unattached, and I try to do my duty well. I try to do my duty as a householder, and I try to do all I can to make my father and mother happy. I neither know your Yoga, nor have I become a Sannyāsin, nor did I go out of the world into a forest; nevertheless, all that you have heard and seen has come to me through the unattached doing of the duty which belongs to my position."

There is a sage in India, a great Yogi, one of the most wonderful men I have ever seen in my life. He is a peculiar man, he will not teach any one; if you ask him a question he will not answer. It is too much for him to take up the position of a teacher, he will not do it. If you ask a question, and wait for some days, in the course of conversation he will bring up the subject, and wonderful light will he throw on it. He told me once the secret of work, "Let the end and the means be joined into one." When you are doing any work, do not think of anything beyond. Do it as worship, as the highest worship, and devote your whole life to it for the time being. Thus, in the story, the Vyādha and the woman did their duty with cheerfulness and whole-heartedness; and the result was that they became illuminated, clearly showing that the right performance of the duties of any station in life, without attachment to results, leads us to the highest realisation of the perfection of the soul.

It is the worker who is attached to results that grumbles about the nature of the duty which has fallen to his lot; to the unattached worker all duties are equally good, and form efficient instruments with which selfishness and sensuality may be killed, and the freedom of the soul secured. We are all apt to think too highly of ourselves. Our duties are determined by our deserts to a much larger extent than we are willing to grant. Competition rouses envy, and it kills the kindliness of the heart. To the grumbler all duties are distasteful; nothing will ever satisfy him, and his whole life is doomed to prove a failure. Let us work on, doing as we go whatever happens to be our duty, and being ever ready to put our shoulders to the wheel. Then surely shall we see the Light!

CHAPTER 5

WE HELP OURSELVES, NOT THE WORLD

Before considering further how devotion to duty helps us in our spiritual progress, let me place before you in a brief compass another aspect of what we in India mean by Karma. In every religion there are three parts: philosophy, mythology, and ritual. Philosophy of course is the essence of every religion; mythology explains and illustrates it by means of the more or less legendary lives of great men, stories and fables of wonderful things, and so on; ritual gives to that philosophy a still more concrete form, so that every one may grasp it—ritual is in fact concretised philosophy. This ritual is Karma; it is necessary in every religion, because most of us cannot understand abstract spiritual things until we grow much spiritually. It is easy for men to think that they can understand anything; but when it comes to practical experience, they find that abstract ideas are often very hard to comprehend. Therefore symbols are of great help, and we cannot dispense with the symbolical method of putting things before us. From time immemorial symbols have been used by all kinds of religions. In one sense we cannot think but in symbols; words themselves are symbols of thought. In another sense everything in the universe may be looked upon as a symbol. The whole universe is a symbol, and God is the essence behind. This kind of symbology is not simply the creation of man; it is not that certain people belonging to a religion sit down together and think out certain symbols, and bring them into existence out of their own minds. The symbols of religion have a natural growth. Otherwise, why is it that certain symbols are associated with certain ideas in the mind of almost every one? Certain symbols are universally prevalent. Many of you may think that the cross first came into existence as a symbol in connection with the Christian religion, but as a matter of fact it existed before Christianity was, before Moses was born, before the Vedas were given out, before there was any human record of human things. The cross may be found to have been in existence among the Aztecs and the Phoenicians; every race seems to have had the cross. Again, the symbol of the crucified Saviour, of a man crucified upon a cross, appears to have been known to almost every nation. The circle has been a great symbol throughout the world. Then there is the most universal of all symbols, the Swastika.

At one time it was thought that the Buddhists carried it all over the world with them, but it has been found out that ages before Buddhism it was used among nations. In Old Babylon and in Egypt it was to be found. What does this show? All these symbols could not have been purely conventional. There must be some reason for them; some natural association between them and the human mind. Language is not the result of convention; it is not that people ever agreed to represent certain ideas by certain words; there never was an idea without a corresponding word or a word without a corresponding idea; ideas and words are in their nature inseparable. The symbols to represent ideas may be sound symbols or colour symbols. Deaf and dumb people have to think with other than sound symbols. Every thought in the mind has a form as its counterpart. This is called in Sanskrit philosophy Nāma-Rupa—name and form. It is as impossible to create by convention a system of symbols as it is to create a language. In the world's ritualistic symbols we have an expression of the religious thought of humanity. It is easy to say that there is no use of rituals and temples and all such paraphernalia; every baby says that in modern times. But it must be easy for all to see that those who worship inside a temple are in many respects different from those who will not worship there. Therefore the association of particular temples, rituals, and other concrete forms with particular religions has a tendency to bring into the minds of the followers of those religions the thoughts for which those concrete things stand as symbols; and it is not wise to ignore rituals and symbology altogether. The study and practice of these things form naturally a part of Karma Yoga.

There are many other aspects of this science of work. One among them is to know the relation between thought and word and what can be achieved by the power of the word. In every religion the power of the word is recognised, so much so that in some of them creation itself is said to have come out of the word. The external aspect of the thought of God is the Word, and as God thought and willed before He created, creation came out of the Word. In this stress and hurry of our materialistic life, our nerves lose sensibility and become hardened. The older we grow, the longer we are knocked about in the world, the more callous we become; and we are apt to neglect things that even happen persistently and prominently around us. Human nature, however, asserts itself sometimes, and we are led to inquire into and wonder at some of these common occurrences; wondering thus is the first step in the acquisition of light. Apart from the higher philosophic and religious value of the Word, we may see that sound symbols play a prominent part in the drama of human life. I am talking to you. I am not touching you; the pulsations of the air caused by my speaking go into your ear, they touch your nerves and produce effects in your minds. You cannot resist this. What can be more wonderful than this? One man calls another a fool, and at this the other stands up and clenches his fist and lands a blow on his nose. Look at the power of the word! There is a woman weeping and miserable; another woman comes along and speaks to her a few gentle words, the doubled up frame of the weeping woman becomes straightened at once, her sorrow is gone and she already begins to smile. Think of the power of words! They are a great force in higher philosophy as well as in common life. Day and night we manipulate this force without thought and without inquiry. To know the nature of this force and to use it well is also a part of Karma Yoga.

Our duty to others means helping others; doing good to the world. Why should we do good to the world? Apparently to help the world, but really to help ourselves. We should always try to help the world, that should be the highest motive in us; but if we consider well, we find that the world does not require our help at all. This world was not made that you or I should come and help it. I once read a sermon in which it was said, "All this beautiful world is very good, because it gives us time and opportunity to help others." Apparently, this is a very beautiful sentiment, but is it not a blasphemy to say that the world needs our help? We cannot deny that there is much misery in it; to go out and help others is, therefore, the best thing we can do, although in the long run, we shall find that helping others is only helping ourselves. As a boy I had some white mice. They were kept in a little box in which there were little wheels, and when the mice tried to cross the wheels, the wheels turned and turned, and the mice never got anywhere. So it is with the world and our helping it. The only help is that we get moral exercise. This world is neither good nor evil; each man manufactures a world for himself. If a blind man begins to think of the world, it is either as soft or hard, or as cold or hot. We are a mass of happiness or misery; we have seen that hundreds of times in our lives. As a rule, the young are optimistic and the old pessimistic. The young have life before them; the old complain their day is gone; hundreds of desires, which they cannot fulfil struggle in their hearts. Both are foolish nevertheless. Life is good or evil according to the state of mind in which we look at it, it is neither by itself. Fire, by itself, is neither good nor evil. When it keeps us warm we say, "How beautiful is fire!" When it burns our fingers, we blame it. Still, in itself it is neither good nor bad. According as we use it, it produces in us the feeling of good or bad; so also is this world. It is perfect. By perfection is meant that it is perfectly fitted to meet its ends. We may all be perfectly sure that it will go on beautifully well without us, and we need not bother our heads wishing to help it.

Yet we must do good; the desire to do good is the highest motive power we have, if we know all the time that it is a privilege to help others. Do not stand on a high pedestal and take five cents in your hand and say, "Here, my poor man," but be grateful that the poor man is there, so that by making a gift to him you are able to help yourself. It is not the receiver that is blessed, but it is the giver. Be thankful that you are allowed to exercise your power of benevolence and mercy in the world, and thus become pure and perfect. All good acts tend to make us pure and perfect. What can we do at best? Build a hospital, make roads, or erect charity asylums. We may organise a charity and collect two or three millions of dollars, build a hospital with one million, with the second give balls and drink champagne, and of the third let the officers steal half, and leave the rest finally to reach the poor; but what are all these? One mighty wind in five minutes can break all your buildings up. What shall we do then? One volcanic eruption may sweep away all our roads and hospitals and cities and buildings. Let us give up all this foolish talk of doing good to the world. It is not waiting for your or my help; yet we must work and constantly do good, because it is a blessing to ourselves. That is the only way we can become perfect. No beggar whom we have helped has ever owed a single cent to us; we owe everything to him, because he has allowed us to exercise our charity on him. It is entirely wrong to think that we have done, or can do, good to the world, or to think that we have helped such and such people. It is a foolish thought, and all foolish thoughts bring misery. We think that we have helped some man and expect him to thank us, and because he does not, unhappiness comes to us. Why should we expect anything in return for what we do? Be grateful to the man you help, think of him as God. Is it not a great privilege to be allowed to worship God by helping our fellow men? If we were really unattached, we should escape all this pain of vain expectation, and could cheerfully do good work in the world. Never will unhappiness or misery come through work done without attachment. The world will go on with its happiness and misery through eternity.

There was a poor man who wanted some money; and somehow he had heard that if he could get hold of a ghost, he might command him to bring money or anything else he liked; so he was very anxious to get hold of a ghost. He went about searching for a man who would give him a ghost, and at last he found a sage with great powers, and besought his help. The sage asked him what he would do with a ghost. "I want a ghost to work for me; teach me how to get hold of one, sir; I desire it very much," replied the man. But the sage said, "Don't disturb yourself, go home." The next day the man went again to the sage and began to weep and pray, "Give me a ghost; I must have a ghost, sir, to help me." At last the sage was disgusted, and said, "Take this charm, repeat this magic word, and a ghost will come, and whatever you say to him he will do. But beware; they are terrible beings, and must be kept continually busy. If you fail to give him work, he will take your life." The man replied, "That is easy; I can give him work for all his life." Then he went to a forest, and after long repetition of the magic word, a huge ghost appeared before him, and said, "I am a ghost. I have been conquered by your magic; but you must keep me constantly employed. The moment you fail to give me work I will kill you." The man said, "Build me a palace," and the ghost said, "It is done; the palace is built." "Bring me money," said the man. "Here is your money," said the ghost. "Cut this forest down, and build a city in its place." "That is done," said the ghost, "anything more?" Now the man began to be frightened and thought he could give him nothing more to do; he did everything in a trice. The ghost said, "Give me something to do or I will eat you up." The poor man could find no further occupation for him, and was frightened. So he ran and ran and at last reached the sage, and said, "Oh, sir, protect my life!" The sage asked him what the matter was, and the man replied, "I have nothing to give the ghost to do. Everything I tell him to do he does in a moment, and he threatens to eat me up if I do not give him work." Just then the ghost arrived, saying, "I'll eat you up," and he would have swallowed the man. The man began to shake, and begged the sage to save his life. The sage said, "I will find you a way out. Look at that dog with a curly tail. Draw your sword quickly and cut the tail off and give it to the ghost to straighten out." The man cut off the dog's tail and gave it to the ghost, saying, "Straighten that out for me." The ghost took it and slowly and carefully straightened it out, but as soon as he let it go, it instantly curled up again. Once more he laboriously straightened it out, only to find it again curled up as soon as he attempted to let go of it. Again he patiently straightened it out, but as soon as he let it go, it curled up again. So he went on for days and days, until he was exhausted and said, "I was never in such trouble before in my life. I am an old veteran ghost, but never before was I in such trouble." "I will make a compromise with you;" he said to the man, "you let me off and I will let you keep all I have given you and will promise not to harm you." The man was much pleased, and accepted the offer gladly.

This world is like a dog's curly tail, and people have been striving to straighten it out for hundreds of years; but when they let it go, it has curled up again. How could it be otherwise? One must first know how to work without attachment, then one will not be a fanatic. When we know that this world is like a dog's curly tail and will never get straightened, we shall not become fanatics. If there were no fanaticism in the world, it would make much more progress than it does now. It is a mistake to think that fanaticism can make for the progress of mankind. On the contrary, it is a retarding element creating hatred and anger, and causing people to fight each other, and making them unsympathetic. We think that whatever we do or possess is the best in the world, and what we do not do or possess is of no value. So, always remember the instance of the curly tail of the dog whenever you have a tendency to become a fanatic. You need not worry or make yourself sleepless about the world; it will go on without you. When you have avoided fanaticism, then alone will you work well. It is the level-headed man, the calm man, of good judgment and cool nerves, of great sympathy and love, who does good work and so does good to himself. The fanatic is foolish and has no sympathy; he can never straighten the world, nor himself become pure and perfect.

To recapitulate the chief points in today's lecture: First, we have to bear in mind that we are all debtors to the world and the world does not owe us anything. It is a great privilege for all of us to be allowed to do anything for the world. In helping the world we really help ourselves. The second point is that there is a God in this universe. It is not true that this universe is drifting and stands in need of help from you and me. God is ever present therein, He is undying and eternally active and infinitely watchful. When the whole universe sleeps, He sleeps not; He is working incessantly; all the changes and manifestations of the world are His. Thirdly, we ought not to hate anyone. This world will always continue to be a mixture of good and evil. Our duty is to sympathise with the weak and to love even the wrongdoer. The world is a grand moral gymnasium wherein we have all to take exercise so as to become stronger and stronger spiritually. Fourthly, we ought not to be fanatics of any kind, because fanaticism is opposed to love. You hear fanatics glibly saying, "I do not hate the sinner. I hate the sin," but I am prepared to go any distance to see the face of that man who can really make a distinction between the sin and the sinner. It is easy to say so. If we can distinguish well between quality and substance, we may become perfect men. It is not easy to do this. And further, the calmer we are and the less disturbed our nerves, the more shall we love and the better will our work be.

CHAPTER 6

NON-ATTACHMENT IS COMPLETE SELF-ABNEGATION

Just as every action that emanates from us comes back to us as reaction, even so our actions may act on other people and theirs on us. Perhaps all of you have observed it as a fact that when persons do evil actions, they become more and more evil, and when they begin to do good, they become stronger and stronger and learn to do good at all times. This intensification of the influence of action cannot be explained on any other ground than that we can act and react upon each other. To take an illustration from physical science, when I am doing a certain action, my mind may be said to be in a certain state of vibration; all minds which are in similar circumstances will have the tendency to be affected by my mind. If there are different musical instruments tuned alike in one room, all of you may have noticed that when one is struck, the others have the tendency to vibrate so as to give the same note. So all minds that have the same tension, so to say, will be equally affected by the same thought. Of course, this influence of thought on mind will vary according to distance and other causes, but the mind is always open to affection. Suppose I am doing an evil act, my mind is in a certain state of vibration, and all minds in the universe, which are in a similar state, have the possibility of being affected by the vibration of my mind. So, when I am doing a good action, my mind is in another state of vibration; and all minds similarly strung have the possibility of being affected by my mind; and this power of mind upon mind is more or less according as the force of the tension is greater or less.

Following this simile further, it is quite possible that, just as light waves may travel for millions of years before they reach any object, so thought waves may also travel hundreds of years before they meet an object with which they vibrate in unison. It is quite possible, therefore, that this atmosphere of ours is full of such thought pulsations, both good and evil. Every thought projected from every brain goes on pulsating, as it were, until it meets a fit object that will receive it. Any mind which is open to receive some of these impulses will take them immediately. So, when a man is doing evil actions, he has brought his mind to a certain state of tension and all the waves which correspond to that state of tension, and which may be said to be already in the atmosphere, will struggle to enter into his mind. That is why an evil-doer generally goes on doing more and more evil. His actions become intensified. Such, also will be the case with the doer of good; he will open himself to all the good waves that are in the atmosphere, and his good actions also will become intensified. We run, therefore, a twofold danger in doing evil: first, we open ourselves to all the evil influences surrounding us; secondly, we create evil which affects others, may be hundreds of years hence. In doing evil we injure ourselves and others also. In doing good we do good to ourselves and to others as well; and, like all other forces in man, these forces of good and evil also gather strength from outside.

According to Karma Yoga, the action one has done cannot be destroyed until it has borne its fruit; no power in nature can stop it from yielding its results. If I do an evil action, I must suffer for it; there is no power in this universe to stop or stay it. Similarly, if I do a good action, there is no power in the universe which can stop its bearing good results. The cause must have its effect; nothing can prevent or restrain this. Now comes a very fine and serious question about Karma Yoga—namely, that these actions of ours, both good and evil, are intimately connected with each other. We cannot put a line of demarcation and say, this action is entirely good and this entirely evil. There is no action which does not bear good and evil fruits at the same time. To take the nearest example: I am talking to you, and some of you, perhaps, think I am doing good; and at the same time I am, perhaps, killing thousands of microbes in the atmosphere; I am thus doing evil to something else. When it is very near to us and affects those we know, we say that it is very good action if it affects them in a good manner. For instance, you may call my speaking to you very good, but the microbes will not; the microbes you do not see, but yourselves you do see. The way in which my talk affects you is obvious to you, but how it affects the microbes is not so obvious. And so, if we analyse our evil actions also, we may find that some good possibly results from them somewhere. He who in good action sees that there is something evil in it, and in the midst of evil sees that there is something good in it somewhere, has known the secret of work.

But what follows from it? That, howsoever we may try, there cannot be any action which is perfectly pure, or any which is perfectly impure, taking purity and impurity in the sense of injury and non-injury. We cannot breathe or live without injuring others, and every bit of the food we eat is taken away from another's mouth. Our very lives are crowding out other lives. It may be men, or animals, or small microbes, but some one or other of these we have to crowd out. That being the case, it naturally follows that perfection can never be attained by work. We may work through all eternity, but there will be no way out of this intricate maze. You may work on, and on, and on; there will be no end to this inevitable association of good and evil in the results of work.

The second point to consider is, what is the end of work? We find the vast majority of people in every country believing that there will be a time when this world will become perfect, when there will be no disease, nor death, nor unhappiness, nor wickedness. That is a very good idea, a very good motive power to inspire and uplift the ignorant; but if we think for a moment, we shall find on the very face of it that it cannot be so. How can it be, seeing that good and evil are the obverse and reverse of the same coin? How can you have good without evil at the same time? What is meant by perfection? A perfect life is a contradiction in terms. Life itself is a state of continuous struggle between ourselves and everything outside. Every moment we are fighting actually with external nature, and if we are defeated, our life has to go. It is, for instance, a continuous struggle for food and air. If food or air fails, we die. Life is not a simple and smoothly flowing thing, but it is a compound effect. This complex struggle between something inside and the external world is what we call life. So it is clear that when this struggle ceases, there will be an end of life.

What is meant by ideal happiness is the cessation of this struggle. But then life will cease, for the struggle can only cease when life itself has ceased. We have seen already that in helping the world we help ourselves. The main effect of work done for others is to purify ourselves. By means of the constant effort to do good to others we are trying to forget ourselves; this forgetfulness of self is the one great lesson we have to learn in life. Man thinks foolishly that he can make himself happy, and after years of struggle finds out at last that true happiness consists in killing selfishness and that no one can make him happy except himself. Every act of charity, every thought of sympathy, every action of help, every good deed, is taking so much of self-importance away from our little selves and making us think of ourselves as the lowest and the least, and, therefore, it is all good. Here we find that Jnāna, Bhakti, and Karma—all come to one point. The highest ideal is eternal and entire self-abnegation, where there is no "I," but all is "Thou"; and whether he is conscious or unconscious of it, Karma Yoga leads man to that end. A religious preacher may become horrified at the idea of an Impersonal God; he may insist on a Personal God and wish to keep up his own identity and individuality, whatever he may mean by that. But his ideas of ethics, if they are really good, cannot but be based on the highest self-abnegation. It is the basis of all morality; you may extend it to men, or animals, or angels, it is the one basic idea, the one fundamental principle running through all ethical systems.

You will find various classes of men in this world. First, there are the God-men, whose self-abnegation is complete, and who do only good to others even at the sacrifice of their own lives. These are the highest of men. If there are a hundred of such in any country, that country need never despair. But they are unfortunately too few. Then there are the good men who do good to others so long as it does not injure themselves. And there is a third class who, to do good to themselves, injure others. It is said by a Sanskrit poet that there is a fourth unnamable class of people who injure others merely for injury's sake.

Just as there are at one pole of existence the highest good men, who do good for the sake of doing good, so, at the other pole, there are others who injure others just for the sake of the injury. They do not gain anything thereby, but it is their nature to do evil.

Here are two Sanskrit words. The one is Pravritti, which means revolving towards, and the other is Nivritti, which means revolving away. The "revolving towards" is what we call the world, the "I and mine"; it includes all those things which are always enriching that "me" by wealth and money and power, and name and fame, and which are of a grasping nature, always tending to accumulate everything in one centre, that centre being "myself". That is the Pravritti, the natural tendency of every human being; taking everything from everywhere and heaping it around one centre, that centre being man's own sweet self. When this tendency begins to break, when it is Nivritti or "going away from," then begin morality and religion. Both Pravritti and Nivritti are of the nature of work: the former is evil work, and the latter is good work. This Nivritti is the fundamental basis of all morality and all religion, and the very perfection of it is entire self-abnegation, readiness to sacrifice mind and body and everything for another being. When a man has reached that state, he has attained to the perfection of Karma Yoga. This is the highest result of good works. Although a man has not studied a single system of philosophy, although he does not believe in any God, and never has believed, although he has not prayed even once in his whole life, if the simple power of good actions has brought him to that state where he is ready to give up his life and all else for others, he has arrived at the same point to which the religious man will come through his prayers and the philosopher through his knowledge; and so you may find that the philosopher, the worker, and the devotee, all meet at one point, that one point being self-abnegation. However much their systems of philosophy and religion may differ, all mankind stand in reverence and awe before the man who is ready to sacrifice himself for others. Here, it is not at all any question of creed, or doctrine—even men who are very much opposed to all religious ideas, when they see one of these acts of complete self-sacrifice, feel that they must revere it. Have you not seen even a most bigoted Christian, when he reads Edwin Arnold's *Light of Asia*, stand in reverence of Buddha, who Preached no God, preached nothing but self-sacrifice? The only thing is that the bigot does not know that his own end and aim in life is exactly the same as that of those from whom he differs. The worshipper, by keeping constantly before him the idea of God and a surrounding of good, comes to the same point at last and says, "Thy will be done," and keeps nothing to himself. That is self-abnegation. The philosopher, with his knowledge, sees that the seeming self is a delusion and easily gives it up. It is self-abnegation. So Karma, Bhakti, and Jnāna all meet here; and this is what was meant by all the great preachers of ancient times, when they taught that God is not the world. There is one thing which is the world and another which is God; and this distinction is very true. What they mean by world is selfishness. Unselfishness is God. One may live on a throne, in a golden palace, and be perfectly unselfish; and then he is in God. Another may live in a hut and wear rags, and have nothing in the world; yet, if he is selfish, he is intensely merged in the world.

To come back to one of our main points, we say that we cannot do good without at the same time doing some evil, or do evil without doing some good. Knowing this, how can we work? There have, therefore, been sects in this world who have in an astoundingly preposterous way preached slow suicide as the only means to get out of the world, because if a man lives, he has to kill poor little animals and plants or do injury to something or some one. So according to them the only way out of the world is to die. The Jains have preached this doctrine as their highest ideal. This teaching seems to be very logical. But the true solution is found in the Gita. It is the theory of non-attachment, to be attached to nothing while doing our work of life. Know that you are separated entirely from the world, though you are in the world, and that whatever you may be doing in it, you are not doing that for your own sake. Any action that you do for yourself will bring its effect to bear upon you. If it is a good action, you will have to take the good effect, and if bad, you will have to take the bad effect; but any action that is not done for your own sake, whatever it be, will have no effect on you. There is to be found a very expressive sentence in our scriptures embodying this idea: "Even if he kill the whole universe (or be himself killed), he is neither the killer nor the killed, when he knows that he is not acting for himself at all." Therefore Karma Yoga teaches, "Do not give up the world; live in the world, imbibe its influences as much as you can; but if it be for your own enjoyment's sake, work not at all." Enjoyment should not be the goal. First kill your self and then take the whole world as yourself; as the old Christians used to say, "The old man must die." This old man is the selfish idea that the whole world is made for our enjoyment. Foolish parents teach their children to pray, "O Lord, Thou hast created this sun for me and this moon for me," as if the Lord has had nothing else to do than to create everything for these babies. Do not teach your children such nonsense. Then again, there are people who are foolish in another way: they teach us that all these animals were created for us to kill and eat, and that this universe is for the enjoyment of men. That is all foolishness. A tiger may say, "Man was created for me" and pray, "O Lord, how wicked are these men who do not come and place themselves before me to be eaten; they are breaking Your law." If the world is created for us, we are also created for the world. That this world is created for our enjoyment is the most wicked idea that holds us down. This world is not for our sake. Millions pass out of it every year; the world does not feel it; millions of others are supplied in their place. Just as much as the world is for us, so we also are for the world.

To work properly, therefore, you have first to give up the idea of attachment. Secondly, do not mix in the fray, hold yourself as a witness and go on working. My master used to say, "Look upon your children as a nurse does." The nurse will take your baby and fondle it and play with it and behave towards it as gently as if it were her own child; but as soon as you give her notice to quit, she is ready to start off bag and baggage from the house. Everything in the shape of attachment is forgotten; it will not give the ordinary nurse the least pang to leave your children and take up other children. Even so are you to be with all that you consider your own. You are the nurse, and if you believe in God, believe that all these things which you consider yours are really His. The greatest weakness often insinuates itself as the greatest good and strength. It is a weakness to think that any one is dependent on me, and that I can do good to another. This belief is the mother of all our attachment, and through this attachment comes all our pain. We must inform our minds that no one in this universe depends upon us; not one beggar depends on our charity; not one soul on our kindness; not one living thing on our help. All are helped on by nature, and will be so helped even though millions of us were not here. The course of nature will not stop for such as you and me; it is, as already pointed out, only a blessed privilege to you and to me that we are allowed, in the way of helping others, to educate ourselves. This is a great lesson to learn in life, and when we have learned it fully, we shall never be unhappy; we can go and mix without harm in society anywhere and everywhere. You may have wives and husbands, and regiments of servants, and kingdoms to govern; if only you act on the principle that the world is not for you and does not inevitably need you, they can do you no harm. This very year some of your friends may have died. Is the world waiting without going on, for them to come again? Is its current stopped? No, it goes on. So drive out of your mind the idea that you have to do something for the world; the world does not require any help from you. It is sheer nonsense on the part of any man to think that he is born to help the world; it is simply pride, it is selfishness insinuating itself in the form of virtue. When you have trained your mind and your nerves to realise this idea of the world's non-dependence on you or on anybody, there will then be no reaction in the form of pain resulting from work. When you give something to a man and expect nothing—do not even expect the man to be grateful—his ingratitude will not tell upon you, because you never expected anything, never thought you had any right to anything in the way of a return. You gave him what he deserved; his own Karma got it for him; your Karma made you the carrier thereof. Why should you be proud of having given away something? You are the porter that carried the money or other kind of gift, and the world deserved it by its own Karma. Where is then the reason for pride in you? There is nothing very great in what you give to the world. When you have acquired the feeling of non-attachment, there will then be neither good nor evil for you. It is only selfishness that causes the difference between good and evil. It is a very hard thing to understand, but you will come to learn in time that nothing in the universe has power over you until you allow it to exercise such a power. Nothing has power over the Self of man, until the Self becomes a fool and loses independence. So, by non-attachment, you overcome and deny the power of anything to act upon you. It is very easy to say that nothing has the right to act upon you until you allow it to do so; but what is the true sign of the man who really does not allow anything to work upon him, who is neither happy nor unhappy when acted upon by the external world? The sign is that good or ill fortune causes no change in his mind: in all conditions he continues to remain the same.

There was a great sage in India called Vyāsa. This Vyāsa is known as the author of the Vedanta aphorisms, and was a holy man. His father had tried to become a very perfect man and had failed. His grandfather had also tried and failed. His great-grandfather had similarly tried and failed. He himself did not succeed perfectly, but his son, Shuka, was born perfect. Vyāsa taught his son wisdom; and after teaching him the knowledge of truth himself, he sent him to the court of King Janaka. He was a great king and was called Janaka Videha. Videha means "without a body". Although a king, he had entirely forgotten that he was a body; he felt that he was a spirit all the time. This boy Shuka was sent to be taught by him. The king knew that Vyāsa's son was coming to him to learn wisdom: so he made certain arrangements beforehand. And when the boy presented himself at the gates of the palace, the guards took no notice of him whatsoever. They only gave him a seat, and he sat there for three days and nights, nobody speaking to him, nobody asking him who he was or whence he was. He was the son of a very great sage, his father was honoured by the whole country, and he himself was a most respectable person; yet the low, vulgar guards of the palace would take no notice of him. After that, suddenly, the ministers of the king and all the big officials came there and received him with the greatest honours. They conducted him in and showed him into splendid rooms, gave him the most fragrant baths and wonderful dresses, and for eight days they kept him there in all kinds of luxury. That solemnly serene face of Shuka did not change even to the smallest extent by the change in the treatment accorded to him; he was the same in the midst of this luxury as when waiting at the door. Then he was brought before the king. The king was on his throne, music was playing, and dancing and other amusements were going on. The king then gave him a cup of milk, full to the brim, and asked him to go seven times round the hall without spilling even a drop. The boy took the cup and proceeded in the midst of the music and the attraction of the beautiful faces. As desired by the king, seven times did he go round, and not a drop of the milk was spilt. The boy's mind could not be attracted by anything in the world, unless he allowed it to affect him. And when he brought the cup to the king, the king said to him, "What your father has taught you, and what you have learned yourself, I can only repeat. You have known the Truth; go home."

Thus the man that has practiced control over himself cannot be acted upon by anything outside; there is no more slavery for him. His mind has become free. Such a man alone is fit to live well in the world. We generally find men holding two opinions regarding the world. Some are pessimists and say, "How horrible this world is, how wicked!" Some others are optimists and say, "How beautiful this world is, how wonderful!" To those who have not controlled their own minds, the world is either full of evil or at best a mixture of good and evil. This very world will become to us an optimistic world when we become masters of our own minds. Nothing will then work upon us as good or evil; we shall find everything to be in its proper place, to be harmonious. Some men, who begin by saying that the world is a hell, often end by saying that it is a heaven when they succeed in the practice of self-control. If we are genuine Karma Yogis and wish to train ourselves to that attainment of this state, wherever we may begin we are sure to end in perfect self-abnegation; and as soon as this seeming self has gone, the whole world, which at first appears to us to be filled with evil, will appear to be heaven itself and full of blessedness. Its very atmosphere will be blessed; every human face there will be god. Such is the end and aim of Karma Yoga, and such is its perfection in practical life.

Our various Yogas do not conflict with each other; each of them leads us to the same goal and makes us perfect. Only each has to be strenuously practiced. The whole secret is in practicing. First you have to hear, then think, and then practice. This is true of every Yoga. You have first to hear about it and understand what it is; and many things which you do not understand will be made clear to you by constant hearing and thinking. It is hard to understand everything at once. The explanation of everything is after all in yourself. No one was ever really taught by another; each of us has to teach himself. The external teacher offers only the suggestion which rouses the internal teacher to work to understand things. Then things will be made clearer to us by our own power of perception and thought, and we shall realise them in our own souls; and that realisation will grow into the intense power of will. First it is feeling, then it becomes willing, and out of that willing comes the tremendous force for work that will go through every vein and nerve and muscle, until the whole mass of your body is changed into an instrument of the unselfish Yoga of work, and the desired result of perfect self-abnegation and utter unselfishness is duly attained. This attainment does not depend on any dogma, or doctrine, or belief. Whether one is Christian, or Jew, or Gentile, it does not matter. Are you unselfish? That is the question. If you are, you will be perfect without reading a single religious book, without going into a single church or temple. Each one of our Yogas is fitted to make man perfect even without the help of the others, because they have all the same goal in view. The Yogas of work, of wisdom, and of devotion are all capable of serving as direct and independent means for the attainment of Moksha. "Fools alone say that work and philosophy are different, not the learned." The learned know that, though apparently different from each other, they at last lead to the same goal of human perfection.

CHAPTER 7

FREEDOM

In addition to meaning work, we have stated that psychologically the word Karma also implies causation. Any work, any action, any thought that produces an effect is called a Karma. Thus the law of Karma means the law of causation, of inevitable cause and sequence. Wheresoever there is a cause, there an effect must be produced; this necessity cannot be resisted, and this law of Karma, according to our philosophy, is true throughout the whole universe. Whatever we see, or feel, or do, whatever action there is anywhere in the universe, while being the effect of past work on the one hand, becomes, on the other, a cause in its turn, and produces its own effect. It is necessary, together with this, to consider what is meant by the word "law". By law is meant the tendency of a series to repeat itself. When we see one event followed by another, or sometimes happening simultaneously with another, we expect this sequence or co-existence to recur. Our old logicians and philosophers of the Nyāya school call this law by the name of Vyāpti. According to them, all our ideas of law are due to association. A series of phenomena becomes associated with things in our mind in a sort of invariable order, so that whatever we perceive at any time is immediately referred to other facts in the mind. Any one idea or, according to our psychology, any one wave that is produced in the mind-stuff, Chitta, must always give rise to many similar waves. This is the psychological idea of association, and causation is only an aspect of this grand pervasive principle of association. This pervasiveness of association is what is, in Sanskrit, called Vyāpti. In the external world the idea of law is the same as in the internal—the expectation that a particular phenomenon will be followed by another, and that the series will repeat itself. Really speaking, therefore, law does not exist in nature. Practically it is an error to say that gravitation exists in the earth, or that there is any law existing objectively anywhere in nature. Law is the method, the manner in which our mind grasps a series of phenomena; it is all in the mind. Certain phenomena, happening one after another or together, and followed by the conviction of the regularity of their recurrence—thus enabling our minds to grasp the method of the whole series—constitute what we call law.

The next question for consideration is what we

mean by law being universal. Our universe is that portion of existence which is characterized by what the Sanskrit psychologists call Desha-kāla-nimitta, or what is known to European psychology as space, time, and causation. This universe is only a part of infinite existence, thrown into a peculiar mould, composed of space, time, and causation. It necessarily follows that law is possible only within this conditioned universe; beyond it there cannot be any law. When we speak of the universe, we only mean that portion of existence which is limited by our mind—the universe of the senses, which we can see, feel, touch, hear, think of, imagine. This alone is under law; but beyond it existence cannot be subject to law, because causation does not extend beyond the world of our minds. Anything beyond the range of our mind and our senses is not bound by the law of causation, as there is no mental association of things in the region beyond the senses, and no causation without association of ideas. It is only when "being" or existence gets moulded into name and form that it obeys the law of causation, and is said to be under law; because all law has its essence in causation. Therefore we see at once that there cannot be any such thing as free will; the very words are a contradiction, because will is what we know, and everything that we know is within our universe, and everything within our universe is moulded by the conditions of space, time, and causation. Everything that we know, or can possibly know, must be subject to causation, and that which obeys the law of causation cannot be free. It is acted upon by other agents, and becomes a cause in its turn. But that which has become converted into the will, which was not the will before, but which, when it fell into this mould of space, time, and causation, became converted into the human will, is free; and when this will gets out of this mould of space, time, and causation, it will be free again. From freedom it comes, and becomes moulded into this bondage, and it gets out and goes back to freedom again.

The question has been raised as to from whom this universe comes, in whom it rests, and to whom it goes; and the answer has been given that from freedom it comes, in bondage it rests, and goes back into that freedom again. So, when we speak of man as no other than that infinite being which is manifesting itself, we mean that only one very small part thereof is man; this body and this mind which we see are only one part of the whole, only one spot of the infinite being. This whole universe is only one speck of the infinite being; and all our laws, our bondages, our joys and our sorrows, our happinesses and our expectations, are only within this small universe; all our progression and digression are within its small compass. So you see how childish it is to expect a continuation of this universe—the creation of our minds—and to expect to go to heaven, which after all must mean only a repetition of this world that we know. You see at once that it is an impossible and childish desire to make the whole of infinite existence conform to the limited and conditioned existence which we know. When a man says that he will have again and again this same thing which he is hating now, or, as I sometimes put it, when he asks for a *comfortable* religion, you may know that he has become so degenerate that he cannot think of anything higher than what he is now; he is just his little present surroundings and nothing more. He has forgotten his infinite nature, and his whole idea is confined to these little joys, and sorrows, and heart-jealousies of the moment. He thinks that this finite thing is the infinite; and not only so, he will not let this foolishness go. He clings on desperately unto Trishnā, and the thirst after life, what the Buddhists call Tanhā and Tissā. There may be millions of kinds of happiness, and beings, and laws, and progress, and causation, all acting outside the little universe that we know; and, after all, the whole of this comprises but one section of our infinite nature.

To acquire freedom we have to get beyond the limitations of this universe; it cannot be found here. Perfect equilibrium, or what the Christians call the peace that passeth all understanding, cannot be had in this universe, nor in heaven, nor in any place where our mind and thoughts can go, where the senses can feel, or which the imagination can conceive. No such place can give us that freedom, because all such places would be within our universe, and it is limited by space, time, and causation. There may be places that are more ethereal than this earth of ours, where enjoyments may be keener, but even those places must be in the universe and, therefore, in bondage to law; so we have to go beyond, and real religion begins where this little universe ends. These little joys, and sorrows, and knowledge of things end there, and the reality begins. Until we give up the thirst after life, the strong attachment to this our transient conditioned existence we have no hope of catching even a glimpse of that infinite freedom beyond. It stands to reason then that there is only one way to attain to that freedom which is the goal of all the noblest aspirations of mankind, and that is by giving up this little life, giving up this little universe, giving up this earth, giving up heaven, giving up the body, giving up the mind, giving up everything that is limited and conditioned. If we give up our attachment to this little universe of the senses or of the mind, we shall be free immediately. The only way to come out of bondage is to go beyond the limitations of law, to go beyond causation.

But it is a most difficult thing to give up the clinging to this universe; few ever attain to that. There are two ways to do that mentioned in our books. One is called the "Neti, Neti" (not this, not this), the other is called "Iti" (this); the former is the negative, and the latter is the positive way. The negative way is the most difficult. It is only possible to the men of the very highest, exceptional minds and gigantic wills who simply stand up and say, "No, I will not have this," and the mind and body obey their will, and they come out successful. But such people are very rare. The vast majority of mankind choose the positive way, the way through the world, making use of all the bondages themselves to break those very bondages. This is also a kind of giving up; only it is done slowly and gradually, by knowing things, enjoying things and thus obtaining experience, and knowing the nature of things until the mind lets them all go at last and becomes unattached. The former way of obtaining non-attachment is by reasoning, and the latter way is through work and experience. The first is the path of Jnāna Yoga, and is characterized by the refusal to do any work; the second is that of Karma Yoga, in which there is no cessation from work. Every one must work in the universe. Only those who are perfectly satisfied with the Self, whose desires do not go beyond the Self, whose mind never strays out of the Self, to whom the Self is all in all, only those do not work. The rest must work. A current rushing down of its own nature falls into a hollow and makes a whirlpool, and, after running a little in that whirlpool, it emerges again in the form of the free current to go on unchecked. Each human life is like that current. It gets into the whirl, gets involved in this world of space, time, and causation, whirls round a little, crying out, "my father, my brother, my name, my fame", and so on, and at last emerges out of it and regains its original freedom. The whole universe is doing that. Whether we know it or not, whether we are conscious or unconscious of it, we are all working to get out of the dream of the world. Man's experience in the world is to enable him to get out of its whirlpool.

What is Karma Yoga? The knowledge of the secret of work. We see that the whole universe is working. For what? For salvation, for liberty; from the atom to the highest being, working for the one end, liberty for the mind, for the body, for the spirit. All things are always trying to get freedom, flying away from bondage. The sun, the moon, the earth, the planets, all are trying to fly away from bondage. The centrifugal and the centripetal forces of nature are indeed typical of our universe. Instead of being knocked about in this universe, and after long delay and thrashing, getting to know things as they are, we learn from Karma Yoga the secret of work, the method of work, the organising power of work. A vast mass of energy may be spent in vain if we do not know how to utilise it. Karma Yoga makes a science of work; you learn by it how best to utilise all the workings of this world. Work is inevitable, it must be so; but we should work to the highest purpose. Karma Yoga makes us admit that this world is a world of five minutes, that it is a something we have to pass through; and that freedom is not here, but is only to be found beyond. To find the way out of the bondages of the world we have to go through it slowly and surely. There may be those exceptional persons about whom I just spoke, those who can stand aside and give up the world, as a snake casts off its skin and stands aside and looks at it. There are no doubt these exceptional beings; but the rest of mankind have to go slowly through the world of work. Karma Yoga shows the process, the secret, and the method of doing it to the best advantage.

What does it say? "Work incessantly, but give up all attachment to work." Do not identify yourself with anything. Hold your mind free. All this that you see, the pains and the miseries, are but the necessary conditions of this world; poverty and wealth and happiness are but momentary; they do not belong to our real nature at all. Our nature is far beyond misery and happiness, beyond every object of the senses, beyond the imagination; and yet we must go on working all the time. "Misery comes through attachment, not through work." As soon as we identify ourselves with the work we do, we feel miserable; but if we do not identify ourselves with it, we do not feel that misery. If a beautiful picture belonging to another is burnt, a man does not generally become miserable; but when his own picture is burnt, how miserable he feels! Why? Both were beautiful pictures, perhaps copies of the same original; but in one case very much more misery is felt than in the other. It is because in one case he identifies himself with the picture, and not in the other. This "I and mine" causes the whole misery. With the sense of possession comes selfishness, and selfishness brings on misery. Every act of selfishness or thought of selfishness makes us attached to something, and immediately we are made slaves. Each wave in the Chitta that says "I and mine" immediately puts a chain round us and makes us slaves; and the more we say "I and mine", the more slavery grows, the more misery increases. Therefore Karma Yoga tells us to enjoy the beauty of all the pictures in the world, but not to identify ourselves with any of them. Never say "mine". Whenever we say a thing is "mine", misery will immediately come. Do not even say "my child" in your mind. Possess the child, but do not say "mine". If you do, then will come the misery. Do not say "my house," do not say "my body". The whole difficulty is there. The body is neither yours, nor mine, nor anybody's. These bodies are coming and going by the laws of nature, but we are free, standing as witness. This body is no more free than a picture or a wall. Why should we be attached so much to a body? If somebody paints a picture, he does it and passes on. Do not project that tentacle of selfishness, "I must possess it". As soon as that is projected, misery will begin.

So Karma Yoga says, first destroy the tendency to project this tentacle of selfishness, and when you have the power of checking it, hold it in and do not allow the mind to get into the ways of selfishness. Then you may go out into the world and work as much as you can. Mix everywhere, go where you please; you will never be contaminated with evil. There is the lotus leaf in the water; the water cannot touch and adhere to it; so will you be in the world. This is called "Vairāgya", dispassion or non-attachment. I believe I have told you that without non-attachment there cannot be any kind of Yoga. Non-attachment is the basis of all the Yogas. The man who gives up living in houses, wearing fine clothes, and eating good food, and goes into the desert, may be a most attached person. His only possession, his own body, may become everything to him; and as he lives he will be simply struggling for the sake of his body. Non-attachment does not mean anything that we may do in relation to our external body, it is all in the mind. The binding link of "I and mine" is in the mind. If we have not this link with the body and with the things of the senses, we are non-attached, wherever and whatever we may be. A man may be on a throne and perfectly non-attached; another man may be in rags and still very much attached. First, we have to attain this state of non-attachment and then to work incessantly. Karma Yoga gives us the method that will help us in giving up all attachment, though it is indeed very hard.

Here are the two ways of giving up all attachment. The one is for those who do not believe in God, or in any outside help. They are left to their own devices; they have simply to work with their own will, with the powers of their mind and discrimination, saying, "I must be non-attached". For those who believe in God there is another way, which is much less difficult. They give up the fruits of work unto the Lord; they work and are never attached to the results. Whatever they see, feel, hear, or do, is for Him. For whatever good work we may do, let us not claim any praise or benefit. It is the Lord's; give up the fruits unto Him. Let us stand aside and think that we are only servants obeying the Lord, our Master, and that every impulse for action comes from Him every moment. Whatever thou worshippest, whatever thou perceivest, whatever thou doest, give up all unto Him and be at rest. Let us be at peace, perfect peace, with ourselves, and give up our whole body and mind and everything as an eternal sacrifice unto the Lord. Instead of the sacrifice of pouring oblations into the fire, perform this one great sacrifice day and night—the sacrifice of your little self. "In search of wealth in this world, Thou art the only wealth I have found; I sacrifice myself unto Thee. In search of some one to be loved, Thou art the only one beloved I have found; I sacrifice myself unto Thee." Let us repeat this day and night, and say, "Nothing for me; no matter whether the thing is good, bad, or indifferent; I do not care for it; I sacrifice all unto Thee." Day and night let us renounce our seeming self until it becomes a habit with us to do so, until it gets into the blood, the nerves, and the brain, and the whole body is every moment obedient to this idea of self-renunciation. Go then into the midst of the battlefield, with the roaring cannon and the din of war, and you will find yourself to be free and at peace.

Karma Yoga teaches us that the ordinary idea of duty is on the lower plane; nevertheless, all of us have to do our duty. Yet we may see that this peculiar sense of duty is very often a great cause of misery. Duty becomes a disease with us; it drags us ever forward. It catches hold of us and makes our whole life miserable. It is the bane of human life. This duty, this idea of duty is the midday summer sun which scorches the innermost soul of mankind. Look at those poor slaves to duty! Duty leaves them no time to say prayers, no time to bathe. Duty is ever on them. They go out and work. Duty is on them! They come home and think of the work for the next day. Duty is on them! It is living a slave's life, at last dropping down in the street and dying in harness, like a horse. This is duty as it is understood. The only true duty is to be unattached and to work as free beings, to give up all work unto God. All our duties are His. Blessed are we that we are ordered out here. We serve our time; whether we do it ill or well, who knows? If we do it well, we do not get the fruits. If we do it ill, neither do we get the care. Be at rest, be free, and work. This kind of freedom is a very hard thing to attain. How easy it is to interpret slavery as duty—the morbid attachment of flesh for flesh as duty! Men go out into the world and struggle and fight for money or for any other thing to which they get attached. Ask them why they do it. They say, "It is a duty". It is the absurd greed for gold and gain, and they try to cover it with a few flowers.

What is duty after all? It is really the impulsion of the flesh, of our attachment; and when an attachment has become established, we call it duty. For instance, in countries where there is no marriage, there is no duty between husband and wife; when marriage comes, husband and wife live together on account of attachment; and that kind of living together becomes settled after generations; and when it becomes so settled, it becomes a duty. It is, so to say, a sort of chronic disease. When it is acute, we call it disease; when it is chronic, we call it nature. It is a disease. So when attachment becomes chronic, we baptise it with the high sounding name of duty. We strew flowers upon it, trumpets sound for it, sacred texts are said over it, and then the whole world fights, and men earnestly rob each other for this duty's sake. Duty is good to the extent that it checks brutality. To the lowest kinds of men, who cannot have any other ideal, it is of some good; but those who want to be Karma Yogis must throw this idea of duty overboard. There is no duty for you and me. Whatever you have to give to the world, do give by all means, but not as a duty. Do not take any thought of that. Be not compelled. Why should you be compelled? *Everything that you do under compulsion goes to build up attachment.* Why should you have any duty? Resign everything unto God. In this tremendous fiery furnace where the fire of duty scorches everybody, drink this cup of nectar and be happy. We are all simply working out His will, and have nothing to do with rewards and punishments. If you want the reward, you must also have the punishment; the only way to get out of the punishment is to give up the reward. The only way of getting out of misery is by giving up the idea of happiness, because these two are linked to each other. On one side there is happiness, on the other there is misery. On one side there is life, on the other there is death. The only way to get beyond death is to give up the love of life. Life and death are the same thing, looked at from different points. So the idea of happiness without misery, or of life without death, is very good for schoolboys and children; but the thinker sees that it is all a contradiction in terms and gives up both. Seek no praise, no reward, for anything you do. No sooner do we perform a good action than we begin to desire credit for it. No sooner do we give money to some charity than we want to see our names blazoned in the papers. Misery must come as the result of such desires. The greatest men in the world have passed away unknown. The Buddhas and the Christs that we know are but second-rate heroes in comparison with the greatest men of whom the world knows nothing. Hundreds of these unknown heroes have lived in every country working silently. Silently they live and silently they pass away; and in time their thoughts find expression in Buddhas or Christs, and it is these latter that become known to us. The highest men do not seek to get any name or fame from their knowledge. They leave their ideas to the world; they put forth no claims for themselves and establish no schools or systems in their name. Their whole nature shrinks from such a thing. They are the pure Sāttvikas, who can never make any stir, but only melt down in love. I have seen one such Yogi who lives in a cave in India. He is one of the most wonderful men I have ever seen. He has so completely lost the sense of his own individuality that we may say that the man in him is completely gone, leaving behind only the all comprehending sense of the divine. If an animal bites one of his arms, he is ready to give it his other arm also, and say that it is the Lord's will. Everything that comes to him is from the Lord. He does not show himself to men, and yet he is a magazine of love and of true and sweet ideas.

Next in order come the men with more Rājas, or activity, combative natures, who take up the ideas of the perfect ones and preach them to the world. The highest kind of men silently collect true and noble ideas, and others—the Buddhas and Christs—go from place to place preaching them and working for them. In the life of Gautama Buddha we notice him constantly saying that he is the twenty-fifth Buddha. The twenty-four before him are unknown to history, although the Buddha known to history must have built upon foundations laid by them. The highest men are calm, silent, and unknown. They are the men who really know the power of thought; they are sure that, even if they go into a cave and close the door and simply think five true thoughts and then pass away, these five thoughts of theirs will live through eternity. Indeed such thoughts will penetrate through the mountains, cross the oceans, and travel through the world. They will enter deep into human hearts and brains and raise up men and women who will give them practical expression in the workings of human life. These Sattvika men are too near the Lord to be active and to fight, to be working, struggling, preaching and doing good, as they say, here on earth to humanity. The active workers, however good, have still a little remnant of ignorance left in them. When our nature has yet some impurities left in it, then alone can we work. It is in the nature of work to be impelled ordinarily by motive and by attachment. In the presence of an ever active Providence who notes even the sparrow's fall, how can man attach any importance to his own work? Will it not be a blasphemy to do so when we know that He is taking care of the minutest things in the world? We have only to stand in awe and reverence before Him saying, "Thy will be done". The highest men cannot work, for in them there is no attachment. Those whose whole soul is gone into the Self, those whose desires are confined in the Self, who have become ever associated with the Self, for them there is no work. Such are indeed the highest of mankind; but apart from them every one else has to work. In so working we should never think that we can help on even the least thing in this universe. We cannot. We only help ourselves in this gymnasium of the world. This is the proper attitude of work. If we work in this way, if we always remember that our present opportunity to work thus is a privilege which has been given to us, we shall never be attached to anything.

Millions like you and me think that we are great people in the world; but we all die, and in five minutes the world forgets us. But the life of God is infinite. "Who can live a moment, breathe a moment, if this all-powerful One does not will it?" He is the ever active Providence. All power is His and within His command. Through His command the winds blow, the sun shines, the earth lives, and death stalks upon the earth. He is the all in all; He is all and in all. We can only worship Him. Give up all fruits of work; do good for its own sake; then alone will come perfect non-attachment. The bonds of the heart will thus break, and we shall reap perfect freedom. This freedom is indeed the goal of Karma Yoga.

CHAPTER 8

THE IDEAL OF KARMA YOGA

The grandest idea in the religion of the Vedanta is that we may reach the same goal by different paths; and these paths I have generalised into four, viz those of work, love, psychology, and knowledge. But you must, at the same time, remember that these divisions are not very marked and quite exclusive of each other. Each blends into the other. But according to the type which prevails, we name the divisions. It is not that you can find men who have no other faculty than that of work, nor that you can find men who are no more than devoted worshippers only, nor that there are men who have no more than mere knowledge. These divisions are made in accordance with the type or the tendency that may be seen to prevail in a man. We have found that, in the end, all these four paths converge and become one. All religions and all methods of work and worship lead us to one and the same goal.

I have already tried to point out that goal. It is freedom as I understand it. Everything that we perceive around us is struggling towards freedom, from the atom to the man, from the insentient, lifeless particle of matter to the highest existence on earth, the human soul. The whole universe is in fact the result of this struggle for freedom. In all combinations every particle is trying to go on its own way, to fly from the other particles; but the others are holding it in check. Our earth is trying to fly away from the sun, and the moon from the earth. Everything has a tendency to infinite dispersion. All that we see in the universe has for its basis this one struggle towards freedom; it is under the impulse of this tendency that the saint prays and the robber robs. When the line of action taken is not a proper one, we call it evil; and when the manifestation of it is proper and high, we call it good. But the impulse is the same, the struggle towards freedom. The saint is oppressed with the knowledge of his condition of bondage, and he wants to get rid of it; so he worships God. The thief is oppressed with the idea that he does not possess certain things, and he tries to get rid of that want, to obtain freedom from it; so he steals. Freedom is the one goal of all nature, sentient or insentient; and consciously or unconsciously, everything is struggling towards that goal. The freedom which the saint seeks is very different from that which the robber seeks; the freedom loved by the saint leads him to the enjoyment of infinite, unspeakable bliss, while that on which the robber has set his heart only forges other bonds for his soul.

There is to be found in every religion the manifestation of this struggle towards freedom. It is the groundwork of all morality, of unselfishness, which means getting rid of the idea that men are the same as their little body. When we see a man doing good work, helping others, it means that he cannot be confined within the limited circle of "me and mine". There is no limit to this getting out of selfishness. All the great systems of ethics preach absolute unselfishness as the goal. Supposing this absolute unselfishness can be reached by a man, what becomes of him? He is no more the little Mr. So-and-so; he has acquired infinite expansion. The little personality which he had before is now lost to him for ever; he has become infinite, and the attainment of this infinite expansion is indeed the goal of all religions and of all moral and philosophical teachings. The personalist, when he hears this idea philosophically put, gets frightened. At the same time, if he preaches morality, he after all teaches the very same idea himself. He puts no limit to the unselfishness of man. Suppose a man becomes perfectly unselfish under the personalistic system, how are we to distinguish him from the perfected ones in other system? He has become one with the universe and to become that is the goal of all; only the poor personalist has not the courage to follow out his own reasoning to its right conclusion. Karma Yoga is the attaining through unselfish work of that freedom which is the goal of all human nature. Every selfish action, therefore, retards our reaching the goal, and every unselfish action takes us towards the goal; that is why the only definition that can be given of morality is this: That which is selfish is immoral, and that which is unselfish is moral.

But, if you come to details, the matter will not be seen to be quite so simple. For instance, environment often makes the details different as I have already mentioned. The same action under one set of circumstances may be unselfish, and under another set quite selfish. So we can give only a general definition, and leave the details to be worked out by taking into consideration the differences in time, place, and circumstances. In one country one kind of conduct is considered moral, and in another the very same is immoral, because the circumstances differ. The goal of all nature is freedom, and freedom is to be attained only by perfect unselfishness; every thought, word, or deed that is unselfish takes us towards the goal, and, as such, is called moral. That definition, you will find, holds good in every religion and every system of ethics. In some systems of thought morality is derived from a Superior Being—God. If you ask why a man ought to do this and not that, their answer is: "Because such is the command of God." But whatever be the source from which it is derived, their code of ethics also has the same central idea—not to think of self but to give up self. And yet some persons, in spite of this high ethical idea, are frightened at the thought of having to give up their little personalities. We may ask the man who clings to the idea of little personalities to consider the case of a person who has become perfectly unselfish, who has no thought for himself, who does no deed for himself, who speaks no word for himself, and then say where his "himself" is. That "himself" is known to him only so long as he thinks, acts, or speaks for himself. If he is only conscious of others, of the universe, and of the all, where is his "himself"? It is gone for ever.

Karma Yoga, therefore, is a system of ethics and religion intended to attain freedom through unselfishness, and by good works. The Karma Yogi need not believe in any doctrine whatever. He may not believe even in God, may not ask what his soul is, nor think of any metaphysical speculation. He has got his own special aim of realising selflessness; and he has to work it out himself. Every moment of his life must be realisation, because he has to solve by mere work, without the help of doctrine or theory, the very same problem to which the Jnāni applies his reason and inspiration and the Bhakta his love.

Now comes the next question: What is this work? What is this doing good to the world? Can we do good to the world? In an absolute sense, no; in a relative sense, yes. No permanent or everlasting good can be done to the world; if it could be done, the world would not be this world. We may satisfy the hunger of a man for five minutes, but he will be hungry again. Every pleasure with which we supply a man may be seen to be momentary. No one can permanently cure this ever-recurring fever of pleasure and pain. Can any permanent happiness be given to the world? In the ocean we cannot raise a wave without causing a hollow somewhere else. The sum total of the good things in the world has been the same throughout in its relation to man's need and greed. It cannot be increased or decreased. Take the history of the human race as we know it today. Do we not find the same miseries and the same happiness, the same pleasures and pains, the same differences in position? Are not some rich, some poor, some high, some low, some healthy, some unhealthy? All this was just the same with the Egyptians, the Greeks, and the Romans in ancient times as it is with the Americans today. So far as history is known, it has always been the same; yet at the same time we find that, running along with all these incurable differences of pleasure and pain, there has ever been the struggle to alleviate them. Every period of history has given birth to thousands of men and women who have worked hard to smooth the passage of life for others. And how far have they succeeded? We can only play at driving the ball from one place to another. We take away pain from the physical plane, and it goes to the mental one. It is like that picture in Dante's hell where the misers were given a mass of gold to roll up a hill. Every time they rolled it up a little, it again rolled down. All our talks about the millennium are very nice as schoolboys' stories, but they are no better than that. All nations that dream of the millennium also think that, of all peoples in the world, they will have the best of it then for themselves. This is the wonderfully unselfish idea of the millennium!

We cannot add happiness to this world; similarly, we

cannot add pain to it either. The sum total of the energies of pleasure and pain displayed here on earth will be the same throughout. We just push it from this side to the other side, and from that side to this, but it will remain the same, because to remain so is its very nature. This ebb and flow, this rising and falling, is in the world's very nature; it would be as logical to hold otherwise as to say that we may have life without death. This is complete nonsense, because the very idea of life implies death and the very idea of pleasure implies pain. The lamp is constantly burning out, and that is its life. If you want to have life, you have to die every moment for it. Life and death are only different expressions of the same thing looked at from different standpoints; they are the falling and the rising of the same wave, and the two form one whole. One looks at the "fall" side and becomes a pessimist another looks at the "rise" side and becomes an optimist. When a boy is going to school and his father and mother are taking care of him, everything seems blessed to him; his wants are simple, he is a great optimist. But the old man, with his varied experience, becomes calmer and is sure to have his warmth considerably cooled down. So, old nations, with signs of decay all around them, are apt to be less hopeful than new nations. There is a proverb in India: "A thousand years a city, and a thousand years a forest." This change of city into forest and vice versa is going on everywhere, and it makes people optimists or pessimists according to the side they see of it.

The next idea we take up is the idea of equality.

These millennium ideas have been great motive powers to work. Many religions preach this as an element in them—that God is coming to rule the universe, and that then there will be no difference at all in conditions. The people who preach this doctrine are mere fanatics, and fanatics are indeed the sincerest of mankind. Christianity was preached just on the basis of the fascination of this fanaticism, and that is what made it so attractive to the Greek and the Roman slaves. They believed that under the millennial religion there would be no more slavery, that there would be plenty to eat and drink; and, therefore, they flocked round the Christian standard. Those who preached the idea first were of course ignorant fanatics, but very sincere. In modern times this millennial aspiration takes the form of equality—of liberty, equality, and fraternity. This is also fanaticism. True equality has never been and never can be on earth. How can we all be equal here? This impossible kind of equality implies total death. What makes this world what it is? Lost balance. In the primal state, which is called chaos, there is perfect balance. How do all the formative forces of the universe come then? By struggling, competition, conflict. Suppose that all the particles of matter were held in equilibrium, would there be then any process of creation? We know from science that it is impossible. Disturb a sheet of water, and there you find every particle of the water trying to become calm again, one rushing against the other; and in the same way all the phenomena which we call the universe—all things therein—are struggling to get back to the state of perfect balance. Again a disturbance comes, and again we have combination and creation. Inequality is the very basis of creation. At the same time the forces struggling to obtain equality are as much a necessity of creation as those which destroy it.

Absolute equality, that which means a perfect balance of all the struggling forces in all the planes, can never be in this world. Before you attain that state, the world will have become quite unfit for any kind of life, and no one will be there. We find, therefore, that all these ideas of the millennium and of absolute equality are not only impossible but also that, if we try to carry them out, they will lead us surely enough to the day of destruction. What makes the difference between man and man? It is largely the difference in the brain. Nowadays no one but a lunatic will say that we are all born with the same brain power. We come into the world with unequal endowments; we come as greater men or as lesser men, and there is no getting away from that pre-natally determined condition. The American Indians were in this country for thousands of years, and a few handfuls of your ancestors came to their land. What difference they have caused in the appearance of the country! Why did not the Indians make improvements and build cities, if all were equal? With your ancestors a different sort of brain power came into the land, different bundles of past impressions came, and they worked out and manifested themselves. Absolute non-differentiation is death. So long as this world lasts, differentiation there will and must be, and the millennium of perfect equality will come only when a cycle of creation comes to its end. Before that, equality cannot be. Yet this idea of realising the millennium is a great motive power. Just as inequality is necessary for creation itself, so the struggle to limit it is also necessary. If there were no struggle to become free and get back to God, there would be no creation either. It is the difference between these two forces that determines the nature of the motives of men. There will always be these motives to work, some tending towards bondage and others towards freedom.

This world's wheel within wheel is a terrible mechanism; if we put our hands in it, as soon as we are caught we are gone. We all think that when we have done a certain duty, we shall be at rest; but before we have done a part of that duty, another is already in waiting. We are all being dragged along by this mighty, complex world-machine. There are only two ways out of it; one is to give up all concerns with the machine, to let it go and stand aside, to give up our desires. That is very easy to say, but is almost impossible to do. I do not know whether in twenty millions of men one can do that. The other way is to plunge into the world and learn the secret of work, and that is the way of Karma Yoga. Do not fly away from the wheels of the world-machine, but stand inside it and learn the secret of work. Through proper work done inside, it is also possible to come out. Through this machinery itself is the way out.

We have now seen what work is. It is a part of natures foundation, and goes on always. Those that believe in God understand this better, because they know that God is not such an incapable being as will need our help. Although this universe will go on always, our goal is freedom, our goal is unselfishness; and according to Karma Yoga, that goal is to be reached through work. All ideas of making the world perfectly happy may be good as motive powers for fanatics; but we must know that fanaticism brings forth as much evil as good. The Karma Yogi asks why you require any motive to work other than the inborn love of freedom. Be beyond the common worldly motives. "To work you have the right, but not to the fruits thereof." Man can train himself to know and to practice that, says the Karma Yogi. When the idea of doing good becomes a part of his very being, then he will not seek for any motive outside. Let us do good because it is good to do good; he who does good work even in order to get to heaven binds himself down, says the Karma Yogi. Any work that is done with any the least selfish motive, instead of making us free, forges one more chain for our feet.

So the only way is to give up all the fruits of work, to be unattached to them. Know that this world is not we, nor are we this world; that we are really not the body; that we really do not work. We are the Self, eternally at rest and at peace. Why should we be bound by anything? It is very good to say that we should be perfectly non-attached, but what is the way to do it? Every good work we do without any ulterior motive, instead of forging a new chain, will break one of the links in the existing chains. Every good thought that we send to the world without thinking of any return, will be stored up there and break one link in the chain, and make us purer and purer, until we become the purest of mortals. Yet all this may seem to be rather quixotic and too philosophical, more theoretical than practical. I have read many arguments against the Bhagavad Gita, and many have said that without motives you cannot work. They have never seen unselfish work except under the influence of fanaticism, and, therefore, they speak in that way.

Let me tell you in conclusion a few words about one man who actually carried this teaching of Karma Yoga into practice. That man is Buddha. He is the one man who ever carried this into perfect practice. All the prophets of the world, except Buddha, had external motives to move them to unselfish action. The prophets of the world, with this single exception, may be divided into two sets, one set holding that they are incarnations of God come down on earth, and the other holding that they are only messengers from God; and both draw their impetus for work from outside, expect reward from outside, however highly spiritual may be the language they use. But Buddha is the only prophet who said, "I do not care to know your various theories about God. What is the use of discussing all the subtle doctrines about the soul? Do good and be good. And this will take you to freedom and to whatever truth there is." He was, in the conduct of his life, absolutely without personal motives; and what man worked more than he? Show me in history one character who has soared so high above all. The whole human race has produced but one such character, such high philosophy, such wide sympathy. This great philosopher, preaching the highest philosophy, yet had the deepest sympathy for the lowest of animals, and never put forth any claims for himself. He is the ideal Karma Yogi, acting entirely without motive, and the history of humanity shows him to have been the greatest man ever born; beyond compare the greatest combination of heart and brain that ever existed, the greatest soul-power that has even been manifested. He is the first great reformer the world has seen. He was the first who dared to say, "Believe not because some old manuscripts are produced, believe not because it is your national belief, because you have been made to believe it from your childhood; but reason it all out, and after you have analysed it, then, if you find that it will do good to one and all, believe it, live up to it, and help others to live up to it." He works best who works without any motive, neither for money, nor for fame, nor for anything else; and when a man can do that, he will be a Buddha, and out of him will come the power to work in such a manner as will transform the world. This man represents the very highest ideal of Karma Yoga.

BHAKTI YOGA

CHAPTER 1

PRAYER

स तन्मयो ह्यमृत ईशसंस्थो ज्ञः सर्वगो भुवनस्यास्य गोप्ता।
य ईशेऽस्य जगतो नित्यमेव नान्यो हेतुर्विद्यत ईशनाय।।
यो ब्रह्माणं विदधाति पूर्व यो वै वेदांश्च प्रहिणोति तस्मै।
तं ह देवं आत्मबुध्दिप्रकाशं मुमुक्षुर्वै शरणमहं प्रपद्ये।।

"He is the Soul of the Universe; He is Immortal; His is the Rulership; He is the All-knowing, the All-pervading, the Protector of the Universe, the Eternal Ruler. None else is there efficient to govern the world eternally. He who at the beginning of creation projected Brahmā (i.e. the universal consciousness), and who delivered the Vedas unto him—seeking liberation I go for refuge unto that effulgent One, whose light turns the understanding towards the Ātman."

Shvetāshvatara-Upanishad, VI. 17-18.

DEFINITION OF BHAKTI

Bhakti Yoga is a real, genuine search after the Lord, a search beginning, continuing, and ending in love. One single moment of the madness of extreme love to God brings us eternal freedom. "Bhakti", says Narada in his explanation of the Bhakti-aphorisms, "is intense love to God"; "When a man gets it, he loves all, hates none; he becomes satisfied for ever"; "This love cannot be reduced to any earthly benefit", because so long as worldly desires last, that kind of love does not come; "Bhakti is greater than karma, greater than Yoga, because these are intended for an object in view, while Bhakti is its own fruition, its own means and its own end."

Bhakti has been the one constant theme of our sages. Apart from the special writers on Bhakti, such as Shāndilya or Narada, the great commentators on the *Vyāsa-Sutras*, evidently advocates of knowledge (Jnāna), have also something very suggestive to say about love. Even when the commentator is anxious to explain many, if not all, of the texts so as to make them import a sort of dry knowledge, the *Sutras*, in the chapter on worship especially, do not lend themselves to be easily manipulated in that fashion.

There is not really so much difference between knowledge (Jnāna) and love (Bhakti) as people sometimes imagine. We shall see, as we go on, that in the end they converge and meet at the same point. So also is it with Rāja Yoga, which when pursued as a means to attain liberation, and not (as unfortunately it frequently becomes in the hands of charlatans and mystery-mongers) as an instrument to hoodwink the unwary, leads us also to the same goal.

The one great advantage of Bhakti is that it is the easiest and the most natural way to reach the great divine end in view; its great disadvantage is that in its lower forms it oftentimes degenerates into hideous fanaticism. The fanatical crew in Hinduism, or Mohammedanism, or Christianity, have always been almost exclusively recruited from these worshippers on the lower planes of Bhakti. That singleness of attachment (Nishthā) to a loved object, without which no genuine love can grow, is very often also the cause of the denunciation of everything else. All the weak and undeveloped minds in every religion or country have only one way of loving their own ideal, i.e. by hating every other ideal. Herein is the explanation of why the same man who is so lovingly attached to his own ideal of God, so devoted to his own ideal of religion, becomes a howling fanatic as soon as he sees or hears anything of any other ideal. This kind of love is somewhat like the canine instinct of guarding the master's property from intrusion; only, the instinct of the dog is better than the reason of man, for the dog never mistakes its master for an enemy in whatever dress he may come before it. Again, the fanatic loses all power of judgment. Personal considerations are in his case of such absorbing interest that to him it is no question at all what a man says—whether it is right or wrong; but the one thing he is always particularly careful to know is who says it. The same man who is kind, good, honest, and loving to people of his own opinion, will not hesitate to do the vilest deeds when they are directed against persons beyond the pale of his own religious brotherhood.

But this danger exists only in that stage of Bhakti which is called the *preparatory* (Gauni). When Bhakti has become ripe and has passed into that form which is called the *supreme* (Parā), no more is there any fear of these hideous manifestations of fanaticism; that soul which is overpowered by this higher form of Bhakti is too near the God of Love to become an instrument for the diffusion of hatred.

It is not given to all of us to be harmonious in the building up of our characters in this life: yet we know that that character is of the noblest type in which all these three—knowledge and love and Yoga—are harmoniously fused. Three things are necessary for a bird to fly—the two wings and the tail as a rudder for steering. Jnāna (Knowledge) is the one wing, Bhakti (Love) is the other, and Yoga is the tail that keeps up the balance. For those who cannot pursue all these three forms of worship together in harmony and take up, therefore, Bhakti alone as their way, it is necessary always to remember that forms and ceremonials, though absolutely necessary for the progressive soul, have no other value than taking us on to that state in which we feel the most intense love to God.

There is a little difference in opinion between the teachers of knowledge and those of love, though both admit the power of Bhakti. The Jnānis hold Bhakti to be an instrument of liberation, the Bhaktas look upon it both as the instrument and the thing to be attained. To my mind this is a distinction without much difference. In fact,

Bhakti, when used as an instrument, really means a lower form of worship, and the higher form becomes inseparable from the lower form of realisation at a later stage. Each seems to lay a great stress upon his own peculiar method of worship, forgetting that with perfect love true knowledge is bound to come even unsought, and that from perfect knowledge true love is inseparable.

Bearing this in mind let us try to understand what the great Vedantic commentators have to say on the subject. In explaining the Sutra Āvrittirasakridupadeshāt*, Bhagavān Shankara says, "Thus people say, 'He is devoted to the king, he is devoted to the Guru'; they say this of him who follows his Guru, and does so, having that following as the one end in view. Similarly they say, 'The loving wife meditates on her loving husband'; here also a kind of eager and continuous remembrance is meant." This is devotion according to Shankara.

"Meditation again is a constant remembrance (of the thing meditated upon) flowing like an unbroken stream of oil poured out from one vessel to another. When this kind of remembering has been attained (in relation to God) all bondages break. Thus it is spoken of in the scriptures regarding constant remembering as a means to liberation. This remembering again is of the same form as seeing, because it is of the same meaning as in the passage, 'When He who is far and near is seen, the bonds of the heart are

---

* Meditation is necessary, that having been often enjoined.

broken, all doubts vanish, and all effects of work disappear' He who is near can be seen, but he who is far can only be remembered. Nevertheless the scripture says that he have to see Him who is near as well as Him who, is far, thereby indicating to us that the above kind of *remembering* is as good as *seeing*. This remembrance when exalted assumes the same form as seeing. . . . Worship is constant remembering as may be seen from the essential texts of scriptures. Knowing, which is the same as repeated worship, has been described as constant remembering. . . . Thus the memory, which has attained to the height of what is as good as direct perception, is spoken of in the Shruti as a means of liberation. 'This Ātman is not to be reached through various sciences, nor by intellect, nor by much study of the Vedas. Whomsoever this Ātman desires, by him is the Ātman attained, unto him this Ātman discovers Himself.' Here, after saying that mere hearing, thinking and meditating are not the means of attaining this Ātman, it is said, 'Whom this Ātman desires, by him the Ātman is attained.' The extremely beloved is desired; by whomsoever this Ātman is extremely beloved, he becomes the most beloved of the Ātman. So that this beloved may attain the Ātman, the Lord Himself helps. For it has been said by the Lord: 'Those who are constantly attached to Me and worship Me with love—I give that direction to their will by which they come to Me.' Therefore it is said that, to whomsoever this remembering, which is of the same form as direct perception, is very dear, because it is dear to the Object of such memory perception, he is desired by the Supreme Ātman, by him the Supreme

Ātman is attained. This constant remembrance is denoted by the word Bhakti." So says Bhagavān Rāmānuja in his commentary on the Sutra Athāto Brahma-jijnāsā*.

In commenting on the Sutra of Patanjali, Ishvara pranidhānādvā, i.e. "Or by the worship of the Supreme Lord"—Bhoja says, "Pranidhāna is that sort of Bhakti in which, without seeking results, such as sense-enjoyments etc., all works are dedicated to that Teacher of teachers." Bhagavān Vyāsa also, when commenting on the same, defines Pranidhana as "the form of Bhakti by which the mercy of the Supreme Lord comes to the Yogi, and blesses him by granting him his desires". According to Shāndilya, "Bhakti is intense love to God." The best definition is, however, that given by the king of Bhaktas, Prahlāda:

या प्रीतिरविवेकानां विषयेष्वनपायिनी।
त्वामनुस्मरतः सा मे हृदयान्मापसर्पतु।।

"That deathless love which the ignorant have for the fleeting objects of the senses—as I keep meditating on Thee—may not that love slip away from my heart!" *Love*! For whom? For the Supreme Lord Ishvara. Love for any other being, however great cannot be Bhakti; for, as Ramanuja says in his *Shri Bhāshya*, quoting an ancient Āchārya, i.e. a great teacher:

---

* Hence follows a dissertation on Brahman.

आब्रह्मस्तम्बपर्यन्ताः जगदन्तर्व्यवस्थिताः।
प्राणिनः कर्मजनितसंसारवशवर्तिनः।।
यतस्ततो न ते ध्याने ध्यानिनामुपकारकाः।
अविद्यान्तर्गतास्सर्वे ते हि संसारगोचराः।।

"From Brahmā to a clump of grass, all things that live in the world are slaves of birth and death caused by Karma; therefore they cannot be helpful as objects of meditation, because they are all in ignorance and subject to change." In commenting on the word Anurakti used by Shāndilya, the commentator Svapneshvara says that it means Anu, after, and Rakti, attachment; i.e. the attachment which comes after the knowledge of the nature and glory of God; else a blind attachment to any one, e.g. to wife or children, would be Bhakti. We plainly see, therefore, that Bhakti is a series or succession of mental efforts at religious realisation beginning with ordinary worship and ending in a supreme intensity of love for Ishvara.

CHAPTER 2

THE PHILOSOPHY OF ISHVARA

Who is Ishvara? Janmādyasya yatah—"From whom is the birth, continuation, and dissolution of the universe,"—He is Ishvara—"the Eternal, the Pure, the Ever-Free, the Almighty, the All-Knowing, the All-Merciful, the Teacher of all teachers"; and above all, Sa Ishvarah anirvachaniya-premasvarupah—"He the Lord is, of His own nature, inexpressible Love." These certainly are the definitions of a Personal God. Are there then two Gods—the "Not this, not this," the Sat-chit-ānanda, the Existence-Knowledge-Bliss of the philosopher, and this God of Love of the Bhakta? No, it is the same Sat-chit-ananda who is also the God of Love, the impersonal and personal in one. It has always to be understood that the Personal God worshipped by the Bhakta is not separate or different from the Brahman. All is Brahman, the One without a second; only the Brahman, as unity or absolute, is too much of an abstraction to be loved and worshipped; so the Bhakta chooses the relative aspect of Brahman, that is, Ishvara, the Supreme Ruler. To use a simile: Brahman is as the clay or substance out of which an infinite variety of articles are fashioned. As clay, they are all one; but form or manifestation differentiates them. Before every one of them was made, they all existed potentially in the clay, and, of course, they are identical substantially; but when formed, and so long as the form remains, they are separate and different; the clay-mouse can never become a clay-elephant, because, as manifestations, form alone makes them what they are, though as unformed clay they are all one. Ishvara is the highest manifestation of the Absolute Reality, or in other words, the highest possible reading of the Absolute by the human mind. Creation is eternal, and so also is Ishvara.

In the fourth Pāda of the fourth chapter of his *Sutras*, after stating the almost infinite power and knowledge which will come to the liberated soul after the attainment of Moksha, Vyāsa makes the remark, in an aphorism, that none, however, will get the power of creating, ruling, and dissolving the universe, because that belongs to God alone. In explaining the Sutra it is easy for the dualistic commentators to show how it is ever impossible for a subordinate soul, Jiva, to have the infinite power and total independence of God. The thorough dualistic commentator Madhvāchārya deals with this passage in his usual summary method by quoting a verse from the *Varāha Purāna.*

In explaining this aphorism the commentator Rāmānuja says, "This doubt being raised, whether among the powers of the liberated souls is included that unique power of the Supreme One, that is, of creation etc. of the universe and even the Lordship of all, or whether, without that, the glory of the liberated consists only in the direct perception of the Supreme One, we get as an argument the following: It is reasonable that the liberated get the Lordship of the universe, because the scriptures say, 'He attains to extreme sameness with the Supreme One and all his desires are realised.' Now extreme sameness and realisation of all desires cannot be attained without the unique power of the Supreme Lord, namely, that of governing the universe. Therefore, to attain the realisation of all desires and the extreme sameness with the Supreme, we must all admit that the liberated get the power of ruling the whole universe. To this we reply, that the liberated get all the powers except that of ruling the universe. Ruling the universe is guiding the form and the life and the desires of all the sentient and the non-sentient beings. The liberated ones from whom all that veils His true nature has been removed, only enjoy the unobstructed perception of the Brahman, but do not possess the power of ruling the universe. This is proved from the scriptural text, 'From whom all these things are born, by which all that are born live, unto whom they, departing, return—ask about it.

That is Brahman.' If this quality of ruling the universe be a quality common even to the liberated then this text would not apply as a definition of Brahman defining Him through His rulership of the universe. The uncommon attributes alone define a thing; therefore in texts like—'My beloved boy, alone, in the beginning there existed the One without a second. That saw and felt, "I will give birth to the many." That projected heat.'—'Brahman indeed alone existed in the beginning. That One evolved. That projected a blessed form, the Kshatra. All these gods are Kshatras: Varuna, Soma, Rudra, Parjanya, Yama, Mrityu, Ishāna.'—'Ātman indeed existed alone in the beginning; nothing else vibrated; He thought of projecting the world; He projected the world after.'—'Alone Nārāyana existed; neither Brahmā, nor Ishana, nor the Dyāvā-Prithivi, nor the stars, nor water, nor fire, nor Soma, nor the sun. He did not take pleasure alone. He after His meditation had one daughter, the ten organs, etc.'—and in others as, 'Who living in the earth is separate from the earth, who living in the Ātman, etc.'—the Shrutis speak of the Supreme One as the subject of the work of ruling the universe. . . . Nor in these descriptions of the ruling of the universe is there any position for the liberated soul, by which such a soul may have the ruling of the universe ascribed to it."

In explaining the next Sutra, Rāmānuja says, "If you say it is not so, because there are direct texts in the Vedas in evidence to the contrary, these texts refer to the glory of the liberated in the spheres of the subordinate deities." This also is an easy solution of the difficulty. Although the system of Ramanuja admits the unity of the total, within that totality of existence there are, according to him, eternal differences. Therefore, for all practical purposes, this system also being dualistic, it was easy for Ramanuja to keep the distinction between the personal soul and the Personal God very clear.

We shall now try to understand what the great representative of the Advaita School has to say on the point. We shall see how the Advaita system maintains all the hopes and aspirations of the dualist intact, and at the same time propounds its own solution of the problem in consonance with the high destiny of divine humanity. Those who aspire to retain their individual mind even after liberation and to remain distinct will have ample opportunity of realising their aspirations and enjoying the blessing of the qualified Brahman. These are they who have been spoken of in the *Bhāgavata Purāna* thus: "O king, such are the, glorious qualities of the Lord that the sages whose only pleasure is in the Self, and from whom all fetters have fallen off, even they love the Omnipresent with the love that is for love's sake." These are they who are spoken of by the Sānkhyas as getting merged in nature in this cycle, so that, after attaining perfection, they may come out in the next as lords of world-systems. But none of these ever becomes equal to God (Ishvara). Those who attain to that state where there is neither creation, nor created, nor creator, where there is neither knower, nor knowable, nor knowledge, where there is neither *I*, nor *thou*, nor *he*, where there is neither subject, nor object, nor relation, "there, who is seen by whom?"—such persons have gone beyond everything to "where words cannot go nor mind", gone to that which the Shrutis declare as "Not this, not this"; but for those who cannot, or will not reach this state, there will inevitably remain the triune vision of the one undifferentiated Brahman as nature, soul, and the interpenetrating sustainer of both—Ishvara. So, when Prahlāda forgot himself, he found neither the universe nor its cause; all was to him one Infinite, undifferentiated by name and form; but as soon as he remembered that he was Prahlada, there was the universe before him and with it the Lord of the universe—"the Repository of an infinite number of blessed qualities". So it was with the blessed Gopis. So long as they had lost sense of their own personal identity and individuality, they were all Krishnas, and when they began again to think of Him as the One to be worshipped, then they were Gopis again, and immediately

तासामाविरभूच्छौरिः स्मयमानमुखाम्बुजः ।
पीताम्बरधरः स्त्रग्वी साखान्मन्मथमन्मथः ।।

> (*Bhagavata*)—"Unto them appeared Krishna with a smile on His lotus face, clad in yellow robes and having garlands on, the embodied conqueror (in beauty) of the god of love."

Now to go back to our Acharya Shankara: "Those", he says, "who by worshipping the qualified Brahman attain conjunction with the Supreme Ruler, preserving their own mind—is their glory limited or unlimited? This doubt arising, we get as an argument: Their glory should be unlimited because of the scriptural texts, 'They attain their own kingdom', 'To him all the gods offer worship', 'Their desires are fulfilled in all the worlds'. As an answer to this, Vyāsa writes, 'Without the power of ruling the universe.' Barring the power of creation etc. of the universe, the other powers such as Animā etc. are acquired by the liberated. As to ruling the universe, that belongs to the eternally perfect Ishvara. Why? Because He is the subject of all the scriptural texts as regards creation etc., and the liberated souls are not mentioned therein in any connection whatsoever. The Supreme Lord indeed is alone engaged in ruling the universe. The texts as to creation etc. all point to Him. Besides, there is given the adjective 'ever-perfect'. Also the scriptures say that the powers Animā etc. of the others are from the search after and the worship of God. Therefore they have no place in the ruling of the universe. Again, on account of their possessing their own minds, it is possible that their wills may differ, and that, whilst one desires creation, another may desire destruction. The only way of avoiding this conflict is to make all wills subordinate to some one will. Therefore the conclusion is that the wills of the liberated are dependent on the will of the Supreme Ruler."

Bhakti, then, can be directed towards Brahman, only in His personal aspect. क्लेशोऽधिकतरस्तेषामव्यक्तासक्तचेतसाम्—"The way is more difficult for those whose mind is attached to the Absolute!" Bhakti has to float on smoothly with the current of our nature. True it is that we cannot have; any idea of the Brahman which is not anthropomorphic, but is it not equally true of everything we know? The greatest psychologist the world has ever known, Bhagavān Kapila, demonstrated ages ago that human consciousness is one of the elements in the make-up of all the objects of our perception and conception, internal as well as external. Beginning with our bodies and going up to Ishvara, we may see that every object of our perception is this consciousness plus something else, whatever that may be; and this unavoidable mixture is what we ordinarily think of as reality. Indeed it is, and ever will be, all of the reality that is possible for the human mind to know. Therefore to say that Ishvara is unreal, because He is anthropomorphic, is sheer nonsense. It sounds very much like the occidentals squabble on idealism and realism, which fearful-looking quarrel has for its foundation a mere play on the word "real". The idea of Ishvara covers all the ground ever denoted and connoted by the word real, and Ishvara is as real as anything else in the universe; and after all, the word real means nothing more than what has now been pointed out. Such is our philosophical conception of Ishvara.

CHAPTER 3

SPIRITUAL REALISATION, THE AIM OF BHAKTI YOGA

To the Bhakta these dry details are necessary only to strengthen his will; beyond that they are of no use to him. For he is treading on a path which is fitted very soon to lead him beyond the hazy and turbulent regions of reason, to lead him to the realm of realisation. He, soon, through the mercy of the Lord, reaches a plane where pedantic and powerless reason is left far behind, and the mere intellectual groping through the dark gives place to the daylight of direct perception. He no more reasons and believes, he almost perceives. He no more argues, he senses. And is not this seeing God, and feeling God, and enjoying God higher than everything else? Nay, Bhaktas have not been wanting who have maintained that it is higher than even Moksha—liberation. And is it not also the highest utility? There are people—and a good many of them too—in the world who are convinced that only that is of use and utility which brings to man creature-comforts. Even religion, God, eternity, soul, none of these is of any use to them, as they do not bring them money or physical comfort. To such, all those things which do not go to gratify the senses and appease the appetites are of no utility. In every mind, utility, however, is conditioned by its own peculiar wants. To men, therefore, who never rise higher than eating, drinking, begetting progeny, and dying, the only gain is in sense enjoyments; and they must wait and go through many more births and reincarnations to learn to feel even the faintest necessity for anything higher. But those to whom the eternal interests of the soul are of much higher value than the fleeting interests of this mundane life, to whom the gratification of the senses is but like the thoughtless play of the baby, to them God and the love of God form the highest and the only utility of human existence. Thank God there are some such still living in this world of too much worldliness.

Bhakti Yoga, as we have said, is divided into the Gauni or the preparatory, and the Parā or the supreme forms. We shall find, as we go on, how in the preparatory stage we unavoidably stand in need of many concrete helps to enable us to get on; and indeed the mythological and symbological parts of all religions are natural growths which early environ the aspiring soul and help it Godward. It is also a significant fact that spiritual giants have been produced only in those systems of religion where there is an exuberant growth of rich mythology and ritualism. The dry fanatical forms of religion which attempt to eradicate all that is poetical, all that is beautiful and sublime, all that gives a firm grasp to the infant mind tottering in its Godward way—the forms which attempt to break down the very ridge-poles of the spiritual roof, and in their ignorant and superstitious conceptions of truth try to drive away all that is life-giving, all that furnishes the formative material to the spiritual plant growing in the human soul—such forms of religion too soon find that all that is left to them is but an empty shell, a contentless frame of words and sophistry with perhaps a little flavour of a kind of social scavengering or the so-called spirit of reform.

The vast mass of those whose religion is like this, are conscious or unconscious materialists—the end and aim of their lives here and hereafter being enjoyment, which indeed is to them the alpha and the omega of human life, and which is their Ishtāpurta; work like street-cleaning and scavengering, intended for the material comfort of man is, according to them, the be-all and end-all of human existence; and the sooner the followers of this curious mixture of ignorance and fanaticism come out in their true colours and join, as they well deserve to do, the ranks of atheists and materialists, the better will it be for the world. One ounce of the practice of righteousness and of spiritual Self-realisation outweighs tons and tons of frothy talk and nonsensical sentiments. Show us one, but one gigantic spiritual genius growing out of all this dry dust of ignorance and fanaticism; and if you cannot, close your mouths, open the windows of your hearts to the clear light of truth, and sit like children at the feet of those who know what they are talking about—the sages of India. Let us then listen attentively to what they say.

CHAPTER 4

THE NEED OF GURU

Every soul is destined to be perfect, and every being, in the end, will attain the state of perfection. Whatever we are now is the result of our acts and thoughts in the past; and whatever we shall be in the future will be the result of what we think and do now. But this, the shaping of our own destinies, does not preclude our receiving help from outside; nay, in the vast majority of cases such help is absolutely necessary. When it comes, the higher powers and possibilities of the soul are quickened, spiritual life is awakened, growth is animated, and man becomes holy and perfect in the end.

This quickening impulse cannot be derived from books. The soul can only receive impulses from another soul, and from nothing else. We may study books all our lives, we may become very intellectual, but in the end we find that we have not developed at all spiritually. It is not true that a high order of intellectual development always goes hand in hand with a proportionate development of the spiritual side in Man. In studying books we are sometimes deluded into thinking that thereby we are being spiritually helped; but if we analyse the effect of the study of books on ourselves, we shall find that at the utmost it is only our intellect that derives profit from such studies, and not our inner spirit. This inadequacy of books to quicken spiritual growth is the reason why, although almost every one of us can *speak* most wonderfully on spiritual matters, when it comes to action and the living of a truly spiritual life, we find ourselves so awfully deficient. To quicken the spirit, the impulse must come from another soul.

The person from whose soul such impulse comes is called the Guru—the teacher; and the person to whose soul the impulse is conveyed is called the Shishya—the student. To convey such an impulse to any soul, in the first place, the soul from which it proceeds must possess the power of transmitting it, as it were, to another; and in the second place, the soul to which it is transmitted must be fit to receive it. The seed must be a living seed, and the field must be ready ploughed; and when both these conditions are fulfilled, a wonderful growth of genuine religion takes place. "The true preacher of religion has to be of wonderful capabilities, and clever shall his hearer be"—आश्चर्यो वक्ता कुशलोऽस्य लब्धा and when both of these are really wonderful and extraordinary, then will a splendid spiritual awakening result, and not otherwise. Such alone are the real teachers, and such alone are also the real students, the real aspirants. All others are only playing with spirituality. They have just a little curiosity awakened, just a little intellectual aspiration kindled in them, but are merely standing on the outward fringe of the horizon of religion. There is no doubt some value even in that, as it may in course of time result in the awakening of a real thirst for religion; and it is a mysterious law of nature that as soon as the field is ready, the seed *must* and does come; as soon as the soul earnestly desires to have religion, the transmitter of the religious force *must* and does appear to help that soul. When the power that attracts the light of religion in the receiving soul is full and strong, the power which answers to that attraction and sends in light does come as a matter of course.

There are, however, certain great dangers in the way. There is, for instance, the danger to the receiving soul of its mistaking momentary emotions for real religious yearning. We may study that in ourselves. Many a time in our lives, somebody dies whom we loved; we receive a blow; we feel that the world is slipping between our fingers, that we want something surer and higher, and that we must become religious. In a few days that wave of feeling has passed away, and we are left stranded just where we were before. We are all of us often mistaking such impulses for real thirst after religion; but as long as these momentary emotions are thus mistaken, that continuous, real craving of the soul for religion will not come, and we shall not find the true transmitter of spirituality into our nature. So whenever we are tempted to complain of our search after the truth that we desire so much, proving vain, instead of so complaining, our first duty ought to be to look into our own souls and find whether the craving in the heart is real. Then in the vast majority of cases it would be discovered that we were not fit for receiving the truth, that there was no real thirst for spirituality.

There are still greater dangers in regard to the *transmitter*, the Guru. There are many who, though immersed in ignorance, yet, in the pride of their hearts, fancy they know everything, and not only do not stop there, but offer to take others on their shoulders; and thus the blind leading the blind, both fall into the ditch.

अविद्यायामन्तरे वर्तमानाः स्वयं धीराः पण्डितम्मन्यमानाः।
दन्द्रम्यमाणाः परियन्ति मूढा अन्धेनैव नीयमाना यथान्धाः।।

— "Fools dwelling in darkness, wise in their own conceit, and puffed up with vain knowledge, go round and round staggering to and fro, like blind men led by the blind."—(Katha Up., I. ii. 5). The world is full of these. Every one wants to be a teacher, every beggar wants to make a gift of a million dollars! Just as these beggars are ridiculous, so are these teachers.

CHAPTER 5

QUALIFICATIONS OF THE ASPIRANT AND THE TEACHER

How are we to know a teacher, then? The sun requires no torch to make him visible, we need not light a candle in order to see him. When the sun rises, we instinctively become aware of the fact, and when a teacher of men comes to help us, the soul will instinctively know that truth has already begun to shine upon it. Truth stands on its own evidence, it does not require any other testimony to prove it true, it is self effulgent. It penetrates into the innermost corners of our nature, and in its presence the whole universe stands up and says, "This is truth." The teachers whose wisdom and truth shine like the light of the sun are the very greatest the world has known, and they are worshipped as God by the major portion of mankind. But we may get help from comparatively lesser ones also; only we ourselves do not possess intuition enough to judge properly of the man from whom we receive teaching and guidance; so there ought to be certain tests, certain conditions, for the teacher to satisfy, as there are also for the taught.

The conditions necessary for the taught are purity, a real thirst after knowledge, and perseverance. No impure soul can be really religious. Purity in thought, speech, and act is absolutely necessary for any one to be religious. As to the thirst after knowledge, it is an old law that we all get whatever we want. None of us can get anything other than what we fix our hearts upon. To pant for religion truly is a very difficult thing, not at all so easy as we generally imagine. Hearing religious talks or reading religious books is no proof yet of a real want felt in the heart; there must be a continuous struggle, a constant fight, an unremitting grappling with our lower nature, till the higher want is actually felt and the victory is achieved. It is not a question of one or two days, of years, or of lives; the struggle may have to go on for hundreds of lifetimes. The success sometimes may come immediately, but we must be ready to wait patiently even for what may look like an infinite length of time. The student who sets out with such a *spirit* of perseverance will surely find success and realisation at last.

In regard to the teacher, we must see that he knows the spirit of the scriptures. The whole world reads Bibles, Vedas, and Korans; but they are all only words, syntax, etymology, philology, the dry bones of religion. The teacher who deals too much in words and allows the mind to be carried away by the force of words loses the spirit. It is the knowledge of the spirit of the scriptures alone that constitutes the true religious teacher. The network of the words of the scriptures is like a huge forest in which the human mind often loses itself and finds no way out. शब्दजालं महारण्यं चित्तभ्रमणकारणम्।— "The network of words is a big forest; it is the cause of a curious wandering of the mind." "The various methods of joining words, the various methods of speaking in beautiful language, the various methods of explaining the diction of the scriptures are only for the disputations and enjoyment of the learned, they do not conduce to the development of spiritual perception"—

वाग्वैखरी शब्दझरी शास्त्रव्याख्यानकौशलम्।
वैदुष्यं विदुषां तद्वद् भुक्तये न तु मुक्तये।।

Those who employ such methods to impart religion to others are only desirous to show off their learning, so that the world may praise them as great scholars. You will find that no one of the great teachers of the world ever went into these various explanations of the text; there is with them no attempt at "text-torturing", no eternal playing upon the meaning of words and their roots. Yet they nobly taught, while others who have nothing to teach have taken up a word sometimes and written a three-volume book on its origin, on the man who used it first, and on what that man was accustomed to eat, and how long he slept, and so on.

Bhagavān Ramakrishna used to tell a story of some men who went into a mango orchard and busied themselves in counting the leaves, the twigs, and the branches, examining their colour, comparing their size, and noting down everything most carefully, and then got up a learned discussion on each of these topics, which were undoubtedly highly interesting to them. But one of them, more sensible than the others, did not care for all these things. and instead thereof, began to eat the mango fruit. And was he not wise? So leave this counting of leaves and twigs and note-taking to others. This kind of work has its proper place, but not here in the spiritual domain. You never see a strong spiritual man among these "leaf counters". Religion, the highest aim, the highest glory of man, does not require so much labour. If you want to be a Bhakta, it is not at all necessary for you to know whether Krishna was born in Mathurā or in Vraja, what he was doing, or just the exact date on which he pronounced the teachings of the Gita. You only require to *feel* the craving for the beautiful lessons of duty and love in the Gita. All the other particulars about it and its author are for the enjoyment of the learned. Let them have what they desire. Say "Shāntih, Shāntih" to their learned controversies, and let *us* "eat the mangoes".

The second condition necessary in the teacher is—sinlessness. The question is often asked, "Why should we look into the character and personality of a teacher? We have only to judge of what he says, and take that up." This is not right. If a man wants to teach me something of dynamics, or chemistry, or any other physical science, he may be anything he likes, because what the physical sciences require is merely an intellectual equipment; but in the spiritual sciences it is impossible from first to last that there can be any spiritual light in the soul that is impure. What religion can an impure man teach? The *sine qua non* of acquiring spiritual truth for one's self or for imparting it to others is the purity of heart and soul. A vision of God or a glimpse of the beyond never comes until the soul is pure. Hence with the teacher of religion we must see first what he is, and then what he says. He must be perfectly pure, and then alone comes the value of his words, because he is only then the true "transmitter". What can he transmit if he has not spiritual power in himself? There must be the worthy vibration of spirituality in the mind of the teacher, so that it may be sympathetically conveyed to the mind of the taught. The function of the teacher is indeed an affair of the transference of something, and not one of mere stimulation of the existing intellectual or other faculties in the taught. Something real and appreciable as an influence comes from the teacher and goes to the taught. Therefore the teacher must be pure.

The third condition is in regard to the motile. The teacher must not teach with any ulterior selfish motive—for money, name, or fame; his work must be simply out of love, out of pure love for mankind at large. The only medium through which spiritual force can be transmitted is love. Any selfish motive, such as the desire for gain or for name, will immediately destroy this conveying median.

God is love, and only he who has known God as love can be a teacher of godliness and God to man.

When you see that in your teacher these conditions are all fulfilled, you are safe; if they are not, it is unsafe to allow yourself to be taught by him, for there is the great danger that, if he cannot convey goodness to your heart, he may convey wickedness. This danger must by all means be guarded against. श्रोत्रियोऽवृजिनोऽकामहतो यो ब्रह्मवित्तमः—"He who is learned in the scriptures, sinless, unpolluted by lust, and is the greatest knower of the Brahman" is the real teacher.

From what has been said, it naturally follows that we cannot be taught to love, appreciate, and assimilate religion everywhere and by everybody. The "books in the running brooks, sermons in stones, and good in everything" is all very true as a poetical figure: but nothing can impart to a man a single grain of truth unless he has the undeveloped germs of it in himself. To whom do the stones and brooks preach sermons? To the human soul, the lotus of whose inner holy shrine is already quick with life. And the light which causes the beautiful opening out of this lotus comes always from the good and wise teacher. When the heart has thus been opened, it becomes fit to receive teaching from the stones or the brooks, the stars, or the sun, or the moon, or from any thing which has its existence in our divine universe; but the unopened heart will see in them nothing but mere stones or mere brooks. A blind man may go to a museum, but he will not profit by it in any way; his eyes must be opened first, and then alone he will be able to learn what the things in the museum can teach.

This eye-opener of the aspirant after religion is the teacher. With the teacher, therefore, our relationship is the same as that between an ancestor and his descendant. Without faith, humility, submission, and veneration in our hearts towards our religious teacher, there cannot be any growth of religion in us; and it is a significant fact that, where this kind of relation between the teacher and the taught prevails, there alone gigantic spiritual men are growing; while in those countries which have neglected to keep up this kind of relation the religious teacher has become a mere lecturer, the teacher expecting his five dollars and the person taught expecting his brain to be filled with the teacher's words, and each going his own way after this much has been done. Under such circumstances spirituality becomes almost an unknown quantity. There is none to transmit it and none to have it transmitted to. Religion with such people becomes business; they think they can obtain it with their dollars. Would to God that religion could be obtained so easily! But unfortunately it cannot be.

Religion, which is the highest knowledge and the highest wisdom, cannot be bought, nor can it be acquired from books. You may thrust your head into all the corners of the world, you may explore the Himalayas, the Alps, and the Caucasus, you may sound the bottom of the sea and pry into every nook of Tibet and the desert of Gobi, you will not find it anywhere until your heart is ready for receiving it and your teacher has come. And when that divinely appointed teacher comes, serve him with childlike confidence and simplicity, freely open your heart to his influence, and see in him God manifested. Those who come to seek truth with such a spirit of love and veneration, to them the Lord of Truth reveals the most wonderful things regarding truth, goodness, and beauty.

CHAPTER 6

INCARNATE TEACHERS AND INCARNATION

Wherever His name is spoken, that very place is holy. How much more so is the man who speaks His name, and with what veneration ought we to approach that man out of whom comes to us spiritual truth! Such great teachers of spiritual truth are indeed very few in number in this world, but the world is never altogether without them. They are always the fairest flowers of human life—अहेतुकदयासिन्धुः—"the ocean ofmercy without any motive". आचार्यं मां विजानीयात्—"Know the Guru to be Me", says Shri Krishna in the *Bhagavata*.

The moment the world is absolutely bereft of these, it becomes a hideous hell and hastens on to its destruction.

Higher and nobler than all ordinary ones are another set of teachers, the Avatāras of Ishvara, in the world. They can transmit spirituality with a touch, even with a mere wish. The lowest and the most degraded characters become in one second saints at their command. They are the Teachers of all teachers, the highest manifestations of God through man. We cannot see God except through them. We cannot help worshipping them; and indeed they are the only ones whom we are bound to worship.

No man can really see God except through these human manifestations. If we try to see God otherwise, we make for ourselves a hideous caricature of Him and believe the caricature to be no worse than the original. There is a story of an ignorant man who was asked to make an image of the God Shiva, and who, after days of hard struggle, manufactured only the image of a monkey. So whenever we try to think of God as He is in His absolute perfection, we invariably meet with the most miserable failure, because as long as we are men, we cannot conceive Him as anything higher than man. The time will come when we shall transcend our human nature and know Him as He is; but as long as we are men, we must worship Him in man and as man. Talk as you may, try as you may, you cannot think of God except as a man. You may deliver great intellectual discourses on God and on all things under the sun, become great rationalists and prove to your satisfaction that all these accounts of the Avataras of God as man are nonsense. But let us come for a moment to practical common sense. What is there behind this kind of remarkable intellect? Zero, nothing, simply so much froth. When next you hear a man delivering a great intellectual lecture against this worship of the Avataras of God, get hold of him and ask what *his* idea of God is, what *he* understands by "omnipotence", "omnipresence", and all similar terms, beyond the spelling of the words. He really means nothing by them; he cannot formulate as their meaning any idea unaffected by his own human nature; he is no better off in this matter than the man in the street who has not read a single book. That man in the street, however, is quiet and does not disturb the peace of the world, while this big talker creates disturbance and misery among mankind. Religion is, after all, realisation, and we must make the sharpest distinction between talk; and intuitive experience. What we experience in the depths of our souls is realisation. Nothing indeed is so uncommon as common sense in regard to this matter.

By our present constitution we are limited and bound to see God as man. If, for instance the buffaloes want to worship God, they will, in keeping with their own nature, see Him as a huge buffalo; if a fish wants to worship God, it will have to form an Idea of Him as a big fish, and man has to think of Him as man. And these various conceptions are not due to morbidly active imagination. Man, the buffalo, and the fish all may be supposed to represent so many different vessels, so to say. All these vessels go to the sea of God to get filled with water, each according to its own shape and capacity; in the man the water takes the shape of man, in the buffalo, the shape of a buffalo and in the fish, the shape of a fish. In each of these vessels there is the same water of the sea of God. When men see Him, they see Him as man, and the animals, if they have any conception of God at all, must see Him as animal each according to its own ideal. So we cannot help seeing God as man, and, therefore, we are bound to worship Him as man. There is no other way.

Two kinds of men do not worship God as man—the human brute who has no religion, and the Paramahamsa who has risen beyond all the weaknesses of humanity and has transcended the limits of his own human nature. To him all nature has become his own Self. He alone can worship God as He is. Here, too, as in all other cases, the two extremes meet. The extreme of ignorance and the other extreme of knowledge—neither of these go through acts of worship. The human brute does not worship because of his ignorance, and the Jivanmuktas (free souls) do not worship because they have realised God in themselves. Being between these two poles of existence, if any one tells you that he is not going to worship God as man, take kindly care of that man; he is, not to use any harsher term, an irresponsible talker; his religion is for unsound and empty brains.

God understands human failings and becomes man to do good to humanity:

यदा यदा हि धर्मस्य ग्लानिर्भवति भारत।
अभ्युत्थानमधर्मस्य तदात्मानं सृजाम्यहम्।।
परित्राणाय साधूनां विनाशाय च दुष्कृताम्।
धर्मसंस्थापनार्थाय सम्भवामि युगे युगे।।

—"Whenever virtue subsides and wickedness prevails, I manifest Myself. To establish virtue, to destroy evil, to save the good I come from Yuga (age) to Yuga."

अवजानन्ति मां मूढा मानुषीं तनुमाश्रितम्।
परं भावमजानन्तो मम भूतमहेश्वरम्।।

—"Fools deride Me who have assumed the human form, without knowing My real nature as the Lord of the universe." Such is Shri Krishna's declaration in the Gita on Incarnation. "When a huge tidal wave comes," says Bhagavān Shri Ramakrishna, "all the little brooks and ditches become full to the brim without any effort or consciousness on their own part; so when an Incarnation comes, a tidal wave of spirituality breaks upon the world, and people feel spirituality almost full in the air."

CHAPTER 7

THE MANTRA: OM: WORD AND WISDOM

But we are now considering not these Mahāpurushas, the great Incarnations, but only the Siddha-Gurus (teachers who have attained the goal); they, as a rule, have to convey the gems of spiritual wisdom to the disciple by means of words (Mantras) to be meditated upon. What are these Mantras? The whole of this universe has, according to Indian philosophy, both name and form (Nāma-Rupa) as its conditions of manifestation. In the human microcosm, there cannot be a single wave in the mind-stuff (Chittavritti) unconditioned by name and form. If it be true that nature is built throughout on the same plan, this kind of conditioning by name and form must also be the plan of the building of the whole of the cosmos. यथा एकेन मृत्पिण्डेन सर्वं मृन्मयं विज्ञातं स्यात्—"As one lump of clay being known, all things of clay are known", so the knowledge of the microcosm must lead to the knowledge of the macrocosm. Now form is the outer crust, of which the name or the idea is the inner essence or kernel. The body is the form, and the mind or the Antahkarana is the name, and sound-symbols are universally associated with Nāma (name) in all beings having the power of speech. In the individual man the thought-waves rising in the limited Mahat or Chitta (mind-stuff), must manifest themselves, first as *words*, and then as the more concrete *forms.*

In the universe, Brahmā or Hiranyagarbha or the cosmic Mahat first manifested himself as name, and then as form, i.e. as this universe. All this expressed sensible universe is the form, behind which stands the eternal inexpressible Sphota, the manifester as *Logos* or Word. This eternal Sphota, the essential eternal material of all ideas or names is the power through which the Lord creates the universe, nay, the Lord first becomes conditioned as the Sphota, and then evolves Himself out as the yet more concrete sensible universe.

This Sphota has one word as its only possible symbol, and this is the ओं (Om).

And as by no possible means of analysis can we separate the word from the idea this Om and the eternal Sphota are inseparable; and therefore, it is out of this holiest of all holy words, the mother of all names and forms, the eternal Om, that the whole universe may be supposed to have been created. But it may be said that, although thought and word are inseparable, yet as there may be various word-symbols for the same thought, it is not necessary that this particular word Om should be the word representative of the thought, out of which the universe has become manifested. To this objection we reply that this Om is the only possible symbol which covers the whole ground, and there is none other like it. The Sphota is the material of all words, yet it is not any definite word in its fully formed state. That is to say, if all the peculiarities which distinguish one word from another be removed, then what remains will be the Sphota; therefore this Sphota is called the Nāda-Brahma, the *Sound-Brahman*.

Now, as every word-symbol, intended to express the inexpressible Sphota, will so particularise it that it will no longer be the Sphota, that symbol which particularises it the least and at the same time most approximately expresses its nature, will be the truest symbol thereof; and this is the Om, and the Om only; because these three letters अ उ म (A.U.M.), pronounced incombination as Om, may well be the generalised symbol of all possible sounds. The letter A is the least differentiated of all sounds, therefore Krishna says in the Gita अक्षराणां अकारोऽस्मि—"I am A among the letters".

Again, all articulate sounds are produced in the space within the mouth beginning with the root of the tongue and ending in the lips—the throat sound is A, and M is the last lip sound, and the U exactly represents the rolling forward of the impulse which begins at the root of the tongue till it ends in the lips. If properly pronounced, this Om will represent the whole phenomenon of sound-production, and no other word can do this; and this, therefore, is the fittest symbol of the Sphota, which is the real meaning of the Om. And as the symbol can never be separated from the thing signified, the Om and the Sphota are one. And as the Sphota, being the finer side of the manifested universe, is nearer to God and is indeed that first manifestation of divine wisdom this Om is truly symbolic of God. Again, just as the "One only" Brahman, the Akhanda-Sachchidānanda, the undivided Existence-Knowledge-Bliss, can be conceived by imperfect human souls only from particular standpoints and associated with particular qualities, so this universe, His body, has also to be thought of along the line of the thinker's mind.

This direction of the worshipper's mind is guided by its prevailing elements or Tattvas. The result is that the same God will be seen in various manifestations as the possessor of various predominant qualities, and the same universe will appear as full of manifold forms. Even as in the case of the least differentiated and the most universal symbol Om, thought and sound-symbol are seen to be inseparably associated with each other, so also this law of their inseparable association applies to the many differentiated views of God and the universe: each of them therefore must have a particular word-symbol to express it. These word-symbols, evolved out of the deepest spiritual perception of sages, symbolise and express, as nearly as possible the particular view of God and the universe they stand for. And as the Om represents the Akhanda, the undifferentiated Brahman, the others represent the Khanda or the differentiated views of the same Being; and they are all helpful to divine meditation and the acquisition of true knowledge.

CHAPTER 8

WORSHIP OF SUBSTITUTES AND IMAGES

The next points to be considered are the worship of Pratikas or of things more or less satisfactory as substitutes for God, and the worship of Pratimās or images. What is the worship of God through a Pratika?

It is अब्रह्मणि ब्रह्मदृष्ट्यऽनुसन्धानम्—"Joining the mind with devotion to that which is not Brahman, taking it to be Brahman"—says Bhagavān Rāmānuja. "Worship the mind as Brahman this is internal; and the Akasha as Brahman, this is with regard to the Devas", says Shankara. The mind is an internal Pratika, the Akasha is an external one, and both have to be worshipped as substitutes of God. He continues, "Similarly—'the Sun is Brahman, this is the command', 'He who worships Name as Brahman'—in all such passages the doubt arises as to the worship of Pratikas." The word Pratika means going towards; and worshipping a Pratika is worshipping something as a substitute which is, in some one or more respects, like Brahman more and more, but is not Brahman. Along with the Pratikas mentioned in the Shrutis there are various others to be found in the Purānas and the Tantras. In this kind of Pratika-worship may be included all the various forms of Pitri-worship and Deva-worship.

Now worshipping Ishvara and Him alone is Bhakti; the worship of anything else—Deva, or Pitri, or any other being—cannot be Bhakti. The various kinds of worship of the various Devas are all to be included in ritualistic Karma, which gives to the worshipper only a particular result in the form of some celestial enjoyment, but can neither give rise to Bhakti nor lead to Mukti. One thing, therefore, has to be carefully borne in mind. If, as it may happen in some cases, the highly philosophic ideal, the supreme Brahman, is dragged down by Pratika-worship to the level of the Pratika, and the Pratika itself is taken to be the Ātman of the worshipper or his Antaryāmin (Inner Ruler), the worshipper gets entirely misled, as no Pratika can really be the Ātman of the worshipper.

But where Brahman Himself is the object of worship, and the Pratika stands only as a substitute or a suggestion thereof, that is to say, where, through the Pratika the omnipresent Brahman is worshipped—the Pratika itself being idealised into the cause of all, Brahman—the worship is positively beneficial; nay, it is absolutely necessary for all mankind until they have all got beyond the primary or preparatory state of the mind in regard to worship. When, therefore, any gods or other beings are worshipped in and for themselves, such worship is only a ritualistic Karma; and as a Vidyā (science) it gives us only the fruit belonging to that particular Vidya; but when the Devas or any other beings are looked upon as Brahman and worshipped, the result obtained is the same as by the worshipping of Ishvara. This explains how, in many cases, both in the Shrutis and the Smritis, a god, or a sage, or some other extraordinary being is taken up and lifted, as it were, out of his own nature and idealised into Brahman, and is then worshipped. Says the Advaitin, "Is not everything Brahman when the name and the form have been removed from it?" "Is not He, the Lord, the innermost Self of every one?" says the Vishishtādvaitin. फलम् आदित्याद्युपासनेषु ब्रह्मैव दास्यति सर्वाध्यक्षत्वात्—"The fruition of even the worship of Adityas etc. Brahman Himself bestows, because He is the Ruler of all." Says Shankara in his *Brahma-Sutra-Bhāsya*—ईदृशं चात्र ब्रह्मण उपास्यत्वं यतः प्रतीकेषु तत्दृष्ट्याध्यारोपणं प्रतिमादिषु इव विष्ण्वादीनाम्। "Here in this way does Brahman become the object of worship, because He, as Brahman, is superimposed on the Pratikas, just as Vishnu etc. are superimposed upon images etc."

The same ideas apply to the worship of the Pratimās as to that of the Pratikas; that is to say, if the image stands for a god or a saint, the worship is not the result of Bhakti, and does not lead lo liberation; but if it stands for the one

God, the worship thereof will bring both Bhakti and Mukti. Of the principal religions of the world we see Vedantism, Buddhism, and certain forms of Christianity freely using images; only two religions, Mohammedanism and Protestantism, refuse such help. Yet the Mohammedans use the grave of their saints and martyrs almost in the place of images; and the Protestants, in rejecting all concrete helps to religion, are drifting away every year farther and farther from spirituality till at present there is scarcely any difference between the advanced Protestants and the followers of August Comte, or agnostics who preach ethics alone. Again, in Christianity and Mohammedanism whatever exists of image worship is made to fall under that category in which the Pratika or the Pratima is worshipped in itself, but not as a "help to the vision" (Drishtisaukaryam) of God; therefore it is at best only of the nature of ritualistic Karmas and cannot produce either Bhakti or Mukti. In this form of image-worship, the allegiance of the soul is given to other things than Ishvara, and, therefore, such use of images, or graves, or temples, or tombs, is real idolatry; it is in itself neither sinful nor wicked—it is a rite—a Karma, and worshippers must and will get the fruit thereof.

CHAPTER 9

THE CHOSEN IDEAL

The next thing to be considered is what we know as Ishta-Nishthā. One who aspires to be a Bhakta must know that "so many opinions are so many ways". He must know that all the various sects of the various religions are the various manifestations of the glory of the same Lord. "They call You by so many names; they divide You, as it were, by different names, yet in each one of these is to be found Your omnipotence . . . . You reach the worshipper through all of these, neither is there any special time so long as the soul has intense love for You. You are so easy of approach; it is my misfortune that I cannot love You." Not only this, the Bhakta must take care not to hate, nor even to criticise those radiant sons of light who are the founders of various sects; he must not even hear them spoken ill of. Very few indeed are those who are at once the possessors of an extensive sympathy and power of appreciation, as well as an intensity of love. We find, as a rule, that liberal and sympathetic sects lose the intensity of religious feeling, and in their hands, religion is apt to degenerate into a kind of politico-social club life. On the other hand, intensely narrow sectaries, whilst displaying a very commendable love of their own ideals, are seen to have acquired every particle of that love by hating every one who is not of exactly the same opinions as themselves. Would to God that this world was full of men who were as intense in their love as worldwide in their sympathies! But such are only few and far between. Yet we know that it is practicable to educate large numbers of human beings into the ideal of a wonderful blending of both the width and the intensity of love; and the way to do that is by this path of the Istha-Nishthā or "steadfast devotion to the chosen ideal". Every sect of every religion presents only one ideal of its own to mankind, but the eternal Vedantic religion opens to mankind an infinite number of doors for ingress into the inner shrine of divinity, and places before humanity an almost inexhaustible array of ideals, there being in each of them a manifestation of the Eternal One. With the kindest solicitude, the Vedanta points out to aspiring men and women the numerous roads, hewn out of the solid rock of the realities of human life, by the glorious sons, or human manifestations, of God, in the past and in the present, and stands with outstretched arms to welcome all—to welcome even those that are yet to be—to that Home of Truth and that Ocean of Bliss, wherein the human soul, liberated from the net of Maya, may transport itself with perfect freedom and with eternal joy.

Bhakti Yoga, therefore, lays on us the imperative command not to hate or deny any one of the various paths that lead to salvation. Yet the growing plant must be hedged round to protect it until it has grown into a tree. The tender plant of spirituality will die if exposed too early to the action of a constant change of ideas and ideals. Many people, in the name of what may be called religious liberalism, may be seen feeding their idle curiosity with a continuous succession of different ideals. With them, hearing new things grows into a kind of disease, a sort of religious drink-mania. They want to hear new things just by way of getting a temporary nervous excitement, and when one such exciting influence has had its effect on them, they are ready for another. Religion is with these people a sort of intellectual opium-eating, and there it ends. "There is another sort of man", says Bhagavān Ramakrishna, "who is like the pearl-oyster of the story. The pearl-oyster leaves its bed at the bottom of the sea, and comes up to the surface to catch the rainwater when the star Svāti is in the ascendant. It floats about on the surface of the sea with its shell wide open, until it has succeeded in catching a drop of the rainwater, and then it dives deep down to its seabed, and there rests until it has succeeded in fashioning a beautiful pearl out of that raindrop."

This is indeed the most poetical and forcible way

in which the theory of Ishta-Nishthā has ever been put. This Eka-Nishthā or devotion to one ideal is absolutely necessary for the beginner in the practice of religious devotion. He must say with Hanuman in the Rāmāyana, "Though I know that the Lord of Shri and the Lord of Jānaki are both manifestations of the same Supreme Being, yet my all in all is the lotus-eyed Rāma." Or, as was said by the sage Tulasidāsa, he must say, "Take the sweetness of all, sit with all, take the name of all, say yea, yea, but keep your seat firm." Then, if the devotional aspirant is sincere, out of this little seed will come a gigantic tree like the Indian banyan, sending out branch after branch and root after root to all sides, till it covers the entire field of religion. Thus will the true devotee realise that He who was his own ideal in life is worshipped in all ideals by all sects, under all names, and through all forms.

CHAPTER 10

THE METHOD AND THE MEANS

In regard to the method and the means of Bhakti Yoga we read in the commentary of Bhagavān Ramanuja on the *Vedanta-Sutras*: "The attaining of That comes through discrimination, controlling the passions, practice, sacrificial work, purity, strength, and suppression of excessive joy." Viveka or discrimination is, according to Ramanuja, discriminating, among other things, the pure food from the impure. According to him, food becomes impure from three causes: (1) by the nature of the food itself, as in the case of garlic etc.; (2) owing to its coming from wicked and accursed persons; and (3) from physical impurities, such as dirt, or hair, etc. The Shrutis say, When the food is pure, the Sattva element gets purified, and the memory becomes unwavering", and Ramanuja quotes this from the Chhāndogya Upanishad.

The question of food has always been one of the most vital with the Bhaktas. Apart from the extravagance into which some of the Bhakti sects have run, there is a great truth underlying this question of food. We must remember that, according to the Sankhya philosophy, the Sattva, Rājas, and Tamas, which in the state of homogeneous equilibrium form the Prakriti, and in the heterogeneous disturbed condition form the universe—are both the substance and the quality of Prakriti. As such they are the materials out of which every human form has been manufactured, and the predominance of the Sattva material is what is absolutely necessary for spiritual development. The materials which we receive through our food into our body-structure go a great way to determine our mental constitution; therefore the food we eat has to be particularly taken care of. However, in this matter, as in others, the fanaticism into which the disciples invariably fall is not to be laid at the door of the masters.

And this discrimination of food is, after all, of secondary importance. The very same passage quoted above is explained by Shankara in his Bhāshya on the Upanishads in a different way by giving an entirely different meaning to the word Āhāra, translated generally as food. According to him, "That which is gathered in is Āhāra. The knowledge of the sensations, such as sound etc., is gathered in for the enjoyment of the enjoyer (self); the purification of the knowledge which gathers in the perception of the senses is the purifying of the food (Āhāra). The word 'purification-of-food' means the acquiring of the knowledge of sensations untouched by the defects of attachment, aversion, and delusion; such is the meaning. Therefore such knowledge or Āhāra being purified, the Sattva material of the possessor it—the internal organ—will become purified, and the Sattva being purified, an unbroken memory of the Infinite One, who has been known in His real nature from scriptures, will result."

These two explanations are apparently conflicting, yet both are true and necessary. The manipulating and controlling of what may be called the finer body, viz the mood, are no doubt higher functions than the controlling of the grosser body of flesh. But the control of the grosser is absolutely necessary to enable one to arrive at the control of the finer. The beginner, therefore, must pay particular attention to all such dietetic rules as have come down from the line of his accredited teachers; but the extravagant, meaningless fanaticism, which has driven religion entirely to the kitchen, as may be noticed in the case of many of our sects, without any hope of the noble truth of that religion ever coming out to the sunlight of spirituality, is a peculiar sort of pure and simple materialism. It is neither Jnāna, nor Bhakti, nor Karma; it is a special kind of lunacy, and those who pin their souls to it are more likely to go to lunatic asylums than to Brahmaloka. So it stands to reason that discrimination in the choice of food is necessary for the attainment of this higher state of mental composition which cannot be easily obtained otherwise.

Controlling the passions is the next thing to be attended to. To restrain the Indriyas (organs) from going towards the objects of the senses, to control them and bring them under the guidance of the will, is the very central virtue in religious culture. Then comes the practice of self-restraint and self-denial. All the immense possibilities of divine realisation in the soul cannot get actualised without struggle and without such practice on the part of the aspiring devotee. "The mind must always think of the Lord." It is very hard at first to compel the mind to think of the Lord always, but with every new effort the power to do so grows stronger in us. "By practice, O son of Kunti, and by non-attachment is it attained", says Shri Krishna in the Gita. And then as to sacrificial work, it is understood that the five great sacrificed* (Panchamahāyajna) have to be performed as usual.

Purity is absolutely the basic work, the bed-rock upon which the whole Bhakti-building rests. Cleansing the external body and discriminating the food are both easy, but without internal cleanliness and purity, these external observances are of no value whatsoever. In the list of qualities conducive to purity, as given by Ramanuja, there are enumerated, Satya, truthfulness; Ārjava, sincerity; Dayā, doing good to others without any gain to one's self; Ahimsā, not injuring others by thought, word, or deed; Anabhidhyā, not coveting others' goods, not thinking vain

* To gods, sages, manes, guests, and all creatures.

thoughts, and not brooding over injuries received from another. In this list, the one idea that deserves special notice is Ahimsā, non-injury to others. This duty of non-injury is, so to speak, obligatory on us in relation to all beings. As with some, it does not simply mean the non-injuring of human beings and mercilessness towards the lower animals; nor, as with some others, does it mean the protecting of cats and dogs and feeding of ants with sugar—with liberty to injure brother-man in every horrible way! It is remarkable that almost every good idea in this world can be carried to a disgusting extreme. A good practice carried to an extreme and worked in accordance with the letter of the law becomes a positive evil. The stinking monks of certain religious sects, who do not bathe lest the vermin on their bodies should be killed, never think of the discomfort and disease they bring to their fellow human beings. They do not, however, belong to the religion of the Vedas!

The test of Ahimsā is absence of jealousy. Any man may do a good deed or make a good gift on the spur of the moment or under the pressure of some superstition or priestcraft; but the real lover of mankind is he who is jealous of none. The so-called great men of the world may all be seen to become jealous of each other for a small name, for a little fame, and for a few bits of gold. So long as this jealousy exists in a heart, it is far away from the perfection of Ahimsā. The cow does not eat meat, nor does the sheep. Are they great Yogis, great non-injurers (Ahimsakas)? Any fool may abstain from eating this or that; surely that gives him no more distinction than to herbivorous animals. The man who will mercilessly cheat widows and orphans and do the vilest deeds for money is worse than any brute even if he lives entirely on grass. The man whose heart never cherishes even the thought of injury to any one, who rejoices at the prosperity of even his greatest enemy, that man is the Bhakta, he is the Yogi, he is the Guru of all, even though he lives every day of his life on the flesh of swine. Therefore we must always remember that external practices have value only as helps to develop internal purity. It is better to have internal purity alone when minute attention to external observances is not practicable. But woe unto the man and woe unto the nation that forgets the real, internal, spiritual essentials of religion and mechanically clutches with death-like grasp at all external forms and never lets them go. The forms have value only so far as they are expressions of the life within. If they have ceased to express life, crush them out without mercy.

The next means to the attainment of Bhakti Yoga is strength (Anavasāda). "This Ātman is not to be attained by the weak", says the Shruti. Both physical weakness and mental weakness are meant here. "The strong, the hardy" are the only fit students. What can puny, little, decrepit things do? They will break to pieces whenever the mysterious forces of the body and mind are even slightly awakened by the practice of any of the Yogas. It is "the young, the healthy, the strong" that can score success. Physical strength, therefore, is absolutely necessary. It is the strong body alone that can bear the shock of reaction resulting from the attempt to control the organs. He who wants to become a Bhakta must be strong, must be healthy. When the miserably weak attempt any of the Yogas, they are likely to get some incurable malady, or they weaken their minds. Voluntarily weakening the body is really no prescription for spiritual enlightenment.

The mentally weak also cannot succeed in attaining the Ātman. The person who aspires to be a Bhakta must be cheerful. In the Western world the idea of a religious man is that he never smiles, that a dark cloud must always hang over his face, which, again, must be long drawn with the jaws almost collapsed. People with emaciated bodies and long faces are fit subjects for the physician, they are not Yogis. It is the cheerful mind that is persevering. It is the strong mind that hews its way through a thousand difficulties. And this, the hardest task of all, the cutting of our way out of the net of Maya, is the work reserved only for giant wills.

Yet at the same time excessive mirth should be avoided (Anuddharsha). Excessive mirth makes us unfit for serious thought. It also fritters away the energies of the mind in vain. The stronger the will, the less the yielding to the sway of the emotions. Excessive hilarity is quite as objectionable as too much of sad seriousness, and all religious realisation is possible only when the mind is in a steady, peaceful condition of harmonious equilibrium.

It is thus that one may begin to learn how to love the Lord.

RĀJA YOGA

PREFACE

Since the dawn of history, various extraordinary phenomena have been recorded as happening amongst human beings. Witnesses are not wanting in modern times to attest to the fact of such events, even in societies living under the full blaze of modern science. The vast mass of such evidence is unreliable, as coming from ignorant, superstitious, or fraudulent persons. In many instances the so-called miracles are imitations. But what do they imitate? It is not the sign of a candid and scientific mind to throw overboard anything without proper investigation. Surface scientists, unable to explain the various extraordinary mental phenomena, strive to ignore their very existence. They are, therefore, more culpable than those who think that their prayers are answered by a being, or beings, above the clouds, or than those who believe that their petitions will make such beings change the course of the universe. The latter have the excuse of ignorance, or at least of a defective system of education, which has taught them dependence upon such beings, a dependence which has become a part of their degenerate nature. The former have no such excuse.

For thousands of years such phenomena have been studied, investigated, and generalised, the whole ground of the religious faculties of man has been analysed, and the practical result is the science of Rāja Yoga. Rāja Yoga does not, after the unpardonable manner of some modern scientists, deny the existence of facts which are difficult to explain; on the other hand, it gently yet in no uncertain terms tells the superstitious that miracles, and answers to prayers, and powers of faith, though true as facts, are not rendered comprehensible through the superstitious explanation of attributing them to the agency of a being, or beings, above the clouds. It declares that each man is only a conduit for the infinite ocean of knowledge and power that lies behind mankind. It teaches that desires and wants are in man, that the power of supply is also in man; and that wherever and whenever a desire, a want, a prayer has been fulfilled, it was out of this infinite magazine that the supply came, and not from any supernatural being. The idea of supernatural beings may rouse to a certain extent the power of action in man, but it also brings spiritual decay. It brings dependence; it brings fear; it brings superstition. It degenerates into a horrible belief in the natural weakness of man. There is no supernatural, says the Yogi, but there are in nature gross manifestations and subtle manifestations. The subtle are the causes, the gross the effects. The gross can be easily perceived by the senses; not so the subtle. The practice of Rāja Yoga will lead to the acquisition of the more subtle perceptions.

All the orthodox systems of India philosophy have one goal in view, the liberation of the soul through perfection. The method is by Yoga. The word Yoga covers an immense ground, but both the Sankhya and the Vedanta Schools point to Yoga in some form or other.

The subject of the present book is that form of Yoga known as Rāja Yoga. The aphorisms of Patanjali are the highest authority on Rāja Yoga, and form its textbook. The other philosophers, though occasionally differing from Patanjali in some philosophical points, have, as a rule, acceded to his method of practice a decided consent. The first part of this book comprises several lectures to classes delivered by the present writer in New York. The second part is a rather free translation of the aphorisms (Sutras) of Patanjali, with a running commentary. Effort has been made to avoid technicalities as far as possible, and to keep to the free and easy style of conversation. In the first part some simple and specific directions are given for the student who want to practise, *but all such are especially and earnestly reminded that, with few exceptions, Yoga can only be safely learnt by direct contact with a teacher.* If these conversations succeed in awakening a desire for further information on the subject, the teacher will not be wanting.

The system of Patanjali is based upon the system of the Sankhyas, the points of difference being very few. The two most important differences are, first, that Patanjali admits a Personal God in the form of a first teacher, while the only God the Sankhyas admit is a nearly perfected being, temporarily in charge of a cycle of creation. Second, the Yogis hold the mind to be equally all-pervading with the soul, or Purusha, and the Sankhyas do not.

—The Author.

Each soul is potentially divine.

The goal is to manifest this Divinity within
by controlling nature, external and internal.

Do this either by work, or worship, or psychic
control, or philosophy—by one, or more,
or all of these—and be free.

This is the whole of religion. Doctrines,
or dogmas, or rituals, or books, or temples, or forms,
are but secondary details.

CHAPTER 1

INTRODUCTORY

All our knowledge is based upon experience. What we call inferential knowledge, in which we go from the less to the more general, or from the general to the particular, has experience as its basis. In what are called the exact sciences, people easily find the truth, because it appeals to the particular experiences of every human being. The scientist does not tell you to believe in anything, but he has certain results which come from his own experiences, and reasoning on them when he asks us to believe in his conclusions, he appeals to some universal experience of humanity. In every exact science there is a basis which is common to all humanity, so that we can at once see the truth or the fallacy of the conclusions drawn therefrom.

Now, the question is: Has religion any such basis or not? I shall have to answer the question both in the affirmative and in the negative.

Religion, as it is generally taught all over the world, is said to be based upon faith and belief, and, in most cases, consists only of different sets of theories, and that is the reason why we find all religions quarrelling with one another. These theories, again, are based upon belief. One man says there is a great Being sitting above the clouds and governing the whole universe, and he asks me to believe that solely on the authority of his assertion. In the same way, I may have my own ideas, which I am asking others to believe, and if they ask a reason, I cannot give them any. This is why religion and metaphysical philosophy have a bad name nowadays. Every educated man seems to say, "Oh, these religions are only bundles of theories without any standard to judge them by, each man preaching his own pet ideas." Nevertheless, there is a basis of universal belief in religion, governing all the different theories and all the varying ideas of different sects in different countries. Going to their basis we find that they also are based upon universal experiences.

In the first place, if you analyse all the various religions of the world, you will find that these are divided into two classes, those with a book and those without a book. Those with a book are the strongest, and have the largest number of followers. Those without books have mostly died out, and the few new ones have very small following. Yet, in all of them we find one consensus of opinion, that the truths they teach are the results of the experiences of particular persons. The Christian asks you to believe in his religion, to believe in Christ and to believe in him as the incarnation of God, to believe in a God, in a soul, and in a better state of that soul. If I ask him for reason, he says he believes in them. But if you go to the fountainhead of Christianity, you will find that it is based upon experience. Christ said he saw God; the disciples said they felt God; and so forth. Similarly, in Buddhism, it is Buddha's experience. He experienced certain truths, saw them, came in contact with them, and preached them to the world. So with the Hindus. In their books the writers, who are called Rishis, or sages, declare they experienced certain truths, and these they preach. Thus it is clear that all the religions of the world have been built upon that one universal and adamantine foundation of all our knowledge—direct experience. The teachers all saw God; they all saw their own souls, they saw their future, they saw their eternity, and what they saw they preached. Only there is this difference that by most of these religions especially in modern times, a peculiar claim is made, namely, that these experiences are impossible at the present day; they were only possible with a few men, who were the first founders of the religions that subsequently bore their names. At the present time these experiences have become obsolete, and, therefore, we have now to take religion on belief. This I entirely deny. If there has been one experience in this world in any particular branch of knowledge, it absolutely follows that that experience has been possible millions of times before, and will be repeated eternally. Uniformity is the rigorous law of nature; what once happened can happen always.

The teachers of the science of Yoga, therefore, declare that religion is not only based upon the experience of ancient times, but that no man can be religious until he has the same perceptions himself. Yoga is the science which teaches us how to get these perceptions. It is not much use to talk about religion until one has felt it. Why is there so much disturbance, so much fighting and quarrelling in the name of God? There has been more bloodshed in the name of God than for any other cause, because people never went to the fountainhead; they were content only to give a mental assent to the customs of their forefathers, and wanted others to do the same. What right has a man to say he has a soul if he does not feel it, or that there is a God if he does not see Him? If there is a God we must see Him, if there is a soul we must perceive it; otherwise it is better not to believe. It is better to be an outspoken atheist than a hypocrite. The modern idea, on the one hand, with the "learned" is that religion and metaphysics and all search after a Supreme Being are futile; on the other hand, with the semi-educated, the idea seems to be that these things really have no basis; their only value consists in the fact that they furnish strong motive powers for doing good to the world. If men believe in a God, they may become good, and moral, and so make good citizens. We cannot blame them for holding such ideas, seeing that all the teaching these men get is simply to believe in an eternal rigmarole of words, without any substance behind them. They are asked to live upon words; can they do it? If they could, I should not have the least regard for human nature. Man wants truth, wants to experience truth for himself; when he has grasped it, realised it, felt it within his heart of hearts, then alone, declare the Vedas, would all doubts vanish, all darkness be scattered, and all crookedness be made straight. "Ye children of immortality, even those who live in the highest sphere, the way is found; there is a way out of all this darkness, and that is by perceiving Him who is beyond all darkness; there is no other way."

The science of Rāja Yoga proposes to put before humanity a practical and scientifically worked out method of reaching this truth. In the first place, every science must have its own method of investigation. If you want to become an astronomer and sit down and cry "Astronomy! Astronomy!" it will never come to you. The same with chemistry. A certain method must be followed. You must go to a laboratory, take different substances, mix them up, compound them, experiment with them, and out of that will come a knowledge of chemistry. If you want to be an astronomer, you must go to an observatory, take a telescope, study the stars and planets, and then you will become an astronomer. Each science must have its own methods. I could preach you thousands of sermons, but they would not make you religious, until you practiced the method. These are the truths of the sages of all countries, of all ages, of men pure and unselfish, who had no motive but to do good to the world. They all declare that they have found some truth higher than what the senses can bring to us, and they invite verification. They ask us to take up the method and practice honestly, and then, if we do not find this higher truth, we will have the right to say there is no truth in the claim, but before we have done that, we are not rational in denying the truth of their assertions. So we must work faithfully using the prescribed methods, and light will come.

In acquiring knowledge we make use of generalisations, and generalisation is based upon observation. We first observe facts, then generalise, and then draw conclusions or principles. The knowledge of the mind, of the internal nature of man, of thought, can never be had until we have first the power of observing the facts that are going on within. It is comparatively easy to observe facts in the external world, for many instruments have been invented for the purpose, but in the internal world we have no instrument to help us. Yet we know we must observe in order to have a real science. Without a proper analysis, any science will be hopeless—mere theorising. And that is why all the psychologists have been quarrelling among themselves since the beginning of time, except those few who found out the means of observation.

The science of Rāja Yoga, in the first place, proposes to give us such a means of observing the internal states. The instrument is the mind itself. The power of attention, when properly guided, and directed towards the internal world, will analyse the mind, and illumine facts for us. The powers of the mind are like rays of light dissipated; when they are concentrated, they illumine. This is our only means of knowledge. Everyone is using it, both in the external and the internal world; but, for the psychologist, the same minute observation has to be directed to the internal world, which the scientific man directs to the external; and this requires a great deal of practice. From our childhood upwards we have been taught only to pay attention to things external, but never to things internal; hence most of us have nearly lost the faculty of observing the internal mechanism. To turn the mind as it were, inside, stop it from going outside, and then to concentrate all its powers, and throw them upon the mind itself, in order that it may know its own nature, analyse itself, is very hard work. Yet that is the only way to anything which will be a scientific approach to the subject.

What is the use of such knowledge? In the first place, knowledge itself is the highest reward of knowledge, and secondly, there is also utility in it. It will take away all our misery. When by analysing his own mind, man comes face to face, as it were, with something which is never destroyed, something which is, by its own nature, eternally pure and perfect, he will no more be miserable, no more unhappy. All misery comes from fear, from unsatisfied desire. Man will find that he never dies, and then he will have no more fear of death. When he knows that he is perfect, he will have no more vain desires, and both these causes being absent, there will be no more misery—there will be perfect bliss, even while in this body.

There is only one method by which to attain this knowledge, that which is called concentration. The chemist in his laboratory concentrates all the energies of his mind into one focus, and throws them upon the materials he is analysing, and so finds out their secrets. The astronomer concentrates all the energies of his mind and projects them through his telescope upon the skies; and the stars, the sun, and the moon, give up their secrets to him. The more I can concentrate my thoughts on the matter on which I am talking to you, the more light I can throw upon you. You are listening to me, and the more you concentrate your thoughts, the more clearly you will grasp what I have to say.

How has all the knowledge in the world been gained but by the concentration of the powers of the mind? The world is ready to give up its secrets if we only know how to knock, how to give it the necessary blow. The strength and force of the blow come through concentration. There is no limit to the power of the human mind. The more concentrated it is, the more power is brought to bear on one point; that is the secret.

It is easy to concentrate the mind on external things, the mind naturally goes outwards; but not so in the case of religion, or psychology, or metaphysics, where the subject and the object, are one. The object is internal, the mind itself is the object, and it is necessary to study the mind itself—mind studying mind. We know that there is the power of the mind called reflection. I am talking to you. At the same time I am standing aside, as it were, a second person, and knowing and hearing what I am talking. You work and think at the same time, while a portion of your mind stands by and sees what you are thinking. The powers of the mind should be concentrated and turned back upon itself, and as the darkest places reveal their secrets before the penetrating rays of the sun, so will this concentrated mind penetrate its own innermost secrets. Thus will we come to the basis of belief, the real genuine religion. We will perceive for ourselves whether we have souls, whether life is of five minutes or of eternity, whether there is a God in the universe or more. It will all be revealed to us. This is what Rāja Yoga proposes to teach. The goal of all its teaching is how to concentrate the minds, then, how to discover the innermost recesses of our own minds, then, how to generalise their contents and form our own conclusions from them. It, therefore, never asks the question what our religion is, whether we are Deists or Atheists, whether Christians, Jews, or Buddhists. We are human beings; that is sufficient. Every human being has the right and the power to seek for religion. Every human being has the right to ask the reason, why, and to have his question answered by himself, if he only takes the trouble.

So far, then, we see that in the study of this Rāja Yoga no faith or belief is necessary. Believe nothing until you find it out for yourself; that is what it teaches us. Truth requires no prop to make it stand. Do you mean to say that the facts of our awakened state require any dreams or imaginings to prove them? Certainly not. This study of Rāja Yoga takes a long time and constant practice. A part of this practice is physical, but in the main it is mental. As we proceed we shall find how intimately the mind is connected with the body. If we believe that the mind is simply a finer part of the body, and that mind acts upon the body, then it stands to reason that the body must react upon the mind. If the body is sick, the mind becomes sick also. If the body is healthy, the mind remains healthy and strong. When one is angry, the mind becomes disturbed. Similarly when the mind is disturbed, the body also becomes disturbed. With the majority of mankind the mind is greatly under the control of the body, their mind being very little developed. The vast mass of humanity is very little removed from the animals. Not only so, but in many instances, the power of control in them is little higher than that of the lower animals. We have very little command of our minds. Therefore to bring that command about, to get that control over body and mind, we must take certain physical helps. When the body is sufficiently controlled, we can attempt the manipulation of the mind. By manipulating the mind, we shall be able to bring it under our control, make it work as we like, and compel it to concentrate its powers as we desire.

According to the Rāja Yogi, the external world is but the gross form of the internal, or subtle. The finer is always the cause, the grosser the effect. So the external world is the effect, the internal the cause. In the same way external forces are simply the grosser parts, of which the internal forces are the finer. The man who has discovered and learned how to manipulate the internal forces will get the whole of nature under his control. The Yogi proposes to himself no less a task than to master the whole universe, to control the whole of nature. He wants to arrive at the point where what we call "nature's laws" will have no influence over him, where he will be able to get beyond them all. He will be master of the whole of nature, internal and external. The progress and civilisation of the human race simply mean controlling this nature.

Different races take to different processes of controlling nature. Just as in the same society some individuals want to control the external nature, and others the internal, so, among races, some want to control the external nature, and others the internal. Some say that by controlling internal nature we control everything. Others that by controlling external nature we control everything. Carried to the extreme both are right, because in nature there is no such division as internal or external. These are fictitious limitations that never existed. The externalists and the internalists are destined to meet at the same point, when both reach the extreme of their knowledge. Just as a physicist, when he pushes his knowledge to its limits, finds it melting away into metaphysics, so a metaphysician will find that what he calls mind and matter are but apparent distinctions, the reality being One.

The end and aim of all science is to find the unity, the One out of which the manifold is being manufactured, that One existing as many. Rāja Yoga proposes to start from the internal world, to study internal nature, and through that, control the whole—both internal and external. It is a very old attempt. India has been its special stronghold, but it was also attempted by other nations. In Western countries it was regarded as mysticism and people who wanted to practice it were either burned or killed as witches and sorcerers. In India, for various reasons, it fell into the hands of persons who destroyed ninety per cent of the knowledge, and tried to make a great secret of the remainder. In modern times many so-called teachers have arisen in the West worse than those of India, because the latter knew something, while these modern exponents know nothing.

Anything that is secret and mysterious in these systems of Yoga should be at once rejected. The best guide in life is strength. In religion, as in all other matters, discard everything that weakens you, have nothing to do with it. Mystery-mongering weakens the human brain. It has well-nigh destroyed Yoga—one of the grandest of sciences. From the time it was discovered, more than four thousand years ago, Yoga was perfectly delineated, formulated, and preached in India. It is a striking fact that the more modern the commentator the greater the mistakes he makes, while the more ancient the writer the more rational he is. Most of the modern writers talk of all sorts of mystery. Thus Yoga fell into the hands of a few persons who made it a secret, instead of letting the full blaze of daylight and reason fall upon it. They did so that they might have the powers to themselves.

In the first place, there is no mystery in what I teach. What little I know I will tell you. So far as I can reason it out I will do so, but as to what I do not know I will simply tell you what the books say. It is wrong to believe blindly. You must exercise your own reason and judgment;

you must practice, and see whether these things happen or not. Just as you would take up any other science, exactly in the same manner you should take up this science for study. There is neither mystery nor danger in it. So far as it is true, it ought to be preached in the public streets, in broad daylight. Any attempt to mystify these things is productive of great danger.

Before proceeding further, I will tell you a little of the Sānkhya philosophy, upon which the whole of Rāja Yoga is based. According to the Sankhya philosophy, the genesis of perception is as follows: the affections of external objects are carried by the outer instruments to their respective brain centres or organs, the organs carry the affections to the mind, the mind to the determinative faculty, from this the Purusha (the soul) receives them, when perception results. Next he gives the order back, as it were, to the motor centres to do the needful. With the exception of the Purusha all of these are material, but the mind is much finer matter than the external instruments. That material of which the mind is composed goes also to form the subtle matter called the Tanmātras. These become gross and make the external matter. That is the psychology of the Sankhya. So that between the intellect and the grosser matter outside there is only a difference in degree. The Purusha is the only thing which is immaterial. The mind is an instrument, as it were, in the hands of the soul, through which the soul catches external objects. The mind is constantly changing and vacillating, and can, when perfected, either attach itself to several organs, to one, or to none. For instance, if I hear the clock with great attention, I will not, perhaps, see anything although my eyes may be open, showing that the mind was not attached to the seeing organ, while it was to the hearing organ. But the perfected mind can be attached to all the organs simultaneously. It has the reflexive power of looking back into its own depths. This reflexive power is what the Yogi wants to attain; by concentrating the powers of the mind, and turning them inward, he seeks to know what is happening inside. There is in this no question of mere belief; it is the analysis arrived at by certain philosophers. Modern physiologists tell us that the eyes are not the organ of vision, but that the organ is in one of the nerve centres of the brain, and so with all the senses; they also tell us that these centres are formed of the same material as the brain itself. The Sankhyas also tell us the same thing The former is a statement on the physical side, and the latter on the psychological side; yet both are the same. Our field of research lies beyond this.

The Yogi proposes to attain that fine state of perception in which he can perceive all the different mental states. There must be mental perception of all of them. One can perceive how the sensation is travelling, how the mind is receiving it, how it is going to the determinative faculty, and how this gives it to the Purusha. As each science requires certain preparations and has its own method, which must be followed before it could be understood, even so in Rāja Yoga.

Certain regulations as to food are necessary; we must

use that food which brings us the purest mind. If you go into a menagerie, you will find this demonstrated at once. You see the elephants, huge animals, but calm and gentle; and if you go towards the cages of the lions and tigers, you find them restless, showing how much difference has been made by food. All the forces that are working in this body have been produced out of food; we see that every day. If you begin to fast, first your body will get weak, the physical forces will suffer; then after a few days, the mental forces will suffer also. First, memory will fail. Then comes a point, when you are not able to think, much less to pursue any course of reasoning. We have, therefore, to take care what sort of food we eat at the beginning, and when we have got strength enough, when our practice is well advanced, we need not be so careful in this respect. While the plant is growing it must be hedged round, lest it be injured; but when it becomes a tree, the hedges are taken away. It is strong enough to withstand all assaults

A Yogi must avoid the two extremes of luxury and austerity. He must not fast, nor torture his flesh. He who does so, says the Gita, cannot be a Yogi: He who fasts, he who keeps awake, he who sleeps much, he who works too much, he who does no work, none of these can be a Yogi (Gita, VI, 16).

CHAPTER 2

THE FIRST STEPS

Rāja Yoga is divided into eight steps. The first is Yama—non-killing, truthfulness, non-stealing, continence, and non-receiving of any gifts. Next is Niyama—cleanliness, contentment, austerity, study, and self-surrender to God. Then comes Āsana, or posture; Pranayama, or control of Prana; Pratyāhāra, or restraint of the senses from their objects; Dhāranā, or fixing the mind on a spot; Dhyāna, or meditation; and Samādhi, or superconsciousness. The Yama and Niyama, as we see, are moral trainings; without these as the basis no practice of Yoga will succeed. As these two become established, the Yogi will begin to realise the fruits of his practice; without these it will never bear fruit. A Yogi must not think of injuring anyone, by thought, word, or deed. Mercy shall not be for men alone, but shall go beyond, and embrace the whole world.

The next step is Āsana, posture. A series of exercises, physical and mental, is to be gone through every day, until certain higher states are reached. Therefore it is quite necessary that we should find a posture in which we can remain long. That posture which is the easiest for one should be the one chosen. For thinking, a certain posture may be very easy for one man, while to another it may be very difficult. We will find later on that during the study of these psychological matters a good deal of activity goes on in the body. Nerve currents will have to be displaced and given a new channel. New sorts of vibrations will begin, the whole constitution will be remodelled as it were. But the main part of the activity will lie along the spinal column, so that the one thing necessary for the posture is to hold the spinal column free, sitting erect, holding the three parts—the chest, neck, and head—in a straight line. Let the whole weight of the body be supported by the ribs, and then you have an easy natural postures with the spine straight. You will easily see that you cannot think very high thoughts with the chest in. This portion of the Yoga is a little similar to the Hatha Yoga which deals entirely with the physical body, its aim being to make the physical body very strong. We have nothing to do with it here, because its practices are very difficult, and cannot be learned in a day, and, after all, do not lead to much spiritual growth. Many of these practices you will find in Delsarte and other teachers, such as placing the body in different postures, but the object in these is physical, not psychological. There is not one muscle in the body over which a man cannot establish a perfect control. The heart can be made to stop or go on at his bidding, and each part of the organism can be similarly controlled.

The result of this branch of Yoga is to make men live long; health is the chief idea, the one goal of the Hatha Yogi. He is determined not to fall sick, and he never does. He lives long; a hundred years is nothing to him; he is quite young and fresh when he is 150, without one hair turned grey. But that is all. A banyan tree lives sometimes 5000 years, but it is a banyan tree and nothing more. So, if a man lives long, he is only a healthy animal. One or two ordinary lessons of the Hatha Yogis are very useful. For instance, some of you will find it a good thing for headaches to drink cold water through the nose as soon as you get up in the morning; the whole day your brain will be nice and cool, and you will never catch cold. It is very easy to do; put your nose into the water, draw it up through the nostrils and make a pump action in the throat.

After one has learned to have a firm erect seat, one has to perform, according to certain schools, a practice called the purifying of the nerves. This part has been rejected by some as not belonging to Rāja Yoga, but as so great an authority as the commentator Shankarāchārya advises it, I think fit that it should be mentioned, and I will quote his own directions from his commentary on the Shvetāshvatara Upanishad: "The mind whose dross has been cleared away by Pranayama, becomes fixed in Brahman; therefore Pranayama is declared. First the nerves are to be purified, then comes the power to practice Pranayama. Stopping the right nostril with the thumb, through the left nostril fill in air, according to capacity; then, without any interval, throw the air out through the right nostril, closing the left one. Again inhaling through the right nostril eject through the left, according to capacity; practicing this three or five times at four hours of the day, before dawn, during midday, in the evening, and at midnight, in fifteen days or a month purity of the nerves is attained; then begins Pranayama."

Practice is absolutely necessary. You may sit down and listen to me by the hour every day, but if you do not practice, you will not get one step further. It all depends on practice. We never understand these things until we experience them. We will have to see and feel them for ourselves. Simply listening to explanations and theories will not do. There are several obstructions to practice. The first obstruction is an unhealthy body: if the body is not in a fit state, the practice will be obstructed. Therefore we have to keep the body in good health; we have to take care of what we eat and drink, and what we do. Always use a mental effort, what is usually called "Christian Science," to keep the body strong. That is all—nothing further of the body. We must not forget that health is only a means to an end. If health were the end, we would be like animals; animals rarely become unhealthy.

The second obstruction is doubt; we always feel doubtful about things we do not see. Man cannot live upon words, however he may try. So, doubt comes to us as to whether there is any truth in these things or not; even the best of us will doubt sometimes: With practice, within a few days, a little glimpse will come, enough to give one encouragement and hope. As a certain commentator on Yoga philosophy says, "When one proof is obtained, however little that may be, it will give us faith in the whole teaching of Yoga." For instance, after the first few months of practice, you will begin to find you can read another's thoughts; they will come to you in picture form. Perhaps you will hear something happening at a long distance, when you concentrate your mind with a wish to hear. These glimpses will come, by little bits at first, but enough to give you faith, and strength, and hope. For instance, if you concentrate your thoughts on the tip of your nose, in a few days you will begin to smell most beautiful fragrance, which will be enough to show you that there are certain mental perceptions that can be made obvious without the contact of physical objects. But we must always remember that these are only the means; the aim, the end, the goal, of all this training is liberation of the soul. Absolute control of nature, and nothing short of it, must be the goal. We must be the masters, and not the slaves of nature; neither body nor mind must be our master, nor must we forget that the body is mine, and not I the body's.

A god and a demon went to learn about the Self from a great sage. They studied with him for a long time. At last the sage told them, "You yourselves are the Being you are seeking." Both of them thought that their bodies were the

Self. They went back to their people quite satisfied and said, "We have learned everything that was to be learned; eat, drink, and be merry; we are the Self; there is nothing beyond us." The nature of the demon was ignorant, clouded; so he never inquired any further, but was perfectly contented with the idea that he was God, that by the Self was meant the body. The god had a purer nature. He at first committed the mistake of thinking: I, this body, am Brahman: so keep it strong and in health, and well dressed, and give it all sorts of enjoyments. But, in a few days, he found out that that could not be the meaning of the sage, their master; there must be something higher. So he came back and said, "Sir, did you teach me that this body was the Self? If so, I see all bodies die; the Self cannot die." The sage said, "Find it out; thou art That." Then the god thought that the vital forces which work the body were what the sage meant. But. after a time, he found that if he ate, these vital forces remained strong, but, if he starved, they became weak. The god then went back to the sage and said, "Sir, do you mean that the vital forces are the Self?" The sage said, "Find out for yourself; thou art That." The god returned home once more, thinking that it was the mind, perhaps, that was the Self. But in a short while he saw that thoughts were so various, now good, again bad; the mind was too changeable to be the Self. He went back to the sage and said, "Sir, I do not think that the mind is the Self; did you mean that?" "No," replied the sage, "thou art That; find out for yourself." The god went home, and at last found that he was the Self, beyond all thought, one without birth or death, whom the sword cannot pierce or the fire burn, whom the air cannot dry or the water melt, the beginningless and endless, the immovable, the intangible, the omniscient, the omnipotent Being; that It was neither the body nor the mind, but beyond them all. So he was satisfied; but the poor demon did not get the truth, owing to his fondness for the body.

This world has a good many of these demoniac natures, but there are some gods too. If one proposes to teach any science to increase the power of sense-enjoyment, one finds multitudes ready for it. If one undertakes to show the supreme goal, one finds few to listen to him. Very few have the power to grasp the higher, fewer still the patience to attain to it. But there are a few also who know that even if the body can be made to live for a thousand years, the result in the end will be the same. When the forces that hold it together go away, the body must fall. No man was ever born who could stop his body one moment from changing. Body is the name of a series of changes. "As in a river the masses of water are changing before you every moment, and new masses are coming, yet taking similar form, so is it with this body." Yet the body must be kept strong and healthy. It is the best instrument we have.

This human body is the greatest body in the universe, and a human being the greatest being. Man is higher than all animals, than all angels; none is greater than man. Even the Devas (gods) will have to come down again and attain to salvation through a human body. Man alone attains to perfection, not even the Devas. According to the Jews and

Mohammedans, God created man after creating the angels and everything else, and after creating man He asked the angels to come and salute him, and all did so except Iblis; so God cursed him and he became Satan. Behind this allegory is the great truth that this human birth is the greatest birth we can have. The lower creation, the animal, is dull, and manufactured mostly out of Tamas. Animals cannot have any high thoughts; nor can the angels, or Devas, attain to direct freedom without human birth. In human society, in the same way, too much wealth or too much poverty is a great impediment to the higher development of the soul. It is from the middle classes that the great ones of the world come. Here the forces are very equally adjusted and balanced.

Returning to our subject, we come next to Pranayarna, controlling the breathing. What has that to do with concentrating the powers of thc mind? Breath is like the flywheel of this machine, the body. In a big engine you find the flywheel first moving, and that motion is conveyed to finer and finer machinery until the most delicate and finest mechanism in the machine is in motion. The breath is that flywheel, supplying and regulating the motive power to everything in this body.

There was once a minister to a great king. He fell into disgrace. The king, as a punishment, ordered him to be shut up in the top of a very high tower. This was done, and the minister was left there to perish. He had a faithful wife, however, who came to the tower at night and called to her husband at the top to know what she could do to help him.

He told her to return to the tower the following night and bring with her a long rope, some stout twine, pack thread, silken thread, a beetle, and a little honey. Wondering much, the good wife obeyed her husband, and brought him the desired articles. The husband directed her to attach the silken thread firmly to the beetle, then to smear its horns with a drop of honey, and to set it free on the wall of the tower, with its head pointing upwards. She obeyed all these instructions, and the beetle started on its long journey. Smelling the honey ahead it slowly crept onwards, in the hope of reaching the honey, until at last it reached the top of the tower, when the minister grasped the beetle, and got possession of the silken thread. He told his wife to tie the other end to the pack thread, and after he had drawn up the pack thread, he repeated the process with the stout twine, and lastly with the rope. Then the rest was easy. The minister descended from the tower by means of the rope, and made his escape. In this body of ours the breath motion is the "silken thread"; by laying hold of and learning to control it we grasp the pack thread of the nerve currents, and from these the stout twine of our thoughts, and lastly the rope of Prana, controlling which we reach freedom.

We do not know anything about our own bodies; we cannot know. At best we can take a dead body, and cut it in pieces, and there are some who can take a live animal and cut it in pieces in order to see what is inside the body. Still, that has nothing to do with our own bodies. We know very little about them. Why do we not? Because our attention is not discriminating enough to catch the very fine movements that are going on within. We can know of them only when the mind becomes more subtle and enters, as it were, deeper into the body. To get the subtle perception we have to begin with the grosser perceptions. We have to get hold of that which is setting the whole engine in motion. That is the Prana, the most obvious manifestation of which is the breath. Then, along with the breath, we shall slowly enter the body, which will enable us to find out about the subtle forces, the nerve currents that are moving all over the body. As soon as we perceive and learn to feel them, we shall begin to get control over them, and over the body. The mind is also set in motion: by these different nerve currents, so at last we shall reach the state of perfect control over the body and the mind, making both our servants. Knowledge is power. We have to get this power. So we must begin at the beginning, with Pranayama, restraining the Prana. This Pranayama is a long subject, and will take several lessons to illustrate it thoroughly. We shall take it part by part.

We shall gradually see the reasons for each exercise and what forces in the body are set in motion. All these things will come to us, but it requires constant practice, and the proof will come by practice. No amount of reasoning which I can give you will be proof to you, until you have demonstrated it for yourselves. As soon as you begin to feel these currents in motion all over you, doubts will vanish, but it requires hard practice every day. You must practice at least twice every day, and the best times are towards the morning and the evening. When night passes into day, and day into night, a state of relative calmness ensues. The early morning and the early evening are the two periods of calmness. Your body will have a like tendency to become calm at those times. We should take advantage of that natural condition and begin then to practice. Make it a rule not to eat until you have practiced; if you do this, the sheer force of hunger will break your laziness. In India they teach children never to eat until they have practiced or worshipped, and it becomes natural to them after a time; a boy will not feel hungry until he has bathed and practiced.

Those of you who can afford it will do better to have a room for this practice alone. Do not sleep in that room, it must be kept holy. You must not enter the room until you have bathed, and are perfectly clean in body and mind. Place flowers in that room always; they are the best surroundings for a Yogi; also pictures that are pleasing. Burn incense morning and evening. Have no quarrelling, nor anger, nor unholy thought in that room. Only allow those persons to enter it who are of the same thought as you. Then gradually there will be an atmosphere of holiness in the room, so that when you are miserable, sorrowful, doubtful, or your mind is disturbed, the very fact of entering that room will make you calm. This was the idea of the temple and the church, and in some temples and churches you will find it even now, but in the majority of them the very idea has been lost. The idea is that by keeping holy vibrations there the place becomes and remains illumined. Those who cannot afford to have a room set apart can practice anywhere they like. Sit in a straight posture, and the first thing to do is to send a current of holy thought to all creation. Mentally repeat, "Let all beings be happy; let all beings be peaceful; let all beings be blissful." So do to the east, south, north and west. The more you do that the better you will feel yourself. You will find at last that the easiest way to make ourselves healthy is to see that others are healthy, and the easiest way to make ourselves happy is to see that others are happy. After doing that, those who believe in God should pray—not for money, not for health, nor for heaven; pray for knowledge and light; every other prayer is selfish. Then the next thing to do is to think of your own body, and see that it is strong and healthy; it is the best instrument you have. Think of it as being as strong as adamant, and that with the help of this body you will cross the ocean of life. Freedom is never to be reached by the weak. Throw away all weakness. Tell your body that it is strong, tell your mind that it is strong, and have unbounded faith and hope in yourself.

CHAPTER 3

PRANA

Pranayama is not, as many think, something about breath; breath indeed has very little to do with it, if anything. Breathing is only one of the many exercises through which we get to the real Pranayama. Pranayama means the control of Prana. According to the philosophers of India, the whole universe is composed of two materials, one of which they call Akasha. It is the omnipresent, all-penetrating existence. Everything that has form, everything that is the result of combination, is evolved out of this Akasha. It is the Akasha that becomes the air, that becomes the liquids, that becomes the solids; it is the Akasha that becomes the sun, the earth, the moon, the stars, the comets; it is the Akasha that becomes the human body, the animal body, the plants, every form that we see, everything that can be sensed, everything that exists. It cannot be perceived; it is so subtle that it is beyond all ordinary perception; it can only be seen when it has become gross, has taken form. At the beginning of creation there is only this Akasha. At the end of the cycle the solids, the liquids, and the gases all melt into the Akasha again, and the next creation similarly proceeds out of this Akasha.

By what power is this Akasha manufactured into this universe? By the power of Prana. Just as Akasha is the infinite, omnipresent material of this universe, so is this Prana the infinite, omnipresent manifesting power of this universe. At the beginning and at the end of a cycle everything becomes Akasha, and all the forces that are in the universe resolve back into the Prana; in the next cycle, out of this Prana is evolved everything that we call energy, everything that we call force. It is the Prana that is manifesting as motion; it is the Prana that is manifesting as gravitation, as magnetism. It is the Prana that is manifesting as the actions of the body, as the nerve currents, as thought force. From thought down to the lowest force, everything is but the manifestation of Prana. The sum total of all forces in the universe, mental or physical, when resolved back to their original state, is called Prana. "When there was neither aught nor naught, when darkness was covering darkness, what existed then? That Akasha existed without motion." The physical motion of the Prana was stopped, but it existed all the same.

At the end of a cycle the energies now displayed in

the universe quiet down and become potential. At the beginning of the next cycle they start up, strike upon the Akasha, and out of the Akasha evolve these various forms, and as the Akasha changes, this Prana changes also into all these manifestations of energy. The knowledge and control of this Prana is really what is meant by Pranayama.

This opens to us the door to almost unlimited power. Suppose, for instance, a man understood the Prana perfectly, and could control it, what power on earth would not be his? He would be able to move the sun and stars out of their places, to control everything in the universe, from the atoms to the biggest suns, because he would control the Prana. This is the end and aim of Pranayama. When the Yogi becomes perfect, there will be nothing in nature not under his control. If he orders the gods or the souls of the departed to come, they will come at his bidding. All the forces of nature will obey him as slaves. When the ignorant see these powers of the Yogi, they call them the miracles. One peculiarity of the Hindu mind is that it always inquires for the last possible generalisation, leaving the details to be worked out afterwards. The question is raised in the Vedas, "What is that, knowing which, we shall know everything?" Thus, all books, and all philosophies that have been written, have been only to prove that by knowing which everything is known. If a man wants to know this universe bit by bit he must know every individual grain of sand, which means infinite time; he cannot know all of them. Then how can knowledge be? How is it possible for a man to be all-knowing through particulars? The Yogis say that behind this particular manifestation there is a generalisation. Behind all particular ideas stands a generalised, an abstract principle; grasp it, and you have grasped everything. Just as this whole universe has been generalised in the Vedas into that One Absolute Existence, and he who has grasped that Existence has grasped the whole universe, so all forces have been generalised into this Prana, and he who has grasped the Prana has grasped all the forces of the universe, mental or physical. He who has controlled the Prana has controlled his own mind, and all the minds that exist. He who has controlled the Prana has controlled his body, and all the bodies that exist, because the Prana is the generalised manifestation of force.

How to control the Prana is the one idea of Pranayama. All the trainings and exercises in this regard are for that one end. Each man must begin where he stands, must learn how to control the things that are nearest to him. This body is very near to us, nearer than anything in the external universe, and this mind is the nearest of all. The Prana which is working this mind and body is the nearest to us of all the Prana in this universe. This little wave of the Prana which represents our own energies, mental and physical, is the nearest to us of all the waves of the infinite ocean of Prana. If we can succeed in controlling that little wave, then alone we can hope to control the whole of Prana. The Yogi who has done this gains perfection; no longer is he under any power. He becomes almost almighty, almost all-knowing. We see sects in every country who have attempted this control of Prana. In this country there are Mind-healers, Faith-healers, Spiritualists, Christian Scientists, Hypnotists, etc., and if we examine these different bodies, we shall find at the back of each this control of the Prana, whether they know it or not. If you boil all their theories down, the residuum will be that. It is the one and the same force they are manipulating, only unknowingly. They have stumbled on the discovery of a force and are using it unconsciously without knowing its nature, but it is the same as the Yogi uses, and which comes from Prana.

The Prana is the vital force in every being. Thought is the finest and highest action of Prana. Thought, again, as we see, is not all. There is also what we call instinct or unconscious thought, the lowest plane of action. If a mosquito stings us, our hand will strike it automatically, instinctively. This is one expression of thought. All reflex actions of the body belong to this plane of thought. There is again the other plane of thought, the conscious. I reason, I judge, I think, I see the pros and cons of certain things, yet that is not all. We know that reason is limited. Reason can go only to a certain extent, beyond that it cannot reach. The circle within which it runs is very very limited indeed. Yet at the same time, we find facts rush into this circle. Like the coming of comets certain things come into this circle; it is certain they come from outside the limit, although our reason cannot go beyond. The causes of the phenomena intruding themselves in this small limit are outside of this limit. The mind can exist on a still higher plane, the superconscious. When the mind has attained to that state, which is called Samādhi—perfect concentration, superconsciousness—it goes beyond the limits of reason, and comes face to face with facts which no instinct or reason can ever know. All manipulations of the subtle forces of the body, the different manifestations of Prana, if trained, give a push to the mind, help it to go up higher, and become superconscious, from where it acts.

In this universe there is one continuous substance on every plane of existence. Physically this universe is one: there is no difference between the sun and you. The scientist will tell you it is only a fiction to say the contrary. There is no real difference between the table and me; the table is one point in the mass of matter, and I another point. Each form represents, as it were, one whirlpool in the infinite ocean of matter, of which not one is constant. Just as in a rushing stream there may be millions of whirlpools, the water in each of which is different every moment, turning round and round for a few seconds, and then passing out, replaced by a fresh quantity, so the whole universe is one constantly changing mass of matter, in which all forms of existence are so many whirlpools. A mass of matter enters into one whirlpool, say a human body, stays there for a period, becomes changed, and goes out into another, say an animal body this time, from which again after a few years, it enters into another whirlpool, called a lump of mineral. It is a constant change. Not one body is constant. There is no such thing as my body, or your body, except in words. Of the one huge mass of matter, one point is called a moon, another a sun, another a man, another the earth, another a plant, another a mineral. Not one is constant, but everything is changing, matter eternally concreting and disintegrating. So it is with the mind. Matter is represented by the ether; when the action of Prana is most subtle, this very ether, in the finer state of vibration, will represent the mind and there it will be still one unbroken mass. If you can simply get to that subtle vibration, you will see and feel that the whole universe is composed of subtle vibrations. Sometimes certain drugs have the power to take us, while as yet in the senses, to that condition. Many of you may remember the celebrated experiment of Sir Humphrey Davy, when the laughing gas overpowered him—how, during the lecture, he remained motionless, stupefied and after that, he said that the whole universe was made up of ideas. For, the time being, as it were, the gross vibrations had ceased, and only the subtle vibrations which he called ideas, were present to him. He could only see the subtle vibrations round him; everything had become thought; the whole universe was an ocean of thought, he and everyone else had become little thought whirlpools.

Thus, even in the universe of thought we find unity, and at last, when we get to the Self, we know that that Self can only be One. Beyond the vibrations of matter in its gross and subtle aspects, beyond motion there is but One. Even in manifested motion there is only unity. These facts can no more be denied. Modern physics also has demonstrated that the sum total of the energies in the universe is the same throughout. It has also been proved that this sum total of energy exists in two forms. It becomes potential, toned down, and calmed, and next it comes out manifested as all these various forces; again it goes back to the quiet state, and again it manifests. Thus it goes on evolving and involving through eternity. The control of this Prana, as before stated, is what is called Pranayama.

The most obvious manifestation of this Prana in the human body is the motion of the lungs. If that stops, as a rule all the other manifestations of force in the body will immediately stop. But there are persons who can train themselves in such a manner that the body will live on, even when this motion has stopped. There are some persons who can bury themselves for days, and yet live without breathing. To reach the subtle we must take the help of the grosser, and so, slowly travel towards the most subtle until we gain our point. Pranayama really means controlling this motion of the lungs and this motion is associated with the breath. Not that breath is producing it; on the contrary it is producing breath. This motion draws in the air by pump action. The Prana is moving the lungs, the movement of the lungs draws in the air. So Pranayama is not breathing, but controlling that muscular power which moves the lungs. That muscular power which goes out through the nerves to the muscles and from them to the lungs, making them move in a certain manner, is the Prana, which we have to control in the practice of Pranayama. When the Prana has become controlled, then we shall immediately find that all the other actions of the Prana in the body will slowly come under control. I myself have seen men who have controlled almost every muscle of the body; and why not? If I have control over certain muscles, why not over every muscle and nerve of the body? What impossibility is there? At present the control is lost, and the motion has become automatic. We cannot move our ears at will, but we know that animals can. We have not that power because we do not exercise it. This is what is called atavism.

Again, we know that motion which has become latent can be brought back to manifestation. By hard work and practice certain motions of the body which are most dormant can be brought back under perfect control. Reasoning thus we find there is no impossibility, but, on the other hand. every probability that each part of the body can be brought under perfect control. This the Yogi does through Pranayama. Perhaps some of you have read that in Pranayama, when drawing in the breath, you must fill your whole body with Prana. In the English translations Prana is given as breath, and you are inclined to ask how that is to be done. The fault is with the translator. Every part of the body can be filled with Prana, this vital force, and when you are able to do that, you can control the whole body. All the sickness and misery felt in the body will be perfectly controlled; not only so, you will be able to control another's body. Everything is infectious in this world, good or bad. If your body be in a certain state of tension, it will have a tendency to produce the same tension in others. If you are strong and healthy, those that live near you will also have the tendency to become strong and healthy, but if you are sick and weak, those around you will have the tendency to become the same. In the case of one man trying to heal another, the first idea is simply transferring his own health to the other. This is the primitive sort of healing. Consciously or unconsciously, health can be transmitted. A very strong man, living with a weak man, will make him a little stronger, whether he knows it or not. When consciously done, it becomes quicker and better in its action. Next come those cases in which a man may not be very healthy himself, yet we know that he can bring health to another. The first man, in such a case, has a little more control over the Prana, and can rouse, for the time being, his Prana, as it were, to a certain state of vibration, and transmit it to another person.

There have been cases where this process has been carried on at a distance, but in reality there is no distance in the sense of a break. Where is the distance that has a break? Is there any break between you and the sun? It is a continuous mass of matter, the sun being one part, and you another. Is there a break between one part of a river and another? Then why cannot any force travel? There is no reason against it. Cases of healing from a distance are perfectly true. The Prana can be transmitted to a very great distance; but to one genuine case, there are hundreds of frauds. This process of healing is not so easy as it is thought to be. In the most ordinary cases of such healing you will find that the healers simply take advantage of the naturally healthy state of the human body. An allopath comes and treats cholera patients, and gives them his medicines. The homoeopath comes and gives his medicines, and cures perhaps more than the allopath does, because the homoeopath does not disturb his patients, but allows nature to deal with them. The Faith-healer cures more still, because he brings the strength of his mind to bear, and rouses, through faith, the dormant Prana of the patient.

There is a mistake constantly made by Faith-healers: they think that faith directly heals a man. But faith alone does not cover all the ground. There are diseases where the worst symptoms are that the patient never thinks that he has that disease. That tremendous faith of the patient is itself one symptom of the disease, and usually indicates that he will die quickly. In such cases the principle that faith cures does not apply. If it were faith alone that cured, these patients also would be cured. It is by the Prana that real curing comes. The pure man, who has controlled the Prana, has the power of bringing it into a certain state of vibration, which can be conveyed to others, arousing in them a similar vibration. You see that in everyday actions. I am talking to you. What am I trying to do? I am, so to say, bringing my mind to a certain state of vibration, and the more I succeed in bringing it to that state, the more you will be affected by what I say. All of you know that the day I am more enthusiastic, the more you enjoy the lecture; and when I am less enthusiastic, you feel lack of interest.

The gigantic will-powers of the world, the world-movers, can bring their Prana into a high state of vibration, and it is so great and powerful that it catches others in a moment, and thousands are drawn towards them, and half the world think as they do. Great prophets of the world had the most wonderful control of the Prana, which gave them tremendous will-power; they had brought their Prana to the highest state of motion, and this is what gave them power to sway the world. All manifestations of power arise from this control. Men may not know the secret, but this is the one explanation. Sometimes in your own body the supply of Prana gravitates more or less to one part; the balance is disturbed, and when the balance of Prana is disturbed, what we call disease is produced. To take away the superfluous Prana, or to supply the Prana that is wanting, will be curing the disease. That again is Pranayama—to learn when there is more or less Prana in one part of the body than there should be. The feelings will become so subtle that the mind will feel that there is less Prana in the toe or the finger than there should be, and will possess the power to supply it. These are among the various functions of Pranayama. They have to be learned slowly and gradually, and as you see, the whole scope of Rāja Yoga is really to teach the control and direction in different planes of the Prana. When a man has concentrated his energies, he masters the Prana that is in his body. When a man is meditating, he is also concentrating the Prana.

In an ocean there are huge waves, like mountains, then smaller waves, and still smaller, down to little bubbles, but back of all these is the infinite ocean. The bubble is connected with the infinite ocean at one end, and the huge wave at the other end. So, one may be a gigantic man, and another a little bubble, but each is connected with that infinite ocean of energy, which is the common birthright of every animal that exists. Wherever there is life, the storehouse of infinite energy is behind it. Starting as some fungus, some very minute, microscopic bubble, and all the time drawing from that infinite store-house of energy, a form is changed slowly and steadily until in course of time it becomes a plant, then an animal, then man, ultimately God. This is attained through millions of aeons, but what is time? An increase of speed, an increase of struggle, is able to bridge the gulf of time. That which naturally takes a long time to accomplish can be shortened by the intensity of the action, says the Yogi. A man may go on slowly drawing in this energy from the infinite mass that exists in the universe, and, perhaps, he will require a hundred thousand years to become a Deva, and then, perhaps, five hundred thousand years to become still higher, and, perhaps, five millions of years to become perfect. Given rapid growth, the time will be lessened. Why is it not possible, with sufficient effort, to reach this very perfection in six months or six years? There is no limit. Reason shows that. If an engine, with a certain amount of coal, runs two miles an hour, it will run the distance in less time with a greater supply of coal. Similarly, why shall not the soul, by intensifying its action, attain perfection in this very life? All beings will at last attain to that goal, we know. But who cares to wait all these millions of aeons? Why not reach it immediately, in this body even, in this human form? Why shall I not get that infinite knowledge, infinite power, now?

The ideal of the Yogi, the whole science of Yoga, is directed to the end of teaching men how, by intensifying the power of assimilation, to shorten the time for reaching perfection, instead of slowly advancing from point to point and waiting until the whole human race has become perfect. All the great prophets, saints, and seers of the world—what did they do? In one span of life they lived the whole life of humanity, traversed the whole length of time that it takes ordinary humanity to come to perfection. In one life they perfect themselves; they have no thought for anything else, never live a moment for any other idea, and thus the way is shortened for them. This is what is meant by concentration, intensifying the power of assimilation, thus shortening the time. Rāja Yoga is the science which teaches us how to gain the power of concentration.

What has Pranayama to do with spiritualism? Spiritualism is also a manifestation of Pranayama. If it be true that the departed spirits exist, only we cannot see them, it is quite probable that there may be hundreds and millions of them about us we can neither see, feel, nor touch. We may be continually passing and repassing through their bodies, and they do not see or feel us. It is a circle within a circle, universe within universe. We have five senses, and we represent Prana in a certain state of vibration. All beings in the same state of vibration will see one another, but if there are beings who represent Prana in a higher state of vibration, they will not be seen. We may increase the intensity of a light until we cannot see it at all, but there may be beings with eyes so powerful that they can see such light. Again, if its vibrations are very low, we do not see a light, but there are animals that may see it, as cats and owls. Our range of vision is only one plane of the vibrations of this

Prana. Take this atmosphere, for instance; it is piled up layer on layer, but the layers nearer to the earth are denser than those above, and as you go higher the atmosphere becomes finer and finer. Or take the case of the ocean; as you go deeper and deeper the pressure of the water increases, and animals which live at the bottom of the sea can never come up, or they will be broken into pieces.

Think of the universe as an ocean of ether, consisting of layer after layer of varying degrees of vibration under the action of Prana; away from the centre the vibrations are less, nearer to it they become quicker and quicker; one order of vibration makes one plane. Then suppose these ranges of vibrations are cut into planes, so many millions of miles one set of vibration, and then so many millions of miles another still higher set of vibration, and so on. It is, therefore, probable, that those who live on the plane of a certain state of vibration will have the power of recognising one another, but will not recognise those above them. Yet, just as by the telescope and the microscope we can increase the scope of our vision, similarly we can by Yoga bring ourselves to the state of vibration of another plane, and thus enable ourselves to see what is going on there. Suppose this room is full of beings whom we do not see. They represent Prana in a certain state of vibration while we represent another. Suppose they represent a quick one, and we the opposite. Prana is the material of which they are composed, as well as we. All are parts of the same ocean of Prana, they differ only in their rate of vibration. If I can bring myself to the quick vibration, this plane will immediately change for me: I shall not see you any more; you vanish and they appear. Some of you, perhaps, know this to be true. All this bringing of the mind into a higher state of vibration is included in one word in Yoga—Samadhi. All these states of higher vibration, superconscious vibrations of the mind, are grouped in that one word, Samadhi, and the lower states of Samadhi give us visions of these beings. The highest grade of Samadhi is when we see the real thing, when we see the material out of which the whole of these grades of beings are composed, and that one lump of clay being known, we know all the clay in the universe.

Thus we see that Pranayama includes all that is true of spiritualism even. Similarly, you will find that wherever any sect or body of people is trying to search out anything occult and mystical, or hidden, what they are doing is really this Yoga, this attempt to control the Prana. You will find that wherever there is any extraordinary display of power, it is the manifestation of this Prana. Even the physical sciences can be included in Pranayama. What moves the steam engine? Prana, acting through the steam. What are all these phenomena of electricity and so forth but Prana? What is physical science? The science of Pranayama, by external means. Prana, manifesting itself as mental power, can only be controlled by mental means. That part of Pranayama which attempts to control the physical manifestations of the Prana by physical means is called physical science, and that part which tries to control the manifestations of the Prana as mental force by mental means is called Rāja Yoga.

CHAPTER 4

THE PSYCHIC PRANA

According to the Yogis, there are two nerve currents in the spinal column, called Pingalā and Idā, and a hollow canal called Sushumna running through the spinal cord. At the lower end of the hollow canal is what the Yogis call the "Lotus of the Kundalini". They describe it as triangular in form in which, in the symbolical language of the Yogis, there is a power called the Kundalini, coiled up. When that Kundalini awakes, it tries to force a passage through this hollow canal, and as it rises step by step, as it were, layer after layer of the mind becomes open and all the different visions and wonderful powers come to the Yogi. When it reaches the brain, the Yogi is perfectly detached from the body and mind; the soul finds itself free.

We know that the spinal cord is composed in a peculiar manner. If we take the figure eight horizontally (∞) there are two parts which are connected in the middle. Suppose you add eight after eight, piled one on top of the other, that will represent the spinal cord. The left is the Ida, the right Pingala, and that hollow canal which runs through the centre of the spinal cord is the Sushumna. Where the spinal cord ends in some of the lumbar vertebrae, a fine fibre issues downwards, and the canal runs up even within that fibre, only much finer. The canal is closed at the lower end, which is situated near what is called the sacral plexus, which, according to modern physiology, is triangular in form. The different plexuses that have their centres in the spinal canal can very well stand for the different "lotuses" of the Yogi.

The Yogi conceives of several centres, beginning with the Mulādhāra, the basic, and ending with the Sahasrāra, the thousand-petalled Lotus in the brain. So, if we take these different plexuses as representing these lotuses, the idea of the Yogi can be understood very easily in the language of modern physiology. We know there are two sorts of actions in these nerve currents, one afferent, the other efferent; one sensory and the other motor; one centripetal, and the other centrifugal. One carries the sensations to the brain, and the other from the brain to the outer body. These vibrations are all connected with the brain in the long run. Several other facts we have to remember, in order to clear the way for the explanation which is to come. This spinal cord, at the brain, ends in a sort of bulb, in the medulla, which is not attached to the brain, but floats in a fluid in the brain, so that if there be a blow on the head the force of that blow will be dissipated in the fluid, and will not hurt the bulb. This is an important fact to remember. Secondly, we have also to know that, of all the centres, we have particularly to remember three, the Muladhara (the basic), the Sahasrara (the thousand-petalled lotus of the brain) and the Manipura (the lotus of the navel).

Next we shall take one fact from physics. We all hear of electricity and various other forces connected with it. What electricity is no one knows, but so far as it is known, it is a sort of motion. There are various other motions in the universe; what is the difference between them and electricity? Suppose this table moves—that the molecules which compose this table are moving in different directions; if they are all made to move in the same direction, it will be through electricity. Electric motion makes the molecules of a body move in the same direction. If all the air molecules in a room are made to move in the same direction, it will make a gigantic battery of electricity of the room. Another point from physiology we must remember, that the centre which regulates the respiratory system, the breathing system, has a sort of controlling action over the system of nerve currents.

Now we shall see why breathing is practised. In the first place, from rhythmical breathing comes a tendency of all the molecules in the body to move in the same direction. When mind changes into will, the nerve currents change into a motion similar to electricity, because the nerves have been proved to show polarity under the action of electric currents. This shows that when the will is transformed into the nerve currents, it is changed into something like electricity. When all the motions of the body have become perfectly rhythmical, the body has, as it were, become a gigantic battery of will. This tremendous will is exactly what the Yogi wants. This is, therefore, a physiological explanation of the breathing exercise. It tends to bring a rhythmic action in the body, and helps us, through the respiratory centre, to control the other centres. The aim of Pranayama here is to rouse the coiled-up power in the Muladhara, called the Kundalini.

Everything that we see, or imagine, or dream, we have to perceive in space. This is the ordinary space, called the Mahākāsha, or elemental space. When a Yogi reads the thoughts of other men, or perceives supersensuous objects he sees them in another sort of space called the Chittākāsha, the mental space. When perception has become objectless, and the soul shines in its own nature, it is called the Chidākāsha, or knowledge space. When the Kundalini is aroused, and enters the canal of the Sushumna, all the perceptions are in the mental space. When it has reached that end of the canal which opens out into the brain, the objectless perception is in the knowledge space. Taking the analogy of electricity, we find that man can send a current only along a wire,* but nature requires no wires to send her

* The reader should remember that this was spoken before the discovery of wireless telegraphy.—Ed.

tremendous currents. This proves that the wire is not really necessary, but that only our inability to dispense with it compels us to use it.

Similarly, all the sensations and motions of the body are being sent into the brain, and sent out of it, through these wires of nerve fibres. The columns of sensory and motor fibres in the spinal cord are the Ida and Pingala of the Yogis. They are the main channels through which the afferent and efferent currents travel. But why should not the mind send news without any wire, or react without any wire? We see this is done in nature. The Yogi says, if you can do that, you have got rid of the bondage of matter. How to do it? If you can make the current pass through the Sushumna, the canal in the middle of the spinal column, you have solved the problem. The mind has made this network of the nervous system, and has to break it, so that no wires will be required to work through. Then alone will all knowledge come to us—no more bondage of body; that is why it is so important that we should get control of that Sushumna. If we can send the mental current through the hollow canal without any nerve fibres to act as wires, the Yogi says, the problem is solved, and he also says it can be done.

This Sushumna is in ordinary persons closed up at the lower extremity; no action comes through it. The Yogi proposes a practice by which it can be opened, and the nerve currents made to travel through. When a sensation is carried to a centre, the centre reacts. This reaction, in the case of automatic centres, is followed by motion; in the case of conscious centres it is followed first by perception, and secondly by motion. All perception is the reaction to action from outside. How, then, do perceptions in dreams arise? There is then no action from outside. The sensory motions, therefore, are coiled up somewhere. For instance, I see a city; the perception of that city is from the reaction to the sensations brought from outside objects comprising that city. That is to say, a certain motion in the brain molecules has been set up by the motion in the incarrying nerves, which again are set in motion by external objects in the city. Now, even after a long time I can remember the city. This memory is exactly the same phenomenon, only it is in a milder form. But whence is the action that sets up even the milder form of similar vibrations in the brain? Not certainly from the primary sensations. Therefore it must be that the sensations are coiled up somewhere, and they, by their acting, bring out the mild reaction which we call dream perception.

Now the centre where all these residual sensations are, as it were, stored up, is called the Muladhara, the root receptacle, and the coiled-up energy of action is Kundalini, "the coiled up". It is very probable that the residual motor energy is also stored up in the same centre, as, after deep study or meditation on external objects, the part of the body where the Muladhara centre is situated (probably the sacral plexus) gets heated. Now, if this coiled-up energy be roused and made active, and then consciously made to travel up the Sushumna canal, as it acts upon centre after centre, a tremendous reaction will set in. When a minute portion of energy travels along a nerve fibre and causes reaction from centres, the perception is either dream or imagination. But when by the power of long internal meditation the vast mass of energy stored up travels along the Sushumna, and strikes the centres, the reaction is tremendous, immensely superior to the reaction of dream or imagination, immensely more intense than the reaction of sense-perception. It is super-sensuous perception. And when it reaches the metropolis of all sensations, the brain, the whole brain, as it were, reacts, and the result is the full blaze of illumination, the perception of the Self. As this Kundalini force travels from centre to centre, layer after layer of the mind, as it were, opens up, and this universe is perceived by the Yogi in its fine, or causal form. Then alone the causes of this universe, both as sensation and reaction, are known as they are, and hence comes all knowledge. The causes being known, the knowledge of the effects is sure to follow.

Thus the rousing of the Kundalini is the one and only way to attaining Divine Wisdom, superconscious perception, realisation of the spirit. The rousing may come in various ways, through love for God, through the mercy of perfected sages, or through the power of the analytic will of the philosopher. Wherever there was any manifestation of what is ordinarily called supernatural power or wisdom, there a little current of Kundalini must have found its way into the Sushumna. Only, in the vast majority of such cases, people had ignorantly stumbled on some practice which set free a minute portion of the coiled-up Kundalini. All worship, consciously or unconsciously, leads to this end. The man who thinks that he is receiving response to his prayers does not know that the fulfilment comes from his own nature, that he has succeeded by the mental attitude of prayer in waking up a bit of this infinite power which is coiled up within himself. What, thus, men ignorantly worship under various names, through fear and tribulation, the Yogi declares to the world to be the real power coiled up in every being, the mother of eternal happiness, if we but know how to approach her. And Rāja Yoga is the science of religion, the rationale of all worship, all prayers, forms, ceremonies, and miracles.

CHAPTER 5

THE CONTROL OF PSYCHIC PRANA

We have now to deal with the exercises in Pranayama. We have seen that the first step, according to the Yogis, is to control the motion of the lungs. What we want to do is to feel the finer motions that are going on in the body. Our minds have become externalised, and have lost sight of the fine motions inside. If we can begin to feel them, we can begin to control them. These nerve currents go on all over the body, bringing life and vitality to every muscle, but we do not feel them. The Yogi says we can learn to do so. How? By taking up and controlling the motion of the lungs; when we have done that for a sufficient length of time, we shall be able to control the finer motions.

We now come to the exercises in Pranayama. Sit upright; the body must be kept straight. The spinal cord, although not attached to the vertebral column, is yet inside of it. If you sit crookedly you disturb this spinal cord, so let it be free. Any time that you sit crookedly and try to meditate you do yourself an injury. The three parts of the body, the chest, the neck, and the head, must be always held straight in one line. You will find that by a little practice this will come to you as easy as breathing. The second thing is to get control of the nerves. We have said that the nerve centre that controls the respiratory organs has a sort of controlling effect on the other nerves, and rhythmical breathing is, therefore, necessary. The breathing that we generally use should not be called breathing at all. It is very irregular. Then there are some natural differences of breathing between men and women.

The first lesson is just to breathe in a measured way, in and out. That will harmonise the system. When you have practiced this for some time, you will do well to join to it the repetition of some word as "Om," or any other sacred word. In India we use certain symbolical words instead of counting one, two, three, four. That is why I advise you to join the mental repetition of the "Om," or some other sacred word to the Pranayama. Let the word flow in and out with the breath, rhythmically, harmoniously, and you will find the whole body is becoming rhythmical. Then you will learn what rest is. Compared with it, sleep is not rest. Once this rest comes the most tired nerves will be calmed down, and you will find that you have never before really rested.

The first effect of this practice is perceived in the change of expression of one's face; harsh lines disappear; with calm thought calmness comes over the face. Next comes beautiful voice. I never saw a Yogi with a croaking voice. These signs come after a few months' practice. After practicing the above mentioned breathing for a few days, you should take up a higher one. Slowly fill the lungs with breath through the Idā, the left nostril, and at the same time concentrate the mind on the nerve current. You are, as it were, sending the nerve current down the spinal column, and striking violently on the last plexus, the basic lotus which is triangular in form, the seat of the Kundalini. Then hold the current there for some time. Imagine that you are slowly drawing that nerve current with the breath through the other side, the Pingalā, then slowly throw it out through the right nostril. This you will find a little difficult to practice. The easiest way is to stop the right nostril with the thumb, and then slowly draw in the breath through the left; then close both nostrils with thumb and forefinger, and imagine that you are sending that current down, and striking the base of the Sushumna; then take the thumb off, and let the breath out through the right nostril. Next inhale slowly through that nostril, keeping the other closed by the forefinger, then close both, as before. The way the Hindus practice this would be very difficult for this country, because they do it from their childhood, and their lungs are prepared for it. Here it is well to begin with four seconds, and slowly increase. Draw in four seconds, hold in sixteen seconds, then throw out in eight seconds. This makes one Pranayama. At the same time think of the basic lotus, triangular in form; concentrate the mind on that centre. The imagination can help you a great deal. The next breathing is slowly drawing the breath in, and then immediately throwing it out slowly, and then stopping the breath out, using the same numbers. The only difference is that in the first case the breath was held in, and in the second, held out. This last is the easier one. The breathing in which you hold the breath in the lungs must not be practiced too much. Do it only four times in the morning, and four times in the evening. Then you can slowly increase the time and number. You will find that you have the power to do so, and that you take pleasure in it. So very carefully and cautiously increase as you feel that you have the power, to six instead of four. It may injure you if you practice it irregularly.

Of the three processes for the purification of the nerves, described above, the first and the last are neither difficult nor dangerous. The more you practice the first one the calmer you will be. Just think of "Om," and you can practice even while you are sitting at your work. You will be all the better for it. Some day, if you practice hard, the Kundalini will be aroused. For those who practice once or twice a day, just a little calmness of the body and mind will come, and beautiful voice; only for those who can go on further with it will Kundalini be aroused, and the whole of nature will begin to change, and the book of knowledge will open. No more will you need to go to books for knowledge; your own mind will have become your book, containing infinite knowledge. I have already spoken of the Ida and Pingala currents, flowing through either side of the spinal column, and also of the Sushumna, the passage through the centre of the spinal cord. These three are present in every animal; whatever being has a spinal column has these three lines of action. But the Yogis claim that in an ordinary man the Sushumna is closed; its action is not evident while that of the other two is carrying power to different parts of the body.

The Yogi alone has the Sushumna open. When this Sushumna current opens, and begins to rise, we get beyond the sense, our minds become supersensuous, superconscious—we get beyond even the intellect, where reasoning cannot reach. To open that Sushumna is the prime object of the Yogi. According to him, along this Sushumna are ranged these centres, or, in more figurative language, these lotuses, as they are called. The lowest one is at the lower end of the spinal cord, and is called Mulādhāra, the next higher is called Svādhishthāna, the third Manipura, the fourth Anāhata, the fifth Vishuddha, the sixth Ājnā and the last, which is in the brain, is the Sahasrāra, or "the thousand-petalled". Of these we have to take cognition just now of two centres only, the lowest, the Muladhara, and the highest, the Sahasrara. All energy has to be taken up from its seat in the Muladhara and brought to the Sahasrara. The Yogis claim that of all the energies that are in the human body the highest is what they call "Ojas". Now this Ojas is stored up in the brain, and the more Ojas is in a man's head, the more powerful he is, the more intellectual, the more spiritually strong. One man may speak beautiful language and beautiful thoughts, but they, do not impress people; another man speaks neither beautiful language nor beautiful thoughts, yet his words charm. Every movement of his is powerful. That is the power of Ojas.

Now in every man there is more or less of this Ojas stored up. All the forces that are working in the body in their highest become Ojas. You must remember that it is only a question of transformation. The same force which is working outside as electricity or magnetism will become changed into inner force; the same forces that are working as muscular energy will be changed into Ojas. The Yogis say that that part of the human energy which is expressed as sex energy, in sexual thought, when checked and controlled, easily becomes changed into Ojas, and as the Muladhara guides these, the Yogi pays particular attention to that centre. He tries to take up all his sexual energy and convert it into Ojas. It is only the chaste man or woman who can make the Ojas rise and store it in the brain; that is why chastity has always been considered the highest virtue. A man feels that if he is unchaste, spirituality goes away, he loses mental vigour and moral stamina. That is why in all the religious orders in the world which have produced spiritual giants you will always find absolute chastity insisted upon. That is why the monks came into existence, giving up marriage. There must be perfect chastity in thought, word, and deed; without it the practice of Rāja Yoga is dangerous, and may lead to insanity. If people practice Rāja Yoga and at the same time lead an impure life, how can they expect to become Yogis?

CHAPTER 6

PRATYAHARA AND DHARANA

The next step is called Pratyāhāra. What is this? You know how perceptions come. First of all there are the external instruments, then the internal organs acting in the body through the brain centres, and there is the mind. When these come together and attach themselves to some external object, then we perceive it. At the same time it is a very difficult thing to concentrate the mind and attach it to one organ only; the mind is a slave.

We hear "Be good," and "Be good," and "Be good," taught all over the world. There is hardly a child, born in any country in the world, who has not been told, "Do not steal," "Do not tell a lie," but nobody tells the child how he can help doing them. Talking will not help him. Why should he not become a thief? We do not teach him how not to steal; we simply tell him, "Do not steal." Only when we teach him to control his mind do we really help him. All actions, internal and external, occur when the mind joins itself to certain centres, called the organs. Willingly or unwillingly it is drawn to join itself to the centres, and that is why people do foolish deeds and feel miserable, which, if the mind were under control, they would not do. What would be the result of controlling the mind? It then would not join itself to the centres of perception, and, naturally, feeling and willing would be under control. It is clear so far. Is it possible? It is perfectly possible. You see it in modern times; the faith-healers teach people to deny misery and pain and evil. Their philosophy is rather roundabout, but it is a part of Yoga upon which they have somehow stumbled. Where they succeed in making a person throw off suffering by denying it, they really use a part of Pratyahara, as they make the mind of the person strong enough to ignore the senses. The hypnotists in a similar manner, by their suggestion, excite in the patient a sort of morbid Pratyahara for the time being. The so-called hypnotic suggestion can only act upon a weak mind. And until the operator, by means of fixed gaze or otherwise, has succeeded in putting the mind of the subject in a sort of passive, morbid condition, his suggestions never work.

Now the control of the centres which is established in a hypnotic patient or the patient of faith-healing, by the operator, for a time, is reprehensible, because it leads to ultimate ruin. It is not really controlling the brain centres by the power of one's own will, but is, as it were, stunning the patient's mind for a time by sudden blows which another's will delivers to it. It is not checking by means of reins and muscular strength the mad career of a fiery team, but rather by asking another to deliver heavy blows on the heads of the horses, to stun them for a time into gentleness. At each one of these processes the man operated upon loses a part of his mental energies, till at last, the mind, instead of gaining the power of perfect control, becomes a shapeless, powerless mass, and the only goal of the patient is the lunatic asylum.

Every attempt at control which is not voluntary, not with the controller's own mind, is not only disastrous, but it defeats the end. The goal of each soul is freedom, mastery—freedom from the slavery of matter and thought, mastery of external and internal nature. Instead of leading towards that, every will-current from another, in whatever form it comes, either as direct control of organs, or as forcing to control them while under a morbid condition, only rivets one link more to the already existing heavy chain of bondage of past thoughts, past superstitions. Therefore, beware how you allow yourselves to be acted upon by others. Beware how you unknowingly bring another to ruin. True, some succeed in doing good to many for a time, by giving a new trend to their propensities, but at the same time, they bring ruin to millions by the unconscious suggestions they throw around, rousing in men and women that morbid, passive, hypnotic condition which makes them almost soulless at last. Whosoever, therefore, asks any one to believe blindly, or drags people behind him by the controlling power of his superior will, does an injury to humanity, though he may not intend it.

Therefore use your own minds, control body and mind yourselves, remember that until you are a diseased person, no extraneous will can work upon you; avoid everyone, however great and good he may be, who asks you to believe blindly. All over the world there have been dancing and jumping and howling sects, who spread like infection when they begin to sing and dance and preach; they also are a sort of hypnotists. They exercise a singular control for the time being over sensitive persons, alas! often, in the long run, to degenerate whole races. Ay, it is healthier for the individual or the race to remain wicked than be made apparently good by such morbid extraneous control. One's heart sinks to think of the amount of injury done to humanity by such irresponsible yet well-meaning religious fanatics. They little know that the minds which attain to sudden spiritual upheaval under their suggestions, with music and prayers, are simply making themselves passive, morbid, and powerless, and opening themselves to any other suggestion, be it ever so evil. Little do these ignorant, deluded persons dream that whilst they are congratulating themselves upon their miraculous power to transform human hearts, which power they think was poured upon them by some Being above the clouds, they are sowing the seeds of future decay, of crime, of lunacy, and of death. Therefore, beware of everything that takes away your freedom. Know that it is dangerous, and avoid it by all the means in your power.

He who has succeeded in attaching or detaching his mind to or from the centres at will has succeeded in Pratyahara, which means, "gathering towards," checking the outgoing powers of the mind, freeing it from the thraldom of the senses. When we can do this, we shall really possess character; then alone we shall have taken a long step towards freedom; before that we are mere machines.

How hard it is to control the mind! Well has it been compared to the maddened monkey. There was a monkey, restless by his own nature, as all monkeys are. As if that were not enough some one made him drink freely of wine, so that he became still more restless. Then a scorpion stung him. When a man is stung by a scorpion, he jumps about for a whole day; so the poor monkey found his condition worse than ever. To complete his misery a demon entered into him. What language can describe the uncontrollable restlessness of that monkey? The human mind is like that monkey, incessantly active by its own nature; then it becomes drunk with the wine of desire, thus increasing its turbulence. After desire takes possession comes the sting of the scorpion of jealousy at the success of others, and last of all the demon of pride enters the mind, making it think itself of all importance. How hard to control such a mind!

The first lesson, then, is to sit for some time and let the mind run on. The mind is bubbling up all the time. It is like that monkey jumping about. Let the monkey jump as much as he can; you simply wait and watch. Knowledge is power, says the proverb, and that is true. Until you know what the mind is doing you cannot control it. Give it the rein; many hideous thoughts may come into it; you will be astonished that it was possible for you to think such thoughts. But you will find that each day the mind's vagaries are becoming less and less violent, that each day it is becoming calmer. In the first few months you will find that the mind will have a great many thoughts, later you will find that they have somewhat decreased, and in a few more months they will be fewer and fewer, until at last the mind will be under perfect control; but we must patiently practice every day. As soon as the steam is turned on, the engine must run; as soon as things are before us we must perceive; so a man, to prove that he is not a machine, must demonstrate that he is under the control of nothing. This controlling of the mind, and not allowing it to join itself to the centres, is Pratyahara. How is this practised? It is a tremendous work, not to be done in a day. Only after a patient, continuous struggle for years can we succeed.

After you have practised Pratyahara for a time, take the next step, the Dhāranā, holding the mind to certain points. What is meant by holding the mind to certain points? Forcing the mind to feel certain parts of the body to the exclusion of others. For instance, try to feel only the hand, to the exclusion of other parts of the body. When the Chitta, or mind-stuff, is confined and limited to a certain place it is Dharana. This Dharana is of various sorts, and along with it, it is better to have a little play of the imagination. For instance, the mind should be made to think of one point in the heart. That is very difficult; an easier way is to imagine a lotus there. That lotus is full of light, effulgent light. Put the mind there. Or think of the lotus in the brain as full of light, or of the different centres in the Sushumna mentioned before.

The Yogi must always practice. He should try to live alone; the companionship of different sorts of people distracts the mind; he should not speak much, because to speak distracts the mind; not work much, because too much work distracts the mind; the mind cannot be controlled after a whole day's hard work. One observing the above rules becomes a Yogi. Such is the power of Yoga that even the least of it will bring a great amount of benefit. It will not hurt anyone, but will benefit everyone. First of all, it will tone down nervous excitement, bring calmness, enable us to see things more clearly. The temperament will be better, and the health will be better. Sound health will be one of the first signs, and a beautiful voice. Defects in the voice will be changed. This will be among the first of the many effects that will come. Those who practise hard will get many other signs. Sometimes there will be sounds, as a peal of bells heard at a distance, commingling, and falling on the ear as one continuous sound. Sometimes things will be seen, little specks of light floating and becoming bigger and bigger; and when these things come, know that you are progressing fast.

Those who want to be Yogis, and practice hard, must take care of their diet at first. But for those who want only a little practice for everyday business sort of life, let them not eat too much; otherwise they may eat whatever they please. For those who want to make rapid progress, and to practice hard, a strict diet is absolutely necessary. They will find it advantageous to live only on milk and cereals for some months. As the organisation becomes finer and finer, it will be found in the beginning that the least irregularity throws one out of balance. One bit of food more or less will disturb the whole system, until one gets perfect control, and then one will be able to eat whatever one likes.

When one begins to concentrate, the dropping of a pin will seem like a thunderbolt going through the brain. As the organs get finer, the perceptions get finer. These are the stages through which we have to pass, and all those who persevere will succeed. Give up all argumentation and other distractions. Is there anything in dry intellectual jargon? It only throws the mind off its balance and disturbs it. Things of subtler planes have to be realised. Will talking do that? So give up all vain talk. Read only those books which have been written by persons who have had realisation.

Be like the pearl oyster. There is a pretty Indian fable to the effect that if it rains when the star Svāti is in the ascendant, and a drop of rain falls into an oyster, that drop becomes a pearl. The oysters know this, so they come to the surface when that star shines, and wait to catch the precious raindrop. When a drop falls into them, quickly the oysters close their shells and dive down to the bottom of the sea, there to patiently develop the drop into the pearl. We should be like that. First hear, then understand, and then, leaving all distractions, shut your minds to outside influences, and devote yourselves to developing the truth within you. There is the danger of frittering away your energies by taking up an idea only for its novelty, and then giving it up for another that is newer. Take one thing up and do it, and see the end of it, and before you have seen the end, do not give it up. He who can become mad with an idea, he alone sees light. Those that only take a nibble here and a nibble there will never attain anything. They may titillate their nerves for a moment, but there it will end. They will be slaves in the hands of nature, and will never get beyond the senses.

Those who really want to be Yogis must give up, once for all, this nibbling at things. Take up one idea. Make that one idea your life—think of it, dream of it, live on that idea. Let the brain, muscles, nerves, every part of your body, be full of that idea, and just leave every other idea alone. This is the way to success, and this is the way great spiritual giants are produced. Others are mere talking machines. If we really want to be blessed, and make others blessed, we must go deeper. The first step is not to disturb the mind, not to associate with persons whose ideas are disturbing. All of you know that certain persons, certain places, certain foods, repel you. Avoid them; and those who want to go to the highest, must avoid all company, good or bad. Practise hard; whether you live or die does not matter. You have to plunge in and work, without thinking of the result. If you are brave enough, in six months you will be a perfect Yogi. But those who take up just a bit of it and a little of everything else make no progress. It is of no use simply to take a course of lessons. To those who are full of Tamas, ignorant and dull—those whose minds never get fixed on any idea, who only crave for something to amuse them—religion and philosophy are simply objects of entertainment. These are the unpersevering. They hear a talk, think it very nice, and then go home and forget all about it. To succeed, you must have tremendous perseverance, tremendous will. "I will drink the ocean," says the persevering soul, "at my will mountains will crumble up." Have that sort of energy, that sort of will, work hard, and you will reach the goal.

CHAPTER 7

DHYANA AND SAMADHI

We have taken a cursory view of the different steps in Rāja Yoga, except the finer ones, the training in concentration, which is the goal to which Rāja Yoga will lead us. We see, as human beings, that all our knowledge which is called rational is referred to consciousness. My consciousness of this table, and of your presence, makes me know that the table and you are here. At the same time, there is a very great part of my existence of which I am not conscious. All the different organs inside the body, the different parts of the brain—nobody is conscious of these.

When I eat food, I do it consciously; when I assimilate it, I do it unconsciously. When the food is manufactured into blood, it is done unconsciously.

When out of the blood all the different parts of my body are strengthened, it is done unconsciously. And yet it is I who am doing all this; there cannot be twenty people in this one body. How do I know that I do it, and nobody else? It may be urged that my business is only in eating and assimilating the food, and that strengthening the body by the food is done for me by somebody else. That cannot be, because it can be demonstrated that almost every action of which we are now unconscious can be brought up to the plane of consciousness. The heart is beating apparently without our control. None of us here can control the heart; it goes on its own way. But by practice men can bring even the heart under control, until it will just beat at will, slowly, or quickly, or almost stop. Nearly every part of the body can be brought under control. What does this show? That the functions which are beneath consciousness are also performed by us, only we are doing it unconsciously. We have, then, two planes in which the human mind works. First is the conscious plane, in which all work is always accompanied with the feeling of egoism. Next comes the unconscious plane, where all work is unaccompanied by the feeling of egoism. That part of mind-work which is unaccompanied with the feeling of egoism is unconscious work, and that part which is accompanied with the feeling of egoism is conscious work. In the lower animals this unconscious work is called instinct. In higher animals, and in the highest of all animals, man, what is called conscious work prevails.

But it does not end here. There is a still higher plane upon which the mind can work. It can go beyond consciousness. Just as unconscious work is beneath consciousness, so there is another work which is above consciousness, and which also is not accompanied with the feeling of egoism. The feeling of egoism is only on the middle plane. When the mind is above or below that line, there is no feeling of "I", and yet the mind works. When the mind goes beyond this line of self-consciousness, it is called Samādhi or superconsciousness. How, for instance, do we know that a man in Samadhi has not gone below consciousness, has not degenerated instead of going higher? In both cases the works are unaccompanied with egoism. The answer is, by the effects, by the results of the work, we know that which is below, and that which is above. When a man goes into deep sleep, he enters a plane beneath consciousness. He works the body all the time, he breathes, he moves the body, perhaps, in his sleep, without any accompanying feeling of ego; he is unconscious, and when he returns from his sleep, he is the same man who went into it. The sum total of the knowledge which he had before he went into the sleep remains the same; it does not increase at all. No enlightenment comes. But when a man goes into Samadhi, if he goes into it a fool, he comes out a sage.

What makes the difference? From one state a man comes out the very same man that he went in, and from another state the man comes out enlightened, a sage, a prophet, a saint, his whole character changed, his life changed, illumined. These are the two effects. Now the effects being different, the causes must be different. As this illumination with which a man comes back from Samadhi is much higher than can be got from unconsciousness, or much higher than can be got by reasoning in a conscious state, it must, therefore, be superconsciousness, and Samadhi is called the superconscious state.

This, in short, is the idea of Samadhi. What is its application? The application is here. The field of reason, or of the conscious workings of the mind, is narrow and limited. There is a little circle within which human reason must move. It cannot go beyond. Every attempt to go beyond is impossible, yet it is beyond this circle of reason that there lies all that humanity holds most dear. All these questions, whether there is an immortal soul, whether there is a God, whether there is any supreme intelligence guiding this universe or not, are beyond the field of reason. Reason can never answer these questions. What does reason say? It says, "I am agnostic; I do not know either yea or nay." Yet these questions are so important to us. Without a proper answer to them, human life will be purposeless. All our ethical theories, all our moral attitudes, all that is good and great in human nature, have been moulded upon answers that have come from beyond the circle. It is very important, therefore, that we should have answers to these questions. If life is only a short play, if the universe is only a "fortuitous combination of atoms," then why should I do good to another? Why should there be mercy, justice, or fellow-feeling? The best thing for this world would be to make hay while the sun shines, each man for himself. If there is no hope, why should I love my brother, and not cut his throat? If there is nothing beyond, if there is no freedom, but only rigorous dead laws, I should only try to make myself happy here. You will find people saying nowadays that they have utilitarian grounds as the basis of morality. What is this basis? Procuring the greatest amount of happiness to the greatest number. Why should I do this? Why should I not produce the greatest unhappiness to the greatest number, if that serves my purpose? How will utilitarians answer this question? How do you know what is right, or what is wrong? I am impelled by my desire for happiness, and I fulfil it, and it is in my nature; I know nothing beyond. I have these desires, and must fulfil them; why should you complain? Whence come all these truths about human life, about morality, about the immortal soul, about God, about love and sympathy, about being good, and, above all, about being unselfish?

All ethics, all human action and all human thought, hang upon this one idea of unselfishness. The whole idea of human life can be put into that one word, unselfishness. Why should we be unselfish? Where is the necessity, the force, the power, of my being unselfish? You call yourself a rational man, a utilitarian; but if you do not show me a reason for utility, I say you are irrational. Show me the reason why I should not be selfish. To ask one to be unselfish may be good as poetry, but poetry is not reason. Show me a reason. Why shall I be unselfish, and why be good? Because Mr. and Mrs. So-and-so say so does not weigh with me. Where is the utility of my being unselfish? My utility is to be selfish if utility means the greatest amount of happiness. What is the answer? The utilitarian can never give it. The answer is that this world is only one drop in an infinite ocean, one link in an infinite chain. Where did those that preached unselfishness, and taught it to the human race, get this idea? We know it is not instinctive; the animals, which have instinct, do not know it. Neither is it reason; reason does not know anything about these ideas. Whence then did they come?

We find, in studying history, one fact held in common by all the great teachers of religion the world ever had. They all claim to have got their truths from beyond, only many of them did not know where they got them from. For instance, one would say that an angel came down in the form of a human being, with wings, and said to him, "Hear, O man, this is the message." Another says that a Deva, a bright being, appeared to him. A third says he dreamed that his ancestor came and told him certain things. He did not know anything beyond that. But this is common that all claim that this knowledge has come to them from beyond, not through their reasoning power. What does the science of Yoga teach? It teaches that they were right in claiming that all this knowledge came to them from beyond reasoning, but that it came from within themselves.

The Yogi teaches that the mind itself has a higher state of existence, beyond reason, a superconscious state, and when the mind gets to that higher state, then this knowledge, beyond reasoning, comes to man. Metaphysical and transcendental knowledge comes to that man. This state of going beyond reason, transcending ordinary human nature, may sometimes come by chance to a man who does not understand its science; he, as it were, stumbles upon it. When he stumbles upon it, he generally interprets it as coming from outside. So this explains why an inspiration, or transcendental knowledge, may be the same in different countries, but in one country it will seem to come through an angel, and in another through a Deva, and in a third through God. What does it mean? It means that the mind brought the knowledge by its own nature, and that the finding of the knowledge was interpreted according to the belief and education of the person through whom it came. The real fact is that these various men, as it were, stumbled upon this superconscious state.

The Yogi says there is a great danger in stumbling upon this state. In a good many cases there is the danger of the brain being deranged, and, as a rule, you will find that all those men, however great they were, who had stumbled upon this superconscious state without understanding it, groped in the dark, and generally had, along with their knowledge, some quaint superstition. They opened themselves to hallucinations. Mohammed claimed that the Angel Gabriel came to him in a cave one day and took him on the heavenly horse, Harak, and he visited the heavens. But with all that, Mohammed spoke some wonderful truths. If you read the Koran, you find the most wonderful truths mixed with superstitions. How will you explain it? That man was inspired, no doubt, but that inspiration was, as it were, stumbled upon. He was not a trained Yogi, and did not know the reason of what he was doing. Think of the good Mohammed did to the world, and think of the great evil that has been done through his fanaticism! Think of the millions massacred through his teachings, mothers bereft of their children, children made orphans, whole countries destroyed, millions upon millions of people killed!

So we see this danger by studying the lives of great teachers like Mohammed and others. Yet we find, at the same time, that they were all inspired. Whenever a prophet got into the superconscious state by heightening his emotional nature, he brought away from it not only some truths, but some fanaticism also, some superstition which injured the world as much as the greatness of the teaching helped. To get any reason out of the mass of incongruity we call human life, we have to transcend our reason, but we must do it scientifically, slowly, by regular practice, and we must cast off all superstition. We must take up the study of the superconscious state just as any other science. On reason we must have to lay our foundation, we must follow reason as far as it leads, and when reason fails, reason itself will show us the way to the highest plane. When you hear a man say, "I am inspired," and then talk irrationally, reject it. Why? Because these three states—instinct, reason, and superconsciousness, or the unconscious, conscious, and superconscious states—belong to one and the same mind. There are not three minds in one man, but one state of it develops into the others. Instinct develops into reason, and reason into the transcendental consciousness; therefore, not one of the states contradicts the others. Real inspiration never contradicts reason, but fulfils it. Just as you find the great prophets saying, "I come not to destroy but to fulfil," so inspiration always comes to fulfil reason, and is in harmony with it.

All the different steps in Yoga are intended to bring us scientifically to the superconscious state, or Samadhi. Furthermore, this is a most vital point to understand, that inspiration is as much in every man's nature as it was in that of the ancient prophets. These prophets were not unique; they were men as you or I. They were great Yogis. They had gained this superconsciousness, and you and I can get the same. They were not peculiar people. The very fact that one man ever reached that state, proves that it is possible for every man to do so. Not only is it possible, but every man must, eventually, get to that state, and that is religion. Experience is the only teacher we have. We may talk and reason all our lives, but we shall not understand a word of truth, until we experience it ourselves. You cannot hope to make a man a surgeon by simply giving him a few books. You cannot satisfy my curiosity to see a country by showing me a map; I must have actual experience. Maps can only create curiosity in us to get more perfect knowledge. Beyond that, they have no value whatever. Clinging to books only degenerates the human mind. Was there ever a more horrible blasphemy than the statement that all the knowledge of God is confined to this or that book? How dare men call God infinite, and yet try to compress Him within the covers of a little book! Millions of people have been killed because they did not believe what the books said, because they would not see all the knowledge of God within the covers of a book. Of course this killing and murdering has gone by, but the world is still tremendously bound up in a belief in books.

In order to reach the superconscious state in a scientific manner it is necessary to pass through the various steps of Rāja Yoga I have been teaching. After Pratyāhāra and Dhāranā, we come to Dhyāna, meditation. When the mind has been trained to remain fixed on a certain internal or external location, there comes to it the power of flowing in an unbroken current, as it were, towards that point. This state is called Dhyana. When one has so intensified the power of Dhyana as to be able to reject the external part of perception and remain meditating only on the internal part, the meaning, that state is called Samadhi. The three—Dharana, Dhyana, and Samadhi—together, are called Samyama. That is, if the mind can first concentrate upon an object, and then is able to continue in that concentration for a length of time, and then, by continued concentration, to dwell only on the internal part of the perception of which the object was the effect, everything comes under the control of such a mind.

This meditative state is the highest state of existence. So long as there is desire, no real happiness can come. It is only the contemplative, witness-like study of objects that brings to us real enjoyment and happiness. The animal has its happiness in the senses, the man in his intellect, and the god in spiritual contemplation. It is only to the soul that has attained to this contemplative state that the world really becomes beautiful. To him who desires nothing, and does not mix himself up with them, the manifold changes of nature are one panorama of beauty and sublimity.

These ideas have to be understood in Dhyana, or meditation. We hear a sound. First, there is the external vibration; second, the nerve motion that carries it to the mind; third, the reaction from the mind, along with which flashes the knowledge of the object which was the external cause of these different changes from the ethereal vibrations to the mental reactions. These three are called in Yoga, Shabda (sound), Artha (meaning), and Jnāna (knowledge). In the language of physics and physiology they are called the ethereal vibration, the motion in the nerve and brain, and the mental reaction. Now these, though distinct processes, have become mixed up in such a fashion as to become quite indistinct. In fact, we cannot now perceive any of these, we only perceive their combined effect, what we call the external object. Every act of perception includes these three, and there is no reason why we should not be able to distinguish them.

When, by the previous preparations, it becomes strong and controlled, and has the power of finer perception, the mind should be employed in meditation. This meditation must begin with gross objects and slowly rise to finer and finer, until it becomes objectless. The mind should first be employed in perceiving the external causes of sensations, then the internal motions, and then its own reaction. When it has succeeded in perceiving the external causes of sensations by themselves, the mind will acquire the power of perceiving all fine material existences, all fine bodies and forms. When it can succeed in perceiving the motions inside by themselves, it will gain the control of all mental waves, in itself or in others, even before they have translated themselves into physical energy; and when he will be able to perceive the mental reaction by itself, the Yogi will acquire the knowledge of everything, as every sensible object, and every thought is the result of this reaction. Then will he have seen the very foundations of his mind, and it will be under his perfect control. Different powers will come to the Yogi, and if he yields to the temptations of any one of these, the road to his further progress will be barred. Such is the evil of running after enjoyments. But if he is strong enough to reject even these miraculous powers, he will attain to the goal of Yoga, the complete suppression of the waves in the ocean of the mind. Then the glory of the soul, undisturbed by the distractions of the mind, or motions of the body, will shine in its full effulgence; and the Yogi will find himself as he is and as he always was, the essence of knowledge, the immortal, the all-pervading.

Samadhi is the property of every human being—nay, every animal. From the lowest animal to the highest angel, some time or other, each one will have to come to that state, and then, and then alone, will real religion begin for him. Until then we only struggle towards that stage. There is no difference now between us and those who have no religion, because we have no experience. What is concentration good for, save to bring us to this experience? Each one of the steps to attain Samadhi has been reasoned out, properly adjusted, scientifically organised, and, when faithfully practiced, will surely lead us to the desired end. Then will all sorrows cease, all miseries vanish; the seeds for actions will be burnt, and the soul will be free for ever.

CHAPTER 8

RĀJA YOGA IN BRIEF

The following is a summary of Rāja Yoga freely translated from the Kurma-Purāna.

The fire of Yoga burns the cage of sin that is around a man. Knowledge becomes purified and Nirvāna is directly obtained. From Yoga comes knowledge; knowledge again helps the Yogi. He who combines in himself both Yoga and knowledge, with him the Lord is pleased. Those that practice Mahayoga, either once a day, or twice a day, or thrice, or always, know them to be gods. Yoga is divided into two parts. One is called Abhāva, and the other, Mahayoga. Where one's self is meditated upon as zero, and bereft of quality, that is called Abhava. That in which one sees the self as full of bliss and bereft of all impurities, and one with God, is called Mahayoga. The Yogi, by each one, realises his Self. The other Yogas that we read and hear of, do not deserve to be ranked with the excellent Mahayoga in which the Yogi finds himself and the whole universe as God. This is the highest of all Yogas.

Yama, Niyama, Āsana, Pranayama, Pratyāhāra, Dhārāna, Dhyāna, and Samādhi are the steps in Rāja Yoga, of which non-injury, truthfulness, non-covetousness, chastity, not receiving anything from another are called Yama. This purifies the mind, the Chitta. Never producing pain by thought, word, and deed, in any living being, is what is called Ahimsā, non-injury. There is no virtue higher than non-injury. There is no happiness higher than what a man obtains by this attitude of non-offensiveness, to all creation. By truth we attain fruits of work. Through truth everything is attained. In truth everything is established. Relating facts as they are—this is truth. Not taking others' goods by stealth or by force, is called Asteya, non-covetousness. Chastity in thought, word, and deed, always, and in all conditions, is what is called Brahmacharya. Not receiving any present from anybody, even when one is suffering terribly, is what is called Aparigraha. The idea is, when a man receives a gift from another, his heart becomes impure, he becomes low, he loses his independence, he becomes bound and attached.

The following are helps to success in Yoga and are called Niyama or regular habits and observances; Tapas, austerity; Svādhyāya, study; Santosha, contentment; Shaucha, purity; Ishvara-pranidhāna, worshipping God.

Fasting, or in other ways controlling the body, is called physical Tapas. Repeating the Vedas and other Mantras, by which the Sattva material in the body is purified, is called study, Svadhyaya. There are three sorts of repetitions of these Mantras. One is called the verbal, another semi-verbal, and the third mental. The verbal or audible is the lowest, and the inaudible is the highest of all. The repetition which is loud is the verbal; the next one is where only the lips move, but no sound is heard. The inaudible repetition of the Mantra, accompanied with the thinking of its meaning, is called the "mental repetition," and is the highest. The sages have said that there are two sorts of purification, external and internal. The purification of the body by water, earth, or other materials is the external purification, as bathing etc. Purification of the mind by truth, and by all the other virtues, is what is called internal purification. Both are necessary. It is not sufficient that a man should be internally pure and externally dirty. When both are not attainable the internal purity is the better, but no one will be a Yogi until he has both. Worship of God is by praise, by thought, by devotion.

We have spoken about Yama and Niyama. The next is Āsana (posture). The only thing to understand about it is leaving the body free, holding the chest, shoulders, and head straight. Then comes Pranayama. Prana means the vital forces in one's own body, Āyāma means controlling them. There are three sorts of Pranayama, the very simple, the middle, and the very high. Pranayama is divided into three parts: filling, restraining, and emptying. When you begin with twelve seconds it is the lowest Pranayama; when you begin with twenty-four seconds it is the middle Pranayama; that Pranayama is the best which begins with thirty-six seconds. In the lowest kind of Pranayama there is perspiration, in the medium kind, quivering of the body, and in the highest Pranayama levitation of the body and influx of great bliss. There is a Mantra called the Gāyatri. It is a very holy verse of the Vedas. "We meditate on the glory of that Being who has produced this universe; may He enlighten our minds." Om is joined to it at the beginning and the end. In one Pranayama repeat three Gayatris. In all books they speak of Pranayama being divided into Rechaka (rejecting or exhaling), Puraka (inhaling), and Kurnbhaka (restraining, stationary). The Indriyas, the organs of the senses, are acting outwards and coming in contact with external objects. Bringing them under the control of the will is what is called Pratyahara or gathering towards oneself. Fixing the mind on the lotus of the heart, or on the centre of the head, is what is called Dharana. Limited to one spot, making that spot the base, a particular kind of mental waves rises; these are not swallowed up by other kinds of waves, but by degrees become prominent, while all the others recede and finally disappear. Next the multiplicity of these waves gives place to unity and one wave only is left in the mind. This is Dhyana, meditation. When no basis is necessary, when the whole of the mind has become one wave, one-formedness, it is called Samadhi. Bereft of all help from places and centres, only the meaning of the thought is present. If the mind can be fixed on the centre for twelve seconds it will be a Dharana, twelve such Dharanas will be a Dhyana, and twelve such Dhyanas will be a Samadhi.

Where there is fire, or in water or on ground which is strewn with dry leaves, where there are many anthills, where there are wild animals, or danger, where four streets meet, where there is too much noise, where there are many wicked persons, Yoga must not be practiced. This applies more particularly to India. Do not practice when the body feels very lazy or ill, or when the mind is very miserable and sorrowful. Go to a place which is well hidden, and where people do not come to disturb you. Do not choose dirty places. Rather choose beautiful scenery, or a room in your own house which is beautiful. When you practice, first salute all the ancient Yogis, and your own Guru, and God, and then begin.

Dhyana is spoken of, and a few examples are given of what to meditate upon. Sit straight, and look at the tip of your nose. Later on we shall come to know how that concentrates the mind, how by controlling the two optic nerves one advances a long way towards the control of the arc of reaction, and so to the control of the will. Here are a few specimens of meditation. Imagine a lotus upon the top of the head, several inches up, with virtue as its centre, and knowledge as its stalk. The eight petals of the lotus are the eight powers of the Yogi. Inside, the stamens and pistils are renunciation. If the Yogi refuses the external powers he will come to salvation. So the eight petals of the lotus are the eight powers, but the internal stamens and pistils are extreme renunciation, the renunciation of all these powers. Inside of that lotus think of the Golden One, the Almighty, the Intangible, He whose name is Om, the Inexpressible, surrounded with effulgent light. Meditate on that. Another meditation is given. Think of a space in your heart, and in the midst of that space think that a flame is burning. Think of that flame as your own soul and inside the flame is another effulgent light, and that is the Soul of your soul, God. Meditate upon that in the heart. Chastity, non-injury, forgiving even the greatest enemy, truth, faith in the Lord, these are all different Vrittis. Be not afraid if you are not perfect in all of these; work, they will come. He who has given up all attachment, all fear, and all anger, he whose whole soul has gone unto the Lord, he who has taken refuge in the Lord, whose heart has become purified, with whatsoever desire he comes to the Lord, He will grant that to him. Therefore worship Him through knowledge, love, or renunciation.

"He who hates none, who is the friend of all, who is merciful to all, who has nothing of his own, who is free from egoism, who is even-minded in pain and pleasure, who is forbearing, who is always satisfied, who works always in Yoga, whose self has become controlled, whose will is firm, whose mind and intellect are given up unto Me, such a one is My beloved Bhakta. From whom comes no disturbance, who cannot be disturbed by others, who is free from joy, anger, fear, and anxiety, such a one is My beloved. He who does not depend on anything, who is pure and active, who does not care whether good comes or evil, and never becomes miserable, who has given up all efforts for himself; who is the same in praise or in blame, with a silent, thoughtful mind, blessed with what little comes in his way, homeless, for the whole world is his home, and who is steady in his ideas, such a one is My beloved Bhakta." Such alone become Yogis.

* * * *

There was a great god-sage called Narada. Just as there are sages among mankind, great Yogis, so there are great Yogis among the gods. Narada was a good Yogi, and very great. He travelled everywhere. One day he was passing through a forest, and saw a man who had been meditating until the white ants had built a huge mound round his body—so long had he been sitting in that position. He said to Narada, "Where are you going?" Narada replied, "I am going to heaven." "Then ask God when He will be merciful to me; when I shall attain freedom." Further on Narada saw another man. He was jumping about, singing, dancing, and said, "Oh, Narada, where are you going?" His voice and his gestures were wild. Narada said, "I am going to heaven." "Then, ask when I shall be free." Narada went on. In the course of time he came again by the same road, and there was the man who had been meditating with the ant-hill round him. He said, "Oh, Narada, did you ask the Lord about me?" "Oh, yes." "What did He say?" "The Lord told me that you would attain freedom in four more births." Then the man began to weep and wail, and said,

"I have meditated until an ant-hill has grown around me, and I have four more births yet!" Narada went to the other man. "Did you ask my question?" "Oh, yes. Do you see this tamarind tree? I have to tell you that as many leaves as there are on that tree, so many times, you shall be born, and then you shall attain freedom." The man began to dance for joy, and said, "I shall have freedom after such a short time!" A voice came, "My child, you will have freedom this minute." That was the reward for his perseverance. He was ready to work through all those births, nothing discouraged him. But the first man felt that even four more births were too long. Only perseverance, like that of the man who was willing to wait aeons brings about the highest result.

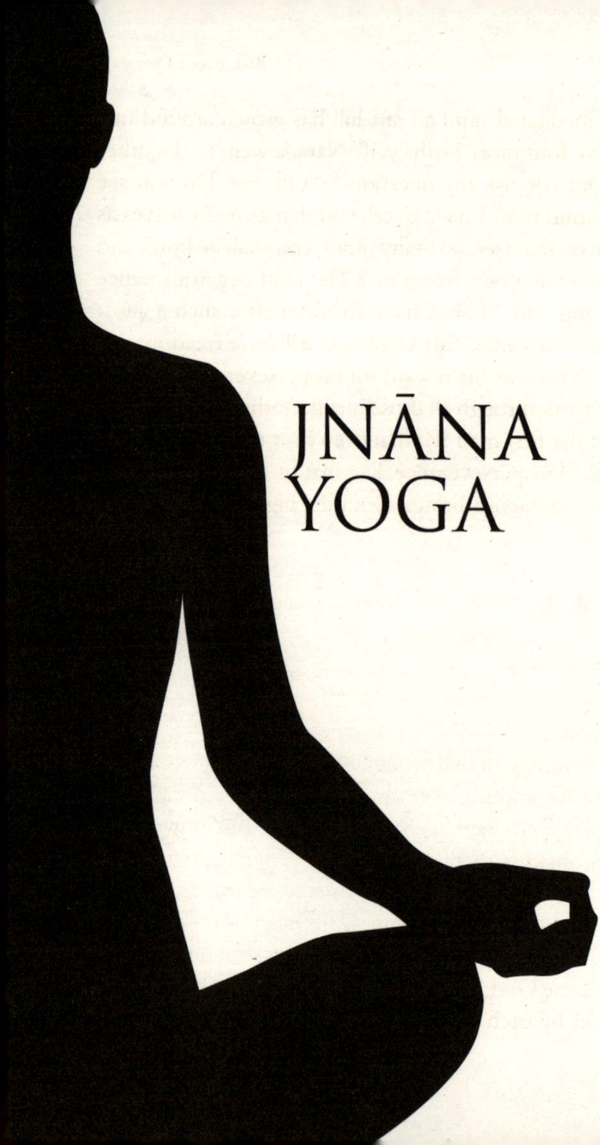

JNĀNA YOGA

CHAPTER 1

THE NECESSITY OF RELIGION

(Delivered in London)

Of all the forces that have worked and are still working to mould the destinies of the human race, none, certainly, is more potent than that, the manifestation of which we call religion. All social organisations have as a background, somewhere, the workings of that peculiar force, and the greatest cohesive impulse ever brought into play amongst human units has been derived from this power. It is obvious to all of us that in very many cases the bonds of religion have proved stronger than the bonds of race, or climate, or even of descent. It is a well-known fact that persons worshipping the same God, believing in the same religion, have stood by each other, with much greater strength and constancy, than people of merely the same descent, or even brothers. Various attempts have been made to trace the beginnings of religion. In all the ancient religions which have come down to us at the present day, we find one claim made—that they are all supernatural, that their genesis is not, as it were, in the human brain, but that they have originated somewhere outside of it.

Two theories have gained some acceptance amongst modern scholars. One is the spirit theory of religion, the other the evolution of the idea of the Infinite. One party maintains that ancestor worship is the beginning of religious ideas; the other, that religion originates in the personification of the powers of nature. Man wants to keep up the memory of his dead relatives and thinks they are living even when the body is dissolved, and he wants to place food for them and, in a certain sense, to worship them. Out of that came the growth we call religion.

Studying the ancient religions of the Egyptians, Babylonians, Chinese, and many other races in America and elsewhere, we find very clear traces of this ancestor worship being the beginning of religion. With the ancient Egyptians, the first idea of the soul was that of a double. Every human body contained in it another being very similar to it; and when a man died, this double went out of the body and yet lived on. But the life of the double lasted only so long as the dead body remained intact, and that is why we find among the Egyptians so much solicitude to keep the body uninjured. And that is why they built those huge pyramids in which they preserved the bodies. For, if any portion of the external body was hurt, the double would be correspondingly injured. This is clearly ancestor worship. With the ancient Babylonians we find the same idea of the double, but with a variation. The double lost all sense of love; it frightened the living to give it food and drink, and to help it in various ways. It even lost all affection for its own children and its own wife. Among the ancient Hindus also, we find traces of this ancestor worship. Among the Chinese, the basis of their religion may also be said to be ancestor worship, and it still permeates the length and breadth of that vast country. In fact, the only religion that can really be said to flourish in China is that of ancestor worship. Thus it seems, on the one hand, a very good position is made out for those who hold the theory of ancestor worship as the beginning of religion.

On the other hand, there are scholars who from the ancient Aryan literature show that religion originated in nature worship. Although in India we find proofs of ancestor worship everywhere, yet in the oldest records there is no trace of it whatsoever. In the Rig Veda Samhitā, the most ancient record of the Aryan race, we do not find any trace of it. Modern scholars think, it is the worship of nature that they find there. The human mind seems to struggle to get a peep behind the scenes. The dawn, the evening, the hurricane, the stupendous and gigantic forces of nature, its beauties, these have exercised the human mind, and it aspires to go beyond, to understand something about them. In the struggle they endow these phenomena with personal attributes, giving them souls and bodies, sometimes beautiful, sometimes transcendent. Every attempt ends by these phenomena becoming abstractions whether personalised or not. So also it is found with the ancient Greeks; their whole mythology is simply this abstracted nature worship. So also with the ancient Germans, the Scandinavians, and all the other Aryan races. Thus, on this side, too, a very strong case has been made out, that religion has its origin in the personification of the powers of nature.

These two views, though they seem to be contradictory, can be reconciled on a third basis, which, to my mind, is the real germ of religion, and that I propose to call the struggle to transcend the limitations of the senses. Either, man goes to seek for the spirits of his ancestors, the spirits of the dead, that is, he wants to get a glimpse of what there is after the body is dissolved, or, he desires to understand the power working behind the stupendous phenomena of nature. Whichever of these is the case, one thing is certain, that he tries to transcend the limitations of the senses. He cannot remain satisfied with his senses; he wants to go beyond them. The explanation need not be mysterious. To me it seems very natural that the first glimpse of religion should come through dreams. The first idea of immortality man may well get through dreams. Is that not a most wonderful state? And we know that children and untutored minds find very little difference between dreaming and their awakened state. What can be more natural than that they find, as natural logic, that even during the sleep state when the body is apparently dead, the mind goes on with all its intricate workings? What wonder that men will at once come to the conclusion that when this body is dissolved for ever, the same working will go on? This, to my mind, would be a more natural explanation of the supernatural, and through this dream idea the human mind rises to higher and higher conceptions. Of course, in time, the vast majority of mankind found out that these dreams are not verified by their waking states, and that during the dream state it is not that man has a fresh existence, but simply that he recapitulates the experiences of the awakened state.

But by this time the search had begun, and the search was inward, arid man continued inquiring more deeply into the different stages of the mind and discovered higher states than either the waking or the dreaming. This state of things we find in all the organised religions of the world, called either ecstasy or inspiration. In all organised religions, their founders, prophets, and messengers are declared to have gone into states of mind that were neither waking nor sleeping, in which they came face to face with a new series of facts relating to what is called the spiritual kingdom. They realised things there much more intensely than we realise facts around us in our waking state. Take, for instance, the religions of the Brahmins. The Vedas are said to be written by Rishis. These Rishis were sages who realised certain facts. The exact definition of the Sanskrit word Rishi is a Seer of Mantras—of the thoughts conveyed in the Vedic hymns. These men declared that they had realised—sensed, if that word can be used with regard to the supersensuous—certain facts, and these facts they proceeded to put on record. We find the same truth declared amongst both the Jews and the Christians.

Some exceptions may be taken in the case of the Buddhists as represented by the Southern sect. It may be asked—if the Buddhists do not believe in any God or soul, how can their religion be derived from the supersensuous state of existence? The answer to this is that even the Buddhists find an eternal moral law, and that moral law was not reasoned out in our sense of the word But Buddha found it, discovered it, in a supersensuous state. Those of you who have studied the life of Buddha even as briefly given in that beautiful poem, *The Light of Asia*, may remember that Buddha is represented as sitting under the Bo-tree until he reached that supersensuous state of mind. All his teachings came through this, and not through intellectual cogitations.

Thus, a tremendous statement is made by all religions; that the human mind, at certain moments, transcends not only the limitations of the senses, but also the power of reasoning. It then comes face to face with facts which it could never have sensed, could never hive reasoned out. These facts are the basis of all the religions of the world. Of course we have the right to challenge these facts, to put them to the test of reason. Nevertheless, all the existing religions of the world claim for the human mind this peculiar power of transcending the limits of the senses and the limits of reason; and this power they put forward as a statement of fact.

Apart from the consideration of tie question how

far these facts claimed by religions are true, we find one characteristic common to them all. They are all abstractions as contrasted with the concrete discoveries of physics, for instance; and in all the highly organised religions they take the purest form of Unit Abstraction, either in the form of an Abstracted Presence, as an Omnipresent Being, as an Abstract Personality called God, as a Moral Law, or in the form of an Abstract Essence underlying every existence. In modern times, too, the attempts made to preach religions without appealing to the supersensuous state if the mind have had to take up the old abstractions of the Ancients and give different names to them as "Moral Law", the "Ideal Unity", and so forth, thus showing that these abstractions are not in the senses. None of us have yet seen an "Ideal Human Being", and yet we are told to believe in it. None of us have yet seen an ideally perfect man, and yet without that ideal we cannot progress. Thus, this one fact stands out from all these different religions, that there is an Ideal Unit Abstraction, which is put before us, either in the form of a Person or an Impersonal Being, or a Law, or a Presence, or an Essence. We are always struggling to raise ourselves up to that ideal. Every human being, whosoever and wheresoever he may be, has an ideal of infinite power. Every human being has an ideal of infinite pleasure. Most of the works that we find around us, the activities displayed everywhere, are due to the struggle for this infinite power or this infinite pleasure. But a few quickly discover that although they are struggling for infinite power, it is not through the senses that it can be reached. They find out very soon that that infinite pleasure is not to be got through the senses, or, in other words, the senses are too limited, and the body is too limited, to express the Infinite. To manifest the Infinite through the finite is impossible, and sooner or later, man learns to give up the attempt to express the Infinite through the finite. This giving up, this renunciation of the attempt, is the background of ethics. Renunciation is the very basis upon which ethics stands. There never was an ethical code preached which had not renunciation for its basis.

Ethics always says, "Not I, but thou." Its motto is, "Not self, but non-self." The vain ideas of individualism, to which man clings when he is trying to find that Infinite Power or that Infinite Pleasure through the senses, have to be given up—say the laws of ethics. You have to put *yourself* last, and others before you. The senses say, "Myself first." Ethics says, "I must hold myself last." Thus, all codes of ethics are based upon this renunciation; destruction, not construction, of the individual on the material plane. That Infinite will never find expression upon the material plane, nor is it possible or thinkable.

So, man has to give up the plane of matter and rise to other spheres to seek a deeper expression of that Infinite. In this way the various ethical laws are being moulded, but all have that one central idea, eternal self-abnegation. Perfect self-annihilation is the ideal of ethics. People are startled if they are asked not to think of their individualities. They seem so very much afraid of losing what they call their individuality. At the same time, the same men would declare the highest ideals of ethics to be right, never for a moment thinking that the scope, the goal, the idea of all ethics is the destruction, and not the building up, of the individual.

Utilitarian standards cannot explain the ethical relations of men, for, in the first place, we cannot derive any ethical laws from considerations of utility. Without the supernatural sanction as it is called, or the perception of the superconscious as I prefer to term it, there can be no ethics. Without the struggle towards the Infinite there can be no ideal. Any system that wants to bind men down to the limits of their own societies is not able to find an explanation for the ethical laws of mankind. The Utilitarian wants us to give up the struggle after the Infinite, the reaching-out for the Supersensuous, as impracticable and absurd, and, in the same breath, asks us to take up ethics and do good to society. Why should we do good? Doing good is a secondary consideration. We must have an ideal. Ethics itself is not the end, but the means to the end. If the end is not there, why should we be ethical? Why should I do good to other men, and not injure them? If happiness is the goal of mankind, why should I not make myself happy and others unhappy? What prevents me? In the second place, the basis of utility is too narrow. All the current social forms and methods are derived from society as it exists, but what right has the Utilitarian to assume that society is eternal? Society did not exist ages ago, possibly will not exist ages hence. Most probably it is one of the passing stages through which we are going towards a higher evolution, and any law that is derived from society alone cannot be eternal, cannot cover the whole ground of man's nature. At best, therefore, Utilitarian theories can only work under present social conditions. Beyond that they have no value. But a morality an ethical code, derived from religion and spirituality, has the whole of infinite man for its scope. It takes up the individual, but its relations are to the Infinite, and it takes up society also—because society is nothing but numbers of these individuals grouped together; and as it applies to the individual and *his* eternal relations, it must necessarily apply to the whole of society, in whatever condition it may be at any given time. Thus we see that there is always the necessity of spiritual religion for mankind. Man cannot always think of matter, however pleasurable it may be.

It has been said that too much attention to things spiritual disturbs our practical relations in this world. As far back as in the days of the Chinese sage Confucius, it was said, "Let us take care of this world: and then, when we have finished with this world, we will take care of other world." It is very well that we should *take care* of this world. But if too much attention to the spiritual may affect a little our practical relations, too much attention to the so-called practical hurts us here and hereafter. It makes us materialistic. For man is not to regard *nature* as his goal, but something higher.

Man is man so long as he is struggling to rise above nature, and this nature is both internal and external. Not only does it comprise the laws that govern the particles of matter outside us and in our bodies, but also the more subtle nature within, which is, in fact, the motive power governing the external. It is good and very grand to conquer external nature, but grander still to conquer our internal nature. It is grand and good to know the laws that govern the stars and planets; it is infinitely grander and better to know the laws that govern the passions, the feelings, the will, of mankind. This conquering of the inner man, understanding the secrets of the subtle workings that are within the human mind, and knowing its wonderful secrets, belong entirely to religion. Human nature—the ordinary human nature, I mean—wants to see big material facts. The ordinary man cannot understand anything that is subtle. Well has it been said that the masses admire the lion that kills a thousand lambs, never for a moment thinking that it is death to the lambs. Although a momentary triumph for the lion; because they find pleasure only in manifestations of physical strength. Thus it is with the ordinary run of mankind. They understand and find pleasure in everything that is external. But in every society there is a section whose pleasures are not in the senses, but beyond, and who now and then catch glimpses of something higher than matter and struggle to reach it. And if we read the history of nations between the lines, we shall always find that the rise of a nation comes with an increase in the number of such men; and the fall begins when this pursuit after the Infinite, however vain Utilitarians may call it, has ceased. That is to say, the mainspring of the strength Of every race lies in its spirituality, and the death of that race begins the day that spirituality wanes and materialism gains ground.

Thus, apart from the solid facts and truths that we may learn from religion, apart from the comforts that we may gain from it, religion, as a science, as a study, is the greatest and healthiest exercise that the human mind can have. This pursuit of the Infinite, this struggle to grasp the Infinite, this effort to get beyond the limitations of the senses—out of matter, as it were—and to evolve the spiritual man—this striving day and night to make the Infinite one with our being—this struggle itself is the grandest and most glorious that man can make. Some persons find the greatest pleasure in eating. We have no right to say that they should not. Others find the greatest pleasure in possessing certain things. We have no right to say that they should not. But they also have no right to say "no" to the man who finds his highest pleasure in spiritual thought. The lower the organisation, the greater the pleasure in the senses. Very few men can eat a meal with the same gusto as a dog or a wolf. But all the pleasures of the dog or the wolf have gone, as it were into the senses. The lower types of humanity in all nations find pleasure in the senses, while the cultured and the educated find it in thought, in philosophy, in arts and sciences. Spirituality is a still higher plane. The subject being infinite, that plane is the highest, and the pleasure there is the highest for those who can appreciate it. So, even on the utilitarian ground that man is to seek for pleasure, he should cultivate religious thought, for it is the highest pleasure that exists. Thus religion, as a study, seems to me to be absolutely necessary.

We can see it in its effects. It is the greatest motive

power that moves the human mind No other ideal can put into us the same mass of energy as the spiritual. So far as human history goes, it is obvious to all of us that this has been the case and that its powers are not dead. I do not deny that men, on simply utilitarian grounds, can be very good and moral. There have been many great men in this world perfectly sound, moral, and good, simply on utilitarian grounds. But the world-movers, men who bring, as it were, a mass of magnetism into the world whose spirit works in hundreds and in thousands, whose life ignites others with a spiritual fire—such men, we always find, have that spiritual background. Their motive power came from religion. Religion is the greatest motive power for realising that infinite energy which is the birthright and nature of every man. In building up character in making for everything that is good and great, in bringing peace to others and peace to one's own self, religion is the highest motive power and, therefore, ought to be studied from that standpoint. Religion must be studied on a broader basis than formerly. All narrow limited, fighting ideas of religion have to go. All sect ideas and tribal or national ideas of religion must be given up. That each tribe or nation should have its own particular God and think that every other is wrong is a superstition that should belong to the past. All such ideas must be abandoned.

As the human mind broadens, its spiritual steps broaden too. The time has already come when a man cannot record a thought without its reaching to all corners of the earth; by merely physical means, we have come into touch with the whole world; so the future religions of the world have to become as universal, as wide.

The religious ideals of the future must embrace all that exists in the world and is good and great, and, at the same time, have infinite scope for future development. All that was good in the past must be preserved; and the doors must be kept open for future additions to the already existing store. Religions must also be inclusive and not look down with contempt upon one another because their particular ideals of God are different. In my life I have seen a great many spiritual men, a great many sensible persons, who did not believe in God at all that is to say, not in our sense of the word. Perhaps they understood God better than we can ever do. The Personal idea of God or the Impersonal, the Infinite, Moral Law, or the Ideal Man—these all have to come under the definition of religion. And when religions have become thus broadened, their power for good will have increased a hundredfold. Religions, having tremendous power in them, have often done more injury to the world than good, simply on account of their narrowness and limitations.

Even at the present time we find many sects and societies, with almost the same ideas, fighting each other, because one does not want to set forth those ideas in precisely the same way as another. Therefore, religions will have to broaden. Religious ideas will have to become universal, vast, and infinite; and then alone we shall have the fullest play of religion, for the power of religion has only just begun to manifest in the world. It is sometimes said that religions are dying out, that spiritual ideas are dying out of the world. To me it seems that they have just begun to grow. The power of religion, broadened and purified, is going to penetrate every part of human life. So long as religion was in the hands of a chosen few or of a body of priests, it was in temples, churches, books, dogmas, ceremonials, forms, and rituals. But when we come to the real, spiritual, universal concept, then, and then alone religion will become real and living; it will come into our very nature, live in our every movement, penetrate every pore of our society, and be infinitely more a power for good than it has ever been before.

What is needed is a fellow-feeling between the different types of religion, seeing that they all stand or fall together, a fellow-feeling which springs from mutual esteem and mutual respect, and not the condescending, patronising, niggardly expression of goodwill, unfortunately in vogue at the present time with many. And above all, this is needed between types of religious expression coming from the study of mental phenomena—unfortunately, even now laying exclusive claim to the name of religion—and those expressions of religion whose heads, as it were, are penetrating more into the secrets of heaven though their feet are clinging to earth, I mean the so-called materialistic sciences.

To bring about this harmony, both will have to make concessions, sometimes very large, nay more, sometimes painful, but each will find itself the better for the sacrifice and more advanced in truth. And in the end, the knowledge which is confined within the domain of time and space will meet and become one with that which is beyond them both, where the mind and senses cannot reach—the Absolute, the Infinite, the One without a second.

CHAPTER 2

THE REAL NATURE OF MAN

(Delivered in London)

Great is the tenacity with which man clings to the senses. Yet, however substantial he may think the external world in which he lives and moves, there comes a time in the lives of individuals and of races when, involuntarily, they ask, "Is this real?" To the person who never finds a moment to question the credentials of his senses, whose every moment is occupied with some sort of sense-enjoyment—even to him death comes, and he also is compelled to ask, "Is this real?" Religion begins with this question and ends with its answer. Even in the remote past, where recorded history cannot help us, in the mysterious light of mythology, back in the dim twilight of civilisation, we find the same question was asked, "What becomes of this? What is real?"

One of the most poetical of the Upanishads, the Katha Upanishad, begins with the inquiry: "When a man dies, there is a dispute. One party declares that he has gone for ever, the other insists that he is still living. Which is true?" Various answers have been given. The whole sphere of metaphysics, philosophy, and religion is really filled with various answers to this question. At the same time, attempts have been made to suppress it, to put a stop to the unrest of mind which asks, "What is beyond? What is real?" But so long as death remains, all these attempts at suppression will always prove to be unsuccessful. We may talk about seeing nothing beyond and keeping all our hopes and aspirations confined to the present moment, and struggle hard not to think of anything beyond the world of senses; and, perhaps, everything outside helps to keep us limited within its narrow bounds. The whole world may combine to prevent us from broadening out beyond the present. Yet, so long as there is death, the question must come again and again, "Is death the end of all these things to which we are clinging, as if they were the most real of all realities, the most substantial of all substances?" The world vanishes in a moment and is gone. Standing on the brink of a precipice beyond which is the infinite yawning chasm, every mind, however hardened, is bound to recoil and ask, "Is this real?" The hopes of a lifetime, built up little by little with all the energies of a great mind, vanish in a second. Are they real? This question must be answered.

Time never lessens its power; on the other hand, it adds strength to it.

Then there is the desire to be happy. We run after everything to make ourselves happy; we pursue our mad career in the external world of senses. If you ask the young man with whom life is successful, he will declare that it is real; and he really thinks so. Perhaps, when the same man grows old and finds fortune ever eluding him, he will then declare that it is fate. He finds at last that his desires cannot be fulfilled. Wherever he goes, there is an adamantine wall beyond which he cannot pass. Every sense-activity results in a reaction. Everything is evanescent. Enjoyment, misery, luxury, wealth, power, and poverty, even life itself, are all evanescent.

Two positions remain to mankind. One is to believe with the nihilists that all is nothing, that we know nothing, that we can never know anything either about the future, the past, or even the present. For we must remember that he who denies the past and the future and wants to stick to the present is simply a madman. One may as well deny the father and mother and assert the child. It would be equally logical. To deny the past and future, the present must inevitably be denied also. This is one position, that of the nihilists. I have never seen a man who could really become a nihilist for one minute. It is very easy to talk.

Then there is the other position—to seek for an explanation, to seek for the real, to discover in the midst of this eternally changing and evanescent world whatever is real. In this body which is an aggregate of molecules of matter, is there anything which is real? This has been the search throughout the history of the, human mind. In the very oldest times, we often find glimpses of light coming into men's minds. We find man, even then, going a step beyond this body, finding something which is not this external body, although very much like it, much more complete, much more perfect, and which remains even when this body is dissolved. We read in the hymns of the Rig Veda, addressed to the God of Fire who is burning a dead body, "Carry him, O Fire, in your arms gently, give him a perfect body, a bright body, carry him where the fathers live, where there is no more sorrow, where there is no more death." The same idea you will find present in every religion. And we get another idea with it. It is a significant fact that all religions, without one exception, hold that man is a degeneration of what he was, whether they clothe this in mythological words, or in the clear language of philosophy, or in the beautiful expressions of poetry. This is the one fact that comes out of every scripture and of every mythology that the man that is, is a degeneration of what he was. This is the kernel of truth within the story of Adam's fall in the Jewish scripture. This is again and again repeated in the scriptures of the Hindus; the dream of a period which they call the Age of Truth, when no man died unless he wished to die, when he could keep his body as long as he liked, and his mind was pure and strong. There was no evil and no misery; and the present age is a corruption of that state of perfection. Side by side with this, we find the story of the deluge everywhere. That story itself is a proof that this present age is held to be a corruption of a former age by every religion. It went on becoming more and more corrupt until the deluge swept away a large portion of mankind, and again the ascending series began. It is going up slowly again to reach once more that early state of purity. You are all aware of the story of the deluge in the Old Testament. The same story was current among the ancient Babylonians, the Egyptians, the Chinese, and the Hindus. Manu, a great ancient sage, was praying on the bank of the Gangā, when a little minnow came to him for protection, and he put it into a pot of water he had before him. "What do you want?" asked Manu. The little minnow declared he was pursued by a bigger fish and wanted protection. Manu carried the little fish to his home, and in the morning he had become as big as the pot and said, "I cannot live in this pot any longer". Manu put him in a tank, and the next day he was as big as the tank and declared he could not live there any more. So Manu had to take him to a river, and in the morning the fish filled the river. Then Manu put him in the ocean, and he declared, "Manu, I am the Creator of the universe. I have taken this form to come and warn you that I will deluge the world. You build an ark and in it put a pair of every kind of animal, and let your family enter the ark, and there will project out of the water my horn. Fasten the ark to it; and when the deluge subsides, come out and people the earth." So the world was deluged, and Manu saved his own family and two of every kind of animal and seeds of every plant. When the deluge subsided, he came and peopled the world; and we are all called "man", because we are the progeny of Manu.

Now, human language is the attempt to express the truth that is within. I am fully persuaded that a baby whose language consists of unintelligible sounds is attempting to express the highest philosophy, only the baby has not the organs to express it nor the means. The difference between the language of the highest philosophers and the utterances of babies is one of degree and not of kind. What you call the most correct, systematic, mathematical language of the present time, and the hazy, mystical, mythological languages of the ancients, differ only in degree. All of them have a grand idea behind, which is, as it were, struggling to express itself; and often behind these ancient mythologies are nuggets of truth; and often, I am sorry to say, behind the fine, polished phrases of the moderns is arrant trash. So, we need not throw a thing overboard because it is clothed in mythology, because it does not fit in with the notions of Mr. So-and-so or Mrs. So-and-so of modern times. If people should laugh at religion because most religions declare that men must believe in mythologies taught by such and such a prophet, they ought to laugh more at these moderns. In modern times, if a man quotes a Moses or a Buddha or a Christ, he is laughed at; but let him give the name of a Huxley, a Tyndall, or a Darwin, and it is swallowed without salt. "Huxley has said it", that is enough for many. We are free from superstitions indeed! That was a religious superstition, and this a scientific superstition; only, in and through that superstition came life-giving ideas of spirituality; in and through this modern superstition come lust and greed. That superstition was worship of God, and this superstition is worship of filthy lucre, of fame or power. That is the difference.

To return to mythology. Behind all these stories we find one idea standing supreme—that man is a degeneration of what he was. Coming to the present times, modern research seems to repudiate this position absolutely. Evolutionists seem to contradict entirely this assertion. According to them, man is the evolution of the mollusc; and, therefore, what mythology states cannot be true. There is in India, however, a mythology which is able to reconcile both these positions. The Indian mythology has a theory of cycles, that all progression is in the form of waves. Every wave is attended by a fall, and that by a rise the next moment, that by a fall in the next, and again another rise The motion is in cycles. Certainly it is true, even on the grounds of modern research, that man cannot be simply an evolution. Every evolution presupposes an involution. The modern scientific man will tell you that you can only get the amount of energy out of a machine which you have previously put into it. Something cannot be produced out of nothing. If a man is an evolution of the mollusc, then the perfect man—the Buddha-man, the Christ-man—was involved in the mollusc. If it is not so, whence come these gigantic personalities? Something cannot come out of nothing. Thus we are in the position of reconciling the scriptures with modern light. That energy which manifests itself slowly through various stages until it becomes the perfect man, cannot come out of nothing. It existed somewhere; and if the mollusc or the protoplasm is the first point to which you can trace it, that protoplasm, somehow or other, must have contained the energy.

There is a great discussion going on as to whether the aggregate of materials we call the body is the cause of manifestation of the force we call the soul, thought, etc., or whether it is the thought that manifests this body. The religions of the world of course hold that the force called thought manifests the body, and not the reverse. There are schools of modern thought which hold that what we call thought is simply the outcome of the adjustment of the parts of the machine which we call body. Taking the second position that the soul or the mass of thought, or however you may call it, is the outcome of this machine, the outcome of the chemical and physical combinations of matter making up the body and brain, leaves the question unanswered. What makes the body? What force combines the molecules into the body form? What force is there which takes up material from the mass of matter around and forms my body one way, another body another way, and so on? What makes these infinite distinctions? To say that the force called soul is the outcome of the combinations of the molecules of the body is putting the cart before the horse. How did the combinations come; where was the force to make them? If you say that some other force was the cause of these combinations, and soul was the outcome of that matter, and that soul—which combined a certain mass of matter—was itself the result of the combinations, it is no answer. That theory ought to be taken which explains most of the facts, if not all, and that without contradicting other existing theories. It is more logical to say that the force which takes up the matter and forms the body is the same which manifests through that body. To say, therefore, that the thought forces manifested by the body are the outcome of the arrangement of molecules and have no independent existence has no meaning; neither can force evolve out of matter. Rather it is possible to demonstrate that what we call matter does not exist at all. It is only a certain state of force. Solidity, hardness, or any other state of matter can be proved to be the result of motion. Increase of vortex motion imparted to fluids gives them the force of solids. A mass of air in vortex motion, as in a tornado, becomes solid-like and by its impact breaks or cuts through solids. A thread of a spider's web, if it could be moved at almost infinite velocity, would be as strong as an iron chain and would cut through an oak tree. Looking at it in this way, it would be easier to prove that what we call matter does not exist. But the other way cannot be proved.

What is the force which manifests itself through the body? It is obvious to all of us, whatever that force be, that it is taking particles up, as it were, and manipulating forms out of them—the human body. None else comes here to manipulate bodies for you and me. I never saw anybody eat food for me. I have to assimilate it, manufacture blood and bones and everything out of that food. What is this mysterious force? Ideas about the future and about the past seem to be terrifying to many. To many they seem to be mere speculation.

We will take the present theme. What is this force which is now working through us? We know how in old times, in all the ancient scriptures, this power, this manifestation of power, was thought to be a bright substance having the form of this body, and which remained even after this body fell. Later on, however, we find a higher idea coming—that this bright body did not represent the force. Whatsoever has form must be the result of combinations of particles and requires something else behind it to move it. If this body requires something which is not the body to manipulate it, the bright body, by the same necessity, will also require something other than itself to manipulate it. So, that something was called the soul, the Ātman in Sanskrit. It was the Ātman which through the bright body, as it were, worked on the gross body outside. The bright body is considered as the receptacle of the mind, and the Ātman is beyond that. It is not the mind even; it works the mind, and through the mind the body. You have an Ātman, I have another each one of us has a separate Ātman and a separate fine body, and through that we work on the gross external body. Questions were then asked about this Ātman about its nature. What is this Ātman, this soul of man which is neither the body nor the mind? Great discussions followed. Speculations were made, various shades of philosophic inquiry came into existence; and I shall try to place before you some of the conclusions that have been reached about this Ātman.

The different philosophies seem to agree that this Ātman, whatever it be, has neither form nor shape, and that which has neither form nor shape must be omnipresent. Time begins with mind, space also is in the mind. Causation cannot stand without time. Without the idea of succession there cannot be any idea of causation. Time, space and causation, therefore, are in the mind, and as this Ātman is beyond the mind and formless, it must be beyond time, beyond space, and beyond causation. Now, if it is beyond time, space, and causation, it must be infinite. Then comes the highest speculation in our philosophy. The infinite cannot be two. If the soul be infinite, there can be only one Soul, and all ideas of various souls—you having one soul, and I having another, and so forth—are not real. The Real Man, therefore, is one and infinite, the omnipresent Spirit. And the apparent man is only a limitation of that Real Man. In that sense the mythologies are true that the apparent man, however great he may be, is only a dim reflection of the Real Man who is beyond. The Real Man, the Spirit, being beyond cause and effect, not bound by time and space, must, therefore, be free. He was never bound, and could not be bound. The apparent man, the reflection, is limited by time, space, and causation, and is, therefore, bound. Or in the language of some of our philosophers, he appears to be bound, but really is not. This is the reality in our souls, this omnipresence, this spiritual nature, this infinity. Every soul is infinite, therefore there is no question of birth and death. Some children were being examined. The examiner put them rather hard questions, and among them was this one: "Why does not the earth fall?" He wanted to evoke answers about gravitation. Most of the children could not answer at all; a few answered that it was gravitation or something. One bright little girl answered it by putting another question: "Where should it fall?" The question is nonsense. Where should the earth fall? There is no falling or rising for the earth. In infinite space there is no up or down; that is only in the relative. Where is the going or coming for the infinite? Whence should it come and whither should it go?

Thus, when people cease to think of the past or future, when they give up the idea of body, because the body comes and goes and is limited, then they have risen to a higher ideal. The body is not the Real Man, neither is the mind, for the mind waxes and wanes. It is the Spirit beyond, which alone can live for ever. The body and mind are continually changing, and are, in fact, only names of series of changeful phenomena, like rivers whose waters are in a constant state of flux, yet presenting the appearance of unbroken streams. Every particle in this body is continually changing; no one has the same body for many minutes together, and yet we think of it as the same body. So with the mind; one moment it is happy, another moment unhappy; one moment strong, another weak; an ever-changing whirlpool. That cannot be the Spirit which is infinite. Change can only be in the limited. To say that the infinite changes in any way is absurd; it cannot be. You can move and I can move, as limited bodies; every particle in this universe is in a constant state of flux, but taking the universe as a unit, as one whole, it cannot move, it cannot change. Motion is always a relative thing. I move in relation to something else. Any particle in this universe can change in relation to any other particle; but take the whole universe as one, and in relation to what can it move? There is nothing besides it. So this infinite Unit is unchangeable, immovable, absolute, and this is the Real Man. Our reality, therefore, consists in the Universal and not in the limited. These are old delusions, however comfortable they are, to think that we are little limited beings, constantly changing. People are frightened when they are told that they are Universal Being, everywhere present. Through everything you work, through every foot you move, through every lip you talk, through every heart you feel.

People are frightened when they are told this. They will again and again ask you if they are not going to keep their individuality. What is individuality? I should like to see it. A baby has no moustache; when he grows to be a man, perhaps he has a moustache and beard. His individuality would be lost, if it were in the body. If I lose one eye, or if I lose one of my hands, my individuality would be lost if it were in the body. Then, a drunkard should not give up drinking because he would lose his individuality. A thief should not be a good man because he would thereby lose his individuality. No man ought to change his habits for fear of this. There is no individuality except in the Infinite. That is the only condition which does not change. Everything else is in a constant state of flux. Neither can individuality be in memory. Suppose, on account of a blow on the head I forget all about my past; then, I have lost all individuality; I am gone. I do not remember two or three years of my childhood, and if memory and existence are one, then whatever I forget is gone. That part of my life which I do not remember, I did not live. That is a very narrow idea of individuality.

We are not individuals yet. We are struggling towards individuality, and that is the Infinite, that is the real nature of man. He alone lives whose life is in the whole universe, and the more we concentrate our lives on limited things, the faster we go towards death. Those moments alone we live when our lives are in the universe, in others; and living this little life is death, simply death, and that is why the fear of death comes. The fear of death can only be conquered when man realises that so long as there is one life in this universe, he is living. When he can say, "I am in everything, in everybody, I am in all lives, I am the universe," then alone comes the state of fearlessness. To talk of immortality in constantly changing things is absurd. Says an old Sanskrit philosopher: It is only the Spirit that is the individual, because it is infinite. No infinity can be divided; infinity cannot be broken into pieces. It is the same one, undivided unit for ever, and this is the individual man, the Real Man. The apparent man is merely a struggle to express, to manifest this individuality which is beyond; and evolution is not in the Spirit. These changes which are going on—the wicked becoming good, the animal becoming man, take them in whatever way you like—

are not in the Spirit. They are evolution of nature and manifestation of Spirit. Suppose there is a screen hiding you from me, in which there is a small hole through which I can see some of the faces before me, just a few faces. Now suppose the hole begins to grow larger and larger, and as it does so, more and more of the scene before me reveals itself and when at last the whole screen has disappeared, I stand face to face with you all. You did not change at all in this case; it was the hole that was evolving, and you were gradually manifesting yourselves. So it is with the Spirit. No perfection is going to be attained. You are already free and perfect. What are these ideas of religion and God and searching for the hereafter? Why does man look for a God? Why does man, in every nation, in every state of society, want a perfect ideal somewhere, either in man, in God, or elsewhere? Because that idea is within you. It was your own heart beating and you did not know; you were mistaking it for something external. It is the God within your own self that is propelling you to seek for Him, to realise Him. After long searches here and there, in temples and in churches, in earths and in heavens, at last you come back, completing the circle from where you started, to your own soul and find that He for whom you have been seeking all over the world, for whom you have been weeping and praying in churches and temples, on whom you were looking as the mystery of all mysteries shrouded in the clouds, is nearest of the near, is your own Self, the reality of your life, body, and soul. That is your own nature. Assert it, manifest it. Not to become pure, you are pure already. You are not to be perfect, you are that already. Nature is like that screen which is hiding the reality beyond. Every good thought that you think or act upon is simply tearing the veil, as it were; and the purity, the Infinity, the God behind, manifests Itself more and more.

This is the whole history of man. Finer and finer becomes the veil, more and more of the light behind shines forth, for it is its nature to shine. It cannot be known; in vain we try to know it. Were it knowable, it would not be what it is, for it is the eternal subject. Knowledge is a limitation, knowledge is objectifying. He is the eternal subject of everything, the eternal witness in this universe, your own Self. Knowledge is, as it were, a lower step, a degeneration. We are that eternal subject already; how can we know it? It is the real nature of every man, and he is struggling to express it in various ways; otherwise, why are there so many ethical codes? Where is the explanation of all ethics? One idea stands out as the centre of all ethical systems, expressed in various forms, namely, doing good to others. The guiding motive of mankind should be charity towards men, charity towards all animals. But these are all various expressions of that eternal truth that, "I am the universe; this universe is one." Or else, where is the reason? Why should I do good to my fellowmen? Why should I do good to others? What compels me? It is sympathy, the feeling of sameness everywhere. The hardest hearts feel sympathy for other beings sometimes. Even the man who gets frightened if he is told that this assumed individuality is really a delusion, that it is ignoble to try to cling to this apparent individuality, that very man will tell you that extreme self-abnegation is the centre of all morality. And what is perfect self-abnegation? It means the abnegation of this apparent self, the abnegation of all selfishness. This idea of "me and mine"—Ahamkāra and Mamatā—is the result of past Superstition, and the more this present self passes away, the more the real Self becomes manifest. This is true self-abnegation, the centre, the basis, the gist of all moral teaching; and whether man knows it or not the whole world is slowly going towards it, practicing it more or less. Only, the vast majority of mankind are doing it unconsciously. Let them do it consciously. Let then make the sacrifice, knowing that this "me and mine" is not the real Self, but only a limitation. But one glimpse of that infinite reality which is behind—but one spark of that infinite fire that is the All—represents the present man; the Infinite is his true nature.

What is the utility, the effect, the result, of this knowledge? In these days, we have to measure everything by utility—by how many pounds shillings, and pence it represents. What right has a person to ask that truth should be judged by the standard of utility or money? Suppose there is no utility, will it be less true? Utility is not the test of truth. Nevertheless, there is the highest utility in this. Happiness, we see is what everyone is seeking for, but the majority seek it in things which are evanescent and not real. No happiness was ever found in the senses. There never was a person who found happiness in the senses or in enjoyment of the senses. Happiness is only found in the Spirit. Therefore the highest utility for mankind is to find this happiness in the Spirit. The next point is that ignorance is the great mother of all misery, and the fundamental ignorance is to think that the Infinite weeps and cries, that He is finite. This is the basis of all ignorance that we, the immortal, the ever pure, the perfect Spirit, think that we are little minds, that we are little bodies; it is the mother of all selfishness. As soon as I think that I am a little body, I want to preserve it, to protect it, to keep it nice, at the expense of other bodies; then you and I become separate. As soon as this idea of separation comes, it opens the door to all mischief and leads to all misery. This is the utility that if a very small fractional part of human beings living today can put aside the idea of selfishness, narrowness, and littleness, this earth will become a paradise tomorrow; but with machines and improvements of material knowledge only, it will never be. These only increase misery, as oil poured on fire increases the flame all the more. Without the knowledge of the Spirit, all material knowledge is only adding fuel to fire, only giving into the hands of selfish man one more instrument to take what belongs to others, to live upon the life of others, instead of giving up his life for them.

Is it practical?—is another question. Can it be practised in modern society? *Truth does not pay homage to any society, ancient or modern.* Society has to pay homage to Truth or die. *Societies should be moulded upon* truth, and truth has not to adjust itself to society. If such a noble truth as unselfishness cannot be practiced in society, it is better for man to give up society and go into the forest. That is the daring man. There are two sorts of courage. One is the courage of facing the cannon. And the other is the courage of spiritual conviction. An Emperor who invaded India was told by his teacher to go and see some of the sages there. After a long search for one, he found a very old man sitting on a block of stone. The Emperor talked with him a little and became very much impressed by his wisdom. He asked the sage to go to his country with him. "No," said the sage, "I am quite satisfied with my forest here." Said the Emperor, "I will give you money, position, wealth. I am the Emperor of the world." "No," replied the man, "I don't care for those things." The Emperor replied, "If you do not go, I will kill you." The man smiled serenely and said, "That is the most foolish thing you ever said, Emperor. You cannot kill me. Me the sun cannot dry, fire cannot burn, sword cannot kill, for I am the birthless, the deathless, the ever-living omnipotent, omnipresent Spirit." This is spiritual boldness, while the other is the courage of a lion or a tiger. In the Mutiny of 1857 there was a Swami, a very great soul, whom a Mohammedan mutineer stabbed severely. The Hindu mutineers caught and brought the man to the Swami, offering to kill him. But the Swami looked up calmly and said, "My brother, thou art He, thou art He!" and expired. This is another instance. What good is it to talk of the strength of your muscles, of the superiority of your Western institutions, if you cannot make Truth square with your society, if you cannot build up a society into which the highest Truth will fit? What is the good of this boastful talk about your grandeur and greatness, if you stand up and say, "This courage is not practical." Is nothing practical but pounds, shillings, and pence? If so, why boast of your society? *That society is the greatest, where the highest truths become practical. That is my opinion; and if society is; not fit for the highest* truths, make it so; and the sooner, the better. Stand up, men and women, in this spirit, dare to believe in the Truth, dare to practice the Truth! The world requires a few hundred bold men and women. Practise that boldness which dares know the Truth, which dares show the Truth in life, which does not quake before death, nay, welcomes death, makes a man know that he, is the Spirit, that, in the whole universe, nothing can kill him. Then you will be free. Then you will know yours real Soul. "This Ātman is first to be heard, then thoughts about and then meditated upon."

There is a great tendency in modern times to talk too much of work and decry thought. Doing is very good, but that comes from thinking. Little manifestations of energy through the muscles are called work. But where there is no thought, there will be no work. Fill the brain, therefore, with high thoughts, highest ideals, place them day and night before you, and out of that will come great work. Talk not about impurity, but say that we are pure. We have hypnotised ourselves into this thought that we are little, that we are born, and that we are going to die, and into a constant state of fear.

There is a story about a lioness, who was big with

young, going about in search of prey; and seeing a flock of sheep, she jumped upon them. She died in the effort; and a little baby lion was born, motherless. It was taken care of by the sheep and the sheep brought it up, and it grew up with them, ate grass, and bleated like the sheep. And although in time it became a big, full-grown lion. It thought it was a sheep. One day another lion came in search of prey and was astonished to find that in the midst of this flock of sheep was a lion, fleeing like the sheep at the approach of danger. He tried to get near the sheep-lion, to tell it that it was not a sheep but a lion; but the poor animal fled at his approach. However, he watched his opportunity and one day found the sheep-lion sleeping. He approached it and said, "You are a lion." "I am a sheep," cried the other lion and could not believe the contrary but bleated. The lion dragged him towards a lake and said, "Look here, here is my reflection and yours." Then came the comparison. It looked at the lion and then at its own reflection, and in a moment came the idea that it was a lion. The lion roared, the bleating was gone. You are lions, you are souls, pure, infinite, and perfect. The might of the universe is within you. "Why weepest thou, my friend? There is neither birth nor death for thee. Why weepest thou? There is no disease nor misery for thee, but thou art like the infinite sky; clouds of various colours come over it, play for a moment, then vanish. But the sky is ever the same eternal blue." Why do we see wickedness? There was a stump of a tree, and in the dark, a thief came that way and said, "That is a policeman." A young man waiting for his beloved saw it and thought that it was his sweetheart. A child who had been told ghost stories took it for a ghost and began to shriek. But all the time it was the stump of a tree. We see the world as we are. Suppose there is a baby in a room with a bag of gold on the table and a thief comes and steals the gold. Would the baby know it was stolen? That which we have inside, we see outside. The baby has no thief inside and sees no thief outside. So with all knowledge. Do not talk of the wickedness of the world and all its sins. Weep that you are bound to see wickedness yet. Weep that you are bound to see sin everywhere, and if you want to help the world, do not condemn it. Do not weaken it more. For what is sin and what is misery, and what are all these, but the results of weakness? The world is made weaker and weaker every day by such teachings. Men are taught from childhood that they are weak and sinners. Teach them that they are all glorious children of immortality, even those who are the weakest in manifestation. Let positive, strong, helpful thought enter into their brains from very childhood. Lay yourselves open to these thoughts, and not to weakening and paralysing ones. Say to your own minds, "I am He, I am He." Let it ring day and night in your minds like a song, and at the point of death declare "I am He." That is the Truth; the infinite strength of the world is yours. Drive out the superstition that has covered your minds. Let us be brave. Know the Truth and practice the Truth. The goal may be distant, but awake, arise, and stop not till the goal is reached.

CHAPTER 3

MAYA AND ILLUSION

(Delivered in London)

Almost all of you have heard of the word Maya. Generally it is used, though incorrectly, to denote illusion, or delusion, or some such thing. But the theory of Maya forms one of the pillars upon which the Vedanta rests; it is, therefore, necessary that it should be properly understood. I ask a little patience of you, for there is a great danger of its being misunderstood. The oldest idea of Maya that we find in Vedic literature is the sense of delusion; but then the real theory had not been reached. We find such passages as, "Indra through his Maya assumed various forms." Here it is true the word Maya means something like magic, and we find various other passages, always taking the same meaning. The word Maya then dropped out of sight altogether. But in the meantime the idea was developing. Later, the question was raised: "Why can't we know this secret of the universe?" And the answer given was very significant: "Because we talk in vain, and because we are satisfied with the things of the senses, and because we are running after desires; therefore, we, as it were, cover the Reality with a mist." Here the word Maya is not used at all, but we get the idea that the cause of our ignorance is a kind of mist that has come between us and the Truth. Much later on, in one of the latest Upanishads, we find the word Maya reappearing, but this time, a transformation has taken place in it, and a mass of new meaning has attached itself to the word. Theories had been propounded and repeated, others had been taken up, until at last the idea of Maya became fixed. We read in the Shvetāshvatara Upanishad, "Know nature to be Maya and the Ruler of this Maya is the Lord Himself." Coming to our philosophers, we find that this word Maya has been manipulated in various fashions, until we come to the great Shankarāchārya. The theory of Maya was manipulated a little by the Buddhists too, but in the hands of the Buddhists it became very much like what is called Idealism, and that is the meaning that is now generally given to the word Maya. When the Hindu says the world is Maya, at once people get the idea that the world is an illusion. This interpretation has some basis, as coming through the Buddhistic philosophers, because there was one section of philosophers who did not believe in the external world at all. But the Maya of the Vedanta, in its last developed form, is neither Idealism nor Realism, nor is it a theory. It is a simple statement of facts—what we are and what we see around us.

As I have told you before, the minds of the people from whom the Vedas came were intent upon following principles, discovering principles. They had no time to work upon details or to wait for them; they wanted to go deep into the heart of things. Something beyond was calling them, as it were, and they could not wait. Scattered through the Upanishads, we find that the details of subjects which we now call modern sciences are often very erroneous, but, at the same time, their principles are correct. For instance, the idea of ether, which is one of the latest theories of modern science, is to be found in our ancient literature in forms much more developed than is the modern scientific theory of ether today, but it was in principle. When they tried to demonstrate the workings of that principle, they made many mistakes. The theory of the all-pervading life principle, of which all life in this universe is but a differing manifestation, was understood in Vedic times; it is found in the Brāhmanas. There is a long hymn in the Samhitās in praise of Prana of which all life is but a manifestation. By the by, it may interest some of you to know that there are theories in the Vedic philosophy about the origin of life on this earth very similar to those which have been advanced by some modern European scientists. You, of course, all know that there is a theory that life came from other planets. It is a settled doctrine with some Vedic philosophers that life comes in this way from the moon.

Coming to the principles, we find these Vedic thinkers

very courageous and wonderfully bold in propounding large and generalised theories. Their solution of the mystery of the universe, from the external world, was as satisfactory as it could be. The detailed workings of modern science do not bring the question one step nearer to solution, because the principles have failed. If the theory of ether failed in ancient times to give a solution of the mystery of the universe, working out the details of that ether theory would not bring us much nearer to the truth. If the theory of all-pervading life failed as a theory of this universe, it would not mean anything more if worked out in detail, for the details do not change the principle of the universe. What I mean is that in their inquiry into the principle, the Hindu thinkers were as bold, and in some cases, much bolder than the moderns. They made some of the grandest generalizations that have yet been reached, and some still remain as theories, which modern science has yet to get even as theories. For instance, they not only arrived at the ether theory, but went beyond and classified mind also as a still more rarefied ether. Beyond that again, they found a still more rarefied ether. Yet that was no solution, it did not solve the problem. No amount of knowledge of the external world could solve the problem. "But", says the scientist, "we are just beginning to know a little: wait a few thousand years and we shall get the solution." "No," says the Vedantist, for he has proved beyond all doubt that the mind is limited, that it cannot go beyond certain limits—beyond time, space, and causation. As no man can jump out of his own self, so no man can go beyond the limits that have been put upon him by the laws of time and space. Every attempt to solve the laws of causation, time, and space would be futile, because the very attempt would have to be made by taking for granted the existence of these three. What does the statement of the existence of the world mean, then? "This world has no existence." What is meant by that? It means that it has no absolute existence. It exists only in relation to my mind, to your mind, and to the mind of everyone else. We see this world with the five senses but if we had another sense, we would see in it something more. If we had yet another sense, it would appear as something still different. It has, therefore, no real existence; it has no unchangeable, immovable, infinite existence. Nor can it be called non-existence, seeing that it exists, and we slave to work in and through it. It is a mixture of existence and non-existence.

Coming from abstractions to the common, everyday details of our lives, we find that our whole life is a contradiction, a mixture of existence and non-existence. There is this contradiction in knowledge. It seems that man can know everything, if he only wants to know; but before he has gone a few steps, he finds an adamantine wall which he cannot pass. All his work is in a circle, and he cannot go beyond that circle. The problems which are nearest and dearest to him are impelling him on and calling, day and night, for a solution, but he cannot solve them, because he cannot go beyond his intellect. And yet that desire is implanted strongly in him. Still we know that the only good is to be obtained by controlling and checking it. With every breath, every impulse of our heart asks us to be selfish. At the same time, there is some power beyond us which says that it is unselfishness alone which is good. Every child is a born optimist; he dreams golden dreams. In youth he becomes still more optimistic. It is hard for a young man to believe that there is such a thing as death, such a thing as defeat or degradation. Old age comes, and life is a mass of ruins. Dreams have vanished into the air, and the man becomes a pessimist. Thus we go from one extreme to another, buffeted by nature, without knowing where we are going. It reminds me of a celebrated song in the *Lalita Vistara*, the biography of Buddha. Buddha was born, says the book, as the saviour of mankind, but he forgot himself in the luxuries of his palace. Some angels came and sang a song to rouse him. And the burden of the whole song is that we are floating down the river of life which is continually changing with no stop and no rest. So are our lives, going on and on without knowing any rest. What are we to do? The man who has enough to eat and drink is an optimist, and he avoids all mention of misery, for it frightens him. Tell not to him of the sorrows and the sufferings of the world; go to him and tell that it is all good. "Yes, I am safe," says he. "Look at me! I have a nice house to live in. I do not fear cold and hunger; therefore do not bring these horrible pictures before me." But, on the other hand, there are others dying of cold and hunger. If you go and teach *them* that it is all good, they will not hear you. How can they wish others to be happy when they are miserable? Thus we are oscillating between optimism and pessimism.

Then, there is the tremendous fact of death. The whole world is going towards death; everything dies. All our progress, our vanities, our reforms, our luxuries, our wealth, our knowledge, have that one end—death. That is all that is certain. Cities come and go, empires rise and fall, planets break into pieces and crumble into dust, to be blown about by the atmospheres of other planets. Thus it has been going on from time without beginning. Death is the end of everything. Death is the end of life, of beauty, of wealth, of power, of virtue too. Saints die and sinners die, kings die and beggars die. They are all going to death, and yet this tremendous clinging on to life exists. Somehow, we do not know why, we cling to life; we cannot give it up. And this is Maya.

The mother is nursing a child with great care; all her soul, her life, is in that child. The child grows, becomes a man, and perchance becomes a blackguard and a brute, kicks her and beats her every day; and yet the mother clings to the child; and when her reason awakes, she covers it up with the idea of love. She little thinks that it is not love, that it is something which has got hold of her nerves, which she cannot shake off; however she may try, she cannot shake off the bondage she is in. And this is Maya.

We are all after the Golden Fleece. Every one of us thinks that this will be his. Every reasonable man sees that his chance is, perhaps, one in twenty millions, yet everyone struggles for it. And this is Maya.

Death is stalking day and night over this earth of ours, but at the same time we think we shall live eternally. A question was once asked of King Yudhishthira, "What is the most wonderful thing on this earth?" And the king replied, "Every day people are dying around us, and yet men think they will never die." And this is Maya.

These tremendous contradictions in our intellect, in our knowledge, yea, in all the facts of our life face us on all sides. A reformer arises and wants to remedy the evils that are existing in a certain nation; and before they have been remedied, a thousand other evils arise in another place. It is like an old house that is falling; you patch it up in one place and the ruin extends to another. In India, our reformers cry and preach against the evils of enforced widowhood. In the West, non-marriage is the great evil. Help the unmarried on one side; they are suffering. Help the widows on the other; they are suffering. It is like chronic rheumatism: you drive from the head, and it goes to the body; you drive it from there, and it goes to the feet. Reformers arise and preach that learning, wealth, and culture should not be in the hands of a select few; and they do their best to make them accessible to all. These may bring more happiness to some, but, perhaps, as culture comes, physical happiness lessens. The knowledge of happiness brings the knowledge of unhappiness. Which way then shall we go? The least amount of material prosperity that we enjoy is causing the same amount of misery elsewhere. This is the law. The young, perhaps, do not see it clearly, but those who have lived long enough and those who have struggled enough will understand it. And this is Maya. These things are going on, day and night, and to find a solution of this problem is impossible. Why should it be so? It is impossible to answer this, because the question cannot be logically formulated. There is neither *how* nor *why* in fact; we only know that it is and that we cannot help it. Even to grasp it, to draw an exact image of it in our own mind, is beyond our power. How can we solve it then?

Maya is a statement of the fact of this universe, of how it is going on. People generally get frightened when these things are told to them. But bold we must be. Hiding facts is not the way to find a remedy. As you all know, a hare hunted by dogs puts its head down and thinks itself safe; so, when we run into optimism; we do just like the hare, but that is no remedy. There are objections against this, but you may remark that they are generally from people who possess many of the good things of life. In this country (England) it is very difficult to become a pessimist. Everyone tells me how wonderfully the world is going on, how progressive; but what he himself is, is his own world. Old questions arise: Christianity must be the only true religion of the world because Christian nations are prosperous! But that assertion contradicts itself, because the prosperity of the Christian nation depends on the misfortune of non-Christian nations. There must be some to prey on. Suppose the whole world were to become Christian, then the Christian nations would become poor, because there would be no non-Christian nations for them to prey upon. Thus the argument kills itself. Animals are living upon plants, men upon animals and, worst of all, upon one another, the strong upon the weak. This is going on everywhere. And this is Maya. What solution do you find for this? We hear every day many explanations, and are told that in the long run all will be good. Taking it for granted that this is possible, why should there be this diabolical way of doing good? Why cannot good be done through good, instead of through these diabolical methods? The descendants of the human beings of today will be happy; but why must there be all this suffering now? There is no solution. This is Maya.

Again, we often hear that it is one of the features of evolution that it eliminates evil, and this evil being continually eliminated from the world, at last only good will remain. That is very nice to hear, and it panders to the vanity of those who have enough of this world's goods, who have not a hard struggle to face every clay and are not being crushed under the wheel of this so-called evolution. It is very good and comforting indeed to such fortunate ones. The common herd may surfer, but they do not care; let them die, they are of no consequence. Very good, yet this argument is fallacious from beginning to end. It takes for granted, in the first place, that manifested good and evil in this world are two absolute realities. In the second place, it make, at still worse assumption that the amount of good is an increasing quantity and the amount of evil is a decreasing quantity. So, if evil is being eliminated in this way by what they call evolution, there will come a time when all this evil will be eliminated and what remains will be all good. Very easy to say, but can it be proved that evil is a lessening quantity? Take, for instance, the man who lives in a forest, who does not know how to cultivate the mind, cannot read a book, has not heard of such a thing as writing. If he is severely wounded, he is soon all right again; while we die if we get a scratch. Machines are making things cheap, making for progress and evolution, but millions are crushed, that one may become rich; while one becomes rich, thousands at the same time become poorer and poorer, and whole masses of human beings are made slaves. That way it is going on. The animal man lives in the senses. If he does not get enough to eat, he is miserable; or if something happens to his body, he is miserable. In the senses both his misery and his happiness begin and end. As soon as this man progresses, as soon as his horizon of happiness increases, his horizon of unhappiness increases proportionately. The man in the forest does not know what it is to be jealous, to be in the law courts, to pay taxes, to be blamed by society, to be ruled over day and night by the most tremendous tyranny that human diabolism ever invented, which pries into the secrets of every human heart. He does not know how man becomes a thousand times more diabolical than any other animal, with all his vain knowledge and with all his pride. Thus it is that, as we emerge out of the senses, we develop higher powers of enjoyment, and at the same time we have to develop higher powers of suffering too. The nerves become finer and capable off more suffering. In every society, we often find that the ignorant, common man, when abused, does not feel much, but he feels a good thrashing. But the gentleman cannot bear a single word of abuse; he has become so finely nerved. Misery has increased with his susceptibility to happiness. This does not go much to prove the evolutionist's case. As we increase our power to be happy, we also increase our power to suffer, and sometimes I am inclined to think that if we increase our power to become happy in arithmetical progression, we shall increase, on the other hand, our power to become miserable in geometrical progression. We who are progressing know that the more we progress, the more avenues are opened to pain as well as to pleasure. And this is Maya.

Thus we find that Maya is not a theory for the explanation of the world; it is simply a statement of facts as they exist, that the very basis of our being is contradiction, that everywhere we have to move through this tremendous contradiction, that wherever there is good, there must also be evil, and wherever there is evil, there must be some good, wherever there is life, death must follow as its shadow, and everyone who smiles will have to weep, and vice versa. Nor can this state of things be remedied. We may verily imagine that there will be a place where there will be only good and no evil, where we shall only smile and never weep. This is impossible in the very nature of things; for the conditions will remain the same. Wherever there is the power of producing a smile in us, there lurks the power of producing tears. Wherever there is the power of producing happiness, there lurks somewhere the power of making us miserable.

Thus the Vedanta philosophy is neither optimistic nor

pessimistic. It voices both these views and takes things as they are. It admits that this world is a mixture of good and evil, happiness and misery, and that to increase the one, one must of necessity increase the other. There will never be a perfectly good or bad world, because the very idea is a contradiction in terms. The great secret revealed by this analysis is that good and bad are not two cut-and-dried, separate existences. There is not one thing in this world of ours which you can label as good and good alone, and there is not one thing in the universe which you can label as bad and bad alone. The very same phenomenon which is appearing to be good now, may appear to be bad tomorrow. The same thing which is producing misery in one, may produce happiness in another. The fire that burns the child, may cook a good meal for a starving man. The same nerves that carry the sensations of misery carry also the sensations of happiness. The only way to stop evil, therefore, is to stop good also; there is no other way. To stop death, we shall have to stop life also. Life without death and happiness without misery are contradictions, and neither can be found alone, because each of them is but a different manifestation of the same thing. What I thought to be good yesterday, I do not think to be good now. When I look back upon my life and see what were my ideals at different times, I final this to be so. At one time my ideal was to drive a strong pair of horses; at another time I thought, if I could make a certain kind of sweetmeat, I should be perfectly happy; later I imagined that I should be entirely satisfied if I had a wife and children and plenty of money. Today I laugh at all these ideals as mere childish nonsense.

The Vedanta says, there must come a time when we shall look back and laugh at the ideals which make us afraid of giving up our individuality. Each one of us wants to keep this body for an indefinite time, thinking we shall be very happy, but there will come a time when we shall laugh at this idea. Now, if such be the truth, we are in a state of hopeless contradiction—neither existence nor non-existence, neither misery nor happiness, but a mixture of them. What, then, is the use of Vedanta and all other philosophies and religions? And, above all, what is the use of doing good work? This is a question that comes to the mind. If it is true that you cannot do good without doing evil, and whenever you try to create happiness there will always be misery, people will ask you, "What is the use of doing good?" The answer is in the first place, that we must work for lessening misery, for that is the only way to make ourselves happy. Every one of us finds it out sooner or later in our lives. The bright ones find it out a little earlier, and the dull ones a little later. The dull ones pay very dearly for the discovery and the bright ones less dearly. In the second place, we must do our part, because that is the only way of getting out of this life of contradiction. Both the forces of good and evil will keep the universe alive for us, until we awake from our dreams and give up this building of mud pies. That lesson we shall have to learn, and it will take a long, long time to learn it.

Attempts have been made in Germany to build a

system of philosophy on the basis that the Infinite has become the finite. Such attempts are also made in England. And the analysis of the position of these philosophers is this, that the Infinite is trying to express itself in this universe, and that there will come a time when the Infinite will succeed in doing so. It is all very well, and we have used the words *Infinite* and *manifestation* and *expression*, and so on, but philosophers naturally ask for a logical fundamental basis for the statement that the finite can fully express the Infinite. The Absolute and the Infinite can become this universe only by limitation. Everything must be limited that comes through the senses, or through the mind, or through the intellect; and for the limited to be the unlimited is simply absurd and can never be. The Vedanta, on the other hand, says that it is true that the Absolute or the Infinite is trying to express itself in the finite, but there will come a time when it will find that it is impossible, and it will then have to beat a retreat, and this beating a retreat means renunciation which is the real beginning of religion. Nowadays it is very hard even to talk of renunciation. It was said of me in America that I was a man who came out of a land that had been dead and buried for five thousand years, and talked of renunciation. So says, perhaps, the English philosopher. Yet it is true that that is the only path to religion. Renounce and give up. What did Christ say? "He that loseth his life for my sake shall find it." Again and again did he preach renunciation as the only way to perfection. There comes a time when the mind awakes from this long and dreary dream—the child gives up its play and wants to go back to its mother. It finds the truth of the statement, "Desire is never satisfied by the enjoyment of desires, it only increases the more, as fire, when butter is poured upon it."

This is true of all sense-enjoyments, of all intellectual enjoyments, and of all the enjoyments of which the human mind is capable. They are nothing, they are within Maya, within this network beyond which we cannot go. We may run therein through infinite time and find no end, and whenever we struggle to get a little enjoyment, a mass of misery falls upon us. How awful is this! And when I think of it, I cannot but consider that this theory of Maya, this statement that it is all Maya, is the best and only explanation. What an amount of misery there is in this world; and if you travel among various nations you will find that one nation attempts to cure its evils by one means, and another by another. The very same evil has been taken up by various races, and attempts have been made in various ways to check it, yet no nation has succeeded. If it has been minimised at one point, a mass of evil has been crowded at another point. Thus it goes. The Hindus, to keep up a high standard of chastity in the race, have sanctioned child-marriage, which in the long run has degraded the race. At the same time, I cannot deny that this child-marriage makes the race more chaste. What would you have? If you want the nation to be more chaste, you weaken men and women physically by child-marriage. On the other hand, are you in England any better off? No, because chastity is the life of a nation. Do you not find in history that the first death-sign of a nation has been unchastity? When that has entered, the end of the race is in sight. Where shall we get a solution of these miseries then? If parents select husbands and wives for their children, then this evil is minimised. The daughters of India are more practical than sentimental. But very little of poetry remains in their lives. Again, if people select their own husbands and wives, that does not seem to bring much happiness. The Indian woman is generally very happy; there are not many cases of quarrelling between husband and wife. On the other hand in the United States, where the greatest liberty obtains, the number of unhappy homes and marriages is large. Unhappiness is here, there, and everywhere. What does it show? That, after all, not much happiness has been gained by all these ideals. We all struggle for happiness and as soon as we get a little happiness on one side, on the other side there comes unhappiness.

Shall we not work to do good then? Yes, with more zest than ever, but what this knowledge will do for us is to break down our fanaticism. The Englishman will no more be a fanatic and curse the Hindu. He will learn to respect the customs of different nations. There will be less of fanaticism and more of real work. Fanatics cannot work, they waste three-fourths of their energy. It is the level-headed, calm, practical man who works. So, the power to work will increase from this idea. Knowing that this is the state of things, there will be more patience. The sight of misery or of evil will not be able to throw us off our balance and make us run after shadows. Therefore, patience will come to us, knowing that the world will have to go on in its own way. If, for instance, all men have become good, the animals will have in the meantime evolved into men, and will have to pass through the same state, and so with the plants. But only one thing is certain; the mighty river is rushing towards the ocean, and all the drops that constitute the stream will in time be drawn into that boundless ocean. So, in this life, with all its miseries and sorrows, its joys and smiles and tears, one thing is certain, that all things are rushing towards their goal, and it: is only a question of time when you and I, and plants and animals, and every particles of life that exists must reach the Infinite Ocean of Perfection, must attain to Freedom, to God.

Let me repeat, once more, that the Vedantic position is neither pessimism nor optimism. It does not say that this world is all evil or all good. It says that our evil is of no less value than our good, and our good of no more value than our evil. They are bound together. This is the world, and knowing this, you work with patience. What for? Why should we work? If this is the state of things, what shall we do? Why not become agnostics? The modern agnostics also know there is no solution of this problem, no getting out of this evil of Maya, as we say in our language; therefore they tell us to be satisfied and enjoy life. Here, again, is a mistake, a tremendous mistake, a most illogical mistake. And it is this. What do you mean by life? Do you mean only the life of the senses? In this, every one of us differs only slightly from the brutes. I am sure that no one is present here whose life is only in the senses. Then, this present life means something more than that. Our feelings, thoughts, and aspirations are all part and parcel of our life; and is not the struggle towards the area, ideal, towards perfection, one of the most important components of what we call life? According to the agnostics, we must enjoy life as it is. But this life means, above all, this search after the ideal; the essence of life is going towards perfection. We must have that, and, therefore, we cannot be agnostics or take the world as it appears. The agnostic position takes this life, minus the ideal component, to be all that exists. And this, the agnostic claims, cannot be reached, therefore he must give up the search. This is what is called Maya—this nature, this universe.

All religions are more or less attempts to get beyond nature—the crudest or the most developed, expressed through mythology or symbology, stories of gods, angels or demons, or through stories of saints or seers, great men or prophets, or through the abstractions of philosophy—all have that one object, all are trying to get beyond these limitations. In one word, they are all struggling towards freedom. Man feels, consciously or unconsciously, that he is bound; he is not what he wants to be. It was taught to him at the very moment he began to look around. That very instant he learnt that he was bound, and be also found that there was something in him which wanted to fly beyond, where the body could not follow, but which was as yet chained down by this limitation. Even in the lowest of religious ideas, where departed ancestors and other spirits—mostly violent and cruel, lurking about the houses of their friends, fond of bloodshed and strong drink—are worshipped, even there we find that one common factor, that of freedom. The man who wants to worship the gods sees in them, above all things, greater freedom than in himself. If a door is closed, he thinks the gods can get through it, and that walls have no limitations for them. This idea of freedom increases until it comes to the ideal of a Personal God, of which the central concept is that He is a Being beyond the limitation of nature, of Maya. I see before me, as it were, that in some of those forest retreats this question is being, discussed by those ancient sages of India; and in one of them, where even the oldest and the holiest fail to reach the solutions a young man stands up in the midst of them, and declares, "Hear, ye children of immortality, hear, who live in the highest places, I have found the way. By knowing Him who is beyond darkness we can go beyond death."

This Maya is everywhere. It is terrible. Yet we have to work through it. The man who says that he will work when the world has become all good and then he will enjoy bliss is as likely to succeed as the man who sits beside the Ganga and says, "I will ford the river when all the water has run into the ocean." The way is not with Maya, but against it. This is another fact to learn. We are not born as helpers of nature, but competitors with nature. We are its bond-masters, but we bind ourselves down. Why is this house here? Nature did not build it. Nature says, go and live in the forest. Man says, I will build a house and fight with nature, and he does so. The whole history of humanity is a continuous fight against the so-called laws of nature, and man gains in the end. Coming to the internal world, there too the same fight is going on, this fight between the animal man and the spiritual man, between light and darkness; and here too man becomes victorious. He, as it were, cuts his way out of nature to freedom.

We see, then, that beyond this Maya the Vedantic philosophers find something which is not bound by Maya; and if we can get there, we shall not be bound by Maya. This idea is in some form or other the common property of all religions. But, with the Vedanta, it is only the beginning of religion and not the end. The idea of a Personal God, the Ruler and Creator of this universe, as He has been styled, the Ruler of Maya, or nature, is not the end of these Vedantic ideas; it is only the beginning. The idea grows and grows until the Vedantist finds that He who, he thought, was standing outside, is he himself and is in reality within. He is the one who is free, but who through limitation thought he was bound.

CHAPTER 4

MAYA AND THE EVOLUTION OF THE CONCEPTION OF GOD

(Delivered in London, 20th October 1896)

We have seen how the idea of Maya, which forms, as it were, one of the basic doctrines of the Advaita Vedanta, is, in its germs, found even in the Samhitās, and that in reality all the ideas which are developed in the Upanishads are to be found already in the Samhitas in some form or other. Most of you are by this time familiar with the idea of Maya, and know that it is sometimes erroneously explained as illusion, so that when the universe is said to be Maya, that also has to be explained as being illusion. The translation of the word is neither happy nor correct. Maya is not a theory; it is simply a statement of facts about the universe as it exists, and to understand

Maya we must go back to the Samhitas and begin with the conception in the germ.

We have seen how the idea of the Devas came. At the same time we know that these Devas were at first only powerful beings, nothing more. Most of you are horrified when reading the old scriptures, whether of the Greeks, the Hebrews, the Persians, or others, to find that the ancient gods sometimes did things which, to us, are very repugnant. But when we read these books, we entirely forget that we are persons of the nineteenth century, and these gods were beings existing thousands of years ago. We also forget that the people who worshipped these gods found nothing incongruous in their characters, found nothing to frighten them, because they were very much like themselves. I may also remark that that is the one great lesson we have to learn throughout our lives. In judging others we always judge them by our own ideals. That is not as it should be. Everyone must be judged according to his own ideal, and not by that of anyone else. In our dealings with our fellow-beings we constantly labour under this mistake, and I am of opinion that the vast majority of our quarrels with one another arise simply from this one cause that we are always trying to judge others' gods by our own, others' ideals by our ideals, and others' motives by our motives. Under certain circumstances I might do a certain thing, and when I see another person taking the same course I think he has also the same motive actuating him, little dreaming that although the effect may be the same, yet many other causes may produce the same thing.

He may have performed the action with quite a different motive from that which impelled me to do it. So in judging of those ancient religions we must not take the standpoint to which we incline, but must put ourselves into the position of thought and life of those early times.

The idea of the cruel and ruthless Jehovah in the Old Testament has frightened many—but why? What right have they to assume that the Jehovah of the ancient Jews must represent the conventional idea of the God of the present day? And at the same time, we must not forget that there will come men after us who will laugh at our ideas of religion and God in the same way that we laugh at those of the ancients. Yet, through all these various conceptions runs the golden thread of unity, and it is the purpose of the Vedanta to discover this thread. "I am the thread that runs through all these various ideas, each one of which is; like a pearl," says the Lord Krishna; and it is the duty of Vedanta to establish this connecting thread, how ever incongruous or disgusting may seem these ideas when judged according to the conceptions of today. These ideas, in the setting of past times, were harmonious and not more hideous than our present ideas. It is only when we try to take them out of their settings and apply to our own present circumstances that the hideousness becomes obvious. For the old surroundings are dead and gone. Just as the ancient Jew has developed into the keen, modern, sharp Jew, and the ancient Aryan into the intellectual Hindu similarly Jehovah has grown, and Devas have grown.

The great mistake is in recognising the evolution

of the worshippers, while we do not acknowledge the evolution of the Worshipped. He is not credited with the advance that his devotees have made. That is to say, you and I, representing ideas, have grown; these gods also, as representing ideas, have grown. This may seem somewhat curious to you—that God can grow. He cannot. He is unchangeable. In the same sense the real man never grows. But man's ideas of God are constantly changing and expanding. We shall see later on how the real man behind each one of these human manifestations is immovable, unchangeable, pure, and always perfect; and in the same way the idea that we form of God is a mere manifestation, our own creation. Behind that is the real God who never changes, the ever pure, the immutable. But the manifestation is always changing revealing the reality behind more and more. When it reveals more of the fact behind, it is called progression, when it hides more of the fact behind, it is called retrogression. Thus, as we grow, so the gods grow. From the ordinary point of view, just as we reveal ourselves as we evolve, so the gods reveal themselves.

We shall now be in a position to understand the theory of Maya. In all the regions of the world the one question they propose to discuss is this: Why is there disharmony in the universe? Why is there this evil in the universe? We do not find this question in the very inception of primitive religious ideas, because the world did not appear incongruous to the primitive man. Circumstances were not inharmonious for him; there was no clash of opinions; to him there was no antagonism of good and evil. There was merely a feeling in his own heart of something which said yea, and something which said nay. The primitive man was a man of impulse. He did what occurred to him, and tried to bring out through his muscles whatever thought came into his mind, and he never stopped to judge, and seldom tried to check his impulses. So with the gods, they were also creatures of impulse. Indra comes and shatters the forces of the demons. Jehovah is pleased with one person and displeased with another, for what reason no one knows or asks. The habit of inquiry had not then arisen, and whatever he did was regarded as right. There was no idea of good or evil. The Devas did many wicked things in our sense of the word; again and again Indra and other gods committed very wicked deeds, but to the worshippers of Indra the ideas of wickedness and evil did not occur, so they did not question them.

With the advance of ethical ideas came the fight. There arose a certain sense in man, called in different languages and nations by different names. Call it the voice of God, or the result of past education, or whatever else you like, but the effect was this that it had a checking power upon the natural impulses of man. There is one impulse in our minds which says, do. Behind it rises another voice which says, do not. There is one set of ideas in our mind which is always struggling to get outside through the channels of the senses, and behind that, although it may be thin and weak, there is an infinitely small voice which says, do not go outside. The two beautiful Sanskrit words for these phenomena are Pravritti and Nivritti, "circling forward" and "circling inward". It is the circling forward which usually governs our actions. Religion begins with this circling inward. Religion begins with this "do not". Spirituality begins with this "do not". When the "do not" is not there, religion has not begun. And this "do not" came, causing men's ideas to grow, despite the fighting gods which they had worshipped.

A little love awoke in the hearts of mankind. It was very small indeed, and even now it is not much greater. It was at first confined to a tribe embracing perhaps members of the same tribe; these gods loved their tribes and each god was a tribal god, the protector of that tribe. And sometimes the members of a tribe would think of themselves as the descendants of their god, just as the clans in different nations think that they are the common descendants of the man who was the founder of the clan. There were in ancient times, and are even now, some people who claim to be descendants not only of these tribal gods, but also of the Sun and the Moon. You read in the ancient Sanskrit books of the great heroic emperors of the solar and the lunar dynasties. They were first worshippers of the Sun and the Moon, and gradually came to think of themselves as descendants of the god of the Sun of the Moon, and so forth. So when these tribal ideas began to grow there came a little love, some slight idea of duty towards each other, a little social organisation. Then, naturally, the idea came: How can we live together without bearing and forbearing? How can one man live with another without having some time or other to check his impulses, to restrain himself, to forbear from doing things which his mind would prompt him to do? It is impossible. Thus comes the idea of restraint. The whole social fabric is based upon that idea of restraint, and we all know that the man or woman who has not learnt the great lesson of bearing and forbearing leads a most miserable life.

Now, when these ideas of religion came, a glimpse of something higher, more ethical, dawned upon the intellect of mankind. The old gods were found to be incongruous—these boisterous, fighting, drinking, beef-eating gods of the ancients—whose delight was in the smell of burning flesh and libations of strong liquor. Sometimes Indra drank so much that he fell upon the ground and talked unintelligibly. These gods could no longer be tolerated. The notion had arisen of inquiring into motives, and the gods had to come in for their share of inquiry. Reason for such-and-such actions was demanded and the reason was wanting. Therefore man gave up these gods, or rather they developed higher ideas concerning them. They took a survey, as it were, of all the actions and qualities of the gods and discarded those which they could not harmonise, and kept those which they could understand, and combined them, labelling them with one name, Deva-deva, the God of gods. The god to be worshipped was no more a simple symbol of power; something more was required than that. He was an ethical god; he loved mankind, and did good to mankind. But the idea of god still remained. They increased his ethical significance, and increased also his power. He became the most ethical being in the universe, as well as almost almighty.

But all this patchwork would not do. As the explanation assumed greater proportions, the difficulty which it sought to solve did the same. If the qualities of the god increased in arithmetical progression, the difficulty and doubt increased in geometrical progression. The difficulty of Jehovah was very little beside the difficulty of the God of the universe, and this question remains to the present day. Why under the reign of an almighty and all-loving God of the universe should diabolical things be allowed to remain? Why so much more misery than happiness, and so much more wickedness than good? We may shut our eyes to all these things, but the fact still remains that this world is a hideous world. At best, it is the hell of Tantalus. Here we are with strong impulses and stronger cravings for sense-enjoyments, but cannot satisfy them. There rises a wave which impels us forward in spite of our own will, and as soon as we move one step, comes a blow. We are all doomed to live here like Tantalus. Ideals come into our head far beyond the limit of our sense-ideals, but when we seek to express them, we cannot do so. On the other hand, we are crushed by the surging mass around us. Yet if I give up all ideality and merely struggle through this world, my existence is that of a brute, and I degenerate and degrade myself. Neither way is happiness. Unhappiness is the fate of those who are content to live in this world, born as they are. A thousand times greater misery is the fate of those who dare to stand forth for truth and for higher things and who dare to ask for something higher than mere brute existence here. These are facts; but there is no explanation—there cannot be any explanation. But the Vedanta shows the way out. You must bear in mind that I have to tell you facts that will frighten you sometimes, but if you remember what I say, think of it, and digest it, it will be yours, it will raise you higher, and make you capable of understanding and living in truth.

Now, it is a statement of fact that this world is a Tantalus's hell, that we do not know anything about this universe, yet at the same time we cannot say that we do not know. I cannot say that this chain exists, when I think that I do not know it. It may be an entire delusion of my brain. I may be dreaming all the time. I am dreaming that I am talking to you, and that you are listening to me. No one can prove that it is not a dream. My brain itself may be a dream, and as to that no one has ever seen his own brain. We all take it for granted. So it is with everything. My own body I take for granted. At the same time I cannot say, I do not know. This standing between knowledge and ignorance, this mystic twilight, the mingling of truth and falsehood—and where they meet—no one knows. We are walking in the midst of a dream. Half sleeping, half waking, passing all our lives in a haze; this is the fate of everyone of us. This is the fate of all sense-knowledge. This is the fate of all philosophy, of all boasted science, of all boasted human knowledge. This is the universe.

What you call matter, or spirit, or mind, or anything else you may like to call them, the fact remains the same:

we cannot say that they are, we cannot say that they are not. We cannot say they are one, we cannot say they are many. This eternal play of light and darkness—indiscriminate, indistinguishable, inseparable—is always there. A fact, yet at the same time not a fact; awake and at the same time asleep. This is a statement of facts, and this is what is called Maya. We are born in this Maya, we live in it, we think in it, we dream in it. We are philosophers in it, we are spiritual men in it, nay, we are devils in this Maya, and we are gods in this Maya. Stretch your ideas as far as you can make them higher and higher, call them infinite or by any other name you please, even these ideas are within this Maya. It cannot be otherwise, and the whole of human knowledge is a generalization of this Maya trying to know it as it appears to be. This is the work of Nāma-Rupa—name and form. Everything that has form, everything that calls up an idea in your mind, is within Maya; for everything that is bound by the laws of time, space, and causation is within Maya.

Let us go back a little to those early ideas of God and see what became of them. We perceive at once that the idea of some Being who is eternally loving us—eternally unselfish and almighty, ruling this universe—could not satisfy. "Where is the just, merciful God?" asked the philosopher. Does He not see millions and millions of His children perish, in the form of men and animals; for who can live one moment here without killing others? Can you draw a breath without destroying thousands of lives? You live, because, millions die. Every moment of your life, every breath that you breathe, is death to thousands;

every movement that you make is death to millions. Every morsel that you eat is death to millions. Why should they die? There is an old sophism that they are very low existences. Supposing they are—which is questionable, for who knows whether the ant is greater than the man, or the man than the ant—who can prove one way or the other? Apart from that question, even taking it for granted that these are very low beings, still why should they die? If they are low, they have more reason to live. Why not? Because they live more in the senses, they feel pleasure and pain a thousandfold more than you or I can do. Which of us eats a dinner with the same gusto as a dog or wolf? None, because our energies are not in the senses; they are in the intellect, in the spirit. But in animals, their whole soul is in the senses, and they become mad and enjoy things which we human beings never dream of, and the pain is commensurate with the pleasure. Pleasure and pain are meted out in equal measure. If the pleasure felt by animals is so much keener than that felt by man, it follows that the animals' sense of pain is as keen, if not keener than man's. So the fact is, the pain and misery men feel in dying is intensified a thousandfold in animals, and yet we kill them without troubling ourselves about their misery. This is Maya. And if we suppose there is a Personal God like a human being, who made everything, these so-called explanations and theories which try to prove that out of evil comes good are not sufficient. Let twenty thousand good things come, but why should they come from evil? On that principle, I might cut the throats of others because I want the full pleasure of my five senses. That is no reason. Why should good come through evil? The question remains to be answered, and it cannot be answered. The philosophy of India was compelled to admit this.

The Vedanta was (and is) the boldest system of religion. It stopped nowhere, and it had one advantage. There was no body of priests who sought to suppress every man who tried to tell the truth. There was always absolute religious freedom. In India the bondage of superstition is a social one; here in the West society is very free. Social matters in India are very strict, but religious opinion is free. In England a man may dress any way he likes, or eat what he lilies—no one objects; but if he misses attending church, then Mrs. Grundy is down on him. He has to conform first to what society says on religion, and then he may think of the truth. In India, on the other hand, if a man dines with one who does not belong to his own caste, down comes society with all its terrible powers and crushes him then and there. If he wants to dress a little differently from the way in which his ancestor dressed ages ago, he is done for. I have heard of a man who was cast out by society because he went several miles to see the first railway train. Well, we shall presume that was not true! But in religion, we find atheists, materialists, and Buddhists, creeds, opinions, and speculations of every phase and variety, some of a most startling character, living side by side. Preachers of all sects go about reaching and getting adherents, and at the very gates of the temples of gods, the Brāhmins—to their credit be it said—allow even the materialists to stand and give forth their opinions.

Buddha died at a ripe old age. I remember a friend of mine, a great American scientist, who was fond of reading his life. He did not like the death of Buddha, because he was not crucified. What a false idea! For a man to be great he must be murdered! Such ideas never prevailed in India. This great Buddha travelled all over India, denouncing her gods and even the God of the universe, and yet he lived to a good old age. For eighty years he lived, and had converted half the country.

Then, there were the Charvakas, who preached horrible things, the most rank, undisguised materialism, such as in the nineteenth century they dare not openly preach. These Charvakas were allowed to preach from temple to temple, and city to city, that religion was all nonsense, that it was priestcraft, that the Vedas were the words and writings of fools, rogues, and demons, and that there was neither God nor an eternal soul. If there was a soul, why did it not come back after death drawn by the love of wife and child. Their idea was that if there was a soul it must still love after death, and want good things to eat and nice dress. Yet no one hurt these Charvakas.

Thus India has always had this magnificent idea of religious freedom, and you must remember that freedom is the first condition of growth. What you do not make free, will never grow. The idea that you can make others grow and help their growth, that you can direct and guide them, always retaining for yourself the freedom of the teacher, is nonsense, a dangerous lie which has retarded the growth of millions and millions of human beings in this world. Let men have the light of liberty. That is the only condition of growth.

We, in India, allowed liberty in spiritual matters, and we have a tremendous spiritual power in religious thought even today. You grant the same liberty in social matters, and so have a splendid social organisation. We have not given any freedom to the expansion of social matters, and ours is a cramped society. You have never given any freedom in religious matters but with fire and sword have enforced your beliefs, and the result is that religion is a stunted, degenerated growth in the European mind. In India, we have to take off the shackles from society; in Europe, the chains must be taken from the feet of spiritual progress. Then will come a wonderful growth and development of man. If we discover that there is one unity running through all these developments, spiritual, moral, and social, we shall find that religion, in the fullest sense of the word, must come into society, and into our everyday life. In the light of Vedanta you will Understand that all sciences are but manifestations of religion, and so is everything that exists in this world.

We see, then, that through freedom the sciences were built; and in them we have two sets of opinions, the one the materialistic and denouncing, and the other the positive and constructive. It is a most curious fact that in every society you find them. Supposing there is an evil in society, you will find immediately one group rise up and denounce it in vindictive fashion, which sometimes degenerates into fanaticism. There are fanatics in every society, and women frequently join in these outcries, because of their impulsive nature. Every fanatic who gets up and denounces something can secure a following. It is very easy to break down; a maniac can break anything he likes, but it would be hard for him to build up anything. These fanatics may do some good, according to their light, but much morn harm. Because social institutions are not made in a day, and to change them means removing the cause. Suppose there is an evil; denouncing it will not remove it, but you must go to work at the root. First find out the cause, then remove it, and the effect will be removed also. Mere outcry not produce any effect, unless indeed it produces misfortune.

There are others who had sympathy in their hearts and who understood the idea that we must go deep into the cause, these were the great saints. One fact you must remember, that all the great teachers of the world have declared that they came not to destroy but to fulfil. Many times his has not been understood, and their forbearance has been thought to be an unworthy compromise with existing popular opinions. Even now, you occasionally hear that these prophets and great teachers were rather cowardly, and dared not say and do what they thought was right; but that was not so. Fanatics little understand the infinite power of love in the hearts of these great sages who looked upon the inhabitants of this world as their children. They were the real fathers, the real gods, filled with infinite sympathy and patience for everyone; they were ready to bear and forbear. They knew how human society should grow, and patiently slowly, surely, went on applying their remedies, not by denouncing and frightening people, but by gently and kindly leading them upwards step by step. Such were the writers of the Upanishads. They knew full well how the old ideas of God were not reconcilable with the advanced ethical ideas of the time; they knew full well that what the atheists were preaching contained a good deal of truth, nay, great nuggets of truth; but at the same time, they understood that those who wished to sever the thread that bound the beads, who wanted to build a new society in the air, would entirely fail.

We never build anew, we simply change places; we cannot have anything new, we only change the position of things. The seed grows into the tree, patiently and gently; we must direct our energies towards the truth and fulfil the truth that exists, not try to make new truths. Thus, instead of denouncing these old ideas of God as unfit for modern times, the ancient sages began to seek out the reality that was in them. The result was the Vedanta philosophy, and out of the old deities, out of the monotheistic God, the Ruler of the universe, they found yet higher and higher ideas in what is called the Impersonal Absolute; they found oneness throughout the universe.

He who sees in this world of manifoldness that One running through all, in this world of death he who finds that One Infinite Life, and in this world of insentience and ignorance he who finds that One Light and Knowledge, unto him belongs eternal peace. Unto none else, unto none else.

CHAPTER 5

MAYA AND FREEDOM

(Delivered in London, 22nd October 1896)

"Trailing clouds of glory we come," says the poet. Not all of us come as trailing clouds of glory; however, some of us come as trailing black fogs; there can be no question about that. But every one of us comes into this world to fight, as on a battlefield. We come here weeping to fight our way, as well as we can, and to make a path for ourselves through this infinite ocean of life; forward we go, having long ages behind us and an immense expanse beyond. So on we go, till death comes and takes us off the field—victorious or defeated, we do not know. And this is Maya.

Hope is dominant in the heart of childhood. The whole world is a golden vision to the opening eyes of the child; he thinks his will is supreme.

As he moves onward, at every step nature stands as an adamantine wall, barring his future progress. He may hurl himself against it again and again, striving to break through. The further he goes, the further recedes the ideal, till death comes, and there is release, perhaps. And this is Maya.

A man of science rises, he is thirsting after knowledge. No sacrifice is too great, no struggle too hopeless for him. He moves onward discovering secret after secret of nature, searching out the secrets from her innermost heart, and what for? What is it all for? Why should we give him glory? Why should he acquire fame? Does not nature do infinitely more than any human being can do?—and nature is dull, insentient. Why should it be glory to imitate the dull, the insentient? Nature can hurl a thunderbolt of any magnitude to any distance. If a man can do one small part as much, we praise him and laud him to the skies. Why? Why should we praise him for imitating nature, imitating death, imitating dullness imitating insentience? The force of gravitation can pull to pieces the biggest mass that ever existed; yet it is insentient. What glory is there in imitating the insentient? Yet we are all struggling after that. And this is Maya.

The senses drag the human soul out. Man is seeking for pleasure and for happiness where it can never be found. For countless ages we are all taught that this is futile and vain, there is no happiness here. But we cannot learn; it is impossible for us to do so, except through our own experiences. We try them, and a blow comes. Do we learn then? Not even then. Like moths hurling themselves against the flame, we are hurling ourselves again and again into sense-pleasures, hoping to find satisfaction there. We return again and again with freshened energy; thus we go on, till crippled and cheated we die. And this is Maya.

So with our intellect. In our desire to solve the mysteries of the universe, we cannot stop our questioning, we feel we must know and cannot believe that no knowledge is to be gained. A few steps, and there arises the wall of beginningless and endless time which we cannot surmount. A few steps, and there appears a wall of boundless space which cannot be surmounted, and the whole is irrevocably bound in by the walls of cause and effect. We cannot go beyond them. Yet we struggle, and still have to struggle. And this is Maya.

With every breath, with every pulsation of the heart with every one of our movements, we think we are free, and the very same moment we are shown that we are not. Bound slaves, nature's bond-slaves, in body, in mind, in all our thoughts, in all our feelings. And this is Maya.

There was never a mother who did not think her child was a born genius, the most extraordinary child that was ever born; she dotes upon her child. Her whole soul is in the child. The child grows up, perhaps becomes a drunkard, a brute, ill-treats the mother, and the more he ill-treats her, the more her love increases. The world lauds it as the unselfish love of the mother, little dreaming that the mother is a born slave, she cannot help it. She would a thousand times rather throw off the burden, but she cannot. So she covers it with a mass of flowers, which she calls wonderful love. And this is Maya.

We are all like this in the world. A legend tells how

once Narada said to Krishna, "Lord, show me Maya." A few days passed away, and Krishna asked Narada to make a trip with him towards a desert, and after walking for several miles, Krishna said, "Narada, I am thirsty; can you fetch some water for me?" "I will go at once, sir, and get you water." So Narada went. At a little distance there was a village; he entered the village in search of water and knocked at a door, which was opened by a most beautiful young girl. At the sight of her he immediately forgot that his Master was waiting for water, perhaps dying for the want of it. He forgot everything and began to talk with the girl. All that day he did not return to his Master. The next day, he was again at the house, talking to the girl. That talk ripened into love; he asked the father for the daughter, and they were married and lived there and had children. Thus twelve years passed. His father-in-law died, he inherited his property. He lived, as he seemed to think, a very happy life with his wife and children, his fields and his cattle and so forth. Then came a flood. One night the river rose until it overflowed its banks and flooded the whole village. Houses fell, men and animals were swept away and drowned, and everything was floating in the rush of the stream. Narada had to escape. With one hand be held his wife, and with the other two of his children; another child was on his shoulders, and he was trying to ford this tremendous flood. After a few steps he found the current was too strong, and the child on his shoulders fell and was borne away. A cry of despair came from Narada. In trying to save that child, he lost his grasp upon one of the others, and it also was lost.

At last his wife, whom he clasped with all his might, was torn away by the current, and he was thrown on the bank, weeping and wailing in bitter lamentation. Behind him there came a gentle voice, "My child, where is the water? You went to fetch a pitcher of water, and I am waiting for you; you have been gone for quite half an hour." "Half an hour!" Narada exclaimed. Twelve whole years had passed through his mind, and all these scenes had happened in half an hour! And this is Maya.

In one form or another, we are all in it. It is a most difficult and intricate state of things to understand. It has been preached in every country, taught everywhere, but only believed in by a few, because until we get the experiences ourselves we cannot believe in it. What does it show? Something very terrible. For it is all futile. Time, the avenger of everything, comes, and nothing is left. He swallows up the saint and the sinner, the king and the peasant, the beautiful and the ugly; he leaves nothing. Everything is rushing towards that one goal destruction. Our knowledge, our arts, our sciences, everything is rushing towards it. None can stem the tide, none can hold it back for a minute. We may try to forget it, in the same way that persons in a plague-striker city try to create oblivion by drinking, dancing, and other vain attempts, and so becoming paralysed. So we are trying to forget, trying to create oblivion by all sorts of sense-pleasures. And this is Maya.

Two ways have been proposed. One method, which everyone knows, is very common, and that is: "It may be very true, but do not think of it. 'Make hay while the sun shines,' as the proverb says. It is all true, it is a fact, but do not mind it. Seize the few pleasures you can, do what little you can, do not look at tile dark side of the picture, but always towards the hopeful, the positive side." There is some truth in this, but there is also a danger. The truth is that it is a good motive power. Hope and a positive ideal are very good motive powers for our lives, but there is a certain danger in them. The danger lies in our giving up the struggle in despair. Such is the case with those who preach, "Take the world as it is, sit down as calmly and comfortably as you can and be contented with all these miseries. When you receive blows, say they are not blows but flowers; and when you are driven about like slaves, say that you are free. Day and night tell lies to others and to your own souls, because that is the only way to live happily." This is what is called practical wisdom, and never was it more prevalent in the world than in this nineteenth century; because never were harder blows hit than at the present time, never was competition keener, never were men so cruel to their fellow-men as now; and, therefore, must this consolation be offered. It is put forward in the strongest way at the present time; but it fails, as it always must fail. We cannot hide a carrion with roses; it is impossible. It would not avail long; for soon the roses would fade, and the carrion would be worse than ever before. So with our lives. We may try to cover our old and festering sores with cloth of gold, but there comes a day when the cloth of gold is removed, and the sore in all its ugliness is revealed.

Is there no hope then? True it is that we are all slaves of Maya, born in Maya, and live in Maya. Is there then no way out, no hope? That we are all miserable, that this world is really a prison, that even our so-called trailing beauty is but a prison-house, and that even our intellects and minds are prison-houses, have been known for ages upon ages. There has never been a man, there has never been a human soul, who has not felt this sometime or other, however he may talk. And the old people feel it most, because in them is the accumulated experience of a whole life, because they cannot be easily cheated by the lies of nature. Is there no way out? We find that with all this, with this terrible fact before us, in the midst of sorrow and suffering, even in this world where life and death are synonymous, even here, there is a still small voice that is ringing through all ages, through every country, and in every heart: "This My Maya is divine, made up of qualities, and very difficult to cross. Yet those that come unto Me, cross the river of life." "Come unto Me all ye that labour and are heavy laden and I will give you rest." This is the voice that is leading us forward. Man has heard it, and is hearing it all through the ages. This voice comes to men when everything seems to be lost and hope has fled, when man's dependence on his own strength has been crushed down and everything seems to melt away between his fingers, and life is a hopeless ruin. Then he hears it. This is called religion.

On the one side, therefore, is the bold assertion that this is all nonsense, that this is Maya, but along with it there is the most hopeful assertion that beyond Maya, there is a way out. On the other hand, practical men tell us, "Don't bother your heads about such nonsense as religion and metaphysics. Live here; this is a very bad world indeed, but make the best of it." Which put in plain language means, live a hypocritical, lying life, a life of continuous fraud, covering all sores in the best way you can. Go on putting patch after patch, until everything is lost, and you are a mass of patchwork. This is what is called practical life. Those that are satisfied with this patchwork will never come to religion. Religion begins with a tremendous dissatisfaction with the present state of things, with our lives, and a hatred, an intense hatred, for this patching up of life, an unbounded disgust for fraud and lies. He alone can be religious who dares say, as the mighty Buddha once said under the Bo-tree, when this idea of practicality appeared before him and he saw that it was nonsense, and yet could not find a way out. When the temptation came to him to give up his search after truth, to go back to the world and live the old life of fraud, calling things by wrong names, telling lies to oneself and to everybody, he, the giant, conquered it and said, "Death is better than a vegetating ignorant life; it is better to die on the battlefield than to live a life of defeat." This is the basis of religion. When a man takes this stand, he is on the way to find the truth, he is on the way to God. That determination must be the first impulse towards becoming religious. I will hew out a way for myself. I will know the truth or give up my life in the attempt. For on this side it is nothing, it is gone, it is vanishing every day. The beautiful, hopeful, young person of today is the veteran of tomorrow. Hopes and joys and pleasures will die like blossoms with tomorrow's frost. That is one side; on the other, there are the great charms of conquest, victories over all the ills of life, victory over life itself, the conquest of the universe. On that side men can stand. Those who dare, therefore, to struggle for victory, for truth, for religion, are in the right way; and that is what the Vedas preach: Be not in despair, the way is very difficult, like walking on the edge of a razor; yet despair not, arise, awake, and find the ideal, the goal.

Now all these various manifestations of religion, in whatever shape and form they have come to mankind, have this one common central basis. It is the preaching of freedom, the way out of this world. They never came to reconcile the world and religion, but to cut the Gordian knot, to establish religion in its own ideal, and not to compromise with the world. That is what every religion preaches, and the duty of the Vedanta is to harmonise all these aspirations, to make manifest the common ground between all the religions of the world, the highest as well as the lowest. What we call the most arrant superstition and the highest philosophy really have a common aim in that they both try to show the way out of the same difficulty, and in most cases this way is through the help of someone who is not himself bound by the laws of nature in one word, someone who is free. In spite of all the difficulties and differences of opinion about the nature of the one free agent, whether he is a Personal God, or a sentient being like man, whether masculine, feminine, or neuter—and the discussions have been endless—the fundamental idea is the same. In spite of the almost hopeless contradictions of the different systems, we find the golden thread of unity running through them all, and in this philosophy, this golden thread has been traced revealed little by little to our view, and the first step to this revelation is the common ground that all are advancing towards freedom.

One curious fact present in the midst of all our joys and sorrows, difficulties and struggles, is that we are surely journeying towards freedom. The question was practically this: "What is this universe? From what does it arise? Into what does it go?" And the answer was: "In freedom it rises, in freedom it rests, and into freedom it melts away." This idea of freedom you cannot relinquish. Your actions, your very lives will be lost without it. Every moment nature is proving us to be slaves and not free. Yet, simultaneously rises the other idea, that still we are free. At every step we are knocked down, as it were, by Maya, and shown that we are bound; and yet at the same moment, together with this blow, together with this feeling that we are bound, comes the other feeling that we are free. Some inner voice tells us that we are free. But if we attempt to realise that freedom, to make it manifest, we find the difficulties almost insuperable Yet, in spite of that it insists on asserting itself inwardly, "I am free, I am free." And if you study all the various religions of the world you will find this idea expressed. Not only religion—you must not take this word in its narrow sense—but the whole life of society is the assertion of that one principle of freedom.

All movements are the assertion of that one freedom. That voice has been heard by everyone, whether he knows it or not, that voice which declares, "Come unto Me all ye that labour and are heavy laden." It may not be in the same language or the same form of speech, but in some form or other, that voice calling for freedom has been with us. Yes, we are born here on account of that voice; every one of our movements is for that. We are all rushing towards freedom, we are all following that voice, whether we know it or not; as the children of the village were attracted by the music of the flute-player, so we are all following the music of the voice without knowing it.

We are ethical when we follow that voice. Not only the human soul, but all creatures, from the lowest to the highest have heard the voice and are rushing towards it; and in the struggle are either combining with each other or pushing each other out of the way. Thus come competition, joys, struggles, life, pleasure, and death, and the whole universe is nothing but the result of this mad struggle to reach the voice. This is the manifestation of nature.

What happens then? The scene begins to shift. As soon as you know the voice and understand what it is, the whole scene changes. The same world which was the ghastly battlefield of Maya is now changed into something good and beautiful. We no longer curse nature, nor say that the world is horrible and that it is all vain; we need no longer weep and wail. As soon as we understand the voice, we see the reassert why this struggle should be here, this fight, this competition, this difficulty, this cruelty, these little pleasures and joys; we see that they are in the nature of things, because without them there would be no going towards the voice, to attain which we are destined, whether we know it or not. All human life, all nature, therefore, is struggling to attain to freedom. The sun is moving towards the goal, so is the earth in circling round the sun, so is the moon in circling round the earth. To that goal the planet is moving, and the air is blowing. Everything is struggling towards that. The saint is going towards that voice—he cannot help it, it is no glory to him. So is the sinner. The charitable man is going straight towards that voice, and cannot be hindered; the miser is also going towards the same destination: the greatest worker of good hears the same voice within, and he cannot resist it, he must go towards the voice; so with the most arrant idler. One stumbles more than another, and him who stumbles more we call bad, him who stumbles less we call good. Good and bad are never two different things, they are one and the same; the difference is not one of kind, but of degree.

Now, if the manifestation of this power of freedom is really governing the whole universe—applying that to religion, our special study—we find this idea has been the one assertion throughout. Take the lowest form of religion where there is the worship of departed ancestors or certain powerful and cruel gods; what is the prominent idea about the gods or departed ancestors? That they are superior to nature, not bound by its restrictions. The worshipper has, no doubt, very limited ideas of nature. He himself cannot pass through a wall, nor fly up into the skies, but the gods whom he worships can do these things. What is meant by that, philosophically? That the assertion of freedom is there, that the gods whom he worships are superior to nature as he knows it. So with those who worship still higher beings. As the idea of nature expands, the idea of the soul which is superior to nature also expands, until we come to what we call monotheism, which holds that there is Maya (nature), and that there is some Being who is the Ruler of this Maya.

Here Vedanta begins, where these monotheistic ideas first appear. But the Vedanta philosophy wants further explanation. This explanation—that there is a Being beyond all these manifestations of Maya, who is superior to and independent of Maya, and who is attracting us towards Himself, and that we are all going towards Him—is very good, says the Vedanta, but yet the perception is not clear, the vision is dim and hazy, although it does not directly contradict reason. Just as in your hymn it is said, "Nearer my God to Thee," the same hymn would be very good to the Vedantin, only he would change a word, and make it, "Nearer my God to me." The idea that the goal is far off, far beyond nature, attracting us all towards it, has to be brought nearer and nearer, without degrading or degenerating it. The God of heaven becomes the God in nature, and the God in nature becomes the God who is nature, and the God who is nature becomes the God within this temple of the body, and the God dwelling in the temple of the body at last becomes the temple itself, becomes the soul and man—and there it reaches the last words it can teach. He whom the sages have been seeking in all these places is in our own hearts; the voice that you heard was right, says the Vedanta, but the direction you gave to the voice was wrong. That ideal of freedom that you perceived was correct, but you projected it outside yourself, and that was your mistake. Bring it nearer and nearer, until you find that it was all the time within you, it was the Self of your own self. That freedom was your own nature, and this Maya never bound you. Nature never has power over you. Like a frightened child you were dreaming that it was throttling you, and the release from this fear is the goal: not only to see it intellectually, but to perceive it, actualise it, much more definitely than we perceive this world. Then we shall know that we are free. Then, and then alone, will all difficulties vanish, then will all the perplexities of heart be smoothed away, all crookedness made straight, then will vanish the delusion of manifoldness and nature; and Maya instead of being a horrible, hopeless dream, as it is now will become beautiful, and this earth, instead of being a prison-house, will become our playground, and even dangers and difficulties, even all sufferings, will become deified and show us their real nature, will show us that behind everything, as the substance of everything, He is standing, and that He is the one real Self.

CHAPTER 6

THE ABSOLUTE AND MANIFESTATION

(Delivered in London, 1896)

The one question that is most difficult to grasp in understanding the Advaita philosophy, and the one question that will be asked again and again and that will always remain is: How has the Infinite, the Absolute, become the finite? I will now take up this question, and, in order to illustrate it, I will use a figure.

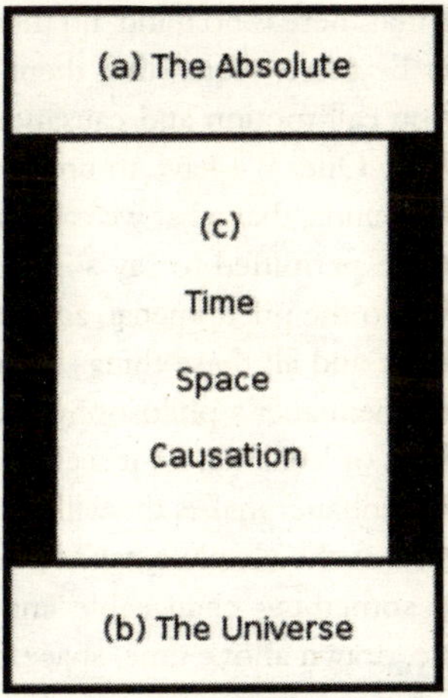

Here is the Absolute (a), and this is the universe (b). The Absolute has become the universe. By this is not only meant the material world, but the mental world, the spiritual world—heavens and earths, and in fact, everything that exists. Mind is the name of a change, and body the name of another change, and so on, and all these changes compose our universe. This Absolute (a) has become the universe (b) by coming through time, space, and causation (c). This is the central idea of Advaita. Time, space, and causation are like the glass through which the Absolute is seen, and when It is seen on the lower side, It appears as the universe. Now we at once gather from this that in the Absolute there is neither time, space, nor causation. The idea of time cannot be there, seeing that there is no mind, no thought. The idea of space cannot be there, seeing that there is no external change. What you call motion and causation cannot exist where there is only One. We have to understand this, and impress it on our minds, that what we call causation begins after, if we may be permitted to say so, the degeneration of the Absolute into the phenomenal, and not before; that our will, our desire and all these things always come after that. I think Schopenhauer's philosophy makes a mistake in its interpretation of Vedanta, for it seeks to make the will everything. Schopenhauer makes the will stand in the place of the Absolute. But the absolute cannot be presented as will, for will is something changeable and phenomenal, and over the line, drawn above time, space, and causation, there is no change, no motion; it is only below the line that external motion and internal motion, called thought begin. There can be no will on the other side, and will therefore, cannot be the cause of this universe. Coming nearer, we see in our own bodies that will is not the cause of every movement. I move this chair; my will is the cause of this movement, and this will becomes manifested as muscular motion at the other end. But the same power that moves the chair is moving the heart, the lungs, and so on, but not through will. Given that the power is the same, it only becomes will when it rises to the plane of consciousness, and to call it will before it has risen to this plane is a misnomer. This makes a good deal of confusion in Schopenhauer's philosophy.

A stone falls and we ask, why? This question is

possible only on the supposition that nothing happens without a cause. I request you to make this very clear in your minds, for whenever we ask why anything happens, we are taking for granted that everything that happens must have a why, that is to say, it must have been preceded by something else which acted as the cause. This precedence and succession are what we call the law of causation. It means that everything in the universe is by turn a cause and an effect. It is the cause of certain things which come after it, and is itself the effect of something else which has preceded it. This is called the law of causation and is a necessary condition of all our thinking. We believe that every particle in the universe, whatever it be, is in relation to every other particle. There has been much discussion as to how this idea arose. In Europe, there have been intuitive philosophers who believed that it was constitutional in humanity, others have believed it came from experience, but the question has never been settled. We shall see later on what the Vedanta has to say about it. But first we have to understand this that the very asking of the question "why" presupposes that everything round us has been preceded by certain things and will be succeeded by certain other things. The other belief involved in this question is that nothing in the universe is independent, that everything is acted upon by something outside itself. Interdependence is the law of the whole universe. In asking what caused the Absolute, what an error we are making! To ask this question we have to suppose that the Absolute also is bound by something, that It is dependent on something; and in making this supposition, we drag the Absolute down to the level of the universe. For in the Absolute there is neither time, space, nor causation; It is all one. That which exists by itself alone cannot have any cause. That which is free cannot have any cause; else it would not be free, but bound. That which has relativity cannot be free. Thus we see the very question, why the Infinite became the finite, is an impossible one, for it is self-contradictory. Coming from subtleties to the logic of our common plane, to common sense, we can see this from another side, when we seek to know how the Absolute has become the relative. Supposing we knew the answer, would the Absolute remain the Absolute? It would have become relative. What is meant by knowledge in our common sense idea? It is only something that has become limited by our mind, that we know, and when it is beyond our mind, it is not knowledge. Now if the Absolute becomes limited by the mind, It is no more Absolute; It has become finite. Everything limited by the mind becomes finite. Therefore to know the Absolute is again a contradiction in terms. That is why this question has never been answered, because if it were answered, there would no more be an Absolute. A God known is no more God; He has become finite like one of us. He cannot be known He is always the Unknowable One.

But what Advaita says is that God is more than knowable. This is a great fact to learn. You must not go home with the idea that God is unknowable in the sense in which agnostics put it. For instance, here is a chair, it is known to us. But what is beyond ether or whether people exist there or not is possibly unknowable. But God is neither known nor unknowable in this sense. He is something still higher than known; that is what is meant by God being unknown and unknowable. The expression is not used in the sense in which it may be said that some questions are unknown ant unknowable. God is more than known. This chair is known, but God is intensely more than that because in and through Him we have to know this chair itself. He is the Witness, the eternal Witness of all knowledge. Whatever we know we have to know in and through Him. He is the Essence of our own Self. He is the Essence of this ego, this I and we cannot know anything excepting in and through that I. Therefore you have to know everything in and through the Brahman. To know the chair you have to know it in and through God. Thus God is infinitely nearer to us than the chair, but yet He is infinitely higher. Neither known, nor unknown, but something infinitely higher than either. He is your Self. "Who would live a second, who would breathe a second in this universe, if that Blessed One were not filling it?" Because in and through Him we breathe, in and through Him we exist. Not the He is standing somewhere and making my blood circulate. What is meant is that He is the Essence of all this, tie Soul of my soul. You cannot by any possibility say you know Him; it would be degrading Him. You cannot get out of yourself, so you cannot know Him. Knowledge is objectification. For instance, in memory you are objectifying many things, projecting them out of yourself. All memory, all the things which I have seen and which I know are in my mind. The pictures, the impressions of all these things, are in my mind, and when I would try to think of them, to know them, the first act of knowledge would be to project them outside. This cannot be done with God, because He is the Essence of our souls, we cannot project Him outside ourselves. Here is one of the profoundest passages in Vedanta: "He that is the Essence of your soul, He is the Truth, He is the Self, thou art That, O Shvetaketu." This is what is meant by "Thou art God." You cannot describe Him by any other language. All attempts of language, calling Him father, or brother, or our dearest friend, are attempts to objectify God, which cannot be done. He is the Eternal Subject of everything. I am the subject of this chair; I see the chair; so God is the Eternal Subject of my soul. How can you objectify Him, the Essence of your souls, the Reality of everything? Thus, I would repeat to you once more, God is neither knowable nor unknowable, but something infinitely higher than either. He is one with us, and that which is one with us is neither knowable nor unknowable, as our own self. You cannot know your own self; you cannot move it out and make it an object to look at, because you are that and cannot separate yourself from it. Neither is it unknowable, for what is better known than yourself? It is really the centre of our knowledge. In exactly the same sense, God is neither unknowable nor known, but infinitely higher than both; for He is our real Self.

First, we see then that the question, "What caused

the Absolute?" is a contradiction in terms; and secondly, we find that the idea of God in the Advaita is this Oneness; and, therefore, we cannot objectify Him, for we are always living and moving in Him, whether we know it or not. Whatever we do is always through Him. Now the question is: What are time, space, and causation? Advaita means non-duality; there are no two, but one. Yet we see that here is a proposition that the Absolute is manifesting Itself as many, through the veil of time, space, and causation. Therefore it seems that here are two, the Absolute and Maya (the sum total of time, space, and causation). It seems apparently very convincing that there are two. To this the Advaitist replies that it cannot be called two. To have two, we must have two absolute independent existences which cannot be caused. In the first place time, space, and causation cannot be said to be independent existences. Time is entirely a dependent existence; it changes with every change of our mind. Sometimes in dream one imagines that one has lived several years, at other times several months were passed as one second. So, time is entirely dependent on our state of mind. Secondly, the idea of time vanishes altogether, sometimes. So with space. We cannot know what space is. Yet it is there, indefinable, and cannot exist separate from anything else. So with causation.

The one peculiar attribute we find in time, space, and causation is that they cannot exist separate from other things. Try to think of space without colour, or limits, or any connection with the things around—just abstract space. You cannot; you have to think of it as the space between two limits or between three objects. It has to be connected with some object to have any existence. So with time; you cannot have any idea of abstract time, but you have to take two events, one preceding and the other succeeding, and join the two events by the idea of succession. Time depends on two events, just as space has to be related to outside objects. And the idea of causation is inseparable from time and space. This is the peculiar thing about them that they have no independent existence. They have not even the existence which the chair or the wall has. They are as shadows around everything which you cannot catch. They have no real existence; yet they are not non-existent, seeing that through them all things are manifesting as this universe. Thus we see, first, that the combination of time, space, and causation has neither existence nor non-existence. Secondly, it sometimes vanishes. To give an illustration, there is a wave on the ocean. The wave is the same as the ocean certainly, and yet we know it is a wave, and as such different from the ocean. What makes this difference? The name and the form, that is, the idea in the mind and the form. Now, can we think of a wave-form as something separate from the ocean? Certainly not. It is always associated with the ocean idea. If the wave subsides, the form vanishes in a moment, and yet the form was not a delusion. So long as the wave existed the form was there, and you were bound to see the form. This is Maya.

The whole of this universe, therefore, is, as it were, a peculiar form; the Absolute is that ocean while you and I, and suns and stars, and everything else are various waves of that ocean. And what makes the waves different? Only the form, and that form is time, space, and causation, all entirely dependent on the wave. As soon as the wave goes, they vanish. As soon as the individual gives up this Maya, it vanishes for him and he becomes free. The whole struggle is to get rid of this clinging on to time, space, and causation, which are always obstacles in our way. What is the theory of evolution? What are the two factors? A tremendous potential power which is trying to express itself, and circumstances which are holding it down, the environments not allowing it to express itself. So, in order to fight with these environments, the power is taking new bodies again and again. An amoeba, in the struggle, gets another body and conquers some obstacles, then gets another body and so on, until it becomes man. Now, if you carry this idea to its logical conclusion, there must come a time when that power that was in the amoeba and which evolved as man will have conquered all the obstructions that nature can bring before it and will thus escape from all its environments. This idea expressed in metaphysics will take this form; there are two components in every action, the one the subject, the other the object and the one aim of life is to make the subject master of the object. For instance, I feel unhappy because a man scolds me. My struggle will be to make myself strong enough to conquer the environment, so that he may scold and I shall not feel. That is how we are all trying to conquer. What is meant by morality? Making the subject strong by attuning it to the

Absolute, so that finite nature ceases to have control over us. It is a logical conclusion of our philosophy that there must come a time when we shall have conquered all the environments, because nature is finite.

Here is another thing to learn. How do you know that nature is finite? You can only know this through metaphysics. Nature is that Infinite under limitations. Therefore it is finite. So, there must come a time when we shall have conquered all environments. And how are we to conquer them? We cannot possibly conquer all the objective environments. We cannot. The little fish wants to fly from its enemies in the water. How does it do so? By evolving wings and becoming a bird. The fish did not change the water or the air; the change was in itself. Change is always subjective. All through evolution you find that the conquest of nature comes by change in the subject. Apply this to religion and morality, and you will find that the conquest of evil comes by the change in the subjective alone. That is how the Advaita system gets its whole force, on the subjective side of man. To talk of evil and misery is nonsense, because they do not exist outside. If I am immune against all anger, I never feel angry. If I am proof against all hatred, I never feel hatred.

This is, therefore, the process by which to achieve that conquest—through the subjective, by perfecting the subjective. I may make bold to say that the only religion which agrees with, and even goes a little further than modern researches, both on physical and moral lines is the Advaita, and that is why it appeals to modern scientists so much. They find that the old dualistic theories are not enough for them, do not satisfy their necessities. A man must have not only faith, but intellectual faith too. Now, in this later part of the nineteenth century, such an idea as that religion coming from any other source than one's own hereditary religion must be false shows that there is still weakness left, and such ideas must be given up. I do not mean that such is the case in this country alone, it is in every country, and nowhere more than in my own. This Advaita was never allowed to come to the people. At first some monks got hold of it and took it to the forests, and so it came to be called the "Forest Philosophy". By the mercy of the Lord, the Buddha came and preached it to the masses, and the whole nation became Buddhists. Long after that, when atheists and agnostics had destroyed the nation again, it was found out that Advaita was the only way to save India from materialism.

Thus has Advaita twice saved India from materialism. Before the Buddha came, materialism had spread to a fearful extent, and it was of a most hideous kind, not like that of the present day, but of a far worse nature. I am a materialist in a certain sense, because I believe that there is only One. That is what the materialist wants you to believe; only he calls it matter and I call it God. The materialists admit that out of this matter all hope, and religion, and everything have come. I say, all these have come out of Brahman. But the materialism that prevailed before Buddha was that crude sort of materialism which taught, "Eat, drink, and be merry; there is no God, soul or heaven; religion is a concoction of wicked priests." It taught the morality that so long as you live, you must try to live happily; eat, though you have to borrow money for the food, and never mind about repaying it. That was the old materialism, and that kind of philosophy spread so much that even today it has got the name of "popular philosophy". Buddha brought the Vedanta to light, gave it to the people, and saved India. A thousand years after his death a similar state of things again prevailed. The mobs, the masses, and various races, had been converted to Buddhism; naturally the teachings of the Buddha became in time degenerated, because most of the people were very ignorant. Buddhism taught no God, no Ruler of the universe, so gradually the masses brought their gods, and devils, and hobgoblins out again, and a tremendous hotchpotch was made of Buddhism in India. Again materialism came to the fore, taking the form of licence with the higher classes and superstition with the lower. Then Shankaracharya arose and once more revivified the Vedanta philosophy. He made it a rationalistic philosophy. In the Upanishads the arguments are often very obscure. By Buddha the moral side of the philosophy was laid stress upon, and by Shankaracharya, the intellectual side. He worked out, rationalised, and placed before men the wonderful coherent system of Advaita.

Materialism prevails in Europe today. You may pray for the salvation of the modern sceptics, but they do not yield, they want reason. The salvation of Europe depends on a rationalistic religion, and Advaita—the non-duality, the Oneness, the idea of the Impersonal God—is the only religion that can have any hold on any intellectual people. It comes whenever religion seems to disappear and irreligion seems to prevail, and that is why it has taken ground in Europe and America.

I would say one thing more in connection with this philosophy. In the old Upanishads we find sublime poetry; their authors were poets. Plato says, inspiration comes to people through poetry, and it seems as if these ancient Rishis, seers of Truth, were raised above humanity to show these truths through poetry. They never preached, nor philosophised, nor wrote. Music came out of their hearts. In Buddha we had the great, universal heart and infinite patience, making religion practical and bringing it to everyone's door. In Shankaracharya we saw tremendous intellectual power, throwing the scorching light of reason upon everything. We want today that bright sun of intellectuality joined with the heart of Buddha, the wonderful infinite heart of love and mercy. This union will give us the highest philosophy. Science and religion will meet and shake hands. Poetry and philosophy will become friends. This will be the religion of the future, and if we can work it out, we may be sure that it will be for all times and peoples. This is the one way that will prove acceptable to modern science, for it has almost come to it. When the scientific teacher asserts that all things are the manifestation of one force, does it not remind you of the God of whom you hear in the Upanishads: "As the one fire entering into the universe expresses itself in various forms, even so that One Soul is expressing Itself in every soul and yet is infinitely more besides?" Do you not see whither science is tending? The Hindu nation proceeded through the study of the mind, through metaphysics and logic. The European nations start from external nature, and now they too are coming to the same results. We find that searching through the mind we at last come to that Oneness, that Universal One, the Internal Soul of everything, the Essence and Reality of everything, the Ever-Free, the Ever-blissful, the Ever-Existing. Through material science we come to the same Oneness. Science today is telling us that all things are but the manifestation of one energy which is the sum total of everything which exists, and the trend of humanity is towards freedom and not towards bondage. Why should men be moral? Because through morality is the path towards freedom, and immorality leads to bondage.

Another peculiarity of the Advaita system is that from its very start it is non-destructive. This is another glory, the boldness to preach, "Do not disturb the faith of any, even of those who through ignorance have attached themselves to lower forms of worship." That is what it says, do not disturb, but help everyone to get higher and higher; include all humanity. This philosophy preaches a God who is a sum total. If you seek a universal religion which can apply to everyone, that religion must not be composed of only the parts, but it must always be their sum total and include all degrees of religious development.

This idea is not clearly found in any other religious system. They are all parts equally struggling to attain to the whole. The existence of the part is only for this. So, from the very first, Advaita had no antagonism with the various sects existing in India. There are dualists existing today, and their number is by far the largest in India, because dualism naturally appeals to less educated minds. It is a very convenient, natural, common sense explanation of the universe. But with these dualists, Advaita has no quarrel. The one thinks that God is outside the universe, somewhere in heaven, and the other, that He is his own Soul, and that it will be a blasphemy to call Him anything more distant. Any idea of separation would be terrible. He is the nearest of the near. There is no word in any language to express this nearness except the word Oneness. With any other idea the Advaitist is not satisfied just as the dualist is shocked with the concept of the Advaita, and thinks it blasphemous. At the same time the Advaitist knows that these other ideas must be, and so has no quarrel with the dualist who is on the right road. From his standpoint, the dualist will have to see many. It is a constitutional necessity of his standpoint. Let him have it. The Advaitist knows that whatever may be his theories, he is going to the same goal as he himself. There he differs entirely from dualist who is forced by his point of view to believe that all differing views are wrong. The dualists all the world over naturally believe in a Personal God who is purely anthropomorphic, who like a great potentate in this world is pleased with some and displeased with others. He is arbitrarily pleased with some people or races and showers blessing upon them. Naturally the dualist comes to the conclusion that God has favourites, and he hopes to be one of them. You will find that in almost every religion is the idea: "We are the favourites of our God, and only by believing as we do, can you be taken into favour with Him." Some dualists are so narrow as to insist that only the few that have been predestined to the favour of God can be saved; the rest may try ever so hard, but they cannot be accepted. I challenge you to show me one dualistic religion which has not more or less of this exclusiveness. And, therefore, in the nature of things, dualistic religions are bound to fight and quarrel with each other, and this they have ever been doing. Again, these dualists win the popular favour by appealing to the vanity of the uneducated. They like to feel that they enjoy exclusive privileges. The dualist thinks you cannot be moral until you have a God with a rod in His hand, ready to punish you. The unthinking masses are generally dualists, and they, poor fellows, have been persecuted for thousands of years in every country; and their idea of salvation is, therefore, freedom from the fear of punishment. I was asked by a clergyman in America, "What! you have no Devil in your religion? How can that be?" But we find that the best and the greatest men that have been born in the world have worked with that high impersonal idea. It is the Man who said, "I and my Father are One", whose power has descended unto millions. For thousands of years it has worked for good. And we know that the same Man, because he was a nondualist, was merciful to others. To the masses who could not conceive of anything higher than a Personal God, he said, "Pray to your Father in heaven." To others who could grasp a higher idea, he said, "I am the vine, ye are the branches," but to his disciples to whom he revealed himself more fully, he proclaimed the highest truth, "I and my Father are One."

It was the great Buddha, who never cared for the dualist gods, and who has been called an atheist and materialist, who yet was ready to give up his body for a poor goat. That Man set in motion the highest moral ideas any nation can have. Whenever there is a moral code, it is ray of light from that Man. We cannot force the great hearts of the world into narrow limits, and keep them there, especially at this time in the history of humanity when there is a degree of intellectual development such as was never dreamed of even a hundred years ago, when a wave of scientific knowledge has arisen which nobody, even fifty years ago, would have dreamed of. By trying to force people into narrow limits you degrade them into animals and unthinking masses. You kill their moral life. What is now wanted is a combination of the greatest heart with the highest intellectuality, of infinite love with infinite knowledge. The Vedantist gives no other attributes to God except these three—that He is Infinite Existence, Infinite Knowledge, and Infinite Bliss, and he regards these three as One. Existence without knowledge and love cannot be; knowledge without love and love without knowledge cannot be. What we want is the harmony of Existence, Knowledge, and Bliss Infinite. For that is our goal. We want harmony, not one-sided development. And it is possible to have the intellect of a Shankara with the heart of a Buddha. I hope we shall all struggle to attain to that blessed combination.

CHAPTER 7

GOD IN EVERYTHING

(Delivered in London, 27th October 1896)

We have seen how the greater portion of our life must of necessity be filled with evils, however we may resist, and that this mass of evil is practically almost infinite for us. We have been struggling to remedy this since the beginning of time, yet everything remains very much the same. The more we discover remedies, the more we find ourselves beset by subtler evils. We have also seen that all religions propose a God, as the one way of escaping these difficulties. All religions tell us that if you take the world as it is, as most practical people would advise us to do in this age, then nothing would be left to us but evil. They further assert that there is something beyond this world. This life in the five senses, life in the material world, is not all; it is only a small portion, and merely superficial. Behind and beyond is the Infinite in which there is no more evil. Some people call It God, some Allah, some Jehovah, Jove, and so on. The Vedantin calls It Brahman.

The first impression we get of the advice given by religions is that we had better terminate our existence. To the question how to cure the evils of life, the answer apparently is, give up life. It reminds one of the old story. A mosquito settled on the head of a man, and a friend, wishing to kill the mosquito, gave it such a blow that he killed both man and mosquito. The remedy of evil seems to suggest a similar course of action. Life is full of ills, the world is full of evils; that is a fact no one who is old enough to know the world can deny.

But what is remedy proposed by all the religions? That this world is nothing. Beyond this world is something which is very real. Here comes the difficulty. The remedy seems to destroy everything. How can that be a remedy? Is there no way out then? The Vedanta says that what all the religions advance is perfectly true, but it should be properly understood. Often it is misunderstood, because the religions are not very clear in their meaning. What we really want is head and heart combined. The heart is great indeed; it is through the heart that come the great inspirations of life. I would a hundred times rather have a little heart and no brain, than be all brains and no heart. Life is possible, progress is possible for him who has heart, but he who has no heart and only brains dies of dryness.

At the same time we know that he who is carried along by his heart alone has to undergo many ills, for now and then he is liable to tumble into pitfalls. The combination of heart and head is what we want. I do not mean that a man should compromise his heart for his brain or vice versa, but let everyone have an infinite amount of heart and feeling, and at the same time an infinite amount of reason. Is there any limit to what we want in this world? Is not the world infinite? There is room for an infinite amount of feeling, and so also for an infinite amount of culture and reason. Let them come together without limit, let them be running together, as it were, in parallel lines each with the other.

Most of the religions understand the fact, but the error into which they all seem to fall is the same; they are carried away by the heart, the feelings. There is evil in the world, give up the world; that is the great teaching, and the only teaching, no doubt. Give up the world. There cannot be two opinions that to understand the truth everyone of us has to give up error. There cannot be two opinions that everyone of us in order to have good must give up evil; there cannot be two opinions that everyone of us to have life must give up what is death.

And yet, what remains to us, if this theory involves giving up the life of the senses, the life as we know it? And what else do we mean by life? If we give this up, what remains?

We shall understand this better, when, later on, we come to the more philosophical portions of the Vedanta. But for the present I beg to state that in Vedanta alone we find a rational solution of the problem. Here I can only lay before you what the Vedanta seeks to teach, and that is the deification of the world. The Vedanta does not in reality denounce the world. The ideal of renunciation nowhere attains such a height as in the teachings of the Vedanta. But, at the same time, dry suicidal advice is not intended; it really means deification of the world—giving up the world as we think of it, as we know it, as it appears to us—and to know what it really is. Deify it; it is God alone. We read at the commencement of one of the oldest of the Upanishads, "Whatever exists in this universe is to be covered with the Lord."

We have to cover everything with the Lord Himself, not by a false sort of optimism, not by blinding our eyes to the evil, but by really seeing God in everything. Thus we have to give up the world, and when the world is given up, what remains? God. What is meant? You can have your wife; it does not mean that you are to abandon her, but that you are to see God in the wife. Give up your children; what does that mean? To turn them out of doors, as some human brutes do in every country? Certainly not. That is diabolism; it is not religion. But see God in your children. So, in everything. In life and in death, in happiness and in misery, the Lord is equally present. The whole world is full of the Lord. Open your eyes and see Him. This is what Vedanta teaches. Give up the world which you have conjectured, because your conjecture was based upon a very partial experience, upon very poor reasoning, and upon your own weakness. Give it up; the world we have been thinking of so long, the world to which we have been clinging so long, is a false world of our own creation. Give that up; open your eyes and see that as such it never existed; it was a dream, Maya. What existed was the Lord Himself. It is He who is in the child, in the wife, and in the husband; it is He who is in the good and in the bad; He is in the sin and in the sinner; He is in life and in death.

A tremendous assertion indeed! Yet that is the theme which the Vedanta wants to demonstrate, to teach, and to preach. This is just the opening theme.

Thus we avoid the dangers of life and its evils. Do not desire anything. What makes us miserable? The cause of all miseries from which we suffer is desire. You desire something, and the desire is not fulfilled; the result is distress. If there is no desire, there is no suffering. But here, too, there is the danger of my being misunderstood. So it is necessary to explain what I mean by giving up desire and becoming free from all misery. The walls have no desire and they never suffer. True, but they never evolve. This chair has no desires, it never suffers; but it is always a chair. There is a glory in happiness, there is a glory in suffering. If I may dare to say so, there is a utility in evil too. The great lesson in misery we all know. There are hundreds of things we have done in our lives which we wish we had never done, but which, at the same time, have been great teachers. As for me, I am glad I have done something good and many things bad; glad I have done something right, and glad I have committed many errors, because every one of them has been a great lesson. I, as I am now, am the resultant of all I have done, all I have thought. Every action and thought have had their effect, and these effects are the sum total of my progress.

We all understand that desires are wrong, but what is meant by giving up desires? How could life go on? It would be the same suicidal advice, killing the desire and the man too. The solution is this. Not that you should not have property, not that you should not have things which are necessary and things which are even luxuries. Have all that you want, and more, only know the truth and realise it. Wealth does not belong to anybody. Have no idea of proprietorship, possessorship. You are nobody, nor am I, nor anyone else. All belongs to the Lord, because the opening verse told us to put the Lord in everything. God is in the wealth that you enjoy. He is in the desire that rises in your mind. He is in the things you buy to satisfy your desire; He is in your beautiful attire, in your beautiful ornaments. This is the line of thought. All will be metamorphosed as soon as you begin to see things in that light. If you put God in your every movement, in your conversation, in your form, in everything, the whole scene changes, and the world, instead of appearing as one of woe and misery, will become a heaven.

"The kingdom of heaven is within you," says Jesus; so says the Vedanta, and every great teacher. "He that hath eyes to see, let him see, and he that hath ears to hear, let him hear." The Vedanta proves that the truth for which we have been searching all this time is present, and was all the time with us. In our ignorance, we thought we had lost it, and went about the world crying and weeping, struggling to find the truth, while all along it was dwelling in our own hearts. There alone can we find it.

If we understand the giving up of the world in its old, crude sense, then it would come to this: that we must not work, that we must be idle, sitting like lumps of earth, neither thinking nor doing anything, but must become fatalists, driven about by every circumstance, ordered about by the laws of nature, drifting from place to place. That would be the result. But that is not what is meant. We must work. Ordinary mankind, driven everywhere by false desire, what do they know of work? The man propelled by his own feelings and his own senses, what does he know about work? He works, who is not propelled by his own desires, by any selfishness whatsoever. He works, who has no ulterior motive in view. He works, who has nothing to gain from work.

Who enjoys the picture, the seller or the seer? The seller is busy with his accounts, computing what his gain will be, how much profit he will realise on the picture. His brain is full of that. He is looking at the hammer, and watching the bids. He is intent on hearing how fast the bids are rising. That man is enjoying the picture who has gone there without any intention of buying or selling. He looks at the picture and enjoys it. So this whole universe is a picture, and when these desires have vanished, men will enjoy the world, and then this buying and selling and these foolish ideas of possession will be ended. The moneylender gone, the buyer gone, the seller gone, this world remains the picture, a beautiful painting. I never read of any more beautiful conception of God than the following: "He is the Great Poet, the Ancient Poet; the whole universe is His poem, coming in verses and rhymes and rhythms, written in infinite bliss." When we have given up desires, then alone shall we be able to read and enjoy this universe of God. Then everything will become deified. Nooks and corners, by-ways and shady places, which we thought dark and unholy, will be all deified. They will all reveal their true nature, and we shall smile at ourselves and think that all this weeping and crying has been but child's play, and we were only standing by, watching.

So, do your work, says the Vedanta. It first advises us how to work—by giving up—giving up the apparent, illusive world. What is meant by that? Seeing God everywhere. Thus do you work. Desire to live a hundred years, have all earthly desires, if you wish, only deify them, convert them into heaven. Have the desire to live a long life of helpfulness, of blissfulness and activity on this earth. Thus working, you will find the way out. There is no other way. If a man plunges headlong into foolish luxuries of the world without knowing the truth, he has missed his footing, he cannot reach the goal. And if a man curses the world, goes into a forest, mortifies his flesh, and kills himself little by little by starvation, makes his heart a barren waste, kills out all feelings, and becomes harsh, stern, and dried-up, that man also has missed the way. These are the two extremes, the two mistakes at either end. Both have lost the way, both have missed the goal.

So work, says the Vedanta, putting God in everything, and knowing Him to be in everything. Work incessantly, holding life as something deified, as God Himself, and knowing that this is all we have to do, this is all we should ask for. God is in everything, where else shall we go to find Him? He is already in every work, in every thought, in every feeling. Thus knowing, we must work—this is the only way, there is no other. Thus the effects of work will not bind us. We have seen how false desires are the cause of all the misery and evil we suffer, but when they are thus deified, purified, through God, they bring no evil, they bring no misery. Those who have not learnt this secret will have to live in a demoniacal world until they discover it. Many do not know what an infinite mine of bliss is in them, around them, everywhere; they have not yet discovered it. What is a demoniacal world? The Vedanta says, ignorance.

We are dying of thirst sitting on the banks of the mightiest river. We are dying of hunger sitting near heaps of food. Here is the blissful universe, yet we do not find it. We are in it all the time, and we are always mistaking it. Religion proposes to find this out for us. The longing for this blissful universe is in all hearts. It has been the search of all nations, it is the one goal of religion, and this ideal is expressed in various languages in different religions. It is only the difference of language that makes all these apparent divergences. One expresses a thought in one way, another a little differently, yet perhaps each is meaning exactly what the other is expressing in a different language.

More questions arise in connection with this. It is very

easy to talk. From my childhood I have heard of seeing God everywhere and in everything, and then I can really enjoy the world, but as soon as I mix with the world, and get a few blows from it, the idea vanishes. I am walking in the street thinking that God is in every man, and a strong man comes along and gives me a push and I fall flat on the footpath. Then I rise up quickly with clenched fist, the blood has rushed to my head, and the reflection goes. Immediately I have become mad. Everything is forgotten; instead of encountering God I see the devil. Ever since we were born we have been told to see God in all. Every religion teaches that—see God in everything and everywhere. Do you not remember in the New Testament how Christ says so? We have all been taught that; but it is when we come to the practical side, that the difficulty begins. You all remember how in *Æesop's Fables* a fine stag is looking at his form reflected in a lake and is saying to his young one, "How powerful I am, look at my splendid head, look at my limbs, how strong and muscular they are; and how swiftly I can run." In the meantime he hears the barking of dogs in the distance, and immediately takes to his heels, and after he has run several miles, he comes back panting. The young one says, "You just told me how strong you were, how was it that when the dog barked, you ran away?" "Yes, my son; but when the dogs bark all my confidence vanishes." Such is the case with us. We think highly of humanity, we feel ourselves strong and valiant, we make grand resolves; but when the "dogs" of trial and temptation bark, we are like the stag in the fable. Then, if such is the case, what is the use of teaching all these things? There is the greatest use. The use is this, that perseverance will finally conquer. Nothing can be done in a day.

"This Self is first to be heard, then to be thought upon, and then meditated upon." Everyone can see the sky, even the very worm crawling upon the earth sees the blue sky, but how very far away it is! So it is with our ideal. It is far away, no doubt, but at the same time, we know that we must have it. We must even have the highest ideal. Unfortunately in this life, the vast majority of persons are groping through this dark life without any ideal at all. If a man with an ideal makes a thousand mistakes, I am sure that the man without an ideal makes fifty thousand. Therefore, it is better to have an ideal. And this ideal we must hear about as much as we can, till it enters into our hearts, into our brains, into our very veins, until it tingles in every drop of our blood and permeates every pore in our body. We must meditate upon it. "Out of the fullness of the heart the mouth speaketh," and out of the fullness of the heart the hand works too.

It is thought which is the propelling force in us. Fill the mind with the highest thoughts, hear them day after day, think them month after month. Never mind failures; they are quite natural, they are the beauty of life, these failures. What would life be without them? It would not be worth having if it were not for struggles. Where would be the poetry of life? Never mind the struggles, the mistakes. I never heard a cow tell a lie, but it is only a cow—never a man. So never mind these failures, these little backslidings;

hold the ideal a thousand times, and if you fail a thousand times, make the attempt once more. The ideal of man is to see God in everything. But if you cannot see Him in everything, see Him in one thing, in that thing which you like best, and then see Him in another. So on you can go. There is infinite life before the soul. Take your time and you will achieve your end.

"He, the One, who vibrates more quickly than mind, who attains to more speed than mind can ever do, whom even the gods reach not, nor thought grasps, He moving, everything moves. In Him all exists. He is moving. He is also immovable. He is near and He is far. He is inside everything. He is outside everything, interpenetrating everything. Whoever sees in every being that same Ātman, and whoever sees everything in that Ātman, he never goes far from that Ātman. When all life and the whole universe are seen in this Ātman, then alone man has attained the secret. There is no more delusion for him. Where is any more misery for him who sees this Oneness in the universe?"

This is another great theme of the Vedanta, this Oneness of life, this Oneness of everything. We shall see how it demonstrates that all our misery comes through ignorance, and this ignorance is the idea of manifoldness, this separation between man and man, between nation and nation, between earth and moon, between moon and sun. Out of this idea of separation between atom and atom comes all misery. But the Vedanta says this separation does not exist, it is not real. It is merely apparent, on the surface. In the heart of things there is Unity still. If you go below the surface, you find that Unity between man and man, between races and races, high and low, rich and poor, gods and men, and men and animals. If you go deep enough, all will be seen as only variations of the One, and he who has attained to this conception of Oneness has no more delusion. What can delude him? He knows the reality of everything, the secret of everything. Where is there any more misery for him? What does he desire? He has traced the reality of everything to the Lord, the Centre, the Unity of everything, and that is Eternal Existence, Eternal Knowledge, Eternal Bliss. Neither death nor disease, nor sorrow, nor misery, nor discontent is there. All is Perfect Union and Perfect Bliss. For whom should he mourn then? In the Reality, there is no death, there is no misery; in the Reality, there is no one to mourn for, no one to be sorry for. He has penetrated everything, the Pure One, the Formless, the Bodiless, the Stainless. He the Knower, He the Great Poet, the Self-Existent, He who is giving to everyone what he deserves. They grope in darkness who worship this ignorant world, the world that is produced out of ignorance, thinking of it as Existence, and those who live their whole lives in this world, and never find anything better or higher, are groping in still greater darkness. But he who knows the secret of nature, seeing That which is beyond nature through the help of nature, he crosses death, and through the help of That which is beyond nature, he enjoys Eternal Bliss. "Thou sun, who hast covered the Truth with thy golden disc, do thou remove the veil, so that I may see the Truth that is within thee. I have known the Truth that is within thee, I have known what is the real meaning of thy rays and thy glory and have seen That which shines in thee; the Truth in thee I see, and That which is within thee is within me, and I am That."

CHAPTER 8

REALISATION

(Delivered in London, 29th October 1896)

I will read to you from one of the Upanishads. It is called the Katha Upanishad. Some of you, perhaps, have read the translation by Sir Edwin Arnold, called the Secret of Death. In our last [i.e. a previous] lecture we saw how the inquiry which started with the origin of the world, and the creation of the universe, failed to obtain a satisfactory answer from without, and how it then turned inwards. This book psychologically takes up that suggestion, questioning into the internal nature of man. It was first asked who created the external world, and how it came into being. Now the question is: What is that in man; which makes him live and move, and what becomes of that when he dies? The first philosophers studied the material substance, and tried to reach the ultimate through that. At the best, they found a personal governor of the universe, a human being immensely magnified, but yet to all intents and purposes a human being. But that could not be the whole of truth; at best, it could be only partial truth. We see this universe as human beings, and our God is our human explanation of the universe.

Suppose a cow were philosophical and had religion it would have a cow universe, and a cow solution of the problem, and it would not be possible that it should see our God. Suppose cats became philosophers, they would see a cat universe and have a cat solution of the problem of the universe, and a cat ruling it. So we see from this that our explanation of the universe is not the whole of the solution. Neither does our conception cover the whole of the universe. It would be a great mistake to accept that tremendously selfish position which man is apt to take. Such a solution of the universal problem as we can get from the outside labours under this difficulty that in the first place the universe we see is our own particular universe, our own view of the Reality. That Reality we cannot see through the senses; we cannot comprehend It. We only know the universe from the point of view of beings with five senses. Suppose we obtain another sense, the whole universe must change for us. Suppose we had a magnetic sense, it is quite possible that we might then find millions and millions of forces in existence which we do not now know, and for which we have no present sense or feeling. Our senses are limited, very limited indeed; and within these limitations exists what we call our universe; and our God is the solution of that universe, but that cannot be the solution of the whole problem. But man cannot stop there. He is a thinking being and wants to find a solution which will comprehensively explain all the universes. He wants to see a world which is at once the world of men, and of gods, and of all possible beings, and to find a solution which will explain all phenomena.

We see, we must first find the universe which includes all universes; we must find something which, by itself, must be the material running through all these various planes of existence, whether we apprehend it through the senses or not. If we could possibly find something which we could know as the common property of the lower as well as of the higher worlds, then our problem would be solved. Even if by the sheer force of logic alone we could understand that there must be one basis of all existence, then our problem might approach to some sort of solution; but this solution certainly cannot be obtained only through the world we see and know, because it is only a partial view of the whole.

Our only hope then lies in penetrating deeper. The early thinkers discovered that the farther they were from the centre, the more marked were the variations and differentiations; and that the nearer they approached the centre, the nearer they were to unity. The nearer we are to the centre of a circle, the nearer we are to the common ground in which all the radii meet; and the farther we are from the centre, the more divergent is our radial line from the others. The external world is far away from the centre, and so there is no common ground in it where all the phenomena of existence can meet. At best, the external world is but one part of the whole of phenomena. There are other parts, the mental, the moral, and the intellectual—the various planes of existence—and to take up only one, and find a solution of the whole out of that one, is simply impossible. We first, therefore, want to find somewhere a centre from which, as it were, all the other planes of existence start, and standing there we should try to find a solution. That is the proposition. And where is that centre? It is within us. The ancient sages penetrated deeper and deeper until they found that in the innermost core of the human soul is the centre of the whole universe. All the planes gravitate towards that one point. That is the common ground, and standing there alone can we find a common solution. So the question who made this world is not very philosophical, nor does its solution amount to anything.

This the Katha Upanishad speaks in very figurative language. There was, in ancient times, a very rich man, who made a certain sacrifice which required that he should give away everything that he had. Now, this man was not sincere. He wanted to get the fame and glory of having made the sacrifice, but he was only giving things which were of no further use to him—old cows, barren, blind, and lame. He had a boy called Nachiketas. This boy saw that his father was not doing what was right, that he was breaking his vow; but he did not know what to say to him. In India, father and mother are living gods to their children. And so the boy approached the father with the greatest respect and humbly inquired of him, "Father, to whom are you going to give me? For your sacrifice requires that everything shall be given away." The father was very much vexed at this question and replied, "What do you mean, boy? A father giving away his own son?" The boy asked the question a second and a third time, and then the angry father answered, "Thee I give unto Death (Yama)." And the story goes on to say that the boy went to Yama, the god of death. Yama was the first man who died. He went to heaven and became the governor of all the Pitris; all the good people who die, go, and live with him for a long time. He is a very pure and holy person, chaste and good, as his name (Yama) implies.

So the boy went to Yama's world. But even gods are sometimes not at home, and three days this boy had to wait there. After the third day Yama returned. "O learned one," said Yama, "you have been waiting here for three days without food, and you are a guest worthy of respect. Salutation to thee, O Brahmin, and welfare to me! I am very sorry I was not at home. But for that I will make amends. Ask three boons, one for each day." And the boy asked, "My first boon is that my father's anger against me may pass away; that he will be kind to me and recognise me when you allow me to depart." Yama granted this fully. The next boon was that he wanted to know about a certain sacrifice which took people to heaven. Now we have seen that the oldest idea which we got in the Samhitā portion of the Vedas was only about heaven where they had bright bodies and lived with the fathers. Gradually other ideas came, but they were not satisfying; there was still need for something higher. Living in heaven would not be very different from life in this world. At best, it would only be a very healthy rich man's life, with plenty of sense-enjoyments and a sound body which knows no disease. It would be this material world, only a little more refined; and we have seen the difficulty that the external material world can never solve the problem. So no heaven can solve the problem. If this world cannot solve the problem, no multiplication of this world can do so, because we must always remember that matter is only an infinitesimal part of the phenomena of nature. The vast part of phenomena which we actually see is not matter. For instance, in every moment of our life what a great part is played by thought and feeling, compared with the material phenomena outside! How vast is this internal world with its tremendous activity! The sense-phenomena are very small compared with it. The heaven solution commits this mistake; it insists that the whole of phenomena is only in touch, taste, sight, etc. So this idea of heaven did not give full satisfaction to all. Yet Nachiketas asks, as the second boon, about some sacrifice through which people might attain to this heaven. There was an idea in the Vedas that these sacrifices pleased the gods and took human beings to heaven.

In studying all religions you will notice the fact that whatever is old becomes holy. For instance, our forefathers in India used to write on birch bark, but in time they learnt how to make paper. Yet the birch bark is still looked upon as very holy. When the utensils in which they used to cook in ancient times were improved upon, the old ones became holy; and nowhere is this idea more kept up than in India. Old methods, which must be nine or ten thousand years old, as of rubbing two sticks together to make fire, are still followed. At the time of sacrifice no other method will do. So with the other branch of the Asiatic Aryans. Their modern descendants still like to obtain fire from lightning, showing that they used to get fire in this way. Even when they learnt other customs, they kept up the old ones, which then became holy. So with the Hebrews. They used to write on parchment. They now write on paper, but parchment is very holy. So with all nations. Every rite which you now consider holy was simply an old custom, and the Vedic sacrifice were of this nature. In course of time, as they found better methods of life, their ideas were much improved; still these old forms remained, and from time to time they were practiced and received a holy significance.

Then, a body of men made it their business to carry on these sacrifices. These were the priests, who speculated on the sacrifices, and the sacrifices became everything to them. The gods came to enjoy the fragrance of the sacrifices, and it was considered that everything in this world could be got by the power of sacrifices. If certain oblations were made, certain hymns chanted, certain peculiar forms of altars made, the gods would grant everything. So Nachiketas asks by what form of sacrifice can a man go to heaven. The second boon was also readily granted by Yama who promised that this sacrifice should henceforth be named after Nachiketas.

Then the third boon comes, and with that the Upanishad proper begins. The boy said, "There is this difficulty: when a man dies some say he is, others that he is not. Instructed by you I desire to understand this." But Yama was frightened. He had been very glad to grant the other two boons. Now he said, "The gods in ancient times were puzzled on this point. This subtle law is not easy to understand. Choose some other boon, O Nachiketas, do not press me on this point, release me."

The boy was determined, and said, "What you have said is true, O Death, that even the gods had doubts on this point, and it is no easy matter to understand. But I cannot obtain another exponent like you and there is no other boon equal to this."

Death said, "Ask for sons and grandsons who will live one hundred years, many cattle, elephants, gold, and horses. Ask for empire on this earth and live as many ears as you like. Or choose any other boon which you think equal to these—wealth and long life. Or be thou a king, O Nachiketas, on the wide earth. I will make thee the enjoyer of all desires. Ask for all those desires which are difficult to obtain in the world. These heavenly maidens with chariots and music, which are not to be obtained by man, are yours. Let them serve you. O Nachiketas, but do not question me as to what comes after death."

Nachiketas said, "These are merely things of a day, O Death, they wear away the energy of all the sense organs.

Even the longest life is very short. These horses and chariots, dances and songs, may remain with Thee. Man cannot be satisfied by wealth. Can we retain wealth when we behold Thee? We shall live only so long as Thou desires. Only the boon which I have asked is chosen by me."

Yama was pleased with this answer and said, "Perfection is one thing and enjoyment another; these two having different ends, engage men differently. He who chooses perfection becomes pure. He who chooses enjoyment misses his true end. Both perfection and enjoyment present themselves to man; the wise man having examined both distinguishes one from the other. He chooses perfection as being superior to enjoyment, but the foolish man chooses enjoyment for the pleasure of his body. O Nachiketas, having thought upon the things which are only apparently desirable, thou hast wisely abandoned them." Death then proceeded to teach Nachiketas.

We now get a very developed idea of renunciation and Vedic morality, that until one has conquered the desires for enjoyment the truth will not shine in him. So long as these vain desires of our senses are clamouring and as it were dragging us outwards every moment, making us slaves to everything outside—to a little colour, a little taste, a little touch—notwithstanding all our pretensions, how can the truth express itself in our hearts?

Yama said, "That which is beyond never rises before the mind of a thoughtless child deluded by the folly of riches. 'This world exists, the other does not,' thinking thus they come again and again under my power. To understand this truth is very difficult. Many, even hearing it continually, do not understand it, for the speaker must be wonderful, so must be the hearer. The teacher must be wonderful, so must be the taught. Neither is the mind to be disturbed By vain arguments, for it is no more a question of argument, it is a question of fact." We have always heard that every religion insists on our having faith. We have been taught to believe blindly. Well, this idea of blind faith is objectionable, no doubt, but analysing it, we find that behind it is a very great truth. What it really means is what we read now. The mind is not to be ruffled by vain arguments, because argument will not help us to know God. It is a question of fact, and not of argument. All argument and reasoning must be based upon certain perceptions. Without these, there cannot be any argument. Reasoning is the method of comparison between certain facts which we have already perceived. If these perceived facts are not there already, there cannot be any reasoning. If this is true of external phenomena, why should it not be so of the internal? The chemist takes certain chemicals and certain results are produced. This is a fact; you see it, sense it, and make that the basis on which to build all your chemical arguments. So with the physicists, so with all other sciences. All knowledge must stand on perception of certain facts, and upon that we have to build our reasoning. But, curiously enough the vast majority of mankind think, especially at the present time, that no such perception is possible in religion, that religion can only be apprehended by vain arguments. Therefore we are told not to disturb the mind by vain arguments. Religion is a question of fact, not of talk. We have to analyse our own souls and to find what is there. We have to understand it and to realise what is understood. That is religion. No amount of talk will make religion. So the question whether there is a God or not can never be proved by argument, for the arguments are as much on one side as on the other. But if there is a God, He is in our own hearts. Have you ever seen Him? The question as to whether this world exists or not has not yet been decided, and the debate between the idealists and the realists is endless. Yet we know that the world exists, that it goes on. We only change the meaning of words. So, with all the questions of life, we must come to facts. There are certain religious facts which, as in external science, have to be perceived, and upon them religion will be built. Of course, the extreme claim that you must believe every dogma of a religion is degrading to the human mind. The man who asks you to believe everything, degrades himself, and, if you believe, degrades you too. The sages of the world have only the right to tell us that they have analysed their minds and have found these facts, and if we do the same we shall also believe, and not before. That is all that there is in religion. But you must always remember this, that as a matter of fact 99.9 per cent of those who attack religion have never analysed their minds, have never struggled to get at the facts. So their arguments do not have any weight against religion, any more than the words of a blind man who cries out, "You are all fools who believe in the sun," would affect us.

This is one great idea to learn and to hold on to, this idea of realisation. This turmoil and fight and difference in religions will cease only when we understand that religion is not in books and temples. It is an actual perception. Only the man who has actually perceived God and soul has religion. There is no real difference between the highest ecclesiastical giant who can talk by the volume, and the lowest, most ignorant materialist. We are all atheists; let us confess it. Mere intellectual assent does not make us religious. Take a Christian, or a Mohammedan, or a follower of any other religion in the world. Any man who truly realised the truth of the Sermon on the Mount would be perfect, and become a god immediately. Yet it is said that there are many millions of Christians in the world. What is meant is that mankind may at some time try to realise that Sermon. Not one in twenty millions is a real Christian.

So, in India, there are said to be three hundred millions of Vedantins. But if there were one in a thousand who had actually realised religion, this world would soon be greatly changed. We are all atheists, and yet we try to fight the man who admits it. We are all in the dark; religion is to us a mere intellectual assent, a mere talk, a mere nothing. We often consider a man religious who can talk well. But this is not religion. "Wonderful methods of joining words, rhetorical powers, and explaining texts of the books in various ways—these are only for the enjoyment of the learned, and not religion." Religion comes when that actual realisation in our own souls begins. That will be the dawn of religion; and then alone we shall be moral. Now we are not much more moral than the animals. We are only held down by the whips of society. If society said today, "I will not punish you if you steal", we should just make a rush for each other's property. It is the policeman that makes us moral. It is social opinion that makes us moral, and really we are little better than animals. We understand how much this is so in the secret of our own hearts. So let us not be hypocrites. Let us confess that we are not religious and have no right to look down on others. We are all brothers and we shall be truly moral when we have realised religion.

If you have seen a certain country, and a man forces you to say that you have not seen it, still in your heart of hearts you know you have. So, when you see religion and God in a more intense sense than you see this external world, nothing will be able to shake your belief. Then you have real faith. That is what is meant by the words in your Gospel, "He who has faith even as a grain of mustard seed." Then you will know the Truth because you have become the Truth.

This is the watchword of the Vedanta—realise religion, no talking will do. But it is done with great difficulty. He has hidden Himself inside the atom, this Ancient One who resides in the inmost recess of every human heart. The sages realised Him through the power of introspection, and got beyond both joy and misery, beyond what we call virtue and vice, beyond good and bad deeds, beyond being and non-being; he who has seen Him has seen the Reality. But what then about heaven? It was the idea of happiness minus unhappiness. That is to say, what we want is the joys of this life minus its sorrows. That is a very good idea, no doubt; it comes naturally; but it is a mistake throughout, because there is no such thing as absolute good, nor any such thing as absolute evil.

You have all heard of that rich man in Rome who learnt one day that he had only about a million pounds of his property left; he said, "What shall I do tomorrow?" and forthwith committed suicide. A million pounds was poverty to him. What is joy, and what is sorrow? It is a vanishing quantity, continually vanishing. When I was a child I thought if I could be a cabman, it would be the very acme of happiness for me to drive about. I do not think so now. To what joy will you cling? This is the one point we must all try to understand, and it is one of the last superstitions to leave us. Everyone's idea of pleasure is different. I have seen a man who is not happy unless he swallows a lump of opium every day. He may dream of a heaven where the land is made of opium. That would be a very bad heaven for me. Again and again in Arabian poetry we read of heaven with beautiful gardens, through which rivers run. I lived much of my life in a country where there is too much water; many villages are flooded and thousands of lives are sacrificed every year. So, my heaven would not have gardens through which rivers flow; I would have a land where very little rain falls. Our pleasures are always changing. If a young man dreams of heaven, he dreams of a heaven where he will have a beautiful wife. When that same man becomes old he does not want a wife. It is our necessities which make our heaven, and the heaven changes with the change of our necessities. If we had a heaven like that desired by those to whom sense-enjoyment is the very end of existence, then we would not progress. That would be the most terrible curse we could pronounce on the soul. Is this all we can come to? A little weeping and dancing, and then to die like a dog! What a curse you pronounce on the head of humanity when you long for these things! That is what you do when you cry after the joys of this world, for you do not know what true joy is. What philosophy insists on is not to give up joys, but to know what joy really is. The Norwegian heaven is a tremendous fighting place where they all sit before Odin; they have a wild boar hunt, and then they go to war and slash each other to pieces. But in some way or other, after a few hours of such fighting, the wounds are all healed up, and they go into a hall where the boar has been roasted, and have a carousal. And then the wild boar takes form again, ready to be hunted the next day. That is much the same thing as our heaven, not a whit worse, only our ideas may be a little more refined. We want to hunt wild boars, and get to a place where all enjoyments will continue, just as the Norwegian imagines that the wild boar is hunted and eaten every day, and recovers the next day.

Now, philosophy insists that there is a joy which is absolute, which never changes. That joy cannot be the joys and pleasures we have in this life, and yet Vedanta shows that everything that is joyful in this life is but a particle of that real joy, because that is the only joy there is. Every moment really we are enjoying the absolute bliss, though covered up, misunderstood, and caricatured. Wherever there is any blessing, blissfulness, or joy, even the joy of the thief in stealing, it is that absolute bliss coming out, only it has become obscured, muddled up, as it were, with all sorts of extraneous conditions, and misunderstood. But to understand that, we have to go through the negation, and then the positive side will begin. We have to give up ignorance and all that is false, and then truth will begin to reveal itself to us. When we have grasped the truth, things which we gave up at first will take new shape and form, will appear to us in a new light, and become deified. They will have become sublimated, and then we shall understand them in their true light. But to understand them, we have first to get a glimpse of truth; we must give them up at first, and then we get them back again, deified. We have to give up all our miseries and sorrows, all our little joys.

"That which all the Vedas declare, which is proclaimed by all penances, seeking which men lead lives of continence, I will tell you in one word—it is 'Om'." You will find this word "Om" praised very much in the Vedas, and it is held to be very sacred.

Now Yama answers the question: "What becomes of a man when the body dies?" "This Wise One never dies, is never born, It arises from nothing, and nothing arises from It. Unborn, Eternal, Everlasting, this Ancient One can never be destroyed with the destruction of the body. If the slayer thinks he can slay, or if the slain thinks he is slain, they both do not know the truth, for the Self neither slays nor is slain." A most tremendous position. I should like to draw your attention to the adjective in the first line, which is "wise". As we proceed we shall find that the ideal of the Vedanta is that all wisdom and all purity are in the soul already, dimly expressed or better expressed—that is all the difference. The difference between man and man, and all things in the whole creation, is not in kind but only in degree. The background, the reality, of everyone is that same Eternal, Ever Blessed, Ever Pure, and Ever Perfect One. It is the Ātman, the Soul, in the saint and the sinner, in the happy and the miserable, in the beautiful and the ugly, in men and in animals; it is the same throughout. It is the shining One. The difference is caused by the power of expression. In some it is expressed more, in others less, but this difference of expression has no effect upon the Ātman. If in their dress one man shows more of his body than another, it does not make any difference in their bodies; the difference is in their dress. We had better remember here that throughout the Vedanta philosophy, there is no such thing as good and bad, they are not two different things; the same thing is good or bad, and the difference is only in degree. The very thing I call pleasurable today, tomorrow under better circumstances I may call pain. The fire that warms us can also consume us; it is not the fault of the fire. Thus, the Soul being pure and perfect, the man who does evil is giving the lie unto himself, he does not know the nature of himself. Even in the murderer the pure Soul is there; It dies not. It was his mistake; he could not manifest It; he had covered It up.

Nor in the man who thinks that he is killed is the Soul killed; It is eternal. It can never be killed, never destroyed. "Infinitely smaller than the smallest, infinitely larger than the largest, this Lord of all is present in the depths of every human heart. The sinless, bereft of all misery, see Him through the mercy of the Lord; the Bodiless, yet dwelling in the body; the Spaceless, yet seeming to occupy space; Infinite, Omnipresent: knowing such to be the Soul, the sages never are miserable."

"This Ātman is not to be realised by the power of speech, nor by a vast intellect, nor by the study of their Vedas." This is a very bold utterance. As I told you before, the sages were very bold thinkers, and never stopped at anything. You will remember that in India these Vedas are regarded in a much higher light than even the Christians regard their Bible. Your idea of revelation is that a man was inspired by God; but in India the idea is that things exist because they are in the Vedas. In and through the Vedas the whole creation has come. All that is called knowledge is in the Vedas. Every word is sacred and eternal, eternal as the soul, without beginning and without end. The whole of the Creator's mind is in this book, as it were. That is the light in which the Vedas are held. Why is this thing moral? Because the Vedas say so. Why is that thing immoral? Because the Vedas say so. In spite of that, look at the boldness of these sages whom proclaimed that the truth is not to be found by much study of the Vedas. "With whom the Lord is pleased, to that man He expresses Himself." But then, the objection may be advanced that this is something like partisanship.

But at Yama explains, "Those who are evil-doers, whose minds are not peaceful, can never see the Light. It is to those who are true in heart, pure in deed, whose senses are controlled, that this Self manifests Itself."

Here is a beautiful figure. Picture the Self to be then rider and this body the chariot, the intellect to be the charioteer, mind the reins, and the senses the horses. He whose horses are well broken, and whose reins are strong and kept well in the hands of the charioteer (the intellect) reaches the goal which is the state of Him, the Omnipresent. But the man whose horses (the senses) are not controlled, nor the reins (the mind) well managed, goes to destruction. This Ātman in all beings does not manifest Himself to the eyes or the senses, but those whose minds have become purified and refined realise Him. Beyond all sound, all sight, beyond form, absolute, beyond all taste and touch, infinite, without beginning and without end, even beyond nature, the Unchangeable; he who realises Him, frees himself from the jaws of death. But it is very difficult. It is, as it were, walking on the edge of a razor; the way is long and perilous, but struggle on, do not despair. Awake, arise, and stop not till the goal is reached.

The one central idea throughout all the Upanishads is that of realisation. A great many questions will arise from time to time, and especially to the modern man. There will be the question of utility, there will be various other questions, but in all we shall find that we are prompted by our past associations. It is association of ideas that has such a tremendous power over our minds. To those who from childhood have always heard of a Personal God and the personality of the mind, these ideas will of course appear very stern and harsh, but if they listen to them and think over them, they will become part of their lives and will no longer frighten them. The great question that generally arises is the utility of philosophy. To that there can be only one answer: if on the utilitarian ground it is good for men to seek for pleasure, why should not those whose pleasure is in religious speculation seek for that? Because sense-enjoyments please many, they seek for them, but there may be others whom they do not please, who want higher enjoyment. The dog's pleasure is only in eating and drinking. The dog cannot understand the pleasure of the scientist who gives up everything, and, perhaps, dwells on the top of a mountain to observe the position of certain stars. The dogs may smile at him and think he is a madman. Perhaps this poor scientist never had money enough to marry even, and lives very simply. May be, the dog laughs at him. But the scientist says, "My dear dog, your pleasure is only in the senses which you enjoy, and you know nothing beyond; but for me this is the most enjoyable life, and if you have the right to seek your pleasure in your own way, so have I in mine." The mistake is that we want to tie the whole world down to our own plane of thought and to make our mind the measure of the whole universe. To you, the old sense-things are, perhaps, the greatest pleasure, but it is not necessary that my pleasure should be the same, and when you insist upon that, I differ from you. That is the difference between the worldly utilitarian and the religious man. The first man says, "See how happy I am. I get money, but do not bother my head about religion. It is too unsearchable, and I am happy without it." So far, so good; good for all utilitarians. But this world is terrible. If a man gets happiness in any way excepting by injuring his fellow-beings, godspeed him; but when this man comes to me and says, "You too must do these things, you will be a fool if you do not," I say, "You are wrong, because the very things, which are pleasurable to you, have not the slightest attraction for me. If I had to go after a few handfuls of gold, my life would not be worth living! I should die." That is the answer the religious man would make. The fact is that religion is possible only for those who have finished with these lower things. We must have our own experiences, must have our full run. It is only when we have finished this run that the other world opens.

The enjoyments of the senses sometimes assume another phase which is dangerous and tempting. You will always hear the idea—in very old times, in every religion—that a time will come when all the miseries of life wills cease, and only its joys and pleasures will remain, and this earth will become a heaven. That I do not believe. This earth will always remain this same world. It is a most terrible thing to say, yet I do not see my way out of it. The misery in the world is like chronic rheumatism in the body; drive it from one part and it goes to another, drive it from there and you will feel it somewhere else. Whatever you do, it is still there. In olden times people lived in forests, and ate each other; in modern times they do not eat each other's flesh, but they cheat one another. Whole countries and cities are ruined by cheating. That does not show much progress. I do not see that what you call progress in the world is other than the multiplication of desires. If one thing is obvious to me it is this that desires bring all misery; it is the state of the beggar, who is always begging for something, and unable to see anything without the wish to possess it, is always longing, longing for more. If the power to satisfy our desires is increased in arithmetical progression, the power of desire is increased in geometrical progression. The sum total of happiness and misery in this world is at least the same throughout. If a wave rises in the ocean it makes a hollow somewhere. If happiness comes to one man, unhappiness comes to another or, perhaps, to some animal. Men are increasing in numbers and some animals are decreasing; we are killing them off, and taking their land; we are taking all means of sustenance from them. How can we say, then, that happiness is increasing? The strong race eats up the weaker, but do you think that the strong race will be very happy? No; they will begin to kill each other. I do not see on practical grounds how this world can become a heaven. Facts are against it. On theoretical grounds also, I see it cannot be.

Perfection is always infinite. We are this infinite already, and we are trying to manifest that infinity. You and I, and all beings, are trying to manifest it. So far it is all right. But from this fact some German philosophers have started a peculiar theory—that this manifestation will become higher and higher until we attain perfect manifestation, until we have become perfect beings. What is meant by perfect manifestation? Perfection means infinity, and manifestation means limit, and so it means that we shall become unlimited limiteds, which is self-contradictory. Such a theory may please children; but it is poisoning their minds with lies, and is very bad for religion. But we know that this world is a degradation, that man is a degradation of God, and that Adam fell. There is no religion today that does not teach that man is a degradation. We have been degraded down to the animal, and are now going up, to emerge out of this bondage. But we shall never be able entirely to manifest the Infinite here. We shall struggle hard, but there will come a time when we shall find that it is impossible to be perfect here, while we are bound by the senses. And then the march back to our original state of Infinity will be sounded.

This is renunciation. We shall have to get out of the difficulty by reversing the process by which we got in, and then morality and charity will begin. What is the watchword of all ethical codes? "Not I, but thou", and this "I" is the outcome of the Infinite behind, trying to manifest Itself on the outside world. This little "I" is the result, and it will have to go back and join the Infinite, its own nature. Every time you say, "Not I, my brother, but thou", you are trying to go back, and every time you say "I, and not thou", you take the false step of trying to manifest the Infinite through the sense-world. That brings struggles and evils into the world, but after a time renunciation must come, eternal renunciation. The little "I" is dead and gone. Why care so much for this little life? All these vain desires of living and enjoying this life, here or in some other place, bring death.

If we are developed from animals, the animals also may be degraded men. How do you know it is not so? You have seen that the proof of evolution is simply this: you find a series of bodies from the lowest to the highest rising in a gradually ascending scale. But from that how can you insist that it is always from the lower upwards, and never from the higher downwards? The argument applies both ways, and if anything is true, I believe it is that the series is repeating itself in going up and down. How can you have evolution without involution? Our struggle for the higher life shows that we have been degraded from a high state. It must be so, only it may vary as to details. I always cling to the idea set forth with one voice by Christ, Buddha, and the Vedanta, that we must all come to perfection in time, but only by giving up this imperfection. This world is nothing. It is at best only a hideous caricature, a shadow of the Reality. We must go to the Reality. Renunciation will take us to It. Renunciation is the very basis of our true life; every moment of goodness and real life that we enjoy is when we do not think of ourselves. This little separate self must die. Then we shall find that we are in the Real, and that Reality is God, and He is our own true nature, and He is always in us and with us. Let us live in Him and stand in Him. It is the only joyful state of existence. Life on the plane of the Spirit is the only life, and let us all try to attain to this realisation.

CHAPTER 9

UNITY IN DIVERSITY

(Delivered in London, 3rd November 1896)

"The Self-existent One projected the senses outwards and, therefore, a man looks outward, not within himself. A certain wise one, desiring immortality, with inverted senses, perceived the Self within." As I have already said, the first inquiry that we find in the Vedas was concerning outward things, and then a new idea came that the reality of things is not to be found in the external world; not by looking outwards, but by turning the eyes, as it is literally expressed, inwards. And the word used for the Soul is very significant: it is He who has gone inward, the innermost reality of our being, the heart centre, the core, from which, as it were, everything comes out; the central sun of which the mind, the body, the sense organs, and everything else we have are but rays going outwards. "Men of childish intellect, ignorant persons, run after desires which are external, and enter the trap of far-reaching death, but the wise, understanding immortality, never seek for the Eternal in this life of finite things." The same idea is here made clear that in this external world, which is full of finite things, it is impossible to see and find the Infinite. The Infinite must be sought in that alone which is infinite, and the only thing infinite about us is that which is within us, our own soul. Neither the body, nor the mind, not even our thoughts, nor the world we see around us, are infinite. The Seer, He to whom they all belong, the Soul of man, He who is awake in the internal man, alone is infinite, and to seek for the Infinite Cause of this whole universe we must go there. In the Infinite Soul alone we can find it. "What is here is there too, and what is there is here also. He who sees the manifold goes from death to death." We have seen how at first there was the desire to go to heaven. When these ancient Aryans became dissatisfied with the world around them, they naturally thought that after death they would go to some place where there would be all happiness without any misery; these places they multiplied and called Svargas—the word may be translated as heavens—where there would be joy for ever, the body would become perfect, and also the mind, and there they would live with their forefathers. But as soon as philosophy came, men found that this was impossible and absurd. The very idea of an infinite in place would be a contradiction in terms, as a place must begin and continue in time. Therefore they had to give up that idea. They found out that the gods who lived in these heavens had once been human beings on earth, who through their good works had become gods, and the godhoods, as they call them, were different states, different positions; none of the gods spoken of in the Vedas are permanent individuals.

For instance, Indra and Varuna are not the names of certain persons, but the names of positions as governors and so on. The Indra who had lived before is not the same person as the Indra of the present day; he has passed away, and another man from earth has filled his place. So with all the other gods These are certain positions, which are filled successively by human souls who have raised themselves to the condition of gods, and yet even they die. In the old Rig Veda we find the word "immortality" used with regard to these gods, but later on it is dropped entirely, for they found that immortality which is beyond time and space cannot be spoken of with regard to any physical form, however subtle it may be. However fine it may be, it must have a beginning in time and space, for the necessary factors that enter into the make-up of form are in space. Try to think of a form without space: it is impossible. Space is one of the materials, as it were, which make up the form, and this is continually changing Space and time are in Maya, and this idea is expressed in the line—"What is hole, that is there too." If there are these gods, they must be bound by the same laws that apply here, and all laws involve destruction and renewal again and again. These laws are moulding matter into different forms, and crushing them out again.

Everything born must die; and so, if there are heavens, the same laws must hold good there.

In this world we find that all happiness is followed by misery as its shadow. Life has its shadow, death. They must go together, because they are not contradictory, not two separate existences, but different manifestations of the same unit, life and death, sorrow and happiness, good and evil. The dualistic conception that good and evil are two separate entities, and that they are both going on eternally is absurd on the face of it. They are the diverse manifestations of one and the same fact, one time appearing as bad, and at another time as good. The difference does not exist in kind, but only in degree. They differ from each other in degree of intensity. We find as a fact that the same nerve systems carry good and bad sensations alike, and when the nerves are injured, neither sensation comes to us. If a certain nerve is paralysed, we do not get the pleasurable feelings that used to come along that wires and at the same time we do not get the painful feelings either. They are never two, but the same. Again. the same thing produces pleasure and pain at different times of life. The same phenomenon will produce pleasure in one, and pain in another. The eating of meat produces pleasure to a man, but pain to the animal which is eaten. There has never been anything which gives pleasure to all alike. Some are pleased, others displeased. So on it will go. Therefore, this duality of existence is denied. And what follows? I told you in my last lecture that we can never have ultimately everything good on this earth and nothing bad. It may have disappointed and frightened some of you, but I cannot help it, and I am open to conviction when I am shown to the contrary; but until that can be proved to me, and I can find that it is true, cannot say so.

The general argument against my statement, and apparently a very convincing one, is this that in the course of evolution, all that is evil in what we see around us is gradually being eliminated, and the result is that if this elimination continues for millions of years, a time will come when all the evil will have been extirpated, and the good alone will remain. This is apparently a very sound argument. Would to God it were true! But there is a fallacy in it, and it is this that it takes for granted that both good and evil are things that are eternally fixed. It takes for granted that there is a definite mass of evil, which may be represented by a hundred, and likewise of good, and that this mass of evil is being diminished every day, leaving only the good. But is it so? The history of the world shows that evil is a continuously increasing quantity, as well as good. Take the lowest man; he lives in the forest. His sense of enjoyment is very small, and so also is his power to suffer. His misery is entirely on the sense-plane. If he does not get plenty of food, he is miserable; but give him plenty of food and freedom to rove and to hunt, and he is perfectly happy. His happiness consists only in the senses, and so does his misery also. But if that man increases in knowledge, his happiness will increase, the intellect will open to him, and his sense-enjoyment will evolve into intellectual enjoyment. He will feel pleasure in reading a beautiful poem, and a mathematical problem will be of absorbing interest to him. But, with these, the inner nerves will become more and more susceptible to miseries of mental pain, of which the savage does not think. Take a very simple illustration. In Tibet there is no marriage, and there is no jealousy, yet we know that marriage is a much higher state. The Tibetans have not known the wonderful enjoyment, the blessing of chastity, the happiness of having a chaste, virtuous wife, or a chaste, virtuous husband. These people cannot feel that. And similarly they do not feel the intense jealousy of the chaste wife or husband, or the misery caused by unfaithfulness on either side, with all the heart-burnings and sorrows which believers in chastity experience. On one side, the latter gain happiness, but on the other, they suffer misery too.

Take your country which is the richest in the world, and which is more luxurious than any other, and see how intense is the misery, how many more lunatics you have, compared with other races, only because the desires are so keen. A man must keep up a high standard of living, and the amount of money he spends in one year would be a fortune to a man in India. You cannot preach to him of simple living because society demands so much of him. The wheel of society is rolling on; it stops not for the widow's tears or the orphans' wails. This is the state of things everywhere. Your sense of enjoyment is developed, your society is very much more beautiful than some others. You have so many more things to enjoy. But those who have fewer have much less misery. You can argue thus throughout, the higher the ideal you have in the brain, the greater is your enjoyment, and the more profound your misery. One is like the shadow of the other. That the evils are being eliminated may be true, but if so, the good also must be dying out. But are not evils multiplying fast, and good diminishing, if I may so put it? If good increases in arithmetical progression, evil increase in geometrical progression. And this is Maya. This is neither optimism nor pessimism. Vedanta does not take he position that this world is only a miserable one. That would be untrue. At the same time, it is a mistake to say that this world is full of happiness and blessings. So it is useless to tell children that this world is all good, all flowers, all milk and honey. That is what we have all dreamt. At the same time it is erroneous to think, because one man has suffered more than another, that all is evil. It is this duality, this play of good and evil that makes our world of experiences. At the same time the Vedanta says, "Do not think that good and evil are two, are two separate essences, for they are one and the same thing, appearing in different degrees and in different guises and producing differences of feeling in the same mind." So, the first thought of the Vedanta is the finding of unity in the external; the One Existence manifesting Itself, however different It may appear in manifestation. Think of the old crude theory of the Persians—two gods creating this world, the good god doing everything that is good, and the bad one, everything bad. On the very face of it, you see the absurdity, for if it be carried out, every law of nature must have two parts, one of which is manipulated by one god, and then he goes away and the other god manipulates the other part. There the difficulty comes that both are working in the same world, and these two gods keep themselves in harmony by injuring one portion and doing good to another. This is a crude case, of course, the crudest way of expressing the duality of existence. But, take the more advanced, the more abstract theory that this world is partly good and partly bad. This also is absurd, arguing from the same standpoint. It is the law of unity that gives us our food, and it is the same law that kills many through accidents or misadventure.

We find, then, that this world is neither optimistic nor pessimistic; it is a mixture of both, and as we go on we shall find that the whole blame is taken away from nature and put upon our own shoulders. At the same time the Vedanta shows the way out, but not by denial of evil, because it analyses boldly the fact as it is and does not seek to conceal anything. It is not hopeless; it is not agnostic. It finds out a remedy, but it wants to place that remedy on adamantine foundations: not by shutting the child's mouth and blinding its eyes with something which is untrue, and which the child will find out in a few days. I remember when I was young, a young man's father died and left him poorly off, with a large family to support, and he found that his father's friends were unwilling to help him. He had a conversation with a clergyman who offered this consolation, "Oh, it is all good, all is sent for our good." That is the old method of trying to put a piece of gold leaf on an old sore. It is a confession of weakness, of absurdity. The young man went away, and six months afterwards a son was born to the clergyman, and he gave a thanksgiving party to which the young man was invited. The clergyman prayed, "Thank God for His mercies." And the young man stood up and said, "Stop, this is all misery." The clergyman asked, "Why?" "Because when my father died you said it was good, though apparently evil; so now, this is apparently good, but really evil." Is this the way to cure the misery of the world? Be good and have mercy on those who suffer. Do not try to patch it up, nothing will cure this world; go beyond it.

This is a world of good and evil. Wherever there is good, evil follows, but beyond and behind all these manifestations, all these contradictions, the Vedanta finds out that Unity. It says, "Give up what is evil and give up what is good." What remains then? Behind good and evil stands something which is yours, the real you, beyond every evil, and beyond every good too, and it is that which is manifesting itself as good and bad. Know that first, and then and then alone you will be a true optimist, and not before; for then you will be able to control everything. Control these manifestations and you will be at liberty to manifest the real "you". First be master of yourself, stand up and be free, go beyond the pale of these laws, for these laws do not absolutely govern you, they are only part of your being. First find out that you are not the slave of nature, never were and never will be; that this nature, infinite as you may think it, is only finite, a drop in the ocean, and your Soul is the ocean; you are beyond the stars, the sun, and the. They are like mere bubbles compared with your infinite being. Know that, and you will control both good and evil. Then alone the whole vision will change and you will stand up and say, "How beautiful is good and how wonderful is evil!"

That is what the Vedanta teaches. It does not propose any slipshod remedy by covering wounds with gold leaf and the more the wound festers, putting on more gold leaf. This life is a hard fact; work your way through it boldly, though it may be adamantine; no matter, the soul is stronger. It lays no responsibility on little gods; for you are the makers of your own fortunes. You make yourselves suffer, you make good and evil, and it is you who put your hands before your eyes and say it is dark. Take your hands away and see the light; you are effulgent, you are perfect already, from the very beginning. We now understand the verse: "He goes from death to death who sees the many here." See that One and be free.

How are we to see it? This mind, so deluded, so weak, so easily led, even this mind can be strong and may catch a glimpse of that knowledge, that Oneness, which saves us from dying again and again. As rain falling upon a mountain flows in various streams down the sides of the mountain, so all the energies which you see here are from that one Unit. It has become manifold falling upon Maya. Do not run after the manifold; go towards the One. "He is in all that moves; He is in all that is pure; He fills the universe; He is in the sacrifice; He is the guest in the house; He is in man, in water, in animals, in truth; He is the Great One. As fire coming into this world is manifesting itself in various forms, even so, that one Soul of the universe is manifesting Himself in all these various forms. As air coming into this universe manifests itself in various forms, even so, the One Soul of all souls, of all beings, is manifesting Himself in all forms." This is true for you when you have understood this Unity, and not before Then is all optimism, because He is seen everywhere. The question is that if all this be true that that Pure One—the Self, the Infinite—has entered all this, how is it that He suffers, how is it that He becomes miserable, impure? He does not, says the Upanishad. "As the sun is the cause of the eyesight of every being, yet is not made defective by the defect in any eye, even so the Self of all is not affected by the miseries of the body, or by any misery that is around you." I may have some disease and see everything yellow, but the sun is not affected by it. "He is the One, the Creator of all, the Ruler of all, the Internal Soul of every being—He who makes His Oneness manifold. Thus sages who realise Him as the Soul of their souls, unto them belongs eternal peace; unto none else, unto none else. He who in this world of evanescence finds Him who never changes, he who in this universe of death finds that One Life, he who in this manifold finds that Oneness, and all those who realise Him as the Soul of their souls, to them belongs eternal peace; unto none else, unto none else. Where to find Him in the external world, where to find Him in the suns, and moons, and stars? There the sun cannot illumine, nor the moon, nor the stars, the flash of lightning cannot illumine the place;

what to speak of this mortal fire? He shining, everything else shines. It is His light that they have borrowed, and He is shining through them." Here is another beautiful simile. Those of you who have been in India and have seen how the banyan tree comes from one root and spreads itself far around, will understand this. He is that banyan tree; He is the root of all and has branched out until He has become this universe, and however far He extends, every one of these trunks and branches is connected.

Various heavens are spoken of in the Brāhmana portions of the Vedas, but the philosophical teaching of the Upanishads gives up the idea of going to heaven. Happiness is not in this heaven or in that heaven, it is in the soul; places do not signify anything. Here is another passage which shows the different states of realisation. "In the heaven of the forefathers, as a man sees things in a dream, so the Real Truth is seen." As in dreams we see things hazy and not so distinct, so we see the Reality there. There is another heaven called the Gandharva, in which it is still less clear; as a man sees his own reflection in the water, so is the Reality seen there. The highest heaven, of which the Hindus conceive is called the Brahmaloka; and in this, the Truth is seen much more clearly, like light and shade, but not yet quite distinctly. But as a man sees his own face in a mirror, perfect, distinct, and clear, so is the Truth shining in the soul of man. The highest heaven, therefore, is in our own souls; the greatest temple of worship is the human soul, greater than all heavens, says the Vedanta; for in no heaven anywhere, can we understand the reality as distinctly and clearly as in this life, in our own soul. Changing places does not help one much. I thought while I was in India that the cave would give me clearer vision. I found it was not so. Then I thought the forest would do so, then, Varanasi. But the same difficulty existed everywhere, because we make our own worlds. If I am evil, the whole world is evil to me. That is what the Upanishad says. And the same thing applies to all worlds. If I die and go to heaven, I should find the same, for until I am pure it is no use going to caves, or forests, or to Varanasi, or to heaven, and if I have polished my mirror, it does not matter where I live, I get the Reality just as It is. So it is useless, running hither and thither, and spending energy in vain, which should be spent only in polishing the mirror. The same idea is expressed again: "None sees Him, none sees His form with the eyes. It is in the mind, in the pure mind, that He is seen, and this immortality is gained."

Those who were at the summer lectures on Rāja Yoga will be interested to know that what was taught then was a different kind of Yoga. The Yoga which we are now considering consists chiefly in controlling the senses. When the senses are held as slaves by the human soul, when they can no longer disturb the mind, then the Yogi has reached the goal. "When all vain desires of the heart have been given up, then this very mortal becomes immortal, then he becomes one with God even here. When all the knots of the heart are cut asunder, then the mortal becomes immortal, and he enjoys Brahman here." Here, on this earth, nowhere else.

A few words ought to be said here. You will generally hear that this Vedanta, this philosophy and other Eastern systems, look only to something beyond, letting go the enjoyments and struggle of this life. This idea is entirely wrong. It is only ignorant people who do not know anything of Eastern thought, and never had brain enough to understand anything of its real teaching, that tell you so. On the contrary, we read in our scriptures that our philosophers do not want to go to other worlds, but depreciate them as places where people weep and laugh for a little while only and then die. As long as we are weak we shall have to go through these experiences; but whatever is true, is here, and that is the human soul. And this also is insisted upon, that by committing suicide, we cannot escape the inevitable; we cannot evade it. But the right path is hard to find. The Hindu is just as practical as the Western, only we differ in our views of life. The one says, build a good house, let us have good clothes and food, intellectual culture, and so on, for this is the whole of life; and in that he is immensely practical. But the Hindu says, true knowledge of the world means knowledge of the soul, metaphysics; and he wants to enjoy that life. In America there was a great agnostic, a very noble man, a very good man, and a very fine speaker. He lectured on religion, which he said was of no use; why bother our heads about other worlds? He employed this simile; we have an orange here, and we want to squeeze all the juice out of it. I met him once and said, "I agree with you entirely. I have some fruit, and I too want to squeeze out the juice. Our difference lies in the choice of the fruit. You want an orange, and I prefer a mango. You think it is enough to live here and eat and drink and have a little scientific knowledge; but you have no right to say that that will suit all tastes. Such a conception is nothing to me. If I had only to learn how an apple falls to the ground, or how an electric current shakes my nerves, I would commit suicide. I want to understand the heart of things, the very kernel itself. Your study is the manifestation of life, mine is the life itself. My philosophy says you must know that and drive out from your mind all thoughts of heaven and hell and all other superstitions, even though they exist in the same sense that this world exists. I must know the heart of this life, its very essence, what it is, not only how it works and what are its manifestations. I want the why of everything, I leave the how to children. As one of your countrymen said, 'While I am smoking a cigarette, if I were to write a book, it would be the science of the cigarette.' It is good and great to be scientific, God bless them in their search; but when a man says that is all, he is talking foolishly, not caring to know the *raison d'être* of life, never studying existence itself. I may argue that all your knowledge is nonsense, without a basis. You are studying the manifestations of life, and when I ask you what life is, you say you do not know. You are welcome to your study, but leave me to mine."

I am practical, very practical, in my own way. So your idea that only the West is practical is nonsense. You are practical in one way, and I in another. There are different types of men and minds. If in the East a man is told that he will find out the truth by standing on one leg all his life, he will pursue that method. If in the West men hear that there is a gold mine somewhere in an uncivilised country, thousands will face the dangers there, in the hope of getting the gold; and, perhaps, only one succeeds. The same men have heard that they have souls but are content to leave the care of them to the church. The first man will not go near the savages, he says it may be dangerous. But if we tell him that on the top of a high mountain lives a wonderful sage who can give him knowledge of the soul, he tries to climb up to him, even if he be killed in the attempt. Both types of men are practical, but the mistake lies in regarding this world as the whole of life. Yours is the vanishing point of enjoyment of the senses—there is nothing permanent in it, it only brings more and more misery—while mine brings eternal peace.

I do not say your view is wrong, you are welcome to it. Great good and blessing come out of it, but do not, therefore, condemn my view. Mine also is practical in its own way. Let us all work on our own plans. Would to God all of us were equally practical on both sides. I have seen some scientists who were equally practical, both as scientists and as spiritual men, and it is my great hope that in course of time the whole of humanity will be efficient in the same manner. When a kettle of water is coming to the boil, if you watch the phenomenon, you find first one bubble rising, and then another and so on, until at last they all join, and a tremendous commotion takes place. This world is very similar. Each individual is like a bubble, and the nations, resemble many bubbles. Gradually these nations are joining, and I am sure the day will come when separation will vanish and that Oneness to which we are all going will become manifest. A time must come when every man will be as intensely practical in the scientific world as in the spiritual, and then that Oneness, the harmony of Oneness, will pervade the whole world. The whole of mankind will become Jivanmuktas—free whilst living. We are all struggling towards that one end through our jealousies and hatreds, through our love and co-operation. A tremendous stream is flowing towards the ocean carrying us all along with it; and though like straws and scraps of paper we may at times float aimlessly about, in the long run we are sure to join the Ocean of Life and Bliss.

CHAPTER 10

THE FREEDOM OF THE SOUL

(Delivered in London, 5th November 1896)

The Katha Upanishad, which we have been studying, was written much later than that to which we now turn—the Chhāndogya. The language is more modern, and the thought more organised. In the older Upanishads the language is very archaic, like that of the hymn portion of the Vedas, and one has to wade sometimes through quite a mass of unnecessary things to get at the essential doctrines. The ritualistic literature about which I told you which forms the second division of the Vedas, has left a good deal of its mark upon this old Upanishad, so that more than half of it is still ritualistic. There is, however, one great gain in studying the very old Upanishads. You trace, as it were, the historical growth of spiritual ideas. In the more recent Upanishads, the spiritual ideas have been collected and brought into one place; as in the Bhagavad Gita, for instance, which we may, perhaps, look upon as the last of the Upanishads, you do not find any inkling of these ritualistic ideas. The Gita is like a bouquet composed of the beautiful flowers of spiritual truths collected from the Upanishads. But in the Gita you cannot study the rise of the spiritual ideas, you cannot trace them to their source. To do that, as has been pointed out by many, you must study the Vedas. The great idea of holiness that has been attached to these books has preserved them, more than any other book in the world, from mutilation. In them, thoughts at their highest and at their lowest have all been preserved, the essential and the non-essential, the most ennobling teachings and the simplest matters of detail stand side by side; for nobody has dared to touch them. Commentators came and tried to smooth them down and to bring out wonderful new ideas from the old things; they tried to find spiritual ideas in even the most ordinary statements, but the texts remained, and as such, they are the most wonderful historical study. We all know that in the scriptures of every religion changes were made to suit the growing spirituality of later times; one word was changed here and another put in there, and so on. This, probably, has not been done with the Vedic literature, or if ever done, it is almost imperceptible. So we have this great advantage, we are able to study thoughts in their original significance, to note how they developed, how from materialistic ideas finer and finer spiritual ideas are evolved, until they attained their greatest height in the Vedanta. Descriptions of some of the old manners and customs are also there, but they do not appear much in the Upanishads. The language used is peculiar, terse, mnemonic.

The writers of these books simply jotted down these lines as helps to remember certain facts which they supposed were already well known. In a narrative, perhaps, which they are telling, they take it for granted that it is well known to everyone they are addressing. Thus a great difficulty arises, we scarcely know the real meaning of any one of these stories, because the traditions have nearly died out, and the little that is left of them has been very much exaggerated. Many new interpretations have been put upon them, so that when you find them in the Purānas they have already become lyrical poems. Just as in the West, we find this prominent fact in the political development of Western races that they cannot bear absolute rule, that they are always trying to prevent any one man from ruling over them, and are gradually advancing to higher and higher democratic ideas, higher and higher ideas of physical liberty, so, in Indian metaphysics, exactly the same phenomenon appears in the development of spiritual life. The multiplicity of gods gave place to one God of the universe, and in the Upanishads there is a rebellion even against that one God. Not only was the idea of many governors of the universe ruling their destinies unbearable, but it was also intolerable that there should be one person ruling this universe. This is the first thing that strikes us. The idea grows and grows, until it attains its climax. In almost all of the Upanishads, we find the climax coming at the last, and that is the dethroning of this God of the universe. The personality of God vanishes, the impersonality comes. God is no more a person, no more a human being, however magnified and exaggerated, who rules this universe, but He has become an embodied principle in every being, immanent in the whole universe. It would be illogical to go from the Personal God to the Impersonal, and at the same time to leave man as a person. So the personal man is broken down, and man as principle is built up. The person is only a phenomenon, the principle is behind it. Thus from both sides, simultaneously, we find the breaking down of personalities and the approach towards principles, the Personal God approaching the Impersonal, the personal man approaching the Impersonal Man. Then come the succeeding stages of the gradual convergence of the two advancing lines of the Impersonal God and the Impersonal Man. And the Upanishads embody the stages through which these two lines at last become one, and the last word of each Upanishad is, "Thou art That". There is but One Eternally Blissful Principle, and that One is manifesting Itself as all this variety.

Then came the philosophers. The work of the Upanishads seems to have ended at that point; the next was taken up by the philosophers. The framework was given them by the Upanishads, and they had to fill in the details. So, many questions would naturally arise. Taking for granted that there is but One Impersonal Principle which is manifesting Itself in all these manifold forms, how is it that the One becomes many? It is another way of putting the same old question which in its crude form comes into the human heart as the inquiry into the cause of evil and so forth. Why does evil exist in the world, and what is its cause? But the same question has now become refined, abstracted. No more is it asked from the platform of the senses why we are unhappy, but from the platform of philosophy. How is it that this One Principle becomes manifold? And the answer, as we have seen, the best answer that India has produced is the theory of Maya which says that It really has not become manifold, that It really has not lost any of Its real nature. Manifoldness is only apparent. Man is only apparently a person, but in reality he is the Impersonal Being. God is a person only apparently, but really He is the Impersonal Being.

Even in this answer there have been succeeding stages, and philosophers have varied in their opinions. All Indian philosophers did not admit this theory of Maya. Possibly most of them did not. There are dualists, with a crude sort of dualism, who would not allow the question to be asked, but stifled it at its very birth. They said, "You have no right to ask such a question, you have no right to ask for an explanation; it is simply the will of God, and we have to submit to it quietly. There is no liberty for the human soul. Everything is predestined—what we shall do, have, enjoy, and suffer; and when suffering comes, it is our duty to endure it patiently; if we do not, we shall be punished all the more. How do we know that? Because the Vedas say so." And thus they have their texts and their meanings and they want to enforce them.

There are others who, though not admitting the Maya theory, stand midway. They say that the whole of this creation forms, as it were, the body of God. God is the Soul of all souls and of the whole of nature. In the case of individual souls, contraction comes from evil doing. When a man does anything evil, his soul begins to contract and his power is diminished and goes on decreasing, until he does good works, when it expands again. One idea seems to be common in all the Indian systems, and I think, in every system in the world, whether they know it or not, and that is what I should call the divinity of man. There is no one system in the world, no real religion, which does not hold the idea that the human soul, whatever it be, or whatever its relation to God, is essentially pure and perfect, whether expressed in the language of mythology, allegory, or philosophy. Its real nature is blessedness and power, not weakness and misery. Somehow or other this misery has come. The crude systems may call it a personified evil, a devil, or an Ahriman, to explain how this misery came. Other systems may try to make a God and a devil in one, who makes some people miserable and others happy, without any reason whatever. Others again, more thoughtful, bring in the theory of Maya and so forth. But one fact stands out clearly, and it is with this that we have to deal. After all, these philosophical ideas and systems are but gymnastics of the mind, intellectual exercises. The one great idea that to me seems to be clear, and comes out through masses of superstition in every country and in every religion, is the one luminous idea that man is divine, that divinity is our nature.

Whatever else comes is a mere superimposition, as the Vedanta calls it. Something has been superimposed, but that divine nature never dies. In the most degraded as well as in the most saintly it is ever present. It has to be called out, and it will work itself out. We have to ask and it will manifest itself. The people of old knew that fire lived in the flint and in dry wood, but friction was necessary to call it out. So this fire of freedom and purity is the nature of every soul, and not a quality, because qualities can be acquired and therefore can be lost. The soul is one with Freedom, and the soul is one with Existence, and the soul is one with Knowledge. The Sat-Chit-Ānanda—Existence-Knowledge-Bliss Absolute—is the nature, the birthright of the Soul, and all the manifestations that we see are Its expressions, dimly or brightly manifesting Itself. Even death is but a manifestation of that Real Existence. Birth and death, life and decay, degeneration and regeneration—are all manifestations of that Oneness. So, knowledge, however it manifests itself, either as ignorance or as learning, is but the manifestation of that same Chit, the essence of knowledge; the difference is only in degree, and not in kind. The difference in knowledge between the lowest worm that crawls under our feet and the highest genius that the world may produce is only one of degree, and not of kind. The Vedantin thinker boldly says that the enjoyments in this life, even the most degraded joys, are but manifestations of that One Divine Bliss, the Essence of the Soul.

This idea seems to be the most prominent in Vedanta, and, as I have said, it appears to me that every religion holds it. I have yet to know the religion which does not. It is the one universal idea working through all religions. Take the Bible for instance. You find there the allegorical statement that the first man Adam was pure, and that his purity was obliterated by his evil deeds afterwards. It is clear from this allegory that they thought that the nature of the primitive man was perfect. The impurities that we see, the weaknesses that we feel, are but superimpositions on that nature, and the subsequent history of the Christian religion shows that they also believe in the possibility, nay, the certainty of regaining that old state. This is the whole history of the Bible, Old and New Testaments together. So with the Mohammedans: they also believed in Adam and the purity of Adam, and through Mohammed the way was opened to regain that lost state. So with the Buddhists: they believe in the state called Nirvana which is beyond this relative world. It is exactly the same as the Brahman of the Vedantins, and the whole system of the Buddhists is founded upon the idea of regaining that lost state of Nirvana. In every system we find this doctrine present, that you cannot get anything which is not yours already. You are indebted to nobody in this universe. You claim your own birthright, as it has been most poetically expressed by a great Vedantin philosopher, in the title of one of his books—"The attainment of our own empire". That empire is ours; we have lost it and we have to regain it. The Māyāvādin, however, says that this losing of the empire was a hallucination; you never lost it. This is the only difference.

Although all the systems agree so far that we had the empire, and that we have lost it, they give us varied advice as to how to regain it. One says that you must perform certain ceremonies, pay certain sums of money to certain idols, eat certain sorts of food, live in a peculiar fashion to regain that empire. Another says that if you weep and prostrate yourselves and ask pardon of some Being beyond nature, you will regain that empire. Again, another says if you love such a Being with all your heart, you will regain that empire. All this varied advice is in the Upanishads. As I go on, you will find it so. But the last and the greatest counsel is that you need not weep at all. You need not go through all these ceremonies, and need not take any notice of how to regain your empire, because you never lost it. Why should you go to seek for what you never lost? You are pure already, you are free already. If you think you are free, free you are this moment, and if you think you are bound, bound you will be. This is a very bold statement, and as I told you at the beginning of this course, I shall have to speak to you very boldly. It may frighten you now, but when you think over it, and realise it in your own life, then you will come to know that what I say is true. For, supposing that freedom is not your nature, by no manner of means can you become free. Supposing you were free and in some way you lost that freedom, that shows that you were not free to begin with. Had you been free, what could have made you lose it? The independent can never be made dependent; if it is really dependent, its independence was a hallucination.

Of the two sides, then, which will you take? If you say that the soul was by its own nature pure and free, it naturally follows that there was nothing in this universe which could make it bound or limited. But if there was anything in nature which could bind the soul, it naturally follows that it was not free, and your statement that it was free is a delusion. So if it is possible for us to attain to freedom, the conclusion is inevitable that the soul is by its nature free. It cannot be otherwise. Freedom means independence of anything outside, and that means that nothing outside itself could work upon it as a cause. The soul is causeless, and from this follow all the great ideas that we have. You cannot establish the immortality of the soul, unless you grant that it is by its nature free, or in other words, that it cannot be acted upon by anything outside. For death is an effect produced by some outside cause. I drink poison and I die, thus showing that my body can be acted upon by something outside that is called poison. But if it be true that the soul is free, it naturally follows that nothing can affect it, and it can never die. Freedom, immortality, blessedness, all depend upon the soul being beyond the law of causation, beyond this Maya. Of these two which will you take? Either make the first a delusion, or make the second a delusion. Certainly I will make the second a delusion. It is more consonant with all my feelings and aspirations. I am perfectly aware that I am free by nature, and I will not admit that this bondage is true and my freedom a delusion.

This discussion goes on in all philosophies, in some form or other. Even in the most modern philosophies you find the same discussion arising. There are two parties. One says that there is no soul, that the idea of soul is a delusion produced by the repeated transit of particles or matter, bringing about the combination which you call the body or brain; that the impression of freedom is the result of the vibrations and motions and continuous transit of these particles. There were Buddhistic sects who held the same view and illustrated it by this example: If young take a torch and whirl it round rapidly, there will be a circle of light. That circle does not really exist, because the torch is changing place every moment. We are but bundles of little particles, which in their rapid whirling produce the delusion of a permanent soul. The other party states that in the rapid succession of thought, matter occurs as a delusion, and does not really exist. So we see one side claiming that spirit is a delusion and the other, that matter is a delusion. Which side will you take? Of course, we will take the spirit and deny matter. The arguments are similar for both, only on the spirit side the argument is little stronger. For nobody has ever seen what matter is. We can only feel ourselves. I never knew a man who could feel matter outside of himself. Nobody was ever able to jump outside of himself. Therefore the argument is a little stronger on the side of the spirit. Secondly, the spirit theory explains the universe, while materialism does not. Hence the materialistic explanation is illogical. If you boil down all the philosophies and analyse them, you will find that they are reduced to one; or the other of these two positions. So here, too, in a more intricate form, in a more philosophical form, we find the same question about natural purity and freedom. Ones side says that the first is a delusion, and the other, that the second is a delusion. And, of course, we side with the second, in believing that our bondage is a delusion.

The solution of the Vedanta is that we are not bound, we are free already. Not only so, but to say or to think that we are bound is dangerous—it is a mistake, it is self-hypnotism. As soon as you say, "I am bound," "I am weak," "I am helpless," woe unto you; you rivet one more chain upon yourself. Do not say it, do not think it. I have heard of a man who lived in a forest and used to repeat day and night, "Shivoham"—I am the Blessed One—and one day a tiger fell upon him and dragged him away to kill him; people on the other side of the river saw it, and heard the voice so long as voice remained in him, saying, "Shivoham"—even in the very jaws of the tiger. There have been many such men. There have been cases of men who, while being cut to pieces, have blessed their enemies. "I am He, I am He; and so art thou. I am pure and perfect and so are all my enemies. You are He, and so am I." That is the position of strength. Nevertheless, there are great and wonderful things in the religions of the dualists; wonderful is the idea of the Personal God apart from nature, whom we worship and love. Sometimes this idea is very soothing. But, says the Vedanta, the soothing is something like the effect that comes from an opiate, not natural. It brings weakness in the long run, and what this world wants today, more than it ever did before, is strength. It is weakness, says the Vedanta, which is the cause of all misery in this world. Weakness is the one cause of suffering. We become miserable because we are weak. We lie, steal, kill, and commit other crimes, because we are weak. We suffer because we are weak. We die because we are weak. Where there is nothing to weaken us, there is no death nor sorrow. We are miserable through delusion. Give up the delusion, and the whole thing vanishes. It is plain and simple indeed. Through all these philosophical discussions and tremendous mental gymnastics we come to this one religious idea, the simplest in the whole world.

The monistic Vedanta is the simplest form in which you can put truth. To teach dualism was a tremendous mistake made in India and elsewhere, because people did not look at the ultimate principles, but only thought of the process which is very intricate indeed. To many, these tremendous philosophical and logical propositions were alarming. They thought these things could not be made universal, could not be followed in everyday practical life, and that under the guise of such a philosophy much laxity of living would arise.

But I do not believe at all that monistic ideas preached to the world would produce immorality and weakness. On the contrary, I have reason to believe that it is the only remedy there is. If this be the truth, why let people drink ditch water when the stream of life is flowing by? If this be the truth, that they are all pure, why not at this moment teach it to the whole world? Why not teach it with the voice of thunder to every man that is born, to saints and sinners, men, women, and children, to the man on the throne and to the man sweeping the streets?

It appears now a very big and a very great undertaking; to many it appears very startling, but that is because of superstition, nothing else. By eating all sorts of bad and indigestible food, or by starving ourselves, we are incompetent to eat a good meal. We have listened to words of weakness from our childhood. You hear people say that they do not believe in ghosts, but at the same time, there are very few who do not get a little creepy sensation in the dark. It is simply superstition. So with all religious superstitions There are people in this country who, if I told them there was no such being as the devil, will think all religion is gone. Many people have said to me, how can there be religion without a devil? How can there be religion without someone to direct us? How can we live without being ruled by somebody? We like to be so treated, because we have become used to it. We are not happy until we feel we have been reprimanded by somebody every day. The same superstition! But however terrible it may seem now, the time will come when we shall look back, each one of us, and smile at every one of those superstitions which covered the pure and eternal soul, and repeat with gladness, with truth, and with strength, I am free, and was free, and always will be free. This monistic idea will come out of Vedanta, and it is the one idea that deserves to live. The scriptures may perish tomorrow. Whether this idea first flashed into the brains of Hebrews or of people living in the Arctic regions, nobody cares. For this is the truth and truth is eternal; and truth itself teaches that it is not the special property of any individual or nation. Men, animals, and gods are all common recipients of this one truth. Let them all receive it. Why make life miserable? Why let people fall into all sorts of superstitions? I will give ten thousand lives, if twenty of them will give up their superstition. Not only in this country, but in the land of its very birth, if you tell people this truth, they are frightened. They say, "This idea is for Sannyāsins who give up the world and live in forests; for them it is all right. But for us poor householders, we must all have some sort of fear, we must have ceremonies," and so on.

Dualistic ideas have ruled the world long enough, and this is the result. Why not make a new experiment? It may take ages for all minds to receive monism, but why not begin now? If we have told it to twenty persons in our lives, we have done a great work.

There is one idea which often militates against it. It is this. It is all very well to say, "I am the Pure, the Blessed," but I cannot show it always in my life. That is true; the ideal is always very hard. Every child that is born sees the sky overhead very far away, but is that any reason why we should not look towards the sky? Would it mend matters to go towards superstition? If we cannot get nectar, would it mend matters for us to drink poison? Would it be any help for us, because we cannot realise the truth immediately, to go into darkness and yield to weakness and superstition?

I have no objection to dualism in many of its forms. I like most of them, but I have objections to every form of teaching which inculcates weakness. This is the one question I put to every man, woman, or child, when they are in physical, mental, or spiritual training. Are you strong? Do you feel strength?—for I know it is truth alone that gives strength. I know that truth alone gives life, and nothing but going towards reality will make us strong, and none will reach truth until he is strong. Every system, therefore, which weakens the mind, makes one superstitious, makes one mope, makes one desire all sorts of wild impossibilities, mysteries, and superstitions, I do not like, because its effect is dangerous. Such systems never bring any good; such things create morbidity in the mind, make it weak, so weak that in course of time it will be almost impossible to receive truth or live up to it. Strength, therefore, is the one thing needful. Strength is the medicine for the world's disease. Strength is the medicine which the poor must have when tyrannised over by the rich. Strength is the medicine that the ignorant must have when oppressed by the learned; and it is the medicine that sinners must have when tyrannised over by other sinners; and nothing gives such strength as this idea of monism. Nothing makes us so moral as this idea of monism. Nothing makes us work so well at our best and highest as when all the responsibility is thrown upon ourselves. I challenge everyone of you. How will you behave if I put a little baby in your hands? Your whole life will be changed for the moment; whatever you may be, you must become selfless for the time being. You will give up all your criminal ideas as soon as responsibility is thrown upon you—your whole character will change. So if the whole responsibility is thrown upon our own shoulders, we shall be at our highest and best; when we have nobody to grope towards, no devil to lay our blame upon, no Personal God to carry our burdens, when we are alone responsible, then we shall rise to our highest and best. I am responsible for my fate, I am the bringer of good unto myself, I am the bringer of evil. I am the Pure and Blessed One. We must reject all thoughts that assert the contrary. "I have neither death nor fear, I have neither caste nor creed, I have neither father nor mother nor brother, neither friend nor foe, for I am Existence, Knowledge, and Bliss Absolute; I am the Blissful One, I am the Blissful One. I am not bound either by virtue or vice, by happiness or misery. Pilgrimages and books and ceremonials can never bind me. I have neither hunger nor thirst; the body is not mine, nor am I subject to the superstitions and decay that come to the body, I am Existence, Knowledge, and Bliss Absolute; I am the Blissful One, I am the Blissful One."

This, says the Vedanta, is the only prayer that we should have. This is the only way to reach the goal, to tell ourselves, and to tell everybody else, that we are divine. And as we go on repeating this, strength comes. He who falters at first will get stronger and stronger, and the voice will increase in volume until the truth takes possession of our hearts, and courses through our veins, and permeates our bodies. Delusion will vanish as the light becomes more and more effulgent, load after load of ignorance will vanish, and then will come a time when all else has disappeared and the Sun alone shines.

CHAPTER 11

THE COSMOS

THE MACROCOSM

(Delivered in New York, 19th January 1896)

The flowers that we see all around us are beautiful, beautiful is the rising of the morning sun, beautiful are the variegated hues of nature. The whole universe is beautiful, and man has been enjoying it since his appearance on earth. Sublime and awe-inspiring are the mountains; the gigantic rushing rivers rolling towards the sea, the trackless deserts, the infinite ocean, the starry heavens—all these are awe-inspiring, sublime, and beautiful indeed. The whole mass of existence which we call nature has been acting on the human mind since time immemorial. It has been acting on the thought of man, and as its reaction has come out the question: What are these, whence are they? As far back as the time of the oldest portion of that most ancient human composition, the Vedas, we find the same question asked: "Whence is this? When there was neither aught nor naught, and darkness was hidden in darkness, who projected this universe? How? Who knows the secret?" And the question has come down to us at the present time. Millions of attempts have been made to answer it, yet millions of times it will have to be answered again. It is not that each answer was a failure; every answer to this question contained a part of truth, and this truth gathers strength as time rolls on. I will try to present before you the outline of the answer that I have gathered from the ancient philosophers of India; in harmony with modern knowledge.

We find that in this oldest of questions a few points had been already solved. The first is that there was a time when there was "neither aught nor naught", when this world did not exist; our mother earth with the seas and oceans, the rivers, and mountains, cities and villages human races, animals, plants, birds, and planets and luminaries, all this infinite variety of creation, had no existence. Are we sure of that? We will try to trace how this conclusion is arrived at. What does man see around him? Take a little plant. He puts a seed in the ground, and later, he finds a plant peep out, lift itself slowly above the ground, and grow and grow, till it becomes a gigantic tree. Then it dies, leaving only the seed. It completes the circle—it comes out of the seed, becomes the tree, and ends in the seed again. Look at a bird, how from the egg it springs, lives its life, and then dies, leaving other eggs, seeds of future birds. So with the animals, so with man. Everything in nature begins, as it were, from certain seeds, certain rudiments, certain fine forms, and becomes grosser and grosser, and develops, going on that way for a certain time, and then again goes back to that fine form, and subsides. The raindrop in which the beautiful sunbeam is playing was drawn in the form of vapour from the ocean, went far away into the air, and reached a region where it changed into water, and dropped down in its present form—to be converted into vapour again. So with everything in nature by which we are surrounded. We know that the huge mountains are being worked upon by glaciers and rivers, which are slowly but surely pounding them and pulverising them into sand, that drifts away into the ocean where it settles down on its bed, layer after layer, becoming hard as rocks, once more to be heaped up into mountains of a future generation. Again they will be pounded and pulverised, and thus the course goes on. From sand rise these mountains; unto sand they go.

If it be true that nature is uniform throughout, if it be true, and so far no human experience has contradicted it, that the same method under which a small grain of sand is created, works in creating the gigantic suns and stars and all this universe, if it be true that the whole of this universe is built on exactly the same plan as the atom, if it be true that the same law prevails throughout the universe, then, as it has been said in the Vedas, "Knowing one lump of clay we know the nature of all the clay that is in the universe." Take up a little plant and study its life, and we know the universe as it is. If we know one grain of sand, we understand the secret of the whole universe. Applying this course of reasoning to phenomena, we find, in the first place, that everything is almost similar at the beginning and the end. The mountain comes from the sand, and goes back to the sand; the river comes out of vapour, and goes back to vapour; plant life comes from the seed, and goes back to the seed; human life comes out of human germs, and goes back to human germs. The universe with its stars and planets has come out of a nebulous state and must go back to it. What do we learn from this? That the manifested or the grosser state is the effect, and the finer state the cause. Thousands of years ago, it was demonstrated by Kapila, the great father of all philosophy, that destruction means going back to the cause. If this table here is destroyed, it will go back to its cause, to those fine forms and particles which, combined, made this form which we call a table. If a man dies, he will go back to the elements which gave him his body; if this earth dies, it will go back to the elements which gave it form. This is what is called destruction, going back to the cause. Therefore we learn that the effect is the same as the cause, not different. It is only in another form. This glass is an effect, and it had its cause, and this cause is present in this form. A certain amount of the material called glass plus the force in the hands of the manufacturer, are the causes, the instrumental and the material, which, combined, produced this form called a glass. The force which was in the hands of the manufacturer is present in the glass as the power of adhesion, without which the particles would fall apart; and the glass material is also present. The glass is only a manifestation of these fine causes in a new shape, and if it be broken to pieces, the force which was present in the form of adhesion will go back and join its own element, and the particles of glass will remain the same until they take new forms.

Thus we find that the effect is never different from the cause. It is only that this effect is a reproduction of the cause in a grosser form. Next, we learn that all these particular forms which we call plants, animals, or men are being repeated *ad infinitum*, rising and falling. The seed produces the tree. The tree produces the seed, which again comes up as another tree, and so on and on; there is no end to it. Water-drops roll down the mountains into the ocean, and rise again as vapour, go back to the mountains and again come down to the ocean. So, rising and falling, the cycle goes on. So with all lives, so with all existence that we can see, feel, hear, or imagine. Everything that is within the bounds of our knowledge is proceeding in the same way, like breathing in and breathing out in the human body. Everything in creation goes on in this form, one wave rising, another falling, rising again, falling again. Each wave has its hollow, each hollow has its wave. The same law must apply to the universe taken as a whole, because of its uniformity. This universe must be resolved into its causes; the sun, moon, stars, and earth, the body and mind, and everything in this universe must return to their finer causes, disappear, be destroyed as it were. But they will live in the causes as fine forms. Out of these fine forms they will emerge again as new earths, suns, moons, and stars.

There is one fact more to learn about this rising and falling. The seed comes out of the tree; it does not immediately become a tree, but has a period of inactivity, or rather, a period of very fine unmanifested action. The seed has to work for some time beneath the soil. It breaks into pieces, degenerates as it were, and regeneration comes out of that degeneration. In the beginning, the whole of this universe has to work likewise for a period in that minute form, unseen and unmanifested, which is called chaos, and; out of that comes a new projection. The whole period of one manifestation of this universe—its going down into the finer form, remaining there for some time, and coming out again—is, in Sanskrit, called a Kalpa or a Cycle. Next comes a very important question especially for modern; times. We see that the finer forms develop slowly and slowly, and gradually becomes grosser and grosser. We have seen that the cause is the same as the effect, and the effect is only the cause in another form. Therefore this whole universe cannot be produced out of nothing. Nothing comes without a cause, and the cause is the effect in another form.

Out of what has this universe been produced then? From a preceding fine universe. Out of what has men been produced? The preceding fine form. Out of what has the tree been produced? Out of the seed; the whole of the tree was there in the seed. It comes out and becomes manifest. So, the whole of this universe has been created out of this very universe existing in a minute form. It has been made manifest now. It will go back to that minute form, and again will be made manifest. Now we find that the fine forms slowly come out and become grosser and grosser until they reach their limit, and when they reach their limit they go back further and further, becoming finer and finer again. This coming out of the fine and becoming gross, simply changing the arrangements of its parts, as it were, is what in modern times called evolution. This is very true, perfectly true; we see it in our lives. No rational man can possibly quarrel with these evolutionists. But we have to learn one thing more. We have to go one step further, and what is that? That every evolution is preceded by an involution. The seed is the father of the tree, but another tree was itself the father of the seed. The seed is the fine form out of which the big tree comes, and another big tree was the form which is involved in that seed. The whole of this universe was present in the cosmic fine universe. The little cell, which becomes afterwards the man, was simply the involved man and becomes evolved as a man. If this is clear, we have no quarrel with the evolutionists, for we see that if they admit this step, instead of their destroying religion, they will be the greatest supporters of it.

We see then, that nothing can be created out of nothing. Everything exists through eternity, and will exist through eternity. Only the movement is in succeeding waves and hollows, going back to fine forms, and coming out into gross manifestations. This involution and evolution is going on throughout the whole of nature. The whole series of evolution beginning with the lowest manifestation of life and reaching up to the highest, the most perfect man, must have been the involution of something else. The question is: The involution of what? What was involved? God. The evolutionist will tell you that your idea that it was God is wrong. Why? Because you see God is intelligent, but we find that intelligence develops much later on in the course of evolution. It is in man and the higher animals that we find intelligence, but millions of years have passed in this world before this intelligence came. This objection of the evolutionists does not hold water, as we shall see by applying our theory. The tree comes out of the seed, goes back to the seed; the beginning and the end are the same. The earth comes out of its cause and returns to it. We know that if we can find the beginning we can find the end. *E converso*, if we find the end we can find the beginning. If that is so, take this whole evolutionary series, from the protoplasm at one end to the perfect man at the other, and this whole series is one life. In the end we find the perfect man, so in the beginning it must have been the same. Therefore, the protoplasm was the involution of the highest intelligence. You may not see it but that involved intelligence is what is uncoiling itself until it becomes manifested in the most perfect man. That can be mathematically demonstrated. If the law of conservation of energy is true, you cannot get anything out of a machine unless you put it in there first. The amount of work that you get out of an engine is exactly the same as you have put into it in the form of water and coal, neither more nor less. The work I am doing now is just what I put into me, in the shape of air, food, and other things. It is only a question of change and manifestation. There cannot be added in the economy of this universe one particle of matter or one foot-pound of force, nor can one particle of matter or one foot-pound of force be taken out. If that be the case, what is this intelligence? If it was not present in the protoplasm, it must have come all of a sudden, something coming out of nothing, which is absurd. It, therefore, follows absolutely that the perfect man, the free man, the God-man, who has gone beyond the laws of nature, and transcended everything, who has no more to go through this process of evolution, through birth and death, that man called the "Christ-man" by the Christians, and the "Buddha-man" by the Buddhists, and the "Free" by the Yogis—that perfect man who is at one end of the chain of evolution was involved in the cell of the protoplasm, which is at the other end of the same chain.

Applying the same reason to the whole of the universe, we see that intelligence must be the Lord of creation, the cause. What is the most evolved notion that man has of this universe? It is intelligence, the adjustment of part to part, the display of intelligence, of which the ancient design theory was an attempt at expression. The beginning was, therefore, intelligence. At the beginning that intelligence becomes involved, and in the end that intelligence gets evolved. The sum total of the intelligence displayed in the universe must, therefore, be the involved universal intelligence unfolding itself. This universal intelligence is what we call God. Call it by any other name, it is absolutely certain that in the beginning there is that Infinite cosmic intelligence. This cosmic intelligence gets involved, and it manifests, evolves itself, until it becomes the perfect man, the "Christ-man," the "Buddha-man." Then it goes back to its own source. That is why all the scriptures say, "In Him we live and move and have our being." That is why all the scriptures preach that we come from God and go back to God. Do not be frightened by theological terms; if terms frighten you, you are not fit to be philosophers. This cosmic intelligence is what the theologians call God.

I have been asked many times, "Why do you use that old word, God?" Because it is the best word for our purpose; you cannot find a better word than that, because all the hopes, aspirations, and happiness of humanity have been centred in that word. It is impossible now to change the word. Words like these were first coined by great saints who realised their import and understood their meaning. But as they become current in society, ignorant people take these words, and the result is that they lose their spirit and glory. The word God has been used from time immemorial, and the idea of this cosmic intelligence, and all that is great and holy, is associated with it. Do you mean to say that because some fool says it is not all right, we should throw it away? Another man may come and say, "Take *my* word," and another again, "Take *my* word." So there will be no end to foolish words. Use the old word, only use it in the true spirit, cleanse it of superstition, and realise fully what this great ancient word means. If you understand the power of the laws of association, you will know that these words are associated with innumerable majestic and powerful ideas; they have been used and worshipped by millions of human souls and associated by them with all that is highest and best, all that is rational, all that is lovable, and all that is great and grand in human nature. And they come as suggestions of these associations, and cannot be given up. If I tried to express all these by only telling you that God created the universe, it would have conveyed no meaning to you. Yet, after all this struggle, we have come back to Him, the Ancient and Supreme One.

We now see that all the various forms of cosmic energy, such as matter, thought, force, intelligence and so forth, are simply the manifestations of that cosmic intelligence, or, as we shall call it henceforth, the Supreme Lord. Everything that you see, feel, or hear, the whole universe, is His creation, or to be a little more accurate, is His projection; or to be still more accurate, is the Lord Himself. It is He who is shining as the sun and the stars, He is the mother earth. He is the ocean Himself. He comes as gentle showers, He is the gentle air that we breathe in, and He it is who is working as force in the body. He is the speech that is uttered, He is the man who is talking. He is the audience that is here. He is the platform on which I stand, He is the light that enables me to see your faces. It is all He. He Himself is both the material and the efficient cause of this universe, and He it is that gets involved in the minute cell, and evolves at the other end and becomes God again. He it is that comes down and becomes the lowest atom, and slowly unfolding His nature, rejoins Himself.

This is the mystery of the universe. "Thou art the man, Thou art the woman, Thou art the strong man walking in the pride of youth, Thou art the old man tottering on crutches, Thou art in everything. Thou art everything, O Lord." This is the only solution of the Cosmos that satisfies the human intellect. In one word, we are born of Him, we live in Him, and unto Him we return.

CHAPTER 12

THE COSMOS

THE MICROCOSM

(Delivered in New York, 26th January 1896)

The human mind naturally wants to get outside, to peer out of the body, as it were, through the channels of the organs. The eye must see, the ear must hear, the senses must sense the external world—and naturally the beauties and sublimities of nature captivate the attention of man first. The first questions that arose in the human soul were about the external world. The solution of the mystery was asked of the sky, of the stars, of the heavenly bodies, of the earth, of the rivers, of the mountains, of the ocean; and in all ancient religions we find traces of how the groping human mind at first caught at everything external. There was a river-god, a sky-god, a cloud-god, a rain-god;

everything external, all of which we now call the powers of nature, became metamorphosed, transfigured, into wills, into gods, into heavenly messengers. As the question went deeper and deeper, these external manifestations failed to satisfy the human mind, and finally the energy turned inward, and the question was asked of man's own soul. From the macrocosm the question was reflected back to the microcosm; from the external world the question was reflected to the internal. From analysing the external nature, man is led to analyse the internal; this questioning of the internal man comes with a higher state of civilisation, with a deeper insight into nature, with a higher state of growth.

The subject of discussion this afternoon is this internal man. No question is so near and dear to man's heart as that of the internal man. How many millions of times, in how many countries has this question been asked! Sages and kings, rich and poor, saints and sinners, every man, every woman, all have from time to time asked this question. Is there nothing permanent in this evanescent human life? Is there nothing, they have asked, which does not die away when this body dies? Is there not something living when this frame crumbles into dust? Is there not something which survives the fire which burns the body into ashes? And if so, what is its destiny? Where does it go? Whence did it come? These questions have been asked again and again, and so long as this creation lasts, so long as there are human brains to think, this question will have to be asked. Yet, it is not that the answer did not come; each time the answer came, and as time rolls on, the answer will gain strength more and more. The question was answered once for all thousands of years ago, and through all subsequent time it is being restated, reillustrated, made clearer to our intellect. What we have to do, therefore, is to make a restatement of the answer. We do not pretend to throw any new light on those all-absorbing problems, but only to put before you the ancient truth in the language of modern times, to speak the thoughts of the ancients in the language of the moderns, to speak the thoughts of the philosophers in the language of the people, to speak the thoughts of the angels in the language of man, to speak the thoughts of God in the language of poor humanity, so that man will understand them; for the same divine essence from which the ideas emanated is ever present in man, and, therefore, he can always understand them.

I am looking at you. How many things are necessary for this vision? First, the eyes. For if I am perfect in every other way, and yet have no eyes, I shall not be able to see you. Secondly, the real organ of vision. For the eyes are not the organs. They are but the instruments of vision, and behind them is the real organ, the nerve centre in the brain. If that centre be injured, a man may have the clearest pair of eyes, yet he will not be able to see anything. So, it is necessary that this centre, or the real organ, be there. Thus, with all our senses. The external ear is but the instrument for carrying the vibration of sound inward to the centre. Yet, that is not sufficient. Suppose in your library you are intently reading a book, and the clock strikes, yet you do not hear it. The sound is there, the pulsations in the air are there, the ear and the centre are also there, and these vibrations have been carried through the ear to the centre, and yet you do not hear it. What is wanting? The mind is not there. Thus we see that the third thing necessary is, that the mind must be there. First the external instruments, then the organ to which this external instrument will carry the sensation, and lastly the organ itself must be joined to the mind. When the mind is not joined to the organ, the organ and the ear may take the impression, and yet we shall not be conscious of it. The mind, too, is only the carrier; it has to carry the sensation still forward, and present it to the intellect. The intellect is the determining faculty and decides upon what is brought to it. Still this is not sufficient. The intellect must carry it forward and present the whole thing before the ruler in the body, the human soul, the king on the throne. Before him this is presented, and then from him comes the order, what to do or what not to do; and the order goes down in the same sequence to the intellect, to the mind, to the organs, and the organs convey it to the instruments, and the perception is complete.

The instruments are in the external body, the gross body of man; but the mind and the intellect are not. They are in what is called in Hindu philosophy the finer body; and what in Christian theology you read of as the spiritual body of man; finer, very much finer than the body, and yet not the soul. This soul is beyond them all. The external body perishes in a few years; any simple cause may disturb and destroy it. The finer body is not so easily perishable; yet it sometimes degenerates, and at other times becomes strong. We see how, in the old man, the mind loses its strength, how, when the body is vigorous, the mind becomes vigorous, how various medicines and drugs affect it, how everything external acts on it, and how it reacts on the external world. Just as the body has its progress and decadence, so also has the mind, and, therefore, the mind is not the soul, because the soul can neither decay nor degenerate. How can we know that? How can we know that there is something behind this mind? Because knowledge which is self-illuminating and the basis of intelligence cannot belong to dull, dead matter. Never was seen any gross matter which had intelligence as its own essence. No dull or dead matter can illumine itself. It is intelligence that illumines all matter. This hall is here only through intelligence because, as a hall, its existence would be unknown unless some intelligence built it. This body is not self-luminous; if it were, it would be so in a dead man also. Neither can the mind nor the spiritual body be self-luminous. They are not of the essence of intelligence. That which is self-luminous cannot decay. The luminosity of that which shines through a borrowed light comes and goes; but that which is light itself, what can make that come and go, flourish and decay? We see that the moon waxes and wanes, because it shines through the borrowed light of the sun. If a lump of iron is put into the fire and made red-hot, it glows and shines, but its light will vanish, because it is borrowed. So, decadence is possible only of that light which is borrowed and is not of its own essence.

Now we see that the body, the external shape, has no light as its own essence, is not self-luminous, and cannot know itself; neither can the mind. Why not? Because the mind waxes and wanes, because it is vigorous at one time and weak at another, because it can be acted upon by anything and everything. Therefore the light which shines through the mind is not its own. Whose is it then? It must belong to that which has it as its own essence, and as such, can never decay or die, never become stronger or weaker; it is self-luminous, it is luminosity itself. It cannot be that the soul knows, it *is* knowledge. It cannot be that the soul has existence, but it is existence. It cannot be that the soul is happy, it is happiness itself. That which is happy has borrowed its happiness; that which has knowledge has received its knowledge; and that which has relative existence has only a reflected existence. Wherever there are qualities these qualities have been reflected upon the substance, but the soul has not knowledge, existence, and blessedness as its qualities, they are the essence of the soul.

Again, it may be asked, why shall we take this for granted? Why shall we admit that the soul has knowledge, blessedness, existence, as its essence, and has not borrowed them? It may be argued, why not say that the soul's luminosity, the soul's blessedness, the soul's knowledge, are borrowed in the same way as the luminosity of the body is borrowed from the mind? The fallacy of arguing in this way will be that there will be no limit. From whom were these borrowed? If we say from some other source, the same question will be asked again. So, at last we shall have to come to one who is self-luminous; to make matters short then, the logical way is to stop where we get self-luminosity, and proceed no further.

We see, then, that this human being is composed first of this external covering, the body; secondly, the finer body, consisting of mind, intellect, and egoism. Behind them is the real Self of man. We have seen that all the qualities and powers of the gross body are borrowed from the mind, and the mind, the finer body, borrows its powers and luminosity from the soul, standing behind.

A great many questions now arise about the nature of this soul. If the existence of the soul is drawn from the argument that it is self-luminous, that knowledge, existence, blessedness are its essence, it naturally follows that this soul cannot have been created. A self-luminous existence, independent of any other existence, could never have been the outcome of anything. It always existed; there was never a time when it did not exist, because if the soul did not exist, where was time? Time is in the soul; it is when the soul reflects its powers on the mind and the mind thinks, that time comes. When there was no soul, certainly there was no thought, and without thought, there was no time. How can the soul, therefore, be said to be existing in time, when time itself exists in the soul? It has neither birth nor death, but it is passing through all these various stages. It is manifesting slowly and gradually from lower to higher, and so on. It is expressing its own grandeur, working through the mind on the body; and through the body it is grasping the external world and understanding it. It takes up a body and uses it; and when that body has failed and is used up, it takes another body; and so on it goes.

Here comes a very interesting question, that question which is generally known as the reincarnation of the soul. Sometimes people get frightened at the idea, and superstition is so strong that thinking men even believe that they are the outcome of nothing, and then, with the grandest logic, try to deduce the theory that although they have come out of zero, they will be eternal ever afterwards. Those that come out of zero will certainly have to go back to zero. Neither you, nor I nor anyone present, has come out of zero, nor will go back to zero. We have been existing eternally, and will exist, and there is no power under the sun or above the sun which can undo your or my existence or send us back to zero. Now this idea of reincarnation is not only not a frightening idea, but is most essential for the moral well-being of the human race. It is the only logical conclusion that thoughtful men can arrive at. If you are going to exist in eternity hereafter, it must be that you have existed through eternity in the past: it cannot be otherwise. I will try to answer a few objections that are generally brought against the theory. Although many of you will think they are very silly objections, still we have to answer them, for sometimes we find that the most thoughtful men are ready to advance the silliest ideas. Well has it been said that there never was an idea so absurd that it did not find philosophers to defend it. The first objection is, why do we not remember our past? Do we remember all our past in this life? How many of you remember what you did when you were babies? None of you remember your early childhood, and if upon memory depends your existence, then this argument proves that you did not exist as babies, because you do not remember your babyhood. It is simply unmitigated nonsense to say that our existence depends on our remembering it. Why should we remember the past? That brain is gone, broken into pieces, and a new brain has been manufactured. What has come to this brain is the resultant, the sum total of the impressions acquired in our past, with which the mind has come to inhabit the new body.

I, as I stand here, am the effect, the result, of all the infinite past which is tacked on to me. And why is it necessary for me to remember all the past? When a great ancient sage, a seer, or a prophet of old, who came face to face with the truth, says something, these modern men stand up and say, "Oh, he was a fool!" But just use another name, "Huxley says it, or Tyndall"; then it must be true, and they take it for granted. In place of ancient superstitions they have erected modern superstitions, in place of the old Popes of religion they have installed modern Popes of science. So we see that this objection as to memory is not valid, and that is about the only serious objection that is raised against this theory. Although we have seen that it is not necessary for the theory that there shall be the memory of past lives, yet at the same time, we are in a position to assert that there are instances which show that this memory does come, and that each one of us will get back this memory in that life in which he will become free. Then alone you will find that this world is but a dream; then alone you will realise in the soul of your soul that you are but actors and the world is a stage; then alone will the idea of non-attachment come to you with the power of thunder; then all this thirst for enjoyment, this clinging on to life and this world will vanish for ever; then the mind will see dearly as daylight how many times all these existed for you, how many millions of times you had fathers and mothers, sons and daughters, husbands and wives, relatives and friends, wealth and power. They came and went. How many times you were on the topmost crest of the wave, and how many times you were down at the bottom of despair! When memory will bring all these to you, then alone will you stand as a hero and smile when the world frowns upon you. Then alone will you stand up and say. "I care not for thee even, O Death, what terrors hast thou for me?" This will come to all.

Are there any arguments, any rational proofs for this reincarnation of the soul? So far we have been giving the negative side, showing that the opposite arguments to disprove it are not valid. Are there any positive proofs? There are; and most valid ones, too. No other theory except that of reincarnation accounts for the wide divergence that we find between man and man in their powers to acquire knowledge. First, let us consider the process by means of which knowledge is acquired. Suppose I go into the street and see a dog. How do I know it is a dog? I refer it to my mind, and in my mind are groups of all my past experiences, arranged and pigeon-holed, as it were. As soon as a new impression comes, I take it up and refer it to some of the old pigeon-holes, and as soon as I find a group of the same impressions already existing, I place it in that group, and I am satisfied. I know it is a dog, because it coincides with the impressions already there. When I do not find the cognates of this new experience inside, I become dissatisfied. When, not finding the cognates of an impression, we become dissatisfied, this state of the mind is called "ignorance"; but, when, finding the cognates of an impression already existing, we become satisfied, this is called "knowledge". When one apple fell, men became dissatisfied. Then gradually they found out the group. What was the group they found? That all apples fell, so they called it "gravitation". Now we see that without a fund of already existing experience, any new experience would be impossible, for there would be nothing to which to refer the new impression. So, if, as some of the European philosophers think, a child came into the world with what they call *tabula rasa*, such a child would never attain to any degree of intellectual power, because he would have nothing to which to refer his new experiences. We see that the power of acquiring knowledge varies in each individual, and this shows that each one of us has come with his own fund of knowledge. Knowledge can only be got in one way, the way of experience; there is no other way to know. If we have not experienced it in this life, we must have experienced it in other lives. How is it that the fear of death is everywhere? A little chicken is just out of an egg and an eagle comes, and the chicken flies in fear to its mother. There is an old explanation (I should hardly dignify it by such a name). It is called instinct. What makes that little chicken just out of the egg afraid to die? How is it that as soon as a duckling hatched by a hen comes near water, it jumps into it and swims? It never swam before, nor saw anything swim. People call it instinct. It is a big word, but it leaves us where we were before. Let us study this phenomenon of instinct. A child begins to play on the piano. At first she must pay attention to every key she is fingering, and as she goes on and on for months and years, the playing becomes almost involuntary, instinctive. What was first done with conscious will does not require later on an effort of the will. This is not yet a complete proof. One half remains, and that is that almost all the actions which are now instinctive can be brought under the control of the will. Each muscle of the body can be brought under control. This is perfectly well known. So the proof is complete by this double method, that what we now call instinct is degeneration of voluntary actions; therefore, if the analogy applies to the whole of creation, if all nature is uniform, then what is instinct in lower animals, as well as in men, must be the degeneration of will.

Applying the law we dwelt upon under macrocosm that each involution presupposes an evolution, and each evolution an involution, we see that instinct is involved reason. What we call instinct in men or animals must therefore be involved, degenerated, voluntary actions, and voluntary actions are impossible without experience. Experience started that knowledge, and that knowledge is there. The fear of death, the duckling taking to the water and all involuntary actions in the human being which have become instinctive, are the results of past experiences. So far we have proceeded very clearly, and so far the latest science is with us. But here comes one more difficulty. The latest scientific men are coming back to the ancient sages, and as far as they have done so, there is perfect agreement. They admit that each man and each animal is born with a fund of experience, and that all these actions in the mind are the result of past experience. "But what," they ask, "is the use of saying that that experience belongs to the soul? Why not say it belongs to the body, and the body alone? Why not say it is hereditary transmission?" This is the last question. Why not say that all the experience with which I am born is the resultant effect of all the past experience of my ancestors? The sum total of the experience from the little protoplasm up to the highest human being is in me, but it has come from body to body in the course of hereditary transmission. Where will the difficulty be? This question is very nice, and we admit some part of this hereditary transmission. How far? As far as furnishing the material. We, by our past actions, conform ourselves to a certain birth in a certain body, and the only suitable material for that body comes from the parents who have made themselves fit to have that soul as their offspring.

The simple hereditary theory takes for granted the most astonishing proposition without any proof, that mental experience can be recorded in matters, that mental experience can be involved in matter. When I look at you in the lake of my mind there is a wave. That wave subsides, but it remains in fine form, as an impression. We understand a physical impression remaining in the body. But what proof is there for assuming that the mental impression can remain in the body, since the body goes to pieces? What carries it? Even granting it were possible for each mental impression to remain in the body, that every impression, beginning from the first man down to my father, was in my father's body, how could it be transmitted to me? Through the bioplasmic cell? How could that be? Because the father's body does not come to the child *in toto*. The same parents may have a number of children; then, from this theory of hereditary transmission, where the impression and the impressed (that is to say, material) are one, it rigorously follows that by the birth of every child the parents must lose a part of their own impressions, or, if the parents should transmit the whole of their impressions, then, after the birth of the first child, their minds would be a vacuum.

Again, if in the bioplasmic cell the infinite amount of impressions from all time has entered, where and how is it? This is a most impossible position, and until these physiologists can prove how and where those impressions live in that cell, and what they mean by a mental impression sleeping in the physical cell, their position cannot be taken for granted. So far it is clear then, that this impression is in the mind, that the mind comes to take its birth and rebirth, and uses the material which is most proper for it, and that the mind which has made itself fit for only a particular kind of body will have to wait until it gets that material. This we understand. The theory then comes to this, that there is hereditary transmission so far as furnishing the material to the soul is concerned. But the soul migrates and manufactures body after body, and each thought we think, and each deed we do, is stored in it in fine forms, ready to spring up again and take a new shape. When I look at you a wave rises in my mind. It dives down, as it were, and becomes finer and finer, but it does not die. It is ready to start up again as a wave in the shape of memory. So all these impressions are in my mind, and when I die the resultant force of them will be upon me. A ball is here, and each one of us takes a mallet in his hands and strikes the ball from all sides; the ball goes from point to point in the room, and when it reaches the door it flies out. What does it carry out with it? The resultant of all these blows. That will give it its direction. So, what directs the soul when the body dies? The resultant, the sum total of all the works it has done, of the thoughts it has thought. If the resultant is such that it has to manufacture a new body for further experience, it will go to those parents who are ready to supply it with suitable material for that body. Thus, from body to body it will go, sometimes to a heaven, and back again to earth, becoming man, or some lower animal. This way it will go on until it has finished its experience, and completed the circle. It then knows its own nature, knows what it is, and ignorance vanishes, its powers become manifest, it becomes perfect; no more is there any necessity for the soul to work through physical bodies, nor is there any necessity for it to work through finer, or mental bodies. It shines in its own light, and is free, no more to be born, no more to die.

We will not go now into the particulars of this. But I will bring before you one more point with regard to this theory of reincarnation. It is the theory that advances the freedom of the human soul. It is the one theory that does not lay the blame of all our weakness upon somebody else, which is a common human fallacy. We do not look at our own faults; the eyes do not see themselves, they see the eyes of everybody else. We human beings are very slow to recognise our own weakness, our own faults, so long as we can lay the blame upon somebody else. Men in general lay all the blame of life on their fellow-men, or, failing that, on God, or they conjure up a ghost, and say it is fate. Where is fate, and who is fate? We reap what we sow. We are the makers of our own fate. None else has the blame, none has the praise. The wind is blowing; those vessels whose sails are unfurled catch it, and go forward on their way, but those which have their sails furled do not catch the wind. Is that the fault of the wind? Is it the fault of the merciful Father, whose wind of mercy is blowing without ceasing, day and night, whose mercy knows no decay, is it His fault that some of us are happy and some unhappy? We make our own destiny. His sun shines for the weak as well as for the strong. His wind blows for saint and sinner alike. He is the Lord of all, the Father of all, merciful, and impartial. Do you mean to say that He, the Lord of creation, looks upon the petty things of our life in the same light as we do? What a degenerate idea of God that would be! We are like little puppies, making life-and-death struggles here, and foolishly thinking that even God Himself will take it as seriously as we do. He knows what the puppies' play means. Our attempts to lay the blame on Him, making Him the punisher, and the rewarder, are only foolish. He neither punishes, nor rewards any. His infinite mercy is open to every one, at all times, in all places, under all conditions, unfailing, unswerving. Upon us depends how we use it. Upon us depends how we utilise it. Blame neither man, nor God, nor anyone in the world. When you find yourselves suffering, blame yourselves, and try to do better.

This is the only solution of the problem. Those that blame others—and, alas! the number of them is increasing every day—are generally miserable with helpless brains; they have brought themselves to that pass through their own mistakes and blame others, but this does not alter their position. It does not serve them in any way. This attempt to throw the blame upon others only weakens them the more. Therefore, blame none for your own faults, stand upon your own feet, and take the whole responsibility upon yourselves. Say, "This misery that I am suffering is of my own doing, and that very thing proves that it will have to be undone by me alone." That which I created, I can demolish; that which is created by some one else I shall never be able to destroy. Therefore, stand up, be bold, be strong. Take the whole responsibility on your own shoulders, and know that you are the creator of your own destiny. All the strength and succour you want is within yourselves. Therefore, make your own future. "Let the dead past bury its dead." The infinite future is before you, and you must always remember that each word, thought, and deed, lays up a store for you and that as the bad thoughts and bad works are ready to spring upon you like tigers, so also there is the inspiring hope that the good thoughts and good deeds are ready with the power of a hundred thousand angels to defend you always and for ever.

CHAPTER 13

IMMORTALITY

(Delivered in America)

What question has been asked a greater number of times, what idea has led men more to search the universe for an answer, what question is nearer and dearer to the human heart, what question is more inseparably connected with our existence, than this one, the immortality of the human soul? It has been the theme of poets and sages, of priests and prophets; kings on the throne have discussed it, beggars in the street have dreamt of it. The best of humanity have approached it, and the worst of men have hoped for it. The interest in the theme has not died yet, nor will it die so long as human nature exists. Various answers have been presented to the world by various minds. Thousands, again, in every period of history have given up the discussion, and yet the question remains fresh as ever. Often in the turmoil and struggle of our lives we seem to forget it, but suddenly some one dies—one, perhaps, whom we loved, one near and dear to our hearts is snatched away from us—and the struggle, the din and turmoil of the world around us, cease for a moment, and the soul asks the old questions "What after this?" "What becomes of the soul?"

All human knowledge proceeds out of experience; we cannot know anything except by experience. All our reasoning is based upon generalised experience, all our knowledge is but harmonised experience. Looking around us, what do we find? A continuous change. The plant comes out of the seed, grows into the tree, completes the circle, and comes back to the seed. The animal comes, lives a certain time, dies, and completes the circle. So does man. The mountains slowly but surely crumble away, the rivers slowly but surely dry up, rains come out of the sea, and go back to the sea. Everywhere circles are being completed, birth, growth, development, and decay following each other with mathematical precision. This is our everyday experience. Inside of it all, behind all this vast mass of what we call life, of millions of forms and shapes, millions upon millions of varieties, beginning from the lowest atom to the highest spiritualised man, we find existing a certain unity. Every day we find that the wall that was thought to be dividing one thing and another is being broken down, and all matter is coming to be recognised by modern science as one substance, manifesting in different ways and in various forms; the one life that runs through all like a continuous chain, of which all these various forms represent the links, link after link, extending almost infinitely, but of the same one chain. This is what is called evolution. It is an old, old idea, as old as human society, only it is getting fresher and fresher as human knowledge is progressing. There is one thing more, which the ancients perceived, but which in modern times is not yet so clearly perceived, and that is involution. The seed is becoming the plant; a grain of sand never becomes a plant. It is the father that becomes a child; a lump of clay never becomes the child. From what does this evolution come, is the question. What was the seed? It was the same as the tree. All the possibilities of a future tree are in that seed; all the possibilities of a future man are in the little baby; all the possibilities of any future life are in the germ. What is this? The ancient philosophers of India called it involution. We find then, that every evolution presupposes an involution. Nothing can be evolved which is not already there. Here, again, modern science comes to our help. You know by mathematical reasoning that the sum total of the energy that is displayed in the universe is the same throughout. You cannot take away one atom of matter or one foot-pound of force. You cannot add to the universe one atom of matter or one foot-pound of force. As such, evolution does not come out of zero; then, where does it come from? From previous involution. The child is the man involved, and the man is the child evolved. The seed is the tree involved, and the tree is the seed evolved. All the possibilities of life are in the germ. The problem becomes a little clearer. Add to it the first idea of continuation of life. From the lowest protoplasm to the most perfect human being there is really but one life. Just as in one life we have so many various phases of expression, the protoplasm developing into the baby, the child, the young man, the old man, so, from that protoplasm up to the most perfect man we get one continuous life, one chain. This is evolution, but we have seen that each evolution presupposes an involution. The whole of this life which slowly manifests itself evolves itself from the protoplasm to the perfected human being—the Incarnation of God on earth—the whole of this series is but one life, and the whole of this manifestation must have been involved in that very protoplasm. This whole life, this very God on earth, was involved in it and slowly came out, manifesting itself slowly, slowly, slowly. The highest expression must have been there in the germ state in minute form; therefore this one force, this whole chain, is the involution of that cosmic life which is everywhere. It is this one mass of intelligence which, from the protoplasm up to the most perfected man, is slowly and slowly uncoiling itself. Not that it grows. Take off all ideas of growth from your mind. With the idea of growth is associated something coming from outside, something extraneous, which would give the lie to the truth that the Infinite which lies latent in every life is independent of all external conditions. It can never grow; It was always there, and only manifests Itself.

The effect is the cause manifested. There is no

essential difference between the effect and the cause. Take this glass, for instance. There was the material, and the material plus the will of the manufacturer made the glass and these two were its causes and are present in it. In what form is the will present? As adhesion. If the force were not here, each particle would fall away. What is the effect then? It is the same as the cause, only taking; different form, a different composition. When the cause is changed and limited for a time, it becomes the effect. We must remember this. Applying it to our idea of life the whole of the manifestation of this one series, from the protoplasm up to the most perfect man, must be the very same thing as cosmic life. First it got involved and became finer; and out of that fine something, which wet the cause, it has gone on evolving, manifesting itself, and becoming grosser.

But the question of immortality is not yet settled. We have seen that everything in this universe is indestructible. There is nothing new; there will be nothing new. The same series of manifestations are presenting themselves alternately like a wheel, coming up and going down. All motion in this universe is in the form of waves, successively rising and falling. Systems after systems are coming out of fine forms, evolving themselves, and taking grosser forms, again melting down, as it were, and going back to the fine forms. Again they rise out of that, evolving for a certain period and slowly going back to the cause. So with all life. Each manifestation of life is coming up and then going back again. What goes down? The form. The form breaks to piccce, but it comes up again. In one sense bodies and forms even are eternal. How? Suppose we take a number of dice and throw them, and they fall in this ratio—6—5—3—4. We take the dice up and throw them again and again; there must be a time when the same numbers will come again; the same combination must come. Now each particle, each atom, that is in this universe, I take for such a die, and these are being thrown out and combined again and again. All these forms before you are one combination. Here are the forms of a glass, a table, a pitcher of water, and so forth. This is one combination; in time, it will all break. But there must come a time when exactly the same combination comes again, when you will be here, and this form will be here, this subject will be talked, and this pitcher will be here. An infinite number of times this has been, and an infinite number of times this will be repeated. Thus far with the physical forms. What do we find? That even the combination of physical forms is eternally repeated.

A most interesting conclusion that follows from this theory is the explanation of facts such as these: Some of you, perhaps, have seen a man who can read the past life of others and foretell the future. How is it possible for any one to see what the future will be, unless there is a regulated future? Effects of the past will recur in the future, and we see that it is so. You have seen the big Ferris Wheel* in Chicago. The wheel revolves, and the little

* An amusement device consisting of a giant power-driven steel wheel, revolvable on its stationary axle, and carrying

rooms in the wheel are regularly coming one after another; one set of persons gets into these, and after they have gone round the circle, they get out, and a fresh batch of people gets in. Each one of these batches is like one of these manifestations, from the lowest animals to the highest man. Nature is like the chain of the Ferris Wheel, endless and infinite, and these little carriages are the bodies or forms in which fresh batches of souls are riding, going up higher and higher until they become perfect and come out of the wheel. But the wheel goes on. And so long as the bodies are in the wheel, it can be absolutely and mathematically foretold where they will go, but not so of the souls. Thus it is possible to read the past and the future of nature with precision. We see, then, that there is recurrence of the same material phenomena at certain periods, and that the same combinations have been taking place through eternity. But that is not the immortality of the soul. No force can die, no matter can be annihilated. What becomes of it? It goes on changing, backwards and forwards, until it returns to the source from which it came. There is no motion in a straight line. Everything moves in a circle; a straight line, infinitely produced, becomes a circle. If that is the case, there cannot be eternal degeneration for any soul. It cannot

---

a number of balanced passenger cars around its rim."—Webster, G. W. G. Ferris erected the first of its kind for the Chicago Exposition of 1893. In India we have a corresponding wooden device very common in fairs.—Ed.

be. Everything must complete the circle, and come back to its source. What are you and I and all these souls? In our discussion of evolution and involution, we have seen that you and I must be part of the cosmic consciousness, cosmic life, cosmic mind, which got involved and we must complete the circle and go back to this cosmic intelligence which is God. This cosmic intelligence is what people call Lord, or God, or Christ, or Buddha, or Brahman, what the materialists perceive as force, and the agnostics as that infinite, inexpressible beyond; and we are all parts of that.

This is the second idea, yet this is not sufficient; there will be still more doubts. It is very good to say that there is no destruction for any force. But all the forces and forms that we see are combinations. This form before us is a composition of several component parts, and so every force that we see is similarly composite. If you take the scientific idea of force, and call it the sum total, the resultant of several forces, what becomes of your individuality? Everything that is a compound must sooner or later go back to its component parts. Whatever in this universe is the result of the combination of matter or force must sooner or later go back to its components. Whatever is the result of certain causes must die, must be destroyed. It gets broken up, dispersed, and resolved back into its components. Soul is not a force; neither is it thought. It is the manufacturer of thought, but not thought itself; it is the manufacturer of the body, but not the body. Why so? We see that the body cannot be the soul. Why not? Because it is not intelligent. A corpse is not intelligent, nor a piece of meat in a butcher's shop. What do we mean by intelligence? Reactive power. We want to go a little more deeply into this. Here is a pitcher; I see it. How? Rays of light from the pitcher enter my eyes, and make a picture in my retina, which is carried to the brain. Yet there is no vision. What the physiologists call the sensory nerves carry this impression inwards. But up to this there is no reaction. The nerve centre in the brain carries the impression to the mind, and the mind reacts, and as soon as this reaction comes, the pitcher flashes before it. Take a more commonplace example. Suppose you are listening to me intently and a mosquito is sitting on the tip of your nose and giving you that pleasant sensation which mosquitoes can give; but you are so intent on hearing me that you do not feel the mosquito at all. What has happened? The mosquito has bitten a certain part of your skin, and certain nerves are there. They have carried a certain sensation to the brain, and the impression is there, but the mind, being otherwise occupied, does not react, so you are not aware of the presence of the mosquito. When a new impression comes, if the mind does not react, we shall not be conscious of it, but when the reaction comes we feel, we see, we hear, and so forth. With this reaction comes illumination, as the Sāmkhya philosophers call it. We see that the body cannot illuminate, because in the absence of attention no sensation is possible. Cases have been known where, under peculiar conditions, a man who had never learnt a particular language was found able to speak it. Subsequent inquiries proved that the man had, when a child, lived among people who spoke that language and the impressions were left in his brain. These impressions remained stored up there, until through some cause the mind reacted, and illumination came, and then the man was able to speak the language. This shows that the mind alone is not sufficient, that the mind itself is an instrument in the hands of someone. In the case of that boy the mind contained that language, yet he did not know it, but later there came a time when he did. It shows that there is someone besides the mind; and when the boy was a baby, that someone did not use the power; but when the boy grew up, he took advantage of it, and used it. First, here is the body, second the mind, or instrument of thought, and third behind this mind is the Self of man. The Sanskrit word is Ātman. As modern philosophers have identified thought with molecular changes in the brain, they do not know how to explain such a case, and they generally deny it. The mind is intimately connected with the brain which dies every time the body changes. The Self is the illuminator, and the mind is the instrument in Its hands, and through that instrument It gets hold of the external instrument, and thus comes perception. The external instruments get hold of the impressions and carry them to the organs, for you must remember always, that the eyes and ears are only receivers—it is the internal organs, the brain centres, which act. In Sanskrit these centres are called Indriyas, and they carry sensations to the mind, and the mind presents them further back to another state of the mind, which in Sanskrit is called Chitta, and there they are organised into will, and all these present them to the King of kings inside, the Ruler on His throne, the Self of man. He then sees and gives His orders. Then the mind immediately acts on the organs, and the organs on the external body. The real Perceiver, the real Ruler, the Governor, the Creator, the Manipulator of all this, is the Self of man.

We see, then, that the Self of man is not the body, neither is It thought. It cannot be a compound. Why not? Because everything that is a compound can be seen or imagined. That which we cannot imagine or perceive, which we cannot bind together, is not force or matter, cause or effect, and cannot be a compound. The domain of compounds is only so far as our mental universe, our thought universe extends. Beyond this it does not hold good; it is as far as law reigns, and if there is anything beyond law, it cannot be a compound at all. The Self of man being beyond the law of causation, is not a compound. It is ever free and is the Ruler of everything that is within law. It will never die, because death means going back to the component parts, and that which was never a compound can never die. It is sheer nonsense to say It dies.

We are now treading on finer and finer ground, and some of you, perhaps, will be frightened. We have seen that this Self, being beyond the little universe of matter and force and thought, is a simple; and as a simple It cannot die. That which does not die cannot live. For life and death are the obverse and reverse of the same coin. Life is another name for death, and death for life. One particular mode of manifestation is what we call life; another particular mode of manifestation of the same thing is what we call death. When the wave rises on the top it is life; and when it falls into the hollow it is death. If anything is beyond death, we naturally see it must also be beyond life. I must remind you of the first conclusion that the soul of man is part of the cosmic energy that exists, which is God. We now find that it is beyond life and death. You were never born, and you will never die. What is this birth and death that we see around us? This belongs to the body only, because the soul is omnipresent. "How can that be?" you may ask. "So many people are sitting here, and you say the soul is omnipresent?" What is there, I ask, to limit anything that is beyond law, beyond causation? This glass is limited; it is not omnipresent, because the surrounding matter forces it to take that form, does not allow it to expand. It is conditioned be everything around it, and is, therefore, limited. But that which is beyond law, where there is nothing to act upon it, how can that be limited? It must be omnipresent. You are everywhere in the universe. How is it then that I am born and I am going to die, and all that? That is the talk of ignorance, hallucination of the brain. You were neither born, nor will you die. You have had neither birth, nor will have rebirth, nor life, nor incarnation, nor anything. What do you mean by coming and going? All shallow nonsense. You are everywhere. Then what is this coming and going? It is the hallucination produced by the change of this fine body which you call the mind. That is going on. Just a little speck of cloud passing before the sky. As it moves on and on, it may create the delusion that the sky moves. Sometimes you see a cloud moving before the moon, and you think that the moon is moving. When you are in a train you think the land is flying, or when you are in a boat, you think the water moves. In reality you are neither going nor coming, you are not being born, nor going to be reborn; you are infinite, ever-present, beyond all causation, and ever-free. Such a question is out of place, it is arrant nonsense. How could there be mortality when there was no birth?

One step more we will have to take to come to a logical conclusion. There is no half-way house. You are metaphysicians, and there is no crying quarter. If then we are beyond all law, we must be omniscient, ever-blessed; all knowledge must be in us and all power and blessedness. Certainly. You are the omniscient. Omnipresent being of the universe. But of such beings can there be many? Can there be a hundred thousand millions of omnipresent beings? Certainly not. Then, what becomes of us all? You are only one; there is only one such Self, and that One Self is you. Standing behind this little nature is what we call the Soul. There is only One Being, One Existence, the ever-blessed, the omnipresent, the omniscient, the birthless, deathless. "Through His control the sky expands, through His control the air breathes, through His control the sun shines, and through His control all live. He is the Reality in nature, He is the Soul of your soul, nay, more, you are He, you are one with Him." Wherever there are two, there is fear, there is danger, there is conflict, there is strife. When it is all One, who is there to hate, who is there to struggle with? When it is all He, with whom can you fight? This explains the true nature of life; this explains the true nature of being. This is perfection, and this is God. As long as you see the many, you are under delusion. "In this world of many he who sees the One, in this ever changing world he who sees Him who never changes, as the Soul of his own soul, as his own Self, he is free, he is blessed, he has reached the goal." Therefore know that thou art He; thou art the God of this universe, "Tat Tvam Asi" (That thou art). All these various ideas that I am a man or a woman, or sick or healthy, or strong or weak, or that I hate or I love, or have a little power, are but hallucinations. Away with them! What makes you weak? What makes you fear? You are the One Being in the universe. What frightens you? Stand up then and be free. Know that every thought and word that weakens you in this world is the only evil that exists. Whatever makes men weak and fear is the only evil that should be shunned. What can frighten you? If the suns come down, and the moons crumble into dust, and systems after systems are hurled into annihilation, what is that to you? Stand as a rock; you are indestructible. You are the Self, the God of the universe. Say—"I am Existence Absolute, Bliss Absolute, Knowledge Absolute, I am He," and like a lion breaking its cage, break your chain and be free for ever. What frightens you, what holds you down? Only ignorance and delusion; nothing else can bind you. You are the Pure One, the Ever-blessed.

Silly fools tell you that you are sinners, and you sit down in a corner and weep. It is foolishness, wickedness, downright rascality to say that you are sinners! You are all God. See you not God and call Him man? Therefore, if you dare, stand on that—mould your whole life on that. If a man cuts your throat, do not say no, for you are cutting your own throat. When you help a poor man, do not feel the least pride. That is worship for you, and not the cause of pride. Is not the whole universe you? Where is there any one that is not you? You are the Soul of this universe. You are the sun, moon, and stars, it is you that are shining everywhere. The whole universe is you. Whom are you going to hate or to fight? Know, then, that thou art He, and model your whole life accordingly; and he who knows this and models his life accordingly will no more grovel in darkness.

CHAPTER 14

THE ĀTMAN

(Delivered in America)

Many of you have read Max Müller's celebrated book, *Three Lectures on the Vedanta Philosophy*, and some of you may, perhaps, have read, in German, Professor Deussen's book on the same philosophy. In what is being written and taught in the West about the religious thought of India, one school of Indian thought is principally represented, that which is called Advaitism, the monistic side of Indian religion; and sometimes it is thought that all the teachings of the Vedas are comprised in that one system of philosophy. There are, however, various phases of Indian thought; and, perhaps, this non-dualistic form is in the minority as compared with the other phases. From the most ancient times there have been various sects of thought in India, and as there never was a formulated or recognised church or any body of men to designate the doctrines which should be believed by each school, people were very free to choose their own form, make their own philosophy and establish their own sects. We, therefore, find that from the most ancient times India was full of religious sects. At the present time, I do not know how many hundreds of sects we have in India, and several fresh ones are coming into existence every year. It seems that the religious activity of that nation is simply inexhaustible.

Of these various sects, in the first place, there can be made two main divisions, the orthodox and the unorthodox. Those that believe in the Hindu scriptures, the Vedas, as eternal revelations of truth, are called orthodox, and those that stand on other authorities, rejecting the Vedas, are the heterodox in India. The chief modern unorthodox Hindu sects are the Jains and the Buddhists. Among the orthodox some declare that the scriptures are of much higher authority than reason; others again say that only that portion of the scriptures which is rational should be taken and the rest rejected.

Of the three orthodox divisions, the Sānkhyas, the Naiyāyikas, and the Mimāmsakas, the former two, although they existed as philosophical schools, failed to form any sect. The one sect that now really covers India is that of the later Mimamsakas or the Vedantists. Their philosophy is called Vedantism. All the schools of Hindu philosophy start from the Vedanta or Upanishads, but the monists took the name to themselves as a speciality, because they wanted to base the whole of their theology and philosophy upon the Vedanta and nothing else. In the course of time the Vedanta prevailed, and all the various sects of India that now exist can be referred to one or other of its schools. Yet these schools are not unanimous in their opinions.

We find that there are three principal variations among the Vedantists. On one point they all agree, and that is that they all believe in God. All these Vedantists also believe the Vedas to be the revealed word of God, not exactly in the same sense, perhaps, as the Christians or the Mohammedans believe, but in a very peculiar sense. Their idea is that the Vedas are an expression of the knowledge of God, and as God is eternal, His knowledge is eternally with Him, and so are the Vedas eternal. There is another common ground of belief: that of creation in cycles, that the whole of creation appears and disappears; that it is projected and becomes grosser and grosser, and at the end of an incalculable period of time it becomes finer and finer, when it dissolves and subsides, and then comes a period of rest. Again it begins to appear and goes through the same process. They postulate the existence of a material which they call Akasha, which is something like the ether of the scientists, and a power which they call Prana. About; this Prana they declare that by its vibration the universe is produced. When a cycle ends, all this manifestation of nature becomes finer and finer and dissolves into that Akasha which cannot be seen or felt, yet out of which everything is manufactured. All the forces that we see in nature, such as gravitation, attraction, and repulsion, or as thought, feeling, and nervous motion—all these various forces resolve into that Prana, and the vibration of the Prana ceases. In that state it remains until the beginning of the next cycle. Prana then begins to vibrate, and that vibration acts upon the Akasha, and all these forms are thrown out in regular succession.

The first school I will tell you about is styled the dualistic school. The dualists believe that God, who is the creator of the universe and its ruler, is eternally separate from nature, eternally separate from the human soul. God is eternal; nature is eternal; so are all souls. Nature and the souls become manifested and change, but God remains the same. According to the dualists, again, this God is personal in that He has qualities, not that He has a body. He has human attributes; He is merciful, He is just, He is powerful, He is almighty, He can be approached, He can be prayed to, He can be loved, He loves in return, and so forth. In one word, He is a human God, only infinitely greater than man; He has none of the evil qualities which men have. "He is the repository of an infinite number of blessed qualities"—that is their definition. He cannot create without materials, and nature is the material out of which He creates the whole universe. There are some non-Vedantic dualists, called "Atomists", who believe that nature is nothing but an infinite number of atoms, and God's will, acting upon these atoms, creates. The Vedantists deny the atomic theory; they say it is perfectly illogical. The indivisible atoms are like geometrical points without parts or magnitude; but something without parts or magnitude, if multiplied an infinite number of times, will remain the same. Anything that has no parts will never make something that has parts; any number of zeros added together will not make one single whole number. So, if these atoms are such that they have no parts or magnitude, the creation of the universe is simply impossible out of such atoms. Therefore, according to the Vedantic dualists, there is what they call indiscrete or undifferentiated nature, and out of that God creates the universe. The vast mass of Indian people are dualists. Human nature ordinarily cannot conceive of anything higher. We find that ninety per cent of the population of the earth who believe in any religion are dualists. All the religions of Europe and Western Asia are dualistic; they have to be. The ordinary man cannot think of anything which is not concrete. He naturally likes to cling to that which his intellect can grasp. That is to say, he can only conceive of higher spiritual ideas by bringing them down to his own level. He can only grasp abstract thoughts by making them concrete. This is the religion of the masses all over the world. They believe in a God who is entirely separate from them, a great king, a high, mighty monarch, as it were. At the same time they make Him purer than the monarchs of the earth; they give Him all good qualities and remove the evil qualities from Him. As if it were ever possible for good to exist without evil; as if there could be any conception of light without a conception of darkness!

With all dualistic theories the first difficulty is, how is it possible that under the rule of a just and merciful God, the repository of an infinite number of good qualities, there can be so many evils in this world? This question arose in all dualistic religions, but the Hindus never invented a Satan as an answer to it. The Hindus with one accord laid the blame on man, and it was easy for them to do so. Why? Because, as I have just now told you, they did not believe that souls were created out of nothing We see in this life that we can shape and form our future every one of us, every day, is trying to shape the morrow; today we fix the fate of the morrow; tomorrow we shall fix the fate of the day after, and so on. It is quite logical that this reasoning can be pushed backward too. If by our own deeds we shape our destiny in the future why not apply the same rule to the past? If, in an infinite chain, a certain number of links are alternately repeated then, if one of these groups of links be explained, we can explain the whole chain. So, in this infinite length of time, if we can cut off one portion and explain that portion and understand it, then, if it be true that nature is uniform, the same explanation must apply to the whole chain of time. If it be true that we are working out our own destiny here within this short space of time if it be true that everything must have a cause as we see it now, it must also be true that that which we are now is the effect of the whole of our past; therefore, no other person is necessary to shape the destiny of mankind but man himself. The evils that are in the world are caused by none else but ourselves. We have caused all this evil; and just as we constantly see misery resulting from evil actions, so can we also see that much of the existing misery in the world is the effect of the past wickedness of man. Man alone, therefore, according to this theory, is responsible. God is not to blame. He, the eternally merciful Father, is not to blame at all. "We reap what we sow."

Another peculiar doctrine of the dualists is, that every soul must eventually come to salvation. No one will be left out. Through various vicissitudes, through various sufferings and enjoyments, each one of them will come out in the end. Come out of what? The one common idea of all Hindu sects is that all souls have to get out of this universe. Neither the universe which we see and feel, nor even an imaginary one, can be right, the real one, because both are mixed up with good and evil. According to the dualists, there is beyond this universe a place full of happiness and good only; and when that place is reached, there will be no more necessity of being born and reborn, of living and dying; and this idea is very dear to them. No more disease there, and no more death. There will be eternal happiness, and they will be in the presence of God for all time and enjoy Him for ever. They believe that all beings, from the lowest worm up to the highest angels and gods, will all, sooner or later, attain to that world where there will be no more misery. But our world will never end; it goes on infinitely, although moving in waves. Although moving in cycles it never ends. The number of souls that are to be saved, that are to be perfected, is infinite. Some are in plants, some are in the lower animals, some are in men, some are in gods, but all of them, even the highest gods, are imperfect, are in bondage. What is the bondage? The necessity of being born and the necessity of dying. Even the highest gods die. What are these gods? They mean certain states, certain offices. For instance, Indra the king of gods, means a certain office; some soul which was very high has gone to fill that post in this cycle, and after this cycle he will be born again as man and come down to this earth, and the man who is very good in this cycle will go and fill that post in the next cycle. So with all these gods; they are certain offices which have been filled alternately by millions and millions of souls, who, after filling those offices, came down and became men. Those who do good works in this world and help others, but with an eye to reward, hoping to reach heaven or to get the praise of their fellow-men, must when they die, reap the benefit of those good works—they become these gods. But that is not salvation; salvation never will come through hope of reward. Whatever man desires the Lord gives him. Men desire power, they desire prestige, they desire enjoyments as gods, and they get these desires fulfilled, but no effect of work can be eternal. The effect will be exhausted after a certain length of time; it may be aeons, but after that it will be gone, and these gods must come down again and become men and get another chance for liberation. The lower animals will come up and become men, become gods, perhaps, then become men again, or go back to animals, until the time when they will get rid of all desire for enjoyment, the thirst for life, this clinging on to the "me and mine". This "me and mine" is the very root of all the evil in the world. If you ask a dualist, "Is your child yours?" he will say, "It is God's. My property is not mine, it is God's." Everything should be held as God's.

Now, these dualistic sects in India are great vegetarians, great preachers of non-killing of animals. But their idea about it is quite different from that of the Buddhist. If you ask a Buddhist, "Why do you preach against killing any animal?" he will answer, "We have no right to take any life;" and if you ask a dualist, "Why do you not kill any animal?" he says, "Because it is the Lord's." So the dualist says that this "me and mine" is to be applied to God and God alone; He is the only "me" and everything is His. When a man has come to the state when he has no "me and mine," when everything is given up to the Lord, when he loves everybody and is ready even to give up his life for an animal, without any desire for reward, then his heart will be purified, and when the heart has been purified, into that heart will come the love of God. God is the centre of attraction for every soul, and the dualist says, "A needle covered up with clay will not be attracted by a magnet, but as soon as the clay is washed off, it will be attracted." God is the magnet and human soul is the needle, and its evil works, the dirt and dust that cover it. As soon as the soul is pure it will by natural attraction come to God and remain with Him for ever, but remain eternally separate. The perfected soul, if it wishes, can take any form; it is able to take a hundred bodies, if it wishes or have none at all, if it so desires. It becomes almost almighty, except that it cannot create; that power belongs to God alone. None, however perfect, can manage the affairs of the universe; that function belongs to God. But all souls, when they become perfect, become happy for ever and live eternally with God. This is the dualistic statement.

One other idea the dualists preach. They protest against the idea of praying to God, "Lord, give me this and give me that." They think that should not be done. If a man must ask some material gift, he should ask inferior beings for it; ask one of these gods, or angels or a perfected being for temporal things. God is only to be loved. It is almost a blasphemy to pray to God, "Lord, give me this, and give me that." According to the dualists, therefore, what a man wants, he will get sooner or later, by praying to one of the gods; but if he wants salvation, he must worship God. This is the religion of the masses of India.

The real Vedanta philosophy begins with those known as the qualified non-dualists. They make the statement that the effect is never different from the cause; the effect is but the cause reproduced in another form. If the universe is the effect and God the cause, it must be God Himself—it cannot be anything but that. They start with the assertion that God is both the efficient and the material cause of the universe; that He Himself is the creator, and He Himself is the material out of which the whole of nature is projected. The word "creation" in your language has no equivalent in Sanskrit, because there is no sect in India which believes in creation, as it is regarded in the West, as something coming out of nothing. It seems that at one time there were a few that had some such idea, but they were very quickly silenced. At the present time I do not know of any sect that believes this. What we mean by creation is projection of that which already existed. Now, the whole universe, according to this sect, is God Himself. He is the material of the universe. We read in the Vedas, "As the Urnanābhi (spider) spins the thread out of its own body, . . . even so the whole universe has come out of the Being."

If the effect is the cause reproduced, the question is: "How is it that we find this material, dull, unintelligent universe produced from a God, who is not material, but who is eternal intelligence? How, if the cause is pure and perfect, can the effect be quite different?" What do these qualified non-dualists say? Theirs is a very peculiar theory. They say that these three existences, God, nature, and the soul, are one. God is, as it were, the Soul, and nature and souls are the body of God. Just as I have a body and I have a soul, so the whole universe and all souls are the body of God, and God is the Soul of souls. Thus, God is the material cause of the universe. The body may be changed—may be young or old, strong or weak—but that does not affect the soul at all. It is the same eternal existence, manifesting through the body. Bodies come and go, but the soul does not change. Even so the whole universe is the body of God, and in that sense it is God. But the change in the universe does not affect God. Out of this material He creates the universe, and at the end of a cycle His body becomes finer, it contracts; at the beginning of another cycle it becomes expanded again, and out of it evolve all these different worlds.

Now both the dualists and the qualified non-dualists admit that the soul is by its nature pure, but through its own deeds it becomes impure. The qualified non-dualists express it more beautifully than the dualists, by saving that the soul's purity and perfection become contracted and again become manifest, and what we are now trying to do is to remanifest the intelligence, the purity, the power which is natural to the soul. Souls have a multitude of qualities, but not that of almightiness or all-knowingness. Every wicked deed contracts the nature of the soul, and every good deed expands it, and these souls, are all parts of God. "As from a blazing fire fly millions of sparks of the same nature, even so from this Infinite Being, God, these souls have come." Each has the same goal. The God of the qualified non-dualists is also a Personal God, the repository of an infinite number of blessed qualities, only He is interpenetrating everything in the universe. He is immanent in everything and everywhere; and when the scriptures say that God is everything, it means that God is interpenetrating everything, not that God has become the wall, but that God is in the wall. There is not a particle, not an atom in the universe where He is not. Souls are all limited; they are not omnipresent. When they get expansion of their powers and become perfect, there is no more birth and death for them; they live with God for ever.

Now we come to Advaitism, the last and, what we think, the fairest flower of philosophy and religion that any country in any age has produced, where human thought attains its highest expression and even goes beyond the mystery which seems to be impenetrable. This is the non-dualistic Vedantism. It is too abstruse, too elevated to be the religion of the masses. Even in India, its birthplace, where it has been ruling supreme for the last three thousand years, it has not been able to permeate the masses. As we go on we shall find that it is difficult for even the most thoughtful man and woman in any country to understand Advaitism. We have made ourselves so weak; we have made ourselves so low. We may make great claims, but naturally we want to lean on somebody else. We are like little, weak plants, always wanting a support. How many times I have been asked for a "comfortable religion!" Very few men ask for the truth, fewer still dare to learn the truth, and fewest of all dare to follow it in all its practical bearings. It is not their fault; it is all weakness of the brain. Any new thought, especially of a high kind, creates a disturbance, tries to make a new channel, as it were, in the brain matter, and that unhinges the system, throws men off their balance. They are used to certain surroundings, and have to overcome a huge mass of ancient superstitions, ancestral superstition, class superstition, city superstition, country superstition, and behind all, the vast mass of superstition that is innate in every human being. Yet there are a few brave souls in the world who dare to conceive the truth, who dare to take it up, and who dare to follow it to the end.

What does the Advaitist declare? He says, if there is a God, that God must be both the material and the efficient cause of the universe. Not only is He the creator, but He is also the created. He Himself is this universe. How can that be? God, the pure, the spirit, has become the universe? Yes; apparently so. That which all ignorant people see as the universe does not really exist. What are you and I and all these things we see? Mere self-hypnotism; there is but one Existence, the Infinite, the Ever-blessed One. In that Existence we dream all these various dreams. It is the Ātman, beyond all, the Infinite, beyond the known, beyond the knowable; in and through That we see the universe. It is the only Reality. It is this table; It is the audience before me; It is the wall; It is everything, minus the name and form. Take away the form of the table, take away the name; what remains is It. The Vedantist does not call It either He or She—these are fictions, delusions of the human brain—there is no sex in the soul. People who are under illusion, who have become like animals, see a woman or a man; living gods do not see men or women. How can they who are beyond everything have any sex idea? Everyone and everything is the Ātman—the Self—the sexless, the pure, the ever-blessed. It is the name, the form, the body, which are material, and they make all this difference. If you take away these two differences of name and form, the whole universe is one; there are no two, but one everywhere. You and I are one. There is neither nature, nor God, nor the universe, only that one Infinite Existence, out of which, through name and form, all these are manufactured. How to know the Knower? It cannot be known. How can you see your own Self? You can only reflect yourself. So all this universe is the reflection of that One Eternal Being, the Ātman, and as the reflection falls upon good or bad reflectors, so good or bad images are cast up. Thus in the murderer, the reflector is bad and not the Self. In the saint the reflector is pure. The Self—the Ātman—is by Its own nature pure. It is the same, the one Existence of the universe that is reflecting Itself from the lowest worm to the highest and most perfect being. The whole of this universe is one Unity, one Existence, physically, mentally, morally and spiritually. We are looking upon this one Existence in different forms and creating all these images upon It. To the being who has limited himself to the condition of man, It appears as the world of man. To the being who is on a higher plane of existence, It may seem like heaven. There is but one Soul in the universe, not two. It neither comes nor goes. It is neither born, nor dies, nor reincarnates. How can It die? Where can It go? All these heavens, all these earths, and all these places are vain imaginations of the mind. They do not exist, never existed in the past, and never will exist in the future.

I am omnipresent, eternal. Where can I go? Where am I not already? I am reading this book of nature. Page after page I am finishing and turning over, and one dream of life after another goes Away. Another page of life is turned over; another dream of life comes, and it goes away, rolling and rolling, and when I have finished my reading, I let it go and stand aside, I throw away the book, and the whole thing is finished. What does the Advaitist preach? He dethrones all the gods that ever existed, or ever will exist in the universe and places on that throne the Self of man, the Ātman, higher than the sun and the moon, higher than the heavens, greater than this great universe itself. No books, no scriptures, no science can ever imagine the glory of the Self that appears as man, the most glorious God that ever was, the only God that ever existed, exists, or ever will exist. I am to worship, therefore, none but myself. "I worship my Self," says the Advaitist. To whom shall I bow down? I salute my Self. To whom shall I go for help? Who can help me, the Infinite Being of the universe? These are foolish dreams, hallucinations; who ever helped any one? None. Wherever you see a weak man, a dualist, weeping and wailing for help from somewhere above the skies, it is because he does not know that the skies also are in him. He wants help from the skies, and the help comes. We see that it comes; but it comes from within himself, and he mistakes it as coming from without. Sometimes a sick man lying on his bed may hear a tap on the door. He gets up and opens it and finds no one there. He goes back to bed, and again he hears a tap. He gets up and opens the door. Nobody is there. At last he finds that it was his own heartbeat which he fancied was a knock at the door. Thus man, after this vain search after various gods outside himself, completes the circle, and comes back to the point from which he started—the human soul, and he finds that the God whom he was searching in hill and dale, whom he was seeking in every brook, in every temple, in churches and heavens, that God whom he was even imagining as sitting in heaven and ruling the world, is his own Self. I am He, and He is I. None but I was God, and this little I never existed.

Yet, how could that perfect God have been deluded?

He never was. How could a perfect God have been dreaming? He never dreamed. Truth never dreams. The very question as to whence this illusion arose is absurd. Illusion arises from illusion alone. There will be no illusion as soon as the truth is seen. Illusion always rests upon illusion; it never rests upon God, the Truth, the Ātman. You are never in illusion; it is illusion that is in you, before you. A cloud is here; another comes and pushes it aside and takes its place. Still another comes and pushes that one away. As before the eternal blue sky, clouds of various hue and colour come, remain for a short time and disappear, leaving it the same eternal blue, even so are you, eternally pure, eternally perfect. You are the veritable Gods of the universe; nay, there are not two—there is but One. It is a mistake to say, "you and I"; say "I". It is I who am eating in millions of mouths; how can I be hungry? It is I who am working through an infinite number of hands; how can I be inactive? It is I who am living the life of the whole universe; where is death for me? I am beyond all life, beyond all death. Where shall I seek for freedom? I am free by my nature. Who can bind me—the God of this universe? The scriptures of the world are but little maps, wanting to delineate my glory, who am the only existence of the universe. Then what are these books to me? Thus says the Advaitist.

"Know the truth and be free in a moment." All the darkness will then vanish. When man has seen himself as one with the Infinite Being of the universe, when all separateness has ceased, when all men and women, an gods and angels, all animals and plants, and the whole universe have melted into that Oneness, then all fear disappears. Can I hurt myself? Can I kill myself? Can I injure myself? Whom to fear? Can you fear yourself? Then will all sorrow disappear. What can cause me sorrow? I am the One Existence of the universe. Then all jealousies will disappear; of whom to be jealous? Of myself? Then all bad feelings disappear. Against whom can I have bad feeling? Against myself? There is none in the universe but I. And this is the one way, says the Vedantist, to Knowledge. Kill out this differentiation, kill out this superstition that there are many. "He who in this world of many sees that One, he who in this mass of insentiency sees that one Sentient Being, he who in this world of shadows catches that Reality, unto him belongs eternal peace, unto none else, unto none else."

These are the salient points of the three steps which Indian religious thought has taken in regard to God. We have seen that it began with the Personal, the extra-cosmic God. It went from the external to the internal cosmic body, God immanent in the universe, and ended in identifying the soul itself with that God, and making one Soul, a unit of all these various manifestations in the universe. This is the last word of the Vedas. It begins with dualism, goes through a qualified monism and ends in perfect monism. We know how very few in this world can come to the last, or even dare believe in it, and fewer still dare act according to it. Yet we know that therein lies the explanation of all ethics, of all morality and all spirituality in the universe. Why is it that every one says, "Do good to others?"

Where is the explanation? Why is it that all great men have preached the brotherhood of mankind, and greater men the brotherhood of all lives? Because whether they were conscious of it or not, behind all that, through all their irrational and personal superstitions, was peering forth the eternal light of the Self denying all manifoldness, and asserting that the whole universe is but one.

Again, the last word gave us one universe, which through the senses we see as matter, through the intellect as souls, and through the spirit as God. To the man who throws upon himself veils, which the world calls wickedness and evil, this very universe will change and become a hideous place; to another man, who wants enjoyments, this very universe will change its appearance and become a heaven, and to the perfect man the whole thing will vanish and become his own Self.

Now, as society exists at the present time, all these three stages are necessary; the one does not deny the other, one is simply the fulfilment of the other. The Advaitist or the qualified Advaitist does not say that dualism is wrong; it is a right view, but a lower one. It is on the way to truth; therefore let everybody work out his own vision of this universe, according to his own ideas. Injure none, deny the position of none; take man where he stands and, if you can, lend him a helping hand and put him on a higher platform, but do not injure and do not destroy. All will come to truth in the long run. "When all the desires of the heart will be vanquished, then this very mortal will become immortal"—then the very man will become God.

CHAPTER 15

THE ĀTMAN: ITS BONDAGE AND FREEDOM

(Delivered in America)

According to the Advaita philosophy, there is only one thing real in the universe, which it calls Brahman; everything else is unreal, manifested and manufactured out of Brahman by the power of Maya. To reach back to that Brahman is our goal. We are, each one of us, that Brahman, that Reality, plus this Maya. If we can get rid of this Maya or ignorance, then we become what we really are. According to this philosophy, each man consists of three parts—the body, the internal organ or the mind, and behind that, what is called the Ātman, the Self. The body is the external coating and the mind is the internal coating of the Ātman who is the real perceiver, the real enjoyer, the being in the body who is working the body by means of the internal organ or the mind.

The Ātman is the only existence in the human body which is immaterial. Because it is immaterial, it cannot be a compound, and because it is not a compound, it does not obey the law of cause and effect, and so it is immortal. That which is immortal can have no beginning because everything with a beginning must have an end. It also follows that it must be formless; there cannot be any fond without matter. Everything that has form must have a beginning and an end. We have none of us seen a form which had not a beginning and will not have an end. A form comes out of a combination of force and matter. This chair has a peculiar form, that is to say a certain quantity of matter is acted upon by a certain amount of force and made to assume a particular shape. The shape is the result of a combination of matter and force. The combination cannot be eternal; there must come to every combination a time when it will dissolve. So all forms have a beginning and an end. We know our body will perish; it had a beginning and it will have an end. But the Self having no form, cannot be bound by the law of beginning and end. It is existing from infinite time; just as time is eternal, so is the Self of man eternal. Secondly, it must be all-pervading. It is only form that is conditioned and limited by space; that which is formless cannot be confined in space. So, according to Advaita Vedanta, the Self, the Ātman, in you, in me, in every one, is omnipresent. You are as much in the sun now as in this earth, as much in England as in America. But the

Self acts through the mind and the body, and where they are, its action is visible.

Each work we do, each thought we think, produces an impression, called in Sanskrit Samskāra, upon the mind and the sum total of these impressions becomes the tremendous force which is called "character". The character of a man is what he has created for himself; it is the result of the mental and physical actions that he has done in his life. The sum total of the Samskaras is the force which gives a man the next direction after death. A man dies; the body falls away and goes back to the elements; but the Samskaras remain, adhering to the mind which, being made of fine material, does not dissolve, because the finer the material, the more persistent it is. But the mind also dissolves in the long run, and that is what we are struggling for. In this connection, the best illustration that comes to my mind is that of the whirlwind. Different currents of air coming from different directions meet and at the meeting-point become united and go on rotating; as they rotate, they form a body of dust, drawing in bits of paper, straw, etc., at one place, only to drop them and go on to another, and so go on rotating, raising and forming bodies out of the materials which are before them. Even so the forces, called Prana in Sanskrit, come together and form the body and the mind out of matter, and move on until the body falls down, when they raise other materials to make another body, and when this falls, another rises, and thus the process goes on. Force cannot travel without matter. So when the body falls down, the mind-stuff remains, Prana in the form of Samskaras acting on it; and then it goes on to another point, raises up another whirl from fresh materials, and begins another motion; and so it travels from place to place until the force is all spent; and then it falls down, ended. So when the mind will end, be broken to pieces entirely, without leaving any Samskara, we shall be entirely free, and until that time we are in bondage; until then the Ātman is covered by the whirl of the mind, and imagines it is being taken from place to place. When the whirl falls down, the Ātman finds that It is all-pervading. It can go where It likes, is entirely free, and is able to manufacture any number of minds or bodies It likes; but until then It can go only with the whirl. This freedom is the goal towards which we are all moving.

Suppose there is a ball in this room, and we each have a mallet in our hands and begin to strike the ball, giving it hundreds of blows, driving it from point to point, until at last it flies out of the room. With what force and in what direction will it go out? These will be determined by the forces that have been acting upon it all through the room. All the different blows that have been given will have their effects. Each one of our actions, mental and physical, is such a blow. The human mind is a ball which is being hit. We are being hit about this room of the world all the time, and our passage out of it is determined by the force of all these blows. In each case, the speed and direction of the ball is determined by the hits it has received; so all our actions in this world will determine our future birth. Our present birth, therefore, is the result of our past. This is one case: suppose I give you an endless chain, in which there is a black link and a white link alternately, without beginning and without end, and suppose I ask you the nature of the chain. At first you will find a difficulty in determining its nature, the chain being infinite at both ends, but slowly you find out it is a chain. You soon discover that this infinite chain is a repetition of the two links, black and white, and these multiplied infinitely become a whole chain. If you know the nature of one of these links, you know the nature of the whole chain, because it is a perfect repetition. All our lives, past, present, and future, form, as it were, an infinite chain, without beginning and without end, each link of which is one life, with two ends, birth and death. What we are and do here is being repeated again and again, with but little variation. So if we know these two links, we shall know all the passages we shall have to pass through in this world. We see, therefore, that our passage into this world has been exactly determined by our previous passages. Similarly we are in this world by our own actions. Just as we go out with the sum total of our present actions upon us, so we see that we come into it with the sum total of our past actions upon us; that which takes us out is the very same thing that brings us in. What brings us in? Our past deeds. What takes us out? Our own deeds *here*, and so on and on we go. Like the caterpillar that takes the thread from its own mouth and builds its cocoon and at last finds itself caught inside the cocoon, we have bound ourselves by our own actions, we have thrown the network of our actions around ourselves. We have set the law of causation in motion, and we find it hard to get ourselves out of it. We have set the wheel in motion, and we are being crushed under it. So this philosophy teaches us that we are uniformly being bound by our own actions, good or bad.

The Ātman never comes nor goes, is never born nor dies. It is nature moving before the Ātman, and the reflection of this motion is on the Ātman; and the Ātman ignorantly thinks it is moving, and not nature. When the Ātman thinks that, it is in bondage; but when it comes to find it never moves, that it is omnipresent, then freedom comes. The Ātman in bondage is called Jiva. Thus you see that when it is said that the Ātman comes and goes, it is said only for facility of understanding, just as for convenience in studying astronomy you are asked to suppose that the sun moves round the earth, though such is not the case. So the Jiva, the soul, comes to higher or lower states. This is the well-known law of reincarnation; and this law binds all creation.

People in this country think it too horrible that man should come up from an animal. Why? What will be the end of these millions of animals? Are they nothing? If we have a soul, so have they, and if they have none, neither have we. It is absurd to say that man alone has a soul, and the animals none. I have seen men worse than animals.

The human soul has sojourned in lower and higher forms, migrating from one to another, according to the Samskaras or impressions, but it is only in the highest form as man that it attains to freedom. The man form is higher than even the angel form, and of all forms it is the highest; man is the highest being in creation, because he attains to freedom.

All this universe was in Brahman, and it was, as it were, projected out of Him, and has been moving on to go back to the source from which it was projected, like the electricity which comes out of the dynamo, completes the circuit, and returns to it. The same is the case with the soul. Projected from Brahman, it passed through all sorts of vegetable and animal forms, and at last it is in man, and man is the nearest approach to Brahman. To go back to Brahman from which we have been projected is the great struggle of life. Whether people know it or not does not matter. In the universe, whatever we see of motion, of struggles in minerals or plants or animals is an effort to come back to the centre and be at rest. There was an equilibrium, and that has been destroyed; and all parts and atoms and molecules are struggling to find their lost equilibrium again. In this struggle they are combining and re-forming, giving rise to all the wonderful phenomena of nature. All struggles and competitions in animal life, plant life, and everywhere else, all social struggles and wars are but expressions of that eternal struggle to get back to that equilibrium.

The going from birth to death, this travelling, is what is called Samsara in Sanskrit, the round of birth and death literally. All creation, passing through this round, will sooner or later become free. The question may be raised that if we all shall come to freedom, why should we *struggle* to attain it? If every one is going to be free, we will sit down and wait. It is true that every being will become free, sooner or later; no one can be lost. Nothing can come to destruction; everything must come up. If that is so, what is the use of our struggling? In the first place, the struggle is the only means that will bring us to the centre, and in the second place, we do not know why we struggle. We have to. "Of thousands of men some are awakened to the idea that they will become free." The vast masses of mankind are content with material things, but there are some who awake, and want to get back, who have had enough of this playing, down here. These struggle consciously, while the rest do it unconsciously.

The alpha and omega of Vedanta philosophy is to "give up the world," giving up the unreal and taking the real. Those who are enamoured of the world may ask, "Why should we attempt to get out of it, to go back to the centre? Suppose we have all come from God, but we find this world is pleasurable and nice; then why should we not rather try to get more and more of the world? Why should we try to get out of it?" They say, look at the wonderful improvements going on in the world every day, how much luxury is being manufactured for it. This is very enjoyable. Why should we go away, and strive for something which is not this? The answer is that the world is certain to die, to be broken into pieces and that many times we have had the same enjoyments. All the forms which we are seeing now have been manifested again and again, and the world in which we live has been here many times before. I have been here and talked to you many times before. You will know that it must be so, and the very words that you have been listening to now, you have heard many times before. And many times more it will be the same. Souls were never different, the bodies have been constantly dissolving and recurring. Secondly, these things periodically occur. Suppose here are three or four dice, and when we throw them, one comes up five, another four, another three, and another two. If you keep on throwing, there must come times when those very same numbers will recur. Go on throwing, and no matter how long may be the interval, those numbers must come again. It cannot be asserted in how many throws they will come again; this is the law of chance. So with souls and their associations. However distant may be the periods, the same combinations and dissolutions will happen again and again. The same birth, eating and drinking, and then death, come round again and again. Some never find anything higher than the enjoyments of the world, but those who want to soar higher find that these enjoyments are never final, are only by the way.

Every form, let us say, beginning from the little worm and ending in man, is like one of the cars of the Chicago Ferris Wheel which is in motion all the time, but the occupants change. A man goes into a car, moves with the wheel, and comes out. The wheel goes on and on. A soul enters one form, resides in it for a time, then leaves it and goes into another and quits that again for a third. Thus the round goes on till it comes out of the wheel and becomes free.

Astonishing powers of reading the past and the future of a man's life have been known in every country and every age. The explanation is that so long as the Ātman is within the realm of causation—though its inherent freedom is not entirely lost and can assert itself, even to the extent of taking the soul out of the causal chain, as it does in the case of men who become free—its actions are greatly influenced by the causal law and thus make it possible for men, possessed with the insight to trace the sequence of effects, to tell the past and the future.

So long as there is desire or want, it is a sure sign that there is imperfection. A perfect, free being cannot have any desire. God cannot want anything. If He desires, He cannot be God. He will be imperfect. So all the talk about God desiring this and that, and becoming angry and pleased by turns is babies' talk, but means nothing. Therefore it has been taught by all teachers, "Desire nothing, give up all desires and be perfectly satisfied."

A child comes into the world crawling and without teeth, and the old man gets out without teeth and crawling. The extremes are alike, but the one has no experience of the life before him, while the other has gone through it all. When the vibrations of ether are very low, we do not see light, it is darkness; when very high, the result is also darkness. The extremes generally appear to be the same, though one is as distant from the other as the poles. The wall has no desires, so neither has the perfect man. But the wall is not sentient enough to desire, while for the perfect man there is nothing to desire. There are idiots who have no desires in this world, because their brain is imperfect. At the same time, the highest state is when we have no desires, but the two are opposite poles of the same existence. One is near the animal, and the other near to God.

CHAPTER 16

THE REAL AND THE APPARENT MAN

(Delivered in New York)

Here we stand, and our eyes look forward sometimes miles ahead. Man has been doing that since he began to think. He is always looking forward, looking ahead. He wants to know where he goes even after the dissolution of his body. Various theories have been propounded, system after system has been brought forward to suggest explanations. Some have been rejected, while others have been accepted, and thus it will go on, so long as man is here, so long as man thinks. There is some truth in each of these systems. There is a good deal of what is not truth in all of them. I shall try to place before you the sum and substance, the result, of the inquiries in this line that have been made in India. I shall try to harmonise the various thoughts on the subject, as they have come up from time to time among Indian philosophers. I shall try to harmonise the psychologists and the metaphysicians, and, if possible, I shall harmonise them with modern scientific thinkers also.

The one theme of the Vedanta philosophy is the search after unity. The Hindu mind does not care for the particular; it is always after the general, nay, the universal. "What is that, by knowing which everything else is to be known?" That is the one theme. "As through the knowledge of one lump of clay all that is of clay is known, so, what is that, by knowing which this whole universe itself will be known?" That is the one search. The whole of this universe, according to the Hindu philosophers, can be resolved into one material, which they call Akasha. Everything that we see around us, feel, touch, taste, is simply a differentiated manifestation of this Akasha. It is all-pervading, fine. All that we call solids, liquids, or gases, figures, forms, or bodies, the earth, sun, moon, and stars—everything is composed of this Akasha.

What force is it which acts upon this Akasha and manufactures this universe out of it? Along with Akasha exists universal power; all that is power in the universe, manifesting as force or attraction—nay, even as thought—is but a different manifestation of that one power which the Hindus call Prana. This Prana, acting on Akasha, is creating the whole of this universe. In the beginning of a cycle, this Prana, as it were, sleeps in the infinite ocean of Akasha. It existed motionless in the beginning. Then arises motion in this ocean of Akasha by the action of this Prana, and as this Prana begins to move, to vibrate, out of this ocean come the various celestial systems, suns, moons, stars, earth, human beings, animals, plants, and the manifestations of all the various forces and phenomena. Every manifestation of power, therefore, according to them, is this Prana. Every material manifestation is Akasha. When this cycle will end, all that we call solid will melt away into the next form, the next finer or the liquid form; that will melt into the gaseous, and that into finer and more uniform heat vibrations, and all will melt back into the original Akasha, and what we now call attraction, repulsion, and motion, will slowly resolve into the original Prana. Then this Prana is said to sleep for a period, again to emerge and to throw out all those forms; and when this period will end, the whole thing will subside again. Thus this process of creation is going down, and coming up, oscillating backwards and forwards. In the language of modern science, it is becoming static during one period, and during another period it is becoming dynamic. At one time it becomes potential, and at the next period it becomes active. This alteration has gone on through eternity.

Yet, this analysis is only partial. This much has been known even to modern physical science. Beyond that, the research of physical science cannot reach. But the inquiry does not stop in consequence. We have not yet found that one, by knowing which everything else will be known. We have resolved the whole universe into two components, into what are called matter and energy, or what the ancient philosophers of India called Akasha and Prana. The next step is to resolve this Akasha and the Prana into their origin. Both can be resolved into the still higher entity which is called mind. It is out of mind, the Mahat, the universally existing thought-power, that these two have been produced. Thought is a still finer manifestation of being than either Akasha or Prana. It is thought that splits itself into these two. The universal thought existed in the beginning, and that manifested, changed, evolved itself into these two Akasha and Prana: and by the combination of these two the whole universe has been produced.

We next come to psychology. I am looking at you. The external sensations are brought to me by the eyes; they are carried by the sensory nerves to the brain. The eyes are not the organs of vision. They are but the external instruments, because if the real organ behind, that which carries the sensation to the brain, is destroyed, I may have twenty eyes, yet I cannot see you. The picture on the retina may be as complete as possible, yet I shall not see you. Therefore, the organ is different from its instruments; behind the instruments, the eyes, there must be the organ So it is with all the sensations. The nose is not the sense of smell; it is but the instrument, and behind it is the organ. With every sense we have, there is first the external instrument in the physical body; behind that in the same physical body, there is the organ; yet these are not sufficient. Suppose I am talking to you, and you are listening to me with close attention. Something happens, say, a bell rings; you will not, perhaps, hear the bell ring. The pulsations of that sound came to your ear, struck the tympanum, the impression was carried by the nerve into the brain; if the whole process was complete up to carrying the impulse to the brain, why did you not hear? Something else was wanting—the mind was not attached to the organ. When the mind detaches itself from the organ, the organ may bring any news to it, but the mind will not receive it. When it attaches itself to the organ, then alone is it possible for the mind to receive the news. Yet, even that does not complete the whole. The instruments may bring the sensation from outside, the organs may carry it inside, the mind may attach itself to the organ, and yet the perception may not be complete. One more factor is necessary; there must be a reaction within. With this reaction comes knowledge. That which is outside sends, as it were, the current of news into my brain. My mind takes it up, and presents it to the intellect, which groups it in relation to pre-received impressions and sends a current of reaction, and with that reaction comes perception. Here, then, is the will. The state of mind which reacts is called Buddhi, the intellect. Yet, even this does not complete the whole. One step more is required. Suppose here is a camera and there is a sheet of cloth, and I try to throw a picture on that sheet. What am I to do? I am to guide various rays of light through the camera to fall upon the sheet and become grouped there. Something is necessary to have the picture thrown upon, which does not move. I cannot form a picture upon something which is moving; that something must be stationary, because the rays of light which I throw on it are moving, and these moving rays of light, must be gathered, unified, co-ordinated, and completed upon something which is stationary. Similar is the case with the sensations which these organs of ours are carrying inside and presenting to the mind, and which the mind in its turn is presenting to the intellect. This process will not be complete unless there is something permanent in the background upon which the picture, as it were, may be formed, upon which we may unify all the different impressions. What is it that gives unity to the changing whole of our being? What is it that keeps up the identity of the moving thing moment after moment? What is it upon which all our different impressions are pieced together, upon which the perceptions, as it were, come together, reside, and form a united whole? We have found that to serve this end there must be something, and we also see that that something must be, relatively to the body and mind, motionless. The sheet of cloth upon which the camera throws the picture is, relatively to the rays of light, motionless, else there will be no picture. That is to say, the perceiver must be an individual. This something upon which the mind is painting all these pictures, this something upon which our sensations, carried by the mind and intellect, are placed and grouped and formed into a unity, is what is called the soul of man.

We have seen that it is the universal cosmic mind that splits itself into the Akasha and Prana, and beyond mind we have found the soul in us. In the universe, behind the universal mind, there is a Soul that exists, and it is called God. In the individual it is the soul of man. In this universe, in the cosmos, just as the universal mind becomes evolved into Akasha and Prana, even so, we may find that the Universal Soul Itself becomes evolved as mind. Is it really so with the individual man? Is his mind the creator of his body, and his soul the creator of his mind? That is to say, are his body, his mind, and his soul three different existences or are they three in one or, again, are they different states of existence of the same unit being? We shall gradually try to find an answer to this question. The first step that we have now gained is this: here is this external body, behind this external body are the organs, the mind, the intellect, and behind this is the soul. At the first step, we have found, as it were, that the soul is separate from the body, separate from the mind itself. Opinions in the religious world become divided at this point, and the departure is this. All those religious views which generally pass under the name of dualism hold that this soul is qualified, that it is of various qualities, that all feelings of enjoyment, pleasure, and pain really belong to the soul. The non-dualists deny that the soul has any such qualities; they say it is unqualified.

Let me first take up the dualists, and try to present to you their position with regard to the soul and its destiny; next, the system that contradicts them; and lastly, let us try to find the harmony which non-dualism will bring to us. This soul of man, because it is separate from the mind and body, because it is not composed of Akasha and Prana, must be immortal. Why? What do we mean by mortality? Decomposition. And that is only possible for things that are the result of composition; anything that is made of two or three ingredients must become decomposed. That alone which is not the result of composition can never become decomposed, and, therefore, can never die. It is immortal. It has been existing throughout eternity; it is uncreate. Every item of creation is simply a composition; no one ever saw creation come out of nothing. All that we know of creation is the combination of already existing things into newer forms. That being so, this soul of man, being simple, must have been existing for ever, and it will exist for ever. When this body falls off, the soul lives on. According to the Vedantists, when this body dissolves, the vital forces of the man go back to his mind and the mind becomes dissolved, as it were, into the Prana, and that Prana enters into the soul of man, and the soul of man comes out, clothed, as it were, with what they call the fine body, the mental body, or spiritual body, as you may like to call it. In this body are the Samskaras of the man. What are the Samskaras? This mind is like a lake, and every thought is like a wave upon that lake. Just as in the lake waves rise and then fall down and disappear, so these thought-waves are continually rising in the mind-stuff and then disappearing, but they do not disappear for ever. They become finer and finer, but they are all there, ready to start up at another time when called upon to do so. Memory is simply calling back into waveform some of those thoughts which have gone into that finer state of existence. Thus, everything that we have thought, every action that we have done, is lodged in the mind; it is all there in fine form, and when a man dies, the sum total of these impressions is in the mind, which again works upon a little fine material as a medium. The soul, clothed, as it were, with these impressions and the fine body, passes out, and the destiny of the soul is guided by the resultant of all the different forces represented by the different impressions. According to us, there are three different goals for the soul.

Those that are very spiritual, when they die, follow the solar rays and reach what is called the solar sphere, through which they reach what is called the lunar sphere, and through that they reach what is called the sphere of lightning, and there they meet with another soul who is already blessed, and he guides the new-comer forward to the highest of all spheres, which is called the Brahmaloka, the sphere of Brahmā. There these souls attain to omniscience and omnipotence, become almost as powerful and all-knowing as God Himself; and they reside there for ever, according to the dualists, or, according to the non-dualists, they become one with the Universal at the end of the cycle. The next class of persons, who have been doing good work with selfish motives, are carried by the results of their good works, when they die, to what is called lunar sphere, where there are various heavens, and there they acquire fine bodies, the bodies of gods. They become gods and live there and enjoy the blessing of heaven for a long period; and after that period is finished, the old Karma is again upon them, and so they fall back again to the earth; they come down through the spheres of air and clouds and all these various regions, and, at last, reach the earth through raindrops. There on the earth they attach themselves to some cereal which is eventually eaten by some man who is fit to supply them with material to make a new body. The last class, namely, the wicked, when they die, become ghosts or demons, and live somewhere midway between the lunar sphere and this earth. Some try to disturb mankind, some are friendly; and after living there for some time they also fall back to the earth and become animals. After living for some time in an animal body they get released, and come back, and become men again, and thus get one more chance to work out their salvation. We see, then, that those who have nearly attained to perfection, in whom only very little of impurity remains, go to the Brahmaloka through the rays of the sun; those who were a middling sort of people, who did some good work here with the idea of going to heaven, go to the heavens in the lunar sphere and there obtain god-bodies; but they have again to become men and so have one more chance to become perfect. Those that are very wicked become ghosts and demons, and then they may have to become animals; after that they become men again and get another chance to perfect themselves. This earth is called the Karma-Bhumi, the sphere of Karma. Here alone man makes his good or bad Karma. When a man wants to go to heaven and does good works for that purpose, he becomes as good and does not as such store up any bad Karma. He just enjoys the effects of the good work he did on earth; and when this good Karma is exhausted, there come, upon him the resultant force of all the evil Karma he had previously stored up in life, and that brings him down again to this earth. In the same way, those that become ghosts remain in that state, not giving rise to fresh Karma, but suffer the evil results of their past misdeeds, and later on remain for a time in an animal body without causing any fresh Karma. When that period is finished, they too become men again. The states of reward and punishment due to good and bad Karmas are devoid of the force generating fresh Karmas; they have only to be enjoyed or suffered. If there is an extraordinarily good or an extraordinarily evil Karma, it bears fruit very quickly. For instance, if a man has been doing many evil things all his life, but does one good act, the result of that good act will immediately appear, but when that result has been gone through, all the evil acts must produce their results also. All men who do certain good and great acts, but the general tenor of whose lives has not been correct, will become gods; and after living for some time in god-bodies, enjoying the powers of gods, they will have again to become men; when the power of the good acts is thus finished, the old evil comes up to be worked out. Those who do extraordinarily evil acts have to put on ghost and devil bodies, and when the effect of those evil actions is exhausted, the little good action which remains associated with them, makes them again become men. The way to Brahmaloka, from which there is no more fall or return, is called the Devayāna, i.e. the way to God; the way to heaven is known as Pitriyāna, i.e. the way to the fathers.

Man, therefore, according to the Vedanta philosophy, is the greatest being that is in the universe, and this world of work the best place in it, because only herein is the greatest and the best chance for him to become perfect. Angels or gods, whatever you may call them, have all to become men, if they want to become perfect. This is the great centre, the wonderful poise, and the wonderful opportunity—this human life.

We come next to the other aspect of philosophy. There are Buddhists who deny the whole theory of the soul that I have just now been propounding. "What use is there," says the Buddhist, "to assume something as the substratum, as the background of this body and mind? Why may we not allow thoughts to run on? Why admit a third substance beyond this organism, composed of mind and body, a third substance called the soul? What is its use? Is not this organism sufficient to explain itself? Why take anew a third something?" These arguments are very powerful. This reasoning is very strong. So far as outside research goes, we see that this organism is a sufficient explanation of itself—at least, many of us see it in that light. Why then need there be a soul as substratum, as a something which is neither mind nor body but stands as a background for both mind and body? Let there be only mind and body. Body is the name of a stream of matter continuously changing. Mind is the name of a stream of consciousness or thought continuously changing. What produces the apparent unity between these two? This unity does not really exist, let us say. Take, for instance, a lighted torch, and whirl it rapidly before you. You see a circle of fire. The circle does not really exist, but because the torch is continually moving, it leaves the appearance of a circle. So there is no unity in this life; it is a mass of matter continually rushing down, and the whole of this matter you may call one unity, but no more. So is mind; each thought is separate from every other thought; it is only the rushing current that leaves behind the illusion of unity; there is no need of a third substance. This universal phenomenon of body and mind is all that really is; do not posit something behind it. You will find that this Buddhist thought has been taken up by certain sects and schools in modern times, and all of them claim that it is new—their own invention. This has been the central idea of most of the Buddhistic philosophies, that this world is itself all-sufficient; that you need not ask for any background at all; all that is, is this sense-universe: what is the use of thinking of something as a support to this universe? Everything is the aggregate of qualities; why should there be a hypothetical substance in which they should inhere? The idea of substance comes from the rapid interchange of qualities, not from something unchangeable which exists behind them. We see how wonderful some of these arguments are, and they appeal easily to the ordinary experience of humanity—in fact, not one in a million can think of anything other than phenomena. To the vast majority of men nature appears to be only a changing, whirling, combining, mingling mass of change. Few of us ever have a glimpse of the calm sea behind. For us it is always lashed into waves; this universe appears to us only as a tossing mass of waves. Thus we find these two opinions. One is that there is something behind both body and mind which is an unchangeable and immovable substance; and the other is that there is no such thing as immovability or unchangeability in the universe; it is all change and nothing but change. The solution of this difference comes in the next step of thought, namely, the non-dualistic.

It says that the dualists are right in finding something behind all, as a background which does not change; we cannot conceive change without there being something unchangeable. We can only conceive of anything that is changeable, by knowing something which is less changeable, and this also must appear more changeable in comparison with something else which is less changeable, and so on and on, until we are bound to admit that there must be something which never changes at all. The whole of this manifestation must have been in a state of non-manifestation, calm and silent, being the balance of opposing forces, so to say, when no force operated, because force acts when a disturbance of the equilibrium comes in. The universe is ever hurrying on to return to that state of equilibrium again. If we are certain of any fact whatsoever, we are certain of this. When the dualists claim that there is a something which does not change, they are perfectly right, but their analysis that it is an underlying something which is neither the body nor the mind, a something separate from both, is wrong. So far as the Buddhists say that the whole universe is a mass of change, they are perfectly right; so long as I am separate from the universe, so long as I stand back and look at something before me, so long as there are two things—the looker-on and the thing looked upon—it will appear always that the universe is one of change, continuously changing all the time. But the reality is that there is both change and changelessness in this universe. It is not that the soul and the mind and the body are three separate existences, for this organism made of these three is really one. It is the same thing which appears as the body, as the mind, and as the thing beyond mind and body, but it is not at the same time all these. He who sees the body does not see the mind even, he who sees the mind does not see that which he calls the soul, and he who sees the soul—for him the body and mind have vanished. He who sees only motion never sees absolute calm, and he who sees absolute calm—for him motion has vanished. A rope is taken for a snake. He who sees the rope as the snake, for him the rope has vanished, and when the delusion ceases and he looks at the rope, the snake has vanished.

There is then but one all-comprehending existence, and that one appears as manifold. This Self or Soul or Substance is all that exists in the universe. That Self or Substance or Soul is, in the language of non-dualism, the Brahman appearing to be manifold by the interposition of name and form. Look at the waves in the sea. Not one wave is really different from the sea, but what makes the wave apparently different? Name and form; the form of the wave and the name which we give to it, "wave". This is what makes it different from the sea. When name and form go, it is the same sea. Who can make any real difference between the wave and the sea? So this whole universe is that one Unit Existence; name and form have created all these various differences. As when the sun shines upon millions of globules of water, upon each particle is seen a most perfect representation of the sun, so the one Soul, the one Self, the one Existence of the universe, being reflected on all these numerous globules of varying names and forms, appears to be various. But it is in reality only one. There is no "I" nor "you"; it is all one. It is either all "I" or all "you". This idea of duality, calf two, is entirely false, and the whole universe, as we ordinarily know it, is the result of this false knowledge. When discrimination comes and man finds there are not two but one, he finds that he is himself this universe. "It is I who am this universe as it now exists, a continuous mass of change. It is I who am beyond all changes, beyond all qualities, the eternally perfect, the eternally blessed."

There is, therefore, but one Ātman, one Self, eternally pure, eternally perfect, unchangeable, unchanged; it has never changed; and all these various changes in the universe are but appearances in that one Self.

Upon it name and form have painted all these dreams; it is the form that makes the wave different from the sea. Suppose the wave subsides, will the form remain? No, it will vanish. The existence of the wave was entirely dependent upon the existence of the sea, but the existence of the sea was not at all dependent upon the existence of the wave. The form remains so long as the wave remains, but as soon as the wave leaves it, it vanishes, it cannot remain. This name and form is the outcome of what is called Maya. It is this Maya that is making individuals, making one appear different from another. Yet it has no existence. Maya cannot be said to exist. Form cannot be said to exist, because it depends upon the existence of another thing. It cannot be said as not to exist, seeing that it makes all this difference. According to the Advaita philosophy, then, this Maya or ignorance—or name and form, or, as it has been called in Europe, "time, space, and causality"—is out of this one Infinite Existence showing us the manifoldness of the universe; in substance, this universe is one. So long as any one thinks that there are two ultimate realities, he is mistaken. When he has come to know that there is but one, he is right. This is what is being proved to us every day, on the physical plane, on the mental plane, and also on the spiritual plane. Today it has been demonstrated that you and I, the sun, the moon, and the stars are but the different names of different spots in the same ocean of matter, and that this matter is continuously changing in its configuration. This particle of energy that was in the sun several months ago may be in the human being now; tomorrow it may be in an animal, the day after tomorrow it may be in a plant. It is ever coming and going. It is all one unbroken, infinite mass of matter, only differentiated by names and forms.

One point is called the sun; another, the moon; another, the stars; another, man; another, animal; another, plant; and so on. And all these names are fictitious; they have no reality, because the whole is a continuously changing mass of matter. This very same universe, from another standpoint, is an ocean of thought, where each one of us is a point called a particular mind. You are a mind, I am a mind, everyone is a mind; and the very same universe viewed from the standpoint of knowledge, when the eyes have been cleared of delusions, when the mind has become pure, appears to be the unbroken Absolute Being, the ever pure, the unchangeable, the immortal.

What then becomes of all this threefold eschatology of the dualist, that when a man dies he goes to heaven, or goes to this or that sphere, and that the wicked persons become ghosts, and become animals, and so forth? None comes and none goes, says the non-dualist. How can you come and go? You are infinite; where is the place for you to go? In a certain school a number of little children were being examined. The examiner had foolishly put all sorts of difficult questions to the little children. Among others there was this question: "Why does not the earth fall?" His intention was to bring out the idea of gravitation or some other intricate scientific truth from these children. Most of them could not even understand the question, and so they gave all sorts of wrong answers. But one bright little girl answered it with another question: "Where shall it fall?" The very question of the examiner was nonsense on the face of it. There is no up and down in the universe; the idea is only relative. So it is with regard to the soul; the very question of birth and death in regard to it is utter nonsense. Who goes and who comes? Where are you not? Where is the heaven that you are not in already? Omnipresent is the Self of man. Where is it to go? Where is it not to go? It is everywhere. So all this childish dream and puerile illusion of birth and death, of heavens and higher heavens and lower worlds, all vanish immediately for the perfect. For the nearly perfect it vanishes after showing them the several scenes up to Brahmaloka. It continues for the ignorant.

How is it that the whole world believes in going to heaven, and in dying and being born? I am studying a book, page after page is being read and turned over. Another page comes and is turned over. Who changes? Who comes and goes? Not I, but the book. This whole nature is a book before the soul, chapter after chapter is being read and turned over, and every now and then a scene opens. That is read and turned over. A fresh one comes, but the soul is ever the same—eternal. It is nature that is changing, not the soul of man. This never changes. Birth and death are in nature, not in you. Yet the ignorant are deluded; just as we under delusion think that the sun is moving and not the earth, in exactly the same way we think that we are dying, and not nature. These are all, therefore, hallucinations. Just as it is a hallucination when we think that the fields are moving and not the railway train, exactly in the same manner is the hallucination of birth and death. When men are in a certain frame of mind, they see this very existence as the earth, as the sun, the moon, the stars; and all those who are in the same state of mind see the same things. Between you and me there may be millions of beings on different planes of existence. They will never see us, nor we them; we only see those who are in the same state of mind and on the same plane with us. Those musical instruments respond which have the same attunement of vibration, as it were; if the state of vibration, which they call "man-vibration", should be changed, no longer would men be seen here; the whole "man-universe" would vanish, and instead of that, other scenery would come before us, perhaps gods and the god-universe, or perhaps, for the wicked man, devils and the diabolic world; but all would be only different views of the one universe. It is this universe which, from the human plane, is seen as the earth, the sun, the moon, the stars, and all such things—it is this very universe which, seen from the plane of wickedness, appears as a place of punishment. And this very universe is seen as heaven by those who want to see it as heaven. Those who have been dreaming of going to a God who is sitting on a throne, and of standing there praising Him all their lives, when they die, will simply see a vision of what they have in their minds; this very universe will simply change into a vast heaven, with all sorts of winged beings flying about and a God sitting on a throne. These heavens are all of man's own making. So what the dualist says is true, says the Advaitin, but it is all simply of his own making. These spheres and devils and gods and reincarnations and transmigrations are all mythology; so also is this human life. The great mistake that men always make is to think that this life alone is true. They understand it well enough when other things are called mythologies, but are never willing to admit the same of their own position. The whole thing as it appears is mere mythology, and the greatest of all lies is that we are bodies, which we never were nor even can be. It is the greatest of all lies that we are mere men; we are the God of the universe. In worshipping God we have been always worshipping our own hidden Self. The worst lie that you ever tell yourself is that you were born a sinner or a wicked man. He alone is a sinner who sees a sinner in another man. Suppose there is a baby here, and you place a bag of gold on the table. Suppose a robber comes and takes the gold away. To the baby it is all the same; because there is no robber inside, there is no robber outside. To sinners and vile men, there is vileness outside, but not to good men. So the wicked see this universe as a hell, and the partially good see it as heaven, while the perfect beings realise it as God Himself. Then alone the veil falls from the eyes, and the man, purified and cleansed, finds his whole vision changed. The bad dreams that have been torturing him for millions of years, all vanish, and he who was thinking of himself either as a man, or a god, or a demon, he who was thinking of himself as living in low places, in high places, on earth, in heaven, and so on, finds that he is really omnipresent; that all time is in him, and that he is not in time; that all the heavens are in him, that he is not in any heaven; and that all the gods that man ever worshipped are in him, and that he is not in any one of those gods. He was the manufacturer of gods and demons, of men and plants and animals and stones, and the real nature of man now stands unfolded to him as being higher than heaven, more perfect than this universe of ours, more infinite than infinite time, more omnipresent than the omnipresent ether. Thus alone man becomes fearless, and becomes free. Then all delusions cease, all miseries vanish, all fears come to an end for ever. Birth goes away and with it death; pains fly, and with them fly away pleasures; earths vanish, and with them vanish heavens; bodies vanish, and with them vanishes the mind also. For that man disappears the whole universe, as it were. This searching, moving, continuous struggle of forces stops for ever, and that which was manifesting itself as force and matter, as struggles of nature, as nature itself, as heavens and earths and plants and animals and men and angels, all that becomes transfigured into one infinite, unbreakable, unchangeable existence, and the knowing man finds that he is one with that existence. "Even as clouds of various colours come before the sky, remain there for a second and then vanish away," even so before this soul are all these visions coming, of earths and heavens, of the moon and the gods, of pleasures and pains; but they all pass away leaving the one infinite, blue, unchangeable sky. The sky never changes; it is the clouds that change. It is a mistake to think that the sky is changed. It is a mistake to think that we are impure, that we are limited, that we are separate. The real man is the one Unit Existence.

Two questions now arise. The first is: "Is it possible

to realise this? So far it is doctrine, philosophy, but is it possible to realise it?" It is. There are men still living in this world for whom delusion has vanished for ever. Do they immediately die after such realisation? Not so soon as we should think. Two wheels joined by one pole are running together. If I get hold of one of the wheels and, with an axe, cut the pole asunder, the wheel which I have got hold of stops, but upon the other wheel is its past momentum, so it runs on a little arid then falls down. This pure and perfect being, the soul, is one wheel, and this external hallucination of body and mind is the other wheel, joined together by the pole of work, of Karma. Knowledge is the axe which will sever the bond between the two, and the wheel of the soul will stop—stop thinking that it is coming and going, living and dying, stop thinking that it is nature and has wants and desires, and will find that it is perfect, desireless. But upon the other wheel, that of the body and mind, will be the momentum of past acts; so it will live for some time, until that momentum of past work is exhausted, until that momentum is worked away, and then the body and mind fall, and the soul becomes free. No more is there any going to heaven and coming back, not even any going to the Brahmaloka, or to any of the highest of the spheres, for where is he to come from, or to go to? The man who has in this life attained to this state, for whom, for a minute at least, the ordinary vision of the world has changed and the reality has been apparent, he is called the "Living Free". This is the goal of the Vedantin, to attain freedom while living.

Once in Western India I was travelling in the desert country on the coast of the Indian Ocean. For days and days I used to travel on foot through the desert, but it was to my surprise that I saw every day beautiful lakes, with trees all round them, and the shadows of the trees upside down and vibrating there. "How wonderful it looks and they call this a desert country!" I said to myself. Nearly a month I travelled, seeing these wonderful lakes and trees and plants. One day I was very thirsty and wanted to have a drink of water, so I started to go to one of these clear, beautiful lakes, and as I approached, it vanished. And with a flash it came to my brain, "This is the mirage about which I have read all my life," and with that came also the idea that throughout the whole of this month, every day, I had been seeing the mirage and did not know it. The next morning I began my march. There was again the lake, but with it came also the idea that it was the mirage and not a true lake. So is it with this universe. We are all travelling in this mirage of the world day after day, month after month, year after year, not knowing that it is a mirage. One day it will break up, but it will come back again; the body has to remain under the power of past Karma, and so the mirage will come back. This world will come back upon us so long as we are bound by Karma: men, women, animals, plants, our attachments and duties, all will come back to us, but not with the same power. Under the influence of the new knowledge the strength of Karma will be broken, its poison will be lost. It becomes transformed, for along with it there comes the idea that we know it now, that the sharp distinction between the reality and the mirage has been known.

This world will not then be the same world as before. There is, however, a danger here. We see in every country people taking up this philosophy and saying, "I am beyond all virtue and vice; so I am not bound by any moral laws; I may do anything I like." You may find many fools in this country at the present time, saying, "I am not bound; I am God Himself; let me do anything I like." This is not right, although it is true that the soul is beyond all laws, physical, mental, or moral. Within law is bondage; beyond law is freedom. It is also true that freedom is of the nature of the soul, it is its birthright: that real freedom of the soul shines through veils of matter in the form of the apparent freedom of man. Every moment of your life you feel that you are free. We cannot live, talk, or breathe for a moment without feeling that we are free; but, at the same time, a little thought shows us that we are like machines and not free. What is true then? Is this idea of freedom a delusion? One party holds that the idea of freedom is a delusion; another says that the idea of bondage is a delusion. How does this happen? Man is really free, the real man cannot but be free. It is when he comes into the world of Maya, into name and form, that he becomes bound. Free will is a misnomer. Will can never be free. How can it be? It is only when the real man has become bound that his will comes into existence, and not before. The will of man is bound, but that which is the foundation of that will is eternally free. So, even in the state of bondage which we call human life or god-life, on earth or in heaven, there yet remains to us that recollection of the freedom which is ours by divine right. And consciously or unconsciously we are all struggling towards it. When a man has attained his own freedom, how can he be bound by any law? No law in this universe can bind him, for this universe itself is his.

He is the whole universe. Either say he is the whole universe or say that to him there is no universe. How can he have then all these little ideas about sex and about country? How can he say, I am a man, I am a woman I am a child? Are they not lies? He knows that they are. How can he say that these are man's rights, and these others are woman's rights? Nobody has rights; nobody separately exists. There is neither man nor woman; the soul is sexless, eternally pure. It is a lie to say that I am a man or a woman, or to say that I belong to this country or that. All the world is my country, the whole universe is mine, because I have clothed myself with it as my body. Yet we see that there are people in this world who are ready to assert these doctrines, and at the same time do things which we should call filthy; and if we ask them why they do so, they tell us that it is our delusion and that they can do nothing wrong. What is the test by which they are to be judged? The test is here.

Though evil and good are both conditioned manifestations of the soul, yet evil is the most external coating, and good is the nearer coating of the real man, the Self. And unless a man cuts through the layer of evil he cannot reach the layer of good, and unless he has passed through both the layers of good and evil he cannot reach the Self. He who reaches the Self, what remains attached to him? A little Karma, a little bit of the momentum of past life, but it is all good momentum. Until the bad momentum is entirely worked out and past impurities are entirely burnt, it is impossible for any man to see and realise truth. So, what is left attached to the man who has reached the Self and seen the truth is the remnant of the good impressions of past life, the good momentum. Even if he lives in the body and works incessantly, he works only to do good; his lips speak only benediction to all; his hands do only good works; his mind can only think good thoughts; his presence is a blessing wherever he goes. He is himself a living blessing. Such a man will, by his very presence, change even the most wicked persons into saints. Even if he does not speak, his very presence will be a blessing to mankind. Can such men do any evil; can they do wicked deeds? There is, you must remember, all the difference of pole to pole between realisation and mere talking. Any fool can talk. Even parrots talk. Talking is one thing, and realising is another. Philosophies, and doctrines, and arguments, and books, and theories, and churches, and sects, and all these things are good in their own way; but when that realisation comes, these things drop away. For instance, maps are good, but when you see the country itself, and look again at the maps, what a great difference you find! So those that have realised truth do not require the ratiocinations of logic and all other gymnastics of the intellect to make them understand the truth; it is to them the life of their lives, concretised, made more than tangible. It is, as the sages of the Vedanta say, "even as a fruit in your hand"; you can stand up and say, it is here. So those that have realised the truth will stand up and say, "Here is the Self". You may argue with them by the year, but they will smile at you; they will regard it all as child's prattle; they will let the child prattle on. They have realised the truth and are full. Suppose you have seen a country, and another man comes to you and tries to argue with you that that country never existed, he may go on arguing indefinitely, but your only attitude of mind towards him must be to hold that the man is fit for a lunatic asylum. So the man of realisation says, "All this talk in the world about its little religions is but prattle; realisation is the soul, the very essence of religion." Religion can be realised. Are you ready? Do you want it? You will get the realisation if you do, and then you will be truly religious. Until you have attained realisation there is no difference between you and atheists. The atheists are sincere, but the man who says that he believes in religion and never attempts to realise it is not sincere.

The next question is to know what comes after realisation. Suppose we have realised this oneness of the universe, that we are that one Infinite Being, and suppose we have realised that this Self is the only Existence and that it is the same Self which is manifesting in all these various phenomenal forms, what becomes of us after that? Shall we become inactive, get into a corner and sit down there and die away? "What good will it do to the world?" That old question! In the first place, why should it do good to the world? Is there any reason why it should? What right has any one to ask the question, "What good will it do to the world?" What is meant by that? A baby likes candies. Suppose you are conducting investigations in connection with some subject of electricity and the baby asks you, "Does it buy candies?" "No" you answer. "Then what good will it do?" says the baby. So men stand up and say, "What good will this do to the world; will it give us money?" "No." "Then what good is there in it?" That is what men mean by doing good to the world. Yet religious realisation does all the good to the world. People are afraid that when they attain to it, when they realise that there is but one, the fountains of love will be dried up, that everything in life will go away, and that all they love will vanish for them, as it were, in this life and in the life to come. People never stop to think that those who bestowed the least thought on their own individualities have been the greatest workers in the world. Then alone a man loves when he finds that the object of his love is not any low, little, mortal thing. Then alone a man loves when he finds that the object of his love is not a clod of earth, but it is the veritable God Himself. The wife will love the husband the more when she thinks that the husband is God Himself. The husband will love the wife the more when he knows that the wife is God Himself. That mother will love the children more who thinks that the children are God Himself. That man will love his greatest enemy who knows that that very enemy is God Himself.

That man will love a holy man who knows that the holy man is God Himself, and that very man will also love the unholiest of men because he knows the background of that unholiest of men is even He, the Lord. Such a man becomes a world-mover for whom his little self is dead and God stands in its place. The whole universe will become transfigured to him. That which is painful and miserable will all vanish; struggles will all depart and go. Instead of being a prison-house, where we every day struggle and fight and compete for a morsel of bread, this universe will then be to us a playground. Beautiful will be this universe then! Such a man alone has the right to stand up and say, "How beautiful is this world!" He alone has the right to say that it is all good. This will be the great good to the world resulting from such realisation, that instead of this world going on with all its friction and clashing, if all mankind today realise only a bit of that great truth, the aspect of the whole world will be changed, and, in place of fighting and quarrelling, there would be a reign of peace. This indecent and brutal hurry which forces us to go ahead of every one else will then vanish from the world. With it will vanish all struggle, with it will vanish all hate, with it will vanish all jealousy, and all evil will vanish away for ever. Gods will live then upon this earth. This very earth will then become heaven, and what evil can there be when gods are playing with gods, when gods are working with gods, and gods are loving gods? That is the great utility of divine realisation. Everything that you see in society will be changed and transfigured then. No more will you think of man as evil; and that is the first great gain. No more will you stand up and sneeringly cast a glance at a poor man or woman who has made a mistake. No more, ladies, will you look down with contempt upon the poor woman who walks the street in the night, because you will see even there God Himself. No more will you think of jealousy and punishments. They will all vanish; and love, the great ideal of love, will be so powerful that no whip and cord will be necessary to guide mankind aright.

If one millionth part of the men and women who live in this world simply sit down and for a few minutes say, "You are all God, O ye men and O ye animals and living beings, you are all the manifestations of the one living Deity!" the whole world will be changed in half an hour. Instead of throwing tremendous bomb-shells of hatred into every corner, instead of projecting currents of jealousy and of evil thought, in every country people will think that it is all He. He is all that you see and feel. How can you see evil until there is evil in you? How can you see the thief, unless he is there, sitting in the heart of your heart? How can you see the murderer until you are yourself the murderer? Be good, and evil will vanish for you. The whole universe will thus be changed. This is the greatest gain to society. This is the great gain to the human organism. These thoughts were thought out, worked out amongst individuals in ancient times in India. For various reasons, such as the exclusiveness of the teachers and foreign conquest, those thoughts were not allowed to spread. Yet they are grand truths; and wherever they have been working, man has become divine. My whole life has been changed by the touch of one of these divine men, about whom I am going to speak to you next Sunday; and the time is coming when these thoughts will be cast abroad over the whole world. Instead of living in monasteries, instead of being confined to books of philosophy to be studied only by the learned, instead of being the exclusive possession of sects and of a few of the learned, they will all be sown broadcast over the whole world, so that they may become the common property of the saint and the sinner, of men and women and children, of the learned and of the ignorant. They will then permeate the atmosphere of the world, and the very air that we breathe will say with every one of its pulsations, "Thou art That". And the whole universe with its myriads of suns and moons, through everything that speaks, with one voice will say, "Thou art That".

Bhagavad Gita

PRAKASH

Reprint 2023

PRAKASH
An imprint of Prakash Books India Pvt. Ltd.

113/A, Darya Ganj,
New Delhi-110 002
Email: info@prakashbooks.com/sales@prakashbooks.com

facebook www.facebook.com/fingerprintpublishing
twitter www.twitter.com/FingerprintP
www.fingerprintpublishing.com

ISBN: 978 93 8943 270 1

Processed & printed in India

Contents

Chapter 01

Arjuna Vishada Yoga

1

धृतराष्ट्र उवाच
धर्मक्षेत्रे कुरुक्षेत्रे समवेता युयुत्सवः ।
मामकाः पाण्डवाश्चैव किमकुर्वत सञ्जय ॥

dhṛtarāṣṭra uvāca
dharma-kṣetre kuru-kṣetre
samavetā yuyutsavaḥ
māmakāḥ pāṇḍavāś caiva
kim akurvata sañjaya

Dhritarashtra said –
After assembling at the sacred ground of Kurukshetra and desiring to fight, what did my sons and Pandu's sons do, Sanjaya?

2

सञ्जय उवाच
दृष्ट्वा तु पाण्डवानीकं व्यूढं दुर्योधनस्तदा ।
आचार्यमुपसङ्गम्य राजा वचनमब्रवीत् ॥

sañjaya uvāca
dṛṣṭvā tu pāṇḍavānīkaṁ
vyūḍhaṁ duryodhanas tadā
ācāryam upasaṅgamya
rājā vacanam abravīt

Sanjaya said –

Observing the formidable formation of the Pandava army, Prince Duryodhan turned towards his guru and spoke these words.

3

पश्यैतां पाण्डुपुत्राणामाचार्य महतीं चमूम् ।
व्यूढां द्रुपदपुत्रेण तव शिष्येण धीमता ॥

paśyaitāṁ pāṇḍu-putrāṇām
ācārya mahatīṁ camūm
vyūḍhāṁ drupada-putreṇa
tava śiṣyeṇa dhīmatā

O' Guru, do you see the excellent military arrangement of the Pandava army, led by none other than your very own gifted disciple, the son of Drupada?

4

अत्र शूरा महेष्वासा भीमार्जुनसमा युधि ।
युयुधानो विराटश्च द्रुपदश्च महारथः ॥

atra śūrā maheṣvāsā
bhīmārjuna-samā yudhi
yuyudhāno virāṭaś ca
drupadaś ca mahā-rathaḥ

Their army is powered by heroes like Bhima and Arjuna and mighty warriors that match their skills, namely Yuyudhana, Virata, and Drupada!

5

धृष्टकेतुश्चेकितानः काशिराजश्च वीर्यवान् ।
पुरुजित्कुन्तिभोजश्च शैब्यश्च नरपुङ्गवः ॥

dhṛṣṭaketuś cekitānaḥ
kāśirājaś ca vīryavān
purujit kuntibhojaś ca
śaibyaś ca nara-puṅgavaḥ

And let's not forget powerful fighters like Dhrishtaketu, Chekitana, and Kashiraja while Purujit, Kuntibhoja, and Saibya are heroes too in society.

6

युधामन्युश्च विक्रान्त उत्तमौजाश्च वीर्यवान् ।
सौभद्रो द्रौपदेयाश्च सर्व एव महारथा: ॥

yudhāmanyuś ca vikrānta
uttamaujāś ca vīryavān
saubhadro draupadeyāś ca
sarva eva mahā-rathāḥ

They also have the worthy Yudhamanyu, the mighty Uttamaujas, the son of Subhadra, and sons of Draupadi, all superior fighters.

7

अस्माकं तु विशिष्टा ये तान्निबोध द्विजोत्तम ।
नायका मम सैन्यस्य संज्ञार्थं तान्ब्रवीमि ते ॥

asmākaṁ tu viśiṣṭā ye
tān nibodha dvijottama
nāyakā mama sainyasya
saṁjñārthaṁ tān bravīmi te

Now, also hear about the distinguished heroes and generals qualified to lead my army.

8

भवान्भीष्मश्च कर्णश्च कृपश्च समितिञ्जय: ।
अश्वत्थामा विकर्णश्च सौमदत्तिस्तथैव च ॥

bhavān bhīṣmaś ca karṇaś ca
kṛpaś ca samitiṁ-jayaḥ
aśvatthāmā vikarṇaś ca
saumadattis tathaiva ca

It has personalities who have never lost a battle, like you, Grandfather Bhishma, Karna, Kripa, Ashwathama, Vikarna, and also the son of Somdatta.

9

अन्ये च बहव: शूरा मदर्थे त्यक्तजीविता: ।
नानाशस्त्रप्रहरणा: सर्वे युद्धविशारदा: ॥

anye ca bahavaḥ śūrā
mad-arthe tyakta-jīvitāḥ
nānā-śastra-praharaṇāḥ
sarve yuddha-viśāradāḥ

There are many more in my army who are experienced in military warfare with expertise in using multiple weapons. Moreover, they will not hesitate to sacrifice their lives for me.

10

अपर्याप्तं तदस्माकं बलं भीष्माभिरक्षितम् ।
पर्याप्तं त्विदमेतेषां बलं भीमाभिरक्षितम् ॥

aparyāptaṁ tad asmākaṁ
balaṁ bhīṣmābhirakṣitam
paryāptaṁ tv idam eteṣāṁ
balaṁ bhīmābhirakṣitam

So, clearly, our strength is fathomless as compared to the limited strength of the Pandavas. We are in safe hands under the protection of Grandfather Bhishma unlike the Pandavas who have only Bhima to protect them.

11

अयनेषु च सर्वेषु यथाभागमवस्थिताः ।
भीष्ममेवाभिरक्षन्तु भवन्तः सर्व एव हि ॥

ayaneṣu ca sarveṣu
yathā-bhāgam avasthitāḥ
bhīṣmam evābhirakṣantu
bhavantaḥ sarva eva hi

I call upon the entire Kaurava army to give utmost support to Grandfather Bhishma throughout the battle.

12

तस्य सञ्जनयन्हर्षं कुरुवृद्धः पितामहः ।
सिंहनादं विनद्योच्चैः शङ्खं दध्मौ प्रतापवान् ॥

tasya sañjanayan harṣaṁ
kuru-vṛddhaḥ pitāmahaḥ
siṁha-nādaṁ vinadyoccaiḥ
śaṅkhaṁ dadhmau pratāpavān

What followed was a loud blowing of the conch by Grandfather Bhishma, the eldest of the Kuru dynasty, sounding like a lion's roar and gladdening the heart of Duryodhan.

13

ततः शङ्खाश्च भेर्यश्च पणवानकगोमुखाः ।
सहसैवाभ्यहन्यन्त स शब्दस्तुमुलोऽभवत् ॥

tataḥ śaṅkhāś ca bheryaś ca
paṇavānaka-gomukhāḥ
sahasaivābhyahanyanta
sa śabdas tumulo 'bhavat

The Kuru army then sounded its conches, kettledrums, trumpets, bugles, and horns, creating a huge uproar.

14

ततः श्वेतैर्हयैर्युक्ते महति स्यन्दने स्थितौ ।
माधवः पाण्डवश्चैव दिव्यौ शङ्खौ प्रदध्मतुः ॥

tataḥ śvetair hayair yukte
mahati syandane sthitau
mādhavaḥ pāṇḍavaś caiva
divyau śaṅkhau pradadhmatuḥ

From the Pandava camp, Madhav and Arjuna blew their divine conches from their glorious chariot drawn by white horses.

15

पाञ्चजन्यं हृषीकेशो देवदत्तं धनञ्जयः ।
पौण्ड्रं दध्मौ महाशङ्खं भीमकर्मा वृकोदरः ॥

pāñcajanyaṁ hṛṣīkeśo
devadattaṁ dhanañjayaḥ
pauṇḍraṁ dadhmau mahā-śaṅkhaṁ
bhīma-karmā vṛkodaraḥ

Hrishikesha blew his conch, Panchajanya. Arjuna blew the Devadutta. Bhima, who ate voraciously and performed great tasks, sounded his mighty conch, Paundra.

16

अनन्तविजयं राजा कुन्तीपुत्रो युधिष्ठिरः ।
नकुलः सहदेवश्च सुघोषमणिपुष्पकौ ॥

anantavijayaṁ rājā
kuntī-putro yudhiṣṭhiraḥ
nakulaḥ sahadevaś ca
sughoṣa-maṇipuṣpakau

Son of Kunti, King Yudhishthir, sounded the Anantavijaya while Nakula and Sahadeva blew the Sughosha and Manipushpak respectively.

17 – 18

काश्यश्च परमेष्वासः शिखण्डी च महारथः ।
धृष्टद्युम्नो विराटश्च सात्यकिश्चापराजितः ॥
द्रुपदो द्रौपदेयाश्च सर्वशः पृथिवीपते ।
सौभद्रश्च महाबाहुः शङ्खान्दध्मुः पृथक्पृथक् ॥

kāśyaś ca parameṣv-āsaḥ
śikhaṇḍī ca mahā-rathaḥ
dhṛṣṭadyumno virāṭaś ca
sātyakiś cāparājitaḥ
drupado draupadeyāś ca
sarvaśaḥ pṛthivī-pate

saubhadraś ca mahā-bāhuḥ
śaṅkhān dadhmuḥ pṛthak pṛthak

Also blowing their conches were the supreme bowmen, the King of Kashi, mighty warrior Shikhandi, Dhrstadyumna, Virata, the invincible Satyaki, together with King Drupada, the sons of Draupadi, and the mighty-armed son of Subhadra.

19

स घोषो धार्तराष्ट्राणां हृदयानि व्यदारयत् ।
नभश्च पृथिवीं चैव तुमुलोऽभ्यनुनादयन् ॥

sa ghoṣo dhārtarāṣṭrāṇāṁ
hṛdayāni vyadārayat
nabhaś ca pṛthivīṁ caiva
tumulo 'bhyanunādayan

The resultant sound vibrations thundered across the sky and earth, filling the hearts of the sons of Dhritarashtra with fear.

20

अथ व्यवस्थितान्दृष्ट्वा धार्तराष्ट्रान्कपिध्वजः ।
प्रवृत्ते शस्त्रसम्पाते धनुरुद्यम्य पाण्डवः ।
हृषीकेशं तदा वाक्यमिदमाह महीपते ॥

atha vyavasthitān dṛṣṭvā
dhārtarāṣṭrān kapi-dhvajaḥ
pravṛtte śastra-sampāte
dhanur udyamya pāṇḍavaḥ
hṛṣīkeśaṁ tadā vākyam
idam āha mahī-pate

Arjuna, the son of Pandu, bearing the insignia of Hanuman on the flag of his chariot, raised his bow in preparation to fight. Looking over the army formation of Dhritarashtra's sons, he spoke to Hrishikesha.

21 – 22

अर्जुन उवाच ।
सेनयोरुभयोर्मध्ये रथं स्थापय मेऽच्युत ॥
यावदेतान्निरीक्षेऽहं योद्धुकामानवस्थितान् ।
कैर्मया सह योद्धव्यमस्मिन्रणसमुद्यमे ॥

arjuna uvāca
senayor ubhayor madhye
rathaṁ sthāpaya me 'cyuta

yāvad etān nirīkṣe 'haṁ
yoddhu-kāmān avasthitān
kair mayā saha yoddhavyam
asmin raṇa-samudyame

Arjuna said –
Do take the chariot in the middle of both the armies so that I can have a good look at those assembled here to fight and compete with me in this battle, O' Infallible One.

23

योत्स्यमानानवेक्षेऽहं य एतेऽत्र समागताः ।
धार्तराष्ट्रस्य दुर्बुद्धेर्युद्धे प्रियचिकीर्षवः ॥

yotsyamānān avekṣe 'haṁ
ya ete 'tra samāgatāḥ
dhārtarāṣṭrasya durbuddher
yuddhe priya-cikīrṣavaḥ

I must see all those who want to fight me and support the wicked sons of Dhritarashtra.

24

सञ्जय उवाच
एवमुक्तो हृषीकेशो गुडाकेशेन भारत ।
सेनयोरुभयोर्मध्ये स्थापयित्वा रथोत्तमम् ॥

sañjaya uvāca
evam ukto hṛṣīkeśo
guḍākeśena bhārata
senayor ubhayor madhye
sthāpayitvā rathottamam

Sanjaya said –

Complying with the instructions of Gudakesha (one who has conquered sleep), Hrishikesha (one who has conquered all senses) pulled the magnificent chariot to the middle of both the armies.

25

भीष्मद्रोणप्रमुखतः सर्वेषां च महीक्षिताम् ।
उवाच पार्थ पश्यैतान्समवेतान्कुरूनिति॥

bhīṣma-droṇa-pramukhataḥ
sarveṣāṁ ca mahī-kṣitām
uvāca pārtha paśyaitān
samavetān kurūn iti

Pointing to Bhishma, Drona, and the kings of the world, Krishna said, 'O' Partha, look! The Kurus are all gathered here.'

26

तत्रापश्यत्स्थितान्पार्थः पितॄनथ पितामहान् ।
आचार्यान्मातुलान्भ्रातॄन्पुत्रान्पौत्रान्सखींस्तथा ।
श्वशुरान्सुहृदश्चैव सेनयोरुभयोरपि ॥

tatrāpaśyat sthitān pārthaḥ
pitṝn atha pitāmahān
ācāryān mātulān bhrātṝn
putrān pautrān sakhīṁs tathā
śvaśurān suhṛdaś caiva
senayor ubhayor api

In both armies, all Arjuna could see was fathers, grandfathers, teachers, maternal uncles, brothers, sons, grandsons, companions, in-laws, and well-wishers.

27

तान्समीक्ष्य स कौन्तेयः सर्वान्बन्धूनवस्थितान् ।
कृपया परयाविष्टो विषीदन्निदमब्रवीत् ॥

tān samīkṣya sa kaunteyaḥ
sarvān bandhūn avasthitān
kṛpayā parayāviṣṭo
viṣīdann idam abravīt

Seeing only the presence of relatives on the battlefield, Kaunteya was overcome with compassion and spoke.

28

अर्जुन उवाच
दृष्ट्वेमं स्वजनं कृष्ण युयुत्सुं समुपस्थितम् ।
सीदन्ति मम गात्राणि मुखं च परिशुष्यति ॥

arjuna uvāca
dṛṣṭvemaṁ sva-janaṁ kṛṣṇa
yuyutsuṁ samupasthitam
sīdanti mama gātrāṇi
mukhaṁ ca pariśuṣyati

Arjuna said –
O' Krishna, my limbs are trembling and my mouth is drying up at the sight of my very own friends and

relatives here on the battlefield, ready to kill each other.

29

वेपथुश्च शरीरे मे रोमहर्षश्च जायते ।
गाण्डीवं स्रंसते हस्तात्त्वक्चैव परिदह्यते ॥

vepathuś ca śarīre me
roma-harṣaś ca jāyate
gāṇḍīvaṁ sraṁsate hastāt
tvak caiva paridahyate

My body is shuddering, my hair is standing on end, Gandiva, my bow is falling off my hand, and my skin burns.

30

न च शक्नोम्यवस्थातुं भ्रमतीव च मे मनः ।
निमित्तानि च पश्यामि विपरीतानि केशव ॥

na ca śaknomy avasthātuṁ
bhramatīva ca me manaḥ
nimittāni ca paśyāmi
viparītāni keśava

O' Keshava, killer of Keshi demon, my mind is reeling in confusion and I see only bad omens bringing misfortune.

31

न च श्रेयोऽनुपश्यामि हत्वा स्वजनमाहवे ।
न काङ्क्षे विजयं कृष्ण न च राज्यं सुखानि च ॥

na ca śreyo 'nupaśyāmi
hatvā sva-janam āhave
na kāṅkṣe vijayaṁ kṛṣṇa
na ca rājyaṁ sukhāni ca

How can there be any merit in killing my own kith and kin? O' Krishna, I have neither a desire for winning this battle nor a desire for kingdom, nor for happiness.

32 – 35

किं नो राज्येन गोविन्द किं भोगैर्जीवितेन वा ।
येषामर्थे काङ्क्षितं नो राज्यं भोगाः सुखानि च ॥
त इमेऽवस्थिता युद्धे प्राणांस्त्यक्त्वा धनानि च ।
आचार्याः पितरः पुत्रास्तथैव च पितामहाः ॥
मातुलाः श्वशुराः पौत्राः श्यालाः सम्बन्धिनस्तथा ।
एतान्न हन्तुमिच्छामि घ्नतोऽपि मधुसूदन ॥

अपि त्रैलोक्यराज्यस्य हेतोः किं नु महीकृते ।
निहत्य धार्तराष्ट्रान्नः का प्रीतिः स्याज्जनार्दन ॥

kiṁ no rājyena govinda
kiṁ bhogair jīvitena vā
yeṣām arthe kāṅkṣitaṁ no
rājyaṁ bhogāḥ sukhāni ca
ta ime 'vasthitā yuddhe
prāṇāṁs tyaktvā dhanāni ca
ācāryāḥ pitaraḥ putrās
tathaiva ca pitāmahāḥ
mātulāḥ śvaśurāḥ pautrāḥ
śyālāḥ sambandhinas tathā
etān na hantum icchāmi
ghnato 'pi madhusūdana
api trailokya-rājyasya
hetoḥ kiṁ nu mahī-kṛte
nihatya dhārtarāṣṭrān naḥ
kā prītiḥ syāj janārdana

What is the use of the kingdom or enjoyment in life, if those we want to share it with are present in this battle itself? O' Govinda, teachers, fathers, sons, grandfathers, maternal uncles, grandsons, fathers-in-law, grand-nephews, brothers-in-law, and other kinsmen have put their lives and wealth on stake here. I refuse to kill them, O' Madhusudan, even if they attack me. Leave alone earth, even if You give me control of all three worlds, I will not fight. What pleasure is there in killing the sons of Dhritarashtra, I ask You, Janardana.

36

पापमेवाश्रयेदस्मान्हत्वैतानाततायिनः ।
तस्मान्नार्हा वयं हन्तुं धार्तराष्ट्रान्सबान्धवान् ।
स्वजनं हि कथं हत्वा सुखिनः स्याम माधव ॥

pāpam evāśrayed asmān
hatvaitān ātatāyinaḥ
tasmān nārhā vayaṁ hantuṁ
dhārtarāṣṭrān sa-bāndhavān
sva-janaṁ hi kathaṁ hatvā
sukhinaḥ syāma mādhava

O' Madhav, killing them will be commiting a sin. Nothing justifies killing the sons of Dhritarashtra and our own friends. Does happiness lie in killing our own family?

37 – 38

यद्यप्येते न पश्यन्ति लोभोपहतचेतस: ।
कुलक्षयकृतं दोषं मित्रद्रोहे च पातकम् ॥
कथं न ज्ञेयमस्माभि: पापादस्मान्निवततुम् ।
कुलक्षयकृतं दोषं प्रपश्यद्भिर्जनार्दन ॥

yady apy ete na paśyanti
lobhopahata-cetasaḥ
kula-kṣaya-kṛtaṁ doṣaṁ
mitra-drohe ca pātakam
kathaṁ na jñeyam asmābhiḥ
pāpād asmān nivartitum
kula-kṣaya-kṛtaṁ doṣaṁ
prapaśyadbhir janārdana

I agree that these people, motivated by greed, see no harm in killing us, their friends and family. But, Janardana, we need not commit the same sin as them being fully aware of the crime.

39

कुलक्षये प्रणश्यन्ति कुलधर्माः सनातनाः ।
धर्मे नष्टे कुलं कृत्स्नमधर्मोऽभिभवत्युत ॥

kula-kṣaye praṇaśyanti
kula-dharmāḥ sanātanāḥ
dharme naṣṭe kulaṁ kṛtsnam
adharmo 'bhibhavaty uta

Irreligious practices increase when dynasties get destroyed and family traditions are lost.

40

अधर्माभिभवात्कृष्ण प्रदुष्यन्ति कुलस्त्रियः ।
स्त्रीषु दुष्टासु वार्ष्णेय जायते वर्णसङ्करः ॥

adharmābhibhavāt kṛṣṇa
praduṣyanti kula-striyaḥ
strīṣu duṣṭāsu vārṣṇeya
jāyate varṇa-saṅkaraḥ

With irreligion, women become immoral producing unwanted children, O' Krishna.

41

सङ्करो नरकायैव कुलघ्नानां कुलस्य च ।
पतन्ति पितरो ह्येषां लुप्तपिण्डोदकक्रियाः ॥

saṅkaro narakāyaiva
kula-ghnānāṁ kulasya ca
patanti pitaro hy eṣāṁ
lupta-piṇḍodaka-kriyāḥ

The unwanted population makes existence a living hell for one and all. Even the ancestors are doomed, being deprived of sacrificial offering of food and water.

42

दोषैरेतैः कुलघ्नानां वर्णसङ्करकारकैः ।
उत्साद्यन्ते जातिधर्माः कुलधर्माश्च शाश्वताः ॥

doṣair etaiḥ kula-ghnānāṁ
varṇa-saṅkara-kārakaiḥ
utsādyante jāti-dharmāḥ
kula-dharmāś ca śāśvatāḥ

The net result is destruction of all dharma, whether related to family or community, merely by the evil act of breaking cultural traditions.

43

उत्सन्नकुलधर्माणां मनुष्याणां जनार्दन ।
नरके नियतं वासो भवतीत्यनुशुश्रुम ॥

utsanna-kula-dharmāṇāṁ
manuṣyāṇāṁ janārdana
narake niyataṁ vāso
bhavatīty anuśuśruma

O' Janardana, I have heard from learned sources that those who mess with family traditions are condemned to hell eternally.

44

अहो बत महत्पापं कर्तुं व्यवसिता वयम् ।
यद्राज्यसुखलोभेन हन्तुं स्वजनमुद्यताः ॥

aho bata mahat pāpaṁ
kartuṁ vyavasitā vayam
yad rājya-sukha-lobhena
hantuṁ sva-janam udyatāḥ

How ironic that we ourselves are trying to commit this sinful act of killing our own family! And for what? Simply to enjoy kingly pleasures?

45

यदि मामप्रतीकारमशस्त्रं शस्त्रपाणयः ।
धार्तराष्ट्रा रणे हन्युस्तन्मे क्षेमतरं भवेत् ॥

yadi mām apratīkāram
aśastraṁ śastra-pāṇayaḥ
dhārtarāṣṭrā raṇe hanyus
tan me kṣemataraṁ bhavet

I would rather die unarmed and without any resistance, when attacked by the weapons of the sons of Dhritarashtra on the battlefield.

46

सञ्जय उवाच
एवमुक्त्वार्जुनः संख्ये रथोपस्थ उपाविशत् ।
विसृज्य सशरं चापं शोकसंविग्नमानसः ॥

sañjaya uvāca
evam uktvārjunaḥ saṅkhye
rathopastha upāviśat
visṛjya sa-śaraṁ cāpaṁ
śoka-saṁvigna-mānasaḥ

Sanjaya said –

With these words, Arjuna put down his bow and arrows and sank to the seat of the chariot with a heart overflowing with grief.

Chapter

02

Sankhya Yoga

1

सञ्जय उवाच
तं तथा कृपयाविष्टमश्रुपूर्णाकुलेक्षणम् ।
विषीदन्तमिदं वाक्यमुवाच मधुसूदनः ॥

sañjaya uvāca
taṁ tathā kṛpayāviṣṭam
aśru-pūrṇākulekṣaṇam
viṣīdantam idaṁ vākyam
uvāca madhusūdanaḥ

Sanjaya said –
Lord Madhusudan addressed Arjuna who was wallowing in pity and shedding tears profusely.

2

श्रीभगवानुवाच
कुतस्त्वा कश्मलमिदं विषमे समुपस्थितम् ।
अनार्यजुष्टमस्वर्ग्यमकीर्तिकरमर्जुन ॥

śrī-bhagavān uvāca
kutas tvā kaśmalam idaṁ
viṣame samupasthitam
anārya-juṣṭam asvargyam
akīrti-karam arjuna

Shri Bhagavan said –

From where have these weaknesses come, O' Arjuna, that too at this hour of danger? It does not befit an Aryan like you who has lived a life of values. This will bring you neither good reputation nor heaven.

3

क्लैब्यं मा स्म गमः पार्थ नैतत्त्वय्युपपद्यते ।
क्षुद्रं हृदयदौर्बल्यं त्यक्त्वोत्तिष्ठ परन्तप ॥

klaibyaṁ mā sma gamaḥ pārtha
naitat tvayy upapadyate
kṣudraṁ hṛdaya-daurbalyaṁ
tyaktvottiṣṭha parantapa

Do not fall prey to this weakness, O' Partha. O' Parantapa, give up this unmanliness and rise to the occasion to fight.

4

अर्जुन उवाच
कथं भीष्ममहं संख्ये द्रोणं च मधुसूदन ।
इषुभि: प्रतियोत्स्यामि पूजार्हावरिसूदन ॥

arjuna uvāca
kathaṁ bhīṣmam ahaṁ saṅkhye
droṇaṁ ca madhusūdana
iṣubhiḥ pratiyotsyāmi
pūjārhāv ari-sūdana

Arjuna said –
O' Madhusudan, how can I possibly attack Bhishma and Drona? How can I shoot arrows at those who I have worshipped? Tell me, O' Killer of Demons!

5

गुरूनहत्वा हि महानुभावान्
श्रेयो भोक्तुं भैक्ष्यमपीह लोके ।
हत्वार्थकामांस्तु गुरूनिहैव
भुञ्जीय भोगान्रुधिरप्रदिग्धान् ॥

gurūn ahatvā hi mahānubhāvān
śreyo bhoktuṁ bhaikṣyam apīha loke
hatvārtha-kāmāṁs tu gurūn ihaiva
bhuñjīya bhogān rudhira-pradigdhān

I'd rather live a life of begging than killing my elders, my teachers, however covetous they may be. After killing them, worldly pleasures will have no significance, tainted with their blood.

6

न चैतद्विद्मः कतरन्नो गरीयो
यद्वा जयेम यदि वा नो जयेयुः ।
यानेव हत्वा न जिजीविषाम-
स्तेऽवस्थिताः प्रमुखे धार्तराष्ट्राः ॥

na caitad vidmaḥ kataran no garīyo
yad vā jayema yadi vā no jayeyuḥ
yān eva hatvā na jijīviṣāmas
te 'vasthitāḥ pramukhe dhārtarāṣṭrāḥ

Right now, I'm not even sure what is better—conquering them or getting conquered? I do not wish to live after killing them. Yet they stand on the side of sons of Dhritarashtra in the battlefield.

7

कार्पण्यदोषोपहतस्वभाव:
पृच्छामि त्वां धर्मसम्मूढचेता: ।
यच्छ्रेय: स्यान्निश्चितं ब्रूहि तन्मे
शिष्यस्तेऽहं शाधि मां त्वां प्रपन्नम् ॥

kārpaṇya-doṣopahata-svabhāvaḥ
pṛcchāmi tvāṁ dharma-saṁmūḍha-cetāḥ
yac chreyaḥ syān niścitaṁ brūhi tan me
śiṣyas te 'haṁ śādhi māṁ tvāṁ prapannam

Overcome by anxiety and weakness, I am confused about my duties. I surrender to You as Your disciple. Please instruct me in my best interest.

8

न हि प्रपश्यामि ममापनुद्याद्
यच्छोकमुच्छोषणमिन्द्रियाणाम् ।
अवाप्य भूमावसपत्नमृद्धं
राज्यं सुराणामपि चाधिपत्यम् ॥

na hi prapaśyāmi mamāpanudyād
yac chokam ucchoṣaṇam indriyāṇām
avāpya bhūmāv asapatnam ṛddhaṁ
rājyaṁ surāṇām api cādhipatyam

Winning a prosperous kingdom on earth or acquiring sovereign powers like that of celestial beings will not be sufficient to nullify the immense grief within that is drying up my senses.

9

सञ्जय उवाच
एवमुक्त्वा हृषीकेशं गुडाकेशः परन्तपः ।
न योत्स्य इति गोविन्दमुक्त्वा तूष्णीं बभूव ह ॥

sañjaya uvāca
evam uktvā hṛṣīkeśaṁ
guḍākeśaḥ parantapaḥ
na yotsya iti govindam
uktvā tūṣṇīṁ babhūva ha

Sanjaya said –

And then Arjuna said to Hrishikesha, 'O' Govinda, I will not fight.' There was silence after that.

10

तमुवाच हृषीकेशः प्रहसन्निव भारत ।
सेनयोरुभयोर्मध्ये विषीदन्तमिदं वचः ॥

tam uvāca hṛṣīkeśaḥ
prahasann iva bhārata
senayor ubhayor madhye
viṣīdantam idaṁ vacaḥ

'O' King,' Hrishikesha then spoke smilingly to the grieving Arjuna, right in the middle of both the armies.

11

श्रीभगवानुवाच
अशोच्यानन्वशोचस्त्वं प्रज्ञावादांश्च भाषसे ।
गतासूनगतासूंश्च नानुशोचन्ति पण्डिताः ॥

śrī-bhagavān uvāca
aśocyān anvaśocas tvaṁ
prajñā-vādāṁś ca bhāṣase
gatāsūn agatāsūṁś ca
nānuśocanti paṇḍitāḥ

Sri Bhagavan said –
Your words are wise but you are lamenting for something that is unworthy. Neither for the living nor for the dead does a wise man lament.

12

न त्वेवाहं जातु नासं न त्वं नेमे जनाधिपा: ।
न चैव न भविष्याम: सर्वे वयमत: परम् ॥

na tv evāhaṁ jātu nāsaṁ
na tvaṁ neme janādhipāḥ
na caiva na bhaviṣyāmaḥ
sarve vayam ataḥ param

There has never been a time when I or you or all these kings were not in existence. And surely, we shall all exist in the future too.

13

देहिनोऽस्मिन्यथा देहे कौमारं यौवनं जरा ।
तथा देहान्तरप्राप्तिर्धीरस्तत्र न मुह्यति ॥

dehino 'smin yathā dehe
kaumāraṁ yauvanaṁ jarā
tathā dehāntara-prāptir
dhīras tatra na muhyati

Childhood, youth, and old age are simply phases in the journey of an embodied soul. The next phase is another body. There is nothing abnormal in this.

14

मात्रास्पर्शास्तु कौन्तेय शीतोष्णसुखदुःखदाः ।
आगमापायिनोऽनित्यास्तांस्तितिक्षस्व भारत ॥

mātrā-sparśās tu kaunteya
śītoṣṇa-sukha-duḥkha-dāḥ
āgamāpāyino 'nityās
tāṁs titikṣasva bhārata

Interaction with sense objects leads to experience of joy and sorrow which are as temporary as the seasons summer and winter that continually come and go, O' son of Kunti. You must adapt to them, tolerate them without losing your balance, O' descendant of Bharata.

15

यं हि न व्यथयन्त्येते पुरुषं पुरुषर्षभ ।
समदुःखसुखं धीरं सोऽमृतत्वाय कल्पते ॥

yaṁ hi na vyathayanty ete
puruṣaṁ puruṣarṣabha
sama-duḥkha-sukhaṁ dhīraṁ
so 'mṛtatvāya kalpate

If one is wise enough to tolerate dualities, to whom joy and sorrow are one and the same, he becomes qualified for eternal life, O' Arjuna, the best of men.

16

नासतो विद्यते भावो नाभावो विद्यते सतः ।
उभयोरपि दृष्टोऽन्तस्त्वनयोस्तत्त्वदर्शिभिः ॥

nāsato vidyate bhāvo
nābhāvo vidyate sataḥ
ubhayor api dṛṣṭo 'ntas
tv anayos tattva-darśibhiḥ

That which is temporary is not the ultimate reality because the ultimate reality is unchangeable and indestructible. This is the conclusion derived by the wise who have pondered on the subject at length.

17

अविनाशि तु तद्विद्धि येन सर्वमिदं ततम् ।
विनाशमव्ययस्यास्य न कश्चित्कर्तुमर्हति ॥

avināśi tu tad viddhi
yena sarvam idaṁ tatam

vināśam avyayasyāsya
na kaścit kartum arhati

Imperishable and indestructible—that is the nature of the soul which pervades the body.

18

अन्तवन्त इमे देहा नित्यस्योक्ताः शरीरिणः ।
अनाशिनोऽप्रमेयस्य तस्माद्युध्यस्व भारत ॥

antavanta ime dehā
nityasyoktāḥ śarīriṇaḥ
anāśino 'prameyasya
tasmād yudhyasva bhārata

What can be destroyed is the external body housing the imperishable and indestructible soul. O' descendant of Bharata, arise and fight.

19

य एनं वेत्ति हन्तारं यश्चैनं मन्यते हतम् ।
उभौ तौ न विजानीतो नायं हन्ति न हन्यते ॥

ya enaṁ vetti hantāraṁ
yaś cainaṁ manyate hatam

ubhau tau na vijānīto
nāyaṁ hanti na hanyate

In ignorance one may think that a soul can slay another soul or a soul gets slayed by another soul but in truth, the learned know that the soul neither kills nor is killed.

20

न जायते म्रियते वा कदाचि-
न्नायं भूत्वा भविता वा न भूयः ।
अजो नित्यः शाश्वतोऽयं पुराणो
न हन्यते हन्यमाने शरीरे ॥

na jāyate mriyate vā kadācin
nāyaṁ bhūtvā bhavitā vā na bhūyaḥ
ajo nityaḥ śāśvato 'yaṁ purāṇo
na hanyate hanyamāne śarīre

There is no birth or death for the soul. Nor does it ever cease to be. It is birthless, ageless, eternal, without a beginning or an end. Even with destruction of the body, the soul is not destroyed.

21

वेदाविनाशिनं नित्यं य एनमजमव्ययम् ।
कथं स पुरुषः पार्थ कं घातयति हन्ति कम् ॥

vedāvināśinaṁ nityaṁ
ya enam ajam avyayam
kathaṁ sa puruṣaḥ pārtha
kaṁ ghātayati hanti kam

Knowing the soul to be birthless, deathless, and indestructible, how will you kill anyone? Or how will anyone be killed, Partha?

22

वासांसि जीर्णानि यथा विहाय
नवानि गृह्णाति नरोऽपराणि ।
तथा शरीराणि विहाय जीर्णा-
न्यन्यानि संयाति नवानि देही ॥

vāsāṁsi jīrṇāni yathā vihāya
navāni gṛhṇāti naro 'parāṇi
tathā śarīrāṇi vihāya jīrṇāny
anyāni saṁyāti navāni dehī

Just as we discard old, worn-out clothes, the soul casts off worn out bodies to enter a new body at the time of death. A body is for the soul what clothes are for us.

23

नैनं छिन्दन्ति शस्त्राणि नैनं दहति पावकः ।
न चैनं क्लेदयन्त्यापो न शोषयति मारुतः ॥

nainaṁ chindanti śastrāṇi
nainaṁ dahati pāvakaḥ
na cainaṁ kledayanty āpo
na śoṣayati mārutaḥ

The soul cannot be wounded by any weapon. It cannot be burnt by fire. Nor moistened by water. Nor can it be blown away by the wind.

24

अच्छेद्योऽयमदाह्योऽयमक्लेद्योऽशोष्य एव च ।
नित्यः सर्वगतः स्थाणुरचलोऽयं सनातनः ॥

acchedyo 'yam adāhyo 'yam
akledyo 'śoṣya eva ca
nityaḥ sarva-gataḥ sthāṇur
acalo 'yaṁ sanātanaḥ

The soul cannot be broken, burnt, dried, or dissolved. It is eternal, unalterable, immovable, and indelible. It is without a beginning.

25

अव्यक्तोऽयमचिन्त्योऽयमविकार्योऽयमुच्यते ।
तस्मादेवं विदित्वैनं नानुशोचितुमर्हसि ॥

avyakto 'yam acintyo 'yam
avikāryo 'yam ucyate
tasmād evaṁ viditvainaṁ
nānuśocitum arhasi

Knowing that the self is invisible, inconceivable, and unchangeable, you should not lament for the body.

26

अथ चैनं नित्यजातं नित्यं वा मन्यसे मृतम् ।
तथापि त्वं महाबाहो नैनं शोचितुमर्हसि ॥

atha cainaṁ nitya-jātaṁ
nityaṁ vā manyase mṛtam
tathāpi tvaṁ mahā-bāho
nainaṁ śocitum arhasi

Even if you wish to believe that the self undergoes constant birth and death, there is still no reason to mourn for it, O' mighty-armed Arjuna.

27

जातस्य हि ध्रुवो मृत्युर्ध्रुवं जन्म मृतस्य च ।
तस्मादपरिहार्येऽर्थे न त्वं शोचितुमर्हसि ॥

jātasya hi dhruvo mṛtyur
dhruvaṁ janma mṛtasya ca
tasmād aparihārye 'rthe
na tvaṁ śocitum arhasi

Because, those born will certainly die one day, and those who die will certainly be born again. Why then grieve over it?

28

अव्यक्तादीनि भूतानि व्यक्तमध्यानि भारत ।
अव्यक्तनिधनान्येव तत्र का परिदेवना ॥

avyaktādīni bhūtāni
vyakta-madhyāni bhārata
avyakta-nidhanāny eva
tatra kā paridevanā

All created beings are unmanifested before birth and after death. They manifest only during life. Why then grieve over it, O' descendant of Bharata?

29

आश्चर्यवत्पश्यति कश्चिदेन-
माश्चर्यवद्वदति तथैव चान्य: ।
आश्चर्यवच्चैनमन्य: शृणोति
श्रुत्वाप्येनं वेद न चैव कश्चित् ॥

āścarya-vat paśyati kaścid enam
āścarya-vad vadati tathaiva cānyaḥ
āścarya-vac cainam anyaḥ śṛṇoti
śrutvāpy enaṁ veda na caiva kaścit

For some the soul is amazing to see, for some it is perplexing to hear, and for some it is a mystery when described. No one has really been able to decode the soul as yet.

30

देही नित्यमवध्योऽयं देहे सर्वस्य भारत ।
तस्मात्सर्वाणि भूतानि न त्वं शोचितुमर्हसि ॥

dehī nityam avadhyo 'yaṁ
dehe sarvasya bhārata
tasmāt sarvāṇi bhūtāni
na tvaṁ śocitum arhasi

Do not grieve for any living being because the soul dwelling within the body is immortal.

31

स्वधर्ममपि चावेक्ष्य न विकम्पितुमर्हसि ।
धर्म्याद्धि युद्धाच्छ्रेयोऽन्यत्क्षत्रियस्य न विद्यते ॥

sva-dharmam api cāvekṣya
na vikampitum arhasi
dharmyād dhi yuddhāc chreyo 'nyat
kṣatriyasya na vidyate

As a warrior, your duty is to fight without fear. There could be nothing more righteous for a Kshatriya than to fight against injustice and *adharma*.

32

यदृच्छया चोपपन्नं स्वर्गद्वारमपावृतम् ।
सुखिनः क्षत्रियाः पार्थ लभन्ते युद्धमीदृशम् ॥

yadṛcchayā copapannaṁ
svarga-dvāram apāvṛtam
sukhinaḥ kṣatriyāḥ pārtha
labhante yuddham īdṛśam

Fighting a battle opens the gates of heavenly abode for warriors. O' Partha, an unsought opportunity like this should make you happy.

33

अथ चेत्त्वमिमं धर्म्यं सङ्ग्रामं न करिष्यसि ।
ततः स्वधर्मं कीर्तिं च हित्वा पापमवाप्स्यसि ॥

atha cet tvam imaṁ dharmyaṁ
saṅgrāmaṁ na kariṣyasi
tataḥ sva-dharmam kīrtiṁ ca
hitvā pāpam avāpsyasi

If you still refuse to fight this *dharmic* battle, you are sinning by not performing your duty. You will lose your reputation too.

34

अकीर्तिं चापि भूतानि कथयिष्यन्ति तेऽव्ययाम् ।
सम्भावितस्य चाकीर्तिर्मरणादतिरिच्यते ॥

akīrtiṁ cāpi bhūtāni
kathayiṣyanti te 'vyayām
sambhāvitasya cākīrtir
maraṇād atiricyate

People will call you a coward. Dishonour is worse than death for a respectable person like you.

35

भयाद्रणादुपरतं मंस्यन्ते त्वां महारथाः ।
येषां च त्वं बहुमतो भूत्वा यास्यसि लाघवम् ॥

bhayād raṇād uparataṁ
maṁsyante tvāṁ mahā-rathāḥ
yeṣāṁ ca tvaṁ bahu-mato
bhūtvā yāsyasi lāghavam

Brave warriors who revere you now will assume you left the battlefield fearing for your life. They will lose all respect for you.

36

अवाच्यवादांश्च बहून्वदिष्यन्ति तवाहिता: ।
निन्दन्तस्तव सामर्थ्यं ततो दु:खतरं नु किम् ॥

avācya-vādāṁś ca bahūn
vadiṣyanti tavāhitāḥ
nindantas tava sāmarthyaṁ
tato duḥkhataraṁ nu kim

Your enemies will humiliate you, even question your abilities. Could there be anything worse than that?

37

हतो वा प्राप्स्यसि स्वर्गं जित्वा वा भोक्ष्यसे महीम् ।
तस्मादुत्तिष्ठ कौन्तेय युद्धाय कृतनिश्चय: ॥

hato vā prāpsyasi svargaṁ
jitvā vā bhokṣyase mahīm
tasmād uttiṣṭha kaunteya
yuddhāya kṛta-niścayaḥ

If you die while fighting, you will experience pleasures in heaven. If you win, you will experience pleasures on earth. It's a win-win situation. So stand up, O' Kaunteya, and fight the battle with determination.

38

सुखदु:खे समे कृत्वा लाभालाभौ जयाजयौ ।
ततो युद्धाय युज्यस्व नैवं पापमवाप्स्यसि ॥

sukha-duḥkhe same kṛtvā
lābhālābhau jayājayau
tato yuddhāya yujyasva
naivaṁ pāpam avāpsyasi

And if you fight because it is your responsibility, disregarding joy, sorrow, profit, loss, victory, or defeat, then there is no sin incurred either.

39

एषा तेऽभिहिता संख्ये बुद्धिर्योगे त्विमां शृणु ।
बुद्ध्या युक्तो यया पार्थ कर्मबन्धं प्रहास्यसि ॥

eṣā te 'bhihitā sāṅkhye
buddhir yoge tv imāṁ śṛṇu
buddhyā yukto yayā pārtha
karma-bandhaṁ prahāsyasi

I have just shared with you the wisdom of *sankhya* yoga also known as analytical knowledge. Now hear well as I tell you about *buddhi* yoga. O' Partha, this wisdom will free you from the bondage of karma.

40

नेहाभिक्रमनाशोऽस्ति प्रत्यवायो न विद्यते ।
स्वल्पमप्यस्य धर्मस्य त्रायते महतो भयात् ॥

nehābhikrama-nāśo 'sti
pratyavāyo na vidyate
sv-alpam apy asya dharmasya
trāyate mahato bhayāt

Following the path of dharma will never go waste. It will never hamper your progress. Whereas even a little advancement will save you from many dangers.

41

व्यवसायात्मिका बुद्धिरेकेह कुरुनन्दन ।
बहुशाखा ह्यनन्ताश्च बुद्धयोऽव्यवसायिनाम् ॥

vyavasāyātmikā buddhir
ekeha kuru-nandana
bahu-śākhā hy anantāś ca
buddhayo 'vyavasāyinām

This path requires resolute determination and focus. If intelligence is irresolute and multi-branched, you will get distracted.

42

यामिमां पुष्पितां वाचं प्रवदन्त्यविपश्चित: ।
वेदवादरता: पार्थ नान्यदस्तीति वादिन: ॥

yām imāṁ puṣpitāṁ vācaṁ
pravadanty avipaścitaḥ
veda-vāda-ratāḥ pārtha
nānyad astīti vādinaḥ

The Vedas advocate rituals by an appealing play of floral words. Men of scanty knowledge get attracted to it and do not look beyond that.

43

कामात्मान: स्वर्गपरा जन्मकर्मफलप्रदाम् ।
क्रियाविशेषबहुलां भोगैश्वर्यगतिं प्रति ॥

kāmātmānaḥ svarga-parā
janma-karma-phala-pradām
kriyā-viśeṣa-bahulāṁ
bhogaiśvarya-gatiṁ prati

For such people, their only goal is material desires and wealth, heavenly planets, or good birth, or power which they hope to achieve through the Vedic rituals.

44

भोगैश्वर्यप्रसक्तानां तयापहृतचेतसाम् ।
व्यवसायात्मिका बुद्धिः समाधौ न विधीयते ॥

bhogaiśvarya-prasaktānāṁ
tayāpahṛta-cetasām
vyavasāyātmikā buddhiḥ
samādhau na vidhīyate

Such strong attachment to worldly powers and sense gratification weakens their determination and they lose out on the path of God.

45

त्रैगुण्यविषया वेदा निस्त्रैगुण्यो भवार्जुन ।
निर्द्वन्द्वो नित्यसत्त्वस्थो निर्योगक्षेम आत्मवान् ॥

trai-guṇya-viṣayā vedā
nistrai-guṇyo bhavārjuna
nirdvandvo nitya-sattva-stho
niryoga-kṣema ātmavān

The Vedas revolve around the three modes of material nature, the *gunas*. But you, Arjuna, you have to rise above the gunas. You have to free yourself from the complexities of the material world and be fixed on the self alone.

46

यावानर्थ उदपाने सर्वतः सम्प्लुतोदके ।
तावान्सर्वेषु वेदेषु ब्राह्मणस्य विजानतः ॥

yāvān artha udapāne
sarvataḥ samplutodake
tāvān sarveṣu vedeṣu
brāhmaṇasya vijānataḥ

Just as a big lake can minimize the importance of a small well, so does the knower of the absolute truth proficient in scriptures serve better than the Vedas.

47

कर्मण्येवाधिकारस्ते मा फलेषु कदाचन ।
मा कर्मफलहेतुर्भूर्मा ते सङ्गोऽस्त्वकर्मणि ॥

karmaṇy evādhikāras te
mā phaleṣu kadācana
mā karma-phala-hetur bhūr
mā te saṅgo 'stv akarmaṇi

Although you are eligible to perform your duties of a Kshatriya, you have no right to the result of that action. Remember that you are not the cause of that result and still you cannot shy away from work.

48

योगस्थ: कुरु कर्माणि सङ्गं त्यक्त्वा धनञ्जय ।
सिद्ध्यसिद्ध्यो: समो भूत्वा समत्वं योग उच्यते ॥

yoga-sthaḥ kuru karmāṇi
saṅgaṁ tyaktvā dhanañjaya
siddhy-asiddhyoḥ samo bhūtvā
samatvaṁ yoga ucyate

O' Dhananjaya, fix your mind on duty, without any thought of the resulting success or failure, and achieve the steadiness of yoga.

49

दूरेण ह्यवरं कर्म बुद्धियोगाद्धनञ्जय ।
बुद्धौ शरणमन्विच्छ कृपणा: फलहेतव: ॥

dūreṇa hy avaraṁ karma
buddhi-yogād dhanañjaya
buddhau śaraṇam anviccha
kṛpaṇāḥ phala-hetavaḥ

Choose to act on the basis of disciplined intelligence rather than desire for enjoyment. Only the miserly cling to the fruits of action, O' conqueror of wealth.

50

बुद्धियुक्तो जहातीह उभे सुकृतदुष्कृते ।
तस्माद्योगाय युज्यस्व योगः कर्मसु कौशलम् ॥

buddhi-yukto jahātīha
ubhe sukṛta-duṣkṛte
tasmād yogāya yujyasva
yogaḥ karmasu kauśalam

Therefore, practise yoga, the art and science of working without attachments. Only that can free you from good and bad reactions.

51

कर्मजं बुद्धियुक्ता हि फलं त्यक्त्वा मनीषिणः ।
जन्मबन्धविनिर्मुक्ताः पदं गच्छन्त्यनामयम् ॥

karma-jaṁ buddhi-yuktā hi
phalaṁ tyaktvā manīṣiṇaḥ
janma-bandha-vinirmuktāḥ
padaṁ gacchanty anāmayam

Endowed with yogic wisdom, the wise decline the fruits of their actions which bind them to the cycle of life and death. Thus liberated, they find peace and freedom from suffering.

52

यदा ते मोहकलिलं बुद्धिर्व्यतितरिष्यति ।
तदा गन्तासि निर्वेदं श्रोतव्यस्य श्रुतस्य च ॥

yadā te moha-kalilaṁ
buddhir vyatitariṣyati
tadā gantāsi nirvedaṁ
śrotavyasya śrutasya ca

Emerging from the forest of illusion, the intelligence becomes detached from what has been heard and what will be heard.

53

श्रुतिविप्रतिपन्ना ते यदा स्थास्यति निश्चला ।
समाधावचला बुद्धिस्तदा योगमवाप्स्यसि ॥

śruti-vipratipannā te
yadā sthāsyati niścalā
samādhāv acalā buddhis
tadā yogam avāpsyasi

Not excited by the floral words of the Vedas, the intelligence is fixed in a spiritual trance, what is called the perfection of yoga.

54

अर्जुन उवाच
स्थितप्रज्ञस्य का भाषा समाधिस्थस्य केशव ।
स्थितधी: किं प्रभाषेत किमासीत व्रजेत किम् ॥

arjuna uvāca
sthita-prajñasya kā bhāṣā
samādhi-sthasya keśava
sthita-dhīḥ kiṁ prabhāṣeta
kim āsīta vrajeta kiṁ

Arjuna said –
O' Keshava, how does one recognize such a person with a steady intellect and divine consciousness? How does he speak, or sit, or move?

55

श्रीभगवानुवाच
प्रजहाति यदा कामान्सर्वान्पार्थ मनोगतान् ।
आत्मन्येवात्मना तुष्ट: स्थितप्रज्ञस्तदोच्यते ॥

śrī-bhagavān uvāca
prajahāti yadā kāmān
sarvān pārtha mano-gatān

ātmany evātmanā tuṣṭaḥ
sthita-prajñas tadocyate

Sri Bhagavan said –
When one is in divine consciousness, one gives up all desires arising from the mind and finds satisfaction in the self alone.

56

दुःखेष्वनुद्विग्नमनाः सुखेषु विगतस्पृहः ।
वीतरागभयक्रोधः स्थितधीर्मुनिरुच्यते ॥

duḥkheṣv anudvigna-manāḥ
sukheṣu vigata-spṛhaḥ
vīta-rāga-bhaya-krodhaḥ
sthita-dhīr munir ucyate

One is neither overjoyed nor agitated in happiness or suffering. Free from desires, cravings for pleasure, fear, and anger, one's mind is tranquil.

57

य: सर्वत्रानभिस्नेहस्तत्तत्प्राप्य शुभाशुभम् ।
नाभिनन्दति न द्वेष्टि तस्य प्रज्ञा प्रतिष्ठिता ॥

yaḥ sarvatrānabhisnehas
tat tat prāpya śubhāśubham
nābhinandati na dveṣṭi
tasya prajñā pratiṣṭhitā

One is of steady wisdom who is unperturbed by material desires and unaffected by joys and sorrows.

58

यदा संहरते चायं कूर्मोऽङ्गानीव सर्वशः ।
इन्द्रियाणीन्द्रियार्थेभ्यस्तस्य प्रज्ञा प्रतिष्ठिता ॥

yadā saṁharate cāyaṁ
kūrmo 'ṅgānīva sarvaśaḥ
indriyāṇīndriyārthebhyas
tasya prajñā pratiṣṭhitā

Like a tortoise pulls his limbs into his shell, one keeps his senses under one's control.

59

विषया विनिवर्तन्ते निराहारस्य देहिनः ।
रसवर्जं रसोऽप्यस्य परं दृष्ट्वा निवर्तते ॥

viṣayā vinivartante
nirāhārasya dehinaḥ
rasa-varjaṁ raso 'py asya
paraṁ dṛṣṭvā nivartate

Often, one may keep the senses under control, but the taste for objects of enjoyment still remains. But one, with divine consciousness, loses the taste for such sensory objects having acquired a higher taste.

60

यततो ह्यपि कौन्तेय पुरुषस्य विपश्चितः ।
इन्द्रियाणि प्रमाथीनि हरन्ति प्रसभं मनः ॥

yatato hy api kaunteya
puruṣasya vipaścitaḥ
indriyāṇi pramāthīni
haranti prasabhaṁ manaḥ

But the sensory objects being immensely powerful can even drag the mind of such a person who has the ability to discriminate, O' Kaunteya.

61

तानि सर्वाणि संयम्य युक्त आसीत मत्परः ।
वशे हि यस्येन्द्रियाणि तस्य प्रज्ञा प्रतिष्ठिता ॥

tāni sarvāṇi saṁyamya
yukta āsīta mat-paraḥ
vaśe hi yasyendriyāṇi
tasya prajñā pratiṣṭhitā

The only way to maintain steady wisdom is to control your senses and absorb your mind in Me.

62

ध्यायतो विषयान्पुंसः सङ्गस्तेषूपजायते ।
सङ्गात्सञ्जायते कामः कामात्क्रोधोऽभिजायते ॥

dhyāyato viṣayān puṁsaḥ
saṅgas teṣūpajāyate
saṅgāt sañjāyate kāmaḥ
kāmāt krodho 'bhijāyate

If you think about sense objects, it will lead to attachment to them. Attachment begets desires and unfulfilled desires cause frustration and anger.

63

क्रोधाद्भवति सम्मोह: सम्मोहात्स्मृतिविभ्रम: ।
स्मृतिभ्रंशाद्बुद्धिनाशो बुद्धिनाशात्प्रणश्यति ॥

krodhād bhavati saṁmohaḥ
saṁmohāt smṛti-vibhramaḥ
smṛti-bhraṁśād buddhi-nāśo
buddhi-nāśāt praṇaśyati

Anger compounds delusion. Delusion leads to loss of memory which in turn destroys the power of discrimination. Loss of discrimination means loss of self and falling to material consciousness again.

64

रागद्वेषविमुक्तैस्तु विषयानिन्द्रियैश्चरन् ।
आत्मवश्यैर्विधेयात्मा प्रसादमधिगच्छति ॥

rāga-dveṣa-vimuktais tu
viṣayān indriyaiś caran
ātma-vaśyair vidheyātmā
prasādam adhigacchati

Self-control over desires and aversions can attract God's grace.

65

प्रसादे सर्वदु:खानां हानिरस्योपजायते ।
प्रसन्नचेतसो ह्याशु बुद्धिः पर्यवतिष्ठते ॥

prasāde sarva-duḥkhānāṁ
hānir asyopajāyate
prasanna-cetaso hy āśu
buddhiḥ paryavatiṣṭhate

God's grace can end all sorrow and the resulting peace fixes the intelligence on God.

66

नास्ति बुद्धिरयुक्तस्य न चायुक्तस्य भावना ।
न चाभावयतः शान्तिरशान्तस्य कुतः सुखम् ॥

nāsti buddhir ayuktasya
na cāyuktasya bhāvanā
na cābhāvayataḥ śāntir
aśāntasya kutaḥ sukham

Only a disciplined person can control his senses and mind, have a clear intelligence, and contemplate on God. Without contemplation on God, there can be no peace and without peace there can be no happiness.

67

इन्द्रियाणां हि चरतां यन्मनोऽनुविधीयते ।
तदस्य हरति प्रज्ञां वायुर्नावमिवाम्भसि ॥

indriyāṇāṁ hi caratāṁ
yan mano 'nuvidhīyate
tad asya harati prajñāṁ
vāyur nāvam ivāmbhasi

If the mind hankers for fulfilment of a desire, any of the wandering senses can carry away the intelligence as easily as the wind blows away a ship from its course in the sea.

68

तस्माद्यस्य महाबाहो निगृहीतानि सर्वशः ।
इन्द्रियाणीन्द्रियार्थेभ्यस्तस्य प्रज्ञा प्रतिष्ठिता ॥

tasmād yasya mahā-bāho
nigṛhītāni sarvaśaḥ
indriyāṇīndriyārthebhyas
tasya prajñā pratiṣṭhitā

Only by withdrawing your senses from the sense objects can you be fixed in transcendental wisdom, O' mighty-armed.

69

या निशा सर्वभूतानां तस्यां जागर्ति संयमी ।
यस्यां जाग्रति भूतानि सा निशा पश्यतो मुनेः ॥

yā niśā sarva-bhūtānāṁ
tasyāṁ jāgarti saṁyamī
yasyāṁ jāgrati bhūtāni
sā niśā paśyato muneḥ

What is darkness for ignorant beings is daylight, a time of awakening, for those with self-control. What is daylight for the ignorant is the dark of night for sages who see.

70

आपूर्यमाणमचलप्रतिष्ठं
समुद्रमापः प्रविशन्ति यद्वत् ।
तद्वत्कामा यं प्रविशन्ति सर्वे
स शान्तिमाप्नोति न कामकामी ॥

āpūryamāṇam acala-pratiṣṭhaṁ
samudram āpaḥ praviśanti yadvat
tadvat kāmā yaṁ praviśanti sarve
sa śāntim āpnoti na kāma-kāmī

Just as the rivers entering the ocean cannot disturb the ocean in any way, desires entering the mind cannot disturb the steady mind of a sage.

71

विहाय कामान्यः सर्वान्पुमांश्चरति निःस्पृहः ।
निर्ममो निरहङ्कारः स शान्तिमधिगच्छति ॥

vihāya kāmān yaḥ sarvān
pumāṁś carati niḥspṛhaḥ
nirmamo nirahaṅkāraḥ
sa śāntim adhigacchati

Peace comes to one who gives up all desires for self-enjoyment, gives up his ego, gives up greed as well as a sense of ownership.

72

एषा ब्राह्मी स्थितिः पार्थ नैनां प्राप्य विमुह्यति ।
स्थित्वास्यामन्तकालेऽपि ब्रह्मनिर्वाणमृच्छति ॥

eṣā brāhmī sthitiḥ pārtha
naināṁ prāpya vimuhyati
sthitvāsyām anta-kāle 'pi
brahma-nirvāṇam ṛcchati

In this enlightened state of consciousness, one never gets confused again. O' Partha, if one attains this consciousness at the time of death, one gets liberated from the cycle of birth and death and all suffering ends by entering the spiritual abode of God.

Chapter

03

Karma Yoga

1

अर्जुन उवाच
ज्यायसी चेत्कर्मणस्ते मता बुद्धिर्जनार्दन ।
तत्किं कर्मणि घोरे मां नियोजयसि केशव ॥

arjuna uvāca
jyāyasī cet karmaṇas te
matā buddhir janārdana
tat kiṁ karmaṇi ghore
māṁ niyojayasi keśava

Arjuna said –
O' Janardana, You say that intelligence is superior to action and yet, O' Keshava, You goad me to fight the war? Why?

2

व्यामिश्रेणेव वाक्येन बुद्धिं मोहयसीव मे ।
तदेकं वद निश्चित्य येन श्रेयोऽहमाप्नुयाम् ॥

vyāmiśreṇeva vākyena
buddhiṁ mohayasīva me
tad ekaṁ vada niścitya
yena śreyo 'ham āpnuyām

My mind is perplexed and unable to decode Your cryptic language. Can You not tell me in simple words which path to take?

3

श्रीभगवानुवाच
लोकेऽस्मिन्द्विविधा निष्ठा पुरा प्रोक्ता मयानघ ।
ज्ञानयोगेन साङ्ख्यानां कर्मयोगेन योगिनाम् ॥

śrī-bhagavān uvāca
loke 'smin dvi-vidhā niṣṭhā
purā proktā mayānagha
jnāna-yogena sāṅkhyānāṁ
karma-yogena yoginām

Sri Bhagavan said –
I have mentioned earlier also that there are two paths to transcendental enlightenment. One is the path of knowledge based on philosophy and contemplation. Other is the path of work or action.

4

न कर्मणामनारम्भान्नैष्कर्म्यं पुरुषोऽश्नुते ।
न च सन्न्यसनादेव सिद्धिं समधिगच्छति ॥

na karmaṇām anārambhān
naiṣkarmyaṁ puruṣo 'śnute
na ca sannyasanād eva
siddhiṁ samadhigacchati

Abstaining from work or physical renunciation is not the answer. Both are inadequate ways to divine enlightenment.

5

न हि कश्चित्क्षणमपि जातु तिष्ठत्यकर्मकृत् ।
कार्यते ह्यवशः कर्म सर्वः प्रकृतिजैर्गुणैः ॥

na hi kaścit kṣaṇam api
jātu tiṣṭhaty akarma-kṛt
kāryate hy avaśaḥ karma
sarvaḥ prakṛti-jair guṇaiḥ

Not for a moment can one live without action. Whether one likes it or not, one is compelled to act, influenced by the three modes of material nature.

6

कर्मेन्द्रियाणि संयम्य य आस्ते मनसा स्मरन् ।
इन्द्रियार्थान्विमूढात्मा मिथ्याचारः स उच्यते ॥

karmendriyāṇi saṁyamya
ya āste manasā smaran
indriyārthān vimūḍhātmā
mithyācāraḥ sa ucyate

It's possible that one restrains one's senses but continues to think of sensual pleasure. He is not really inactive. He is but a hypocrite.

7

यस्त्विन्द्रियाणि मनसा नियम्यारभतेऽर्जुन ।
कर्मेन्द्रियैः कर्मयोगमसक्तः स विशिष्यते ॥

yas tv indriyāṇi manasā
niyamyārabhate 'rjuna
karmendriyaiḥ karma-yogam
asaktaḥ sa viśiṣyate

Far better is one who controls his senses through the mind and engages oneself in karma without attachment, O' Arjuna.

8

नियतं कुरु कर्म त्वं कर्म ज्यायो ह्यकर्मणः ।
शरीरयात्रापि च ते न प्रसिद्ध्येदकर्मणः ॥

niyataṁ kuru karma tvaṁ
karma jyāyo hy akarmaṇaḥ
śarīra-yātrāpi ca te
na prasiddhyed akarmaṇaḥ

Choose to act, choose to do your duties, over inactivity, or not doing your duties. Without action we cannot even maintain our own body.

9

यज्ञार्थात्कर्मणोऽन्यत्र लोकोऽयं कर्मबन्धनः ।
तदर्थं कर्म कौन्तेय मुक्तसङ्गः समाचर ॥

yajñārthāt karmaṇo 'nyatra
loko 'yaṁ karma-bandhanaḥ
tad-arthaṁ karma kaunteya
mukta-saṅgaḥ samācara

Remember, Kaunteya, that to liberate oneself from the bondage of existence, action has to be done as a sacrifice to the Lord. All other actions are binding. So, Arjuna, work without attachment.

10

सहयज्ञाः प्रजाः सृष्ट्वा पुरोवाच प्रजापतिः ।
अनेन प्रसविष्यध्वमेष वोऽस्त्विष्टकामधुक् ॥

saha-yajñāḥ prajāḥ sṛṣṭvā
purovāca prajāpatiḥ
anena prasaviṣyadhvam
eṣa vo 'stv iṣṭa-kāma-dhuk

The creator Prajapati blessed all mankind at the beginning of existence to perform sacrifices that would please the Lord and usher in prosperity.

11

देवान्भावयतानेन ते देवा भावयन्तु वः ।
परस्परं भावयन्तः श्रेयः परमवाप्स्यथ ॥

devān bhāvayatānena
te devā bhāvayantu vaḥ
parasparaṁ bhāvayantaḥ
śreyaḥ param avāpsyatha

Sacrifices please the *devatas* who then satisfy those who have performed the sacrifice. This reciprocation between gods and mankind benefits all.

12

इष्टान्भोगान्हि वो देवा दास्यन्ते यज्ञभाविताः ।
तैर्दत्तानप्रदायैभ्यो यो भुङ्क्ते स्तेन एव सः ॥

iṣṭān bhogān hi vo devā
dāsyante yajña-bhāvitāḥ
tair dattān apradāyaibhyo
yo bhuṅkte stena eva saḥ

When pleased, the gods supply gifts that are necessities for life. But using those necessities without performing sacrifices in gratitude, is as good as theft.

13

यज्ञशिष्टाशिनः सन्तो मुच्यन्ते सर्वकिल्बिषैः ।
भुञ्जते ते त्वघं पापा ये पचन्त्यात्मकारणात् ॥

yajña-śiṣṭāśinaḥ santo
mucyante sarva-kilbiṣaiḥ
bhuñjate te tv agham pāpā
ye pacanty ātma-kāraṇāt

Pious people habitually take food that is first offered to God and by doing so, they are relieved of their sins. But the wicked eat only for their enjoyment and simply by eating they are sinning.

14

अन्नाद्भवन्ति भूतानि पर्जन्यादन्नसम्भवः ।
यज्ञाद्भवति पर्जन्यो यज्ञः कर्मसमुद्भवः ॥

annād bhavanti bhūtāni
parjanyād anna-sambhavaḥ
yajñād bhavati parjanyo
yajñaḥ karma-samudbhavaḥ

Living beings are dependent on grains. Grains are produced by rain. Rains are a result of performing sacrifices one does as prescribed duty.

15

कर्म ब्रह्मोद्भवं विद्धि ब्रह्माक्षरसमुद्भवम् ।
तस्मात्सर्वगतं ब्रह्म नित्यं यज्ञे प्रतिष्ठितम् ॥

karma brahmodbhavaṁ viddhi
brahmākṣara-samudbhavam
tasmāt sarva-gataṁ brahma
nityaṁ yajñe pratiṣṭhitam

The prescribed duties to be followed are listed in the Vedas, the sacred literature which is directly spoken by God. Thus all sacrifices revolve around the absolute Lord.

16

एवं प्रवर्तितं चक्रं नानुवर्तयतीह यः ।
अघायुरिन्द्रियारामो मोघं पार्थ स जीवति ॥

evaṁ pravartitaṁ cakraṁ
nānuvartayatīha yaḥ
aghāyur indriyārāmo
moghaṁ pārtha sa jīvati

Ignoring the cycle of duties as given in the Vedas is living a life of sin and irresponsibility. A life of sensual pleasure is a waste of life, Partha.

17

यस्त्वात्मरतिरेव स्यादात्मतृप्तश्च मानवः ।
आत्मन्येव च सन्तुष्टस्तस्य कार्यं न विद्यते ॥

yas tv ātma-ratir eva syād
ātma-tṛptaś ca mānavaḥ
ātmany eva ca santuṣṭas
tasya kāryaṁ na vidyate

However, the prescribed duties do not apply to one who is illuminated and fully self-realized.

18

नैव तस्य कृतेनार्थो नाकृतेनेह कश्चन ।
न चास्य सर्वभूतेषु कश्चिदर्थव्यपाश्रयः ॥

naiva tasya kṛtenārtho
nākṛteneha kaścana
na cāsya sarva-bhūteṣu
kaścid artha-vyapāśrayaḥ

A self-realized person has no attachment to the results of prescribed actions. He has no motivation to perform them because he has nothing to gain or lose.

19

तस्मादसक्तः सततं कार्यं कर्म समाचर ।
असक्तो ह्याचरन्कर्म परमाप्नोति पूरुषः ॥

tasmād asaktaḥ satataṁ
kāryaṁ karma samācara
asakto hy ācaran karma
param āpnoti pūruṣaḥ

So perform your duties, work without attachment to the fruits of your actions. Only this can lead you to realization of God.

20

कर्मणैव हि संसिद्धिमास्थिता जनकादय: ।
लोकसङ्ग्रहमेवापि सम्पश्यन्कर्तुमर्हसि ॥

karmaṇaiva hi saṁsiddhim
āsthitā janakādayaḥ
loka-saṅgraham evāpi
sampaśyan kartum arhasi

This is how King Janak and others have attained perfection. By action without attachment to results. You should also set an example for others by proper actions.

21

यद्यदाचरति श्रेष्ठस्तत्तदेवेतरो जन: ।
स यत्प्रमाणं कुरुते लोकस्तदनुवर्तते ॥

yad yad ācarati śreṣṭhas
tat tad evetaro janaḥ
sa yat pramāṇaṁ kurute
lokas tad anuvartate

Actions of a great man are followed by the world. The standards he sets are emulated by the world.

22

न मे पार्थास्ति कर्तव्यं त्रिषु लोकेषु किञ्चन ।
नानवाप्तमवाप्तव्यं वर्त एव च कर्मणि ॥

na me pārthāsti kartavyaṁ
triṣu lokeṣu kiñcana
nānavāptam avāptavyaṁ
varta eva ca karmaṇi

O' Partha, even though I have no duties to perform in any of the three worlds, I still do my duties.

23

यदि ह्यहं न वर्तेयं जातु कर्मण्यतन्द्रितः ।
मम वर्त्मानुवर्तन्ते मनुष्याः पार्थ सर्वशः ॥

yadi hy ahaṁ na varteyaṁ
jātu karmaṇy atandritaḥ
mama vartmānuvartante
manuṣyāḥ pārtha sarvaśaḥ

Because, Partha, if I do not do my duties, people can use that as an example for not doing their duties.

24

उत्सीदेयुरिमे लोका न कुर्यां कर्म चेदहम् ।
सङ्करस्य च कर्ता स्यामुपहन्यामिमाः प्रजाः ॥

utsīdeyur ime lokā
na kuryāṁ karma ced aham
saṅkarasya ca kartā syām
upahanyām imāḥ prajāḥ

If I do not act dutifully, the world will suffer and I will be responsible for that. There will be chaos, destroying peace for humanity, all because of Me.

25

सक्ताः कर्मण्यविद्वांसो यथा कुर्वन्ति भारत ।
कुर्याद्विद्वांस्तथासक्तश्चिकीर्षुर्लोकसङ्ग्रहम् ॥

saktāḥ karmaṇy avidvāṁso
yathā kurvanti bhārata
kuryād vidvāṁs tathāsaktaś
cikīrṣur loka-saṅgraham

O' scion of Bharata, the ignorant act attached to the results of their action whilst the wise act without those attachments, thereby inspiring the masses.

26

न बुद्धिभेदं जनयेदज्ञानां कर्मसङ्गिनाम् ।
जोषयेत्सर्वकर्माणि विद्वान्युक्तः समाचरन् ॥

na buddhi-bhedaṁ janayed
ajñānāṁ karma-saṅginām
joṣayet sarva-karmāṇi
vidvān yuktaḥ samācaran

The wise should not confuse the ignorant lest they stop work altogether. They should inspire them to act on their duties in an enlightened way.

27

प्रकृतेः क्रियमाणानि गुणैः कर्माणि सर्वशः ।
अहङ्कारविमूढात्मा कर्ताहमिति मन्यते ॥

prakṛteḥ kriyamāṇāni
guṇaiḥ karmāṇi sarvaśaḥ
ahaṅkāra-vimūḍhātmā
kartāham iti manyate

It is the three modes of material nature that perform all activities. But the ignorant, deluding himself to be the body, thinks that he is the doer.

28

तत्त्ववित्तु महाबाहो गुणकर्मविभागयोः ।
गुणा गुणेषु वर्तन्त इति मत्वा न सज्जते ॥

tattva-vit tu mahā-bāho
guṇa-karma-vibhāgayoḥ
guṇā guṇeṣu vartanta
iti matvā na sajjate

O' mighty-armed Arjuna, a knowledgeable person knows all about the soul, karma, and gunas. He does not get entangled with attachments or sense gratification.

29

प्रकृतेर्गुणसम्मूढाः सज्जन्ते गुणकर्मसु ।
तानकृत्स्नविदो मन्दान्कृत्स्नविन्न विचालयेत् ॥

prakṛter guṇa-saṁmūḍhāḥ
sajjante guṇa-karmasu
tān akṛtsna-vido mandān
kṛtsna-vin na vicālayet

But those influenced by gunas remain attached to material objects and enjoyment. The wise should not perplex such ignorant souls.

30

मयि सर्वाणि कर्माणि सन्न्यस्याध्यात्मचेतसा ।
निराशीर्निर्ममो भूत्वा युध्यस्व विगतज्वरः ॥

mayi sarvāṇi karmāṇi
sannyasyādhyātma-cetasā
nirāśīr nirmamo bhūtvā
yudhyasva vigata-jvaraḥ

The answer to this diseased condition is to meditate on Me and surrender unto Me in full knowledge. Free from desires, free from ego, free from grief, and then fight!

31

ये मे मतमिदं नित्यमनुतिष्ठन्ति मानवाः ।
श्रद्धावन्तोऽनसूयन्तो मुच्यन्ते तेऽपि कर्मभिः ॥

ye me matam idaṁ nityam
anutiṣṭhanti mānavāḥ
śraddhāvanto 'nasūyanto
mucyante te 'pi karmabhiḥ

Practising my teachings faithfully and without envy, will bring freedom from karmic bondage.

32

ये त्वेतदभ्यसूयन्तो नानुतिष्ठन्ति मे मतम् ।
सर्वज्ञानविमूढांस्तान्विद्धि नष्टानचेतसः ॥

ye tv etad abhyasūyanto
nānutiṣṭhanti me matam
sarva-jñāna-vimūḍhāṁs tān
viddhi naṣṭān acetasaḥ

And those who do not follow my teachings out of ignorance and envy, will live in bondage and misery for life.

33

सदृशं चेष्टते स्वस्याः प्रकृतेर्ज्ञानवानपि ।
प्रकृतिं यान्ति भूतानि निग्रहः किं करिष्यति ॥

sadṛśaṁ ceṣṭate svasyāḥ
prakṛter jñānavān api
prakṛtiṁ yānti bhūtāni
nigrahah kiṁ kariṣyati

Both the wise and the ignorant act as per their nature. Nothing is achieved by suppressing one's innate natural tendencies.

34

इन्द्रियस्येन्द्रियस्यार्थे रागद्वेषौ व्यवस्थितौ ।
तयोर्न वशमागच्छेत्तौ ह्यस्य परिपन्थिनौ ॥

indriyasyendriyasyārthe
rāga-dveṣau vyavasthitau
tayor na vaśam āgacchet
tau hy asya paripanthinau

It is the senses which affect desires and aversions. Do not let them be in control as they are enemies that block the path of self-realization.

35

श्रेयान्स्वधर्मो विगुण: परधर्मात्स्वनुष्ठितात् ।
स्वधर्मे निधनं श्रेय: परधर्मो भयावह: ॥

śreyān sva-dharmo viguṇaḥ
para-dharmāt sva-nuṣṭhitāt
sva-dharme nidhanaṁ śreyaḥ
para-dharmo bhayāvahaḥ

It is advisable to act according to one's own nature and duties. Even if it is not done perfectly, it is still better than doing another's duty. Better to die while engaged in one's own duties than be engaged in another's path which is downright dangerous for the soul.

36

अर्जुन उवाच
अथ केन प्रयुक्तोऽयं पापं चरति पूरुषः ।
अनिच्छन्नपि वार्ष्णेय बलादिव नियोजितः ॥

arjuna uvāca
atha kena prayukto 'yaṁ
pāpaṁ carati pūruṣaḥ
anicchann api vārṣṇeya
balād iva niyojitaḥ

Arjuna said –
What is it that makes one act sinfully and improperly, against his will, as if by an overpowering force?

37

श्रीभगवानुवाच
काम एष क्रोध एष रजोगुणसमुद्भवः ।
महाशनो महापाप्मा विद्ध्येनमिह वैरिणम् ॥

śrī-bhagavān uvāca
kāma eṣa krodha eṣa

rajo-guṇa-samudbhavaḥ
mahā-śano mahā-pāpmā
viddhy enam iha vairiṇam

Sri Bhagavan said –
It is lust and lust alone which is the biggest enemy of the whole world. A product of the mode of passion, it eventually transforms into anger.

38

धूमेनाव्रियते वह्निर्यथादर्शो मलेन च ।
यथोल्बेनावृतो गर्भस्तथा तेनेदमावृतम् ॥

dhūmenāvriyate vahnir
yathādarśo malena ca
yatholbenāvṛto garbhas
tathā tenedam āvṛtam

Excessive desire can cover mind's clarity just as smoke covers fire, dust covers a mirror, and womb covers a foetus.

39

आवृतं ज्ञानमेतेन ज्ञानिनो नित्यवैरिणा ।
कामरूपेण कौन्तेय दुष्पूरेणानलेन च ॥

āvṛtaṁ jñānam etena
jñānino nitya-vairiṇā
kāma-rūpeṇa kaunteya
duṣpūreṇānalena ca

Even the wise and learned are seen to be covered by this force of lust which is insatiable like a raging fire.

40

इन्द्रियाणि मनो बुद्धिरस्याधिष्ठानमुच्यते ।
एतैर्विमोहयत्येष ज्ञानमावृत्य देहिनम् ॥

indriyāṇi mano buddhir
asyādhiṣṭhānam ucyate
etair vimohayaty eṣa
jñānam āvṛtya dehinam

Overwhelming the embodied soul and clouding its knowledge, lust takes charge through the senses, mind, and intelligence.

41

तस्मात्त्वमिन्द्रियाण्यादौ नियम्य भरतर्षभ ।
पाप्मानं प्रजहि ह्येनं ज्ञानविज्ञाननाशनम् ॥

tasmāt tvam indriyāṇy ādau
niyamya bharatarṣabha
pāpmānaṁ prajahi hy enaṁ
jñāna-vijñāna-nāśanam

O' best of the Bharatas, waste no time in controlling the senses and killing this sinful demon called lust that destroys knowledge and self-realization.

42

इन्द्रियाणि पराण्याहुरिन्द्रियेभ्यः परं मनः ।
मनसस्तु परा बुद्धिर्यो बुद्धेः परतस्तु सः ॥

indriyāṇi parāṇy āhur
indriyebhyaḥ paraṁ manaḥ
manasas tu parā buddhir
yo buddheḥ paratas tu saḥ

The senses are superior to gross objects, the mind is superior to the senses, higher than the mind is the intelligence, and superior to the intellect stands the soul.

43

एवं बुद्धेः परं बुद्ध्वा संस्तभ्यात्मानमात्मना ।
जहि शत्रुं महाबाहो कामरूपं दुरासदम् ॥

evaṁ buddheḥ paraṁ buddhvā
saṁstabhyātmānam ātmanā
jahi śatruṁ mahā-bāho
kāma-rūpaṁ durāsadam

The soul being superior, can control the material senses, mind, and intelligence. O' mighty-armed Arjuna, use spiritual power to destroy the unconquerable enemy known as lust.

Chapter

04

Jnana Karma Sannyasa Yoga

1

श्रीभगवानुवाच
इमं विवस्वते योगं प्रोक्तवानहमव्ययम् ।
विवस्वान्मनवे प्राह मनुरिक्ष्वाकवेऽब्रवीत् ॥

śrī-bhagavān uvāca
imaṁ vivasvate yogaṁ
proktavān aham avyayam
vivasvān manave prāha
manur ikṣvākave 'bravīt

Sri Bhagavan said –
I taught this eternal yogic science to Vivasvan who shared it with Manu and Manu passed it on to Ikshvaku.

2

एवं परम्पराप्राप्तमिमं राजर्षयो विदुः ।
स कालेनेह महता योगो नष्टः परन्तप ॥

evaṁ paramparā-prāptam
imaṁ rājarṣayo viduḥ
sa kāleneha mahatā
yogo naṣṭaḥ parantapa

The supreme science in this way was handed down to kings in continuous tradition. But Arjuna, with time, the link was broken and the yogic science got lost.

3

स एवायं मया तेऽद्य योगः प्रोक्तः पुरातनः ।
भक्तोऽसि मे सखा चेति रहस्यं ह्येतदुत्तमम् ॥

sa evāyaṁ mayā te 'dya
yogaḥ proktaḥ purātanaḥ
bhakto 'si me sakhā ceti
rahasyaṁ hy etad uttamam

Today, I am revealing to you the same ancient science of yoga. It is a secret science that you being my friend and devotee are qualified to hear and understand.

4

अर्जुन उवाच
अपरं भवतो जन्म परं जन्म विवस्वतः ।
कथमेतद्विजानीयां त्वमादौ प्रोक्तवानिति ॥

arjuna uvāca
aparaṁ bhavato janma
paraṁ janma vivasvataḥ
katham etad vijānīyāṁ
tvam ādau proktavān iti

Arjuna said –
How is it possible that You instructed Vivasvan when the fact is that Vivasvan was born long before You?

5

श्रीभगवानुवाच
बहूनि मे व्यतीतानि जन्मानि तव चार्जुन ।
तान्यहं वेद सर्वाणि न त्वं वेत्थ परन्तप ॥

śrī-bhagavān uvāca
bahūni me vyatītāni
janmāni tava cārjuna
tāny ahaṁ veda sarvāṇi
na tvaṁ vettha parantapa

Sri Bhagavan said –
O' destroyer of enemies, both you and I have taken many births before. I remember them all whereas you do not.

6

अजोऽपि सन्नव्ययात्मा भूतानामीश्वरोऽपि सन् ।
प्रकृतिं स्वामधिष्ठाय सम्भवाम्यात्ममायया ॥

ajo 'pi sann avyayātmā
bhūtānām īśvaro 'pi san
prakṛtiṁ svām adhiṣṭhāya
sambhavāmy ātma-māyayā

I am the controller of all beings. Although I am birthless and eternal, yet I appear in the material world by the power of my energies.

7

यदा यदा हि धर्मस्य ग्लानिर्भवति भारत ।
अभ्युत्थानमधर्मस्य तदात्मानं सृजाम्यहम् ॥

yadā yadā hi dharmasya
glānir bhavati bhārata
abhyutthānam adharmasya
tadātmānaṁ sṛjāmy aham

Whenever there is gross decline in dharma and escalation of adharma, I appear Myself, O' descendant of Bharata.

8

परित्राणाय साधूनां विनाशाय च दुष्कृताम् ।
धर्मसंस्थापनार्थाय सम्भवामि युगे युगे ॥

paritrāṇāya sādhūnāṁ
vināśāya ca duṣkṛtām
dharma-saṁsthāpanārthāya
sambhavāmi yuge yuge

I appear in every millennium to protect the pious, to destroy the wicked, and to establish dharma again.

9

जन्म कर्म च मे दिव्यमेवं यो वेत्ति तत्त्वत: ।
त्यक्त्वा देहं पुनर्जन्म नैति मामेति सोऽर्जुन ॥

janma karma ca me divyam
evaṁ yo vetti tattvataḥ
tyaktvā dehaṁ punar janma
naiti mām eti so 'rjuna

O' Arjuna, he reaches my spiritual abode and does not take birth again in this world, if he sees divinity in my birth and activities.

10

वीतरागभयक्रोधा मन्मया मामुपाश्रिताः ।
बहवो ज्ञानतपसा पूता मद्भावमागताः ॥

vīta-rāga-bhaya-krodhā
man-mayā mām upāśritāḥ
bahavo jñāna-tapasā
pūtā mad-bhāvam āgatāḥ

Many have reached Me in the past by surrendering to Me, being free of attachments, fear, anger, their mind absorbed in Me and purified in the fire of knowledge.

11

ये यथा मां प्रपद्यन्ते तांस्तथैव भजाम्यहम् ।
मम वर्त्मानुवर्तन्ते मनुष्याः पार्थ सर्वशः ॥

ye yathā māṁ prapadyante
tāṁs tathaiva bhajāmy aham
mama vartmānuvartante
manuṣyāḥ pārtha sarvaśaḥ

In whatever way people surrender to Me, I reciprocate accordingly. O' son of Prtha, whatever the circumstances, everyone is on my path only.

12

काङ्क्षन्तः कर्मणां सिद्धिं यजन्त इह देवताः ।
क्षिप्रं हि मानुषे लोके सिद्धिर्भवति कर्मजा ॥

kāṅkṣantaḥ karmaṇāṁ siddhiṁ
yajanta iha devatāḥ
kṣipraṁ hi mānuṣe loke
siddhir bhavati karma-jā

Those who desire material success in the world, perform sacrifices and worship the devatas. It is easier to achieve material rewards from them.

13

चातुर्वर्ण्यं मया सृष्टं गुणकर्मविभागशः ।
तस्य कर्तारमपि मां विद्ध्यकर्तारमव्ययम् ॥

cātur-varṇyaṁ mayā sṛṣṭaṁ
guṇa-karma-vibhāgaśaḥ
tasya kartāram api māṁ
viddhy akartāram avyayam

The four socio-religious divisions are created by Me. The division is based on the three gunas and karmas. And though I am the creator, I am eternal and transcendental to it.

14

न मां कर्माणि लिम्पन्ति न मे कर्मफले स्पृहा ।
इति मां योऽभिजानाति कर्मभिर्न स बध्यते ॥

na māṁ karmāṇi limpanti
na me karma-phale spṛhā
iti māṁ yo 'bhijānāti
karmabhir na sa badhyate

I am not affected by any action, nor do I desire the fruits of action. Just understanding this truth about Me will free one from karmic bondage.

15

एवं ज्ञात्वा कृतं कर्म पूर्वैरपि मुमुक्षुभिः ।
कुरु कर्मैव तस्मात्त्वं पूर्वैः पूर्वतरं कृतम् ॥

evaṁ jñātvā kṛtaṁ karma
pūrvair api mumukṣubhiḥ
kuru karmaiva tasmāt tvaṁ
pūrvaiḥ pūrvataraṁ kṛtam

Ancient seekers of liberation knew this and performed actions. You too should follow their example and perform your duty.

16

किं कर्म किमकर्मेति कवयोऽप्यत्र मोहिताः ।
तत्ते कर्म प्रवक्ष्यामि यज्ज्ञात्वा मोक्ष्यसेऽशुभात् ॥

kiṁ karma kim akarmeti
kavayo 'py atra mohitāḥ
tat te karma pravakṣyāmi
yaj jñātvā mokṣyase 'śubhāt

What is action and what is inaction, is a most confusing subject. Now hear my explanation on what action is all about and free yourself from the bondage of sinful reactions.

17

कर्मणो ह्यपि बोद्धव्यं बोद्धव्यं च विकर्मणः ।
अकर्मणश्च बोद्धव्यं गहना कर्मणो गतिः ॥

karmaṇo hy api boddhavyaṁ
boddhavyaṁ ca vikarmaṇaḥ
akarmaṇaś ca boddhavyaṁ
gahanā karmaṇo gatiḥ

Even the wise are confused in understanding what is prescribed action, wrong action, and inaction. Karma is a deeply profound and mystical subject.

18

कर्मण्यकर्म यः पश्येदकर्मणि च कर्म यः ।
स बुद्धिमान्मनुष्येषु स युक्तः कृत्स्नकर्मकृत् ॥

karmaṇy akarma yaḥ paśyed
akarmaṇi ca karma yaḥ
sa buddhimān manuṣyeṣu
sa yuktaḥ kṛtsna-karma-kṛt

The wise can identify action in inaction and inaction in action. They are yogis who have mastered their actions.

19

यस्य सर्वे समारम्भाः कामसङ्कल्पवर्जिताः ।
ज्ञानाग्निदग्धकर्माणं तमाहुः पण्डितं बुधाः ॥

yasya sarve samārambhāḥ
kāma-saṅkalpa-varjitāḥ
jñānāgni-dagdha-karmāṇaṁ
tam āhuḥ paṇḍitaṁ budhāḥ

Such a wise person is a sage who acts without any desires and his karmic reactions are burnt in the fire of knowledge.

20

त्यक्त्वा कर्मफलासङ्गं नित्यतृप्तो निराश्रयः ।
कर्मण्यभिप्रवृत्तोऽपि नैव किञ्चित्करोति सः ॥

tyaktvā karma-phalāsaṅgaṁ
nitya-tṛpto nirāśrayaḥ
karmaṇy abhipravṛtto 'pi
naiva kiñcit karoti saḥ

Detached from the results of actions, he is always satisfied and independent. He is active without any fruitive activity.

21

निराशीर्यतचित्तात्मा त्यक्तसर्वपरिग्रहः ।
शारीरं केवलं कर्म कुर्वन्नाप्नोति किल्बिषम् ॥

nirāśīr yata-cittātmā
tyakta-sarva-parigrahaḥ
śārīraṁ kevalaṁ karma
kurvan nāpnoti kilbiṣam

He is in control of his mind and intelligence with no perception of possession, performing only necessary actions that incur no sin.

22

यदृच्छालाभसन्तुष्टो द्वन्द्वातीतो विमत्सरः ।
समः सिद्धावसिद्धौ च कृत्वापि न निबध्यते ॥

yadṛcchā-lābha-santuṣṭo
dvandvātīto vimatsaraḥ
samaḥ siddhāv asiddhau ca
kṛtvāpi na nibadhyate

He is content; free of envy and duality; steady in success and failure. Thus, he is free of karmic reactions even when constantly engaged in work.

23

गतसङ्गस्य मुक्तस्य ज्ञानावस्थितचेतसः ।
यज्ञायाचरतः कर्म समग्रं प्रविलीयते ॥

gata-saṅgasya muktasya
jñānāvasthita-cetasaḥ
yajñāyācarataḥ karma
samagraṁ pravilīyate

He who is detached and firmly in transcendental knowledge, is released from all karma and is himself transcendental.

24

ब्रह्मार्पणं ब्रह्म हविर्ब्रह्माग्नौ ब्रह्मणा हुतम् ।
ब्रह्मैव तेन गन्तव्यं ब्रह्मकर्मसमाधिना ॥

brahmārpaṇaṁ brahma havir
brahmāgnau brahmaṇā hutam
brahmaiva tena gantavyaṁ
brahma-karma-samādhinā

For one whose thoughts are completely absorbed in God, all his offerings are also of spiritual nature. It is easy for him to attain God.

25

दैवमेवापरे यज्ञं योगिनः पर्युपासते ।
ब्रह्माग्नावपरे यज्ञं यज्ञेनैवोपजुह्वति ॥

daivam evāpare yajñaṁ
yoginaḥ paryupāsate
brahmāgnāv apare yajñaṁ
yajñenaivopajuhvati

Some prefer to make material offerings to devatas while a few sacrifice themselves in the fire of the Supreme.

26

श्रोत्रादीनीन्द्रियाण्यन्ये संयमाग्निषु जुह्वति ।
शब्दादीन्विषयानन्य इन्द्रियाग्निषु जुह्वति ॥

śrotrādīnīndriyāṇy anye
saṁyamāgniṣu juhvati
śabdādīn viṣayān anya
indriyāgniṣu juhvati

In the fire of the controlled mind, some sacrifice their sense of hearing. While some sacrifice objects of sense gratification at the fire of senses.

27

सर्वाणीन्द्रियकर्माणि प्राणकर्माणि चापरे ।
आत्मसंयमयोगाग्नौ जुह्वति ज्ञानदीपिते ॥

sarvāṇīndriya-karmāṇi
prāṇa-karmāṇi cāpare
ātma-saṁyama-yogāgnau
juhvati jñāna-dīpite

Some offer the functions of their organs and the vital air in the fire of self-control.

28

द्रव्ययज्ञास्तपोयज्ञा योगयज्ञास्तथापरे ।
स्वाध्यायज्ञानयज्ञाश्च यतय: संशितव्रता: ॥

dravya-yajñās tapo-yajñā
yoga-yajñās tathāpare
svādhyāya-jñāna-yajñāś ca
yatayaḥ saṁśita-vratāḥ

Some sacrifice their wealth in charity, some offer austerities. Some follow *ashtanga* yoga and some take vows to study Vedas and cultivate knowledge.

29

अपाने जुह्वति प्राणं प्राणेऽपानं तथापरे ।
प्राणापानगती रुद्ध्वा प्राणायामपरायणा: ।
अपरे नियताहारा: प्राणान्प्राणेषु जुह्वति ॥

apāne juhvati prāṇaṁ
prāṇe 'pānaṁ tathāpare
prāṇāpāna-gatī ruddhvā
prāṇāyāma-parāyaṇāḥ
apare niyatāhārāḥ
prāṇān prāṇeṣu juhvati

Some practice breath control by sacrificing inhalation unto exhalation and exhalation unto inhalation. Some restrain both inhalation and exhalation to reach a state of trance. And some give up intake of food, sacrificing their vital force.

30

सर्वेऽप्येते यज्ञविदो यज्ञक्षपितकल्मषाः ।
यज्ञशिष्टामृतभुजो यान्ति ब्रह्म सनातनम् ॥

sarve 'py ete yajña-vido
yajña-kṣapita-kalmaṣāḥ
yajña-śiṣṭāmṛta-bhujo
yānti brahma sanātanam

Such sacrificial acts have the power to cleanse impurities. Enjoying the sacrificial remnants, they attain the supreme abode.

31

नायं लोकोऽस्त्ययज्ञस्य कुतोऽन्यः कुरुसत्तम ॥

nāyaṁ loko 'sty ayajñasya
kuto 'nyaḥ kuru-sattama

O' best of Kurus, without a life of sacrifice, it's impossible to be happy in this life, leave alone the next.

32

एवं बहुविधा यज्ञा वितता ब्रह्मणो मुखे ।
कर्मजान्विद्धि तान्सर्वानेवं ज्ञात्वा विमोक्ष्यसे ॥

evaṁ bahu-vidhā yajñā
vitatā brahmaṇo mukhe
karma-jān viddhi tān sarvān
evaṁ jñātvā vimokṣyase

The Vedas describe different sacrifices suitable for different categories of work. Know them and be liberated from material bondage.

33

श्रेयान्द्रव्यमयाद्यज्ञाज्ज्ञानयज्ञः परन्तप ।
सर्वं कर्माखिलं पार्थ ज्ञाने परिसमाप्यते ॥

śreyān dravya-mayād yajñāj
jñāna-yajñaḥ parantapa
sarvaṁ karmākhilaṁ pārtha
jñāne parisamāpyate

O' conqueror of enemies! O' Partha, higher than material sacrifice is sacrifice performed in knowledge because that work concludes with transcendental knowledge.

34

तद्विद्धि प्रणिपातेन परिप्रश्नेन सेवया ।
उपदेक्ष्यन्ति ते ज्ञानं ज्ञानिनस्तत्त्वदर्शिनः ॥

tad viddhi praṇipātena
paripraśnena sevayā
upadekṣyanti te jñānaṁ
jñāninas tattva-darśinaḥ

The wise who are self-realized can impart these truths to you if you approach them with humility in a mood of submissive curiosity and genuine service.

35

यज्ज्ञात्वा न पुनर्मोहमेवं यास्यसि पाण्डव ।
येन भूतान्यशेषाणि द्रक्ष्यस्यात्मन्यथो मयि ॥

yaj jñātvā na punar moham
evaṁ yāsyasi pāṇḍava
yena bhūtāny aśeṣāṇi
drakṣyasy ātmany atho mayi

Enlightened by a guru, you will be free of all ignorance and see all living beings as sharing a common spiritual core, being in Me, a part of Me, O' son of Pandu.

36

अपि चेदसि पापेभ्यः सर्वेभ्यः पापकृत्तमः ।
सर्वं ज्ञानप्लवेनैव वृजिनं सन्तरिष्यसि ॥

api ced asi pāpebhyaḥ
sarvebhyaḥ pāpa-kṛt-tamaḥ
sarvaṁ jñāna-plavenaiva
vṛjinaṁ santariṣyasi

This boat of transcendental knowledge can help you cross the ocean of material existence, however big a sinner you may be.

37

यथैधांसि समिद्धोऽग्निर्भस्मसात्कुरुतेऽर्जुन ।
ज्ञानाग्निः सर्वकर्माणि भस्मसात्कुरुते तथा ॥

yathaidhāṁsi samiddho 'gnir
bhasma-sāt kurute 'rjuna
jñānāgniḥ sarva-karmāṇi
bhasma-sāt kurute tathā

O' Arjuna, just as a fire burns wood to ashes, so does knowledge burn away all karmic reactions.

38

न हि ज्ञानेन सदृशं पवित्रमिह विद्यते ।
तत्स्वयं योगसंसिद्धः कालेनात्मनि विन्दति ॥

na hi jñānena sadṛśaṁ
pavitram iha vidyate
tat svayaṁ yoga-saṁsiddhaḥ
kālenātmani vindati

Nothing is more purifying than this divine knowledge. A mind purified by yoga receives this knowledge with time.

39

श्रद्धावाँल्लभते ज्ञानं तत्परः संयतेन्द्रियः ।
ज्ञानं लब्ध्वा परां शान्तिमचिरेणाधिगच्छति ॥

śraddhāvāl labhate jñānaṁ
tat-paraḥ saṁyatendriyaḥ
jñānaṁ labdhvā parāṁ śāntim
acireṇādhigacchati

Faith and self-control lead to success in this endeavour and once successful, one attains everlasting peace.

40

अज्ञश्चाश्रद्दधानश्च संशयात्मा विनश्यति ।
नायं लोकोऽस्ति न परो न सुखं संशयात्मनः ॥

ajñaś cāśraddadhānaś ca
saṁśayātmā vinaśyati
nāyaṁ loko 'sti na paro
na sukhaṁ saṁśayātmanaḥ

The faithless doubting the scriptures, perish eternally. They remain lost, finding happiness nowhere in this world or the other world.

41

योगसन्न्यस्तकर्माणं ज्ञानसञ्छिन्नसंशयम् ।
आत्मवन्तं न कर्माणि निबध्नन्ति धनञ्जय ॥

yoga-sannyasta-karmāṇaṁ
jñāna-sañchinna-saṁśayam
ātmavantaṁ na karmāṇi
nibadhnanti dhanañjaya

One becomes free of karmic bondage, O' Dhananjaya, when one renounces fruitive actions, dispels doubts by knowledge, and is self-realized.

42

तस्मादज्ञानसम्भूतं हृत्स्थं ज्ञानासिनात्मनः ।
छित्त्वैनं संशयं योगमातिष्ठोत्तिष्ठ भारत ॥

tasmād ajñāna-sambhūtaṁ
hṛt-sthaṁ jñānāsinātmanaḥ
chittvainaṁ saṁśayaṁ yogam
ātiṣṭhottiṣṭha bhārata

O' scion of Bharata, slash your doubts with the sword of knowledge and stand up once again to fight equipped with yogic knowledge.

Chapter

05

Karma Sannyasa Yoga

~ **1** ~

अर्जुन उवाच
सन्न्यासं कर्मणां कृष्ण पुनर्योगं च शंससि ।
यच्छ्रेय एतयोरेकं तन्मे ब्रूहि सुनिश्चितम् ॥

arjuna uvāca
sannyāsaṁ karmaṇāṁ kṛṣṇa
punar yogaṁ ca śaṁsasi
yac chreya etayor ekaṁ
tan me brūhi suniścitam

Arjuna said –
O' Krishna, You suggested renunciation of action first. You followed up by encouraging practising karma yoga. Without any ambiguity, please tell me which is the better of the two.

~ **2** ~

श्रीभगवानुवाच
सन्न्यासः कर्मयोगश्च निःश्रेयसकरावुभौ ।
तयोस्तु कर्मसन्न्यासात्कर्मयोगो विशिष्यते ॥

śrī-bhagavān uvāca
sannyāsaḥ karma-yogaś ca
niḥśreyasa-karāv ubhau

tayos tu karma-sannyāsāt
karma-yogo viśiṣyate

Sri Bhagavan said –
Both paths I suggested lead to the supreme goal. But the path of karma yoga or action without attachment to results is better than renunciation of action to acquire knowledge.

3

ज्ञेयः स नित्यसन्न्यासी यो न द्वेष्टि न काङ्क्षति ।
निर्द्वन्द्वो हि महाबाहो सुखं बन्धात्प्रमुच्यते ॥

jñeyaḥ sa nitya-sannyāsī
yo na dveṣṭi na kāṅkṣati
nirdvandvo hi mahā-bāho
sukhaṁ bandhāt pramucyate

A karma yogi is considered to be renounced because he is free of desires and aversions pertaining to results of action. Free from all material bondages, he attains liberation easily.

4

सांख्ययोगौ पृथग्बाला: प्रवदन्ति न पण्डिता: ।
एकमप्यास्थित: सम्यगुभयोर्विन्दते फलम् ॥

sāṅkhya-yogau pṛthag bālāḥ
pravadanti na paṇḍitāḥ
ekam apy āsthitaḥ samyag
ubhayor vindate phalam

It is ignorance to believe karma yoga to be different from sankhya yoga or contemplation. The wise know that they are not different from each other, leading to the same destination.

5

यत्सांख्यै: प्राप्यते स्थानं तद्योगैरपि गम्यते ।
एकं सांख्यं च योगं च य: पश्यति स पश्यति ॥

yat sāṅkhyaiḥ prāpyate sthānaṁ
tad yogair api gamyate
ekaṁ sāṅkhyaṁ ca yogaṁ ca
yaḥ paśyati sa paśyati

Only a person with clarity of vision understands this. Karma yoga and work in renunciation are one and the same, yielding the same results with the same destination.

6

सन्न्यासस्तु महाबाहो दुःखमाप्तुमयोगतः ।
योगयुक्तो मुनिर्ब्रह्म न चिरेणाधिगच्छति ॥

sannyāsas tu mahā-bāho
duḥkham āptum ayogataḥ
yoga-yukto munir brahma
na cireṇādhigacchati

But renunciation of work in the absence of karma yoga or work in devotion is difficult. Only when one practises work in devotion, does one easily attain the Absolute, O' mighty-armed Arjuna.

7

योगयुक्तो विशुद्धात्मा विजितात्मा जितेन्द्रियः ।
सर्वभूतात्मभूतात्मा कुर्वन्नपि न लिप्यते ॥

yoga-yukto viśuddhātmā
vijitātmā jitendriyaḥ
sarva-bhūtātma-bhūtātmā
kurvann api na lipyate

With the help of karma yoga, one purifies the senses, mind, and intelligence, and with such self-control he feels compassion for all living beings. Although continuously working, he is free of all entanglements.

8 – 9

नैव किञ्चित्करोमीति युक्तो मन्येत तत्त्ववित् ।
पश्यन्स्पृशञ्जिघ्रन्नश्नन्गच्छन्स्वपन्श्वसन् ॥
प्रलपन्विसृजन्गृह्णन्नुन्मिषन्निमिषन्नपि ।
इन्द्रियाणीन्द्रियार्थेषु वर्तन्त इति धारयन् ॥

naiva kiñcit karomīti
yukto manyeta tattva-vit
paśyañ śṛṇvan spṛśañ jighrann
aśnan gacchan svapan śvasan
pralapan visṛjan gṛhṇann
unmiṣan nimiṣann api
indriyāṇīndriyārtheṣu
vartanta iti dhārayan

A person of such consciousness knows that he is not the doer. Even when he sees, hears, touches, smells, eats, walks, sleeps, breathes, talks, evaluates, he knows that it is not him but the material senses that are doing this by interacting with the sense objects.

10

ब्रह्मण्याधाय कर्माणि सङ्गं त्यक्त्वा करोति यः ।
लिप्यते न स पापेन पद्मपत्रमिवाम्भसा ॥

brahmaṇy ādhāya karmāṇi
saṅgaṁ tyaktvā karoti yaḥ
lipyate na sa pāpena
padma-patram ivāmbhasā

He is free from sinful reactions of work if he dedicates his work to the Supreme God and works without any attachment. Just like a lotus leaf that is untouched by water even when surrounded by it.

11

कायेन मनसा बुद्ध्या केवलैरिन्द्रियैरपि ।
योगिनः कर्म कुर्वन्ति सङ्गं त्यक्त्वात्मशुद्धये ॥

kāyena manasā buddhyā
kevalair indriyair api
yoginaḥ karma kurvanti
saṅgaṁ tyaktvātma-śuddhaye

A karma yogi still acts, using his body, mind, and intelligence only to get purified. Although he has no attachment to his work.

12

युक्त: कर्मफलं त्यक्त्वा शान्तिमाप्नोति नैष्ठिकीम् ।
अयुक्त: कामकारेण फले सक्तो निबध्यते ॥

yuktaḥ karma-phalaṁ tyaktvā
śāntim āpnoti naiṣṭhikīm
ayuktaḥ kāma-kāreṇa
phale sakto nibadhyate

A karma yogi who has dedicated his work to God and renounced the results of his actions, gains peace. Whereas those who work without dedicating their acts to God, motivated by their own desires, get entangled.

13

सर्वकर्माणि मनसा सन्न्यस्यास्ते सुखं वशी ।
नवद्वारे पुरे देही नैव कुर्वन्न कारयन् ॥

sarva-karmāṇi manasā
sannyasyāste sukhaṁ vaśī
nava-dvāre pure dehī
naiva kurvan na kārayan

With this kind of detachment, the embodied soul lives happily in the city of nine gates, neither being the doer nor the cause.

14

न कर्तृत्वं न कर्माणि लोकस्य सृजति प्रभुः ।
न कर्मफलसंयोगं स्वभावस्तु प्रवर्तते ॥

na kartṛtvaṁ na karmāṇi
lokasya sṛjati prabhuḥ
na karma-phala-saṁyogaṁ
svabhāvas tu pravartate

It is factually the modes of material nature and not the soul that creates the urge to act or the resultant fruits of those actions.

15

नादत्ते कस्यचित्पापं न चैव सुकृतं विभुः ।
अज्ञानेनावृतं ज्ञानं तेन मुह्यन्ति जन्तवः ॥

nādatte kasyacit pāpaṁ
na caiva sukṛtaṁ vibhuḥ
ajñānenāvṛtaṁ jñānaṁ
tena muhyanti jantavaḥ

It is not God who is responsible for pious or wicked deeds. It is the responsibility of the living being who is conditioned by material nature and covered by ignorance.

16

ज्ञानेन तु तदज्ञानं येषां नाशितमात्मन: ।
तेषामादित्यवज्ज्ञानं प्रकाशयति तत्परम् ॥

jñānena tu tad ajñānaṁ
yeṣāṁ nāśitam ātmanaḥ
teṣām āditya-vaj jñānaṁ
prakāśayati tat param

When ignorance is destroyed by true knowledge, God is revealed. Just as the sun heralds visibility in the daytime.

17

तद्बुद्धयस्तदात्मानस्तन्निष्ठास्तत्परायणा: ।
गच्छन्त्यपुनरावृत्तिं ज्ञाननिर्धूतकल्मषा: ॥

tad-buddhayas tad-ātmānas
tan-niṣṭhās tat-parāyaṇāḥ
gacchanty apunar-āvṛttiṁ
jñāna-nirdhūta-kalmaṣāḥ

Absorbed in God, with faith and intelligence fixed in God, with sins destroyed by knowledge, he takes the path of liberation where there is no rebirth.

18

विद्याविनयसम्पन्ने ब्राह्मणे गवि हस्तिनि ।
शुनि चैव श्वपाके च पण्डिता: समदर्शिन: ॥

vidyā-vinaya-sampanne
brāhmaṇe gavi hastini
śuni caiva śva-pāke ca
paṇḍitāḥ sama-darśinaḥ

A brahmana, a cow, a dog, and a dog-eater are all the same for a man in knowledge.

19

इहैव तैजत: सर्गो येषां साम्ये स्थितं मन: ।
निर्दोषं हि समं ब्रह्म तस्माद्‌ब्रह्मणि ते स्थिता: ॥

ihaiva tair jitaḥ sargo
yeṣāṁ sāmye sthitaṁ manaḥ
nirdoṣaṁ hi samaṁ brahma
tasmād brahmaṇi te sthitāḥ

This vision of equality and impartiality helps conquer the cycle of birth and death. By sharing the qualities of God, men in knowledge are in a transcendental situation themselves.

20

न प्रहृष्येत्प्रियं प्राप्य नोद्विजेत्प्राप्य चाप्रियम् ।
स्थिरबुद्धिरसम्मूढो ब्रह्मविद्ब्रह्मणि स्थित: ॥

na prahṛṣyet priyaṁ prāpya
nodvijet prāpya cāpriyam
sthira-buddhir asammūḍho
brahma-vid brahmaṇi sthitaḥ

Being transcendental and fixed in God, they are free of delusions and unaffected by pleasure or pain.

21

बाह्यस्पर्शेष्वसक्तात्मा विन्दत्यात्मनि यत्सुखम् ।
स ब्रह्मयोगयुक्तात्मा सुखमक्षयमश्नुते ॥

bāhya-sparśeṣv asaktātmā
vindaty ātmani yat sukham
sa brahma-yoga-yuktātmā
sukham akṣayam aśnute

Rejecting external sensual pleasures, they find joy within. Uniting with God, they find infinite happiness.

22

ये हि संस्पर्शजा भोगा दुःखयोनय एव ते ।
आद्यन्तवन्तः कौन्तेय न तेषु रमते बुधः ॥

ye hi saṁsparśajā bhogā
duḥkha-yonaya eva te
ādy-antavantaḥ kaunteya
na teṣu ramate budhaḥ

O' Kaunteya, pleasure coming from sense organs is actually a source of pain. The wise do not care for them because such pleasures have a beginning and end soon.

23

शक्नोतीहैव यः सोढुं प्राक्शरीरविमोक्षणात् ।
कामक्रोधोद्भवं वेगं स युक्तः स सुखी नरः ॥

śaknotīhaiva yaḥ soḍhuṁ
prāk śarīra-vimokṣaṇāt
kāma-krodhodbhavaṁ vegaṁ
sa yuktaḥ sa sukhī naraḥ

Only by tolerating the agitations arising from desires and anger can one become happy. He alone is a yogi.

24

योऽन्तःसुखोऽन्तरारामस्तथान्तर्ज्योतिरेव यः ।
स योगी ब्रह्मनिर्वाणं ब्रह्मभूतोऽधिगच्छति ॥

yo 'ntaḥ-sukho 'ntar-ārāmas
tathāntar-jyotir eva yaḥ
sa yogī brahma-nirvāṇaṁ
brahma-bhūto 'dhigacchati

A yogi is happy within himself. He sees God within himself. He is flooded with self-enlightenment. He attains liberation from material existence and unites with God.

25

लभन्ते ब्रह्मनिर्वाणमृषयः क्षीणकल्मषाः ।
छिन्नद्वैधा यतात्मानः सर्वभूतहिते रताः ॥

labhante brahma-nirvāṇam
ṛṣayaḥ kṣīṇa-kalmaṣāḥ
chinna-dvaidhā yatātmānaḥ
sarva-bhūta-hite ratāḥ

He is free from sins. He has no doubts. He is self-controlled and engaged in welfare of others. He is liberated and attains God.

26

कामक्रोधविमुक्तानां यतीनां यतचेतसाम् ।
अभितो ब्रह्मनिर्वाणं वर्तते विदितात्मनाम् ॥

kāma-krodha-vimuktānāṁ
yatīnāṁ yata-cetasām
abhito brahma-nirvāṇaṁ
vartate viditātmanām

He renounces anger and desires. His mind is under his control. He is self-realized. He gets liberation in this world and the next.

27 – 28

स्पर्शान्कृत्वा बहिर्बाह्यांश्चक्षुश्चैवान्तरे भ्रुवो: ।
प्राणापानौ समौ कृत्वा नासाभ्यन्तरचारिणौ ॥
यतेन्द्रियमनोबुद्धिर्मुनिर्मोक्षपरायण: ।
विगतेच्छाभयक्रोधो य: सदा मुक्त एव स: ॥

sparśān kṛtvā bahir bāhyāṁś
cakṣuś caivāntare bhruvoḥ
prāṇāpānau samau kṛtvā
nāsābhyantara-cāriṇau
yatendriya-mano-buddhir
munir mokṣa-parāyaṇaḥ

vigatecchā-bhaya-krodho
yaḥ sadā mukta eva saḥ

Purging out thoughts of sensual enjoyment, concentrating between the brows, equalizing the breath in inhalation and exhalation, controlling the mind and intelligence, giving up desires and fears. This is the way to liberation.

29

भोक्तारं यज्ञतपसां सर्वलोकमहेश्वरम् ।
सुहृदं सर्वभूतानां ज्ञात्वा मां शान्तिमृच्छति ॥

bhoktāraṁ yajña-tapasāṁ
sarva-loka-maheśvaram
suhṛdaṁ sarva-bhūtānāṁ
jñātvā māṁ śāntim ṛcchati

Only when one understands that I am the enjoyer of end results of all sacrifices and austerities, I control everything in this world and I am a friend to everyone, only then peace is attained.

Chapter

06

Dhyana Yoga

1

श्रीभगवानुवाच
अनाश्रित: कर्मफलं कार्यं कर्म करोति य: ।
स सन्न्यासी च योगी च न निरग्निर्न चाक्रिय: ॥

śrī-bhagavān uvāca
anāśritaḥ karma-phalaṁ
kāryaṁ karma karoti yaḥ
sa sannyāsī ca yogī ca
na niragnir na cākriyaḥ

Sri Bhagavan said –

A true yogi or a true renunciant is one who performs his duties renouncing attachment to results and not one who abandons work and the sacrificial fire.

2

यं सन्न्यासमिति प्राहुर्योगं तं विद्धि पाण्डव ।
न ह्यसन्न्यस्तसङ्कल्पो योगी भवति कश्चन ॥

yaṁ sannyāsam iti prāhur
yogaṁ taṁ viddhi pāṇḍava
na hy asannyasta-saṅkalpo
yogī bhavati kaścana

O' son of Pandu, yoga cannot be separated from renunciation because to become a yogi, one must renounce all desires.

3

आरुरुक्षोर्मुनेर्योगं कर्म कारणमुच्यते ।
योगारूढस्यतस्यैव शमः कारणमुच्यते ॥

ārurukṣor muner yogaṁ
karma kāraṇam ucyate
yogārūḍhasya tasyaiva
śamaḥ kāraṇam ucyate

To become a yogi, work without attachment is recommended. Only for an elevated yogi, giving up work is recommended.

4

यदा हि नेन्द्रियार्थेषु न कर्मस्वनुषज्जते ।
सर्वसङ्कल्पसन्न्यासी योगारूढस्तदोच्यते ॥

yadā hi nendriyārtheṣu
na karmasv anuṣajjate
sarva-saṅkalpa-sannyāsī
yogārūḍhas tadocyate

Work without desires, without sense gratification, and without any attachment to results leads to attainment of yoga.

5

उद्धरेदात्मनात्मानं नात्मानमवसादयेत् ।
आत्मैव ह्यात्मनो बन्धुरात्मैव रिपुरात्मनः ॥

uddhared ātmanātmānaṁ
nātmānam avasādayet
ātmaiva hy ātmano bandhur
ātmaiva ripur ātmanaḥ

The mind can act as a friend to elevate oneself or it can also work like an enemy to degrade oneself.

6

बन्धुरात्मात्मनस्तस्य येनात्मैवात्मना जितः ।
अनात्मनस्तु शत्रुत्वे वर्तेतात्मैव शत्रुवत् ॥

bandhur ātmātmanas tasya
yenātmaivātmanā jitaḥ
anātmanas tu śatrutve
vartetātmaiva śatru-vat

When the mind is conquered, it becomes a friend. Left unconquered, it is an enemy.

7

जितात्मनः प्रशान्तस्य परमात्मा समाहितः ।
शीतोष्णसुखदुःखेषु तथा मानापमानयोः ॥

jitātmanaḥ praśāntasya
paramātmā samāhitaḥ
śītoṣṇa-sukha-duḥkheṣu
tathā mānāpamānayoḥ

For a conquered mind, joy, sorrow, heat, cold, pain, pleasure, all are the same. Such a yogi attains peace and realization of the Supreme Soul.

8

ज्ञानविज्ञानतृप्तात्मा कूटस्थो विजितेन्द्रियः ।
युक्त इत्युच्यते योगी समलोष्ट्राश्मकाञ्चनः ॥

jñāna-vijñāna-tṛptātmā
kūṭa-stho vijitendriyaḥ
yukta ity ucyate yogī
sama-loṣṭrāśma-kāñcanaḥ

A self-realized yogi, steeped in transcendental knowledge and controlled senses, sees stones, mud, and gold as equal.

9

सुहृन्मित्रार्युदासीनमध्यस्थद्वेष्यबन्धुषु ।
साधुष्वपि च पापेषु समबुद्धिर्विशिष्यते ॥

suhṛn-mitrāry-udāsīna-madhyastha-
dveṣya-bandhuṣu
sādhuṣv api ca pāpeṣu
sama-buddhir viśiṣyate

An advanced yogi sees a friend and an enemy equally and is impartial to all, be it saint or sinner.

10

योगी युञ्जीत सततमात्मानं रहसि स्थितः ।
एकाकी यतचित्तात्मा निराशीरपरिग्रहः ॥

yogī yuñjīta satatam
ātmānaṁ rahasi sthitaḥ
ekākī yata-cittātmā
nirāśīr aparigrahaḥ

A yogi should live in seclusion, be free from material desires and possessions, regulate the mind and meditate on the Supreme.

11

शुचौ देशे प्रतिष्ठाप्य स्थिरमासनमात्मनः ।
नात्युच्छ्रितं नातिनीचं चैलाजिनकुशोत्तरम् ॥

śucau deśe pratiṣṭhāpya
sthiram āsanam ātmanaḥ
nāty-ucchritaṁ nāti-nīcaṁ
cailājina-kuśottaram

The yogi should practice in a clean and secluded place on a seat made of kusha grass, covered by deer skin and a cloth over it. The asana should neither be too low nor too high.

12

तत्रैकाग्रं मनः कृत्वा यतचित्तेन्द्रियक्रियः ।
उपविश्यासने युञ्ज्याद्योगमात्मविशुद्धये ॥

tatraikāgraṁ manaḥ kṛtvā
yata-cittendriya-kriyaḥ
upaviśyāsane yuñjyād
yogam ātma-viśuddhaye

Seated on this asana, he should begin the practice of purifying the heart by controlling his thoughts and by single-point meditation.

13

समं कायशिरोग्रीवं धारयन्नचलं स्थिरः ।
सम्प्रेक्ष्य नासिकाग्रं स्वं दिशश्चानवलोकयन् ॥

samaṁ kāya-śiro-grīvaṁ
dhārayann acalaṁ sthiraḥ
samprekṣya nāsikāgraṁ svaṁ
diśaś cānavalokayan

He sits straight with head, neck, and back aligned in a straight line with his gaze steadily concentrated on the tip of his nose.

14

प्रशान्तात्मा विगतभीर्ब्रह्मचारिव्रते स्थितः ।
मनः संयम्य मच्चित्तो युक्त आसीत मत्परः ॥

prasāntātmā vigata-bhīr
brahmacāri-vrate sthitaḥ
manaḥ saṁyamya mac-citto
yukta āsīta mat-paraḥ

The yogi meditates on Me with a serene and fearless mind, on a vow of celibacy, holding Me as his supreme goal of life.

15

युञ्जन्नेवं सदात्मानं योगी नियतमानसः ।
शान्तिं निर्वाणपरमां मत्संस्थामधिगच्छति ॥

yuñjann evaṁ sadātmānaṁ
yogī niyata-mānasaḥ
śāntiṁ nirvāṇa-paramām
mat-saṁsthām adhigacchati

With a disciplined mind and body and totally absorbed in Me, the yogi transcends material existence to reach the spiritual kingdom.

16

नात्यश्नतस्तु योगोऽस्ति न चैकान्तमनश्नतः ।
न चातिस्वप्नशीलस्य जाग्रतो नैव चार्जुन ॥

nāty-aśnatas tu yogo 'sti
na caikāntam anaśnataḥ
na cāti-svapna-śīlasya
jāgrato naiva cārjuna

O' Arjuna, those who eat or sleep too much or too little, cannot be successful in yoga.

17

युक्ताहारविहारस्य युक्तचेष्टस्य कर्मसु ।
युक्तस्वप्नावबोधस्य योगो भवति दुःखहा ॥

yuktāhāra-vihārasya
yukta-ceṣṭasya karmasu
yukta-svapnāvabodhasya
yogo bhavati duḥkha-hā

Balanced eating, sleeping, working, and recreation is necessary for yoga practice to overcome all difficulties in life.

18

यदा विनियतं चित्तमात्मन्येवावतिष्ठते ।
निस्पृह: सर्वकामेभ्यो युक्त इत्युच्यते तदा ॥

yadā viniyataṁ cittam
ātmany evāvatiṣṭhate
nispṛhaḥ sarva-kāmebhyo
yukta ity ucyate tadā

He is a successful yogi who withdraws his mind from desires and focuses only on the transcendental.

19

यथा दीपो निवातस्थो नेङ्गते सोपमा स्मृता ।
योगिनो यतचित्तस्य युञ्जतो योगमात्मन: ॥

yathā dīpo nivāta-stho
neṅgate sopamā smṛtā
yogino yata-cittasya
yuñjato yogam ātmanaḥ

The unwavering mind of a yogi is like an unflickering lamp in a windless place.

20 – 21

यत्रोपरमते चित्तं निरुद्धं योगसेवया ।
यत्र चैवात्मनात्मानं पश्यन्नात्मनि तुष्यति ॥
सुखमात्यन्तिकं यत्तद्बुद्धिग्राह्यमतीन्द्रियम् ।
वेत्ति यत्र न चैवायं स्थितश्चलति तत्त्वतः ॥

yatroparamate cittaṁ
niruddhaṁ yoga-sevayā
yatra caivātmanātmānaṁ
paśyann ātmani tuṣyati
sukham ātyantikaṁ yat tad
buddhi-grāhyam atīndriyam
vetti yatra na caivāyaṁ
sthitaś calati tattvataḥ

On attaining perfection, the yogi sees the soul through the purified mind and experiences inner joy. In this joyous state of pure bliss or samadhi, which is beyond comprehension of the senses, he never wavers from the path.

22 – 23

यं लब्ध्वा चापरं लाभं मन्यते नाधिकं ततः ।
यस्मिन्स्थितो न दुःखेन गुरुणापि विचाल्यते ॥
तं विद्याद्दुःखसंयोगवियोगं योगसंज्ञितम् ॥

yam labdhva capram labham
manyate nadhikam tatah
yasmin sthito na dukhena
gurunapi vicalyate
taṁ vidyād duḥkha-saṁyoga-viyogaṁ
yoga-saṁjñitam

Once he attains this state of samadhi, he knows there's nothing greater left to achieve. He is not perturbed by anything, come what may. He is free of all miseries. This state is achieved only by practising yoga with determination and optimism.

24

स निश्चयेन योक्तव्यो योगोऽनिर्विण्णचेतसा ।
सङ्कल्पप्रभवान्कामांस्त्यक्त्वा सर्वानशेषतः ।
मनसैवेन्द्रियग्रामं विनियम्य समन्ततः ॥

sa niścayena yoktavyo
yogo 'nirviṇṇa-cetasā
saṅkalpa-prabhavān kāmāṁs

tyaktvā sarvān aśeṣataḥ
manasaivendriya-grāmaṁ
viniyamya samantataḥ

From controlling the mind and senses from all sides to relinquishing all cravings, the practice of yoga needs steadfast determination without any deviation.

25

शनैः शनैरुपरमेद्बुद्ध्या धृतिगृहीतया ।
आत्मसंस्थं मनः कृत्वा न किञ्चिदपि चिन्तयेत् ॥

śanaiḥ śanair uparamed
buddhyā dhṛti-gṛhītayā
ātma-saṁsthaṁ manaḥ kṛtvā
na kiñcid api cintayet

He progresses step by step to make the mind still, the intelligence being absorbed in a trance and the mind situated in the Self.

26

यतो यतो निश्चलति मनश्चञ्चलमस्थिरम् ।
ततस्ततो नियम्यैतदात्मन्येव वशं नयेत् ॥

yato yato niścalati
manaś cañcalam asthiram
tatas tato niyamyaitad
ātmany eva vaśaṁ nayet

The unsteady mind may wander again and again, here and there, but the yogi always pulls it back to focus on God and keeps it under control.

27

प्रशान्तमनसं ह्येनं योगिनं सुखमुत्तमम् ।
उपैति शान्तरजसं ब्रह्मभूतमकल्मषम् ॥

praśānta-manasaṁ hy enaṁ
yoginaṁ sukham uttamam
upaiti śānta-rajasaṁ
brahma-bhūtam akalmaṣam

In return, the yogi experiences ultimate bliss when his mind is still, his passions are under control, and he is free of sinful reactions.

28

युञ्जन्नेवं सदात्मानं योगी विगतकल्मषः ।
सुखेन ब्रह्मसंस्पर्शमत्यन्तं सुखमश्नुते ॥

yuñjann evaṁ sadātmānaṁ
yogī vigata-kalmaṣaḥ
sukhena brahma-saṁsparśam
atyantaṁ sukham aśnute

The yogic practice frees him from material contamination and by connecting with God, he reaches ultimate happiness.

29

सर्वभूतस्थमात्मानं सर्वभूतानि चात्मनि ।
ईक्षते योगयुक्तात्मा सर्वत्र समदर्शनः ॥

sarva-bhūta-stham ātmānaṁ
sarva-bhūtāni cātmani
īkṣate yoga-yuktātmā
sarvatra sama-darśanaḥ

The yogi sees all beings existing in Me and he sees Me existing in all beings. He sees all with equal vision.

30

यो मां पश्यति सर्वत्र सर्वं च मयि पश्यति ।
तस्याहं न प्रणश्यामि स च मे न प्रणश्यति ॥

yo māṁ paśyati sarvatra
sarvaṁ ca mayi paśyati
tasyāhaṁ na praṇaśyāmi
sa ca me na praṇaśyati

A yogi who sees Me everywhere and sees everything in Me, never loses Me nor do I lose him.

31

सर्वभूतस्थितं यो मां भजत्येकत्वमास्थित: ।
सर्वथा वर्तमानोऽपि स योगी मयि वर्तते ॥

sarva-bhūta-sthitaṁ yo māṁ
bhajaty ekatvam āsthitaḥ
sarvathā vartamāno 'pi
sa yogī mayi vartate

A yogi who worships Me knowing Me to be the Super Soul within all living beings, lives in Me always.

32

आत्मौपम्येन सर्वत्र समं पश्यति योऽर्जुन ।
सुखं वा यदि वा दुःखं स योगी परमो मतः ॥

ātmaupamyena sarvatra
samaṁ paśyati yo 'rjuna
sukhaṁ vā yadi vā duḥkhaṁ
sa yogī paramo mataḥ

O' Arjuna, the perfect yogi responds to the pains and pleasures of others as if they were his own.

33

अर्जुन उवाच
योऽयं योगस्त्वया प्रोक्तः साम्येन मधुसूदन ।
एतस्याहं न पश्यामि चञ्चलत्वात्स्थितिं स्थिराम् ॥

arjuna uvāca
yo 'yaṁ yogas tvayā proktaḥ
sāmyena madhusūdana
etasyāhaṁ na paśyāmi
cañcalatvāt sthitiṁ sthirām

Arjuna said –
O' Madhusudan, given that the mind is restless and wavering, this practice of yoga is highly unrealistic and impossible to do.

34

चञ्चलं हि मनः कृष्ण प्रमाथि बलवद्दृढम् ।
तस्याहं निग्रहं मन्ये वायोरिव सुदुष्करम् ॥

cañcalaṁ hi manaḥ kṛṣṇa
pramāthi balavad dṛḍham
tasyāhaṁ nigrahaṁ manye
vāyor iva su-duṣkaram

O' Krishna, it is far simpler to control the wind than the mind which is stubborn, wavering, dominating, and agitated.

35

श्रीभगवानुवाच
असंशयं महाबाहो मनो दुर्निग्रहं चलम् ।
अभ्यासेन तु कौन्तेय वैराग्येण च गृह्यते ॥

śrī-bhagavān uvāca
asaṁśayaṁ mahā-bāho
mano durnigrahaṁ calam
abhyāsena tu kaunteya
vairāgyeṇa ca gṛhyate

Sri Bhagavan said –

Rightly said, O' mighty-armed Arjuna. The restless mind is indeed difficult to control but it can surely be done by practice and detachment.

36

असंयतात्मना योगो दुष्प्राप इति मे मतिः ।
वश्यात्मना तु यतता शक्योऽवाप्तुमुपायतः ॥

asaṁyatātmanā yogo
duṣprāpa iti me matiḥ
vaśyātmanā tu yatatā
śakyo 'vāptum upāyataḥ

Yoga is difficult for one whose mind is out of control. But in my opinion, once the mind is controlled, yoga can be perfected.

37

अर्जुन उवाच
अयतिः श्रद्धयोपेतो योगाच्चलितमानसः ।
अप्राप्य योगसंसिद्धिं कां गतिं कृष्ण गच्छति ॥

arjuna uvāca
ayatiḥ śraddhayopeto

yogāc calita-mānasaḥ
aprāpya yoga-saṁsiddhiṁ
kāṁ gatiṁ kṛṣṇa gacchati

Arjuna said –

O' Krishna, what happens to the yogi who begins in good faith but falters in between because of worldly desires and goes off the path?

38

कच्चिन्नोभयविभ्रष्टश्छिन्नाभ्रमिव नश्यति ।
अप्रतिष्ठो महाबाहो विमूढो ब्रह्मण: पथि ॥

kaccin nobhaya-vibhraṣṭaś
chinnābhram iva naśyati
apratiṣṭho mahā-bāho
vimūḍho brahmaṇaḥ pathi

Lost from his original path, is he not like a wandering cloud, with neither material success nor spiritual success, O' mighty-armed Krishna?

39

एतन्मे संशयं कृष्ण छेत्तुमर्हस्यशेषतः ।
त्वदन्यः संशयस्यास्य छेत्ता न ह्युपपद्यते ॥

etan me saṁśayaṁ kṛṣṇa
chettum arhasy aśeṣataḥ
tvad-anyaḥ saṁśayasyāsya
chettā na hy upapadyate

Krishna, these are my doubts and only You can dispel them completely.

40

श्रीभगवानुवाच
पार्थ नैवेह नामुत्र विनाशस्तस्य विद्यते ।
न हि कल्याणकृत्कश्चिद्दुर्गतिं तात गच्छति ॥

śrī-bhagavān uvāca
pārtha naiveha nāmutra
vināśas tasya vidyate
na hi kalyāṇa-kṛt kaścid
durgatiṁ tāta gacchati

Sri Bhagavan said –
A person on this auspicious path will never meet misfortune. Not in this world, not in the spiritual world. He is never defeated by evil forces.

41

प्राप्य पुण्यकृतां लोकानुषित्वा शाश्वती: समा: ।
शुचीना श्रीमतां गेहे योगभ्रष्टोऽभिजायते ॥

prāpya puṇya-kṛtāṁ lokān
uṣitvā śāśvatīḥ samāḥ
śucīnāṁ śrīmatāṁ gehe
yoga-bhraṣṭo 'bhijāyate

On death, the unsuccessful yogi goes to heaven and enjoys in virtuous company. After a long period of enjoyment, he takes birth again in a spiritual or wealthy family.

42

अथवा योगिनामेव कुले भवति धीमताम् ।
एतद्धि दुर्लभतरं लोके जन्म यदीदृशम् ॥

atha vā yoginām eva
kule bhavati dhīmatām
etad dhi durlabhataraṁ
loke janma yad īdṛśam

Or in very rare cases, he may be born in the family of an exalted transcendentalist.

43

तत्र तं बुद्धिसंयोगं लभते पौर्वदेहिकम् ।
यतते च ततो भूयः संसिद्धौ कुरुनन्दन ॥

tatra taṁ buddhi-saṁyogaṁ
labhate paurva-dehikam
yatate ca tato bhūyaḥ
saṁsiddhau kuru-nandana

On birth, once again he takes up a yogic life and strives for spiritual perfection by reawakening the consciousness of his previous life.

44

पूर्वाभ्यासेन तेनैव ह्रियते ह्यवशोऽपि सः ।
जिज्ञासुरपि योगस्य शब्दब्रह्मातिवर्तते ॥

pūrvābhyāsena tenaiva
hriyate hy avaśo 'pi saḥ
jijñāsur api yogasya
śabda-brahmātivartate

In this life, he acquires a spontaneous attraction for God. On the strength of past practice, he can transcend and rise above the Vedic ritualistic practice.

45

प्रयत्नाद्यतमानस्तु योगी संशुद्धकिल्बिषः ।
अनेकजन्मसंसिद्धस्ततो याति परां गतिम् ॥

prayatnād yatamānas tu
yogī saṁśuddha-kilbiṣaḥ
aneka-janma-saṁsiddhas
tato yāti parāṁ gatim

By renewing his efforts in controlling the mind, he makes further progress. After many births of practice, he becomes free of material desires and achieves the supreme goal.

46

तपस्विभ्योऽधिको योगी ज्ञानिभ्योऽपि मतोऽधिकः ।
कर्मिभ्यश्चाधिको योगी तस्माद्योगी भवार्जुन ॥

tapasvibhyo 'dhiko yogī
jñānibhyo 'pi mato 'dhikaḥ
karmibhyaś cādhiko yogī
tasmād yogī bhavārjuna

O' Arjuna, be a yogi because he is better than all three—the ascetic, the *gyani*, and the ritualistic materialist.

47

योगिनामपि सर्वेषां मद्गतेनान्तरात्मना ।
श्रद्धावान्भजते यो मां स मे युक्ततमो मतः ॥

yogināṁ api sarveṣāṁ
mad-gatenāntar-ātmanā
śraddhāvān bhajate yo māṁ
sa me yuktatamo mataḥ

That yogi is best who imposes full faith in Me, worships Me in full devotion and is most intimately united with Me.

Chapter

07

Jnyana Vijnyana Yoga

1

श्रीभगवानुवाच
मय्यासक्तमना: पार्थ योगं युञ्जन्मदाश्रय: ।
असंशयं समग्रं मां यथा ज्ञास्यसि तच्छृणु ॥

śrī-bhagavān uvāca
mayy āsakta-manāḥ pārtha
yogaṁ yuñjan mad-āśrayaḥ
asaṁśayaṁ samagraṁ māṁ
yathā jñāsyasi tac chṛṇu

Sri Bhagavan said –
Now listen, Arjuna, to how you can know Me completely. It is only by practising yoga, by fixing your mind on Me and taking shelter in Me, you will know Me, without any doubts.

2

ज्ञानं तेऽहं सविज्ञानमिदं वक्ष्याम्यशेषत: ।
यज्ज्ञात्वा नेह भूयोऽन्यज्ज्ञातव्यमवशिष्यते ॥

jñānaṁ te 'haṁ sa-vijñānam
idaṁ vakṣyāmy aśeṣataḥ
yaj jñātvā neha bhūyo 'nyaj
jñātavyam avaśiṣyate

I give you now both knowledge and realization after which you will know everything there is to know.

3

मनुष्याणां सहस्रेषु कश्चिद्यतति सिद्धये ।
यततामपि सिद्धानां कश्चिन्मां वेत्ति तत्त्वतः ॥

manuṣyāṇāṁ sahasreṣu
kaścid yatati siddhaye
yatatām api siddhānāṁ
kaścin māṁ vetti tattvataḥ

Only one out of thousands of men, strives for perfection. Even amongst those who have attained perfection, hardly a soul understands Me in essence.

4

भूमिरापोऽनलो वायुः खं मनो बुद्धिरेव च ।
अहङ्कार इतीयं मे भिन्ना प्रकृतिरष्टधा ॥

bhūmir āpo 'nalo vāyuḥ
khaṁ mano buddhir eva ca
ahaṅkāra itīyaṁ me
bhinnā prakṛtir aṣṭadhā

Earth, water, fire, air, ether, mind, intellect, and ego are eight of my material energies.

5

अपरेयमितस्त्वन्यां प्रकृतिं विद्धि मे पराम् ।
जीवभूतां महाबाहो ययेदं धार्यते जगत् ॥

apareyam itas tv anyāṁ
prakṛtiṁ viddhi me parām
jīva-bhūtāṁ mahā-bāho
yayedaṁ dhāryate jagat

O' mighty-armed Arjuna, these are my inferior energies whereas my superior energy comprising souls, maintains the universe.

6

एतद्योनीनि भूतानि सर्वाणीत्युपधारय ।
अहं कृत्स्नस्य जगतः प्रभवः प्रलयस्तथा ॥

etad-yonīni bhūtāni
sarvāṇīty upadhāraya
ahaṁ kṛtsnasya jagataḥ
prabhavaḥ pralayas tathā

These two energies, the material and spiritual, are the source of origin of all living beings. And I am both, the creator and the destroyer of the entire world.

7

मत्तः परतरं नान्यत्किञ्चिदस्ति धनञ्जय ।
मयि सर्वमिदं प्रोतं सूत्रे मणिगणा इव ॥

mattaḥ parataraṁ nānyat
kiñcid asti dhanañjaya
mayi sarvam idaṁ protaṁ
sūtre maṇi-gaṇā iva

Nothing is higher than Me. O' Dhananjaya, like a string that holds pearls, I hold everything together.

8

रसोऽहमप्सु कौन्तेय प्रभास्मि शशिसूर्ययोः ।
प्रणवः सर्ववेदेषु शब्दः खे पौरुषं नृषु ॥

raso 'ham apsu kaunteya
prabhāsmi śaśi-sūryayoḥ
praṇavaḥ sarva-vedeṣu
śabdaḥ khe pauruṣaṁ nṛṣu

I am the taste in water, the brilliance of the sun and moon, mantra Om of the Vedic mantras, the sound in ether, and the ability in man.

9

पुण्यो गन्धः पृथिव्यां च तेजश्चास्मि विभावसौ ।
जीवनं सर्वभूतेषु तपश्चास्मि तपस्विषु ॥

puṇyo gandhaḥ pṛthivyāṁ ca
tejaś cāsmi vibhāvasau
jīvanaṁ sarva-bhūteṣu
tapaś cāsmi tapasviṣu

I am the aroma of earth, the warmth of fire, the life of all that is living and penance of the ascetics.

10

बीजं मां सर्वभूतानां विद्धि पार्थ सनातनम् ।
बुद्धिर्बुद्धिमतामस्मि तेजस्तेजस्विनामहम् ॥

bījaṁ māṁ sarva-bhūtānāṁ
viddhi pārtha sanātanam
buddhir buddhimatām asmi
tejas tejasvinām aham

The original seed of the entire existence, wisdom of the intelligent, the might of the mighty, that's Me, O' Partha.

11

बलं बलवतां चाहं कामरागविवर्जितम् ।
धर्माविरुद्धो भूतेषु कामोऽस्मि भरतर्षभ ॥

balaṁ balavatāṁ cāhaṁ
kāma-rāga-vivarjitam
dharmāviruddho bhūteṣu
kāmo 'smi bharatarṣabha

I give strength to the strong, bereft of desire and attachment. I am love aligned with injunctions of scriptures, O' Arjuna.

12

ये चैव सात्त्विका भावा राजसास्तामसाश्च ये ।
मत्त एवेति तान्विद्धि न त्वहं तेषु ते मयि ॥

ye caiva sāttvikā bhāvā
rājasās tāmasāś ca ye
matta eveti tān viddhi
na tv ahaṁ teṣu te mayi

The three modes of material existence, goodness, passion and ignorance, are manifestations of my energy alone. Though they be in Me, I am beyond them.

13

त्रिभिर्गुणमयैर्भावैरेभिः सर्वमिदं जगत् ।
मोहितं नाभिजानाति मामेभ्यः परमव्ययम् ॥

tribhir guṇa-mayair bhāvair
ebhiḥ sarvam idaṁ jagat
mohitaṁ nābhijānāti
mām ebhyaḥ param avyayam

Influenced by the three modes of nature, none can understand Me; that I am eternal and unaffected by the gunas.

14

दैवी ह्येषा गुणमयी मम माया दुरत्यया ।
मामेव ये प्रपद्यन्ते मायामेतां तरन्ति ते ॥

daivī hy eṣā guṇa-mayī
mama māyā duratyayā
mām eva ye prapadyante
māyām etāṁ taranti te

Maya, my divine energy comprising the three gunas is difficult to overcome. But certainly not difficult for those who surrender to Me.

15

न मां दुष्कृतिनो मूढाः प्रपद्यन्ते नराधमाः ।
माययापहृतज्ञाना आसुरं भावमाश्रिताः ॥

na māṁ duṣkṛtino mūḍhāḥ
prapadyante narādhamāḥ
māyayāpahṛta-jñānā
āsuraṁ bhāvam āśritāḥ

Those who do not surrender to Me are grossly foolish, the lowest rung of mankind, covered by illusion and atheistic demoniacs.

16

चतुर्विधा भजन्ते मां जनाः सुकृतिनोऽर्जुन ।
आर्तो जिज्ञासुरर्थार्थी ज्ञानी च भरतर्षभ ॥

catur-vidhā bhajante māṁ
janāḥ sukṛtino 'rjuna
ārto jijñāsur arthārthī
jñānī ca bharatarṣabha

O' Arjuna, four kinds of pious men surrender to Me—those in distress, those seeking wealth, those out of curiosity, and those desiring to know the Absolute Truth.

17

तेषां ज्ञानी नित्ययुक्त एकभक्तिर्विशिष्यते ।
प्रियो हि ज्ञानिनोऽत्यर्थमहं स च मम प्रियः ॥

teṣāṁ jñānī nitya-yukta
eka-bhaktir viśiṣyate
priyo hi jñānino 'tyartham
ahaṁ sa ca mama priyaḥ

Out of these, the one in knowledge and engaged in my devotional service, is the best. Who loves Me is dear to Me.

18

उदाराः सर्व एवैते ज्ञानी त्वात्मैव मे मतम् ।
आस्थितः स हि युक्तात्मा मामेवानुत्तमां गतिम् ॥

udārāḥ sarva evaite
jñānī tv ātmaiva me matam
āsthitaḥ sa hi yuktātmā
mām evānuttamāṁ gatim

All those who come to Me are no doubt noble souls. But one who is self-realized, meditating upon Me, will find Me, the highest of all goals.

19

बहूनां जन्मनामन्ते ज्ञानवान्मां प्रपद्यते ।
वासुदेवः सर्वमिति स महात्मा सुदुर्लभः ॥

bahūnāṁ janmanām ante
jñānavān māṁ prapadyate
vāsudevaḥ sarvam iti
sa mahātmā sudurlabhaḥ

After many births of self-realization, a person eventually surrenders to Me knowing Me to be the cause of everything. Such a soul is very rare indeed.

20

कामैस्तैस्तैर्हृतज्ञाना: प्रपद्यन्तेऽन्यदेवता: ।
तं तं नियममास्थाय प्रकृत्या नियता: स्वया ॥

kāmais tais tair hṛta-jñānāḥ
prapadyante 'nya-devatāḥ
taṁ taṁ niyamam āsthāya
prakṛtyā niyatāḥ svayā

Carried away by material desires, some souls surrender to devatas, following rituals of worship as per their gunas.

21

यो यो यां यां तनुं भक्त: श्रद्धयार्चितुमिच्छति ।
तस्य तस्याचलां श्रद्धां तामेव विदधाम्यहम् ॥

yo yo yāṁ yāṁ tanuṁ bhaktaḥ
śraddhayārcitum icchati
tasya tasyācalāṁ śraddhāṁ
tām eva vidadhāmy aham

If one desires to worship any particular devata, I Myself give him steady faith to do so sincerely.

22

स तया श्रद्धया युक्तस्तस्याराधनमीहते ।
लभते च ततः कामान्मयैव विहितान्हितान् ॥

sa tayā śraddhayā yuktas
tasyārādhanam īhate
labhate ca tataḥ kāmān
mayaiva vihitān hi tān

With that faith, he worships and fulfills his desires through devatas, only because I have arranged for it.

23

अन्तवत्तु फलं तेषां तद्भवत्यल्पमेधसाम् ।
देवान्देवयजो यान्ति मद्भक्ता यान्ति मामपि ॥

antavat tu phalaṁ teṣāṁ
tad bhavaty alpa-medhasām
devān deva-yajo yānti
mad-bhaktā yānti mām api

But worshipping devatas is not a sign of intelligence because those results are temporary. Those who worship devatas, reach the devatas; those who worship Me, reach Me.

24

अव्यक्तं व्यक्तिमापन्नं मन्यन्ते मामबुद्धयः ।
परं भावमजानन्तो ममाव्ययमनुत्तमम् ॥

avyaktaṁ vyaktim āpannaṁ
manyante mām abuddhayaḥ
paraṁ bhāvam ajānanto
mamāvyayam anuttamam

The ignorant think of Me as formless, to have become embodied now. Only the intelligent know Me as eternal and Supreme.

25

नाहं प्रकाशः सर्वस्य योगमायासमावृतः ।
मूढोऽयं नाभिजानाति लोको मामजमव्ययम् ॥

nāhaṁ prakāśaḥ sarvasya
yoga-māyā-samāvṛtaḥ
mūḍho 'yaṁ nābhijānāti
loko mām ajam avyayam

I am invisible, covered by my illusory energy, the *yoga-maya*. The foolish and the unintelligent never realize that I am unborn and imperishable.

26

वेदाहं समतीतानि वर्तमानानि चार्जुन ।
भविष्याणि च भूतानि मां तु वेद न कश्चन ॥

vedāhaṁ samatītāni
vartamānāni cārjuna
bhaviṣyāṇi ca bhūtāni
māṁ tu veda na kaścana

I know everything not only about present but also about past and future. O' Arjuna, I know about all living beings but no one knows about Me.

27

इच्छाद्वेषसमुत्थेन द्वन्द्वमोहेन भारत ।
सर्वभूतानि सम्मोहं सर्गे यान्ति परन्तप ॥

icchā-dveṣa-samutthena
dvandva-mohena bhārata
sarva-bhūtāni sammohaṁ
sarge yānti parantapa

O' descendant of Bharata, all living beings are deluded by the dualities of desires and aversions. They are born as such, O' Parantapa.

28

येषां त्वन्तगतं पापं जनानां पुण्यकर्मणाम् ।
ते द्वन्द्वमोहनिर्मुक्ता भजन्ते मां दृढव्रताः ॥

yeṣāṁ tv anta-gataṁ pāpaṁ
janānāṁ puṇya-karmaṇām
te dvandva-moha-nirmuktā
bhajante māṁ dṛḍha-vratāḥ

A pious life in the past and a pious life in the present can free them from delusions of duality after which they worship and serve Me with great determination.

29

जरामरणमोक्षाय मामाश्रित्य यतन्ति ये ।
ते ब्रह्म तद्विदुः कृत्स्नमध्यात्मं कर्म चाखिलम् ॥

jarā-maraṇa-mokṣāya
mām āśritya yatanti ye
te brahma tad viduḥ kṛtsnam
adhyātmaṁ karma cākhilam

Those with intelligence aspire for liberation from old age and death, taking shelter of Me because they have knowledge of both, transcendental and material activities.

30

साधिभूताधिदैवं मां साधियज्ञं च ये विदुः ।
प्रयाणकालेऽपि च मां ते विदुर्युक्तचेतसः ॥

sādhibhūtādhidaivaṁ māṁ
sādhiyajñaṁ ca ye viduḥ
prayāṇa-kāle 'pi ca māṁ
te vidur yukta-cetasaḥ

Even at the time of death, they know Me as Adhibhuta, Adhidaivam, and Adhiyagyam (the principal force behind the material creation, the devatas, and all sacrifices).

Chapter

08

Akshara Brahma Yoga

1

अर्जुन उवाच
किं तद्ब्रह्म किमध्यात्मं किं कर्म पुरुषोत्तम ।
अधिभूतं च किं प्रोक्तमधिदैवं किमुच्यते ॥

arjuna uvāca
kiṁ tad-brahma kim adhyātmaṁ
kiṁ karma puruṣottama
adhibhūtaṁ ca kiṁ proktam
adhidaivaṁ kim ucyate

Arjuna said –
O' Purushottam, please explain to me what is Brahman, what is Adhyatma, what is Karma, what is Adhibhutam, and what is Adhidaivam?

2

अधियज्ञः कथं कोऽत्र देहेऽस्मिन्मधुसूदन ।
प्रयाणकाले च कथं ज्ञेयोऽसि नियतात्मभिः ॥

adhiyajñaḥ kathaṁ ko 'tra
dehe 'smin madhusūdana
prayāṇa-kāle ca kathaṁ
jñeyo 'si niyatātmabhiḥ

Also who is Adhiyagya and how is he situated in the body? How does one serving You know You at the time of death?

3

श्रीभगवानुवाच
अक्षरं ब्रह्म परमं स्वभावोऽध्यात्ममुच्यते ।
भूतभावोद्भवकरो विसर्गः कर्मसंज्ञितः ॥

śrī-bhagavān uvāca
akṣaraṁ brahma paramaṁ
svabhāvo 'dhyātmam ucyate
bhūta-bhāvodbhava-karo
visargaḥ karma-saṁjñitaḥ

Sri Bhagavan said –

Brahman is the supreme, indestructible, and transcendental living entity. The material nature of a living entity is called Adhyatma. Karma is the fruitive action that results in the material body of living beings.

4

अधिभूतं क्षरो भावः पुरुषश्चाधिदैवतम् ।
अधियज्ञोऽहमेवात्र देहे देहभृतां वर ॥

adhibhūtaṁ kṣaro bhāvaḥ
puruṣaś cādhidaivatam
adhiyajño 'ham evātra
dehe deha-bhṛtāṁ vara

Adhibhuta is the material nature in constant flux. Adhidaiva is the universal form of the Lord that includes all devatas, and I situated in every heart, the Lord of all sacrifices, am called Adhiyagya.

5

अन्तकाले च मामेव स्मरन्मुक्त्वा कलेवरम् ।
यः प्रयाति स मद्भावं याति नास्त्यत्र संशयः ॥

anta-kāle ca mām eva
smaran muktvā kalevaram
yaḥ prayāti sa mad-bhāvaṁ
yāti nāsty atra saṁśayaḥ

Those who remember Me alone at their time of death, attain Me, without doubt.

6

यं यं वापि स्मरन्भावं त्यजत्यन्ते कलेवरम् ।
तं तमेवैति कौन्तेय सदा तद्भावभावित: ॥

yaṁ yaṁ vāpi smaran bhāvaṁ
tyajaty ante kalevaram
taṁ tam evaiti kaunteya
sadā tad-bhāva-bhāvitaḥ

O' son of Kunti, whatever one is absorbed in at the time of death, is the state one attains in the next life.

7

तस्मात्सर्वेषु कालेषु मामनुस्मर युध्य च ।
मय्यर्पितमनोबुद्धिर्मामेवैष्यस्यसंशय: ॥

tasmāt sarveṣu kāleṣu
mām anusmara yudhya ca
mayy arpita-mano buddhir
mām evaiṣyasy asaṁśayaḥ

So keep Me always in your thoughts and yet carry on with your duty of fighting. With your mind and intelligence absorbed in Me and surrendered to Me, you will reach Me certainly.

8

अभ्यासयोगयुक्तेन चेतसा नान्यगामिना ।
परमं पुरुषं दिव्यं याति पार्थानुचिन्तयन् ॥

abhyāsa-yoga-yuktena
cetasā nānya-gāminā
paramaṁ puruṣaṁ divyaṁ
yāti pārthānucintayan

By practising to constantly fix your thoughts on Me and by remaining devoted to Me, you will surely come to Me.

9

कविं पुराणमनुशासितार-
मणोरणीयांसमनुस्मरेद्यः ।
सर्वस्य धातारमचिन्त्यरूप-
मादित्यवर्णं तमसः परस्तात् ॥

kaviṁ purāṇam anuśāsitāram
aṇor aṇīyāṁsam anusmared yaḥ
sarvasya dhātāram acintya-rūpam
āditya-varṇaṁ tamasaḥ parastāt

God is omniscient, the oldest, the controller, smaller than an atom, sustainer of everything, inconceivable, transcendental, a personality as effulgent as the sun and driving away all the darkness.

10

प्रयाणकाले मनसाचलेन
भक्त्या युक्तो योगबलेन चैव ।
भ्रुवोर्मध्ये प्राणमावेश्य सम्यक्
स तं परं पुरुषमुपैति दिव्यम् ॥

prayāṇa-kāle manasācalena
bhaktyā yukto yoga-balena caiva
bhruvor madhye prāṇam āveśya samyak
sa taṁ paraṁ puruṣam upaiti divyam

By practice of yoga, if one can fix the life air between eyebrows and meditate on God without deviating at the time of death, he will surely attain Him.

11

यदक्षरं वेदविदो वदन्ति
विशन्ति यद्यतयो वीतरागाः ।
यदिच्छन्तो ब्रह्मचर्यं चरन्ति
तत्ते पदं सङ्ग्रहेण प्रवक्ष्ये ॥

yad akṣaraṁ veda-vido vadanti
viśanti yad yatayo vīta-rāgāḥ
yad icchanto brahmacaryaṁ caranti
tat te padaṁ saṅgraheṇa pravakṣye

I will now speak about the path which leads to the goal of liberation. It is the goal described by Vedic scholars. It is the goal desired by ascetics for which they practice detachment and celibacy.

12

सर्वद्वाराणि संयम्य मनो हृदि निरुध्य च ।
मूर्ध्न्याधायात्मनः प्राणमास्थितो योगधारणाम् ॥

sarva-dvārāṇi saṁyamya
mano hṛdi nirudhya ca
mūrdhny ādhāyātmanaḥ prāṇam
āsthito yoga-dhāraṇām

One is on the path of yoga by shutting down the doors of sense organs, fixing the mind on the heart and the life air in the head. This is the path of detachment.

13

ॐ इत्येकाक्षरं ब्रह्म व्याहरन्मामनुस्मरन् ।
यः प्रयाति त्यजन्देहं स याति परमां गतिम् ॥

oṁ ity ekākṣaraṁ brahma
vyāharan mām anusmaran
yaḥ prayāti tyajan dehaṁ
sa yāti paramāṁ gatim

On this path, if one leaves the body while remembering Me and chanting the sacred mantra Om, he achieves the supreme destination.

14

अनन्यचेताः सततं यो मां स्मरति नित्यशः ।
तस्याहं सुलभः पार्थ नित्ययुक्तस्य योगिनः ॥

ananya-cetāḥ satataṁ
yo māṁ smarati nityaśaḥ
tasyāhaṁ sulabhaḥ pārtha
nitya-yuktasya yoginaḥ

O' Partha, for a true yogi who is absorbed in Me and remembers Me uninterrupted, I am easily available.

15

मामुपेत्य पुनर्जन्म दुःखालयमशाश्वतम् ।
नाप्नुवन्ति महात्मानः संसिद्धिं परमां गताः ॥

mām upetya punar janma
duḥkhālayam aśāśvatam
nāpnuvanti mahātmānaḥ
saṁsiddhiṁ paramāṁ gatāḥ

These great souls who achieve Me, get freedom from the cycle of birth and death and never return to the material world which is a place of misery. They experience ultimate bliss of perfection.

16

आब्रह्मभुवनाल्लोकाः पुनरावर्तिनोऽर्जुन ।
मामुपेत्य तु कौन्तेय पुनर्जन्म न विद्यते ॥

ā-brahma-bhuvanāl lokāḥ
punar āvartino 'rjuna
mām upetya tu kaunteya
punar janma na vidyate

O' Arjuna, rebirth is a reality for those in the highest planet Brahmaloka to the lowest planet in the material world. Only when you reach my spiritual abode, you never take birth again.

17

सहस्रयुगपर्यन्तमहर्यद्ब्रह्मणो विदुः ।
रात्रिं युगसहस्रान्तां तेऽहोरात्रविदो जनाः ॥

sahasra-yuga-paryantam
ahar yad brahmaṇo viduḥ
rātriṁ yuga-sahasrāntāṁ
te 'ho-rātra-vido janāḥ

As per human timelines, a day of Lord Brahma comprises a thousand *yugas* and his night comprises another thousand yugas.

18

अव्यक्ताद् व्यक्तय: सर्वा: प्रभवन्त्यहरागमे ।
रात्र्यागमे प्रलीयन्ते तत्रैवाव्यक्तसंज्ञके ॥

avyaktād vyaktayaḥ sarvāḥ
prabhavanty ahar-āgame
rātry-āgame pralīyante
tatraivāvyakta-saṁjñake

All living beings come into existence during Lord Brahma's day and they all dissolve into non-existence with the arrival of his night.

19

भूतग्राम: स एवायं भूत्वा भूत्वा प्रलीयते ।
रात्र्यागमेऽवश: पार्थ प्रभवत्यहरागमे ॥

bhūta-grāmaḥ sa evāyaṁ
bhūtvā bhūtvā pralīyate
rātry-āgame 'vaśaḥ pārtha
prabhavaty ahar-āgame

With the advent of every day and every night of Brahma, the living beings are repeatedly manifested and destroyed, O' Partha.

20

परस्तस्मात्तु भावोऽन्योऽव्यक्तोऽव्यक्तात्सनातनः ।
यः स सर्वेषु भूतेषु नश्यत्सु न विनश्यति ॥

paras tasmāt tu bhāvo 'nyo
'vyakto 'vyaktāt sanātanaḥ
yaḥ sa sarveṣu bhūteṣu
naśyatsu na vinaśyati

Beyond this creation and destruction is another superior and higher world that never ceases to exist all through this.

21

अव्यक्तोऽक्षर इत्युक्तस्तमाहुः परमां गतिम् ।
यं प्राप्य न निवर्तन्ते तद्धाम परमं मम ॥

avyakto 'kṣara ity uktas
tam āhuḥ paramāṁ gatim
yaṁ prāpya na nivartante
tad dhāma paramaṁ mama

That other world is the infallible supreme destination, my supreme abode. From here, one never returns to the material world.

22

पुरुषः स परः पार्थ भक्त्या लभ्यस्त्वनन्यया ।
यस्यान्तःस्थानि भूतानि येन सर्वमिदं ततम् ॥

puruṣaḥ sa paraḥ pārtha
bhaktyā labhyas tv ananyayā
yasyāntaḥ-sthāni bhūtāni
yena sarvam idaṁ tatam

The greatest personality, the Supreme Lord is only attained through pure devotion. He is all-pervading and everything is situated in Him.

23

यत्र काले त्वनावृत्तिमावृत्तिं चैव योगिनः ।
प्रयाता यान्ति तं कालं वक्ष्यामि भरतर्षभ ॥

yatra kāle tv anāvṛttim
āvṛttiṁ caiva yoginaḥ
prayātā yānti taṁ kālaṁ
vakṣyāmi bharatarṣabha

Now I will explain how the time of death determines whether the yogi achieves liberation or is reborn.

24

अग्निर्ज्योतिरहः शुक्लः षण्मासा उत्तरायणम् ।
तत्र प्रयाता गच्छन्ति ब्रह्म ब्रह्मविदो जनाः ॥

agnir jyotir ahaḥ śuklaḥ
ṣaṇ-māsā uttarāyaṇam
tatra prayātā gacchanti
brahma brahma-vido janāḥ

One who knows the Brahman, passes away during the sun's northern course, the bright fortnight of the moon, in the presence of *agni* and at an auspicious moment of the bright part of the day, reaching Brahman as his destination.

25

धूमो रात्रिस्तथा कृष्णः षण्मासा दक्षिणायनम् ।
तत्र चान्द्रमसं ज्योतिर्योगी प्राप्य निवर्तते ॥

dhūmo rātris tathā kṛṣṇaḥ
ṣaṇ-māsā dakṣiṇāyanam
tatra cāndramasaṁ jyotir
yogī prāpya nivartate

The ritualistic who pass away during the sun's southern course, the dark fortnight of the moon, the time of smoke, the night, attain the moon planet for a certain period of enjoyment and return.

26

शुक्लकृष्णे गती ह्येते जगतः शाश्वते मते ।
एकया यात्यनावृत्तिमन्ययावर्तते पुनः ॥

śukla-kṛṣṇe gatī hy ete
jagataḥ śāśvate mate
ekayā yāty anāvṛttim
anyayāvartate punaḥ

Vedas describe two paths of leaving the world—the path of light and the path of darkness. On the path of light, one does not return. On the path of darkness, one returns.

27

नैते सृती पार्थ जानन्योगी मुह्यति कश्चन ।
तस्मात्सर्वेषु कालेषु योगयुक्तो भवार्जुन ॥

naite sṛtī pārtha jānan
yogī muhyati kaścana
tasmāt sarveṣu kāleṣu
yoga-yukto bhavārjuna

Knowledge of these two paths clears all confusion, O' Arjuna. Therefore, be fixed in yoga always.

28

वेदेषु यज्ञेषु तपःसु चैव
दानेषु यत्पुण्यफलं प्रदिष्टम् ।
अत्येति तत्सर्वमिदं विदित्वा
योगी परं स्थानमुपैति चाद्यम् ॥

vedeṣu yajñeṣu tapaḥsu caiva
dāneṣu yat puṇya-phalaṁ pradiṣṭam
atyeti tat sarvam idaṁ viditvā
yogī paraṁ sthānam upaiti cādyam

A yogi who performs devotional service, transcends the fruits of Vedic study, austerities, sacrifices, charity, and piety. He attains my supreme eternal abode.

Chapter

09

Raja Vidya Rajaguhya Yoga

1

श्रीभगवानुवाच
इदं तु ते गुह्यतमं प्रवक्ष्याम्यनसूयवे ।
ज्ञानं विज्ञानसहितं यज्ज्ञात्वा मोक्ष्यसेऽशुभात् ॥

śrī-bhagavān uvāca
idaṁ tu te guhyatamaṁ
pravakṣyāmy anasūyave
jñānaṁ vijñāna-sahitaṁ
yaj jñātvā mokṣyase 'śubhāt

Sri Bhagavan said –
Because you have no envy for Me, Arjuna, I will share with you secret knowledge and its realized application which will immunize you from all inauspiciousness of material existence.

2

राजविद्या राजगुह्यं पवित्रमिदमुत्तमम् ।
प्रत्यक्षावगमं धर्म्यं सुसुखं कर्तुमव्ययम् ॥

rāja-vidyā rāja-guhyaṁ
pavitram idam uttamam
pratyakṣāvagamaṁ dharmyaṁ
su-sukhaṁ kartum avyayam

This secret is the king of all secrets, the most profound knowledge and deeply purifying. Easy and joyful to practise, it is the topmost rung of dharma for self-realization.

3

अश्रद्दधानाः पुरुषा धर्मस्यास्य परन्तप ।
अप्राप्य मां निवर्तन्ते मृत्युसंसारवर्त्मनि ॥

aśraddadhānāḥ puruṣā
dharmasyāsya parantapa
aprāpya māṁ nivartante
mṛtyu-saṁsāra-vartmani

I am not attainable to those who lack faith in this dharma. They will be born again and again to stay in the cycle of life and death, O' Parantapa.

4

मया ततमिदं सर्वं जगदव्यक्तमूर्तिना ।
मत्स्थानि सर्वभूतानि न चाहं तेष्ववस्थितः ॥

mayā tatam idaṁ sarvaṁ
jagad avyakta-mūrtinā
mat-sthāni sarva-bhūtāni
na cāhaṁ teṣv avasthitaḥ

The entire cosmic world is perfused by my invisible force. The living beings are dependent on Me while I am independent of them.

5

न च मत्स्थानि भूतानि पश्य मे योगमैश्वरम् ।
भूतभृन्न च भूतस्थो ममात्मा भूतभावनः ॥

na ca mat-sthāni bhūtāni
paśya me yogam aiśvaram
bhūta-bhṛn na ca bhūta-stho
mamātmā bhūta-bhāvanaḥ

But not necessarily, the living beings live in Me. This is the wonder of my mystical powers. I, the creator and maintainer of everything, cannot be influenced by anything material.

6

यथाकाशस्थितो नित्यं वायुः सर्वत्रगो महान् ।
तथा सर्वाणि भूतानि मत्स्थानीत्युपधारय ॥

yathākāśa-sthito nityaṁ
vāyuḥ sarvatra-go mahān
tathā sarvāṇi bhūtāni
mat-sthānīty upadhāraya

All living beings are found in Me just as the mighty wind that blows all over is always found in the sky.

7

सर्वभूतानि कौन्तेय प्रकृतिं यान्ति मामिकाम् ।
कल्पक्षये पुनस्तानि कल्पादौ विसृजाम्यहम् ॥

sarva-bhūtāni kaunteya
prakṛtiṁ yānti māmikām
kalpa-kṣaye punas tāni
kalpādau visṛjāmy aham

Every material being enters into Me at the end of every cycle of *kalpa*, or millennium. O' Kaunteya, I send them back again at the beginning of the next cycle of kalpa.

8

प्रकृतिं स्वामवष्टभ्य विसृजामि पुनः पुनः ।
भूतग्राममिमं कृत्स्नमवशं प्रकृतेर्वशात् ॥

prakṛtiṁ svām avaṣṭabhya
visṛjāmi punaḥ punaḥ
bhūta-grāmam imaṁ kṛtsnam
avaśaṁ prakṛter vaśāt

I alone rule the material energy and by my will, I create and destroy material forms as per their nature.

9

न च मां तानि कर्माणि निबध्नन्ति धनञ्जय ।
उदासीनवदासीनमसक्तं तेषु कर्मसु ॥

na ca māṁ tāni karmāṇi
nibadhnanti dhanañjaya
udāsīnavad āsīnam
asaktaṁ teṣu karmasu

My actions are not binding, O' Dhananjaya. I am only an observer—indifferent and detached.

10

मयाध्यक्षेण प्रकृतिः सूयते सचराचरम् ।
हेतुनानेन कौन्तेय जगद्विपरिवर्तते ॥

mayādhyakṣeṇa prakṛtiḥ
sūyate sa-carācaram
hetunānena kaunteya
jagad viparivartate

O' Kaunteya, it is only by my direction that this material world of animate and inanimate objects is in a constant flux of creation, maintenance, and destruction.

11

अवजानन्ति मां मूढा मानुषीं तनुमाश्रितम् ।
परं भावमजानन्तो मम भूतमहेश्वरम् ॥

avajānanti māṁ mūḍhā
mānuṣīṁ tanum āśritam
paraṁ bhāvam ajānanto
mama bhūta-maheśvaram

They are fools who do not see my divinity when I descend in human form. They do not know that I am the Supreme Lord of all that exists.

12

मोघाशा मोघकर्माणो मोघज्ञाना विचेतसः ।
राक्षसीमासुरीं चैव प्रकृतिं मोहिनीं श्रिताः ॥

moghāśā mogha-karmāṇo
mogha-jñānā vicetasaḥ
rākṣasīm āsurīṁ caiva
prakṛtiṁ mohinīṁ śritāḥ

They come under the spell of material energy embracing demonic and atheistic beliefs. Alas, all their hopes for liberation, their fruitive actions, and their knowledge are a total waste.

13

महात्मानस्तु मां पार्थ दैवीं प्रकृतिमाश्रिताः ।
भजन्त्यनन्यमनसो ज्ञात्वा भूतादिमव्ययम् ॥

mahātmānas tu māṁ pārtha
daivīṁ prakṛtim āśritāḥ
bhajanty ananya-manaso
jñātvā bhūtādim avyayam

But those who are mahatmas, surrender to divine energy and accept Me as the singular source of all existence. They remain absorbed in Me with mind and intelligence.

14

सततं कीर्तयन्तो मां यतन्तश्च दृढव्रताः ।
नमस्यन्तश्च मां भक्त्या नित्ययुक्ता उपासते ॥

satataṁ kīrtayanto māṁ
yatantaś ca dṛḍha-vratāḥ
namasyantaś ca māṁ bhaktyā
nitya-yuktā upāsate

In such absorption, they sing my glories constantly. With steadfast devotion, they only desire to worship Me.

15

ज्ञानयज्ञेन चाप्यन्ये यजन्तो मामुपासते ।
एकत्वेन पृथक्त्वेन बहुधा विश्वतोमुखम् ॥

jñāna-yajñena cāpy anye
yajanto mām upāsate
ekatvena pṛthaktvena
bahudhā viśvato-mukham

Some others worship Me by cultivating knowledge. They may either think of Me as one with them or separate from them or believe in my cosmic form.

16

अहं क्रतुरहं यज्ञः स्वधाहमहमौषधम् ।
मन्त्रोऽहमहमेवाज्यमहमग्निरहं हुतम् ॥

aham̐ kratur aham̐ yajñaḥ
svadhāham aham auṣadham
mantro 'ham aham evājyam
aham agnir aham̐ hutam

I am the Vedic ritual, the sacrifice, the oblation, the medicinal herb, the transcendental mantra, the ghee, the sacrificial fire. I am the act of offering itself.

17

पिताहमस्य जगतो माता धाता पितामहः ।
वेद्यं पवित्रम् ॐकार ऋक् साम यजुरेव च ॥

pitāham asya jagato
mātā dhātā pitāmahaḥ
vedyam̐ pavitram om̐kāra
ṛk sāma yajur eva ca

I represent the father, mother, grandfather, and the maintainer of this universe. I am the knowledge, the purifier, the mantra Om. I am the Vedas, Rg, Sama, and Yajur.

18

गतिर्भर्ता प्रभुः साक्षी निवासः शरणं सुहृत् ।
प्रभवः प्रलयः स्थानं निधानं बीजमव्ययम् ॥

gatir bhartā prabhuḥ sākṣī
nivāsaḥ śaraṇaṁ suhṛt
prabhavaḥ pralayaḥ sthānaṁ
nidhānaṁ bījam avyayam

I am the goal, supporter, master, witness, abode, shelter, well-wisher, creation, destruction, maintenance, the reservoir, and the eternal seed.

19

तपाम्यहमहं वर्षं निगृह्णाम्युत्सृजामि च ।
अमृतं चैव मृत्युश्च सदसच्चाहमर्जुन ॥

tapāmy aham ahaṁ varṣaṁ
nigṛhṇāmy utsṛjāmi ca
amṛtaṁ caiva mṛtyuś ca
sad asac cāham arjuna

O' Arjuna, heat and rain, immortality and death, matter and spirit, all are in my power.

20

त्रैविद्या मां सोमपाः पूतपापा
यज्ञैरिष्ट्वा स्वर्गतिं प्रार्थयन्ते ।
ते पुण्यमासाद्य सुरेन्द्रलोक-
मश्नन्ति दिव्यान्दिवि देवभोगान् ॥

trai-vidyā māṁ soma-pāḥ pūta-pāpā
yajñair iṣṭvā svar-gatiṁ prārthayante
te puṇyam āsādya surendra-lokam
aśnanti divyān divi deva-bhogān

The pious who perform Vedic rituals and drink the nectar of *soma*, seek heavenly planets of King Indra. They enjoy pleasures enjoyed by devatas having done pious activities.

21

ते तं भुक्त्वा स्वर्गलोकं विशालं
क्षीणे पुण्ये मर्त्यलोकं विशन्ति ।
एवं त्रयीधर्ममनुप्रपन्ना
गतागतं कामकामा लभन्ते ॥

te taṁ bhuktvā svarga-lokaṁ viśālaṁ
kṣīṇe puṇye martya-lokaṁ viśanti
evaṁ trayī-dharmam anuprapannā
gatāgataṁ kāma-kāmā labhante

When they exhaust their piety, they return to the planet of mortals. The Vedic rituals can give you only so much of fleeting pleasures followed by entanglement in cycle of life and death again.

22

अनन्याश्चिन्तयन्तो मां ये जनाः पर्युपासते ।
तेषां नित्याभियुक्तानां योगक्षेमं वहाम्यहम् ॥

ananyāś cintayanto māṁ
ye janāḥ paryupāsate
teṣāṁ nityābhiyuktānāṁ
yoga-kṣemaṁ vahāmy aham

But those who worship Me and meditate exclusively on Me, I fulfill what they need and preserve what they already have.

23

येऽप्यन्यदेवताभक्ता यजन्ते श्रद्धयान्विताः ।
तेऽपि मामेव कौन्तेय यजन्त्यविधिपूर्वकम् ॥

ye 'py anya-devatā-bhaktā
yajante śraddhayānvitāḥ
te 'pi mām eva kaunteya
yajanty avidhi-pūrvakam

O' Kaunteya, when one worships any other devata, he is in fact worshipping Me indirectly but incorrectly.

24

अहं हि सर्वयज्ञानां भोक्ता च प्रभुरेव च ।
न तु मामभिजानन्ति तत्त्वेनातश्च्यवन्ति ते ॥

ahaṁ hi sarva-yajñānāṁ
bhoktā ca prabhur eva ca
na tu mām abhijānanti
tattvenātaś cyavanti te

Those who do not understand that I am the real enjoyer and the Supreme Lord of each and every sacrifice, they fall down and remain in the cycle of life and death.

25

यान्ति देवव्रता देवान्पितृन्यान्ति पितृव्रताः ।
भूतानि यान्ति भूतेज्या यान्ति मद्याजिनोऽपि माम् ॥

yānti deva-vratā devān
pitṝn yānti pitṛ-vratāḥ
bhūtāni yānti bhūtejyā
yānti mad-yājino 'pi mām

Those worshipping devatas will be born amongst devatas. Those worshipping ancestors, reach the ancestors. Those worshipping ghosts live amongst ghosts. Those worshipping Me, attain Me.

26

पत्रं पुष्पं फलं तोयं यो मे भक्त्या प्रयच्छति ।
तदहं भक्त्युपहृतमश्नामि प्रयतात्मनः ॥

patraṁ puṣpaṁ phalaṁ toyaṁ
yo me bhaktyā prayacchati

tad ahaṁ bhakty-upahṛtam
aśnāmi prayatātmanaḥ

I accept an offering of a leaf, a flower, a fruit, or water if it is offered with love and devotion.

27

यत्करोषि यदश्नासि यज्जुहोषि ददासि यत् ।
यत्तपस्यसि कौन्तेय तत्कुरुष्व मदर्पणम् ॥

yat karoṣi yad aśnāsi
yaj juhoṣi dadāsi yat
yat tapasyasi kaunteya
tat kuruṣva mad arpaṇam

Everything that you do, everything that you eat, everything you offer, everything you give in charity, every austerity that you perform, do it as an offering to Me, O' son of Kunti.

28

शुभाशुभफलैरेवं मोक्ष्यसे कर्मबन्धनैः ।
सन्न्यासयोगयुक्तात्मा विमुक्तो मामुपैष्यसि ॥

śubhāśubha-phalair evaṁ
mokṣyase karma-bandhanaiḥ
sannyāsa-yoga-yuktātmā
vimukto mām upaiṣyasi

By doing so, you will be free from good and bad effects of karmic bondage. By being absorbed in Me, you break free from the effects of your actions and reach Me.

29

समोऽहं सर्वभूतेषु न मे द्वेष्योऽस्ति न प्रियः ।
ये भजन्ति तु मां भक्त्या मयि ते तेषु चाप्यहम् ॥

samo 'haṁ sarva-bhūteṣu
na me dveṣyo 'sti na priyaḥ
ye bhajanti tu māṁ bhaktyā
mayi te teṣu cāpy aham

I am impartial. I like or dislike no one. But one who worships Me faithfully, is my friend and I am his friend.

30

अपि चेत्सुदुराचारो भजते मामनन्यभाक् ।
साधुरेव स मन्तव्यः सम्यग्व्यवसितो हि सः ॥

api cet su-durācāro
bhajate mām ananya-bhāk
sādhur eva sa mantavyaḥ
samyag vyavasito hi saḥ

Even a sinner can be considered saintly if he worships Me because he is on the right path.

31

क्षिप्रं भवति धर्मात्मा शश्वच्छान्तिं निगच्छति ।
कौन्तेय प्रतिजानीहि न मे भक्तः प्रणश्यति ॥

kṣipraṁ bhavati dharmātmā
śaśvac-chāntiṁ nigacchati
kaunteya pratijānīhi
na me bhaktaḥ praṇaśyati

He will soon become virtuous and will be at peace. O' Kaunteya, state this boldly to the whole world that my devotee never perishes.

32

मां हि पार्थ व्यपाश्रित्य येऽपि स्युः पापयोनयः ।
स्त्रियो वैश्यास्तथा शूद्रास्तेऽपि यान्ति परां गतिम् ॥

māṁ hi pārtha vyapāśritya
ye 'pi syuḥ pāpa-yonayaḥ
striyo vaiśyās tathā śūdrās
te 'pi yānti parāṁ gatim

All those who seek my protection, attain the supreme goal, O' Partha, irrespective of their gender, caste, or qualities.

33

किं पुनर्ब्राह्मणाः पुण्या भक्ता राजर्षयस्तथा ।
अनित्यमसुखं लोकमिमं प्राप्य भजस्व माम् ॥

kiṁ punar brāhmaṇāḥ puṇyā
bhaktā rājarṣayas tathā
anityam asukhaṁ lokam
imaṁ prāpya bhajasva mām

The brahmanas, kings, and devotees are thus more predisposed to worshipping Me in this temporary and joyless world.

34

मन्मना भव मद्भक्तो मद्याजी मां नमस्कुरु ।
मामेवैष्यसि युक्त्वैवमात्मानं मत्परायण: ॥

man-manā bhava mad-bhakto
mad-yājī māṁ namaskuru
mām evaiṣyasi yuktvaivam
ātmānaṁ mat-parāyaṇaḥ

Always think of Me, be devoted to Me, offer obeisance and worship Me always. Showing such devotion, you will surely reach Me.

Chapter

10

Vibhuti Yoga

1

श्रीभगवानुवाच
भूय एव महाबाहो शृणु मे परमं वचः ।
यत्तेऽहं प्रीयमाणाय वक्ष्यामि हितकाम्यया ॥

śrī-bhagavān uvāca
bhūya eva mahā-bāho
śṛṇu me paramaṁ vacaḥ
yat te 'haṁ prīyamāṇāya
vakṣyāmi hita-kāmyayā

Sri Bhagavan said –
Listen, O' mighty-armed Arjuna, to my ultimate advice. Because you are so dear to me, I give you this advice for your own good.

2

न मे विदुः सुरगणाः प्रभवं न महर्षयः ।
अहमादिर्हि देवानां महर्षीणां च सर्वशः ॥

na me viduḥ sura-gaṇāḥ
prabhavaṁ na maharṣayaḥ
aham ādir hi devānāṁ
maharṣīṇāṁ ca sarvaśaḥ

Both devatas and great *rishis* have no knowledge about my origin. In fact, I am the source of their origin.

3

यो मामजमनादिं च वेत्ति लोकमहेश्वरम् ।
असम्मूढः स मर्त्येषु सर्वपापैः प्रमुच्यते ॥

yo mām ajam anādiṁ ca
vetti loka-maheśvaram
asammūḍhaḥ sa martyeṣu
sarva-pāpaiḥ pramucyate

Only he who is free of illusions knows Me as unborn, without a beginning and as the Supreme Lord of the universe. He is then at once freed from all sins.

4 – 5

बुद्धिर्ज्ञानमसम्मोहः क्षमा सत्यं दमः शमः ।
सुखं दुःखं भवोऽभावो भयं चाभयमेव च ॥
अहिंसा समता तुष्टिस्तपो दानं यशोऽयशः ।
भवन्ति भावा भूतानां मत्त एव पृथग्विधाः ॥

buddhir jñānam asammohaḥ
kṣamā satyaṁ damaḥ śamaḥ
sukhaṁ duḥkhaṁ bhavo 'bhāvo
bhayaṁ cābhayam eva ca
ahiṁsā samatā tuṣṭis
tapo dānaṁ yaśo 'yaśaḥ

bhavanti bhāvā bhūtānāṁ
matta eva pṛthag-vidhāḥ

I am the source of all qualities seen in humans—intelligence, knowledge, clarity of thoughts, forgiveness, truthfulness, sense control, mind control, joy, sorrow, birth, death, fear, valour, non-violence, equanimity, contentment, austerity, charity, fame, and infamy.

6

महर्षयः सप्त पूर्वे चत्वारो मनवस्तथा ।
मद्भावा मानसा जाता येषां लोक इमाः प्रजाः ॥

maharṣayaḥ sapta pūrve
catvāro manavas tathā
mad-bhāvā mānasā jātā
yeṣāṁ loka imāḥ prajāḥ

The seven great sages, preceded by the four Kumaras and the Manus from whom all creatures have originated, took birth from my mind.

7

एतां विभूतिं योगं च मम यो वेत्ति तत्त्वतः ।
सोऽविकल्पेन योगेन युज्यते नात्र संशयः ॥

etāṁ vibhūtiṁ yogaṁ ca
mama yo vetti tattvataḥ
so 'vikalpena yogena
yujyate nātra saṁśayaḥ

There is no doubt that those who know my extraordinary powers and opulence, unite with Me by yoga of devotion.

8

अहं सर्वस्य प्रभवो मत्तः सर्वं प्रवर्तते ।
इति मत्वा भजन्ते मां बुधा भावसमन्विताः ॥

ahaṁ sarvasya prabhavo
mattaḥ sarvaṁ pravartate
iti matvā bhajante māṁ
budhā bhāva-samanvitāḥ

Everything material and spiritual originates from Me. I am the source of everything. The wise who are aware of this, worship me wholeheartedly.

9

मच्चित्ता मद्गतप्राणा बोधयन्तः परस्परम् ।
कथयन्तश्च मां नित्यं तुष्यन्ति च रमन्ति च ॥

mac-cittā mad-gata-prāṇā
bodhayantaḥ parasparam
kathayantaś ca māṁ nityaṁ
tuṣyanti ca ramanti ca

My devotees fix their mind and consciousness in Me and surrender their life to Me. Their only satisfaction lies in constantly discussing about Me and enlightening each other.

10

तेषां सततयुक्तानां भजतां प्रीतिपूर्वकम् ।
ददामि बुद्धियोगं तं येन मामुपयान्ति ते ॥

teṣāṁ satata-yuktānāṁ
bhajatāṁ prīti-pūrvakam
dadāmi buddhi-yogaṁ taṁ
yena māṁ upayānti te

Because they are constantly worshipping Me with love and are so devoted to Me, I give them the knowledge by which they can return to Me.

11

तेषामेवानुकम्पार्थमहमज्ञानजं तमः ।
नाशयाम्यात्मभावस्थो ज्ञानदीपेन भास्वता ॥

teṣām evānukampārtham
aham ajñāna-jaṁ tamaḥ
nāśayāmy ātma-bhāva-stho
jñāna-dīpena bhāsvatā

I care for them so much that I enter their hearts to destroy their ignorance just like a bright lamp of knowledge destroys darkness.

12 – 13

अर्जुन उवाच
परं ब्रह्म परं धाम पवित्रं परमं भवान् ।
पुरुषं शाश्वतं दिव्यमादिदेवमजं विभुम् ॥
आहुस्त्वामृषयः सर्वे देवर्षिर्नारदस्तथा ।
असितो देवलो व्यासः स्वयं चैव ब्रवीषि मे ॥

arjuna uvāca
paraṁ brahma paraṁ dhāma
pavitraṁ paramaṁ bhavān
puruṣaṁ śāśvataṁ divyam
ādi-devam ajaṁ vibhum
āhus tvām ṛṣayaḥ sarve

devarṣir nāradas tathā
asito devalo vyāsaḥ
svayaṁ caiva bravīṣi me

Arjuna said –

I hail the supreme Brahman, the supreme abode, the supreme purifier, the eternal truth, the primal being, the unborn, and the omnipresent. Exalted sages such as Narada, Asita, Devala, and Vyasa accept this and now You Yourself have confirmed this.

14

सर्वमेतदृतं मन्ये यन्मां वदसि केशव ।
न हि ते भगवन्व्यक्तिं विदुर्देवा न दानवाः ॥

sarvam etad ṛtaṁ manye
yan māṁ vadasi keśava
na hi te bhagavan vyaktiṁ
vidur devā na dānavāḥ

I accept Your words as the ultimate truth, O' Keshava. Devatas and demons can never understand Your divine personality.

15

स्वयमेवात्मनात्मानं वेत्थ त्वं पुरुषोत्तम ।
भूतभावन भूतेश देवदेव जगत्पते ॥

svayam evātmanātmānaṁ
vettha tvaṁ puruṣottama
bhūta-bhāvana bhūteśa
deva-deva jagat-pate

O' Supreme Being, Lord of All Beings, Lord of the Universe, Lord of Devatas, only You can know Yourself by Your inconceivable potency.

16

वक्तुमर्हस्यशेषेण दिव्या ह्यात्मविभूतय: ।
याभिर्विभूतिभिर्लोकानिमांस्त्वं व्याप्य तिष्ठसि ॥

vaktum arhasy aśeṣeṇa
divyā hy ātma-vibhūtayaḥ
yābhir vibhūtibhir lokān
imāṁs tvaṁ vyāpya tiṣṭhasi

Please narrate and enlighten me about Your divine opulences by which You manifest and pervade the entire planetary system.

17

कथं विद्यामहं योगिंस्त्वां सदा परिचिन्तयन् ।
केषु केषु च भावेषु चिन्त्योऽसि भगवन्मया ॥

kathaṁ vidyām ahaṁ yogiṁs
tvāṁ sadā paricintayan
keṣu keṣu ca bhāveṣu
cintyo 'si bhagavan mayā

How may I know You and keep You in my thoughts? In which form can I meditate on You? Please tell me, O' Bhagavan and Supreme Master.

18

विस्तरेणात्मनो योगं विभूतिं च जनार्दन ।
भूयः कथय तृप्तिर्हि शृण्वतो नास्ति मेऽमृतम् ॥

vistareṇātmano yogaṁ
vibhūtiṁ ca janārdana
bhūyaḥ kathaya tṛptir hi
śṛṇvato nāsti me 'mṛtam

O' Janardana, tell me every detail of Your majestic power and opulences. I can go on and on hearing the nectarine stream of Your words.

19

श्रीभगवानुवाच
हन्त ते कथयिष्यामि दिव्या ह्यात्मविभूतय: ।
प्राधान्यत: कुरुश्रेष्ठ नास्त्यन्तो विस्तरस्य मे ॥

śrī-bhagavān uvāca
hanta te kathayiṣyāmi
divyā hy ātma-vibhūtayaḥ
prādhānyataḥ kuru-śreṣṭha
nāsty anto vistarasya me

Sri Bhagavan said –
O' best of Kurus, I will certainly explain to you some exemplary aspects of my manifestation because there is no end to my infinite opulence.

20

अहमात्मा गुडाकेश सर्वभूताशयस्थित: ।
अहमादिश्च मध्यं च भूतानामन्त एव च ॥

aham ātmā guḍākeśa
sarva-bhūtāśaya-sthitaḥ
aham ādiś ca madhyaṁ ca
bhūtānām anta eva ca

O' Gudakesha, I am situated in the heart of every living entity as the Self. I am the beginning, the middle, and the end of all living beings.

21

आदित्यानामहं विष्णुर्ज्योतिषां रविरंशुमान ।
मरीचिर्मरुतामस्मि नक्षत्राणामहं शशी ॥

ādityānām ahaṁ viṣṇur
jyotiṣāṁ ravir aṁśumān
marīcir marutām asmi
nakṣatrāṇām ahaṁ śaśī

Amongst the Adityas, I am Vishnu. Amongst illuminaries, I am the sun. I am Marici amongst Maruts, and the moon amongst heavenly bodies.

22

वेदानां सामवेदोऽस्मि देवानामस्मि वासवः ।
इन्द्रियाणां मनश्चास्मि भूतानामस्मि चेतना ॥

vedānāṁ sāma-vedo 'smi
devānām asmi vāsavaḥ
indriyāṇāṁ manaś cāsmi
bhūtānām asmi cetanā

I am Sama-Veda amongst the Vedas. I am Indra amongst the devatas. Amongst the senses I am the mind and amongst all living beings I am the consciousness.

23

रुद्राणां शङ्करश्चास्मि वित्तेशो यक्षरक्षसाम् ।
वसूनां पावकश्चास्मि मेरुः शिखरिणामहम् ॥

rudrāṇāṁ śaṅkaraś cāsmi
vitteśo yakṣa-rakṣasām
vasūnāṁ pāvakaś cāsmi
meruḥ śikhariṇām aham

Amongst Rudras I am Shankar, amongst the *rakshasas* I am Kuber, amongst Vasus I am Agni, and amongst mountains I am Meru.

24

पुरोधसां च मुख्यं मां विद्धि पार्थ बृहस्पतिम् ।
सेनानीनामहं स्कन्दः सरसामस्मि सागरः ॥

purodhasāṁ ca mukhyaṁ māṁ
viddhi pārtha bṛhaspatim

senānīnām ahaṁ skandaḥ
sarasām asmi sāgaraḥ

O' Partha, of priests I am Brihaspati. Of military chiefs I am Skanda, and of water bodies I am ocean.

25

महर्षीणां भृगुरहं गिरामस्म्येकमक्षरम् ।
यज्ञानां जपयज्ञोऽस्मि स्थावराणां हिमालयः ॥

maharṣīṇāṁ bhṛgur ahaṁ
girām asmy ekam akṣaram
yajñānāṁ japa-yajño 'smi
sthāvarāṇāṁ himālayaḥ

Amongst exalted sages I am Brighu. Amongst sound vibrations I am the transecnendental sound Om. I am *japa* amongst all sacrifices and I am Himalaya amongst the immovables.

26

अश्वत्थ: सर्ववृक्षाणां देवर्षीणां च नारद: ।
गन्धर्वाणां चित्ररथ: सिद्धानां कपिलो मुनि: ॥

aśvatthaḥ sarva-vṛkṣāṇāṁ
devarṣīṇāṁ ca nāradaḥ
gandharvāṇāṁ citrarathaḥ
siddhānāṁ kapilo muniḥ

I am Banyan amongst trees. I am Narada amongst the celestial sages. Amongst Gandharvas I am Chitraratha and amongst perfect beings I am Kapila.

27

उच्चै:श्रवसमश्वानां विद्धि माममृतोद्भवम् ।
ऐरावतं गजेन्द्राणां नराणां च नराधिपम् ॥

uccaiḥśravasam aśvānāṁ
viddhi mām amṛtodbhavam
airāvataṁ gajendrāṇāṁ
narāṇāṁ ca narādhipam

Amongst horses, I am Uccaihsrava, born from the nectar of immortality while churning the ocean. Amongst elephants I am Airavata. Amongst men I am king.

28

आयुधानामहं वज्रं धेनूनामस्मि कामधुक् ।
प्रजनश्चास्मि कन्दर्पः सर्पाणामस्मि वासुकिः ॥

āyudhānām ahaṁ vajraṁ
dhenūnām asmi kāmadhuk
prajanaś cāsmi kandarpaḥ
sarpāṇām asmi vāsukiḥ

Amongst weapons I am Vajra (thunderbolt). Amongst cows, I am Kamadhenu. I am Cupid, the root of procreation and I am Vasuki, chief of serpents.

29

अनन्तश्चास्मि नागानां वरुणो यादसामहम् ।
पितृणामर्यमा चास्मि यमः संयमतामहम् ॥

anantaś cāsmi nāgānāṁ
varuṇo yādasām aham
pitṝṇām aryamā cāsmi
yamaḥ saṁyamatām aham

I am Ananta amongst *nagas*, I am Varun amongst aquatics. Amongst ancestors, I am Aryama and I am Yama, the god of death, amongst dispensers of justice.

30

प्रह्लादश्चास्मि दैत्यानां कालः कलयतामहम् ।
मृगाणां च मृगेन्द्रोऽहं वैनतेयश्च पक्षिणाम् ॥

prahlādaś cāsmi daityānāṁ
kālaḥ kalayatām aham
mṛgāṇāṁ ca mṛgendro 'haṁ
vainateyaś ca pakṣiṇām

I am Prahlada amongst demons. I am time amongst controllers. Of animals, I am lion and of birds, I am Garuda.

31

पवनः पवतामस्मि रामः शस्त्रभृतामहम् ।
झषाणां मकरश्चास्मि स्रोतसामस्मि जाह्नवी ॥

pavanaḥ pavatām asmi
rāmaḥ śastra-bhṛtām aham
jhaṣāṇāṁ makaraś cāsmi
srotasām asmi jāhnavī

Amongst purifiers, I am the wind. Amongst weapon fighters I am Rama. A shark amongst fishes and Ganga amongst flowing rivers.

32

सर्गाणामादिरन्तश्च मध्यं चैवाहमर्जुन ।
अध्यात्मविद्या विद्यानां वादः प्रवदतामहम् ॥

sargāṇām ādir antaś ca
madhyaṁ caivāham arjuna
adhyātma-vidyā vidyānāṁ
vādaḥ pravadatām aham

I am the beginning, the middle, and the end of all creation. O' Arjuna, I am the spiritual science of self amongst knowledge and the concluding truth of every argument.

33

अक्षराणामकारोऽस्मि द्वन्द्वः सामासिकस्य च ।
अहमेवाक्षयः कालो धाताहं विश्वतोमुखः ॥

akṣarāṇām akāro 'smi
dvandvaḥ sāmāsikasya ca
aham evākṣayaḥ kālo
dhātāhaṁ viśvato-mukhaḥ

Amongst alphabets, I am letter A. Of compound words, I am the dual word. I am eternal time and I am the creator Brahma.

34

मृत्युः सर्वहरश्चाहमुद्भवश्च भविष्यताम् ।
कीर्तिः श्रीर्वाक्च नारीणां स्मृतिर्मेधा धृतिः क्षमा ॥

mṛtyuḥ sarva-haraś cāham
udbhavaś ca bhaviṣyatām
kīrtiḥ śrīr vāk ca nārīṇāṁ
smṛtir medhā dhṛtiḥ kṣamā

I am the all-destructive death. I am the origin of all things yet to be in future. In women, I am fame, prosperity, speech, memory, intelligence, courage, and patience.

35

बृहत्साम तथा साम्नां गायत्री छन्दसामहम् ।
मासानां मार्गशीर्षोऽहमृतूनां कुसुमाकरः ॥

bṛhat-sāma tathā sāmnāṁ
gāyatrī chandasām aham
māsānāṁ mārga-śīrṣo 'ham
ṛtūnāṁ kusumākaraḥ

Amongst hymns I am Brhat-sama; amongst mantras I am Gayatri; amongst months I am Margashirsha (November and December); and amongst seasons I am the blossom of spring.

36

द्यूतं छलयतामस्मि तेजस्तेजस्विनामहम् ।
जयोऽस्मि व्यवसायोऽस्मि सत्त्वं सत्त्ववतामहम् ॥

dyūtaṁ chalayatām asmi
tejas tejasvinām aham
jayo 'smi vyavasāyo 'smi
sattvaṁ sattvavatām aham

Amongst cheaters, I am a gambler. I am the energy of the energetic. I am victory, effort, and goodness of the virtuous.

37

वृष्णीनां वासुदेवोऽस्मि पाण्डवानां धनञ्जयः ।
मुनीनामप्यहं व्यासः कवीनामुशना कविः ॥

vṛṣṇīnāṁ vāsudevo 'smi
pāṇḍavānāṁ dhanañjayaḥ
munīnām apy ahaṁ vyāsaḥ
kavīnām uśanā kaviḥ

I am Vasudeva amongst Vrsnis and Arjuna amongst Pandavas. Amongst sages, I am Vyasa and amongst poets I am Ushana.

38

दण्डो दमयता मस्मि नीतिरस्मि जिगीषताम् ।
मौनं चैवास्मि गुह्यानां ज्ञानं ज्ञानवतामहम् ॥

daṇḍo damayatām asmi
nītir asmi jigīṣatām
maunaṁ caivāsmi guhyānāṁ
jñānaṁ jñānavatām aham

I am the rod that punishes; I am morality in victory. Of secrets, I am silence and of wise, I am wisdom.

39

यच्चापि सर्वभूतानां बीजं तदहमर्जुन ।
न तदस्ति विना यत्स्यान्मया भूतं चराचरम् ॥

yac cāpi sarva-bhūtānāṁ
bījaṁ tad aham arjuna
na tad asti vinā yat syān
mayā bhūtaṁ carācaram

I am the seed of all that exists. O' Arjuna, there is nothing moving or non-moving that can exist in my absence.

40

नान्तोऽस्ति मम दिव्यानां विभूतीनां परन्तप ।
एष तूद्देशतः प्रोक्तो विभूतेर्विस्तरो मया ॥

nānto 'sti mama divyānāṁ
vibhūtīnāṁ parantapa
eṣa tūddeśataḥ prokto
vibhūter vistaro mayā

O' Parantapa, this is not the end of all my divine manifestations. It is only a speck of my infinite opulence.

41

यद्यद्विभूतिमत्सत्त्वं श्रीमदूर्जितमेव वा ।
तत्तदेवावगच्छ त्वं मम तेजोंऽशसम्भवम् ॥

yad yad vibhūtimat sattvaṁ
śrīmad ūrjitam eva vā
tat tad evāvagaccha tvaṁ
mama tejo'ṁśa-sambhavam

Whatever you see to be beautiful, powerful, and extraordinary around you, all of it originates from my stupendous power.

42

अथवा बहुनैतेन किं ज्ञातेन तवार्जुन ।
विष्टभ्याहमिदं कृत्स्नमेकांशेन स्थितो जगत् ॥

atha vā bahunaitena
kiṁ jñātena tavārjuna
viṣṭabhyāham idaṁ kṛtsnam
ekāṁśena sthito jagat

O' Arjuna, what is the need to know all this? Suffice it to know that just a fragment of Me can pervade and sustain the entire cosmos.

Chapter

11

Vishvarupa Darshan Yoga

1

अर्जुन उवाच
मदनुग्रहाय परमं गुह्यमध्यात्मसंज्ञितम् ।
यत्त्वयोक्तं वचस्तेन मोहोऽयं विगतो मम ॥

arjuna uvāca
mad-anugrahāya paramaṁ
guhyam adhyātma-saṁjñitam
yat tvayoktaṁ vacas tena
moho 'yaṁ vigato mama

Arjuna said –
Because of Your kindness, I have heard your words on the supremely confidential knowledge and now I have no illusions whatsoever.

2

भवाप्ययौ हि भूतानां श्रुतौ विस्तरशो मया ।
त्वत्तः कमलपत्राक्ष माहात्म्यमपि चाव्ययम् ॥

bhavāpyayau hi bhūtānāṁ
śrutau vistaraśo mayā
tvattaḥ kamala-patrākṣa
māhātmyam api cāvyayam

You have discussed the appearance and disappearance of living beings at length as well as Your magnificent glories, O' Lotus-eyed One.

3

एवमेतद्यथात्थ त्वमात्मानं परमेश्वर ।
द्रष्टुमिच्छामि ते रूपमैश्वरं पुरुषोत्तम ॥

evam etad yathāttha tvam
ātmānaṁ parameśvara
draṣṭum icchāmi te rūpam
aiśvaraṁ puruṣottama

I see Your form, the one you spoke of, O' Supreme Lord. But I desire to see that form which pervades the cosmos, O' Greatest of All.

4

मन्यसे यदि तच्छक्यं मया द्रष्टुमिति प्रभो ।
योगेश्वर ततो मे त्वं दर्शयात्मानमव्ययम् ॥

manyase yadi tac chakyaṁ
mayā draṣṭum iti prabho
yogeśvara tato me tvaṁ
darśayātmānam avyayam

Show me Your cosmic form, O' Lord, if You think I am capable of beholding it.

5

श्रीभगवानुवाच
पश्य मे पार्थ रूपाणि शतशोऽथ सहस्रशः ।
नानाविधानि दिव्यानि नानावर्णाकृतीनि च ॥

śrī-bhagavān uvāca
paśya me pārtha rūpāṇi
śataśo 'tha sahasraśaḥ
nānā-vidhāni divyāni
nānā-varṇākṛtīni ca

Sri Bhagavan said –
O' Partha, here are my numerous forms in hundreds and thousands, all multi-coloured and multi-shaped.

6

पश्यादित्यान्वसून्रुद्रानश्विनौ मरुतस्तथा ।
बहून्यदृष्टपूर्वाणि पश्याश्चर्याणि भारत ॥

paśyādityān vasūn rudrān
aśvinau marutas tathā
bahūny adṛṣṭa-pūrvāṇi
paśyāścaryāṇi bhārata

See the Adityas, Vasus, Rudra, Ashvinis, Maruts, and other devatas. No one must have ever heard or seen any of this before.

7

इहैकस्थं जगत्कृत्स्नं पश्याद्य सचराचरम् ।
मम देहे गुडाकेश यच्चान्यद्द्रष्टुमिच्छसि ॥

ihaika-sthaṁ jagat kṛtsnaṁ
paśyādya sa-carācaram
mama dehe guḍākeśa
yac cānyad draṣṭum icchasi

O' Gudakesha, see the entire universe, everything moving and non-moving in Me. You can see whatever your heart desires, from the present or the future.

8

न तु मां शक्यसे द्रष्टुमनेनैव स्वचक्षुषा ।
दिव्यं ददामि ते चक्षुः पश्य मे योगमैश्वरम् ॥

na tu māṁ śakyase draṣṭum
anenaiva sva-cakṣuṣā
divyaṁ dadāmi te cakṣuḥ
paśya me yogam aiśvaram

Oh, but your material eyes cannot see my cosmic form. To see my grand opulence, I will give you special vision.

9

सञ्जय उवाच
एवमुक्त्वा ततो राजन्महायोगेश्वरो हरिः ।
दर्शयामास पार्थाय परमं रूपमैश्वरम् ॥

sañjaya uvāca
evam uktvā tato rājan
mahā-yogeśvaro hariḥ
darśayām āsa pārthāya
paramaṁ rūpam aiśvaram

Sanjaya said –

O' King, the Supreme Lord, the Lord of All Yoga, then flashed his divine and opulent form to Arjuna.

10 – 11

अनेकवक्त्रनयनमनेकाद्भुतदर्शनम् ।
अनेकदिव्याभरणं दिव्यानेकोद्यतायुधम् ॥
दिव्यमाल्याम्बरधरं दिव्यगन्धानुलेपनम् ।
सर्वाश्चर्यमयं देवमनन्तं विश्वतोमुखम् ॥

aneka-vaktra-nayanam
anekādbhuta-darśanam
aneka-divyābharaṇaṁ
divyānekodyatāyudham
divya-mālyāmbara-dharaṁ
divya-gandhānulepanam
sarvāścarya-mayaṁ devam
anantaṁ viśvato-mukham

Arjuna saw in the cosmic form, many wonderful faces, eyes, ornaments, weapons, and garments. It was anointed with divine fragrances and wearing heavenly garlands. The form was awe-inspiring, majestic, and infinite.

12

दिवि सूर्यसहस्रस्य भवेद्युगपदुत्थिता ।
यदि भाः सदृशी सा स्याद्भासस्तस्य महात्मनः ॥

divi sūrya-sahasrasya
bhaved yugapad utthitā
yadi bhāḥ sadṛśī sā syād
bhāsas tasya mahātmanaḥ

The cosmic form was so dazzling that it could outshine thousands of blazing suns.

13

तत्रैकस्थं जगत्कृत्स्नं प्रविभक्तमनेकधा ।
अपश्यद्देवदेवस्य शरीरे पाण्डवस्तदा ॥

tatraikasthaṁ jagat kṛtsnaṁ
pravibhaktam anekadhā
apaśyad deva-devasya
śarīre pāṇḍavas tadā

Arjuna, the son of Pandu, sighted the entire universe held together in one place, within God.

14

ततः स विस्मयाविष्टो हृष्टरोमा धनञ्जयः ।
प्रणम्य शिरसा देवं कृताञ्जलिरभाषत ॥

tataḥ sa vismayāviṣṭo
hṛṣṭa-romā dhanañjayaḥ
praṇamya śirasā devaṁ
kṛtāñjalir abhāṣata

Captivated by what he saw, Arjuna had goosebumps all over. He folded his palms and bowed down his head in veneration.

15

अर्जुन उवाच
पश्यामि देवांस्तव देव देहे
सर्वांस्तथा भूतविशेषसङ्घान् ।
ब्रह्माणमीशं कमलासनस्थ-
मृषींश्च सर्वानुरगांश्च दिव्यान् ॥

arjuna uvāca
paśyāmi devāṁs tava deva dehe
sarvāṁs tathā bhūta-viśeṣa-saṅghān
brahmāṇam īśaṁ kamalāsana-stham
ṛṣīṁś ca sarvān uragāṁś ca divyān

Arjuna said –

O' Lord, within Your body I see an assembly of celestial beings. I see Lord Brahma and Lord Shiva seated on lotus flowers as well as sages and celestial serpents.

16

अनेकबाहूदरवक्त्रनेत्रं
पश्यामि त्वां सर्वतोऽनन्तरूपम् ।
नान्तं न मध्यं न पुनस्तवादिं
पश्यामि विश्वेश्वर विश्वरूप ॥

aneka-bāhūdara-vaktra-netraṁ
paśyāmi tvāṁ sarvato 'nanta-rūpam
nāntaṁ na madhyaṁ na punas tavādiṁ
paśyāmi viśveśvara viśva-rūpa

I see innumerable arms, bellies, mouths, and eyes in this expansive form. O' Vishveshvara, there is no beginning, no middle, and no end to it.

17

किरीटिनं गदिनं चक्रिणं च
तेजोराशिं सर्वतो दीप्तिमन्तम् ।
पश्यामि त्वां दुर्निरीक्ष्यं समन्ता-
द्दीप्तानलार्कद्युतिमप्रमेयम् ॥

kirīṭinaṁ gadinaṁ cakriṇaṁ ca
tejo-rāśiṁ sarvato dīptimantam
paśyāmi tvāṁ durnirīkṣyaṁ samantād
dīptānalārka-dyutim aprameyam

Though difficult to see Your form blinded by Your fiery and radiating halo, I see You with crowns, holding clubs and discs.

18

त्वमक्षरं परमं वेदितव्यं
त्वमस्य विश्वस्य परं निधानम् ।
त्वमव्ययः शाश्वतधर्मगोप्ता
सनातनस्त्वं पुरुषो मतो मे ॥

tvam akṣaraṁ paramaṁ veditavyaṁ
tvam asya viśvasya paraṁ nidhānam
tvam avyayaḥ śāśvata-dharma-goptā
sanātanas tvaṁ puruṣo mato me

You are infallible, the supreme object of knowledge, maintainer of eternal dharma and in my opinion, the Supreme, transcendental personality.

19

अनादिमध्यान्तमनन्तवीर्य-
मनन्तबाहुं शशिसूर्यनेत्रम्।
पश्यामि त्वां दीप्तहुताशवक्त्रं
स्वतेजसा विश्वमिदं तपन्तम् ॥

anādi-madhyāntam ananta-vīryam
ananta-bāhuṁ śaśi-sūrya-netram
paśyāmi tvāṁ dīpta-hutāśa-vaktraṁ
sva-tejasā viśvam idaṁ tapantam

You are unlimited with no beginning, no middle, no end. With arms infinite. The sun and moon are Your eyes and fire blazes from Your mouth that warms the entire universe.

20

द्यावापृथिव्योरिदमन्तरं हि
व्याप्तं त्वयैकेन दिशश्च सर्वाः ।
दृष्ट्वाद्भुतं रूपमुग्रं तवेदं
लोकत्रयं प्रव्यथितं महात्मन् ॥

dyāv āpṛthivyor idam antaraṁ hi
vyāptaṁ tvayaikena diśaś ca sarvāḥ
dṛṣṭvādbhutaṁ rūpam ugraṁ tavedaṁ
loka-trayaṁ pravyathitaṁ mahātman

O' Great One, You pervade the space between the planets and the three worlds tremble in fear on beholding Your wondrous and terrible form.

21

अमी हि त्वां सुरसङ्घा विशन्ति
केचिद्भीताः प्राञ्जलयो गृणन्ति ।
स्वस्तीत्युक्त्वा महर्षिसिद्धसङ्घाः
स्तुवन्ति त्वां स्तुतिभिः पुष्कलाभिः ॥

amī hi tvāṁ sura-saṅghā viśanti
kecid bhītāḥ prāñjalayo gṛṇanti
svastīty uktvā maharṣi-siddha-saṅghāḥ
stuvanti tvāṁ stutibhiḥ puṣkalābhiḥ

With folded hands, a stream of devatas entering Your cosmic form surrender unto You, praying for peace. Sages and Siddhas chant hymns praising You.

22

रुद्रादित्या वसवो ये च साध्या
विश्वेऽश्विनौ मरुतश्चोष्मपाश्च ।
गन्धर्वयक्षासुरसिद्धसङ्घा
वीक्षन्ते त्वां विस्मिताश्चैव सर्वे ॥

rudrādityā vasavo ye ca sādhyā
viśve 'śvinau marutaś coṣmapāś ca
gandharva-yakṣāsura-siddha-saṅghā
vīkṣante tvāṁ vismitāś caiva sarve

The Rudras, Adityas, Vasus, Sadhyas, Vishvadevas, Ashvinis, Maruts, ancestors, Gandharvas, Yakshas, Asuras, and Siddhas are all stunned with Your form.

23

रूपं महत्ते बहुवक्त्रनेत्रं
महाबाहो बहुबाहूरुपादम् ।
बहूदरं बहुदंष्ट्राकरालं
दृष्ट्वा लोका: प्रव्यथितास्तथाहम् ॥

rūpaṁ mahat te bahu-vaktra-netraṁ
mahā-bāho bahu-bāhūru-pādam
bahūdaraṁ bahu-daṁṣṭrā-karālaṁ
dṛṣṭvā lokāḥ pravyathitās tathāham

The whole world is cowering in fear at the sight of Your terrible form of multiple mouths, faces, eyes, ears, arms, bellies, thighs, feet, and the fearsome teeth. And so am I, O' Mighty-armed One.

24

नभ:स्पृशं दीप्तमनेकवर्णं
व्यात्ताननं दीप्तविशालनेत्रम् ।
दृष्ट्वा हि त्वां प्रव्यथितान्तरात्मा
धृतिं न विन्दामि शमं च विष्णो ॥

nabhaḥ spṛśaṁ dīptam aneka-varṇaṁ
vyāttānanaṁ dīpta-viśāla-netram
dṛṣṭvā hi tvāṁ pravyathitāntar-ātmā
dhṛtiṁ na vindāmi śamaṁ ca viṣṇo

I have lost my composure and peace of mind as I tremble with fear beholding Your fiery form touching the sky, Your gruesome mouth and raging large eyes.

25

दंष्ट्राकरालानि च ते मुखानि
दृष्ट्वैव कालानलसन्निभानि ।
दिशो न जाने न लभे च शर्म
प्रसीद देवेश जगन्निवास ॥

daṁṣṭrā-karālāni ca te mukhāni
dṛṣṭvaiva kālānala-sannibhāni
diśo na jāne na labhe ca śarma
prasīda deveśa jagan-nivāsa

Fearing from all directions, I have lost my mental equilibrium. Your deathly faces and hideous teeth that spew fire give me no comfort. O' Lord of all Lords, You are the abode for the universe, please have mercy on me.

26 – 27

अमी च त्वां धृतराष्ट्रस्य पुत्राः
सर्वे सहैवावनिपालसङ्घैः ।
भीष्मो द्रोणः सूतपुत्रस्तथासौ
सहास्मदीयैरपि योधमुख्यैः ॥
वक्त्राणि ते त्वरमाणा विशन्ति
दंष्ट्राकरालानि भयानकानि ।
केचिद्विलग्ना दशनान्तरेषु
सन्दृश्यन्ते चूर्णितैरुत्तमाङ्गैः ॥

amī ca tvāṁ dhṛtarāṣṭrasya putrāḥ
sarve sahaivāvani-pāla-saṅghaiḥ
bhīṣmo droṇaḥ sūta-putras tathāsau
sahāsmadīyair api yodha-mukhyaiḥ
vaktrāṇi te tvaramāṇā viśanti
daṁṣṭrā-karālāni bhayānakāni
kecid vilagnā daśanāntareṣu
sandṛśyante cūrṇitair uttamāṅgaiḥ

I see all the sons of Dhritarashtra and their supporting kings, with Bhishma, Drona, Karna, and also our soldiers, hurtling helplessly into Your sinister mouth. Your terrible teeth crushing their heads.

28

यथा नदीनां बहवोऽम्बुवेगाः
समुद्रमेवाभिमुखा द्रवन्ति।
तथा तवामी नरलोकवीरा
विशन्ति वक्त्राण्यभिविज्वलन्ति ॥

yathā nadīnāṁ bahavo 'mbu-vegāḥ
samudram evābhimukhā dravanti
tathā tavāmī nara-loka-vīrā
viśanti vaktrāṇy abhivijvalanti

Like rivers flow rapidly into the sea, these warriors are gushing into Your flaming mouth to meet their end.

29

यथा प्रदीप्तं ज्वलनं पतङ्गा
विशन्ति नाशाय समृद्धवेगाः ।
तथैव नाशाय विशन्ति लोका-
स्तवापि वक्त्राणि समृद्धवेगाः ॥

yathā pradīptaṁ jvalanaṁ pataṅgā
viśanti nāśāya samṛddha-vegāḥ
tathaiva nāśāya viśanti lokās
tavāpi vaktrāṇi samṛddha-vegāḥ

Like moths fly into the fire and get destroyed, these warriors enter Your mouth to meet their destruction.

30

लेलिह्यसे ग्रसमानः समन्ता-
ल्लोकान्समग्रान्वदनैर्ज्वलद्भिः।
तेजोभिरापूर्य जगत्समग्रं
भासस्तवोग्राः प्रतपन्ति विष्णो ॥

lelihyase grasamānaḥ samantāl
lokān samagrān vadanair jvaladbhiḥ
tejobhir āpūrya jagat samagraṁ
bhāsas tavogrāḥ pratapanti viṣṇo

You devour and lick everyone with Your fiery mouth while Your brilliant rays surround and scorch the entire cosmos.

31

आख्याहि मे को भवानुग्ररूपो
नमोऽस्तु ते देववर प्रसीद ।
विज्ञातुमिच्छामि भवन्तमाद्यं
न हि प्रजानामि तव प्रवृत्तिम् ॥

ākhyāhi me ko bhavān ugra-rūpo
namo 'stu te deva-vara prasīda
vijñātum icchāmi bhavantam ādyaṁ
na hi prajānāmi tava pravṛttim

Who are You? What is Your purpose? I pay my obeisance to You. Please show me mercy. O' Lord of Lords, I do not understand Your ferocious form and actions.

32

श्रीभगवानुवाच
कालोऽस्मि लोकक्षयकृत्प्रवृद्धो
लोकान्समाहर्तुमिह प्रवृत्तः ।
ऋतेऽपि त्वां न भविष्यन्ति सर्वे
येऽवस्थिताः प्रत्यनीकेषु योधाः ॥

śrī-bhagavān uvāca
kālo 'smi loka-kṣaya-kṛt pravṛddho
lokān samāhartum iha pravṛttaḥ
ṛte 'pi tvāṁ na bhaviṣyanti sarve
ye 'vasthitāḥ pratyanīkeṣu yodhāḥ

Sri Bhagavan said –

I am time, a force that destroys everything and everyone. Whether you fight or not, everyone in the war except the Pandavas, will be destroyed.

33

तस्मात्त्वमुत्तिष्ठ यशो लभस्व
जित्वा शत्रून्भुङ्क्ष्व राज्यं समृद्धम् ।
मयैवैते निहता: पूर्वमेव
निमित्तमात्रं भव सव्यसाचिन् ॥

tasmāt tvam uttiṣṭha yaśo labhasva
jitvā śatrūn bhuṅkṣva rājyaṁ samṛddham
mayaivaite nihatāḥ pūrvam eva
nimitta-mātraṁ bhava savya-sācin

Therefore stand up and fight. Kill your enemies and rule your kingdom. Your enemies are already destined to be killed by Me, O' Savyasachi, but you can be my instrument.

34

द्रोणं च भीष्मं च जयद्रथं च
कर्णं तथान्यानपि योधवीरान् ।
मया हतांस्त्वं जहि मा व्यथिष्ठा
युध्यस्व जेतासि रणे सपत्नान् ॥

droṇaṁ ca bhīṣmaṁ ca jayadrathaṁ ca
karṇaṁ tathānyān api yodha-vīrān
mayā hatāṁs tvaṁ jahi mā vyathiṣṭhā
yudhyasva jetāsi raṇe sapatnān

Fight without any fear because I have already killed Drona, Bhishma, Jayadratha, and other stalwarts. You will win if you fight.

35

सञ्जय उवाच
एतच्छ्रुत्वा वचनं केशवस्य
कृताञ्जलिर्वेपमानः किरीटी ।
नमस्कृत्वा भूय एवाह कृष्णं
सगद्गदं भीतभीतः प्रणम्य ॥

sañjaya uvāca
etac chrutvā vacanaṁ keśavasya
kṛtāñjalir vepamānaḥ kirītī
namaskṛtvā bhūya evāha kṛṣṇaṁ
sagadgadaṁ bhīta-bhītaḥ praṇamya

Sanjaya said –
Arjuna continued to tremble in fear even after hearing the words of Keshava. With folded hands, he offered Him obeisance and spoke in a faltering voice.

36

अर्जुन उवाच
स्थाने हृषीकेश तव प्रकीर्त्या
जगत्प्रहृष्यत्यनुरज्यते च ।
रक्षांसि भीतानि दिशो द्रवन्ति
सर्वे नमस्यन्ति च सिद्धसङ्घाः ॥

arjuna uvāca
sthāne hṛṣīkeśa tava prakīrtyā
jagat prahṛṣyaty anurajyate ca
rakṣāṁsi bhītāni diśo dravanti
sarve namasyanti ca siddha-saṅghāḥ

Arjuna said –
Your name and glories brings cheer to the world while striking terror in demons who flee in fear. While the sages rightfully bow down to You, O' Hrishikesha.

37

कस्माच्च ते न नमेरन्महात्मन्
गरीयसे ब्रह्मणोऽप्यादिकर्त्रे ।
अनन्त देवेश जगन्निवास
त्वमक्षरं सदसत्तत्परं यत् ॥

kasmāc ca te na nameran mahātman
garīyase brahmaṇo 'py ādi-kartre

ananta deveśa jagan-nivāsa
tvam akṣaraṁ sad-asat tat paraṁ yat

And why should they not bow down to You, the one who is greater than Brahma, the indestructable, the infinite, the abode of the universe, and that which transcends the visible and the invisible?

38

त्वमादिदेवः पुरुषः पुराण-
स्त्वमस्य विश्वस्य परं निधानम् ।
वेत्तासि वेद्यं च परं च धाम
त्वया ततं विश्वमनन्तरूप ॥

tvam ādi-devaḥ puruṣaḥ purāṇas
tvam asya viśvasya paraṁ nidhānam
vettāsi vedyaṁ ca paraṁ ca dhāma
tvayā tataṁ viśvam ananta-rūpa

You are the original and supreme person, a shelter for the entire world. You are the supreme abode. You are both the knower and knowledge. You transcend the material nature to pervade the cosmos in Your infinite form.

39

वायुर्यमोऽग्निर्वरुण: शशाङ्क:
प्रजापतिस्त्वं प्रपितामहश्च ।
नमो नमस्तेऽस्तु सहस्रकृत्व:
पुनश्च भूयोऽपि नमो नमस्ते ॥

vāyur yamo 'gnir varuṇaḥ śaśāṅkaḥ
prajāpatis tvaṁ prapitāmahaś ca
namo namas te 'stu sahasra-kṛtvaḥ
punaś ca bhūyo 'pi namo namas te

You are Vayu, Yamaraja, Agni, Varuna, Chandra; You are the progenitor and the great-grandfather. I pay homage to You thousands of times, again and again and again.

40

नम: पुरस्तादथ पृष्ठतस्ते
नमोऽस्तु ते सर्वत एव सर्व ।
अनन्तवीर्यामितविक्रमस्त्वं
सर्वं समाप्नोषि ततोऽसि सर्व: ॥

namaḥ purastād atha pṛṣṭhatas te
namo 'stu te sarvata eva sarva
ananta-vīryāmita-vikramas tvaṁ
sarvaṁ samāpnoṣi tato 'si sarvaḥ

I salute You from the front, behind, and from all sides. Your strength is infinite. Your courage is absolute. You pervade everything and You are everything!

41 – 42

सखेति मत्वा प्रसभं यदुक्तं
हे कृष्ण हे यादव हे सखेति ।
अजानता महिमानं तवेदं
मया प्रमादात्प्रणयेन वापि ॥
यच्चावहासार्थमसत्कृतोऽसि
विहारशय्यासनभोजनेषु ।
एकोऽथ वाप्यच्युत तत्समक्षं
तत्क्षामये त्वामहमप्रमेयम् ॥

sakheti matvā prasabhaṁ yad uktaṁ
he kṛṣṇa he yādava he sakheti
ajānatā mahimānaṁ tavedaṁ
mayā pramādāt praṇayena vāpi
yac cāvahāsārtham asat-kṛto 'si
vihāra-śayyāsana-bhojaneṣu
eko 'tha vāpy acyuta tat-samakṣaṁ
tat kṣāmaye tvām aham aprameyam

Forgive my ignorance and foolishness for addressing You as 'Krishna,' 'Yadava,' 'friend' as I was unaware of Your majestic stature. Forgive me for joking with You while playing, sitting, resting, and eating together with You privately or publicly.

43

पितासि लोकस्य चराचरस्य
त्वमस्य पूज्यश्च गुरुर्गरीयान् ।
न त्वत्समोऽस्त्यभ्यधिकः कुतोऽन्यो
लोकत्रयेऽप्यप्रतिमप्रभाव ॥

pitāsi lokasya carācarasya
tvam asya pūjyaś ca gurur garīyān
na tvat-samo 'sty abhyadhikaḥ kuto 'nyo
loka-traye 'py apratima-prabhāva

O' father of all things living and non-living in the universe! O' Reverant Supreme! O' Spiritual Master! O' Superpower! When none is equal to You in all three worlds then how can anyone be greater than You?

44

तस्मात्प्रणम्य प्रणिधाय कायं
प्रसादये त्वामहमीशमीड्यम् ।
पितेव पुत्रस्य सखेव सख्युः
प्रियः प्रियायार्हसि देव सोढुम् ॥

tasmāt praṇamya praṇidhāya kāyaṁ
prasādaye tvām aham īśam īḍyam
piteva putrasya sakheva sakhyuḥ
priyaḥ priyāyārhasi deva soḍhum

By prostrating before You, my Supreme God, I beg for Your mercy. Please overlook my indiscretions like a father tolerates a son's behaviour, like a friend forgives a friend or a lover forgives his beloved.

45

अदृष्टपूर्वं हृषितोऽस्मि दृष्ट्वा
भयेन च प्रव्यथितं मनो मे ।
तदेव मे दर्शय देव रूपं
प्रसीद देवेश जगन्निवास ॥

adṛṣṭa-pūrvaṁ hṛṣito 'smi dṛṣṭvā
bhayena ca pravyathitaṁ mano me
tad eva me darśaya deva rūpaṁ
prasīda deveśa jagan-nivāsa

I feel immense joy and disturbing fear at the same time at the sight of Your cosmic form that I had never seen before. How I long to see Your original pleasing form once again. Please be kind on me, O' shelter of the entire world.

46

किरीटिनं गदिनं चक्रहस्त-
मिच्छामि त्वां द्रष्टुमहं तथैव ।
तेनैव रूपेण चतुर्भुजेन
सहस्रबाहो भव विश्वमूर्ते ॥

kirīṭinaṁ gadinaṁ cakra-hastam
icchāmi tvāṁ draṣṭum ahaṁ tathaiva
tenaiva rūpeṇa catur-bhujena
sahasra-bāho bhava viśva-mūrte

I am eager to see Your crowned form holding a mace, disc, conch, and lotus. O' Thousand-armed One, let me see Your four-armed form.

47

श्रीभगवानुवाच
मया प्रसन्नेन तवार्जुनेदं
रूपं परं दर्शितमात्मयोगात् ।
तेजोमयं विश्वमनन्तमाद्यं
यन्मे त्वदन्येन न दृष्टपूर्वम् ॥

śrī-bhagavān uvāca
mayā prasannena tavārjunedaṁ
rūpaṁ paraṁ darśitam ātma-yogāt
tejomayaṁ viśvam anantam ādyaṁ
yan me tvad-anyena na dṛṣṭa-pūrvam

Sri Bhagavan said –
O' Arjuna, I gave you vision of my infinite, dazzling, fulgent form which no one has seen before.

48

न वेदयज्ञाध्ययनैर्न दानै-
र्न च क्रियाभिर्न तपोभिरुग्रैः ।
एवंरूपः शक्य अहं नृलोके
द्रष्टुं त्वदन्येन कुरुप्रवीर ॥

na veda-yajñādhyayanair na dānair
na ca kriyābhir na tapobhir ugraiḥ

evaṁ rūpaḥ śakya ahaṁ nṛ-loke
draṣṭuṁ tvad-anyena kuru-pravīra

I can be seen neither by study of the Vedas, nor by sacrifices. Nor by charity, nor by pious deeds nor austerities. None has seen this, O' best of the Kurus.

49

मा ते व्यथा मा च विमूढभावो
दृष्ट्वा रूपं घोरमीदृङ्ममेदम् ।
व्यपेतभीः प्रीतमनाः पुनस्त्वं
तदेव मे रूपमिदं प्रपश्य ॥

mā te vyathā mā ca vimūḍha-bhāvo
dṛṣṭvā rūpaṁ ghoram īdṛṅ mamedam
vyapetabhīḥ prīta-manāḥ punas tvaṁ
tad eva me rūpam idaṁ prapaśya

Let go of the fear you feel from this terrible form and set your eyes on the form you so long to see with a peaceful heart.

50

सञ्जय उवाच
इत्यर्जुनं वासुदेवस्तथोक्त्वा
स्वकं रूपं दर्शयामास भूयः ।
आश्वासयामास च भीतमेनं
भूत्वा पुनः सौम्यवपुर्महात्मा ॥

sañjaya uvāca
ity arjunaṁ vāsudevas tathoktvā
svakaṁ rūpaṁ darśayām āsa bhūyaḥ
āśvāsayām āsa ca bhītam enaṁ
bhūtvā punaḥ saumya-vapur mahatma

Sanjaya said –
With these words, the kind-hearted Lord assumed His four-handed form. He consoled Arjuna further by returning to His gentle two-handed form.

51

अर्जुन उवाच
दृष्ट्वेदं मानुषं रूपं तव सौम्यं जनार्दन ।
इदानीमस्मि संवृत्तः सचेताः प्रकृतिं गतः ॥

arjuna uvāca
dṛṣṭvedaṁ mānuṣaṁ rūpaṁ
tava saumyaṁ janārdana

idānīm asmi saṁvṛttaḥ
sa-cetāḥ prakṛtiṁ gataḥ

Seeing his friend Krishna in front of him again, Arjuna said, 'O' Janardana, I am relieved and in good consciousness to see You back in Your human likeness.'

52

श्रीभगवानुवाच
सुदुर्दर्शमिदं रूपं दृष्टवानसि यन्मम ।
देवा अप्यस्य रूपस्य नित्यं दर्शनकाङ्क्षिणः ॥

śrī-bhagavān uvāca
sudurdarśam idaṁ rūpaṁ
dṛṣṭavān asi yan mama
devā apy asya rūpasya
nityaṁ darśana-kāṅkṣiṇaḥ

Sri Bhagavan said –

This current form which you love is a very rare sight. A sight even devatas hanker to see.

53

नाहं वेदैर्न तपसा न दानेन न चेज्यया ।
शक्य एवंविधो द्रष्टुं दृष्टवानसि मां यथा ॥

nāhaṁ vedair na tapasā
na dānena na cejyayā
śakya evaṁ-vidho drașṭuṁ
dṛṣṭavān asi māṁ yathā

You have seen a form that can never be seen just by understanding the Vedas, or by austerities, charity, sarifices, and penance. None of this works when it comes to seeing Me.

54

भक्त्या त्वनन्यया शक्य अहमेवंविधोऽर्जुन ।
ज्ञातुं द्रष्टुं च तत्त्वेन प्रवेष्टुं च परन्तप ॥

bhaktyā tv ananyayā śakya
aham evaṁ-vidho 'rjuna
jñātuṁ drașṭuṁ ca tattvena
praveṣṭuṁ ca parantapa

O' Arjuna, by devotion alone I can be seen directly as I stand before you. By devotion alone I can be understood and attained, O' Parantapa.

55

मत्कर्मकृन्मत्परमो मद्भक्तः सङ्गवर्जितः ।
निर्वैरः सर्वभूतेषु यः स मामेति पाण्डव ॥

mat-karma-kṛn mat-paramo
mad-bhaktaḥ saṅga-varjitaḥ
nirvairaḥ sarva-bhūteṣu
yaḥ sa mām eti pāṇḍava

O' Pandava, anyone who engages in my devotional activities, free from fruitive activities, free from attachments, friendly to all, can easily come to Me.

Chapter

12

Bhakti Yoga

1

अर्जुन उवाच
एवं सततयुक्ता ये भक्तास्त्वां पर्युपासते ।
ये चाप्यक्षरमव्यक्तं तेषां के योगवित्तमाः ॥

arjuna uvāca
evaṁ satata-yuktā ye
bhaktās tvāṁ paryupāsate
ye cāpy akṣaram avyaktaṁ
teṣāṁ ke yoga-vittamāḥ

Arjuna said –
In Your opinion, who is better? A devotee who worships You, engaged in serving You or one who worships the impersonal form?

2

श्रीभगवानुवाच
मय्यावेश्य मनो ये मां नित्ययुक्ता उपासते ।
श्रद्धया परयोपेतास्ते मे युक्ततमा मताः ॥

śrī-bhagavān uvāca
mayy āveśya mano ye māṁ
nitya-yuktā upāsate
śraddhayā parayopetās
te me yuktatamā matāḥ

Sri Bhagavan said –

In my opinion, the devotee who worships Me with steady faith, always absorbed in Me, engaged in my service, he is the best yogi.

3 – 4

ये त्वक्षरमनिर्देश्यमव्यक्तं पर्युपासते ।
सर्वत्रगमचिन्त्यं च कूटस्थमचलं ध्रुवम् ॥
सन्नियम्येन्द्रियग्रामं सर्वत्र समबुद्धयः ।
ते प्राप्नुवन्ति मामेव सर्वभूतहिते रताः ॥

ye tv akṣaram anirdeśyam
avyaktaṁ paryupāsate
sarvatra-gam acintyaṁ ca
kūṭastham acalaṁ dhruvam
sanniyamyendriya-grāmaṁ
sarvatra sama-buddhayaḥ
te prāpnuvanti mām eva
sarva-bhūta-hite ratāḥ

Yet, those who worship the impersonal form that is indestructible, unmanifest, and all-pervading, they will attain Me too.

5

क्लेशोऽधिकतरस्तेषामव्यक्तासक्तचेतसाम् ।
अव्यक्ता हि गतिर्दुःखं देहवद्भिरवाप्यते ॥

kleśo 'dhikataras teṣām
avyaktāsakta-cetasām
avyaktā hi gatir duḥkhaṁ
dehavadbhir avāpyate

However, they will face more difficulties on their path and their progress will be slow. For embodied beings, the path of impersonal worship is a hardship.

6 – 7

ये तु सर्वाणि कर्माणि मयि सन्न्यस्य मत्पराः ।
अनन्येनैव योगेन मां ध्यायन्त उपासते ॥
तेषामहं समुद्धर्ता मृत्युसंसारसागरात् ।
भवामि न चिरात्पार्थ मय्यावेशितचेतसाम् ॥

ye tu sarvāṇi karmāṇi
mayi sannyasya mat-parāḥ
ananyenaiva yogena
māṁ dhyāyanta upāsate
teṣām ahaṁ samuddhartā
mṛtyu-saṁsāra-sāgarāt
bhavāmi na cirāt pārtha
mayy āveśita-cetasām

O' Partha, only those who worship Me and meditate on Me exclusively, surrender to Me with mind and body, them I deliver quickly from the cyclic ocean of birth and death.

8

मय्येव मन आधत्स्व मयि बुद्धिं निवेशय ।
निवसिष्यसि मय्येव अत ऊर्ध्वं न संशयः ॥

mayy eva mana ādhatsva
mayi buddhiṁ niveśaya
nivasiṣyasi mayy eva
ata ūrdhvaṁ na saṁśayaḥ

If you fasten your mind and intelligence to Me, you will undoubtedly, always live with Me.

9

अथ चित्तं समाधातुं न शक्नोषि मयि स्थिरम् ।
अभ्यासयोगेन ततो मामिच्छाप्तुं धनञ्जय ॥

atha cittaṁ samādhātuṁ
na śaknoṣi mayi sthiram
abhyāsa-yogena tato
mām icchāptuṁ dhanañjaya

If you cannot fasten your mind and intelligence to Me, then follow the path and principles of yoga of devotional service which is the right path to attain Me, O' Dhananjaya.

10

अभ्यासेऽप्यसमर्थोऽसि मत्कर्मपरमो भव ।
मदर्थमपि कर्माणि कुर्वन्सिद्धिमवाप्स्यसि ॥

abhyāse 'py asamartho 'si
mat-karma-paramo bhava
mad-artham api karmāṇi
kurvan siddhim avāpsyasi

If you cannot follow the path of devotion, then work for Me following my instructions. Even with this you will attain the stage of perfection.

11

अथैतदप्यशक्तोऽसि कर्तुं मद्योगमाश्रितः ।
सर्वकर्मफलत्यागं ततः कुरु यतात्मवान् ॥

athaitad apy aśakto 'si
kartuṁ mad-yogam āśritaḥ
sarva-karma-phala-tyāgaṁ
tataḥ kuru yatātmavān

At least give up attachment to the fruits of your actions if you cannot work for Me. By such self-control and detached work, be self-realized.

12

श्रेयो हि ज्ञानमभ्यासाज्ज्ञानाद्ध्यानं विशिष्यते ।
ध्यानात्कर्मफलत्यागस्त्यागाच्छान्तिरनन्तरम् ॥

śreyo hi jñānam abhyāsāj
jñānād dhyānaṁ viśiṣyate
dhyānāt karma-phala-tyāgas
tyāgāc chāntir anantaram

If that is also not possible, then acquire knowledge of the self. Better than acquiring knowledge is meditation and better than meditation is renunciation of fruits of actions which brings peace through self-realization.

13 – 14

अद्वेष्टा सर्वभूतानां मैत्रः करुण एव च ।
निर्ममो निरहङ्कारः समदुःखसुखः क्षमी ॥
सन्तुष्टः सततं योगी यतात्मा दृढनिश्चयः ।
मय्यर्पितमनोबुद्धिर्यो मद्भक्तः स मे प्रियः ॥

advesṭā sarva-bhūtānāṁ
maitraḥ karuṇa eva ca
nirmamo nirahaṅkāraḥ
sama-duḥkha-sukhaḥ kṣamī
santuṣṭaḥ satataṁ yogī
yatātmā dṛḍha-niścayaḥ
mayy-arpita-mano-buddhir
yo mad-bhaktaḥ sa me priyaḥ

Free from malice, compassion for all, equipoised in pain and pleasure, tolerant, content, determined, self-controlled, consistent in devotional service, mind, and intelligence attached to Me. These are qualities of devotees who are dear to Me.

15

यस्मान्नोद्विजते लोको लोकान्नोद्विजते च यः ।
हर्षामर्षभयोद्वेगैर्मुक्तो यः स च मे प्रियः ॥

yasmān nodvijate loko
lokān nodvijate ca yaḥ
harṣāmarṣa-bhayodvegair
mukto yaḥ sa ca me priyaḥ

He who never agitates anyone and is never disturbed by anyone, he who is unaffected by pleasure, fear, or distress, he is very dear to Me.

16

अनपेक्षः शुचिर्दक्ष उदासीनो गतव्यथः ।
सर्वारम्भपरित्यागी यो मद्भक्तः स मे प्रियः ॥

anapekṣaḥ śucir dakṣa
udāsīno gata-vyathaḥ
sarvārambha-parityāgī
yo mad-bhaktaḥ sa me priyaḥ

He who does not depend on the results of his actions, he who is pure, impartial, skillful, selfless, without anxieties, that devotee is very dear to Me.

17

यो न हृष्यति न द्वेष्टि न शोचति न काङ्क्षति ।
शुभाशुभपरित्यागी भक्तिमान्य: स मे प्रिय: ॥

yo na hṛṣyati na dveṣṭi
na śocati na kāṅkṣati
śubhāśubha-parityāgī
bhaktimān yaḥ sa me priyaḥ

He who neither rejoices, laments nor desires, he who renounces the auspicious and the evil, that devotee is very dear to Me.

18 – 19

सम: शत्रौ च मित्रे च तथा मानापमानयो: ।
शीतोष्णसुखदु:खेषु सम: सङ्गविवर्जित: ॥
तुल्यनिन्दास्तुतिर्मौनी सन्तुष्टो येन केनचित् ।
अनिकेत: स्थिरमतिर्भक्तिमान्मे प्रियो नर: ॥

samaḥ śatrau ca mitre ca
tathā mānāpamānayoḥ
śītoṣṇa-sukha-duḥkheṣu
samaḥ saṅga-vivarjitaḥ
tulya-nindā-stutir maunī
santuṣṭo yena kenacit

aniketaḥ sthira-matir
bhaktimān me priyo naraḥ

He who has equal vision for friends and enemies, is unaffected by honour and dishonour, criticism and praise, happiness and grief, heat and cold, is always in favourable association, is silent, content, unconcerned about residence, whose intelligence is fixed in Me, mind absorbed in my service, he is very dear to Me.

20

ये तु धर्मामृतमिदं यथोक्तं पर्युपासते ।
श्रद्दधाना मत्परमा भक्तास्तेऽतीव मे प्रियाः ॥

ye tu dharmāmṛtam idaṁ
yathoktaṁ paryupāsate
śraddadhānā mat-paramā
bhaktās te 'tīva me priyāḥ

By following this path of devotional service faithfully and focusing on Me as the ultimate goal, he becomes my most loved devotee.

Chapter 13

Ksetra Ksetrajna Vibhaga Yoga

1

अर्जुन उवाच
प्रकृतिं पुरुषं चैव क्षेत्रं क्षेत्रज्ञमेव च ।
एतद्वेदितुमिच्छामि ज्ञानं ज्ञेयं च केशव ॥

arjuna uvāca
prakṛtiṁ puruṣaṁ caiva
kṣetraṁ kṣetra-jñam eva ca
etad veditum icchāmi
jñānaṁ jñeyaṁ ca keśava

Arjuna said –

O' Keshava, what is meant by *prakriti*? What is meant by *purush*? What is *kshetra* and *kshetragya*? I want to know what true knowledge is and what the goal of true knowledge is.

2

श्रीभगवानुवाच
इदं शरीरं कौन्तेय क्षेत्रमित्यभिधीयते ।
एतद्यो वेत्ति तं प्राहुः क्षेत्रज्ञ इति तद्विदः ॥

śrī-bhagavān uvāca
idaṁ śarīraṁ kaunteya
kṣetram ity abhidhīyate
etad yo vetti taṁ prāhuḥ
kṣetra-jñaḥ iti tad-vidaḥ

Sri Bhagavan said –
O' Kaunteya, the body, the field of action, is called kshetra. One who knows the field is the knower of the field or kshetragya.

3

क्षेत्रज्ञं चापिमां विद्धि सर्वक्षेत्रेषु भारत ।
क्षेत्रक्षेत्रज्ञयोर्ज्ञानं यत्तज्ज्ञानं मतं मम ॥

kṣetra-jñaṁ cāpi māṁ viddhi
sarva-kṣetreṣu bhārata
kṣetra-kṣetrajñayor jñānaṁ
yat taj jñānaṁ mataṁ mama

I am the knower of all bodies and simply knowing the body and its owner is real knowledge in my opinion.

4

तत्क्षेत्रं यच्च यादृक्च यद्विकारि यतश्च यत् ।
स च यो यत्प्रभावश्च तत्समासेन मे शृणु ॥

tat kṣetraṁ yac ca yādṛk ca
yad vikāri yataś ca yat
sa ca yo yat prabhāvaś ca
tat samāsena me śṛṇu

Now please hear Me explain to you about the nature of the field. Its origin, its constitution, the changes it goes through, its knower, and its influence.

5

ऋषिभिर्बहुधा गीतं छन्दोभिर्विविधैः पृथक् ।
ब्रह्मसूत्रपदैश्चैव हेतुमद्भिर्विनिश्चितैः ॥

ṛṣibhir bahudhā gītaṁ
chandobhir vividhaih pṛthak
brahma-sūtra-padaiś caiva
hetumadbhir viniścitaiḥ

The Vedic literature, especially Brahmasutra gives detailed knowledge on the field of activity and the knower of the field with sound logical reasoning by sages.

6 – 7

महाभूतान्यहङ्कारो बुद्धिरव्यक्तमेव च ।
इन्द्रियाणि दशैकं च पञ्च चेन्द्रियगोचराः ॥
इच्छा द्वेषः सुखं दुःखं सङ्घातश्चेतना धृतिः ।
एतत्क्षेत्रं समासेन सविकारमुदाहृतम् ॥

mahā-bhūtāny ahaṅkāro
buddhir avyaktam eva ca
indriyāṇi daśaikaṁ ca
pañca cendriya-gocarāḥ
icchā dveṣaḥ sukhaṁ duḥkhaṁ
saṅghātaś cetanā dhṛtiḥ
etat kṣetraṁ samāsena
sa-vikāram udāhṛtam

Briefly put, kshetra or the field of activities comprises the five elements of nature, ego, intellect, the unmanifest matter, five sense organs, five sense objects (desire, hatred, pleasure, pain, the aggregate), consciousness, and will.

8 – 12

अमानित्वमदम्भित्वमहिंसा क्षान्तिरार्जवम् ।
आचार्योपासनं शौचं स्थैर्यमात्मविनिग्रहः ॥
इन्द्रियार्थेषु वैराग्यमनहङ्कार एव च ।
जन्ममृत्युजराव्याधिदुःखदोषानुदर्शनम् ॥
असक्तिरनभिष्वङ्गः पुत्रदारगृहादिषु ।
नित्यं च समचित्तत्वमिष्टानिष्टोपपत्तिषु ॥
मयि चानन्ययोगेन भक्तिरव्यभिचारिणी ।
विविक्तदेशसेवित्वमरतिर्जनसंसदि ॥
अध्यात्मज्ञाननित्यत्वं तत्त्वज्ञानार्थदर्शनम् ।
एतज्ज्ञानमिति प्रोक्तमज्ञानं यदतोऽन्यथा ॥

amānitvam adambhitvam
ahiṁsā kṣāntir ārjavam
ācāryopāsanaṁ śaucaṁ
sthairyam ātma-vinigrahaḥ
indriyārtheṣu vairāgyam
anahaṅkāra eva ca
janma-mṛtyu-jarā-vyādhi
duḥkha-doṣānudarśanam
asaktir anabhiṣvaṅgaḥ
putra-dāra-gṛhādiṣu
nityaṁ ca sama-cittatvam
iṣṭāniṣṭopapattiṣu
mayi cānanya-yogena
bhaktir avyabhicāriṇī
vivikta-deśa-sevitvam

aratir jana-saṁsadi
adhyātma-jñāna-nityatvaṁ
tattva-jñānārtha-darśanam
etaj jñānam iti proktam
ajñānaṁ yad ato 'nyathā

Knowledge includes humility, modesty, non-violence, forbearance, simplicity, serving the guru, cleanliness, persistence, self-control, abstaining from sense objects, rejecting the ego, understanding the futility of birth, death, old age, disease, detachment from materialism, detachment from family affairs, balanced mind in the midst of desires, firm devotion to Me, living in seclusion, uninterested in social affairs, prioritizing self-realization, awareness of philosophical truths. Anything contrasting this is ignorance.

13

ज्ञेयं यत्तत्प्रवक्ष्यामि यज्ज्ञात्वामृतमश्नुते ।
अनादिमत्परं ब्रह्म न सत्तन्नासदुच्यते ॥

jñeyaṁ yat tat pravakṣyāmi
yaj jñātvāmṛtam aśnute
anādi mat-paraṁ brahma
na sat tan nāsad ucyate

I will now disclose to you that which is to be known, the knowable, knowing which you will realize eternality. The Brahman is without a beginning, beyond the cause and effects of material nature, and under my control.

14

सर्वतः पाणिपादं तत्सर्वतोऽक्षिशिरोमुखम् ।
सर्वतः श्रुतिमल्लोके सर्वमावृत्य तिष्ठति ॥

sarvataḥ pāṇi-pādaṁ tat
sarvato 'kṣi-śiro-mukham
sarvataḥ śrutimal loke
sarvam āvṛtya tiṣṭhati

His hands, legs, eyes, face, ears are everywhere. He exists everywhere. He is all-pervading.

15

सर्वेन्द्रियगुणाभासं सर्वेन्द्रियविवर्जितम् ।
असक्तं सर्वभृच्चैव निर्गुणं गुणभोक्तृ च ॥

sarvendriya-guṇābhāsaṁ
sarvendriya-vivarjitam
asaktaṁ sarva-bhṛc caiva
nirguṇaṁ guṇa-bhoktṛ ca

He is the original source of all senses but he himself has no senses. Though detached, he maintains all existence. Though controller of all three modes of material nature, he is beyond the modes.

16

बहिरन्तश्च भूतानामचरं चरमेव च ।
सूक्ष्मत्वात्तदविज्ञेयं दूरस्थं चान्तिके च तत् ॥

bahir antaś ca bhūtānām
acaraṁ caram eva ca
sūkṣmatvāt tad avijñeyaṁ
dūra-sthaṁ cāntike ca tat

He exists inside and outside of everything moving and non-moving. He is beyond material comprehension or recognition. He is far, and also near.

17

अविभक्तं च भूतेषु विभक्तमिव च स्थितम् ।
भूतभर्तृ च तज्ज्ञेयं ग्रसिष्णु प्रभविष्णु च ॥

avibhaktaṁ ca bhūteṣu
vibhaktam iva ca sthitam
bhūta-bhartṛ ca taj jñeyaṁ
grasiṣṇu prabhaviṣṇu ca

He is indivisible though he appears divided in all living beings. He is the supreme creator, maintainer, and annihilator.

18

ज्योतिषामपि तज्ज्योतिस्तमसः परमुच्यते ।
ज्ञानं ज्ञेयं ज्ञानगम्यं हृदि सर्वस्य विष्ठितम् ॥

jyotiṣām api taj jyotis
tamasaḥ param ucyate
jñānaṁ jñeyaṁ jñāna-gamyaṁ
hṛdi sarvasya viṣṭhitam

He is the source of light for all luminaries. Beyond the darkness of ignorance. He is knowledge, the object of knowledge, and also the goal of knowledge. He lives in everyone's heart.

19

इति क्षेत्रं तथा ज्ञानं ज्ञेयं चोक्तं समासतः ।
मद्भक्त एतद्विज्ञाय मद्भावायोपपद्यते ॥

iti kṣetraṁ tathā jñānaṁ
jñeyaṁ coktuṁ samāsataḥ
mad-bhakta etad vijñāya
mad-bhāvāyopapadyate

A devotee alone understands what I have said about field of activity, knowledge, and object of knowledge, and he is the one who attains Me.

20

प्रकृतिं पुरुषं चैव विद्ध्यनादी उभावपि ।
विकारांश्च गुणांश्चैव विद्धि प्रकृतिसम्भवान् ॥

prakṛtiṁ puruṣaṁ caiva
viddhyanādī ubhāv api
vikārāṁś ca guṇāṁś caiva
viddhi prakṛti-sambhavān

Prakriti or material nature and purusha or living entity, both are without a beginning. All transformations and material modes arise from material nature.

21

कार्यकारणकर्तृत्वे हेतुः प्रकृतिरुच्यते ।
पुरुषः सुखदुःखानां भोक्तृत्वे हेतुरुच्यते ॥

kārya-kāraṇa-kartṛtve
hetuḥ prakṛtir ucyate
puruṣaḥ sukha-duḥkhānāṁ
bhoktṛtve hetur ucyate

Prakriti is responsible for material cause and effect. Purusha is responsible for experiences of suffering and enjoyment.

22

पुरुषः प्रकृतिस्थो हि भुङ्क्ते प्रकृतिजान्गुणान् ।
कारणं गुणसङ्गोऽस्य सदसद्योनिजन्मसु ॥

puruṣaḥ prakṛti-stho hi
bhuṅkte prakṛti-jān guṇān
kāraṇaṁ guṇa-saṅgo'sya
sad-asad-yoni-janmasu

Purusha, in association with prakriti, lives under the influence of the three gunas becoming good or bad according to the gunas.

23

उपद्रष्टानुमन्ता च भर्ता भोक्ता महेश्वरः ।
परमात्मेति चाप्युक्तो देहेऽस्मिन्पुरुषः परः ॥

upadraṣṭānumantā ca
bhartā bhoktā maheśvaraḥ—
paramātmeti cāpy ukto
dehe'smin puruṣaḥ paraḥ

Within the body is another Witness, Permitter, Supporter, the Supreme Soul. It is the Supreme Controller and Enjoyer called the Super Soul.

24

य एवं वेत्ति पुरुषं प्रकृतिं च गुणैः सह ।
सर्वथा वर्तमानोऽपि न स भूयोऽभिजायते ॥

ya evaṁ vetti puruṣaṁ
prakṛtiṁ ca guṇaiḥ saha
sarvathā vartamāno'pi
na sa bhūyo 'bhijāyate

For liberation, one only needs to understand material nature, the individual soul and its interaction with the material modes. Understanding this, one will surely be liberated from the cycle of birth and death.

25

ध्यानेनात्मनि पश्यन्ति केचिदात्मानमात्मना ।
अन्ये साङ्ख्येन योगेन कर्मयोगेन चापरे ॥

dhyānenātmani paśyanti
kecid ātmānam ātmanā
anye sāṅkhyena yogena
karma-yogena cāpare

One can try to understand the Supreme Soul through meditation, by acquiring knowledge, or by work without expectations of result.

26

अन्ये त्वेवमजानन्तः श्रुत्वान्येभ्य उपासते ।
तेऽपि चातितरन्त्येव मृत्युं श्रुतिपरायणाः ॥

anye tv evam ajānantaḥ
śrutvānyebhya upāsate
te'pi cātitaranty eva
mṛtyuṁ śruti-parāyaṇāḥ

Some others worship the Supreme Soul by hearing from saintly persons although they have no spiritual knowledge and they too transcend the cycle of birth and death.

27

यावत्सञ्जायते किञ्चित्सत्त्वं स्थावरजङ्गमम्।
क्षेत्रक्षेत्रज्ञसंयोगात्तद्विद्धि भरतर्षभ ॥

yāvat sanjayate kiṅcit
sattvaṁ sthāvara-jaṅgamam
kṣetra-kṣetrajña-saṁyogāt
tad viddhi bharatarṣabha

O' Arjuna, the world that you see exists because of the combined interaction of the field of activities and the knower of the field.

28

समं सर्वेषु भूतेषु तिष्ठन्तं परमेश्वरम् ।
विनश्यत्स्वविनश्यन्तं यः पश्यति स पश्यति ॥

samaṁ sarveṣu bhūteṣu
tiṣṭhantaṁ parameśvaram
vinaśyatsv avinaśyantaṁ
yaḥ paśyati sa paśyati

Knowing that the Super Soul resides besides the soul in every being and that both are undestroyable, is true insight.

29

समं पश्यन्हि सर्वत्र समवस्थितमीश्वरम् ।
न हिनस्त्यात्मनात्मानं ततो याति परां गतिम् ॥

samaṁ paśyan hi sarvatra
samavasthitam īśvaram
na hinasty ātmanātmānaṁ
tato yāti parāṁ gatim

By knowing the Super Soul to be equally present everywhere and in everyone, the mind remains in a higher consciousness and attains the supreme goal of life.

30

प्रकृत्यैव च कर्माणि क्रियमाणानि सर्वशः ।
यः पश्यति तथात्मानमकर्तारं स पश्यति ॥

prakṛtyaiva ca karmāṇi
kriyamāṇāni sarvaśaḥ
yaḥ paśyati tathātmānam
akartāraṁ sa paśyati

One who is aware that activities are carried out not by the soul but by the body borne out of material nature, he truly sees.

31

यदा भूतपृथग्भावमेकस्थमनुपश्यति ।
तत एव च विस्तारं ब्रह्म सम्पद्यते तदा ॥

yadā bhūta-pṛthag-bhāvam
eka-stham anupaśyati
tata eva ca vistāraṁ
brahma sampadyate tadā

When one sees the diversity of living beings coming from a singular source of material nature, one attains Brahman.

32

अनादित्वान्निर्गुणत्वात्परमात्मायमव्ययः ।
शरीरस्थोऽपि कौन्तेय न करोति न लिप्यते ॥

anāditvān nirguṇatvāt
paramātmāyam avyayaḥ
śarīra-stho 'pi kaunteya
na karoti na lipyate

O' Kaunteya, the Supreme Soul is transcendental, imperishable, and beginningless. It neither acts nor gets entangled even in proximity with material nature.

33

यथा सर्वगतं सौक्ष्म्यादाकाशं नोपलिप्यते ।
सर्वत्रावस्थितो देहे तथात्मा नोपलिप्यते ॥

yathā sarva-gataṁ saukṣmyād
ākāśaṁ nopalipyate
sarvatrāvasthito dehe
tathātmā nopalipyate

The all-pervading sky does not get contaminated by anything that it holds. This is true also for the soul which does not mix with the body although it pervades the body.

34

यथा प्रकाशयत्येकः कृत्स्नं लोकमिमं रविः ।
क्षेत्रं क्षेत्री तथा कृत्स्नं प्रकाशयति भारत ॥

yathā prakāśayaty ekaḥ
kṛtsnaṁ lokam imaṁ raviḥ
kṣetraṁ kṣetrī tathā kṛtsnaṁ
prakāśayati bhārata

Like the sun illuminates the entire cosmos, the soul illuminates the entire body, O' scion of Bharata.

35

क्षेत्रक्षेत्रज्ञयोरेवमन्तरं ज्ञानचक्षुषा ।
भूतप्रकृतिमोक्षं च ये विदुर्यान्ति ते परम् ॥

kṣetra-kṣetrajñayor evam
antaraṁ jñāna-cakṣuṣā
bhūta-prakṛti-mokṣaṁ ca
ye vidur yānti te param

By differentiating between the field and the knower of the field, one automatically realizes how to become free from material nature and reach the supreme goal.

Chapter 14

Guna Traya Vibhaga Yoga

1

श्रीभगवानुवाच
परं भूयः प्रवक्ष्यामि ज्ञानानां ज्ञानमुत्तमम् ।
यज्ज्ञात्वा मुनयः सर्वे परां सिद्धिमितो गताः ॥

śrī-bhagavān uvāca
paraṁ bhūyaḥ pravakṣyāmi
jñānānāṁ jñānam uttamam
yaj jñātvā munayaḥ sarve
parāṁ siddhim ito gatāḥ

Sri Bhagavan said –
I will continue now to share with you the supreme wisdom on the basis of which great sages have attained the highest perfection of life.

2

इदं ज्ञानमुपाश्रित्य मम साधर्म्यमागताः ।
सर्गेऽपि नोपजायन्ते प्रलये न व्यथन्ति च ॥

idaṁ jñānam upāśritya
mama sādharmyam āgatāḥ
sarge'pi nopajāyante
pralaye na vyathanti ca

By accepting this wisdom, one comes to Me and is saved from birth and death at the time of creation and annihilation.

3

मम योनिर्महद्ब्रह्म तस्मिन्गर्भं दधाम्यहम् ।
सम्भवः सर्वभूतानां ततो भवति भारत ॥

mama yonir mahad-brahma
tasmin garbhaṁ dadhāmy aham
sambhavaḥ sarva-bhūtānāṁ
tato bhavati bhārata

My material energy Brahman is the womb that I impregnate, giving birth to all living beings, O' descendant of Bharata.

4

सर्वयोनिषु कौन्तेय मूर्तयः सम्भवन्ति याः ।
तासां ब्रह्म महद्योनिरहं बीजप्रदः पिता ॥

sarva-yoniṣu kaunteya
mūrtayaḥ sambhavanti yāḥ
tāsāṁ brahma mahad yonir
ahaṁ bīja-pradaḥ pitā

O' son of Kunti, all species of life are borne from the womb of Mother Nature and I am the seed-giving Father.

~ **5** ~

सत्त्वं रजस्तम इति गुणाः प्रकृतिसम्भवाः ।
निबध्नन्ति महाबाहो देहे देहिनमव्ययम् ॥

sattvaṁ rajas tama iti
guṇāḥ prakṛti-sambhavāḥ
nibadhnanti mahā-bāho
dehe dehinam avyayam

The material nature comprises three modes—*sattvic* (goodness), *rajasic* (passion), and *tamasic* (ignorance) which bind the soul to the body, O' mighty-armed Arjuna.

6

तत्र सत्त्वं निर्मलत्वात्प्रकाशकमनामयम् ।
सुखसङ्गेन बध्नाति ज्ञानसङ्गेन चानघ ॥

tatra sattvaṁ nirmalatvāt
prakāśakam anāmayam
sukha-saṅgena badhnāti
jñāna-saṅgena cānagha

The mode of goodness is the purest amongst these, being enlightened and free from sorrow. People in mode of goodness are attached to happiness and knowledge.

7

रजो रागात्मकं विद्धि तृष्णासङ्गसमुद्भवम् ।
तन्निबध्नाति कौन्तेय कर्मसङ्गेन देहिनम् ॥

rajo rāgātmakaṁ viddhi
tṛṣṇā-saṅga-samudbhavam
tan nibadhnāti kaunteya
karma-saṅgena dehinam

The mode of passion is the cause of infinite desires and cravings, and pushes the conditioned soul to perform fruitive activities, O' Kaunteya.

8

तमस्त्वज्ञानजं विद्धि मोहनं सर्वदेहिनाम् ।
प्रमादालस्यनिद्राभिस्तन्निबध्नाति भारत ॥

tamas tv ajñāna-jaṁ viddhi
mohanaṁ sarva-dehinām
pramādālasya-nidrābhis
tan nibadhnāti bhārata

The mode of ignorance incites the embodied soul into an illusion which is seen as laziness, sleepiness, and deluded madness.

9

सत्त्वं सुखे सञ्जयति रजः कर्मणि भारत ।
ज्ञानमावृत्य तु तमः प्रमादे सञ्जयत्युत ॥

sattvaṁ sukhe sañjayati
rajaḥ karmaṇi bhārata
jñānam āvṛtya tu tamaḥ
pramāde sañjayaty uta

Sattva guna binds one to happiness, *rajas* guna to fruitive activity, and *tamas* guna to madness.

10

रजस्तमश्चाभिभूय सत्त्वं भवति भारत ।
रजः सत्त्वं तमश्चैव तमः सत्त्वं रजस्तथा ॥

rajas tamaś cābhibhūya
sattvaṁ bhavati bhārata
rajaḥ sattvaṁ tamaś caiva
tamaḥ sattvaṁ rajas tathā

In a battle for supremacy, sometimes goodness reigns supreme defeating passion and ignorance, sometimes passion takes over beating goodness and ignorance, and sometimes ignorance dominates prevailing over goodness and passion, O' son of Bharata.

11

सर्वद्वारेषु देहेऽस्मिन्प्रकाश उपजायते ।
ज्ञानं यदा तदा विद्याद्विवृद्धं सत्त्वमित्युत ॥

sarva-dvāreṣu dehe'smin
prakāśa upajāyate
jñānaṁ yadā tadā vidyād
vivṛddhaṁ sattvam ity uta

When the gates of the body are enlightened with knowledge, sattva is the active mode.

12

लोभ: प्रवृत्तिरारम्भ: कर्मणामशम: स्पृहा ।
रजस्येतानि जायन्ते विवृद्धे भरतर्षभ ॥

lobhaḥ pravṛttir ārambhaḥ
karmaṇām aśamaḥ spṛhā
rajasy etāni jāyante
vivṛddhe bharatarṣabha

Attachments, yearnings, fruitive activities are symptomatic of rajasic guna, O' Arjuna.

13

अप्रकाशोऽप्रवृत्तिश्च प्रमादो मोह एव च ।
तमस्येतानि जायन्ते विवृद्धे कुरुनन्दन ॥

aprakāśo 'pravṛttiś ca
pramādo moha eva ca
tamasy etāni jāyante
vivṛddhe kuru-nandana

Darkness, inactivity, and illusions indicate dominance of tamas guna, O' descendant of the Kurus.

14

यदा सत्त्वे प्रवृद्धे तु प्रलयं याति देहभृत् ।
तदोत्तमविदां लोकानमलान्प्रतिपद्यते ॥

yadā sattve pravṛddhe tu
pralayaṁ yāti deha-bhṛt
tadottama-vidāṁ lokān
amalān pratipadyate

In the mode of goodness, one goes to higher planets, on death.

15

रजसि प्रलयं गत्वा कर्मसङ्गिषु जायते ।
तथा प्रलीनस्तमसि मूढयोनिषु जायते ॥

rajasi pralayaṁ gatvā
karma-saṅgiṣu jāyate
tathā pralīnas tamasi
mūḍha-yoniṣu jāyate

When death is in the mode of passion, one takes birth amongst those driven by fruitive activities. Death in the mode of ignorance obtains birth amongst animals.

16

कर्मणः सुकृतस्याहुः सात्त्विकं निर्मलं फलम् ।
रजसस्तु फलं दुःखमज्ञानं तमसः फलम् ॥

karmaṇaḥ sukṛtasyāhuḥ
sāttvikaṁ nirmalaṁ phalam
rajasas tu phalaṁ duḥkham
ajñānaṁ tamasaḥ phalam

Pious actions in mode of goodness result in purity. Actions in mode of passion beget suffering while actions in mode of ignorance result in foolhardiness.

17

सत्त्वात्सञ्जायते ज्ञानं रजसो लोभ एव च ।
प्रमादमोहौ तमसो भवतोऽज्ञानमेव च ॥

sattvāt sañjāyate jñānaṁ
rajaso lobha eva ca
pramāda-mohau tamaso
bhavato 'jñānam eva ca

Knowledge comes from sattva mode. Greed from rajas, and nescience and foolishness from tamas.

18

ऊर्ध्वं गच्छन्ति सत्त्वस्था मध्ये तिष्ठन्ति राजसाः ।
जघन्यगुणवृत्तिस्था अधो गच्छन्ति तामसाः ॥

ūrdhvaṁ gacchanti sattva-sthā
madhye tiṣṭhanti rājasāḥ
jaghanya-guṇa-vṛtti-sthā
adho gacchanti tāmasāḥ

Sattva takes you to higher planets. Rajas keeps you on earthly planets. Tamas spirals you down to hellish planets.

19

नान्यं गुणेभ्यः कर्तारं यदा द्रष्टानुपश्यति ।
गुणेभ्यश्च परं वेत्ति मद्भावं सोऽधिगच्छति ॥

nānyaṁ guṇebhyaḥ kartāraṁ
yadā draṣṭānupaśyati
guṇebhyaś ca paraṁ vetti
mad-bhāvaṁ so 'dhigacchati

Understanding that it is only these three modes of material nature that are involved in all activities and not the Supreme Lord, takes you to the spiritual platform.

20

गुणानेतानतीत्य त्रीन्देही देहसमुद्भवान् ।
जन्ममृत्युजरादुःखैर्विमुक्तोऽमृतमश्नुते ॥

gunạ̄n etān atītya trīn
dehī deha-samudbhavān
janma-mṛtyu-jarā-duḥkhair
vimukto 'mṛtam aśnute

By transcending the modes of nature, you can release yourself from miseries of birth, death, and old age to enjoy eternally.

21

अर्जुन उवाच
कैर्लिङ्गैस्त्रीन्गुणानेतानतीतो भवति प्रभो ।
किमाचारः कथं चैतांस्त्रीन्गुणानतिवर्तते ॥

arjuna uvāca
kair liṅgais trīn guṇān etān
atīto bhavati prabho
kim ācāraḥ kathaṁ caitāṁs
trīn guṇān ativartate

Arjuna said –
Prabhu, how does one transcend the three modes? How is he recognized and how does he behave?

22 – 25

श्रीभगवानुवाच
प्रकाशं च प्रवृत्तिं च मोहमेव च पाण्डव ।
न द्वेष्टि सम्प्रवृत्तानि न निवृत्तानि काङ्क्षति ॥
उदासीनवदासीनो गुणैर्यो न विचाल्यते ।
गुणा वर्तन्त इत्येवं योऽवतिष्ठति नेङ्गते ॥
समदुःखसुखः स्वस्थः समलोष्टाश्मकाञ्चनः ।
तुल्यप्रियाप्रियो धीरस्तुल्यनिन्दात्मसंस्तुतिः ॥
मानापमानयोस्तुल्यस्तुल्यो मित्रारिपक्षयोः ।
सर्वारम्भपरित्यागी गुणातीतः स उच्यते ॥

śrī-bhagavān uvāca
prakāśaṁ ca pravṛttiṁ ca
moham eva ca pāṇḍava
na dveṣṭi sampravṛttāni
na nivṛttāni kāṅkṣati
udāsīnavad āsīno
guṇair yo na vicālyate
guṇā vartanta ity evaṁ
yo 'vatiṣṭhati neṅgate
sama-duḥkha-sukhaḥ svasthaḥ
sama-loṣṭāśma-kāñcanaḥ
tulya-priyāpriyo dhīras
tulya-nindātma-saṁstutiḥ
mānāpamānayos tulyas
tulyo mitrāri-pakṣayoḥ

sarvārambha-parityāgī
guṇātītaḥ sa ucyate

Sri Bhagavan said –
O' Arjuna, one who has transcended the three modes of material nature has no hatred for knowledge, attachment, and delusion, nor does he long for them when absent. He is indifferent and undisturbed by the acts of the modes of nature, remaining steady and composed in joy and sorrow. He views mud, stone, and gold, all equally. He does not differentiate between what he likes and what he dislikes, praise or blame, honour or dishonour, friends or foes and has renounced all result-oriented activities.

26

मां च योऽव्यभिचारेण भक्तियोगेन सेवते ।
स गुणान्समतीत्यैतान्ब्रह्मभूयाय कल्पते ॥

māṁ ca yo 'vyabhicāreṇa
bhakti-yogena sevate
sa guṇān samatītyaitān
brahma-bhūyāya kalpate

When one serves Me constantly with devotion irrespective of circumstances, one rises above the three modes of nature and reaches the Brahman platform.

27

ब्रह्मणो हि प्रतिष्ठाहममृतस्याव्ययस्य च ।
शाश्वतस्य च धर्मस्य सुखस्यैकान्तिकस्य च ॥

brahmaṇo hi pratiṣṭhāham
amṛtasyāvyayasya ca
śāśvatasya ca dharmasya
sukhasyaikāntikasya ca

I am the basis of that absolute bliss coming from the eternal, indestructive, formless, and immortal Brahman.

Chapter

15

Purushottama Yoga

1

श्रीभगवानुवाच
ऊर्ध्वमूलमध:शाखमश्वत्थं प्राहुरव्ययम् ।
छन्दांसि यस्य पर्णानि यस्तं वेद स वेदवित् ॥

śrī-bhagavān uvāca
ūrdhva-mūlam adhaḥ-śākham
aśvatthaṁ prāhur avyayam
chandāṁsi yasya parṇāni
yas taṁ veda sa veda-vit

Sri Bhagavan said –
There exists a banyan tree which has roots growing upwards, branches downwards, and its leaves are the Vedic hymns. If one can understand this eternal tree, one can understand the Vedas.

2

अधश्चोर्ध्वं प्रसृतास्तस्य शाखा
गुणप्रवृद्धा विषयप्रवाला: ।
अधश्च मूलान्यनुसन्ततानि
कर्मानुबन्धीनि मनुष्यलोके ॥

adhaś cordhvaṁ prasṛtās tasya śākhā
guṇa-pravṛddhā viṣaya-pravālāḥ

adhaś ca mūlāny anusantatāni
karmānubandhīni manuṣya-loke

Nurtured by the three gunas, the branches spread across downwards and upwards. The twigs are the sense objects. The roots are bound by karma, the fruitive activities of human beings.

3 – 4

न रूपमस्येह तथोपलभ्यते
नान्तो न चादिर्न च सम्प्रतिष्ठा ।
अश्वत्थमेनं सुविरूढमूल-
मसङ्गशस्त्रेण दृढेन छित्त्वा ॥
ततः पदं तत्परिमार्गितव्यं
यस्मिन्गता न निवर्तन्ति भूयः ।
तमेव चाद्यं पुरुषं प्रपद्ये
यतः प्रवृत्तिः प्रसृता पुराणी ॥

na rūpam asyeha tathopalabhyate
nānto na cādir na ca sampratiṣṭhā
aśvattham enaṁ su-virūḍha-mūlam
asaṅga-śastreṇa dṛḍhena chittvā
tataḥ padaṁ tat parimārgitavyaṁ
yasmin gatā na nivartanti bhūyaḥ
tam eva cādyaṁ puruṣaṁ prapadye
yataḥ pravṛttiḥ prasṛtā purāṇī

This tree is covert, its beginning, its end, and even its foundation is not easily perceptible in this world. But one has to still cut this deep-rooted tree with determination and detachment. Having done that, one must search for a higher destination, the Supreme God, the reservoir of all activity and all existence. Once he surrenders to Him, he never comes back to this world again.

5

निर्मानमोहा जितसङ्गदोषा
अध्यात्मनित्या विनिवृत्तकामाः ।
द्वन्द्वैर्विमुक्ताः सुखदुःखसंज्ञै-
र्गच्छन्त्यमूढाः पदमव्ययं तत् ॥

nirmāna-mohā jita-saṅga-doṣā
adhyātma-nityā vinivṛtta-kāmāḥ
dvandvair vimuktāḥ sukha-duḥkha-saṁjñair
gacchanty amūḍhāḥ padam avyayaṁ tat

One who surrenders to the Supreme God, has humility, uninfluenced by illusions or bad association, without lust and free from dualities of joy and sorrow, he attains my spiritual abode.

6

न तद्भासयते सूर्यो न शशाङ्को न पावकः ।
यद्गत्वा न निवर्तन्ते तद्धाम परमं मम ॥

na tad bhāsayate sūryo
na śaśāṅko na pāvakaḥ
yad gatvā na nivartante
tad dhāma paramaṁ mama

My supreme abode needs no illumination by the sun, moon, or fire. From there, one will never return to the material world.

7

ममैवांशो जीवलोके जीवभूतः सनातनः ।
मनःषष्ठानीन्द्रियाणि प्रकृतिस्थानि कर्षति ॥

mamaivāṁśo jīva-loke
jīva-bhūtaḥ sanātanaḥ
manaḥ ṣaṣṭhānīndriyāṇi
prakṛti-sthāni karṣati

The embodied souls are my fragments, my parts and parcel. But conditioned and bound by the material nature, they are still struggling with the six senses including the mind.

8

शरीरं यदवाप्नोति यच्चाप्युत्क्रामतीश्वरः ।
गृहीत्वैतानि संयाति वायुर्गन्धानिवाशयात् ॥

śarīraṁ yad avāpnoti
yac cāpy utkrāmatīśvaraḥ
gṛhītvaitāni saṁyāti
vāyur gandhān ivāśayāt

As the air carries fragrance from place to place, so does the soul carries its mind and perceptions from body to body.

9

श्रोत्रं चक्षुः स्पर्शनं च रसनं घ्राणमेव च ।
अधिष्ठाय मनश्चायं विषयानुपसेवते ॥

śrotraṁ cakṣuḥ sparśanaṁ ca
rasanaṁ ghrāṇam eva ca
adhiṣṭhāya manaś cāyaṁ
viṣayān upasevate

When acquiring a new body, the soul obtains a particular mental framework and sense organs to help it enjoy correspondingly.

10

उत्क्रामन्तं स्थितं वाऽपि भुञ्जानं वा गुणान्वितम्।
विमूढा नानुपश्यन्ति पश्यन्ति ज्ञानचक्षुष:॥

utkrāmantaṁ sthitaṁ vāpi
bhuñjānaṁ vā guṇānvitam
vimūḍhā nānupaśyanti
paśyanti jñāna-cakṣuṣaḥ

The ignorant enjoy the sense objects under the influence of three modes of material nature, grossly unaware of the nature of the soul within. Only the eyes of knowledge can see the truth.

11

यतन्तो योगिनश्चैनं पश्यन्त्यात्मन्यवस्थितम् ।
यतन्तोऽप्यकृतात्मानो नैनं पश्यन्त्यचेतस: ॥

yatanto yoginaś cainaṁ
paśyanty ātmany avasthitam
yatanto 'py akṛtātmāno
nainaṁ paśyanty acetasaḥ

The self-realized and those striving from transcendence can see the soul within the body. For others not self-realized, with no ability of discrimination, cannot see this even if they try.

12

यदादित्यगतं तेजो जगद्भासयतेऽखिलम् ।
यच्चन्द्रमसि यच्चाग्नौ तत्तेजो विद्धि मामकम् ॥

yad āditya-gataṁ tejo
jagad bhāsayate 'khilam
yac candramasi yac cāgnau
tat tejo viddhi māmakam

The luminescence of the sun that illuminates the world, the brilliance of the moon, the dazzle of fire, all originate from Me.

13

गामाविश्य च भूतानि धारयाम्यहमोजसा ।
पुष्णामि चौषधीः सर्वाः सोमो भूत्वा रसात्मकः ॥

gām āviśya ca bhūtāni
dhārayāmy aham ojasā
puṣṇāmi cauṣadhīḥ sarvāḥ
somo bhūtvā rasātmakaḥ

My enegy permeates each planet to sustain it. It is my energy in the moon that nourishes plants and vegetables.

14

अहं वैश्वानरो भूत्वा प्राणिनां देहमाश्रित: ।
प्राणापानसमायुक्त: पचाम्यन्नं चतुर्विधम् ॥

ahaṁ vaiśvānaro bhūtvā
prāṇināṁ deham āśritaḥ
prāṇāpāna-samāyuktaḥ
pacāmy annaṁ catur-vidham

I am the fire of digestion. I am the incoming and outgoing life breath required to digest the four kinds of food.

15

सर्वस्य चाहं हृदि सन्निविष्टो
मत्त: स्मृतिर्ज्ञानमपोहनं च ।
वेदैश्च सर्वैरहमेव वेद्यो
वेदान्तकृद्वेदविदेव चाहम्॥

sarvasya cāhaṁ hṛdi sanniviṣṭo
mattaḥ smṛtir jñānam apohanaṁ ca
vedaiś ca sarvair aham eva vedyo
vedānta-kṛd veda-vid eva cāham

Seated in the hearts of all living beings, from Me come memory, remembrance, and forgetfulness. I am the conclusion of the Vedas and I alone am to be known from the Vedas. I am also the compiler as well as the knower of the Vedas.

16

द्वाविमौ पुरुषौ लोके क्षरश्चाक्षर एव च ।
क्षरः सर्वाणि भूतानि कूटस्थोऽक्षर उच्यते ॥

dvāv imau puruṣau loke
kṣaraś cākṣara eva ca
kṣaraḥ sarvāṇi bhūtāni
kūṭa-stho 'kṣara ucyate

There are two classes of entities as given in the Vedas—the fallible who are found in the material world and the infallible present in the spiritual world.

17

उत्तमः पुरुषस्त्वन्यः परमात्मेत्युदाहृतः ।
यो लोकत्रयमाविश्य बिभर्त्यव्यय ईश्वरः ॥

uttamaḥ puruṣas tv anyaḥ
paramātmety udāhṛtaḥ
yo loka-trayam āviśya
bibharty avyaya īśvaraḥ

Higher than these two is the greatest entity, the Supreme Soul, the eternal Lord Himself who pervades and maintains the three worlds.

18

यस्मात्क्षरमतीतोऽहमक्षरादपि चोत्तमः ।
अतोऽस्मि लोके वेदे च प्रथितः पुरुषोत्तमः ॥

yasmāt kṣaram atīto 'ham
akṣarād api cottamaḥ
ato 'smi loke vede ca
prathitaḥ puruṣottamaḥ

I am described in the Vedas as the Supreme Being because I am transcendental, the best of all and above the fallible and infallible.

19

यो मामेवमसम्मूढो जानाति पुरुषोत्तमम् ।
स सर्वविद्भजति मां सर्वभावेन भारत ॥

yo mām evam asammūḍho
jānāti puruṣottamam
sa sarva-vid bhajati māṁ
sarva-bhāvena bhārata

Recognizing Me as the Supreme Being is knowing everything that needs to be known. Without doubt, he then serves Me in full devotion, O' descendant of Bharata.

20

इति गुह्यतमं शास्त्रमिदमुक्तं मयानघ ।
एतद्बुद्ध्वा बुद्धिमान्स्यात्कृतकृत्यश्च भारत ॥

iti guhyatamaṁ śāstram
idam uktaṁ mayānagha
etad buddhvā buddhimān syāt
kṛta-kṛtyaś ca bhārata

I have opened for you the secret principle of the Vedas. O' sinless Arjuna, this knowledge will make you wise and take you to the perfection of your life.

Chapter 16

Daivasura Sampada Vibhaga Yoga

1 – 3

श्रीभगवानुवाच
अभयं सत्त्वसंशुद्धिर्ज्ञानयोगव्यवस्थितिः ।
दानं दमश्च यज्ञश्च स्वाध्यायस्तप आर्जवम् ॥
अहिंसा सत्यमक्रोधस्त्यागः शान्तिरपैशुनम् ।
दया भूतेष्वलोलुप्त्वं मार्दवं ह्रीरचापलम् ॥
तेजः क्षमा धृतिः शौचमद्रोहो नातिमानिता ।
भवन्ति सम्पदं दैवीमभिजातस्य भारत ॥

śrī-bhagavān uvāca
abhayaṁ sattva-saṁśuddhir
jñāna-yoga-vyavasthitiḥ
dānaṁ damaś ca yajñaś ca
svādhyāyas tapa ārjavam
ahiṁsā satyam akrodhas
tyāgaḥ śāntir apaiśunam
dayā bhūteṣv aloluptvaṁ
mārdavaṁ hrīr acāpalam
tejaḥ kṣamā dhṛtiḥ śaucam
adroho nātimānitā
bhavanti sampadaṁ daivīm
abhijātasya bhārata

O' Arjuna, these are qualities of saintly and divine beings—fearlessness, purity, spiritual knowledge, charity, control over senses, sacrifice, Vedic study, austerity, simplicity, non-violence, truthfulness, want of anger, renunciation, tranquillity, dislike for criticism, compassion, absence of greed, gentleness, modesty, determination, vigour, forgiveness, fortitude, cleanliness, non-enviousness, and indifference to honour.

4

दम्भो दर्पोऽभिमानश्च क्रोधः पारुष्यमेव च ।
अज्ञानं चाभिजातस्य पार्थ सम्पदमासुरीम् ॥

dambho darpo 'bhimānaś ca
krodhaḥ pāruṣyam eva ca
ajñānaṁ cābhijātasya
pārtha sampadam āsurīm

O' Partha, the qualities of demonic beings are—arrogance, pride, conceit, anger, harsh speech, and ignorance.

5

दैवी सम्पद्विमोक्षाय निबन्धायासुरी मता ।
मा शुचः सम्पदं दैवीमभिजातोऽसि पाण्डव ॥

daivī sampad vimokṣāya
nibandhāyāsurī matā
mā śucaḥ sampadaṁ daivīm
abhijāto 'si pāṇḍava

The divine qualities propel you to liberation and the demonic qualities to bondage. O' son of Pandu, you have no cause for concern because your divine qualities are inborn.

6

द्वौ भूतसर्गौ लोकेऽस्मिन्दैव आसुर एव च ।
दैवो विस्तरशः प्रोक्त आसुरं पार्थ मे शृणु ॥

dvau bhūta-sargau loke 'smin
daiva āsura eva ca
daivo vistaraśaḥ prokta
āsuraṁ pārtha me śṛṇ

Divine and demonic are the two kinds of beings in the world. I have enumerated the qualities of divine beings, now hear about the demonic ones.

7

प्रवृत्तिं च निवृत्तिं च जना न विदुरासुराः ।
न शौचं नापि चाचारो न सत्यं तेषु विद्यते ॥

pravṛttiṁ ca nivṛttiṁ ca
janā na vidur āsurāḥ
na śaucaṁ nāpi cācāro
na satyaṁ teṣu vidyate

Those with demonic qualities are ignorant about how to act and how not to. They are devoid of cleanliness, truthfulness, and good behaviour.

8

असत्यमप्रतिष्ठं ते जगदाहुरनीश्वरम् ।
अपरस्परसम्भूतं किमन्यत्कामहैतुकम् ॥

asatyam apratiṣṭhaṁ te
jagad āhur anīśvaram
aparaspara-sambhūtaṁ
kim anyat kāma-haitukam

They believe the world to be an illusion, without any role of God. Simply a product of sensual desires culminating in sexual union.

9

एतां दृष्टिमवष्टभ्य नष्टात्मानोऽल्पबुद्धयः ।
प्रभवन्त्युग्रकर्माणः क्षयाय जगतोऽहिताः ॥

etāṁ dṛṣṭim avaṣṭabhya
naṣṭātmāno 'lpa-buddhayaḥ
prabhavanty ugra-karmāṇaḥ
kṣayāya jagato 'hitāḥ

These are souls with inadequate intelligence and inappropriate beliefs, indulging in heinous acts destructive for the world.

10

काममाश्रित्य दुष्पूरं दम्भमानमदान्विताः ।
मोहाद्गृहीत्वासद्ग्राहान्प्रवर्तन्तेऽशुचिव्रताः ॥

kāmam āśritya duṣpūraṁ
dambha-māna-madānvitāḥ
mohād gṛhītvāsad-grāhān
pravartante 'śuci-vratāḥ

Soaked in lust, pride, and arrogance, the demonic stick to their beliefs of impermanence and act in unclean ways.

11 – 12

चिन्तामपरिमेयां च प्रलयान्तामुपाश्रिताः ।
कामोपभोगपरमा एतावदिति निश्चिताः ॥
आशापाशशतैर्बद्धाः कामक्रोधपरायणाः ।
ईहन्ते कामभोगार्थमन्यायेनार्थसञ्चयान् ॥

cintām aparimeyāṁ ca
pralayāntām upāśritāḥ
kāmopabhoga-paramā
etāvad iti niścitāḥ
āśā-pāśa-śatair baddhāḥ
kāma-krodha-parāyaṇāḥ
īhante kāma-bhogārtham
anyāyenārtha-sañcayān

Satisfying sensual desires is their primary goal in life. Their numerous desires, bound by lust and anger, lead to endless anxiety. To satisfy their lust, they acquire illegal wealth.

13 – 15

इदमद्य मया लब्धमिमं प्राप्स्ये मनोरथम् ।
इदमस्तीदमपि मे भविष्यति पुनर्धनम्॥
असौ मया हतः शत्रुर्हनिष्ये चापरानपि ।
ईश्वरोऽहमहं भोगी सिद्धोऽहं बलवान्सुखी॥
आढ्योऽभिजनवानस्मि कोऽन्योऽस्ति सदृशो मया ।
यक्ष्ये दास्यामि मोदिष्य इत्यज्ञानविमोहिताः ॥

idam adya mayā labdham
imaṁ prāpsye manoratham
idam astīdam api me
bhaviṣyati punar dhanam
asau mayā hataḥ śatrur
haniṣye cāparān api
īśvaro 'ham ahaṁ bhogī
siddho 'haṁ balavān sukhī
āḍhyo 'bhijanavān asmi
ko'nyo'sti sadṛśo mayā
yakṣye dāsyāmi modiṣya
ity ajñāna-vimohitāḥ

The ungodly think, 'I have so much wealth today and I will acquire much more tomorrow. It's mine and it will increase in future. My enemies will suffer, destroyed by me. I am the Lord and enjoyer. I am powerful and happy. None is equal to me. By sacrifices and charities, I will enjoy my life.' This is their delusion in the mode of ignorance.

16

अनेकचित्तविभ्रान्ता मोहजालसमावृताः ।
प्रसक्ताः कामभोगेषु पतन्ति नरकेऽशुचौ ॥

aneka-citta-vibhrāntā
moha-jāla-samāvṛtāḥ
prasaktāḥ kāma-bhogeṣu
patanti narake 'śucau

Trapped in a mesh of illusions, they are confused and attached to sense gratification. Thus they live in hell.

17

आत्मसम्भाविताः स्तब्धा धनमानमदान्विताः ।
यजन्ते नामयज्ञैस्ते दम्भेनाविधिपूर्वकम् ॥

ātma-sambhāvitāḥ stabdhā
dhana-māna-madānvitāḥ
yajante nāma-yajñais te
dambhenāvidhi-pūrvakam

Because of pride, obstinacy, and delusion of wealth, they perform sacrifices as per their own whims without following Vedic guidelines and regulations.

18

अहङ्कारं बलं दर्पं कामं क्रोधं च संश्रिताः ।
मामात्मपरदेहेषु प्रद्विषन्तोऽभ्यसूयकाः ॥

ahaṅkāraṁ balaṁ darpaṁ
kāmaṁ krodhaṁ ca saṁśritāḥ
mām ātma-para-deheṣu
pradviṣanto 'bhyasūyakāḥ

They even envy the Supreme Lord who exists in their own and others' hearts, blinded as they are with power, arrogance, lust, anger, and ego.

19

तानहं द्विषतः क्रूरान्संसारेषु नराधमान् ।
क्षिपाम्यजस्रमशुभानासुरीष्वेव योनिषु ॥

tān ahaṁ dviṣataḥ krūrān
saṁsāreṣu narādhamān
kṣipāmy ajasram aśubhān
āsurīṣv eva yoniṣu

The envious, the wicked, the lowest amongst men, I cast them into the wombs of demonic species to take repeated births.

20

आसुरीं योनिमापन्ना मूढा जन्मनि जन्मनि ।
मामप्राप्यैव कौन्तेय ततो यान्त्यधमां गतिम् ॥

āsurīṁ yonim āpannā
mūḍhā janmani janmani
māṁ aprāpyaiva kaunteya
tato yānty adhamāṁ gatim

Born as demonic beings in the material world, they get degraded lower and lower and never attain Me, O' son of Kunti.

21

त्रिविधं नरकस्येदं द्वारं नाशनमात्मनः ।
कामः क्रोधस्तथा लोभस्तस्मादेतत्त्रयं त्यजेत् ॥

tri-vidhaṁ narakasyedaṁ
dvāraṁ nāśanam ātmanaḥ
kāmaḥ krodhas tathā lobhas
tasmād etat trayaṁ tyajet

Lust, anger, and greed are the three gates that open into hell. If not given up, they degrade the soul.

22

एतैर्विमुक्तः कौन्तेय तमोद्वारैस्त्रिभिर्नरः ।
आचरत्यात्मनः श्रेयस्ततो याति परां गतिम् ॥

etair vimuktaḥ kaunteya
tamo-dvārais tribhir naraḥ
ācaraty ātmanaḥ śreyas
tato yāti parāṁ gatim

The further one is from the three gates, the closer he is to self-realization and supreme destination.

23

यः शास्त्रविधिमुत्सृज्य वर्तते कामकारतः ।
न स सिद्धिमवाप्नोति न सुखं न परां गतिम् ॥

yaḥ śāstra-vidhim utsṛjya
vartate kāma-kārataḥ
na sa siddhim avāpnoti
na sukhaṁ na parāṁ gatim

Impulsive actions disregarding scriptural directions bring neither happiness, nor the stage of perfection, nor achievement of the supreme goal of life.

24

तस्माच्छास्त्रं प्रमाणं ते कार्याकार्यव्यवस्थितौ ।
ज्ञात्वा शास्त्रविधानोक्तं कर्म कर्तुमिहार्हसि ॥

tasmāc chāstraṁ pramāṇaṁ te
kāryākārya-vyavasthitau
jñātvā śāstra-vidhānoktaṁ
karma kartum ihārhasi

It is best advisable to discern dos and don'ts as per scriptural authority and then implement them to achieve gradual elevation.

Chapter

17

Shraddha Tarya Vibhaga Yoga

1

अर्जुन उवाच
ये शास्त्रविधिमुत्सृज्य यजन्ते श्रद्धयान्विताः ।
तेषां निष्ठा तु का कृष्ण सत्त्वमाहो रजस्तमः ॥

arjuna uvāca
ye śāstra-vidhim utsṛjya
yajante śraddhayānvitāḥ
teṣāṁ niṣṭhā tu kā kṛṣṇa
sattvam āho rajas tamaḥ

Arjuna said –

O' Krishna, what is the fate of those who do not adhere to scriptural instructions but worship as per their own fancies. Is their faith in goodness, passion, or ignorance?

2

श्रीभगवानुवाच
त्रिविधा भवति श्रद्धा देहिनां सा स्वभावजा ।
सात्त्विकी राजसी चैव तामसी चेति तां शृणु ॥

śrī-bhagavān uvāca
tri-vidhā bhavati śraddhā
dehināṁ sā svabhāva-jā

sāttvikī rājasī caiva
tāmasī ceti tāṁ śṛṇu

Sri Bhagavan said –
Faith in embodied beings depends on the predominant guna, whether it is sattvic, rajasic, or tamasic.

3

सत्त्वानुरूपा सर्वस्य श्रद्धा भवति भारत ।
श्रद्धामयोऽयं पुरुषो यो यच्छ्रद्धः स एव सः ॥

sattvānurūpā sarvasya
śraddhā bhavati bhārata
śraddhā-mayo 'yaṁ puruṣo
yo yac-chraddhaḥ sa eva saḥ

Faith evolves as per the modes of nature and according to the modes a living being has acquired, he will evolve to a particular faith, O' son of Bharata.

4

यजन्ते सात्त्विका देवान्यक्षरक्षांसि राजसाः ।
प्रेतान्भूतगणांश्चान्ये यजन्ते तामसा जनाः ॥

yajante sāttvikā devān
yakṣa-rakṣāṁsi rājasāḥ
pretān bhūta-gaṇāṁś cānye
yajante tāmasā janāḥ

In the mode of goodness, living beings worship devatas. In the mode of passion, they worship demons. In the mode of ignorance, they worship ghosts and spirits.

5 – 6

अशास्त्रविहितं घोरं तप्यन्ते ये तपो जनाः ।
दम्भाहङ्कारसंयुक्ताः कामरागबलान्विताः ॥
कर्षयन्तः शरीरस्थं भूतग्राममचेतसः ।
मां चैवान्तः शरीरस्थं तान्विद्ध्यासुरनिश्चयान् ॥

aśāstra-vihitaṁ ghoraṁ
tapyante ye tapo janāḥ
dambhāhaṅkāra-saṁyuktāḥ
kāma-rāga-balānvitāḥ
karṣayantaḥ śarīra-sthaṁ
bhūta-grāmam acetasaḥ

māṁ caivāntaḥ śarīra-sthaṁ
tān viddhy āsura-niścayān

Some perform severe austerities not recommended in the scriptures but motivated by ego, lust, pride, and attachments. They torture not only themselves but also the Super Soul within and are considered to be demons.

7

आहारस्त्वपि सर्वस्य त्रिविधो भवति प्रियः ।
यज्ञस्तपस्तथा दानं तेषां भेदमिमं शृणु ॥

āhāras tv api sarvasya
tri-vidho bhavati priyaḥ
yajñas tapas tathā dānaṁ
teṣāṁ bhedam imaṁ śṛṇu

The food that you eat, the sacrifices, austerities, and charities you perform, all are of three types, depending on the three modes of nature. I will tell you how to differentiate them.

8

आयुः सत्त्वबलारोग्यसुखप्रीतिविवर्धनाः ।
रस्याः स्निग्धाः स्थिरा हृद्या आहाराः सात्त्विकप्रियाः ॥

āyuḥ sattva-balārogyasukha-
prīti-vivardhanāḥ
rasyāḥ snigdhāḥ sthirā hṛdyā
āhārāḥ sāttvika-priyāḥ

Food in sattva guna is healthy and nourishing. It prolongs life, purifies existence, and brings happiness and satisfaction. The juicy, wholesome, and fatty food in sattva guna gives pleasure to those in goodness mode.

9

कट्वम्ललवणात्युष्णतीक्ष्णरूक्षविदाहिनः ।
आहारा राजसस्येष्टा दुःखशोकामयप्रदाः ॥

kaṭv-amla-lavaṇāty-uṣṇa-tīkṣṇa-
rūkṣa-vidāhinaḥ
āhārā rājasasyeṣṭā
duḥkha-śokāmaya-pradāḥ

Rajasic food is extremely bitter, sour, salty, hot, pungent, dry, and burning, liked by those in mode of passion. This kind of food brings pain, disease, and suffering.

10

यातयामं गतरसं पूति पर्युषितं च यत् ।
उच्छिष्टमपि चामेध्यं भोजनं तामसप्रियम् ॥

yāta-yāmaṁ gata-rasaṁ
pūti paryuṣitaṁ ca yat
ucchiṣṭam api cāmedhyaṁ
bhojanaṁ tāmasa-priyam

Those in tamas are attracted to food that is stale, tasteless, overcooked, rotten, unhygienic, remnants of others, and unfit for offering.

11

अफलाकाङ्क्षिभिर्यज्ञो विधिदिष्टो य इज्यते ।
यष्टव्यमेवेति मनः समाधाय स सात्त्विकः ॥

aphalākāṇkṣibhir yajño
vidhi-dṛṣṭo ya ijyate
yaṣṭavyam eveti manaḥ
samādhāya sa sāttvikaḥ

That sacrifice which is performed in alignment with scriptures as one's duties and not for any reward, is sacrifice in mode of goodness.

12

अभिसन्धाय तु फलं दम्भार्थमपि चैव यत् ।
इज्यते भरतश्रेष्ठ तं यज्ञं विद्धि राजसम् ॥

abhisandhāya tu phalaṁ
dambhārtham api caiva yat
ijyate bharata-śreṣṭha
taṁ yajñaṁ viddhi rājasam

Sacrifice performed out of pride, to show off, or to acquire material benefits, is the domain of passion, O' Arjuna.

13

विधिहीनमसृष्टान्नं मन्त्रहीनमदक्षिणम् ।
श्रद्धाविरहितं यज्ञं तामसं परिचक्षते ॥

vidhi-hīnam asṛṣṭānnaṁ
mantra-hīnam adakṣiṇam
śraddhā-virahitaṁ yajñam
tāmasaṁ paricakṣate

Sacrifices that defy scriptural instructions, without distribution of *prasadam*, without offering of food, without chanting of Vedic hymns, without alms and without faith are in the mode of ignorance.

14

देवद्विजगुरुप्राज्ञपूजनं शौचमार्जवम् ।
ब्रह्मचर्यमहिंसा च शारीरं तप उच्यते ॥

deva-dvija-guru-prājña
pūjanaṁ śaucam ārjavam
brahmacaryam ahiṁsā ca
śārīraṁ tapa ucyate

Austerity of the body includes worshipping God, the brahmanas, the wise, and the spiritual master. It also includes hygiene, celibacy, non-violence, and simple living.

15

अनुद्वेगकरं वाक्यं सत्यं प्रियहितं च यत् ।
स्वाध्यायाभ्यसनं चैव वाङ्मयं तप उच्यते ॥

anudvega-karaṁ vākyaṁ
satyaṁ priya-hitaṁ ca yat

svādhyāyābhyasanaṁ caiva
vāṅ-mayaṁ tapa ucyate

Words and speech that is truthful, pleasing, beneficial, non-distressing, and based on the scriptures, is considered austerity of speech.

16

मन:प्रसाद: सौम्यत्वं मौनमात्मविनिग्रह: ।
भावसंशुद्धिरित्येतत्तपो मानसमुच्यते ॥

manaḥ-prasādaḥ saumyatvaṁ
maunam ātma-vinigrahaḥ
bhāva-saṁśuddhir ity etat
tapo mānasam ucyate

Satisfaction, silence, self-control, peace of mind, and purity of thoughts are austerities of the mind.

17

श्रद्धया परया तप्तं तपस्तत्त्रिविधं नरै: ।
अफलाकाङ्‍क्षिभिर्युक्तै: सात्त्विकं परिचक्षते ॥

śraddhayā parayā taptaṁ
tapas tat tri-vidhaṁ naraiḥ

aphalākāṅkṣibhir yuktaiḥ
sāttvikaṁ paricakṣate

The three austerities of the body, speech, and mind, are in the mode of goodness when they are practised without hankering for selfish materialistic benefits but out of devotion to the Supreme Lord for the purpose of pleasing Him.

18

सत्कारमानपूजार्थं तपो दम्भेन चैव यत् ।
क्रियते तदिह प्रोक्तं राजसं चलमध्रुवम् ॥

satkāra-māna-pūjārtham
tapo dambhena caiva yat
kriyate tad iha proktaṁ
rājasaṁ calam adhruvam

Austerities performed for show in the hope of getting honour and respect are in the mode of passion. It is not a steady or long-term endeavour.

19

मूढग्राहेणात्मनो यत्पीडया क्रियते तपः ।
परस्योत्सादनार्थं वा तत्तामसमुदाहृतम् ॥

mūḍha-grāheṇātmanaḥ yat
pīḍayā kriyate tapaḥ
parasyotsādanārthaṁ vā
tat tāmasam udāhṛtam

Austerities performed thoughtlessly to destroy self or to torture others are in the mode of ignorance.

20

दातव्यमिति यद्दानं दीयतेऽनुपकारिणे ।
देशे काले च पात्रे च तद्दानं सात्त्विकं स्मृतम् ॥

dātavyam iti yad dānaṁ
dīyate 'nupakāriṇe
deśe kāle ca pātre ca
tad dānaṁ sāttvikaṁ smṛtam

Charity given to a worthy person, at the right time and place, without any selfish motive but as a matter of duty, that charity is declared to be in mode of goodness.

21

यत्तु प्रत्युपकारार्थं फलमुद्दिश्य वा पुनः ।
दीयते च परिक्लिष्टं तद्दानं राजसं स्मृतम् ॥

yat tu pratyupakārārthaṁ
phalam uddiśya vā punaḥ
dīyate ca parikliṣṭaṁ
tad dānaṁ rājasaṁ smṛtam

In mode of passion, charity is given reluctantly, expecting some reward for it or with a greedy desire to enjoy the fruit of it.

22

अदेशकाले यद्दानमपात्रेभ्यश्च दीयते ।
असत्कृतमवज्ञातं तत्तामसमुदाहृतम् ॥

adeśa-kāle yad dānam
apātrebhyaś ca dīyate
asatkṛtam avajñātaṁ
tat tāmasam udāhṛtam

Charity given with disrespect and disdain to unworthy persons at an inauspicious time at an impure place is said to be in the mode of ignorance.

23

ॐ तत्सदिति निर्देशो ब्रह्मणस्त्रिविधः स्मृतः ।
ब्राह्मणास्तेन वेदाश्च यज्ञाश्च विहिताः पुरा ॥

om-tat-sad iti nirdeśo
brahmaṇas tri-vidhaḥ smṛtaḥ
brāhmaṇās tena vedāś ca
yajñāś ca vihitāḥ purā

The Supreme Truth is represented by the three syllables 'Om Tat Sat.' From the beginning of creation, these syllables were used by brahmanas while chanting from the Vedas and performing sacrifices.

24

तस्माद्ॐ इत्युदाहृत्य यज्ञदानतपःक्रियाः ।
प्रवर्तन्ते विधानोक्ताः सततं ब्रह्मवादिनाम् ॥

tasmād om ity udāhṛtya
yajña-dāna-tapaḥ-kriyāḥ
pravartante vidhānoktāḥ
satataṁ brahma-vādinām

To obtain the Supreme, spiritualists chant the syllable 'Om' before beginning any sacrifice, austerity, or charity as per the Vedic standard.

25

तदित्यनभिसन्धाय फलं यज्ञतप:क्रिया: ।
दानक्रियाश्च विविधा: क्रियन्ते मोक्षकाङ्क्षिभि: ॥

tad ity anabhisandhāya
phalaṁ yajña-tapaḥ-kriyāḥ
dāna-kriyāś ca vividhāḥ
kriyante mokṣa-kāṅkṣibhiḥ

To achieve liberation from material shackles, one must chant the syllable 'Tat' before beginning any sacrifice, austerity, or charity.

26 – 27

सद्भावे साधुभावे च सदित्येतत्प्रयुज्यते ।
प्रशस्ते कर्मणि तथा सच्छब्द: पार्थ युज्यते ॥
यज्ञे तपसि दाने च स्थिति: सदिति चोच्यते ।
कर्म चैव तदर्थीयं सदित्येवाभिधीयते ॥

sad-bhāve sādhu-bhāve ca
sad ity etat prayujyate
praśaste karmaṇi tathā
sac-chabdaḥ pārtha yujyate
yajñe tapasi dāne ca
sthitiḥ sad iti cocyate

karma caiva tad-arthīyaṁ
sad ity evābhidhīyate

O' Partha, to obtain the objective of devotional service, the Supreme Truth, one must chant the syllable 'Sat' before beginning any sacrifice, austerity, or charity. 'Sat' is indicative of the Supreme Lord.

28

अश्रद्धया हुतं दत्तं तपस्तप्तं कृतं च यत् ।
असदित्युच्यते पार्थ न च तत्प्रेत्य नो इह ॥

aśraddhayā hutaṁ dattaṁ
tapas taptaṁ kṛtaṁ ca yat
asad ity ucyate pārtha
na ca tat pretya no iha

Any sacrifice, austerity, or charity done without faith in God is called 'Asat.' Any such act is impermanent and useless in this life and next.

Chapter 18

Moksha Sannyasa Yoga

1

अर्जुन उवाच
सन्न्यासस्य महाबाहो तत्त्वमिच्छामि वेदितुम् ।
त्यागस्य च हृषीकेश पृथक्केशिनिषूदन ॥

arjuna uvāca
sannyāsasya mahābāho
tattvam icchāmi veditum
tyāgasya ca hṛṣīkeśa
pṛthak keśī-niṣūdana

Arjuna said –
O' mighty-armed Krishna, O' killer of Keshi demon, I want to know about renunciation of action (*tyaga*) and renunciation as an order of life (*sanyas*). Please tell me the difference between the two, O' Hrishikesha.

2

श्रीभगवानुवाच
काम्यानां कर्मणां न्यासं सन्न्यासं कवयो विदुः ।
सर्वकर्मफलत्यागं प्राहुस्त्यागं विचक्षणाः ॥

śrī-bhagavān uvāca
kāmyānāṁ karmaṇāṁ nyāsaṁ
sannyāsaṁ kavayo viduḥ

sarva-karma-phala-tyāgaṁ
prāhus tyāgaṁ vicakṣaṇāḥ

Sri Bhagavan said –
Renunciation of action or tyaga is giving up the fruits of all actions. Whereas sanyas is a state of detachment; giving up all activities that are motivated by material desires.

3

त्याज्यं दोषवदित्येके कर्म प्राहुर्मनीषिण: ।
यज्ञदानतप:कर्म न त्याज्यमिति चापरे ॥

tyājyaṁ doṣavad ity eke
karma prāhur manīṣiṇaḥ
yajña-dāna-tapaḥ-karma
na tyājyam iti cāpare

It is claimed by those learned that activities that qualify as evil should be abandoned. Some others claim that activities like sacrifice, charity, and austerities should never be abandoned.

4

निश्चयं शृणु मे तत्र त्यागे भरतसत्तम ।
त्यागो हि पुरुषव्याघ्र त्रिविधः सम्प्रकीर्तितः ॥

niścayaṁ śṛṇu me tatra
tyāge bharata-sattama
tyāgo hi puruṣa-vyāghra
tri-vidhaḥ samprakīrtitaḥ

Now hear what I have to say, O' best of Bharatas. Scriptures describe three types of renunciation, O' tiger amongst humans.

5

यज्ञदानतपःकर्म न त्याज्यं कार्यमेव तत् ।
यज्ञो दानं तपश्चैव पावनानि मनीषिणाम् ॥

yajña-dāna-tapaḥ-karma
na tyājyaṁ kāryam eva tat
yajño dānaṁ tapaś caiva
pāvanāni manīṣiṇām

Great beings are purified by acts of sacrifice, charity, and austerity. These are simply a must and can never be given up.

6

एतान्यपि तु कर्माणि सङ्गं त्यक्त्वा फलानि च ।
कर्तव्यानीति मे पार्थ निश्चितं मतमुत्तमम् ॥

etāny api tu karmāṇi
saṅgaṁ tyaktvā phalāni ca
kartavyānīti me pārtha
niścitaṁ matam uttamam

O' Partha, these must be performed as a matter of duty, without attachments or expectations. This is my firm opinion.

7

नियतस्य तु सन्न्यासः कर्मणो नोपपद्यते ।
मोहात्तस्य परित्यागस्तामसः परिकीर्तितः ॥

niyatasya tu sannyāsaḥ
karmaṇo nopapadyate
mohāt tasya parityāgas
tāmasaḥ parikīrtitaḥ

Overcome by illusion, if one renounces prescribed duties, it is renunciation in the mode of ignorance. Prescribed and recommended duties should never be abandoned.

8

दुःखमित्येव यत्कर्म कायक्लेशभयात्त्यजेत् ।
स कृत्वा राजसं त्यागं नैव त्यागफलं लभेत् ॥

duḥkham ity eva yat karma
kāya-kleśa-bhayāt tyajet
sa kṛtvā rājasaṁ tyāgaṁ
naiva tyāga-phalaṁ labhet

Renouncing prescribed duties out of physical discomfort or fear, is renunciation in the mode of passion which does not yield any elevating outcome.

9

कार्यमित्येव यत्कर्म नियतं क्रियतेऽर्जुन ।
सङ्गं त्यक्त्वा फलं चैव स त्यागः सात्त्विको मतः ॥

kāryam ity eva yat karma
niyataṁ kriyate 'rjuna
saṅgaṁ tyaktvā phalaṁ caiva
sa tyāgaḥ sāttviko mataḥ

But renunciation of all attachments and results of actions while acting with a sense of duty is indicative of mode of goodness, O' Arjuna.

10

न द्वेष्ट्यकुशलं कर्म कुशले नानुषज्जते ।
त्यागी सत्त्वसमाविष्टो मेधावी छिन्नसंशयः ॥

na dveṣṭy akuśalaṁ karma
kuśale nānuṣajjate
tyāgī sattva-samāviṣṭo
medhāvī chinna-saṁśayaḥ

A renunciate in the mode of goodness does not avoid unfavourable activities or aspire to perform favourable activities. He has no doubts as to his prescribed duties.

11

न हि देहभृता शक्यं त्यक्तुं कर्माण्यशेषतः ।
यस्तु कर्मफलत्यागी स त्यागीत्यभिधीयते ॥

na hi deha-bhṛtā śakyaṁ
tyaktuṁ karmāṇy aśeṣataḥ
yas tu karma-phala-tyāgī
sa tyāgīty abhidhīyate

To give up all activities is impossible for an embodied being. To give up fruits of action is itself true renunciation.

12

अनिष्टमिष्टं मिश्रं च त्रिविधं कर्मणः फलम् ।
भवत्यत्यागिनां प्रेत्य न तु सन्न्यासिनां क्वचित् ॥

anisṭam iṣṭaṁ miśraṁ ca
tri-vidhaṁ karmaṇaḥ phalam
bhavaty atyāgināṁ pretya
na tu sannyāsināṁ kvacit

The three consequences of actions—auspicious, inauspicious, and mixed—await those who do not renounce. The renounced will have no such experience of suffering or enjoying.

13

पञ्चैतानि महाबाहो कारणानि निबोध मे ।
सांख्ये कृतान्ते प्रोक्तानि सिद्धये सर्वकर्मणाम् ॥

pañcaitāni mahā-bāho
kāraṇāni nibodha me
sāṅkhye kṛtānte proktāni
siddhaye sarva-karmaṇām

According to Sankhya philosophy, there are five causative factors that complete all actions. O' Arjuna, now learn about this.

14

अधिष्ठानं तथा कर्ता करणं च पृथग्विधम् ।
विविधाश्च पृथक्चेष्टा दैवं चैवात्र पञ्चमम् ॥

adhiṣṭhānaṁ tathā kartā
karaṇaṁ ca pṛthag-vidham
vividhāś ca pṛthak ceṣṭā
daivaṁ caivātra pañcamam

The five factors are the place of action (body), the person executing the action, the senses, effort and finally, the Super Soul.

15

शरीरवाङ्मनोभिर्यत्कर्म प्रारभते नरः ।
न्याय्यं वा विपरीतं वा पञ्चैते तस्य हेतवः ॥

śarīra-vāṅ-manobhir yat
karma prārabhate naraḥ
nyāyyaṁ vā viparītaṁ vā
pañcaite tasya hetavaḥ

Every action performed by the body, mind, or speech, whether right or wrong, is the result of these five factors.

16

तत्रैवं सति कर्तारमात्मानं केवलं तु यः ।
पश्यत्यकृतबुद्धित्वान्न स पश्यति दुर्मतिः ॥

tatraivaṁ sati kartāram
ātmānaṁ kevalaṁ tu yaḥ
paśyaty akṛta-buddhitvān
na sa paśyati durmatiḥ

Only a fool considers himself as the doer and disregards the five factors.

17

यस्य नाहङ्कृतो भावो बुद्धिर्यस्य न लिप्यते ।
हत्वापि स इमाँल्लोकान्न हन्ति न निबध्यते ॥

yasya nāhaṅkṛto bhāvo
buddhir yasya na lipyate
hatvāpi sa imāl̐ lokān
na hanti na nibadhyate

But a person who has surrendered his ego as the doer and whose intelligence is clear, is not bound by his actions. Even if he kills people, he does not really kill.

18

ज्ञानं ज्ञेयं परिज्ञाता त्रिविधा कर्मचोदना ।
करणं कर्म कर्तेति त्रिविधः कर्मसङ्ग्रहः ॥

jñānaṁ jñeyaṁ parijñātā
tri-vidhā karma-codanā
karaṇaṁ karma karteti
tri-vidhaḥ karma saṅgrahaḥ

Motivating triggers for action are knowledge, object of knowledge, and the knower. Senses, the object, and the doer are triple integrated components of action.

19

ज्ञानं कर्म च कर्ता च त्रिधैव गुणभेदतः ।
प्रोच्यते गुणसंख्याने यथावच्छृणु तान्यपि ॥

jñānaṁ karma ca kartā ca
tridhaiva guṇa-bhedataḥ
procyate guṇa-saṅkhyāne
yathāvac chṛṇu tāny api

Knowledge, action, and doer are also of three kinds, subjective to the three modes of material nature. Listen now as I explain.

20

सर्वभूतेषु येनैकं भावमव्ययमीक्षते ।
अविभक्तं विभक्तेषु तज्ज्ञानं विद्धि सात्त्विकम् ॥

sarva-bhūteṣu yenaikaṁ
bhāvam avyayam īkṣate
avibhaktaṁ vibhakteṣu
taj jñānaṁ viddhi sāttvikam

When one sees the undivided Supreme God divided equally in all living beings, it is knowledge in the mode of goodness.

21

पृथक्त्वेन तु यज्ज्ञानं नानाभावान्पृथग्विधान् ।
वेत्ति सर्वेषु भूतेषु तज्ज्ञानं विद्धि राजसम् ॥

pṛthaktvena tu yaj jñānaṁ
nānā-bhāvān pṛthag-vidhān
vetti sarveṣu bhūteṣu
taj jñānaṁ viddhi rājasam

When one sees different living beings as separate and unconnected entities, it is knowledge in the mode of passion.

22

यत्तु कृत्स्नवदेकस्मिन्कार्ये सक्तमहैतुकम् ।
अतत्त्वार्थवदल्पं च तत्तामसमुदाहृतम् ॥

yat tu kṛtsna-vad ekasmin
kārye saktam ahaitukam
atattvārthavad alpaṁ ca
tat tāmasam udāhṛtam

And when one is attached to a certain kind of work, with indifference to truth, that knowledge is in the mode of ignorance.

23

नियतं सङ्गरहितमरागद्वेषतः कृतम् ।
अफलप्रेप्सुना कर्म यत्तत्सात्त्विकमुच्यते ॥

niyataṁ saṅga-rahitam
arāga-dveṣataḥ kṛtam
aphala-prepsunā karma
yat tat sāttvikam ucyate

Dutiful action as per scriptural recommendations, without attachment or aversion, without any expectation of results, is action in the mode of goodness.

24

यत्तु कामेप्सुना कर्म साहङ्कारेण वा पुनः ।
क्रियते बहुलायासं तद्राजसमुदाहृतम् ॥

yat tu kāmepsunā karma
sāhaṅkāreṇa vā punaḥ
kriyate bahulāyāsaṁ
tad rājasam udāhṛtam

Acts of repeated effort, motivated by false ego and sense gratification are said to be in the mode of passion.

25

अनुबन्धं क्षयं हिंसामनपेक्ष्य च पौरुषम् ।
मोहादारभ्यते कर्म यत्तत्तामसमुच्यते ॥

anubandhaṁ kṣayaṁ hiṁsām
anapekṣya ca pauruṣam
mohād ārabhyate karma
yat tat tāmasam ucyate

And actions under madness, dismissing the Vedic injunctions, disregarding future consequences, causing hurt to others, are in the mode of ignorance.

26

मुक्तसङ्गोऽनहंवादी धृत्युत्साहसमन्वितः ।
सिद्ध्यसिद्ध्योर्निर्विकारः कर्ता सात्त्विक उच्यते ॥

mukta-saṅgo 'nahaṁ-vādī
dhṛty-utsāha-samanvitaḥ
siddhy-asiddhyor nirvikāraḥ
kartā sāttvika ucyate

The qualities of a worker in the mode of goodness are enthusiasm, determination, detachment, unaffected by success or failure, and without the trappings of false ego.

27

रागी कर्मफलप्रेप्सुर्लुब्धो हिंसात्मकोऽशुचिः ।
हर्षशोकान्वितः कर्ता राजसः परिकीर्तितः ॥

rāgī karma-phala-prepsur
lubdho hiṁsātmako 'śuciḥ
harṣa-śokānvitaḥ kartā
rājasaḥ parikīrtitaḥ

In passion, the doer is greedy, violent, impure, easily moved by joy and sorrow, and desires rewards of his actions.

28

अयुक्तः प्राकृतः स्तब्धः शठो नैष्कृतिकोऽलसः ।
विषादी दीर्घसूत्री च कर्ता तामस उच्यते ॥

ayuktaḥ prākṛtaḥ stabdhaḥ
śaṭho naiṣkṛtiko 'lasaḥ
viṣādī dīrgha-sūtrī ca
kartā tāmasa ucyate

Undisciplined, arrogant, lazy, obstinate, despondent, deceitful, procrastinating, and going against the scriptures, are workers in the mode of ignorance.

29

बुद्धेर्भेदं धृतेश्चैव गुणतस्त्रिविधं शृणु ।
प्रोच्यमानमशेषेण पृथक्त्वेन धनञ्जय ॥

buddher bhedaṁ dhṛteś caiva
guṇatas tri-vidhaṁ śṛṇu
procyamānam aśeṣeṇa
pṛthaktvena dhanañjaya

Now listen, Dhananjaya, to the three kinds of intelligence and determination borne out of the three modes of nature.

30

प्रवृत्तिं च निवृत्तिं च कार्याकार्ये भयाभये ।
बन्धं मोक्षं च या वेत्ति बुद्धिः सा पार्थ सात्त्विकी ॥

pravṛttiṁ ca nivṛttiṁ ca
kāryākārye bhayābhaye
bandhaṁ mokṣaṁ ca yā vetti
buddhiḥ sā pārtha sāttvikī

In the mode of goodness, O' Partha, the intelligence knows what is to be done and what need not be done, what is to be feared and what need not be feared, what is liberating and what is binding.

31

यया धर्ममधर्मं च कार्यं चाकार्यमेव च ।
अयथावत्प्रजानाति बुद्धिः सा पार्थ राजसी ॥

yayā dharmam adharmaṁ ca
kāryaṁ cākāryam eva ca
ayathāvat prajānāti
buddhiḥ sā pārtha rājasī

And in the mode of passion, the intelligence fails to understand the difference between religion and irreligion or right and wrong, O' Partha.

32

अधर्मं धर्ममिति या मन्यते तमसावृता ।
सर्वार्थान्विपरीतांश्च बुद्धिः सा पार्थ तामसी ॥

adharmaṁ dharmam iti yā
manyate tamasāvṛtā
sarvārthān viparītāṁś ca
buddhiḥ sā pārtha tāmasī

Intelligence in the mode of ignorance is veiled by darkness and illusion, misunderstanding right to be wrong and irreligion to be religion, thereby veering in the wrong direction.

33

धृत्या यया धारयते मनःप्राणेन्द्रियक्रियाः ।
योगेनाव्यभिचारिण्या धृतिः सा पार्थ सात्त्विकी ॥

dhṛtyā yayā dhārayate
manaḥ prāṇendriya-kriyāḥ
yogenāvyabhicāriṇyā
dhṛtiḥ sā pārtha sāttvikī

Determination that remains steady by dint of yoga and controls the mind and the senses is in the mode of goodness, O' Partha.

34

यया तु धर्मकामार्थान्धृत्या धारयतेऽर्जुन ।
प्रसङ्गेन फलाकाङ्क्षी धृतिः सा पार्थ राजसी ॥

yayā tu dharma-kāmārthān
dhṛtyā dhārayate 'rjuna
prasaṅgena phalākāṅkṣī
dhṛtiḥ sā pārtha rājasī

The will with which one strives for material gains in religion, economic prosperity, and sensual gratification is in the mode of passion, O' Partha.

35

यया स्वप्नं भयं शोकं विषादं मदमेव च ।
न विमुञ्चति दुर्मेधा धृतिः सा पार्थ तामसी ॥

yayā svapnaṁ bhayaṁ śokaṁ
viṣādaṁ madam eva ca
na vimuñcati durmedhā
dhṛtiḥ sā pārtha tāmasī

And the will by which one is irrationally adamant on sleeping, fearing, lamenting, being depressed, being ill-humoured, that determination is in the mode of ignorance, O' Partha.

36

सुखं त्विदानीं त्रिविधं शृणु मे भरतर्षभ ।
अभ्यासाद्रमते यत्र दुःखान्तं च निगच्छति ॥

sukhaṁ tv idānīṁ tri-vidhaṁ
śṛṇu me bharatarṣabha
abhyāsād ramate yatra
duḥkhāntaṁ ca nigacchati

Hear now as I describe the three kinds of happiness experienced by conditioned souls which can mitigate suffering, O' descendant of Bharata.

37

यत्तदग्रे विषमिव परिणामेऽमृतोपमम् ।
तत्सुखं सात्त्विकं प्रोक्तमात्मबुद्धिप्रसादजम् ॥

yat tad agre viṣam iva
pariṇāme 'mṛtopamam
tat sukhaṁ sāttvikaṁ proktam
ātma-buddhi-prasāda-jam

What may seem like poison initially but eventually takes shape of nectar is happiness in the mode of goodness, that awakens self-realization.

38

विषयेन्द्रियसंयोगाद्यत्तदग्रेऽमृतोपमम् ।
परिणामे विषमिव तत्सुखं राजसं स्मृतम् ॥

viṣayendriya-saṁyogād
yat tad agre 'mṛtopamam
pariṇāme viṣam iva
tat sukhaṁ rājasaṁ smṛtam

Happiness arising from interaction between senses and sense objects seems like nectar first but is actually poison, that happiness is in the mode of passion.

39

यदग्रे चानुबन्धे च सुखं मोहनमात्मनः ।
निद्रालस्यप्रमादोत्थं तत्तामसमुदाहृतम् ॥

yad agre cānubandhe ca
sukhaṁ mohanam ātmanaḥ
nidrālasya-pramādotthaṁ
tat tāmasam udāhṛtam

Happiness in the mode of ignorance is delusional, derived from sleep and laziness and blocking the path of self-realization.

40

न तदस्ति पृथिव्यां वा दिवि देवेषु वा पुनः ।
सत्त्वं प्रकृतिजैर्मुक्तं यदेभिः स्यात्त्रिभिर्गुणैः ॥

na tad asti pṛthivyāṁ vā
divi deveṣu vā punaḥ
sattvaṁ prakṛti-jair muktaṁ
yad ebhiḥ syāt tribhir guṇaiḥ

No living being on earth, or on other planets, including the devatas, are free from the three modes of material nature.

41

ब्राह्मणक्षत्रियविशां शूद्राणां च परन्तप ।
कर्माणि प्रविभक्तानि स्वभावप्रभवैर्गुणैः ॥

brāhmaṇa-kṣatriya-viśāṁ
śūdrāṇāṁ ca parantapa
karmāṇi pravibhaktāni
svabhāva-prabhavair guṇaiḥ

The duties of Brahmanas, Kshatriyas, Vaishyas, and Sudras are allocated according to qualities acquired as per the dominant mode of material nature, O' Parantapa.

42

शमो दमस्तपः शौचं क्षान्तिरार्जवमेव च ।
ज्ञानं विज्ञानमास्तिक्यं ब्रह्मकर्म स्वभावजम् ॥

śamo damas tapaḥ śaucaṁ
kṣāntir ārjavam eva ca
jñānaṁ vijñānam āstikyaṁ
brahma-karma svabhāva-jam

The inbuilt qualities of Brahmanas are tranquillity, self-control, austerity, purity, tolerance, honesty, wisdom, and faith in God.

43

शौर्यं तेजो धृतिर्दाक्ष्यं युद्धे चाप्यपलायनम् ।
दानमीश्वरभावश्च क्षात्रं कर्म स्वभावजम् ॥

śauryaṁ tejo dhṛtir dākṣyaṁ
yuddhe cāpy apalāyanam
dānam īśvara-bhāvaś ca
kṣātraṁ karma svabhāva-jam

The qualities ingrained in Kshatriyas are heroism, power, determination, resourcefulness, courage to fight, generosity, and leadership.

44

कृषिगोरक्ष्यवाणिज्यं वैश्यकर्म स्वभावजम् ।
परिचर्यात्मकं कर्म शूद्रस्यापि स्वभावजम् ॥

kṛṣi-go-rakṣya-vāṇijyaṁ
vaiśya-karma svabhāva-jam
paricaryātmakaṁ karma
śūdrasyāpi svabhāva-jam

Farming, cattle raising, trading are the natural propensities in Vaishyas, while labour and service is the intrinsic nature of Sudras.

45

स्वे स्वे कर्मण्यभिरतः संसिद्धिं लभते नरः ।
स्वकर्मनिरतः सिद्धिं यथा विन्दति तच्छृणु ॥

sve sve karmaṇy abhirataḥ
saṁsiddhiṁ labhate naraḥ
sva-karma-nirataḥ siddhiṁ
yathā vindati tac chṛṇu

Please hear now how everyone can attain perfection by following their natural calling for work.

46

यत: प्रवृत्तिर्भूतानां येन सर्वमिदं ततम् ।
स्वकर्मणा तमभ्यर्च्य सिद्धिं विन्दति मानव: ॥

yataḥ pravṛttir bhūtānāṁ
yena sarvam idaṁ tatam
sva-karmaṇā tam abhyarcya
siddhiṁ vindati mānavaḥ

By performing their duties, they are in effect worshipping the all-pervading God, and are on their way to attain perfection.

47

श्रेयान्स्वधर्मो विगुण: परधर्मात्स्वनुष्ठितात् ।
स्वभावनियतं कर्म कुर्वन्नाप्नोति किल्बिषम् ॥

śreyān sva-dharmo viguṇaḥ
para-dharmāt sv-anuṣṭhitāt
svabhāva-niyataṁ karma
kurvan nāpnoti kilbiṣam

Performing one's own prescribed duties even if imperfectly, is better than performing another's duty perfectly because following dharma will never accrue a sinful reaction.

48

सहजं कर्म कौन्तेय सदोषमपि न त्यजेत् ।
सर्वारम्भा हि दोषेण धूमेनाग्निरिवावृताः ॥

saha-jaṁ karma kaunteya
sa-doṣam api na tyajet
sarvārambhā hi doṣeṇa
dhūmenāgnir ivāvṛtāḥ

Every action may have a concomitant defect in it just as smoke accompanies and covers fire. That should still not be reason to give up one's instinctive prescribed duty, O' son of Kunti.

49

असक्तबुद्धिः सर्वत्र जितात्मा विगतस्पृहः ।
नैष्कर्म्यसिद्धिं परमां सन्न्यासेनाधिगच्छति ॥

asakta-buddhiḥ sarvatra
jitātmā vigata-spṛhaḥ
naiṣkarmya-siddhiṁ paramāṁ
sannyāsenādhigacchati

The stage of perfection or the end result of renunciation can be obtained simply by self-control and disentangling from material things and pleasures.

50

सिद्धिं प्राप्तो यथा ब्रह्म तथाप्नोति निबोध मे ।
समासेनैव कौन्तेय निष्ठा ज्ञानस्य या परा ॥

siddhiṁ prāpto yathā brahma
tathāpnoti nibodha me
samāsenaiva kaunteya
niṣṭhā jñānasya yā parā

Now hear how one can achieve the Supreme Brahman after attaining perfection, O' Kaunteya.

51 – 53

बुद्ध्या विशुद्धया युक्तो धृत्यात्मानं नियम्य च ।
शब्दादीन्विषयांस्त्यक्त्वा रागद्वेषौ व्युदस्य च ॥
विविक्तसेवी लघ्वाशी यतवाक्कायमानसः ।
ध्यानयोगपरो नित्यं वैराग्यं समुपाश्रितः ॥
अहङ्कारं बलं दर्पं कामं क्रोधं परिग्रहम् ।
विमुच्य निर्ममः शान्तो ब्रह्मभूयाय कल्पते ॥

buddhyā viśuddhayā yukto
dhṛtyātmānaṁ niyamya ca
śabdādīn viṣayāṁs tyaktvā
rāga-dveṣau vyudasya ca
vivikta-sevī laghv-āśī
yata-vāk-kāya-mānasaḥ

dhyāna-yoga-paro nityaṁ
vairāgyaṁ samupāśritaḥ
ahaṅkāraṁ balaṁ darpaṁ
kāmaṁ krodhaṁ parigraham
vimucya nirmamaḥ śānto
brahma-bhūyāya kalpate

One gets elevated to the platform of Brahman by—purifying the intelligence, controlling the mind with determination, forsaking the objects of sense gratification, giving up likes and dislikes, residing in a secluded place, eating less, regulating speech and body, following yogic trance, detaching from egotism, lust, anger and belongings, being selfless and at peace.

54

ब्रह्मभूतः प्रसन्नात्मा न शोचति न काङ्क्षति ।
समः सर्वेषु भूतेषु मद्भक्तिं लभते पराम् ॥

brahma-bhūtaḥ prasannātmā
na śocati na kāṅkṣati
samaḥ sarveṣu bhūteṣu
mad-bhaktiṁ labhate parām

Having realized the Brahman, he is free from hankerings and lamentation, equally disposed towards all living beings and attains transcendental devotion for me.

55

भक्त्या मामभिजानाति यावान्यश्चास्मि तत्त्वतः ।
ततो मां तत्त्वतो ज्ञात्वा विशते तदनन्तरम् ॥

bhaktyā mām abhijānāti
yāvān yaś cāsmi tattvataḥ
tato māṁ tattvato jñātvā
viśate tad-anantaram

Worshipping with devotion is essential to understand Me, the supreme person, and enter my kingdom.

56

सर्वकर्माण्यपि सदा कुर्वाणो मद्व्यपाश्रयः ।
मत्प्रसादादवाप्नोति शाश्वतं पदमव्ययम् ॥

sarva-karmāṇy api sadā
kurvāṇo mad-vyapāśrayaḥ
mat-prasādād avāpnoti
śāśvataṁ padam avyayam

With my mercy and blessings, my devotee is protected and reaches my eternal abode, regardless of the activities he is engaged in.

57

चेतसा सर्वकर्माणि मयि सन्न्यस्य मत्परः ।
बुद्धियोगमुपाश्रित्य मच्चित्तः सततं भव ॥

cetasā sarva-karmāṇi
mayi sannyasya mat-paraḥ
buddhi-yogam upāśritya
mac-cittaḥ satataṁ bhava

Seek my protection. Surrender unto Me. Absorb your consciousness in Me. In every endeavour and activity.

58

मच्चित्तः सर्वदुर्गाणि मत्प्रसादात्तरिष्यसि ।
अथ चेत्त्वमहङ्कारान्न श्रोष्यसि विनङ्क्ष्यसि ॥

mac-cittaḥ sarva-durgāṇi
mat-prasādāt tariṣyasi
atha cet tvam ahaṅkārān
na śroṣyasi vinaṅkṣyasi

With such absorption in Me, you can overcome all hurdles in life. If you remain absorbed in your self and your ego, you will be lost.

59

यदहङ्कारमाश्रित्य न योत्स्य इति मन्यसे ।
मिथ्यैष व्यवसायस्ते प्रकृतिस्त्वां नियोक्ष्यति ॥

yad ahaṅkāram āśritya
na yotsya iti manyase
mithyaiṣa vyavasāyas te
prakṛtis tvāṁ niyokṣyati

Ignoring my advice if you decide not to fight, your decision will be misguided by your mind going against your material nature. You will surely end up fighting other insignificant battles as is your nature.

60

स्वभावजेन कौन्तेय निबद्धः स्वेन कर्मणा ।
कर्तुं नेच्छसि यन्मोहात्करिष्यस्यवशोऽपि तत् ॥

svabhāva-jena kaunteya
nibaddhaḥ svena karmaṇā
kartuṁ necchasi yan mohāt
kariṣyasy avaśo 'pi tat

Your decision of not fighting is delusional. Sooner or later you will be driven to war because that is your innate nature that binds you, O' Kaunteya.

61

ईश्वरः सर्वभूतानां हृद्देशेऽर्जुन तिष्ठति ।
भ्रामयन्सर्वभूतानि यन्त्रारूढानि मायया ॥

īśvaraḥ sarva-bhūtānāṁ
hṛd-deśe 'rjuna tiṣṭhati
bhrāmayan sarva-bhūtāni
yantrārūḍhāni māyayā

The living entity, while seated on a Maya-made machine, is guided in every activity by God who is present in every heart.

62

तमेव शरणं गच्छ सर्वभावेन भारत ।
तत्प्रसादात्परां शान्तिं स्थानं प्राप्स्यसि शाश्वतम् ॥

tam eva śaraṇaṁ gaccha
sarva-bhāvena bhārata
tat-prasādāt parāṁ śāntiṁ
sthānaṁ prāpsyasi śāśvatam

By His grace, you will find transcendental serenity and His eternal and supreme abode, O' descendant of Bharata. Surrender totally unto Him.

63

इति ते ज्ञानमाख्यातं गुह्याद्गुह्यतरं मया ।
विमृश्यैतदशेषेण यथेच्छसि तथा कुरु ॥

iti te jñānam ākhyātaṁ
guhyād guhyataraṁ mayā
vimṛśyaitad aśeṣeṇa
yathecchasi tathā kuru

I have fully explained to you the most confidential knowledge. Now it is up to you to meditate on it and decide what it is that you wish to do.

64

सर्वगुह्यतमं भूयः शृणु मे परमं वचः ।
इष्टोऽसि मे दृढमिति ततो वक्ष्यामि ते हितम् ॥

sarva-guhyatamaṁ bhūyaḥ
śṛṇu me paramaṁ vacaḥ
iṣṭo 'si me dṛḍham iti
tato vakṣyāmi te hitam

I have only given you my topmost secret because you are my dear friend. Hear it again because I only want good for you.

65

मन्मना भव मद्भक्तो मद्याजी मां नमस्कुरु ।
मामेवैष्यसि सत्यं ते प्रतिजाने प्रियोऽसि मे ॥

man-manā bhava mad-bhakto
mad-yājī māṁ namaskuru
mām evaiṣyasi satyaṁ te
pratijāne priyo 'si me

Focus your mind on Me. Become my devotee. Worship Me. Offer your obeisance to Me. Then certainly you will attain Me. It's my promise to you because you are very dear to Me.

66

सर्वधर्मान्परित्यज्य मामेकं शरणं व्रज ।
अहं त्वां सर्वपापेभ्यो मोक्षयिष्यामि मा शुचः ॥

sarva-dharmān parityajya
mām ekaṁ śaraṇaṁ vraja
ahaṁ tvāṁ sarva-pāpebhyo
mokṣayiṣyāmi mā śucaḥ

Reject every other dharma that you know of and surrender to Me exclusively. I will free you from the most sinful reactions, have no fear.

67

इदं ते नातपस्काय नाभक्ताय कदाचन ।
न चाशुश्रूषवे वाच्यं न च मां योऽभ्यसूयति ॥

idaṁ te nātapaskāya
nābhaktāya kadācana
na cāśuśrūṣave vācyaṁ
na ca māṁ yo 'bhyasūyati

Never speak of this knowledge to those who are not my devotees, neither to those who are not austere, or to those who envy Me and do not want to hear.

68

य इदं परमं गुह्यं मद्भक्तेष्वभिधास्यति ।
भक्तिं मयि परां कृत्वा मामेवैष्यत्यसंशयः ॥

ya idaṁ paramaṁ guhyaṁ
mad-bhakteṣv abhidhāsyati
bhaktiṁ mayi parāṁ kṛtvā
mām evaiṣyaty asaṁśayaḥ

But sharing this topmost secret qualifies as the highest form of work in devotion and such a devotee will surely come back to Me.

69

न च तस्मान्मनुष्येषु कश्चिन्मे प्रियकृत्तमः ।
भविता न च मे तस्मादन्यः प्रियतरो भुवि ॥

na ca tasmān manuṣyeṣu
kaścin me priya-kṛttamaḥ
bhavitā na ca me tasmād
anyaḥ priyataro bhuvi

No one is more dear to Me nor will anyone be more dear to me in this world than one who shares this knowledge with others.

70

अध्येष्यते च य इमं धर्म्यं संवादमावयोः ।
ज्ञानयज्ञेन तेनाहमिष्टः स्यामिति मे मतिः ॥

adhyeṣyate ca ya imaṁ
dharmyaṁ saṁvādam āvayoḥ
jñāna-yajñena tenāham
iṣṭaḥ syām iti me matiḥ

Moreover, I proclaim that the study of this dharmic conversation between us is akin to worshipping Me with intelligence.

71

श्रद्धावाननसूयश्च शृणुयादपि यो नरः ।
सोऽपि मुक्तः शुभाँल्लोकान्प्राप्नुयात्पुण्यकर्मणाम् ॥

śraddhāvān anasūyaś ca
śṛṇuyād api yo naraḥ
so 'pi muktaḥ śubhāl lokān
prāpnuyāt puṇya-karmaṇām

Simply by hearing this conversation faithfully and without envy will free one from all past sins and deliver one to auspicious heavenly planets.

72

कच्चिदेतच्छ्रुतं पार्थ त्वयैकाग्रेण चेतसा ।
कच्चिदज्ञानसम्मोहः प्रणष्टस्ते धनञ्जय ॥

kaccid etac chrutaṁ pārtha
tvayaikāgreṇa cetasā
kaccid ajñāna-sammohaḥ
praṇaṣṭas te dhanañjaya

O' Partha, have you been hearing my words with concentration? Is your ignorance and illusion destroyed as yet, O' Dhanajaya?

73

अर्जुन उवाच
नष्टो मोहः स्मृतिर्लब्धा त्वत्प्रसादान्मयाच्युत ।
स्थितोऽस्मि गतसन्देहः करिष्ये वचनं तव ॥

arjuna uvāca
naṣṭo mohaḥ smṛtir labdhā
tvat-prasādān mayācyuta
sthito 'smi gata-sandehaḥ
kariṣye vacanaṁ tava

Arjuna said –

Oh yes, Krishna, my illusion is destroyed and my memory regained! By Your mercy, I have no doubts as to what I should do. I will follow Your instructions in totality.

74

सञ्जय उवाच
इत्यहं वासुदेवस्य पार्थस्य च महात्मनः ।
संवादमिममश्रौषमद्भुतं रोमहर्षणम् ॥

sañjaya uvāca
ity ahaṁ vāsudevasya
pārthasya ca mahātmanaḥ
saṁvādam imam aśrauṣam
adbhutaṁ roma-harṣaṇam

Sanjaya said –

I have been blessed to hear this conversation between Vasudeva and Partha. My hair stands on ends with so mesmerizing a dialogue.

75

व्यासप्रसादाच्छुतवानेतद्गुह्यमहं परम् ।
योगं योगेश्वरात्कृष्णात्साक्षात्कथयतः स्वयम् ॥

vyāsa-prasādāc chrutavān
etad guhyam ahaṁ param
yogaṁ yogeśvarāt kṛṣṇāt
sākṣāt kathayataḥ svayam

This confidential conversation I could hear directly from the mouth of the Yoga master, Krishna, by the grace of Vyasa.

76

राजन्संस्मृत्य संस्मृत्य संवादमिममद्भुतम् ।
केशवार्जुनयोः पुण्यं हृष्यामि च मुहुर्मुहुः ॥

rājan saṁsmṛtya saṁsmṛtya
saṁvādam imam adbhutam
keśavārjunayoḥ puṇyaṁ
hṛṣyāmi ca muhur muhuḥ

I feel the thrill again and again just remembering the sacred and transcendental dialogue between Keshava and Arjuna, O' King.

77

तच्च संस्मृत्य संस्मृत्य रूपमत्यद्भुतं हरेः ।
विस्मयो मे महान्राजन्हृष्यामि च पुनः पुनः ॥

tac ca saṁsmṛtya saṁsmṛtya
rūpam aty-adbhutaṁ hareḥ
vismayo me mahān rājan
hṛṣyāmi ca punaḥ punaḥ

I am awestruck recollecting the astounding form of Hari, experiencing continuous ecstasy.

78

यत्र योगेश्वरः कृष्णो यत्र पार्थो धनुर्धरः ।
तत्र श्रीर्विजयो भूतिर्ध्रुवा नीतिर्मतिर्मम ॥

yatra yogeśvaraḥ kṛṣṇo
yatra pārtho dhanur-dharaḥ
tatra śrīr vijayo bhūtir
dhruvā nītir matir mama

Victory, wealth, righteousness, and power will follow wherever there is the master of Yoga, Krishna, and the supreme archer Arjuna. This is my conclusion.

Reprint 2023

PRAKASH
An imprint of Prakash Books India Pvt. Ltd.

113/A, Darya Ganj,
New Delhi-110 002
Email: info@prakashbooks.com/sales@prakashbooks.com

facebook www.facebook.com/fingerprintpublishing
twitter www.twitter.com/FingerprintP
www.fingerprintpublishing.com

ISBN: 978 93 8971 732 7

Processed & printed in India

This volume is reverently dedicated to all seekers of truth and lovers of wisdom

Contents

PREFACE

The translator's idea of rendering the Upanishads into clear simple English, accessible to Occidental readers, had its origin in a visit paid to a Boston friend in 1909. The gentleman, then battling with a fatal malady, took from his library shelf a translation of the Upanishads and, opening it, expressed deep regret that the obscure and unfamiliar form shut from him what he felt to be profound and vital teaching.

The desire to unlock the closed doors of this ancient treasure house, awakened at that time, led to a series

of classes on the Upanishads at The Vedanta Centre of Boston during its early days in St. Botolph Street. The translation and commentary then given were transcribed and, after studious revision, were published in the Centre's monthly magazine, "The Message of the East," in 1913 and 1914. Still further revision has brought it to its present form.

So far as was consistent with a faithful rendering of the Sanskrit text, the Swami throughout his translation has sought to eliminate all that might seem obscure and confusing to the modern mind. While retaining in remarkable measure the rhythm and archaic force of the lines, he has tried not to sacrifice directness and simplicity of style. Where he has been obliged to use the Sanskrit term for lack of an exact English equivalent, he has invariably interpreted it by a familiar English word in brackets; and everything has been done to remove the sense of strangeness in order that

the Occidental reader may not feel himself an alien in the new regions of thought opened to him.

Even more has the Swami striven to keep the letter subordinate to the spirit. Any Scripture is only secondarily an historical document. To treat it as an object of mere intellectual curiosity is to cheat the world of its deeper message. If mankind is to derive the highest benefit from a study of it, its appeal must be primarily to the spiritual consciousness; and one of the salient merits of the present translation lies in this, that the translator approaches his task not only with the grave concern of the careful scholar, but also with the profound reverence and fervor of the true devotee.

Editor

Boston – March, 1919

INTRODUCTION

The Upanishads represent the loftiest heights of ancient Indo-Aryan thought and culture. They form the wisdom portion or Gnana-Kanda of the Vedas, as contrasted with the Karma-Kanda or sacrificial portion. In each of the four great Vedas—known as Rik, Yajur, Sama and Atharva—there is a large portion which deals predominantly with rituals and ceremonials, and which has for its aim to show man how by the path of right action he may prepare himself for higher attainment. Following this in each Veda is another portion called the Upanishad, which

deals wholly with the essentials of philosophic discrimination and ultimate spiritual vision. For this reason the Upanishads are known as the Vedanta, that is, the end or final goal of wisdom (Veda, wisdom; anta, end).

The name Upanishad has been variously interpreted. Many claim that it is a compound Sanskrit word Upa-ni-shad, signifying "sitting at the feet or in the presence of a teacher"; while according to other authorities it means "to shatter" or "to destroy" the fetters of ignorance. Whatever may have been the technical reason for selecting this name, it was chosen undoubtedly to give a picture of aspiring seekers "approaching" some wise Seer in the seclusion of an Himalayan forest, in order to learn of him the profoundest truths regarding the cosmic universe and God. Because these teachings were usually given in the stillness of some distant retreat, where the noises of the world could not disturb the tranquillity of

the contemplative life, they are known also as Aranyakas, Forest Books. Another reason for this name may be found in the fact that they were intended especially for the Vanaprasthas (those who, having fulfilled all their duties in the world, had retired to the forest to devote themselves to spiritual study).

The form which the teaching naturally assumed was that of dialogue, a form later adopted by Plato and other Greek philosophers. As nothing was written and all instruction was transmitted orally, the Upanishads are called Srutis, "what is heard." The term was also used in the sense of revealed, the Upanishads being regarded as direct revelations of God; while the Smritis, minor Scriptures "recorded through memory," were traditional works of purely human origin. It is a significant fact that nowhere in the Upanishads is mention made of any author or recorder.

No date for the origin of the Upanishads

can be fixed, because the written text does not limit their antiquity. The word Sruti makes that clear to us. The teaching probably existed ages before it was set down in any written form. The text itself bears evidence of this, because not infrequently in a dialogue between teacher and disciple the teacher quotes from earlier Scriptures now unknown to us. As Professor Max Müller states in his lectures on the Vedanta Philosophy: "One feels certain that behind all these lightning-flashes of religious and philosophic thought there is a distant past, a dark background of which we shall never know the beginning." Some scholars place the Vedic period as far back as 4000 or 5000 B.C.; others from 2000 to 1400 B.C. But even the most conservative admit that it antedates, by several centuries at least, the Buddhistic period which begins in the sixth century B.C.

The value of the Upanishads, however, does not rest upon their antiquity, but upon the

vital message they contain for all times and all peoples. There is nothing peculiarly racial or local in them. The ennobling lessons of these Scriptures are as practical for the modern world as they were for the Indo-Aryans of the earliest Vedic age. Their teachings are summed up in two Maha-Vakyam or "great sayings":—Tat twamasi (That thou art) and Aham Brahmasmi (I am Brahman). This oneness of Soul and God lies at the very root of all Vedic thought, and it is this dominant ideal of the unity of all life and the oneness of Truth which makes the study of the Upanishads especially beneficial at the present moment.

One of the most eminent of European Orientalists writes: "If we fix our attention upon it (this fundamental dogma of the Vedanta system) in its philosophical simplicity as the identity of God and the Soul, the Brahman and the Atman, it will be found to possess a significance reaching far beyond the Upanishads, their time

and country; nay, we claim for it an inestimable value for the whole race of mankind.

Whatever new and unwonted paths the philosophy of the future may strike out, this principle will remain permanently unshaken and from it no deviation can possibly take place. If ever a general solution is reached of the great riddle . . . the key can only be found where alone the secret of nature lies open to us from within, that is to say, in our innermost self. It was here that for the first time the original thinkers of the Upanishads, to their immortal honor, found it . . ."

The first introduction of the Upanishads to the Western world was through a translation into Persian made in the seventeenth century. More than a century later the distinguished French scholar, Anquetil Duperron, brought a copy of the manuscript from Persia to France and translated it into French and Latin. Publishing only the Latin text. Despite the distortions

which must have resulted from transmission through two alien languages, the light of the thought still shone with such brightness that it drew from Schopenhauer the fervent words: "How entirely does the Oupnekhat (Upanishad) breathe throughout the holy spirit of the Vedas! How is every one, who by a diligent study of its Persian Latin has become familiar with that incomparable book, stirred by that spirit to the very depth of his Soul! From every sentence deep, original and sublime thoughts arise, and the whole is pervaded by a high and holy and earnest spirit." Again he says: "The access to (the Vedas) by means of the Upanishads is in my eyes the greatest privilege which this still young century (1818) may claim before all previous centuries." This testimony is borne out by the thoughtful American scholar, Thoreau, who writes: "What extracts from the Vedas I have read fall on me like the light of a higher and purer luminary which describes a loftier course

through a purer stratum free from particulars, simple, universal."

The first English translation was made by a learned Hindu, Raja Ram Mohun Roy (1775-1833). Since that time there have been various European translations—French, German, Italian and English. But a mere translation, however accurate and sympathetic, is not sufficient to make the Upanishads accessible to the Occidental mind. Professor Max Müller after a lifetime of arduous labor in this field frankly confesses: "Modern words are round, ancient words are square, and we may as well hope to solve the quadrature of the circle, as to express adequately the ancient thought of the Vedas in modern English."

Without a commentary it is practically impossible to understand either the spirit or the meaning of the Upanishads. They were never designed as popular Scriptures. They grew up essentially as text books of God-knowledge

and Self-knowledge, and like all text books they need interpretation. Being transmitted orally from teacher to disciple, the style was necessarily extremely condensed and in the form of aphorisms. The language also was often metaphorical and obscure. Yet if one has the perseverance to penetrate beneath these mere surface difficulties, one is repaid a hundredfold; for these ancient Sacred Books contain the most precious gems of spiritual thought.

Every Upanishad begins with a Peace Chant (Shanti-patha) to create the proper atmosphere of purity and serenity. To study about God the whole nature must be prepared, so unitedly and with loving hearts teacher and disciples prayed to the Supreme Being for His grace and protection. It is not possible to comprehend the subtle problems of life unless the thought is tranquil and the energy concentrated. Until our mind is withdrawn from the varied distractions and agitations of worldly affairs, we

cannot enter into the spirit of higher religious study. No study is of avail so long as our inner being is not attuned. We must hold a peaceful attitude towards all living things; and if it is lacking, we must strive fervently to cultivate it through suggestion by chanting or repeating some holy text. The same lesson is taught by Jesus the Christ when He says: "If thou bring thy gift to the altar and there rememberest that thy brother hath aught against thee; leave there thy gift before the altar and go thy way; first be reconciled to thy brother, and then come and offer thy gift."

Bearing this lofty ideal of peace in our minds, let us try to make our hearts free from prejudice, doubt and intolerance, so that from these sacred writings we may draw in abundance inspiration, love and wisdom.

Paramananda

Isa-Upanishad

This Upanishad desires its title from the opening words Isa-vasya, "God-covered." The use of Isa (Lord)—a more personal name of the Supreme Being than Brahman, Atman or Self, the names usually found in the Upanishads—constitutes one of its peculiarities. It forms the closing chapter of the Yajur-Veda, known as Shukla (White).

Oneness of the Soul and God, and the value of both faith and works as means of ultimate attainment are the leading themes of this Upanishad. The general teaching of the Upanishads is that works alone, even the highest, can bring only temporary happiness and must inevitably bind a man unless through them he gains knowledge of his real Self. To help him acquire this knowledge is the aim of this and all Upanishads.

ISA-UPANISHAD
Peace Chant

OM! That (the Invisible-Absolute) is whole; whole is this (the visible phenomenal); from the Invisible Whole comes forth the visible whole. Though the visible whole has come out from that Invisible Whole, yet the Whole remains unaltered.

OM! PEACE! PEACE! PEACE!

The indefinite term "That" is used in the Upanishads to designate the Invisible-Absolute, because no word or name can fully define It. A finite object, like a table or a tree, can be defined; but God, who is infinite and unbounded, cannot be expressed by finite language. Therefore the Rishis or Divine Seers, desirous not to limit the Unlimited, chose the indefinite term "That" to designate the Absolute.

In the light of true wisdom the phenomenal

and the Absolute are inseparable. All existence is in the Absolute; and whatever exists, must exist in It; hence all manifestation is merely a modification of the One Supreme Whole, and neither increases nor diminishes It. The Whole therefore remains unaltered.

I

All this, whatsoever exists in the universe, should be covered by the Lord. Having renounced (the unreal), enjoy (the Real). Do not covet the wealth of any man.

We cover all things with the Lord by perceiving the Divine Presence everywhere. When the consciousness is firmly fixed in God, the conception of diversity naturally drops away; because the One Cosmic Existence shines through all things. As we gain the light of

wisdom, we cease to cling to the unrealities of this world and we find all our joy in the realm of Reality.

The word "enjoy" is also interpreted by the great commentator Sankaracharya as "protect," because knowledge of our true Self is the greatest protector and sustainer. If we do not have this knowledge, we cannot be happy; because nothing on this external plane of phenomena is permanent or dependable. He who is rich in the knowledge of the Self does not covet external power or possession.

II

If one should desire to live in this world a hundred years, one should live performing Karma (righteous deeds). Thus thou mayest live; there is no other way. By doing this, Karma (the fruits of thy actions) will not defile thee.

If a man still clings to long life and earthly possessions, and is therefore unable to follow the path of Self-knowledge (Gnana-Nishta) as prescribed in the first Mantram (text), then he may follow the path of right action (Karma-Nishta). Karma here means actions performed without selfish motive, for the sake of the Lord alone. When a man performs actions clinging blindly to his lower desires, then his actions bind him to the plane of ignorance or the plane of birth and death; but when the same actions are performed with surrender to God, they purify and liberate him.

III

After leaving their bodies, they who have killed the Self go to the worlds of the Asuras, covered with blinding ignorance.

The idea of rising to bright regions as a reward for well-doers, and of falling into realms of darkness as a punishment for evil-doers is common to all great religions. But Vedanta claims that this condition of heaven and hell is only temporary; because our actions, being finite, can produce only a finite result.

What does it mean "to kill the Self?" How can the immortal Soul ever be destroyed? It cannot be destroyed, it can only be obscured. Those who hold themselves under the sway of ignorance, who serve the flesh and neglect the Atman or the real Self, are not able to perceive the effulgent and indestructible nature of their Soul; hence they fall into the realm where the Soul light does not shine. Here the

Upanishad shows that the only hell is absence of knowledge. As long as man is overpowered by the darkness of ignorance, he is the slave of Nature and must accept whatever comes as the fruit of his thoughts and deeds. When he strays into the path of unreality, the Sages declare that he destroys himself; because he who clings to the perishable body and regards it as his true Self must experience death many times.

IV

That One, though motionless, is swifter than the mind. The senses can never overtake It, for It ever goes before. Though immovable, It travels faster than those who run. By It the all-pervading air sustains all living beings.

This verse explains the character of the Atman or Self. A finite object can be taken

from one place and put in another, but it can only occupy one space at a time. The Atman, however, is present everywhere; hence, though one may run with the greatest swiftness to overtake It, already It is there before him.

Even the all-pervading air must be supported by this Self, since It is infinite; and as nothing can live without breathing air, all living things must draw their life from the Cosmic Self.

V

It moves and It moves not. It is far and also It is near. It is within and also It is without all this.

It is near to those who have the power to understand It, for It dwells in the heart of every one; but It seems far to those whose mind is covered by the clouds of sensuality and self-delusion. It is within, because It is the

innermost Soul of all creatures; and It is without as the essence of the whole external universe, infilling it like the all-pervading ether.

VI

He who sees all beings in the Self and the Self in all beings, he never turns away from It (the Self).

VII

He who perceives all beings as the Self for him how can there be delusion or grief, when he sees this oneness (everywhere)?

He who perceives the Self everywhere never shrinks from anything, because through his

higher consciousness he feels united with all life. When a man sees God in all beings and all beings in God, and also God dwelling in his own Soul, how can he hate any living thing? Grief and delusion rest upon a belief in diversity, which leads to competition and all forms of selfishness. With the realization of oneness, the sense of diversity vanishes and the cause of misery is removed.

VIII

He (the Self) is all-encircling, resplendent, bodiless, spotless, without sinews, pure, untouched by sin, all-seeing, all-knowing, transcendent, self-existent; He has disposed all things duly for eternal years.

This text defines the real nature of the Self. When our mind is cleansed from the dross

of matter, then alone can we behold the vast, radiant, subtle, ever-pure and spotless Self, the true basis of our existence.

IX

They enter into blind darkness who worship Avidya (ignorance and delusion); they fall, as it were, into greater darkness who worship Vidya (knowledge).

X

By Vidya one end is attained; by Avidya, another. Thus we have heard from the wise men who taught this.

XI

He who knows at the same time both Vidya and Avidya, crosses over death by Avidya and attains immortality through Vidya.

Those who follow or "worship" the path of selfishness and pleasure (Avidya), without knowing anything higher, necessarily fall into darkness; but those who worship or cherish Vidya (knowledge) for mere intellectual pride and satisfaction, fall into greater darkness, because the opportunity which they misuse is greater.

In the subsequent verses Vidya and Avidya are used in something the same sense as "faith" and "works" in the Christian Bible; neither alone can lead to the ultimate goal, but when taken together they carry one to the Highest. Work done with unselfish motive purifies the mind and enables man to perceive his undying nature. From this he gains inevitably a knowledge of

God, because the Soul and God are one and inseparable; and when he knows himself to be one with the Supreme and Indestructible Whole, he realizes his immortality.

XII

They fall into blind darkness who worship the Unmanifested and they fall into greater darkness who worship the manifested.

XIII

By the worship of the Unmanifested one end is attained; by the worship of the manifested, another. Thus we have heard from the wise men who taught us this.

XIV

He who knows at the same time both the Unmanifested (the cause of manifestation) and the destructible or manifested, he crosses over death through knowledge of the destructible and attains immortality through knowledge of the First Cause (Unmanifested).

This particular Upanishad deals chiefly with the Invisible Cause and the visible manifestation, and the whole trend of its teaching is to show that they are one and the same, one being the outcome of the other hence no perfect knowledge is possible without simultaneous comprehension of both. The wise men declare that he who worships in a one-sided way, whether the visible or the invisible, does not reach the highest goal. Only he who has a co-ordinated understanding of both the visible and the invisible, of matter and spirit, of activity and that which is behind activity,

conquers Nature and thus overcomes death. By work, by making the mind steady and by following the prescribed rules given in the Scriptures, a man gains wisdom. By the light of that wisdom he is able to perceive the Invisible Cause in all visible forms. Therefore the wise man sees Him in every manifested form. They who have a true conception of God are never separated from Him. They exist in Him and He in them.

XV

The face of Truth is hidden by a golden disk. O Pushan (Effulgent Being)! Uncover (Thy face) that I, the worshipper of Truth, may behold Thee.

XVI

O Pushan! O Sun, sole traveller of the heavens, controller of all, son of Prajapati, withdraw Thy rays and gather up Thy burning effulgence. Now through Thy Grace I behold Thy blessed and glorious form. The Purusha (Effulgent Being) who dwells within Thee, I am He.

Here the sun, who is the giver of all light, is used as the symbol of the Infinite, giver of all wisdom. The seeker after Truth prays to the Effulgent One to control His dazzling rays, that his eyes, no longer blinded by them, may behold the Truth. Having perceived It, he proclaims: "Now I see that that Effulgent Being and I are one and the same, and my delusion is destroyed." By the light of Truth he is able to discriminate between the real and the unreal, and the knowledge thus gained convinces him that he is one with the Supreme; that there is no difference between himself and the Supreme

Truth; or as Christ said, "I and my Father are one."

XVII

May my life-breath go to the all-pervading and immortal Prana, and let this body be burned to ashes. Om! O mind, remember thy deeds! O mind, remember, remember thy deeds! Remember!

Seek not fleeting results as the reward of thy actions, O mind! Strive only for the Imperishable. This Mantram or text is often chanted at the hour of death to remind one of the perishable nature of the body and the eternal nature of the Soul. When the clear vision of the distinction between the mortal body and the immortal Soul dawns in the heart, then all craving for physical pleasure or material possession drops away;

and one can say, let the body be burned to ashes that the Soul may attain its freedom; for death is nothing more than the casting-off of a worn-out garment.

XVIII

O Agni (Bright Being)! Lead us to blessedness by the good path. O Lord! Thou knowest all our deeds, remove all evil and delusion from us. To Thee we offer our prostrations and supplications again and again.

HERE ENDS THIS UPANISHAD

This Upanishad is called Isa-Vasya-Upanishad, that which gives Brahma-Vidya or knowledge of the All-pervading Deity. The dominant thought running through it is that we cannot enjoy life or realize true happiness unless we consciously "cover" all with the Omnipresent Lord. If we are not fully conscious of that which sustains our life, how can we live wisely and perform our duties? Whatever we see, movable or immovable, good or bad, it is all "That." We must not divide our conception of the universe; for in dividing it, we have only fragmentary knowledge and we thus limit ourselves.

He who sees all beings in his Self and his Self in all beings, he never suffers; because when he sees all creatures within his true Self, then jealousy, grief and hatred vanish. He alone can love. That AH-pervading One is self-effulgent, birthless, deathless, pure, untainted by sin and sorrow. Knowing this, he becomes free from the bondage of matter and

transcends death. Transcending death means realizing the difference between body and Soul and identifying oneself with the Soul. When we actually behold the undecaying Soul within us and realize our true nature, we no longer identify ourself with the body which dies and we do not die with the body.

Self-knowledge has always been the theme of the Sages; and the Upanishads deal especially with the knowledge of the Self and also with the knowledge of God, because there is no difference between the Self and God. They are one and the same. That which comes out of the Infinite Whole must also be infinite; hence the Self is infinite. That is the ocean, we are the drops. So long as the drop remains separate from the ocean, it is small and weak; but when it is one with the ocean, then it has all the strength of the ocean. Similarly, so long as man believes himself to be separate from the Whole, he is helpless; but when he identifies himself with It,

then he transcends all weakness and partakes of Its omnipotent qualities.

Katha-Upanishad

The Katha-Upanishad is probably the most widely known of all the Upanishads. It was early translated into Persian and through this rendering first made its way into Europe. Later Raja Ram Mohun Roy brought out an English version. It has since appeared in various languages; and English, German and French writers are all agreed in pronouncing it one of the most perfect expressions of the religion and philosophy of the Vedas. Sir Edwin Arnold popularized it by his metrical rendering under the name of "The Secret of Death," and Ralph Waldo Emerson gives its story in brief at the close of his essay on "Immortality."

There is no consensus of opinion regarding the place of this Upanishad in Vedic literature. Some authorities declare it to belong to the Yajur-Veda,

others to the Sama-Veda, while a large number put it down as a part of the Atharva-Veda. The story is first suggested in the Rig-Veda; it is told more definitely in the Yajur-Veda; and in the Katha-Upanishad it appears fully elaborated and interwoven with the loftiest Vedic teaching. There is nothing however, to indicate the special place of this final version, nor has any meaning been found for the name Katha.

The text presents a dialogue between an aspiring disciple, Nachiketas, and the Ruler of Death regarding the great Hereafter.

KATHA-UPANISHAD
Peace Chant

May He (the Supreme Being) protect us both, teacher and taught. May He be pleased with us. May we acquire strength. May our study bring us illumination. May there be no enmity among us.

OM! PEACE! PEACE! PEACE!

PART FIRST

I

Vahasrava, being desirous of heavenly rewards (at the Viswajit sacrifice), made a gift of all that he possessed. He had a son by the name of Nachiketas.

II

When the offerings were being distributed, faith (Shraddha) entered (the heart of) Nachiketas, who, though young, yet resected:

III

These cows have drunk water, eaten grass and given milk for the last time, and their senses have lost all vigour. He who gives these undoubtedly goes to joyless realms.

In India the idea of sacrifice has always been to give freely for the joy of giving, without asking anything in return; and the whole purpose and merit of the sacrifice is lost, if the giver entertains the least thought of name, fame or individual benefit. The special Viswajit sacrifice which Vajasrava was making required

of him to give away all that he possessed. When, however, the gifts were brought forward to be offered, his son Nachiketas, although probably a lad about twelve years of age, observed how worthless were the animals which his father was offering. His heart at once became filled with Shraddha. There is no one English word which can convey the meaning of this Sanskrit term. It is more than mere faith. It also implies self-reliance, an independent sense of right and wrong, and the courage of one's own conviction. As a boy of tender age, Nachiketas had no right to question his father's action; yet, impelled by the sudden awakening of his higher nature, he could not but reflect: "By merely giving these useless cows, my father cannot gain any merit. If he has vowed to give all his possessions, then he must also give me. Otherwise his sacrifice will not be complete and fruitful." Therefore, anxious for his father's welfare, he approached him gently and reverently.

IV

He said to his father: Dear father, to whom wilt thou give me?

He said it a second time, then a third time. The father replied:

I shall give thee unto Death.

Nachiketas, being a dutiful son and eager to atone for his father's inadequate sacrifice, tried to remind him thus indirectly that he had not fulfilled his promise to give away all his possessions, since he had not yet offered his own son, who would be a worthier gift than useless cattle. His father, conscious that he was not making a true sacrifice, tried to ignore the boy's questions; but irritated by his persistence, he at last impatiently made answer: "I give thee to Yama, the Lord of Death." The fact that anger could so quickly rise in his heart proved that he had not the proper attitude of a sacrificer, who must always be tranquil, uplifted and free from egoism.

V

Nachiketas thought: Among many (of my father's pupils) I stand first; among many (others) I stand in the middle (but never last). What will be accomplished for my father by my going this day to Yama?

It was not conceit which led Nachiketas to consider his own standing and importance. He was weighing his value as a son and pupil in order to be able to judge whether or not he had merit enough to prove a worthy gift. Although he realized that his father's harsh reply was only the expression of a momentary outburst of anger; yet he believed that greater harm might befall his father, if his word was not kept. Therefore he sought to strengthen his father's resolution by reminding him of the transitory condition of life. He said:

VI

Look back to those who lived before and look to those who live now. Like grain the mortal decays and like grain again springs up (is reborn).

All things perish, Truth alone remains. Why then fear to sacrifice me also; Thus Nachiketas convinced his father that he should remain true to his word and send him to Yama, the Ruler of Death. Then Nachiketas went to the abode of Death, but Yama was absent and the boy waited without food or drink for three days. On Yama's return one of his household said to him:

VII

Like fire a Brahmana guest enters into houses. That fire is quenched by an offering. (Therefore) O Vaivaswata, bring water.

VIII

The foolish man in whose house a Brahmana guest remains without food, all his hopes and expectations, all the merit gained by his association with the holy, by his good words and deeds, all his sons and cattle, are destroyed.

According to the ancient Vedic ideal a guest is the representative of God and should be received with due reverence and honor. Especially is this the case with a Brahmana or a Sannyasin whose life is wholly consecrated to God. Any one who fails to give proper care to a holy guest brings misfortune on himself and his household. When Yama returned, therefore, one of the members of his household anxiously informed him of Nachiketas' presence and begged him to bring water to wash his feet, this being always the first service to an arriving guest.

IX

Yama said: O Brahmana! Revered guest! My salutations to thee. As thou hast remained three nights in my house without food, therefore choose three boons, O Brahmana.

X

Nachiketas said: May Gautama, my father, be free from anxious thought (about me). May he lose all anger (towards me) and be pacified in heart. May he know and welcome me when I am sent back by thee. This, O Death, is the first of the three boons I choose.

XI

Yama replied: Through my will Auddalaki Aruni (thy father) will know thee, and be again towards thee as before. He will sleep in peace at night. He will be free from wrath when he sees thee released from the mouth of death.

XII

Nachiketas said: In the realm of heaven there is no fear, thou (Death) art not there; nor is there fear of old age. Having crossed beyond both hunger and thirst and being above grief, (they) rejoice in heaven.

XIII

Thou knowest, O Death, the fire-sacrifice that leads to heaven.

Tell this to me, who am full of Shraddha (faith and yearning).

They who live in the realm of heaven enjoy freedom from death.

This I beg as my second boon.

XIV

Yama replied: I know well that fire which leads to the realm of heaven. I shall tell it to thee. Listen to me. Know, O Nachiketas, that this is the means of attaining endless worlds and their support. It is hidden in the heart of all beings.

XV

Yama then told him that fire-sacrifice, the beginning of all the worlds; what bricks, how many and how laid for the altar. Nachiketas repeated all as it was told to him. Then Death, being pleased with him, again said:

XVI

The great-soured Yama, being well pleased, said to him (Nachiketas): I give thee now another boon. This fire (sacrifice) shall be named after thee. Take also this garland of many colours.

XVII

He who performs this Nachiketa fire-sacrifice three times, being united with the three (mother, father and teacher), and who fulfills the three-fold duty (study of the Vedas, sacrifice and alms-giving) crosses over birth and death. Knowing this worshipful shining fire, born of Brahman, and realizing Him, he attains eternal peace.

XVIII

He who knows the three-fold Nachiketa fire and performs the Nachiketa fire-sacrifice with three-fold knowledge, having cast off the fetters of death and being beyond grief, he rejoices in the realm of heaven.

XIX

O Nachiketas, this is thy fire that leads to heaven, which thou hast chosen as thy second boon. People will call this fire after thy name. Ask the third boon, Nachiketas.

Fire is regarded as "the foundation of all the worlds," because it is the revealer of creation. If there were no fire or light, no manifested form would be visible. We read in the Semitic Scriptures, "In the beginning the Lord said, 'Let there be light.'" Therefore, that which stands in the external universe as one of the purest symbols of the Divine, also dwells in subtle form in the heart of every living being as the vital energy, the life-force or cause of existence.

Yama now tells Nachiketas how, by performing sacrifice with the three-fold knowledge, he may transcend grief and death and reach heaven. The three-fold knowledge referred to is regarding the preparation of the

altar and fire. Nachiketas being eager to learn, listened with wholehearted attention and was able to repeat all that was told him. This so pleased Yama that he granted him the extra boon of naming the fire-sacrifice after him and gave him a garland set with precious stones.

Verses XVI-XVIII are regarded by many as an interpolation, which would account for certain obscurities and repetitions in them.

XX

Nachiketas said: There is this doubt regarding what becomes of a man after death. Some say he exists, others that he does not exist. This knowledge I desire, being instructed by thee. Of the boons this is the third boon.

XXI

Yama replied: Even the Devas (Bright Ones) of old doubted regarding this. It is not easy to know; subtle indeed is this subject. O Nachiketas, choose another boon. Do not press me. Ask not this boon of me.

XXII

Nachiketas said: O Death, thou sayest that even the Devas had doubts about this, and that it is not easy to know. Another teacher like unto thee is not to be found. Therefore no other boon can be equal to this one.

XXIII

Yama said: Ask for sons and grandsons who shall live a hundred years, many cattle, elephants, gold and horses. Ask for lands of vast extent and live thyself as many autumns as thou desirest.

XXIV

If thou thinkest of any other boon equal to this, ask for wealth and long life; be ruler over the wide earth. O Nachiketas, I shall make thee enjoyer of all desires.

XXV

Whatsoever objects of desire are difficult to obtain in the realm of mortals, ask them all as thou desirest; these lovely maidens with their chariots and musical instruments, such as are not obtainable by mortals—be served by these whom I give to thee. O Nachiketas, do not ask regarding death.

The third boon asked by Nachiketas concerning the great Hereafter was one which could be granted only to those who were freed from all mortal desires and limitations, therefore Yama first tested Nachiketas to see whether he was ready to receive such knowledge. "Do not press me regarding this secret," he said. "Even wise men cannot understand it and thou art a mere lad. Take, rather, long life, wealth, whatever will give thee happiness on the mortal plane." But the boy proved his strength and worthiness by

remaining firm in his resolution to know the great secret of life and death.

XXVI

Nachiketas said: O Death, these are fleeting; they weaken the vigour of all the senses in man. Even the longest life is short. Keep thou thy chariots, dance and music.

XXVII

Man cannot be satisfied by wealth. Shall we possess wealth when we see thee (Death)? Shall we continue to live as long as thou rulest? Therefore that boon alone is to be chosen by me.

XXVIII

What man dwelling on the decaying mortal plane, having approached the undecaying immortal one, and having reflected upon the nature of enjoyment through beauty and sense pleasure, would delight in long life?

XXIX

O Death, that regarding which there is doubt, of the great Hereafter, tell us. Nachiketas asks for no other boon than that which penetrates this hidden secret.

PART SECOND

I

Yama said: The good is one thing and the pleasant another. These two, having different ends, bind a man. It is well with him who chooses the good. He who chooses the pleasant misses the true end.

II

The good and the pleasant approach man; the wise examines both and discriminates between them; the wise prefers the good to the pleasant, but the foolish man chooses the pleasant through love of bodily pleasure.

III

O Nachiketas after wise reflection thou hast renounced the pleasant and all pleasing forms. Thou hast not accepted this garland of great value for which many mortals perish.

IV

Wide apart are these two,—ignorance and what is known as wisdom, leading in opposite directions. I believe Nachiketas to be one who longs for wisdom, since many tempting objects have not turned thee aside.

With this second part, the Ruler of Death begins his instructions regarding the great Hereafter. There are two paths,—one leading Godward, the other leading to worldly pleasure. He who follows one inevitably goes away from

the other; because, like light and darkness they conflict. One leads to the imperishable spiritual realm; the other to the perishable physical realm. Both confront a man at every step of life. The discerning man distinguishing between the two, chooses the Real and Eternal, and he alone attains the highest, while the ignorant man, preferring that which brings him immediate and tangible results, misses the true purpose of his existence. Although Yama put before Nachiketas many temptations to test his sincerity and earnestness, he judging them at their real value, refused them all, saying "I have come from the mortal realm, shall I ask for what is mortal? I desire only that which is eternal." Then Death said to him: "I now see that thou art a sincere desirer of Truth. I offered thee vast wealth, long life and every form of pleasure which tempts and deludes men; but thou hast proved thy worthiness by rejecting them all."

V

Fools dwelling in ignorance, yet imagining themselves wise and learned, go round and round in crooked ways, like the blind led by the blind.

VI

The Hereafter never rises before the thoughtless child (the ignorant), deluded by the glamour of wealth. "This world alone is, there is none other": thinking thus, he falls under my sway again and again.

There are many in the world, who, puffed up with intellectual conceit, believe that they are capable of guiding others. But although they may possess a certain amount of worldly wisdom, they are devoid of deeper

understanding; therefore all that they say merely increases doubt and confusion in the minds of those who hear them. Hence they are likened to blind men leading the blind.

The Hereafter does not shine before those who are lacking in the power of discrimination and are easily carried away therefore by the charm of fleeting objects. As children are tempted by toys, so they are tempted by pleasure, power, name and fame. To them these seem the only realities. Being thus attached to perishable things, they come many times under the dominion of death. There is one part of us which must die; there is another part which never dies. When a man can identify himself with his undying nature, which is one with God, then he overcomes death.

VII

He about whom many are not even able to hear, whom many cannot comprehend even after hearing: wonderful is the teacher, wonderful is he who can receive when taught by an able teacher.

Throughout the Vedic Scriptures it is declared that no one can impart spiritual knowledge unless he has realization. What is meant by realization? It means knowledge based on direct perception. In India often the best teachers have no learning, but their character is so shining that every one learns merely by coming in contact with them. In one of the Scriptures we read: Under a banyan tree sat a youthful teacher and beside him an aged disciple. The mind of the disciple was full of doubts and questions, but although the teacher continued silent, gradually every doubt vanished from the disciple's mind. This signifies that the

conveying of spiritual teaching does not depend upon words only. It is the life, the illumination, which counts. Such God-enlightened men, however, cannot easily be found; but even with such a teacher, the knowledge of the Self cannot be gained unless the heart of the disciple is open and ready for the Truth. Hence Yama says both teacher and taught must be wonderful.

VIII

When taught by a man of inferior understanding, this Atman cannot be truly known, even though frequently thought upon. There is no way (to know It) unless it is taught by another (an illumined teacher), for it is subtler than the subtle and beyond argument.

IX

O Dearest, this Atman cannot be attained by argument; It is truly known only when taught by another (a wise teacher). O Nachiketas, thou hast attained It. Thou art fixed in Truth. May we ever, find a questioner like thee.

Knowledge of the Atman or Self cannot be attained when it is taught by those who themselves lack in real understanding of It; and who therefore, having no definite conviction of their own, differ among themselves as to its nature and existence. Only he who has been able to perceive the Self directly, through the unfoldment of his higher nature, can proclaim what It actually is; and his words alone carry weight and bring illumination. It is too subtle to be reached by argument. This secret regarding the Hereafter cannot be known through reasoning or mere intellectual gymnastics. It is

to be attained only in a state of consciousness which transcends the boundary line of reason.

X

I know that (earthly) treasure is transitory, for the eternal can never be attained by things which are non-eternal. Hence the Nachiketa fire (sacrifice) has been performed by me with perishable things and yet I have attained the eternal.

XI

O Nachiketas, thou hast seen the fulfillment of all desires, the basis of the universe, the endless fruit of sacrificial rites, the other shore where

there is no fear, that which is praiseworthy, the great and wide support; yet, being wise, thou hast rejected all with firm resolve.

The teacher, saying that the imperishable cannot be attained by the perishable, shows that no amount of observance of rituals and ceremonies can earn the imperishable and eternal. Although the Nachiketa fire-sacrifice may bring results which seem eternal to mortals because of their long duration, yet they too must come to an end; therefore this sacrifice cannot lead to the final goal. Yama praises Nachiketas because, when all heavenly and earthly pleasures, as well as knowledge of all realms and their enjoyments were offered him, yet he cast them aside and remained firm in his desire for Truth alone.

XII

The wise, who by means of the highest meditation on the Self knows the Ancient One, difficult to perceive, seated in the innermost recess, hidden in the cave of the heart, dwelling in the depth of inner being, (he who knows that One) as God, is liberated from the fetters of joy and sorrow.

XIII

A mortal, having heard and fully grasped this, and having realized through discrimination the subtle Self, rejoices, because he has obtained that which is the source of all joy. I think the abode (of Truth) is open to Nachiketas.

The Scriptures give three stages in all spiritual attainment. The aspirant must first hear

about the Truth from an enlightened teacher; next he must reflect upon what he has heard; then by constant practice of discrimination and meditation he realizes it; and with realization comes the fulfilment of every desire, because it unites him with the source of all. Having beheld this, a man learns that all sense pleasures are but fragmentary reflections of that one supreme joy, which can be found in the true Self alone. Yama assures Nachiketas that there is no doubt of his realizing the Truth, because he has shown the highest discrimination as well as fixity of purpose.

XIV

Nachiketas said: That which thou seest, which is neither virtue nor vice, neither cause nor effect, neither past nor future (but beyond these), tell me That.

XV

Yama replied: That goal which all the Vedas glorify, which all austerities proclaim, desiring which (people) practice Brahmacharya (a life of continence and service), that goal I tell thee briefly—it is Aum.

What name can man give to God? How can the Infinite be bound by any finite word? All that language can express must be finite, since it is itself finite. Yet it is very difficult for mortals to think or speak of anything without calling it

by a definite name. Knowing this, the Sages gave to the Supreme the name A-U-M which stands as the root of all language. The first letter "A" is the mother-sound, being the natural sound uttered by every creature when the throat is opened, and no sound can be made without opening the throat. The last letter "M," spoken by closing the lips, terminates all articulation. As one carries the sound from the throat to the lips, it passes through the sound "U." These three sounds therefore cover the whole field of possible articulate sound. Their combination is called the Akshara or the imperishable word, the Sound-Brahman or the Word God, because it is the most universal name which can be given to the Supreme. Hence it must be the word which was "in the beginning" and corresponds to the Logos of Christian theology. It is because of the all-embracing significance of this name that it is used so universally in the Vedic Scriptures to designate the Absolute.

XVI

This Word is indeed Brahman. This Word is indeed the Supreme.

He who knows this Word obtains whatever he desires.

XVII

This is the best Support, This is the highest Support; he who knows this Support is glorified in the world of Brahman.

This sacred Word is the highest symbol of the Absolute. He who through meditating on It grasps Its full significance, realizes the glory of God and at once has all his desires satisfied, because God is the fulfilment of all desires.

XVIII

This Self is never born, nor does It die. It did not spring from anything, nor did anything spring from It. This Ancient One is unborn, eternal, everlasting. It is not slain even though the body is slain.

XIX

If the slayer thinks that he slays, or if the slain thinks that he is slain, both of these know not. For It neither slays nor is It slain.

XX

The Self is subtler than the subtle, greater than the great; It dwells in the heart of each living being. He who is free from desire and free from grief, with mind and senses tranquil, beholds the glory of the Atman.

Although this Atman dwells in the heart of every living being, yet It is not perceived by ordinary mortals because of Its subtlety. It cannot be perceived by the senses; a finer spiritual sight is required. The heart must be pure and freed from every unworthy selfish desire; the thought must be indrawn from all external objects; mind and body must be under control; when the whole being thus becomes calm and serene, then it is possible to perceive that effulgent Atman. It is subtler than the subtle, because It is the invisible essence of every thing; and It is greater than the great because It is the boundless, sustaining power

of the whole universe; that upon which all existence rests.

XXI

Though sitting, It travels far; though lying, It goes everywhere. Who else save me is fit to know that God, who is (both) joyful and joyless?

The Self is all-pervading, hence It is that which sits still and that which travels, that which is active and that which is inactive. It is both stationary and moving, and It is the basis of all forms of existence; therefore whatever exists in the universe, whether joy or joylessness, pleasure or pain, must spring from It. Who is better able to know God than I myself, since He resides in my heart and is the very essence of my being? Such should be the attitude of one who is seeking.

XXII

The wise who know the Self, bodiless, seated within perishable bodies, great and all-pervading, grieve not.

Then a wise man through the practice of discrimination has seen clearly the distinction between body and Soul, he knows that his true Self is not the body, though It dwells in the body. Thus realizing the indestructible, all-pervading nature of his real Self, he surmounts all fear of death or loss, and is not moved even by the greatest sorrow.

XXIII

This Self cannot be attained by study of the Scriptures, nor by intellectual perception, nor by frequent hearing (of It); He whom the Self

chooses, by him alone is It attained. To him the Self reveals Its true nature.

We may imagine that by much study we can find out God; but merely hearing about a thing and gaining an intellectual comprehension of it does not mean attaining true knowledge of it. Knowledge only comes through direct perception, and direct perception of God is possible for those alone who are pure in heart and spiritually awakened. Although He is alike to all beings and His mercy is on all, yet the impure and worldy-minded do not get the blessing, because they do not know how to open their hearts to it. He who longs for God, him the Lord chooses; because to him alone can He reveal His true nature.

XXIV

He who has not turned away from evil conduct, whose senses are uncontrolled, who is not tranquil, whose mind is not at rest, he can never attain this Atman even by knowledge.

Yama having first described what the Atman is, now tells us how to attain It. A man must try to subdue his lower nature and gain control over the body and senses. He must conquer the impure selfish desires which now disturb the serenity of his mind, that it may grow calm and peaceful. In other words, he must live the life and develop all spiritual qualities in order to perceive the Atman.

XXV

Who then can know where is this mighty Self? He (that Self) to whom the Brahmanas and Kshatriyas are but food and death itself a condiment.

This text proclaims the glory and majesty of the Supreme. The Brahmanas stand for spiritual strength, the Kshatriyas for physical strength, yet both are overpowered by His mightiness. Life and death alike are food for Him. As the light of the great sun swallows up all the lesser lights of the universe, similarly all worlds are lost in the effulgence of the Eternal Omnipresent Being.

PART THIRD

I

There are two who enjoy the fruits of their good deeds in the world, having entered into the cave of the heart, seated (there) on the highest summit. The knowers of Brahman call them shadow and light. So also (they are called) by householders who perform five fire-sacrifices or three Nachiketa fire-sacrifices.

Here the two signify the Higher Self and the lower self, dwelling in the innermost cave of the heart. The Seers of Truth, as well as householders who follow the path of rituals and outer forms with the hope of enjoying the fruits of their good deeds, both proclaim that the Higher Self is like a light and the lower self like a shadow. When the Truth shines clearly in the heart of the knower, then he surmounts

the apparent duality of his nature and becomes convinced that there is but One, and that all outer manifestations are nothing but reflections or projections of that One.

II

May we be able to learn that Nachiketa fire-sacrifice, which is a bridge for those who perform sacrifice. May we also know the One, who is the highest imperishable Brahman for those who desire to cross over to the other shore which is beyond fear.

The significance of this text is May we acquire the knowledge of Brahman, the Supreme, in both manifested and unmanifested form. He is manifested as the Lord of sacrifice for those who follow the path of ritual He is the unmanifested, eternal, universal Supreme Being

for those who follow the path of wisdom. The "other shore," being the realm of immortality, is said to be beyond fear; because disease, death, and all that which mortals fear, cease to exist there. It is believed by many that these two opening verses were a later interpolation.

III

Know the Atman (Self) as the lord of the chariot, and the body as the chariot. Know also the intellect to be the driver and mind the reins.

IV

The senses are called the horses; the sense objects are the roads; when the Atman is united

with body, senses and mind, then the wise call Him the enjoyer.

In the third chapter Yama defines what part of our being dies and what part is deathless, what is mortal and what is immortal. But the Atman, the Higher Self, is so entirely beyond human conception that it is impossible to give a direct definition of It. Only through similies can some idea of It be conveyed. That is the reason why all the great Teachers of the world have so often taught in the form of parables. So here the Ruler of Death represents the Self as the lord of this chariot of the body. The intellect or discriminative faculty is the driver, who controls these wild horses of the senses by holding firmly the reins of the mind. The roads over which these horses travel are made up of all the external objects which attract or repel the senses:—the sense of smelling follows the path of sweet odours, the sense of seeing the way of beautiful sights. Thus each sense, unless

restrained by the discriminative faculty, seeks to go out towards its special objects. When the Self is joined with body, mind and senses, It is called the intelligent enjoyer; because It is the one who wills, feels, perceives and does everything.

V

He who is without discrimination and whose mind is always uncontrolled, his senses are unmanageable, like the vicious horses of a driver.

VI

But he who is full of discrimination and whose mind is always controlled, his senses are manageable, like the good horses of a driver.

The man whose intellect is not discriminative and who fails to distinguish right from wrong, the real from the unreal, is carried away by his sense passions and desires, just as a driver is carried away by vicious horses over which he has lost control. But he who clearly distinguishes what is good from what is merely pleasant, and controls all his out-going forces from running after apparent momentary pleasures, his senses obey and serve him as good horses obey their driver.

VII

He who does not possess discrimination, whose mind is uncontrolled and always impure, he does not reach that goal, but falls again into Samsara (realm of birth and death).

VIII

But he who possesses right discrimination, whose mind is under control and always pure, he reaches that goal, from which he is not born again.

IX

The man who has a discriminative intellect for the driver, and a controlled mind for the reins, reaches the end of the journey, the highest place of Vishnu (the All-pervading and Unchangeable One).

A driver must possess first a thorough knowledge of the road; next he must understand how to handle the reins and control his horses. Then will he drive safely to his destination. Similarly in this journey of life, our mind and senses must be wholly under the control of our higher discriminative faculty; for only when all our forces work in unison can we hope to reach the goal—the abode of Absolute Truth.

X

Beyond the senses are the objects, beyond the objects is the mind, beyond the mind is the intellect, beyond the intellect is the great Atman.

XI

Beyond the great Atman is the Unmanifested; beyond the Unmanifested is the Purusha (the Cosmic Soul); beyond the Purusha there is nothing. That is the end, that is the final goal.

In these two verses the Teacher shows the process of discrimination, by which one attains knowledge of the subtle Self. Beginning with the sense-organs, he leads up to the less and less gross, until he reaches that which is subtlest of all, the true Self of man. The senses are dependent on sense-objects, because without these the

senses would have no utility. Superior to sense-objects is the mind, because unless these objects affect the mind, they cannot influence the senses. Over the mind the determinative faculty exercises power; this determinative faculty is governed by the individual Self; beyond this Self is the undifferentiated creative energy known as Avyaktam; and above this is the Purusha or Supreme Self. Than this there is nothing higher. That is the goal, the Highest Abode of Peace and Bliss.

XII

This Atman (Self), hidden in all beings, does not shine forth; but It is seen by subtle seers through keen and subtle understanding.

If It dwells in all living beings, why do we not see It? Because the ordinary man's

vision is too dull and distracted. It is visible to those alone whose intellect has been purified by constant thought on the Supreme, and whose sight therefore has become refined and sharpened. This keenness of vision comes only when all our forces have been made one-pointed through teadfast practice of concentration and meditation.

XIII

A wise man should control speech by mind, mind by intellect, intellect by the great Atman, and that by the Peaceful One (the Paramatman or Supreme Self).

Here Yama gives the practical method to be followed if one wishes to realize the Supreme. The word "speech" stands for all the senses. First, therefore, a man must control his outgoing

senses by the mind. Then the mind must be brought under the control of the discriminative faculty; that is, it must be withdrawn from all sense-objects and cease to waste its energies on nonessential things. The discriminative faculty in turn must be controlled by the higher individual intelligence and this must be governed wholly by the Supreme Intelligence.

XIV

A rise! Awake! Having reached the Great Ones (illumined Teachers), gain understanding. The path is as sharp as a razor, impassable and difficult to travel, so the wise declare.

This is the eternal call of the wise: Awake from the slumber of ignorance! Arise and seek out those who know the Truth, because only those who have direct vision of Truth are

capable of teaching It. Invoke their blessing with a humble spirit and seek to be instructed by them. The path is very difficult to tread. No thoughtless or lethargic person can safely travel on it. One must be strong, wakeful and persevering.

XV

Knowing That which is soundless, touchless, formless, undecaying; also tasteless, odorless, and eternal; beginningless, endless and immutable; beyond the Unmanifested: (knowing That) man escapes from the mouth of death.

The Ruler of Death defines here the innermost essence of our being. Because of its extreme subtlety, it cannot be heard or felt or smelled or tasted like any ordinary object.

It never dies. It has no beginning or end. It is unchangeable. Realizing this Supreme Reality, man escapes from death and attains everlasting life. Thus the Teacher has gradually led Nachiketas to a point where he can reveal to him the secret of death. The boy had thought that there was a place where he could stay and become immortal. But Yama shows him that immortality is a state of consciousness and is not gained so long as man clings to name and form, or to perishable objects. What dies? Form. Therefore the formful man dies; but not that which dwells within. Although inconceivably subtle, the Sages have always made an effort through similies and analogies to give some idea of this inner Self or the God within. They have described It as beyond mind and speech; too subtle for ordinary perception, but not beyond the range of purified vision.

XVI

The intelligent man, who has heard and repeated the ancient story of Nachiketas, told by the Ruler of Death, is glorified in the world of Brahman.

XVII

He who with devotion recites this highest secret of immortality before an assembly of Brahmanas (pious men) or at the time of Shraddha (funeral ceremonies), gains everlasting reward, he gains everlasting reward.

PART FOURTH

I

The Self-existent created the senses out-going; for this reason man sees the external, but not the inner Atman (Self). Some wise man, however, desiring immortality, with eyes turned away (from the external) sees the Atman within.

In the last chapter the Ruler of Death instructed Nachiketas regarding the nature and glory of the Self. Now he shows the reason why the Self is not seen by the majority. It is because man's mind is constantly drawn outward through the channels of his senses, and this prevents his seeing the inner Self (Pratyagatman); but now and then a seeker, wiser than others, goes within and attains the vision of the undying Self.

II

Children (the ignorant) pursue external pleasures; (thus) they fall into the wide-spread snare of death. But the wise, knowing the nature of immortality, do not seek the permanent among fleeting things.

Those who are devoid of discrimination and fail to distinguish between real and unreal, the fleeting and the permanent, set their hearts on the changeable things of this world; hence they entangle themselves in the net of insatiable desire, which leads inevitably to disappointment and suffering. To such, death must seem a reality because they identify themselves with that which is born and which dies. But the wise, who see deeper into the nature of things, are no longer deluded by the charm of the phenomenal world and do not seek for permanent happiness among its passing enjoyments.

III

That by which one knows form, taste, smell, sound, touch and sense enjoyments, by That also one knows whatever remains (to be known). This verily is That (which thou hast asked to know).

IV

That by which a mortal perceives, both in dream and in waking, by knowing that great all-pervading Atman the wise man grieves no more.

In these verses the teacher tries to make plain that all knowledge, as well as all sense perception, in every state of consciousness—sleeping, dreaming or waking—is possible only because the Self exists. There can be no knowledge or perception independent of

the Self. Wise men, aware of this, identify themselves with their Higher Self and thus transcend the realm of grief.

V

He who knows this Atman, the honey-eater (perceiver and enjoyer of objects), ever near, as the lord of the past and future, fears no more. This verily is That.

VI

He who sees Him seated in the five elements, born of Tapas (fire of Brahman), born before water; who, having entered the cave of the heart, abides therein—this verily is That.

This verse indicates that He, the Great Self, is the cause of all created objects. According to the Vedas, His first manifestation was Brahma, the Personal God or Creator, born of the fire of wisdom. He existed before the evolution of the five elements—earth, water, fire, air and ether; hence He was "born before water." He is the Self dwelling in the hearts of all creatures.

VII

He who knows Aditi, who rises with Prana (the Life Principle), existent in all the Devas; who, having entered into the heart, abides there; and who was born from the elements—this verily is That.

This verse is somewhat obscure and seems like an interpolated amplification of the preceding verse.

VIII

The all-seeing fire which exists hidden in the two sticks, as the foetus is well-guarded in the womb by the mother, (that fire) is to be worshipped day after day by wakeful seekers (after wisdom), as well as by sacrificers. This verily is That.

Fire is called all-seeing because its light makes everything visible. In Vedic sacrifices the altar fire was always kindled by rubbing together two sticks of a special kind of wood called Arani. Because fire was regarded as one of the most perfect symbols of Divine wisdom, it was to be worshipped by all seekers after Truth, whether they followed the path of meditation or the path of rituals.

IX

From whence the sun rises, and whither it goes at setting, upon That all the Devas depend. No one goes beyond That. This verily is That.

X

What is here (in the visible world), that is there (in the invisible); he who sees difference (between visible and invisible) goes from death to death.

XI

By mind alone this is to be realized. There is no difference whatever (between visible and

invisible). He who sees difference here (between these) goes from death to death.

In the sight of true wisdom, there is no difference between the creator and the created. Even physical science has come to recognize that cause and effect are but two aspects of one manifestation of energy. He who fails to see this, being engrossed in the visible only, goes from death to death; because he clings to external forms which are perishable. Only the essence which dwells within is unchangeable and imperishable. This knowledge of the oneness of visible and invisible, however, cannot be acquired through sense-perception. It can only be attained by the purified mind.

XII

The Purusha (Self), of the size of a thumb, resides in the middle of the body as the lord of the past and the future, (he who knows Him) fears no more. This verily is That.

The seat of the Purusha is said to be the heart, hence It "resides in the middle of the body." Although It is limitless and all-pervading, yet in relation to Its abiding-place It is represented as limited in extension, "the size of a thumb." This refers really to the heart, which in shape may be likened to a thumb. Its light is everywhere, yet we see it focused in a lamp and believe it to be there only; similarly, although the life-current flows everywhere in the body, the heart is regarded as peculiarly its seat.

XIII

That Purusha, of the size of a thumb, is like a light without smoke, lord of the past and the future. He is the same today and tomorrow. This verily is That.

In this verse the teacher defines the effulgent nature of the Soul, whose light is pure like a flame without smoke. He also answers the question put by Nachiketas as to what happens after death, by declaring that no real change takes place, because the Soul is ever the same.

XIV

As rain water, (falling) on the mountain top, runs down over the rocks on all sides; similarly, he who sees difference (between visible forms) runs after them in various directions.

XV

O Gautama (Nachiketas), as pure water poured into pure water becomes one, so also is it with the Self of an illumined Knower (he becomes one with the Supreme).

PART FIFTH

I

The city of the Unborn, whose knowledge is unchanging, has eleven gates. Thinking on Him, man grieves no more; and being freed (from ignorance), he attains liberation. This verily is That.

This human body is called a city with eleven gates, where the eternal unborn Spirit dwells. These gates are the two eyes, two ears, two nostrils, the mouth, the navel, the two lower apertures, and the imperceptible opening at the top of the head. The Self or Atman holds the position of ruler in this city; and being above the modifications of birth, death and all human imperfections, It is not affected by the changes of the physical organism. As the intelligent man through constant thought and meditation

realizes the splendour of this Supreme Spirit, he becomes free from that part of his nature which grieves and suffers, and thus he attains liberation.

II

He is the sun dwelling in the bright heaven; He is the air dwelling in space; He is the fire burning on the altar; He is the guest dwelling in the house. He dwells in man. He dwells in those greater than man. He dwells in sacrifice. He dwells in the ether. He is (all that is) born in water, (all that) is born in earth, (all that) is born in sacrifice, (all that) is born on mountains. He is the True and the Great.

III

He it is who sends the (in-coming) Prana (life-breath) upward and throws the (out-going) breath downward. Him all the senses worship, the adorable Atman, seated in the centre (the heart).

IV

When this Atman, which is seated in the body, goes out (from the body), what remains then? This verily is That.

V

No mortal lives by the in-coming breath (Prana) or by the out-going breath (Apana), but he lives by another on which these two depend.

VI

O Gautama (Nachiketas), I shall declare unto thee the secret of the eternal Brahman and what happens to the Self after death.

VII

Some Jivas (individual Souls) enter wombs to be embodied; others go into immovable forms, according to their deeds and knowledge.

This text shows the application of the law of cause and effect to all forms of life. The thoughts and actions of the present life determine the future birth and environment.

VIII

The Being who remains awake while all sleep, who grants all desires, That is pure, That is Brahman, That alone is said to be immortal. On That all the worlds rest. None goes beyond That. This verily is That.

IX

As fire, though one, having entered the world, becomes various according to what it burns, so

does the Atman (Self) within all living beings, though one, become various according to what it enters. It also exists outside.

X

As air, though one, having entered the world, becomes various according to what it enters, so does the Atman within all living beings, though one, become various according to what it enters. It also exists outside.

By using these similies of fire and air, the teacher tries to show Nachiketas the subtle quality of the great Self, who, although one and formless like air and fire, yet assumes different shapes according to the form in which It dwells. But, being all-pervading and unlimited, It cannot be confined to these forms; therefore it is said that It also exists outside all forms.

XI

As the sun, the eye of the whole world, is not defiled by external impurities seen by the eyes, thus the one inner Self of all living beings is not defiled by the misery of the world, being outside it.

The sun is called the eye of the world because it reveals all objects. As the sun may shine on the most impure object, yet remain uncontaminated by it, so the Divine Self within is not touched by the impurity or suffering of the physical form in which it dwells, the Self being beyond all bodily limitations.

XII

There is one ruler, the Self of all living beings, who makes the one form manifold; the wise

who perceive Him seated within their Self, to them belongs eternal bliss, not to others.

XIII

Eternal among the changing, consciousness of the conscious, who, though one, fulfils the desires of many: the wise who perceive Him seated within their Self, to them belongs eternal peace, not to others.

XIV

They (the wise) perceive that indescribable highest bliss, saying, This is That. How am I to know It? Does It shine (by Its own light) or does It shine (by reflected light)?

XV

The sun does not shine there, nor the moon, nor the stars; nor do these lightnings shine there, much less this fire. When He shines, everything shines after Him; by His light all is lighted.

PART SIXTH

I

This ancient Aswattha tree has its root above and branches below.

That is pure, That is Brahman, That alone is called the Immortal.

All the worlds rest in That. None goes beyond That. This verily is That.

This verse indicates the origin of the tree of creation (the Samsara-Vriksha), which is rooted above in Brahman, the Supreme, and sends its branches downward into the phenomenal world. Heat and cold, pleasure and pain, birth and death, and all the shifting conditions of the mortal realm—these are the branches; but the origin of the tree, the Brahman, is eternally pure, unchanging, free and deathless. From the highest angelic form to the minutest atom, all

created things have their origin in Him. He is the foundation of the universe. There is nothing beyond Him.

II

Whatever there is in the universe is evolved from Prana and vibrates in Prana. That is a mighty terror, like an upraised thunderbolt. They who know That become immortal.

III

From fear of Him the fire burns, from fear of Him the sun shines. From fear of Him Indra and Vayu and Death, the fifth, speed forth.

Just as the body cannot live or act without

the Soul, similarly nothing in the created world can exist independent of Brahman, who is the basis of all existence. His position is like that of a king whom all must obey; hence it is said that the gods of sun, moon, wind, rain, do His bidding. He is likened to an upraised thunderbolt, because of the impartial and inevitable nature of His law, which all powers, great or small, must obey absolutely.

IV

If a man is not able to know Him before the dissolution of the body, then he becomes embodied again in the created worlds.

As soon as a man acquires knowledge of the Supreme, he is liberated; but if he fails to attain such knowledge before his Soul is separated from the body, then he must take other bodies

and return again and again to this realm of birth and death, until through varied experience he realizes the nature of the Supreme and his relation to Him.

V

As in a mirror, so is He seen within oneself; as in a dream, so (is He seen) in the world of the fathers (departed spirits); as in water, so (is He seen) in the world of Gandharvas (the angelic realm). As light and shadow, so (is He seen) in the world of Brahma (the Creator).

When by means of a purified understanding one beholds God within, the image is distinct as in a polished mirror; but one cannot have clear vision of the Supreme by attaining to the various realms known as heavens, where one reaps the fruit of his good deeds. It is only by

developing one's highest consciousness here in this life that perfect God-vision can be attained.

VI

Knowing that the senses are distinct (from the Atman) and their rising and setting separate (from the Atman), a wise man grieves no more.

A wise man never confounds the Atman, which is birthless and deathless, with that which has beginning and end. Therefore, when he sees his senses and is physical organism waxing and waning, he knows that his real Self within can never be affected by these outer changes, so he remains unmoved.

VII

Higher than the senses is the mind, higher than the mind is the intellect, higher than the intellect is the great Atman, higher than the Atman is the Unmanifested.

VIII

Beyond the Unmanifested is the all-pervading and imperceptible Being (Purusha). By knowing Him, the mortal is liberated and attains immortality.

This division of the individual into senses, mind, intellect, self-consciousness, undifferentiated creative energy and the Absolute Self is explained in the commentary of verse XI, Part Third.

IX

His form is not to be seen. No one can see Him with the eye. He is perceived by the heart, by the intellect and by the mind. They who know this become immortal.

The Supreme, being formless, cannot be discerned by the senses, hence all knowledge of Him must be acquired by the subtler faculties of heart, intellect and mind, which are developed only through the purifying practice of meditation.

X

When the five organs of perception become still, together with the mind, and the intellect ceases to be active: that is called the highest state.

The teacher now shows Nachiketas the

process by which the transcendental vision can be attained. he out-going senses,—seeing, hearing, smelling, touching, tasting; the restless mind and the intellect: all must be indrawn and quieted. The state of equilibrium thus attained is called the highest state, because all the forces of one's being become united and focused; and this inevitably leads to supersensuous vision.

XI

This firm holding back of the senses is what is known as Yoga.

Then one should become watchful, for Yoga comes and goes.

Yoga literally means to join or to unite the lower self with the Higher Self, the object with the subject, the worshipper with God. In order to gain this union, however, one must

first disunite oneself from all that scatters the physical, mental and intellectual forces; so the outgoing perceptions must be detached from the external world and indrawn. When this is accomplished through constant practice of concentration and meditation, the union takes place of its own accord. But it may be lost again, unless one is watchful.

XII

He cannot be attained by speech, by mind, or by the eye. How can That be realized except by him who says "He is"?

XIII

He should be realized as "He is" and also as the reality of both (visible and invisible). He who knows Him as "He is," to him alone His real nature is revealed.

This supersensuous vision cannot be gained through man's ordinary faculties. By mind, eye, or speech the manifested attributes of the Divine can be apprehended; but only one who has acquired the supersensuous sight can directly perceive God's existence and declare definitely that "He is," that He alone exists in both the visible and the invisible world.

XIV

When all desires dwelling in the heart cease, then the mortal becomes immortal and attains Brahman here.

XV

When all the ties of the heart are cut asunder here, then the mortal becomes immortal. Such is the teaching.

XVI

There are a hundred and one nerves of the heart. One of them penetrates the centre of the head. Going upward through it, one

attains immortality. The other (hundred nerve-courses) lead, in departing, to different worlds.

The nervous system of the body provides the channels through which the mind travels; the direction in which it moves is determined by its desires and tendencies. When the mind becomes pure and desireless, it takes the upward course and at the time of departing passes out through the imperceptible opening at the crown of the head; but as long as it remains full of desires, its course is downward towards the realms where those desires can be satisfied.

XVII

The Purusha, the inner Self, of the size of a thumb, is ever seated in the heart of all living beings. With perseverance man should draw Him out from his body as one draws the

inner stalk from a blade of grass. One should know Him as pure and deathless, as pure and deathless.

As has been explained in Part Fourth, verse XII, the inner Self, although unlimited, is described as "the size of a thumb" because of its abiding-place in the heart, often likened to a lotus-bud which is similar to a thumb in size and shape. Through the process of steadfast discrimination, one should learn to differentiate the Soul from the body, just as one separates the pith from a reed.

XVIII

Thus Nachiketas, having acquired this wisdom taught by the Ruler of Death, together with all the rules of Yoga, became free from impurity and death and attained Brahman (the Supreme).

So also will it be with another who likewise knows the nature of the Self.

Peace Chant

May He (the Supreme Being) protect us both. May He be pleased with us. May we acquire strength. May our study bring us illumination. May there be no enmity among us.

OM! PEACE! PEACE! PEACE!

HERE ENDS THIS UPANISHAD

Kena-Upanishad

Like the Isavasya, this Upanishad derives its name from the opening word of the text, Kena-ishitam, "by whom directed." It is also known as the Talavakara-Upanishad because of its place as a chapter in the Talavakara-Brahmana of the Sama-Veda.

Among the Upanishads it is one of the most analytical and metaphysical, its purpose being to lead the mind from the gross to the subtle, from effect to cause. By a series of profound questions and answers, it seeks to locate the source of man's being; and to expand his self-consciousness until it has become identical with God-Consciousness.

KENA-UPANISHAD
Peace Chant

May my limbs, speech, Prana (life-force), sight, hearing, strength and all my senses, gain in vigor. All is the Brahman (Supreme Lord) of the Upanishads. May I never deny the Brahman. May the Brahman never deny me. May there be no denial of the Brahman. May there be no separation from the Brahman. May all the virtues declared in the sacred Upanishads be manifest in me, who am devoted to the Atman (Higher Self). May they be manifest in me.

OM! PEACE! PEACE! PEACE!

PART FIRST

I

By whom commanded and directed does the mind go towards its objects? Commanded by whom does the life-force, the first (cause), move? At whose will do men utter speech? What power directs the eye and the ear?

Thus the disciple approached the Master and inquired concerning the cause of life and human activity. Having a sincere longing for Truth he desired to know who really sees and hears, who actuates the apparent physical man. He perceived all about him the phenomenal world, the existence of which he could prove by his senses; but he sought to know the invisible causal world, of which he was now only vaguely conscious. Is mind all-pervading and all-powerful, or is it impelled by some other force,

he asked. Who sends forth the vital energy, without which nothing can exist? The teacher replies:

II

It is the ear of the ear, the mind of the mind, the speech of the speech, the life of the life, the eye of the eye. The wise, freed (from the senses and from mortal desires), after leaving this world, become immortal.

An ordinary man hears, sees, thinks, but he is satisfied to know only as much as can be known through the senses; he does not analyze and try to find that which stands behind the ear or eye or mind. He is completely identified with his external nature. His conception does not go beyond the little circle of his bodily life, which concerns the outer man only. He has no

consciousness of that which enables his senses and organs to perform their tasks.

There is a vast difference between the manifested form and That which is manifested through the form. When we know That, we shall not die with the body. One who clings to the senses and to things that are ephemeral, must die many deaths, but that man who knows the eye of the eye, the ear of the eye, having severed himself from his physical nature, becomes immortal. Immortality is attained when man transcends his apparent nature and finds that subtle, eternal and inexhaustible essence which is within him.

III

There the eye does not go, nor speech, nor mind. We do not know That; we do not understand

how It can be taught. It is distinct from the known and also It is beyond the unknown. Thus we have heard from the ancient (teachers) who told us about It.

These physical eyes are unable to perceive that subtle essence. Nor can it be expressed by finite language or known by finite intelligence, because it is infinite. Our conception of knowing finite things is to know their name and form; but knowledge of God must be distinct from such knowledge. This is why some declare God to be unknown and unknowable; because He is far more than eye or mind or speech can perceive, comprehend or express. The Upanishad does not say that He cannot be known. He is unknowable to man's finite nature. How can a finite mortal apprehend the Infinite Whole? But He can be known by man's God-like nature.

IV

That which speech does not illumine, but which illumines speech: know that alone to be the Brahman (the Supreme Being), not this which people worship here.

V

That which cannot be thought by mind, but by which, they say, mind is able to think: know that alone to be the Brahman, not this which people worship here.

VI

That which is not seen by the eye, but by which the eye is able to see: know that alone to be the Brahman, not this which people worship here.

VII

That which cannot be heard by the ear, but by which the ear is able to hear: know that alone to be Brahman, not this which people worship here.

VIII

That which none breathes with the breath, but by which breath is in-breathed: know that

alone to be the Brahman, not this which people worship here.

Ordinarily we know three states of consciousness only,—waking, dreaming and sleeping. There is, however, a fourth state, the superconscious, which transcends these. In the first three states the mind is not clear enough to save us from error; but in the fourth state it gains such purity of vision that it can perceive the Divine. If God could be known by the limited mind and senses, then God-knowledge would be like any other knowledge and spiritual science like any physical science. He can be known, however, by the purified mind only. Therefore to know God, man must purify himself. The mind described in the Upanishads is the superconscious mind. According to the Vedic Sages the mind in its ordinary state is only another sense organ. This mind is limited, but when it becomes illumined by the light of the Cosmic Intelligence, or the "mind of the mind,"

then it is able to apprehend the First Cause or That which stands behind all external activities.

PART SECOND

I

If thou thinkest "I know It well," then it is certain that thou knowest but little of the Brahman (Absolute Truth), or in what form He (resideth) in the Devas (minor aspects of Deity). Therefore I think that what thou thinkest to be known is still to be sought after.

Having given the definition of the real Self or Brahman, by which mortals are able to see, hear, feel and think, the teacher was afraid that the disciple, after merely hearing about It, might conclude that he knew It. So he said to him: "You have heard about It, but that is not enough. You must experience It. Mere intellectual recognition will not give you true knowledge of It. Neither can It be taught to you. The teacher can only show the way. You must find It for yourself."

Knowledge means union between subject and object. To gain this union one must practice, theory cannot help us. The previous chapter has shown that the knowledge of Brahman is beyond sense-perception: "There the eye does not go, nor speech, nor mind." "That is distinct from known and also It is beyond the unknown." Therefore it was necessary for the teacher to remind the disciple that knowledge based on sense-perception or intellectual apprehension should not be confounded with supersensuous knowledge. Although the disciple had listened to the teacher with unquestioning mind and was intellectually convinced of the truth of his words, it was now necessary for him to prove by his own experience what he had heard. Guided by the teacher, he sought within himself through meditation the meaning of Brahman; and having gained a new vision, he approached the teacher once more.

II

The disciple said: I do not think I know It well, nor do I think that I do not know It. He among us who knows It truly, knows (what is meant by) "I know" and also what is meant by "I know It not."

This appears to be contradictory, but it is not. In the previous chapter we learned that Brahman is "distinct from the known" and "beyond the unknown." The disciple, realizing this, says: "So far as mortal conception is concerned, I do not think I know, because I understand that It is beyond mind and speech; yet from the higher point of view, I cannot say that I do not know; for the very fact that I exist, that I can seek It, shows that I know; for It is the source of my being. I do not know, however, in the sense of knowing the whole Infinite Ocean of existence." The word knowledge is used ordinarily to signify acquaintance with

phenomena only, but man must transcend this relative knowledge before he can have a clear conception of God. One who wishes to attain Soul-consciousness must rise above matter.

The observation of material science being confined to the sense plane, it ignores what is beyond. Therefore it must always be limited and subject to change. It discovered atoms, then it went further and discovered electrons, and when it had found the one, it had to drop the other; so this kind of knowledge can never lead to the ultimate knowledge of the Infinite, because it is exclusive and not inclusive. Spiritual science is not merely a question of mind and brain, it depends on the awakening of our latent higher consciousness.

III

He who thinks he knows It not, knows It. He who thinks he knows It, knows It not. The true knowers think they can never know It (because of Its infinitude), while the ignorant think they know It.

By this text the teacher confirms the idea that Brahman is unthinkable, because unconditioned. Therefore he says: He who considers It beyond thought, beyond sense-perception, beyond mind and speech, he alone has a true understanding of Brahman. They who judge a living being from his external form and sense faculties, know him not; because the real Self of man is not manifested in his seeing, hearing, speaking. His real Self is that within by which he hears and speaks and sees. In the same way he knows not Brahman who thinks he knows It by name and form. The arrogant and foolish man thinks he knows everything;

but the true knower is humble. He says: "How can I know Thee, who art Infinite and beyond mind and speech?" In the last portion of the text, the teacher draws an impressive contrast between the attitude of the wise man who knows, but thinks he does not know; and that of the ignorant who does not know, but thinks he knows.

IV

It (Brahman) is known, when It is known in every state of consciousness. (Through such knowledge) one attains immortality. By attaining this Self, man gains strength; and by Self-knowledge immortality is attained.

We have learned from the previous text that the Brahman is unknown to those whose knowledge is limited to sense experience; but

He is not unknown to those whose purified intelligence perceives Him as the basis of all states of consciousness and the essence of all things. By this higher knowledge a man attains immortality, because he knows that although his body may decay and die, the subtle essence of his being remains untouched. Such an one also acquires unlimited strength, because he identifies himself with the ultimate Source. The strength which comes from one's own muscle and brain or from one's individual power must be limited and mortal and therefore cannot lift one beyond death; but through the strength which Atma-gnana or Self-knowledge gives, immortality is reached. Whenever knowledge is based on direct perception of this undying essence, one transcends all fear of death and becomes immortal.

V

If one knows It here, that is Truth; if one knows It not here, then great is his loss. The wise seeing the same Self in all beings, being liberated from this world, become immortal.

PART THIRD

I

The Brahman once won a victory for the Devas. Through that victory of the Brahman, the Devas became elated. They thought, "This victory is ours. This glory is ours."

Brahman here does not mean a personal Deity. There is a Brahma, the first person of the Hindu Trinity; but Brahman is the Absolute, the One without a second, the essence of all. There are different names and forms which represent certain personal aspects of Divinity, such as Brahma the Creator, Vishnu the Preserver and Siva the Transformer; but no one of these can fully represent the Whole. Brahman is the vast ocean of being, on which rise numberless ripples and waves of manifestation. From the smallest atomic form to a Deva or an angel, all

spring from that limitless ocean of Brahman, the inexhaustible Source of life. No manifested form of life can be independent of its source, just as no wave, however mighty, can be independent of the ocean. Nothing moves without that Power. He is the only Doer. But the Devas thought: "This victory is ours, this glory is ours."

II

The Brahman perceived this and appeared before them. They did not know what mysterious form it was.

III

They said to Fire: "O Jataveda (All-knowing)! Find out what mysterious spirit this is." He said: "Yes."

IV

He ran towards it and He (Brahman) said to him: "Who art thou?"

"I am Agni, I am Jataveda," he (the Fire-god) replied.

V

Brahman asked: "What power resides in thee?" Agni replied: "I can burn up all whatsoever exists on earth."

VI

Brahman placed a straw before him and said: "Burn this." He (Agni) rushed towards it with all speed, but was not able to burn it. So he returned from there and said (to the Devas): "I was not able to find out what this great mystery is."

VII

Then they said to Vayu (the Air-god): "Vayu! Find out what this mystery is." He said: "Yes."

VIII

He ran towards it and He (Brahman) said to him: "Who art thou?" "I am Vayu, I am Matarisva (traveller of Heaven)," he (Vayu) said.

IX

Then the Brahman said: "What power is in thee?" Vayu replied: "I can blow away all whatsoever exists on earth."

X

Brahman placed a straw before him and said: "Blow this away." He (Vayu) rushed towards it with all speed, but was not able to blow it away. So he returned from there and said (to the Devas): "I was not able to find out what this great mystery is."

XI

Then they said to Indra: "O Maghavan (Worshipful One)! Find out what this mystery is." He said: "Yes"; and ran towards it, but it disappeared before him.

XII

Then he saw in that very space a woman beautifully adorned, Uma of golden hue, daughter of Haimavat (Himalaya). He asked: "What is this great mystery?"

Here we see how the Absolute assumes concrete form to give knowledge of Himself to the earnest seeker. Brahman, the impenetrable mystery, disappeared and in His place appeared a personal form to represent Him. This is a subtle way of showing the difference between the Absolute and the personal aspects of Deity. The Absolute is declared to be unknowable and unthinkable, but He assumes deified personal aspects to make Himself known to His devotees. Thus Uma, daughter of the Himalaya, represents that personal aspect as the offspring of the Infinite Being; while the Himalaya stands as the symbol of the Eternal, Unchangeable One.

PART FOURTH

I

She (Uma) said: "It is Brahman. It is through the victory of Brahman that ye are victorious." Then from her words, he (Indra) knew that it (that mysterious form) was Brahman.

Uma replied to Indra, "It is to Brahman that you owe your victory. It is through His power that you live and act. He is the agent and you are all only instruments in His hands. Therefore your idea that 'This victory is ours, this glory is ours,' is based on ignorance." At once Indra saw their mistake. The Devas, being puffed up with vanity, had thought they themselves had achieved the victory, whereas it was Brahman; for not even a blade of grass can move without His command.

II

Therefore these Devas,—Agni, Vayu and Indra—excel other Devas, because they came nearer to Brahman. It was they who first knew this spirit as Brahman.

III

Therefore Indra excels all other Devas, because he came nearest to Brahman, and because he first (before all others) knew this spirit as Brahman.

Agni, Vayu and Indra were superior to the other Devas because they gained a closer vision; and they were able to do this because they were purer; while Indra stands as the head of the Devas, because he realized the Truth directly, he reached Brahman. The significance of this

is that whoever comes in direct touch with Brahman or the Supreme is glorified.

IV

Thus the teaching of Brahman is here illustrated in regard to the Devas. He dashed like lightning, and appeared and disappeared just as the eye winks.

The teaching as regards the Devas was that Brahman is the only Doer. He had appeared before them in a mysterious form; but the whole of the unfathomable Brahman could not be seen in any definite form; so at the moment of vanishing, He manifested more of His immeasurable glory and fleetness of action by a sudden dazzling flash of light.

V

Next (the teaching) is regarding Adhyatman (the embodied Soul). The mind seems to approach Him (Brahman). By this mind (the seeker) again and again remembers and thinks about Brahman.

Only by the mind can the seeker after knowledge approach Brahman, whose nature in glory and speed has been described as like unto a flash of lightning. Mind alone can picture the indescribable Brahman; and mind alone, being swift in its nature, can follow Him. It is through the help of this mind that we can think and meditate on Brahman; and when by constant thought of Him the mind becomes purified, then like a polished mirror it can reflect His Divine Glory.

VI

That Brahman is called Tadvanam (object of adoration). He is to be worshipped by the name Tadvanam. He who knows Brahman thus, is loved by all beings.

Brahman is the object of adoration and the goal of all beings. For this reason he should be worshipped and meditated upon as Tadvanam. Whoever knows Him in this aspect becomes one with Him, and serves as a clear channel through which the blessings of Brahman flow out to others. The knower of God partakes of all His lovable qualities and is therefore loved by all true devotees.

VII

The disciple asked: O Master, teach me the Upanishad. (The teacher replied:) The Upanishad has been taught thee. We have certainly taught thee the Upanishad about Brahman.

VIII

The Upanishad is based on tapas (practice of the control of body, mind and senses), dama (subjugation of the senses), karma (right performance of prescribed actions). The Vedas are its limbs. Truth is its support.

IX

He who knows this (wisdom of the Upanishad), having been cleansed of all sin, becomes established in the blissful, eternal and highest abode of Brahman, in the highest abode of Brahman.

HERE ENDS THIS UPANISHAD

This Upanishad is called Kena, because it begins with the inquiry: "By whom" (Kena) willed or directed does the mind go towards its object? From whom comes life? What enables man to speak, to hear and see? And the teacher in reply gives him the definition of Brahman, the Source and Basis of existence. The spirit of the Upanishads is always to show that no matter where we look or what we see or feel in the visible world, it all proceeds from one Source.

The prevailing note of all Vedic teaching is this: One tremendous Whole becoming the world, and again the world merging in that Whole. It also strives in various ways to define that Source, knowing which all else is known and without which no knowledge can be well established. So here the teacher replies: That which is the eye of the eye, the ear of the ear, that is the inexhaustible river of being which flows on eternally; while bubbles of creation rise on the surface, live for a time, then burst.

The teacher, however, warns the disciple that this eye, ear, mind, can never perceive It; for It is that which illumines speech and mind, which enables eye and ear and all sense-faculties to perform their tasks. "It is distinct from the known and also It is beyond the unknown." He who thinks he knows It, knows It not; because It is never known by those who believe that It can be grasped by the intellect or by the senses;

but It can be known by him who knows It as the basis of all consciousness.

The knower of Truth says, "I know It not," because he realizes the unbounded, infinite nature of the Supreme. "Thou art this (the visible), Thou art That (the invisible), and Thou art all that is beyond," he declares. The ordinary idea of knowledge is that which is based on sense preceptions; but the knowledge of an illumined Sage is not confined to his senses. He has all the knowledge that comes from the senses and all that comes from Spirit.

The special purpose of this Upanishad is to give us the knowledge of the Real, that we may not come under the dominion of the ego by identifying ourselves with our body, mind and senses. Mortals become mortals because they fall under the sway of ego and depend on their own limited physical and mental strength. The lesson of the parable of the Devas and Brahman is that there is no real power, no real doer

except God. He is the eye of the eye, the ear of the ear; and eyes, ears, and all our faculties have no power independent of Him. When we thus realize Him as the underlying Reality of our being, we transcend death and become immortal.

OM! PEACE! PEACE! PEACE!